AUTHORS' LETTER

014596775 Liverpool Univ

KT-148-329

University of Liverpool

Withdrawn from stock

Dear Reader:

We understand today's students are **different**!

Today's students—often referred to as 'Millennials' or "Digital Natives'—have grown up in a constantly connected world. They are highly social and work well in teams. They multi-task, have dynamic attention spans, and want to stay connected. They are optimistic and determined to make the world better. Finally, they are kinesthetic and visual learners.

The unmet needs and desires of today's millennial students can be grouped into three categories:

Visual and Collaborative Learning:

Millennials prefer to be engaged visually. They prefer interactive media, videos and textbooks with an emphasis on useful exhibits, photos, maps and other visual learning aids. Millennials prefer content that they can read or digitally access at a time and place of their choosing. They prefer self-paced learning. They enjoy group tasks.

Relevant Knowledge and Job Related Skills:

Millennials want relevant company examples, more concise foundational course content and tools that develop specific IB skills that will better prepare them for jobs as they enter the global working community.

Focus on Contemporary Issues that Matter to Millennials:

Millennials desire content with a strong emphasis on **culture, ethics, corporate social responsibility, sustainability, governance, social trends and other contemporary issues that matter to them.**

The new 4th edition of our textbook, *International Business: The New Realities©*, and the MyManagementLab® online assessment and preparation solution, have been completely redesigned and rewritten to address these unmet needs and desires.

This new 4th edition has been carefully crafted to:

- **Engage students**—make them want to learn more about international business
- **Ensure students are prepared to learn the material** by using collaborative learning and realistic experiences that enable interaction, demonstration, and social networking
- **Show students how to apply the material** by incorporating content on contemporary issues that matter to millennials which will better prepare them as they enter the global working community.
- **Enable students to acquire critical thinking and problem-solving skills**

Specifically, here is what the 4th edition offers:

VISUAL AND COLLABORATIVE LEARNING

Reduced number of chapters from 20 to 17. Market research with educators indicates that the ideal number of chapters for comprehensive course coverage is 17. The authors have condensed the writing and eliminated certain non-essential content in this new edition to address these needs.

Writing style and comprehension enhancement. The authors have utilized a writing style in the 4th edition to optimize reading and comprehension. Average sentence length is approximately 12 words per sentence. The reading level is fully accessible to Millennials.

New chapter organization designed to optimize student learning. Each chapter objective is linked to a specific CKR Learning Module© that can be read in approximately 20 minutes.

171 new and updated Exhibits designed to improve understanding and retention with specific links to chapter content. This is more than double the number of exhibits found in competing textbooks.

New and updated Maps specifically designed for the Millennial student learning style. This is double the number of maps as in competing textbooks.

Videos. The new *Watch It* feature links most chapters to one or two custom-designed videos on international business that clarify complex material and facilitate learning.

RELEVANT KNOWLEDGE AND JOB RELATED SKILLS

More concise foundational content development based upon marketing research from professors. The 4th edition puts more focus on foundational content. The authors have streamlined the narrative, emphasizing simplified explanations that have been classroom-tested.

Currency of examples and references. More than 70 percent of the references in the new edition are from 2008 or later, as compared to about 30 percent in leading competing textbooks. We have included company examples that are exciting and relevant to today's student.

ALWAYS LEARNING

Career Toolbox—IB Skills Building. IB Skill Building Exercises facilitate the development of specific and relevant international business expertise that prepare Millennials for the work world. IB Skill Building Exercises are unique to the 4th edition.

GlobalEDGE Internet Exercises in each chapter provide instructors a basis for student assignments and projects. The GlobalEDGE™ knowledge portal was developed under the direction of co-author S. Tamer Cavusgil while at Michigan State University.

You Can Do It—Recent Grads in IB. This edition offers nine biographies of real university graduates who have embarked on fascinating careers in international business. These inspiring stories, three of them new to this edition, bring the prospect of an exciting IB career to life.

FOCUS ON CONTEMPORARY ISSUES THAT MATTER

Emphasis on the new IB environment. Compared to leading competing texts, the new 4th edition presents more current and deeper coverage of contemporary IB topics such as emerging markets, developing economies, growth of the service sector, risks in IB, globalization and technology, women in IB and other important trends.

Ethics, CSR, Sustainability and Governance chapter. The authors have rewritten, updated and expanded the chapter to include the most current topics, issues and company examples.

Ethical dilemmas throughout the book. Ethical dilemmas are presented in the majority of chapters and focus on the dilemmas that managers encounter at the boundary of ethical norms and business practice. Students can apply the CKR Ethical Framework© from Chapter 4 to address each dilemma.

Group project on corporate social responsibility. The 4th edition contains a new, comprehensive activity in which students debate corporate social responsibility in international business. In this extended classroom-tested exercise, located in the *Instructor's Manual*, students debate the merits and consequences of CSR as 'executives,' 'consumers', and 'activists.'

Culture chapter expanded, updated and rewritten to address the issues and topics of greatest importance and interest to Millennials and professors.

Dedicated chapter on emerging markets and developing economies. The only leading IB text with a specific chapter devoted to emerging markets and developing economies.

Women in international business. Women comprise about 50 percent of the undergraduate enrollment in business degree programs. Women increasingly pursue careers in international business. The 4th edition is the only text with a dedicated section devoted to the unique needs and challenges women face in international business.

Balanced coverage of multinational enterprises, small and medium size enterprises and born globals.

Unlike numerous other IB textbooks, the 4th edition features substantial content on the variety of firms active in international business today.

Balanced focus. The 4th edition offers a global perspective, avoiding excessive focus on specific nations or regions.

PERSONALIZED LEARNING

MyManagementLab delivers online assessment and preparation material that helps students study and prepare actively for class. Chapter-by-chapter activities, including pre-tests, post-tests, and video and critical-thinking exercises, emphasize content that students need to review and learn to succeed.

The Pearson eText lets students access their textbook anytime, anywhere, and any way they want—including online or downloading to tablet computers.

A **personalized study plan** for each student promotes better critical thinking skills and helps students succeed in the course and beyond.

INSTRUCTOR SUPPORT

AACSB tagging accompanies all end-of-chapter exercises to help instructors identify the AACSB learning goals that each exercise supports and to aid in measuring student learning of course content within AACSB guidelines. All test bank items are tagged as well.

Instructor's Manual. The Instructor's Manual is authored by Marta Szabo White of Georgia State University, winner of numerous teaching awards. The cutting-edge Manual provides numerous resources for each chapter such as exercises, critical-thinking assignments, debate topics, and research assignments.

Test Item File, authored by an assessment expert with extensive experience in test authoring. It includes approximately 100 questions per chapter, all reviewed and edited by the authors to ensure accuracy and appropriateness. TestGen Test Generating software is also available.

Newly prepared PowerPoint slides and an **Image Library** contain all of the exhibits from the textbook. All PowerPoints have been developed and classroom-tested by the authors. These are available electronically for instructors to download.

International Business

The New Realities

Global Edition

Fourth Edition

S. Tamer Cavusgil

Fuller E. Callaway Professorial Chair, Georgia State University

Gary Knight

Helen Simpson Jackson Chair in International Management,
Willamette University

John R. Riesenberger

President, Consilium Partners
Thunderbird School of Global Management (retired)

PEARSON

Boston Columbus Indianapolis New York San Francisco Amsterdam Cape Town
Dubai London Madrid Milan Munich Paris Montréal Toronto Delhi
Mexico City São Paulo Sydney Hong Kong Seoul Singapore Taipei Tokyo

Vice President, Business Publishing: Donna Battista
Editor-in-Chief: Stephanie Wall
Acquisitions Editor: Emily Tamburri
Program Manager Team Lead: Ashley Santora
Program Manager: Sarah Holle/Denise Weiss
Editorial Assistant: Eric Santucci
Editorial Assistant, Global Editions: Alice Dazley
Associate Project Editor, Global Edition: Amrita Kar
Project Manager, Global Editions: Nikhil Rakshit
Manager, Media Production, Global Edition: Vikram Kumar
Senior Manufacturing Controller, Production, Global Edition:
    Trudy Kimber
Vice President, Product Marketing: Maggie Moylan
Director of Marketing, Digital Services and Products: Jeanette Koskinas
Field Marketing Manager: Lenny Ann Raper
Product Marketing Assistant: Jessica Quazza
Project Manager Team Lead: Jeff Holcomb
Project Manager: Meghan DeMaio

Operations Specialist: Carol Melville
Creative Director: Blair Brown
Senior Art Director: Janet Slowik
Cover Designer: Lumina Datamatics Ltd
Cover Image: sakhorn/Shutterstock
**Vice President, Director of Digital
    Strategy & Assessment:** Paul Gentile
Manager of Learning Applications: Paul Deluca
Digital Editor: Brian Surette
Digital Studio Manager: Diane Lombardo
Digital Studio Project Manager: Robin Lazrus
Digital Studio Project Manager: Alana Coles
Digital Studio Project Manager: Monique Lawrence
Digital Studio Project Manager: Regina DaSilva
Full-Service Project Management and Composition: Integra
Printer/Binder: Vivar, Malsysia
Cover Printer: Vivar, Malsysia
Text Font: 10/12, Times LT Pro Roman

Microsoft and/or its respective suppliers make no representations about the suitability of the information contained in the documents and related graphics published as part of the services for any purpose. All such documents and related graphics are provided as-is without warranty of any kind. Microsoft and/or its respective suppliers hereby disclaim all warranties and conditions with regard to this information, including all warranties and conditions of merchantability, whether express, implied, or statutory, fitness for a particular purpose, title and non-infringement. In no event shall Microsoft and/or its respective suppliers be liable for any special, indirect or consequential damages or any damages whatsoever resulting from loss of use, data or profits, whether in an action of contract, negligence or other tortious action, arising out of or in connection with the use or performance of information available from the services.

The documents and related graphics contained herein could include technical inaccuracies or typographical errors. Changes are periodically added to the information herein. Microsoft and/or its respective suppliers may make improvements and/or changes in the product(s) and/or the program(s) described herein at any time. Partial screen shots may be viewed in full within the software version specified.

Trademarks
Microsoft® Windows®, and Microsoft Office® are registered trademarks of the Microsoft corporation in the U.S.A. and other countries. This book is not sponsored or endorsed by or affiliated with the Microsoft corporation.

Pearson Education Limited
Edinburgh Gate
Harlow
Essex CM20 2JE
England

and Associated Companies throughout the world

Visit us on the World Wide Web at:
www.pearsonglobaleditions.com

© Pearson Education Limited 2017

The rights of S. Tamer Cavusgil, Gary Knight and John R. Riesenberger to be identified as the authors of this work have been asserted by them in accordance with the Copyright, Designs and Patents Act 1988.

Authorized adaptation from the United States edition, entitled International Business: The New Realities, Fourth Edition, ISBN 978-0-13-432483-8 by S. Tamer Cavusgil, Gary Knight and John R. Riesenberger, published by Pearson Education © 2017.

All rights reserved. No part of this publication may be reproduced, stored in a retrieval system, or transmitted in any form or by any means, electronic, mechanical, photocopying, recording or otherwise, without either the prior written permission of the publisher or a license permitting restricted copying in the United Kingdom issued by the Copyright Licensing Agency Ltd, Saffron House, 6–10 Kirby Street, London EC 1N 8TS.

All trademarks used herein are the property of their respective owners. The use of any trademark in this text does not vest in the author or publisher any trademark ownership rights in such trademarks, nor does the use of such trademarks imply any affiliation with or endorsement of this book by such owners.

ISBN-10: 1-292-15283-4
ISBN-13: 978-1-292-15283-7

British Library Cataloguing-in-Publication Data
A catalogue record for this book is available from the British Library

20 19 18 17
10 9 8 7 6 5 4 3 2

Typeset in Times LT Pro Roman by Integra
Printed and bound by Vivar in Malaysia

Dedicated to...

This book is dedicated to all those who feel passionate about cross-border business, our readers around the world. I trust that this edition will inspire and help you discover the magic of international business. Since any journey is much more rewarding when you are accompanied by others, I also dedicate this edition to my students of four decades whom I had the opportunity to mentor over the years.

S. Tamer Cavusgil
Atlanta, Georgia

This book is dedicated to my wife, Mari, for her intellect, patience, and adventurous spirit; to Bill and Audrey, and to Hiroshi and Hisako, for being great parents and role models; and to the many students I have had the good fortune to influence over the years.

Gary Knight
Portland, Oregon

This book is dedicated to my parents, Richard and Marie Riesenberger, for their example, many sacrifices, and love. To my wife and best friend, Pat, for her enthusiasm and loving support. To my daughters, Chris and Jen, and their husbands, Byron and Martijn, of whom I am so very proud and thankful. To my amazing grandchildren, Ryan, Paige, Ethan, and Emma—the future of the New Realities.

John R. Riesenberger
Basking Ridge, New Jersey

> About the Authors

S. Tamer Cavusgil

Georgia State University, Fuller E. Callaway Professorial Chair

Executive Director, Center for International Business Education and Research (CIBER), J. Mack Robinson College of Business

Professor Cavusgil has been mentoring students, executives, and educators in international business for the past four decades. A native of Turkey, his professional work has taken him to numerous other emerging markets.

Tamer serves as Fuller E. Callaway Professorial Chair at Georgia State University's Robinson College of Business. He is also a visiting professor at Leeds University Business School, U.K.; University of South Australia; and Xi'an Jiaotong University.

Previously, Tamer served as *Senior Fulbright Scholar* to Australia and taught at Monash University. Tamer also served as a visiting professor at Manchester Business School and held the Gianni and Joan Montezemolo Visiting Chair at the University of Cambridge, United Kingdom, where he is also an Honorary Fellow of Sidney Sussex College. At Michigan State University, where he served for 21 years, he was the inaugural holder of the John Byington Chair in Global Marketing and Founding Director of CIBER.

Professor Cavusgil is an elected Fellow of the Academy of International Business, a distinction earned by a select group of intellectual leaders in international business. He also served as Vice President of the AIB, and on the Board of Directors of the American Marketing Association.

Tamer was named International Trade Educator of the Year in 1996 by the National Association of Small Business International Trade Educators (NASBITE). Most recently, he was inducted as Doctor Honoris Causa (Honorary Doctorate) by the Universiteit Hasselt, Belgium, "in recognition of seminal research in, and groundbreaking contributions to the field of international marketing and international business performance."

Tamer has authored more than two dozen books and some 200 refereed journal articles. His work is among the most cited contributions in international business. He is the founding editor of the *Journal of International Marketing* and *Advances in International Marketing*. He serves on the editorial review boards of a dozen professional journals.

Tamer holds a Bachelor of Science degree in business and economics from the Middle East Technical University in Ankara, Turkey. He earned his MBA and PhD degrees in business from the University of Wisconsin.

Gary Knight

Willamette University, Professor of Global Management and Helen Simpson Jackson Chair in International Management

University of Southern Denmark, Visiting Professor

Professor Gary Knight has been teaching international business for more than 20 years. A native of the United States, he has lived and worked in many countries around the world.

Gary has been Helen Simpson Jackson Chair in International Management at Willamette University since 2012. He is also Visiting Professor at the University of Southern Denmark, Odense. He was professor at Florida State University for 15 years where he directed the school's International Business Program.

Gary has been an invited speaker at institutions worldwide and developed study abroad programs in Asia, Europe, and Latin America. He has won several awards, including the Jerry Hudson Award for Excellence in Teaching, Willamette University, and Best Teacher in the MBA Program, Florida State University.

Gary has co-authored six books and more than 100 refereed articles in academic journals and conference proceedings. His research emphasizes international business strategy, international services, emerging markets, and internationalization of small and medium-sized firms.

Gary won the Hans Thorelli Best Paper Award for his article "Entrepreneurship and Strategy: The SME Under Globalization." Along with S. Tamer Cavusgil, he won the 2014 Decade Award at the *Journal of International Business Studies* for their article on born global firms.

Gary is ranked in the top five percent of scholars who have published in the *Journal of International Business Studies* since 1995, based on number of articles published. He recently was ranked one of the top 10 scholars in the United States, and top 15 worldwide, in international business research impact based on Google Scholar citation data. He is on the editorial review boards of several international journals. He has provided expert testimony on global commerce and small business to the U.S. House of Representatives.

Gary is Chair of the Academy of International Business, Western United States Chapter. Prior to joining academia, he was Export Manager of a medium-sized enterprise, directing the firm's operations in Canada, Europe, Japan, and Mexico and supervising some 50 distributors. He enjoyed a brief career in banking and as a teacher in Japan.

Gary earned his MBA at the University of Washington and PhD at Michigan State University, both in international business. Earlier degrees were in finance and modern languages. He also attended the University of Paris in France and Sophia University in Japan and is fluent in French, Japanese, and Spanish.

John R. Riesenberger
President, Consilium Partners
Thunderbird School of Global Management, Clinical Professor of Executive Development, Corporate Learning Group (retired)

Professor Riesenberger's teaching activities centered on leadership and global project management at the Thunderbird School of Global Management, Corporate Learning Group. His passion is to help students and young professionals develop the managerial skills frequently required of new graduates entering careers in international business.

John is an accomplished author, consultant, and international executive with senior executive positions in major pharmaceutical firms, biotechnology firms, and pharmaceutical agencies. John's international business career spans more than three decades in the global pharmaceutical industry. He has conducted business transactions in 21 countries.

Currently, he also serves as the president of Consilium Partners, Inc., a pharmaceutical consulting firm with clients in pharmaceutical, biotechnology, and pharmaceutical agency firms.

He worked for 30 years with Pharmacia & Upjohn and The Upjohn Company as a senior international executive. His experience covered a diverse range of divisional, geographic, and functional accountabilities. His most recent position was as vice president of Global Business Management. He also served as corporate vice president and Chief Commercialization Officer for a biotechnology firm and as the executive vice president of a pharmaceutical science agency.

John serves as a member of the board of directors of the Ontario Institute for Cancer Research. He was a member of the Global Advisory Board of the American Marketing Association. He served as an executive in residence at the Michigan State University Center for International Business Education and Research. He served on the editorial review board of the *Journal of International Marketing*. He served as chairman of the Industry Advisory Board's Value of Marketing Program, SEI Center for the Advanced Studies in Management at the Wharton School of the University of Pennsylvania. He is the former chairman of the Pharmaceutical Manufacturing Association Marketing

Practices Committee. Professor Riesenberger is the coauthor, with Robert T. Moran, of *The Global Challenge: Building the New Worldwide Enterprise* (McGraw-Hill, London).

John holds a Bachelor of Science degree in Economics–Business and an MBA in Management from Hofstra University. He attended the Harvard Business School's International Senior Management Program.

> Brief Contents

> Contents

6 Political and Legal Systems in National Environments   172

10 Financial Management and Accounting in the Global Firm   286

Part 4 Entering and Working in International Markets   374

13 Exporting and Global Sourcing   374

Part 5 Functional Area Excellence   464

16 Marketing in the Global Firm   464

> Preface

Today's students are *different!*

The current generation of college students are Millennials. In creating the fourth edition of Cavusgil, Knight, and Riesenberger (CKR 4e), we have designed a textbook with this important group in mind. Millennials share distinctive characteristics:

- Dynamic attention spans
- Tendency to multitask
- Visual learners accessing content from exhibits, photos, maps, and digital content, usually
- Through high-tech devices
- Need to stay connected through social media and their networks
- Work well in teams
- Sheltered and special
- Optimistic
- Need to achieve
- Bear increased pressure to perform

Millennials are the most diverse and educated generation to date. They prefer learning with a heart that is empathic and responds to their hopes and needs. They often experience the world through multimedia. Those starting college today have never known a time without the Internet.

Millennial college graduates face an evolving economic environment. In Europe, Japan, North America, Australia, New Zealand, and other advanced economies, many confront new challenges and an increasingly competitive job market.

Millennials have been shaped by technology. Revolutionary developments in computers and information technology have coincided with Millennials' coming of age. More than any previous generation, they use tablets, smartphones, and similar devices to acquire information and knowledge. High technology has shaped how they learn and relate to their world. Technology has affected their expectations about innovation and creativity in their own work lives. Millennials prefer realistic experiences.

Millennials are oriented to achievement and their communities. Many yearn to play meaningful roles in their communities and the world at large. More than previous generations, they value ethical behavior, sustainability, and social responsibility. They want to learn how internationally active companies and other organizations employ ethics, sustainability, and social responsibility to foster a better world.

When it comes to work and career, Millennials want to be successful. They want to acquire skills in their coursework that they can use to obtain meaningful jobs and excel in their careers. They view creativity and critical thinking as important qualities for the job market. Today's college students seek interesting careers with opportunities for advancement. Millennial women are sophisticated. They value equality, fairness, and attaining rewarding careers that leverage their resourcefulness and creativity.

To address the characteristics of the Millennial generation, we have designed CKR 4e to emphasize the following features:

- *Visual learning* CKR 4e puts more emphasis on interactive media and videos as well as exhibits, maps, and other visual learning aids. The MyManagementLab portal provides access to a wide array of additional visual resources.
- *Collaborative learning* Millennials are connected through networks of friends and associates with whom they communicate continually. Most prefer learning in the company of their peers, frequently working in groups. Learning is facilitated through information technology, the Internet, and social media. CKR 4e has been developed accordingly.
- *Relevant knowledge and job-related skills* CKR 4e includes more relevant examples and activities, concise foundational course content, and tools that develop specific international business (IB) skills that will prepare Millennials for the work world.

- *Digital platform* Millennials prefer content that they can read or access digitally at a time and place of their choosing. Digital learning enhances engagement, self-pacing, and the ability to customize content to individual needs. Digital platforms help ensure timely, up-to-date content and the ability to collaborate with peers. In these and other ways, CKR 4e provides such digital options.
- *Contemporary issues that matter to Millennials* CKR 4e emphasizes the new IB environment. Compared to the leading competitor, the fourth edition presents more current and more in-depth coverage of contemporary IB topics such as emerging markets, developing economies, growth of the service sector, risks in IB, globalization and technology, women in IB, and other important trends.
- *Meaningful content* CKR 4e provides substantial content oriented to ethics, corporate social responsibility, and sustainability in international business.

In addition, CKR 4e has the following features:

- Highly accessible writing and explanations that engage students. Opening and closing cases appeal to students, featuring firms and subjects such as Apple, Disney, Facebook, Harley-Davidson, H&M, born global firms, social media in China, and the global movie industry. The content stimulates student desire to learn more about international business.
- Content that helps ensure that students are prepared to learn the material by using collaborative learning and realistic experiences that enable interaction, demonstration, and social networking.
- More content on contemporary issues that matter to Millennials and will prepare them better as they enter the global working community.
- More exercises and activities that enable students to acquire critical thinking and problem-solving skills.
- Fewer chapters and greater focus on essential foundational content. We have streamlined the narrative, improved readability and clarity, and simplified some explanations.
- New and improved organization of chapters. We have improved the organization of each chapter, in part by aligning learning objectives more systematically with individual sections within chapters.
- More exhibits that enhance readability and explanatory value. CKR 4e contains 171 exhibits (about three times more than leading competitors). Students like exhibits because they help clarify complex material and facilitate reading the chapters.
- More videos that enrich the learning process. Through the new Watch It feature, each chapter links to one or two custom-designed videos on international business that clarify and provide real-world context to concepts and explanations.
- Simulations that enhance and reinforce learning. Most chapters link to a simulation that reinforces key material and learning enjoyment.
- Career Toolbox exercises, a new feature in CKR 4e designed to simulate real-world decision-making. Nearly every chapter contains a Career Toolbox exercise, intended to familiarize students with key managerial challenges and decisions that professionals encounter in international business. Students can complete Career Toolbox exercises individually or in teams.
- Group project on international corporate social responsibility. CKR 4e contains a new, comprehensive activity in which students debate corporate social responsibility (CSR) in international business. In this extended exercise, located in the *Instructor's Manual*, students debate the merits and consequences of CSR as executives, consumers, or activists.
- You Can Do It—Recent Grad in IB biographies. CKR 4e offers nine biographies (three new to this edition) of actual university graduates who have embarked on fascinating careers in international business. These inspiring stories bring the prospect of an exciting IB career to life.
- Content that is contemporary, reflecting international business conditions today. CKR 4e presents more current and more in-depth, globally balanced coverage of material, examples, cases, and exercises. More than 70 percent of the references in CKR 4e are from 2008 or later (versus only about 30 percent in the leading competitor).

Learning Goals and Standards

This book supports Association to Advance Collegiate Schools of Business (AACSB) international accreditation. In every chapter, next to each end-of-chapter exercise, we provide a specific AACSB tagging logo to help instructors identify which AACSB learning goals that activity supports. We also provide AACSB tagging for all the questions in the Test Item File that accompanies the textbook.

WHAT ARE AACSB LEARNING STANDARDS? One of the criteria for AACSB accreditation is the quality of the curricula. Although no specific courses are required, the AACSB expects a curriculum to include learning experiences in such areas as:

- Communication abilities
- Ethical understanding and reasoning abilities
- Analytic skills
- Use of information technology
- Dynamics of the global economy
- Multicultural and diversity understanding
- Reflective thinking skills

These seven categories are AACSB Learning Standards. Questions that test skills relevant to these standards are tagged with the appropriate standard. For example, a question testing the moral questions associated with externalities would receive the ethical understanding and reasoning abilities tag.

HOW CAN I USE THESE TAGS? Tagged exercises help you measure whether students are grasping the course content that aligns with AACSB guidelines noted previously. In addition, the tagged exercises may help identify potential applications of these skills. This, in turn, may suggest enrichment activities or other educational experiences to help students achieve these goals.

Supplements

At the Instructor Resource Center, www.pearsonglobaleditions.com/Cavusgil, instructors can easily register to gain access to a variety of instructor resources available with this text in downloadable format. If assistance is needed, our dedicated technical support team is ready to help with the media supplements that accompany this text. Visit http://247.pearsoned.com for answers to frequently asked questions and toll-free user support phone numbers.

The following supplements are available with this text:

- *Instructor's Resource Manual*
- Test Bank
- TestGen® Computerized Test Bank
- PowerPoint Presentation

> Acknowledgments

Our Reviewers

Through numerous drafts of the manuscript, we received guidance and insights at several critical junctures from many trusted reviewers who provided specific recommendations on how to improve and refine the content, presentation, and organization. Their contributions were invaluable in crystallizing our thinking. We extend our gratitude to:

Anil Agarwal, University of Arizona
Raj Aggarwal, University of Akron
Anshu Arora, Savannah State University
Richard Ajayi, University of Central Florida
Hamid Ali, Chicago State University
Allen Amason, University of Georgia
Gary Anders, Arizona State University
Robert Armstrong, University of North Alabama
Mathias Arrfelt, Arizona State University
Bulent Aybar, Southern New Hampshire University
Nizamettin Aydin, Suffolk University
Peter Banfe, Ohio Northern University
Eric Baumgardner, Xavier University
Mack Bean, Franklin Pierce University
Lawrence Beer, Arizona State University
Enoch Beraho, South Carolina State University
David Berg, University of Wisconsin–Milwaukee
Jean Boddewyn, Baruch College, City University of New York
Henry Bohleke, Owens Community College
Santanu Borah, University of Northern Alabama
Darrell Brown, Indiana University, Purdue University, Indianapolis
Linda Brown, Scottsdale Community College
Diana Bullen, Mesa Community College
Nancy Bush, Wingate University
Kirt Butler, Michigan State University
Michael Campo, Regis University
Tom Cary, City University, Seattle
Erin Cavusgil, University of Michigan–Flint
Kalyan Chakravarty, California State University, Northridge
Aruna Chandra, Indiana State University
Kent Cofoid, Seminole State College
Tim Curran, University of South Florida
Madeline Calabrese Damkar, California State University–East Bay
Donna Davisson, Cleveland State University
Seyda Deligonul, St. John Fisher College
Peter Dowling, Latrobe University, Australia

Juan España, National University
Bradley Farnsworth, University of Michigan, Ann Arbor
Aysun Ficici, Southern New Hampshire University
John Finley, Columbus State University
Ian Gladding, Lewis University
Jorge Gonzalez, University of Texas–Pan American
Tom Head, Roosevelt University
Bruce Heiman, San Francisco State University
David Hrovat, Northern Kentucky University
Douglas Johansen, Jacksonville University
Paul Jones, Regis University
Ali Kara, Pennsylvania State University–University Park
Bruce Keillor, Youngstown University
Daekwan Kim, Florida State University
Ki Hee Kim, William Patterson University
Konghee Kim, St. Cloud State University
Ahmet Kirca, Michigan State University
Leonard Kloft, Wright State University
Peter Knight, Santa Clara University
Anthony Koh, University of Toledo
Stephanie Kontrim-Baumann, Missouri Baptist University
Tatiana Kostova, University of South Carolina
Chuck Kwok, University of South Carolina
Ann Langlois, Palm Beach Atlantic University
Romas Laskauskas, Stevenson University
Yikuan Lee, San Francisco State University
Bijou Lester, Drexel University
Phil Lewis, Eastern Michigan University
Charles Main, Northern Arizona University
Minghua Li, Franklin Pierce University
Peter Liesch, University of Queensland
Bob McNeal, Alabama State University–Montgomery
Bulent Menguc, Kadir Has University
Janis Miller, Clemson University
Barbara Moebius, Waukesha County Technical College
Bruce Money, Brigham Young University
Bill Murray, University of San Francisco
Paul Myer, University of Maine

Matthew B. Myers, University of Tennessee

Max Grunbaum Nagiel, Daytona State College

Kuei-Hsien Niu, Sacramento State University

Bernard O'Rourke, Caldwell College

Braimoh Oseghale, Fairleigh Dickinson University

Jeffrey W. Overby, Belmont University

Susan Peterson, Scottsdale Community College

Iordanis Petsas, University of Scranton

Zahir Quraeshi, Western Michigan University

Roberto Ragozzino, University of Central Florida

Brandon Randolph-Seng, Texas Tech University

Michelle Reina, Wisconsin Lutheran College

Elizabeth Rose, University of Otago

Michael Rubach, University of Central Arkansas

Carol Sanchez, Grand Valley State University

Hakan Saraoglu, Bryant University

Jeff Sarbaum, University of North Carolina at Greensboro

Amit Sen, Xavier University

Deepak Sethi, Old Dominion University

Karen Sneary, Northwestern Oklahoma State University

Kurt Stanberry, University of Houston–Downtown

John Stanbury, George Mason University

William Streeter, Olin Business School, Washington University in Saint Louis

Philip Sussan, University of Central Florida

Charles Ray Taylor, Villanova University

Deanna Teel, Houston Community College

Gladys Torres-Baumgarten, Ramapo College of New Jersey

Kimberly Townsend, Syracuse University

Thuhang Tran, Middle Tennessee State University

Joseph Trendowski, Old Dominion University

Sameer Vaidya, Texas Wesleyan University

Chandu Valluki, St. Mary's University of Minnesota

Cheryl Van Deusen, University of North Florida

Linn Van Dyne, Michigan State University

Davina Vora, State University of New York–New Paltz

William Walker, University of Houston

Paula Weber, St. Cloud State University

Mindy West, Arizona State University

Sidney Wheeler, Embry-Riddle Aeronautical University

Marta Szabo White, Georgia State University

Richard Wilson, Hofstra University

Yim-Yu Wong, San Francisco State University

Jennifer Woolley, Santa Clara University

Alan Wright, Troy University

Alex Xu, University of Michigan–Flint

Attila Yaprak, Wayne State University

Betty Yobaccio, Bryant University

Pierre Yourougou, Whitman School of Management, Syracuse University

Bashar Zakaria, California State University–Sacramento

Anatoly Zhuplev, Loyola Marymount University

Focus Group Participants

We were also fortunate that so many colleagues generously gave their time and offered perspectives on our teaching resources. We met with these colleagues in person, teleconferenced with them, or otherwise received their input. The insights and recommendations of these educators were instrumental in the design and format of our teaching system. We extend our gratitude and thanks to the following reviewers and colleagues.

David Ahlstrom, The Chinese University of Hong Kong

Yusaf Akbar, Southern New Hampshire University

Victor Alicea, Normandale Community College

Gail Arch, Curry College

Anke Arnaud, University of Central Florida

Choton Basu, University of Wisconsin–Whitewater

Eric Baumgardner, Xavier University

Mark Bean, Franklin Pierce College

Enoch Beraho, South Carolina State University

Paula Bobrowski, Auburn University

Teresa Brosnan, City University, Bellevue

Darrell Brown, Indiana University, Purdue University–Indianapolis

Nichole Castater, Clark Atlanta University

Aruna Chandra, Indiana State University

Mike C. H. (Chen-Ho) Chao, Baruch College, City University of New York

David Chaplin, Waldorf College

Dong Chen, Loyola Marymount University

Chen Oi Chin, Lawrence Technological University

Patrick Chinon, Syracuse University

Farok J. Contractor, Rutgers University

Angelica Cortes, University of Texas–Pan American

Michael Deis, Clayton State University

Les Dlabay, Lake Forest College

Gary Donnelly, Casper College

Gideon Falk, Purdue University–Calumet

Marc Fetscherin, Rollins College

Charles Fishel, San Jose State University

Frank Flauto, Austin Community College

Georgine K. Fogel, Salem International University

Frank Franzak, Virginia Commonwealth University

Debbie Gilliard, Metropolitan State College

Robert Goddard, Appalachian State University

Andy Grein, Baruch College, City University of New York

Andrew C. Gross, Cleveland State University

David Grossman, Goucher College

Seid Hassan, Murray State University

Wei He, Indiana State University

Xiaohong He, Quinnipiac University

Christina Heiss, University of Missouri–Kansas City

Pol Herrmann, Iowa State University

Guy Holburn, University of Western Ontario

Anisul Islam, University of Houston–Downtown

Basil Janavaras, Minnesota State University

Raj Javalgi, Cleveland State University

Ruihua Jiang, Oakland University

Yikuan Jiang, California State University–East Bay

James Kennelly, Skidmore College

Ken Kim, University of Toledo

Leonard Kloft, Wright State University

Anthony C. Koh, The University of Toledo

Ann Langlois, Palm Beach Atlantic University

Michael La Rocco, University of Saint Francis

Romas A. Laskauskas, Villa Julie College

Shaomin Li, Old Dominion University

Ted London, University of Michigan

Peter Magnusson, Saint Louis University

Charles Mambula, Suffolk University

David McArthur, Utah Valley State College

Ofer Meilich, Bradley University

Lauryn Migenes, University of Central Florida

Mortada Mohamed, Austin Community College

Robert T. Moran, Thunderbird

Carolyn Mueller, Stetson University

Kelly J. Murphrey, Texas A&M University

Lilach Nachum, Baruch College, CUNY

William Newburry, Florida International University

Stanley Nollen, Georgetown University

Augustine Nwabuzor, Florida A&M University

Bernard O'Rourke, Caldwell College

David Paul, California State University–East Bay

Christine Cope Pence, University of California Riverside

Heather Pendarvis-McCord, Bradley University

Kathleen Rehbein, Marquette University

Liesl Riddle, George Washington University

John Rushing, Barry University

Mary Saladino, Montclair State University

Carol Sanchez, Grand Valley State University

Camille Schuster, California State University–San Marcos

Eugene Seeley, Utah Valley State College

Deepak Sethi, Old Dominion University

Mandep Singh, Western Illinois University

Rajendra Sinhaa, Des Moines Area Community College

John E. Spillan, Pennsylvania State University–DuBois

Uday S. Tate, Marshall University

Janell Townsend, Oakland University

Sameer Vaidya, Texas Wesleyan University

Robert Ware, Savannah State University

Marta Szabo White, Georgia State University

Steve Williamson, University of North Florida

Lynn Wilson, Saint Leo University

Attila Yaprak, Wayne State University

Rama Yelkur, University of Wisconsin–Eau Claire

Minyuan Zhao, University of Michigan

Christopher Ziemnowicz, Concord University

Our Colleagues, Doctoral Students, and Practitioners

Numerous individuals have contributed to our thinking over the years. Through conversations, conferences, seminars, and writings, we have greatly benefited from the views and experience of international business educators and professionals from around the world. We also have had many rich conversations with the doctoral students whom we have mentored over the years.

Their names appear below if they have not been previously mentioned. Directly or indirectly, their thoughtful ideas and suggestions have had a significant impact on the development of this book. Our appreciation goes to many individuals, including:

John Abbott, The Upjohn Company

Billur Akdeniz, University of New Hampshire

Catherine N. Axinn, Ohio University

Nizam Aydin, Suffolk University

Ted Bany, The Upjohn Company

Christopher Bartlett, Harvard Business School

Vicky Bamiatzi, Leeds University

Simon Bell, University of Melbourne

Daniel C. Bello, Georgia State University

Muzaffer Bodur, Bogazici University

Jacobus Boers, Georgia State University

Nakiye Boyacigiller, Sabanci University

John Brawley, The Upjohn Company

David Bruce, Georgia State University

Kostas Bozos, Leeds University

Peter Buckley, Leeds University

Susan Caolo, Georgia State University

Jorge Carneiro, PUC–Rio, Brazil

Pedro Carrillo, Georgia State University

Erin Cavusgil, University of Michigan–Flint

Brian Chabowski, University of Tulsa

Emin Civi, University of New Brunswick, St. John, Canada

Mourad Dakhli, Georgia State University

Tevfik Dalgic, University of Texas at Dallas

Guillermo D'Andrea, Universidad Austral–Argentina

Angela da Rocha, PUC–Rio Brazil

Seyda Deligonul, St. John Fisher College

Fernando Doria, Georgia State University

Rick Della Guardia, The Upjohn Company

Deniz Erden, Bogazici University

Felicitas Evangelista, University of Western Sydney, Australia

Cuneyt Evirgen, Sabanci University

J. Betty Feng, Farmingdale State College (SUNY)

Carol Finnegan, University of Colorado at Colorado Springs

Harold Fishkin, The Upjohn Company

Michael Fishkin, Stony Brook University

Richard Fletcher, University of Western Sydney, Australia

Susan Freeman, University of South Australia

Esra Gencturk, Ozyegin University

Pervez Ghauri, Kings College London

Tracy Gonzalez-Padron, University of Colorado at Colorado Springs

David Grossman, Goucher College

Qian Gu, Georgia State University

Bill Hahn, Science Branding Communications

Tomas Hult, Michigan State University

Bryan Jean, National Cheng-Chi University

Raj Javalgi, Cleveland State University

Destan Kandemir, Bilkent University

Ilke Kardes, Georgia State University

George Kaufman, The Upjohn Company

Ihsen Ketata, Georgia State University

Irem Kiyak, Michigan State University

Tunga Kiyak, Michigan State University

Yener Kandogan, University of Michigan–Flint

Tuba Koc, Georgia State University

Phillip Kotler, Northwestern University

David Kuhlmeier, Valdosta State University

John Lavaca, Pearson Prentice Hall

Tiger Li, Florida International University

Karen Loch, Georgia State University

Mushtaq Luqmani, Western Michigan University

Robert McCarthy, The Upjohn Company

Ellen Miller, The Upjohn Company

Myron Miller, Michigan State University (ret.)

Vincent Mongello, The Upjohn Company

Robert T. Moran, Thunderbird

G. M. Naidu, University of Wisconsin–Whitewater (ret.)

John R. Nevin, University of Wisconsin

Sushil Nifadkar, Georgia State University

Gregory Osland, Butler University

Erkan Ozkaya, California Polytechnic University-Pomona

Aysegul Ozsomer, Koc University

Ayse Ozturk, Georgia State University

Ed Perper, Science Branding Communications

Morys Perry, University of Michigan–Flint

Penny Prime, Georgia State University

Hussain Rammal, University of South Australia

Vivas Reyes, Georgia State University

Alex Rialp, Universidad Autonoma de Barcelona, Spain

Tony Roath, University of Bath

Carol Sanchez, Grand Valley State University

Hakan Saraoglu, Bryant University

Michael Savitt, The Upjohn Company

Peter Seaver, The Upjohn Company

Oktay Sekercisoy, Binghamton University

Linda Hui Shi, University of Victoria

Rudolf R. Sinkovics, The University of Manchester

Carl Arthur Solberg, Norwegian School of Management, Norway

Elif Sonmez-Persinger, Eastern Michigan University

Douglas Squires, The Upjohn Company of Canada

Barbara Stoettinger, Wirtschaftuniversität, Wien, Austria

Detmar Straub, Georgia State University

Berk Talay, University of Massachusetts–Lowell

Cherian Thachenkary, Georgia State University

David Tse, University of Hong Kong

Mithat Uner, Gazi University

Nukhet Vardar, Yeditepe University

Marta Szabo White, Georgia State University

Joachim Wolf, University of Kiel

Peter Wright, University of Melbourne

Fang Wu, University of Texas–Dallas

Shichun (Alex) Xu, University of Michigan–Flint

Goksel Yalcinkaya, University of New Hampshire

Attila Yaprak, Wayne State University

Ugur Yavas, East Tennessee State University

Sengun Yeniyurt, Rutgers University

Poh-Lin Yeoh, Bentley College

Eden Yin, University of Cambridge

Chun Zhang, University of Vermont

Shaoming Zou, University of Missouri

Contributors

Mamoun Benmamoun, St. Louis University

Susan Leshnower, Midland College

Marta Szabo White, Georgia State Universtiy

Our Pearson Team

This book would not have been possible without the tireless efforts of many dedicated professionals at our publisher, Pearson. We are especially grateful to Emily Tamburri, Acquisitions Editor, Stephanie Wall, Editor-in-Chief; Eric Santucci, Editorial Assistant; Jessica Quazza, Product Marketing Assistant; Denise Weiss, Program Manager; and Meghan DeMaio, Project Manager. Our appreciation goes to many other individuals at Pearson, including Jeff Holcomb, Maggie Moylan, Kris Ellis-Levy, Sarah Holle, and Ashley Santora.

Pearson Education wishes to acknowledge and thank Jon and Diane Sutherland, Stefania Paladini (Coventry University), Krish Saha (Coventry University), Neil Pyper (Coventry University), Chin Tee Suan (Multimedia University), Bernard Bouwman (Avans Hogeschool Breda), Fuad Aliyev (Khazar University), Hamed Shamma (The American University in Cairo), Suresh George (Coventry University), and Jacques Couvas (Bilkent University) for contributing to the Global Edition, and Alice Shiu (Hong Kong Polytechnic University), Loik Allain (ESG Rennes), Anna Rosinus (University of Applied Sciences), Suresh George (Coventry University) and Panagiota Sapouna (Glasgow Caledonian University) for reviewing the Global Edition.

Chapter 1

Introduction: What Is International Business?

Learning Objectives *After studying this chapter, you should be able to:*

1.1 Describe the key concepts in international business.

1.2 Understand how international business differs from domestic business.

1.3 Identify major participants in international business.

1.4 Describe why firms internationalize.

1.5 Appreciate why you should study international business.

China Globalises London's Black Cabs

Globalisation refers to international transactions, co-operation, and competition among firms. China has become one of the most active trading nations in an increasingly globalised world. China's pursuit in transforming itself into an industrial economy gave birth to a thriving automobile industry and Geely Automobile Holdings Limited was founded in 1986. Geely is a subsidiary of Li Shufu's Zhejiang Geely Group. They began with motorcycle production and eventually started manufacturing cars in 1997. Geely's moto of 'Happy Life, Geely Drive' encompasses its customers, suppliers and human resource to manufacture safe, environmental friendly and god value automobiles. Relentless pursuit of better technology, foreign brands and oversees market resulted in Geely's European acquisition of Volvo cars in 2010 and London Taxi Company (LTC) in 2012.

London Taxi Company is the manufacturer of the iconic London Black Cabs. Coventry has been the home of the company for last 70 years. Coventry city is the birth place of British motor industry and has long tradition of manufacturing iconic automobile brands like Jaguar, Rover, Triumph, and Armstrong Siddeley. The FX4 model taxis rolled out in 1959 from Coventry plant set the quintessential shape for the black cabs. They formed partnership with Geely in 2006 which finally acquired the taxi maker in 2012 for £11.4 million after it went into administration. London Taxi Company's current annual production is approximately 2000 taxis. Geely has been constantly investing to increase capacity and competitiveness since acquisition. The company has recently announced a £250 million investment to build a new factory with a production capacity of approximately 36000 cars annually. This new investment is celebrated locally and nationally due to 1000 new jobs creation and boost to the local economy. Geely's ambition to put iconic London taxis in all major cities in the world require lots of innovation in emission technology and globalising the

Source: aslysun/Shutterstock

London taxi experience. The current technology is not suitable for bigger cities due to high emission, less fuel efficiency and bulky weight. The company has pledged to invest a further £80 million in research and development of TX5 model with hybrid engines. Hybrid and electric taxis are expected to roll out from the new factory in 2018.

Western manufacturers are also developing strong manufacturing bases in China to tap the opportunities presented by the increasing purchasing powers of Chinese people. Competition from foreign manufacturer, cost pressures due to stringent regulatory requirements at home and volatility in some export markets are some of the current challenges for Geely. The management is searching for new opportunities to overcome these challenges.

The Chinese state extended its support to fund Geely's oversees ambitions. China EXIM bank is offering a 20 billion yuan credit line to Geely. This is exciting news for privately owned enterprises in China as favourable credit lines were mostly available for the state owned enterprises (SOEs) until recently. This is an expected move from new Chinese leadership team under chronic overcapacity and mounting losses of the State Owned Enterprises.

Geely's ownership of London Taxi Company is an example of multinational corporations (MNCs) from emerging economies acquisition in the industrial hearts of developed countries. This is a fairly new phenomenon in international business which becoming more and more common with growing powers of emerging economies.

Questions

1-1. What might be the underlying motivations of emerging markets MNCs like Geely's acquisition of foreign auto brand?

1-2. How does cooperation in international business offer competitiveness?

1-3. What role can the government play in promoting internationalisation?

SOURCES: Geely warns of growing international pressure on Chinese brands' *The Financial Times*, March 19, 2014 [www.ft.com]; 'London Taxi Company Coventry plant to create 1,000 jobs' *BBC*, March 26, 2015 [www.bbc.co.uk]; The London Taxi Company official website [London-taxis.co.uk]; 'Coventry's Motor Industry, Warwickshire' *Warwickshire Life*, February 07, 2010 [www.warwickshirelife.co.uk]; Geely official website [www.global.geely.com]; 'London's Black Cabs. A Resilient, Iconic Industry In A Time Of Upheaval' *Huffington Post*, February 20, 2015 [www.huffingtonpost.co.uk]; China ExIm Bank official website [English.eximbank.gov.cn]. 'China SOE's restructuring leaves state ownership intact' *The Financial Times*, March 12, 2015 [www.ft.com].

International business
Performance of trade and investment activities by firms across national borders.

As revealed in the opening case, international business touches our daily experiences. **International business** refers to firms' performance of trade and investment activities across national borders. Because it emphasizes crossing national boundaries, we also refer to international business as *cross-border business*. Firms organize, source, manufacture, market, and conduct other value-adding activities on an international scale. They seek foreign customers and engage in collaborative relationships with foreign business partners. Although international business is performed mainly by individual firms, governments and international agencies also conduct international business activities.[1] Firms and nations exchange many physical and intellectual assets, including products, services, capital, technology, know-how, and labor. In this book, we are mainly concerned with the international business activities of the individual firm.

International business is characterized by six major dimensions, as illustrated in Exhibit 1.1. Firms' growing international activities give rise to the globalization of markets. As they venture abroad, firms undertake international trade and investment activities. In doing so, they encounter various types of risks and challenges that occur to a lesser degree, or not at all, in the home country. Participants in international business are diverse and include firms, distribution channel intermediaries, and facilitators. When they expand abroad, firms employ such international market entry strategies as exporting and direct investment. We explore each of the six dimensions in detail in this chapter.

EXHIBIT 1.1

Elements of International Business

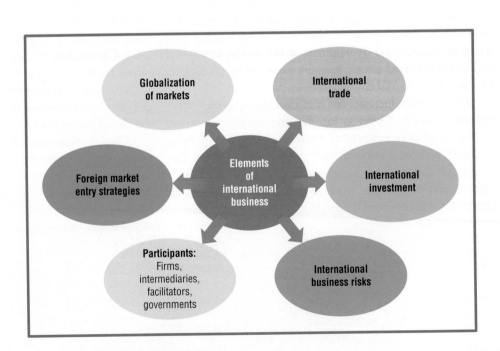

Although trading across borders has been around for centuries, contemporary international business has gained much momentum and complexity over the past four decades. Firms seek international market opportunities more than ever before. Like Vodafone, international business affects the everyday lives of people worldwide. Daily activities such as shopping, listening to music, watching a movie, or surfing the Internet involve interactions and transactions that connect you to the global economy. Internationalization of business gives you access to products and services from around the world. It profoundly affects your quality of life and economic well-being.

Modern online platforms such as Amazon, Alibaba, Facebook, and Instagram are also expressions of ongoing economic integration and growing interdependency of countries worldwide, known as the **globalization of markets**. Globalization is a macro-trend of intense economic interconnectedness among the nations of the world. A parallel trend is the ongoing internationalization of countless firms and dramatic growth in the volume and variety of cross-border transactions in goods, services, and capital flows. **Internationalization** refers to the tendency of companies to deepen their international business activities systematically. It has led to widespread diffusion of products, technology, and knowledge worldwide.

> **The globalization of markets is evident in several related trends.**
>
> - *Unprecedented growth of international trade.* In 1960, cross-border trade was modest—about $100 billion per year. Today, it accounts for a substantial proportion of the world economy, with world exports alone amounting to some $18 trillion annually—that is, $18,000,000,000,000!
> - *Trade between nations, accompanied by substantial flows of capital, technology, and knowledge.*
> - *Development of highly sophisticated global financial systems and mechanisms* that facilitate the cross-border flow of products, money, technology, and knowledge.
> - *Greater collaboration among nations* through multilateral regulatory agencies such as the World Trade Organization (WTO, www.wto.org) and the International Monetary Fund (IMF, www.imf.org).
>
> *Source:* UNCTAD, *World Investment Report*, New York: United Nations (2015), www.unctad.org; World Trade Organization, *World Trade Report*, Geneva: World Trade Organization (2015), www.wto.org.

Globalization both compels and facilitates firms to expand abroad. Simultaneously, company internationalization has become easier than ever before. A few decades ago, international business was largely the domain of large, multinational firms. Recent developments have created a more level playing field that allows all types of firms to benefit from active participation in international business. In this book, you will read about the international activities of smaller firms and those of large, multinational enterprises. You will learn about companies in the services sector that are internationalizing in such industries as banking, engineering, insurance, and retailing.

What Are the Key Concepts in International Business?

International trade describes the exchange of products (merchandise) and services (intangibles) across national borders. Exchange can occur through **exporting**, the sale of products or services to customers located abroad from a base in the home country or a third country. Exchange also can take the form of **importing or global sourcing**—the procurement of products or services from suppliers located abroad for consumption in the home country or a third country. While exporting represents the outbound flow of products and services, importing is an inbound activity. Both finished products and intermediate goods (for example, raw materials and components) can be imported and exported.

Globalization of markets
Ongoing economic integration and growing interdependency of *countries* worldwide.

Internationalization
The tendency of *companies* to deepen their international business activities systematically.

International trade
Exchange of products and services across national borders, typically through exporting and importing.

Exporting
Sale of products or services to customers located abroad from a base in the home country or a third country.

1.1 Describe the key concepts in international business

Importing or global sourcing
Procurement of products or services from suppliers located abroad for consumption in the home country or a third country.

International investment
The transfer of assets to another country or the acquisition of assets in that country.

International portfolio investment
Passive ownership of foreign securities such as stocks and bonds to generate financial returns.

Foreign direct investment (FDI)
An internationalization strategy in which the firm establishes a physical presence abroad through acquisition of productive assets such as capital, technology, labor, land, plant, and equipment.

International investment refers to the transfer of assets to another country or the acquisition of assets in that country. Economists refer to such assets as *factors of production*; they include capital, technology, managerial talent, and manufacturing infrastructure. Trade implies that products and services cross national borders. By contrast, investment implies that the firm itself crosses borders to secure ownership of assets located abroad.

The two essential types of cross-border investment are international portfolio investment and foreign direct investment. **International portfolio investment** refers to the passive ownership of foreign securities such as stocks and bonds to gain financial returns. It does not entail active management or control over these assets. The foreign investor has a relatively short-term interest in the ownership of these assets.

Foreign direct investment (FDI) is an internationalization strategy in which the firm establishes a physical presence abroad through acquisition of productive assets such as land, plant, equipment, capital, and technology. It is a foreign-market entry strategy that gives investors partial or full ownership of a productive enterprise typically dedicated to manufacturing, marketing, or management activities. Investing such resources abroad is generally for the long term and involves extensive planning.

The Nature of International Trade

Overall, export growth has outpaced the growth of domestic production during the past few decades, illustrating the fast pace of globalization. Exhibit 1.2 contrasts the growth of total world exports with the growth of total world *gross domestic product (GDP)* since 1980. GDP is defined as the total value of products and services produced in a country in the course of a year. Following a 27-year boom, world trade declined in 2009 due to the global recession. However, trade revived and returned to normal levels by 2012. Trade was a key factor reducing the impact of the global recession.[2] What is remarkable is that, since 2008, the annual rate of growth in world exports surpassed that of world GDP by almost a factor of two (5.4 versus 2.8 percent).

Three factors have been especially notable in explaining why trade growth has long outpaced GDP growth. First is the rise of emerging markets during the past three decades. These rapidly developing economies are home to swiftly growing middle-class households possessing substantial disposable income. Second, advanced (or developed) economies such as the United States and the European Union are now sourcing many of the products they consume from such low-cost manufacturing locations as China, India, and Mexico. Third, advances in information

EXHIBIT 1.2

Comparing the Growth Rates of World GDP and World Exports

Source: Based on data from the International Monetary Fund, *World Economic Outlook Database April 2015*, http://www.imf.org/external/pubs/ft/weo/2015/01/weodata/index.aspx.

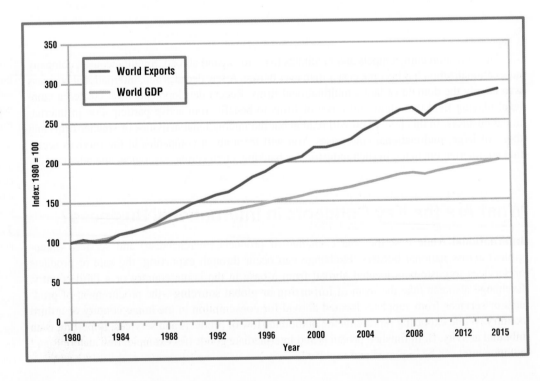

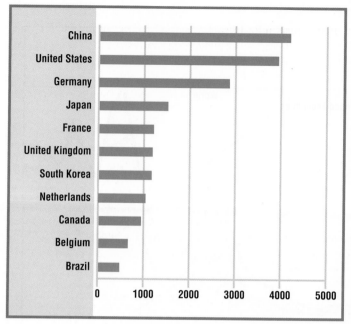

(a) Total annual value of products trade (exports + imports) in billions of U.S. dollars

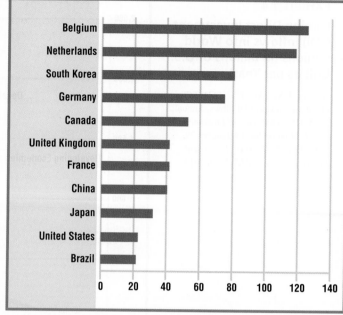

(b) Total annual value of products trade (exports + imports) as a percentage of nation's GDP

and transportation technologies, decline of trade barriers, and liberalization of markets all contribute to rapid growth of trade among nations.

Exhibit 1.3 identifies leading nations in merchandise exports (not services). Panel (a) shows the total annual value of merchandise exports and imports in billions of U.S. dollars. Panel (b) shows the annual value of products traded as a percentage of each nation's GDP. During the recent global recession, China surpassed the United States to become the world's leading exporter in total dollar terms. Trade accounts for about 45 percent of China's GDP as opposed to 23 percent for the United States. Merchandise trade is a much larger component of economic activity in countries such as Belgium (125 percent) and the Netherlands (118 percent). These percentages suggest that some countries depend very heavily on international trade relative to the value of all goods and services they produce domestically.

How can the magnitude of trade activity surpass 100 percent of a nation's GDP? How can trade activity be a multiple of national value added? The answer is that countries such as Singapore, Hong Kong, and the Netherlands are known as *entrepôt* economies. *Entrepôt* is from the French for "intermediate depot." Such countries import a large volume of products, some of which they process into higher value-added products and some they simply re-export to other destinations. For example, Singapore is a major *entrepôt* for petroleum products it receives from the Middle East, which it then exports to China and other destinations in Asia.

The Nature of International Investment

Of the two types of investment flows—portfolio investment versus foreign direct investment—we are concerned primarily with foreign direct investment (FDI) in this text because it is the ultimate form of internationalization and encompasses the widest range of international business involvement. FDI is the foreign entry strategy practiced by the most internationally active firms. Companies usually undertake FDI for the long term and retain partial or complete ownership of the assets they acquire. In the process, the firm establishes a new legal business entity in the host country, subject to the regulations of the host government.

FDI is especially common among large, resourceful companies with substantial international operations. For example, many European and U.S. firms have invested in China, India, and Russia to establish plants to manufacture or assemble products, taking advantage of low-cost labor or natural resources in these countries. At the same time, companies from these rapidly developing economies have begun to invest in Western markets. In 2008, the Turkish company Yildiz acquired the premium chocolate maker Godiva from U.S.-based Campbell

EXHIBIT 1.3

Leading Countries in International Merchandise Trade

Sources: Based on data from the World Bank, *World Development Indicators*, World Bank, Washington, DC, 2015 (www.worldbank.org); World Trade Organization, *Statistics Database*, Geneva: World Trade Organization (2015), www.wto.org; UNCTAD, *World Investment Report*, New York: United Nations (2015), www.unctad.org.

EXHIBIT 1.4

Foreign Direct Investment (FDI) Inflows into World Regions (in Billions of U.S. Dollars per Year)

Sources: UNCTAD, *UNCTADSTAT Database*, Inward FDI Flows, Annual, 2015; UNCTAD, *Global Investment Trends Monitor No. 18*, January 29, 2015; UNCTAD, *World Investment Prospects Survey 2013–2015*, 2013.

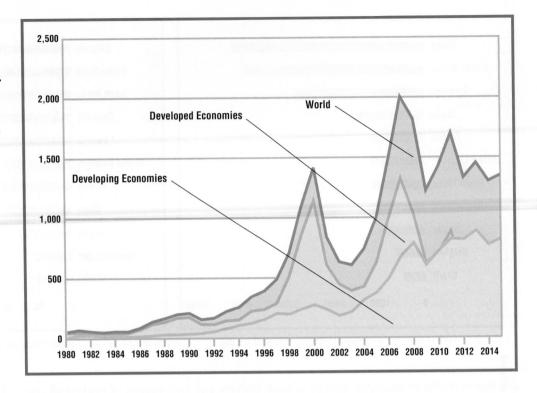

Soup Company in a deal valued at $850 million. In 2014, it paid more than $3 billion dollars to acquire British-based cookie and snack maker United Biscuits.[3]

Exhibit 1.4 illustrates the dramatic growth of FDI since the 1980s. The exhibit reveals that the dollar volume of FDI has grown immensely since the 1980s, especially in developed (advanced) economies such as Japan, Europe, and North America. FDI inflows to the developing economies began to surpass those to the advanced economies in about 2010. FDI inflows were interrupted in 2001 as investors panicked following the September 11 terrorist attacks in the United States. The inflows were interrupted again in 2008 by the global recession. These dips underscore the importance of maintaining stability in the world economy. Despite these setbacks, the overall trend remains strong and growing over time. Particularly significant is the growth of FDI into developing economies, much of which results from their need for modern industrial infrastructure. It reflects the growing importance of developing economies and emerging markets as target markets and sourcing bases.

Services as Well as Products

Historically, international trade and investment were mainly the domain of companies that make and sell products—tangible merchandise such as clothing, computers, and motor vehicles. Today, firms that produce *services* (intangibles) are key international business players as well. Services are deeds, performances, or efforts performed directly by people working in banks, consulting firms, hotels, construction companies, retailers, and countless other firms in the services sector. International trade in services accounts for about one-quarter of all international trade and is growing rapidly.

Vodafone in the opening case is a leading services firm that has internationalized rapidly. If you own a house, your mortgage might be underwritten by the Dutch bank ABN Amro. Perhaps you eat lunch in a cafeteria owned by the French firm Sodexho, which manages the food and beverage operations on numerous university campuses. Recently, Riot Games expanded its operations into Germany, Ireland, China, and Turkey to meet rapidly rising demand for its online video games. Demand for the firm's *League of Legends* game has spread rapidly, prompting the need to establish offices at gamer locations worldwide. The 2015 League of Legends World Championship attracted fans from around the world for two weeks of competition and more than 100 hours of live content broadcast in 19 languages.[4]

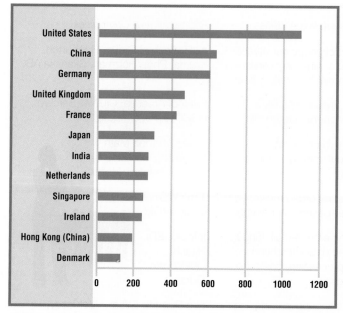

(a) Total annual value of services trade (exports + imports) in billions of U.S. dollars

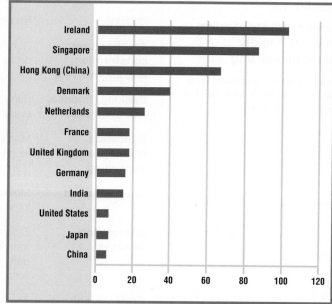

(b) Total annual value of services trade (exports + imports) as a percentage of nation's GDP

EXHIBIT 1.5

Countries Leading in International Services Trade

Sources: Based on data from the World Bank, *World Development Indicators*, Washington, DC: World Bank (2015), www.worldbank.org; World Trade Organization, *Statistics Database*, Geneva: World Trade Organization (2015), www.wto.org; UNCTAD, *World Investment Report*, New York: United Nations (2015), www.unctad. org.

Exhibit 1.5 identifies countries leading in total international services trade. Panel (a) shows the total annual value of services exports and imports in billions of U.S. dollars. Panel (b) shows the total annual value of services trade as a percentage of each nation's GDP. As with products, larger advanced economies account for most world services trade. This is expected because services typically comprise more than two-thirds of the GDPs of these countries. Recently, the emerging markets of China and India have gained strong reputations in this area. Ireland has emerged as the leader in world services trade as a percentage of GDP. Compare the value of merchandise trade in Exhibit 1.3 with the value of services trade in Exhibit 1.5 for each country. Although services trade is growing rapidly, the value of merchandise trade is still much larger. One reason is that services face greater challenges and barriers in cross-border trade than merchandise goods do.

Not all services can be exported. Examples are repair work done on your car or the experience of eating a meal in a restaurant. Although some services can be digitized and moved across borders, most service providers can operate internationally only by establishing a physical presence abroad through direct investment. Firms invest abroad to set up restaurants, retail stores, and other physical facilities through which they sell billions of dollars' worth of services every year.

There are numerous industries in the services sector with strong potential for internationalization. The giant Internet retailer eBay earned more than $75 billion in 2014, of which more than 50 percent came from international sales. The company expects that most future revenue growth will come from abroad. When developing its business in India, eBay acquired the Mumbai-based e-retailer Baazee, which followed eBay's expansion into China, Korea, and Europe.[5] Exhibit 1.6 illustrates the diversity of service sectors that are internationalizing, extending their reach beyond the countries where they are based. If you are considering a career in international business, keep these industries in mind.

The International Financial Services Sector

International banking and financial services are among the most internationally active service industries. Explosive growth of investment and financial flows has led to the emergence of capital markets worldwide. It resulted from two main factors: the internationalization of banks and the massive flow of money across national borders into pension funds and portfolio investments. In the developing economies, banks and other financial institutions have fostered economic activity by increasing the availability of local investment capital, which stimulates the development of financial markets and encourages locals to save money.

EXHIBIT 1.6

Service Industry Sectors That Are Rapidly Internationalizing

Source: Based on International Trade Administration, Washington, DC: U.S. Department of Commerce.

Industry	Representative Activities	Representative Companies
Architectural, construction, and engineering	Construction, power utilities, design, engineering services, for airports, hospitals, dams	ABB, Bechtel Group, Halliburton, Kajima, Philip Holzman, Skanska AB
Banking, finance, and insurance	Banks, insurance, risk evaluation, management	Bank of America, CIGNA, Barclays, HSBC, Ernst & Young
Education, training, and publishing	Management training, technical training, language training	Berlitz, Kumon Math & Reading Centers, NOVA, Pearson, Elsevier
Entertainment	Movies, recorded music, Internet-based entertainment	Time Warner, Sony, Virgin, MGM
Information services	E-commerce, e-mail, funds transfer, data interchange, data processing, computer services	Infosys, EDI, Hitachi, Qualcomm, Cisco
Professional business services	Accounting, advertising, legal, management consulting	Leo Burnett, EYLaw, McKinsey, A.T. Kearney, Booz Allen Hamilton
Transportation	Aviation, ocean shipping, railroads, trucking, airports	Maersk, Santa Fe, Port Authority of New Jersey, SNCF (French railroads)
Travel and tourism	Transportation, lodging, food and beverage, aircraft travel, ocean carriers, railways	Carlson Wagonlit, Marriott, British Airways

International banking is flourishing in the Middle East. For example, the return on equity in Saudi Arabia often exceeds 20 percent (compared to 15 percent in the United States and much less in France and Germany). National Commercial Bank, the biggest bank in the region, calculates that non-interest-bearing deposits comprise nearly 50 percent of total deposits in Saudi Arabia. Banks lend this free money to companies and consumers at high margins. By structuring loans as partnerships, they comply with Islamic rules that forbid banks to pay interest.[6]

1.2 Understand how international business differs from domestic business

How Does International Business Differ from Domestic Business?

Firms operate in countries characterized by distinctive economic, cultural, and political conditions. For example, the economic environment of Colombia differs sharply from that of Canada, the legal environment of Saudi Arabia does not resemble that of Japan, and the cultural environment of China is very distinct from that of Kenya. Not only does the firm find itself in unfamiliar surroundings, it encounters many *uncontrollable variables*—factors over which management has little control. These factors introduce new or elevated business risks. As exemplified by Vodafone in the opening case, distinctive conditions in each country require firms to adapt their products and approaches from country to country.

The Four Risks in Internationalization

Globalization is not without risks. When companies undertake international business, they are routinely exposed to four major types of risk, as illustrated in Exhibit 1.7. These are cross-cultural risk, country risk, currency risk, and commercial risk. The firm must manage these risks to avoid financial loss or product failures.

EXHIBIT 1.7

The Four Risks of International Business

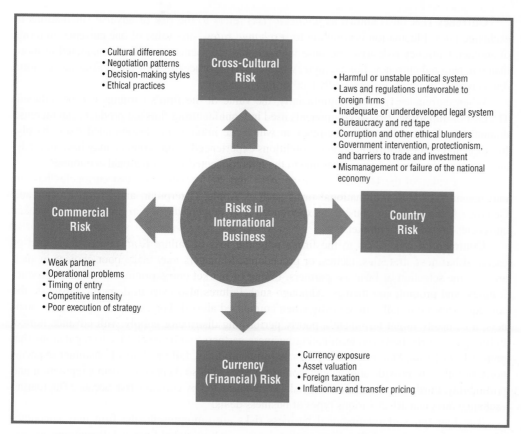

- Cultural differences
- Negotiation patterns
- Decision-making styles
- Ethical practices

Cross-Cultural Risk

- Harmful or unstable political system
- Laws and regulations unfavorable to foreign firms
- Inadequate or underdeveloped legal system
- Bureaucracy and red tape
- Corruption and other ethical blunders
- Government intervention, protectionism, and barriers to trade and investment
- Mismanagement or failure of the national economy

Commercial Risk

Risks in International Business

Country Risk

- Weak partner
- Operational problems
- Timing of entry
- Competitive intensity
- Poor execution of strategy

Currency (Financial) Risk

- Currency exposure
- Asset valuation
- Foreign taxation
- Inflationary and transfer pricing

Cross-cultural risk occurs when a cultural misunderstanding puts some human value at stake. Cross-cultural risk arises from differences in language, lifestyles, mind-sets, customs, and religion. Values unique to a culture tend to be long lasting and transmitted from one generation to the next. Values influence the mind-set and work style of employees and the shopping patterns of buyers. Foreign customer characteristics can differ significantly from those of buyers in the home market.

Language is a critical dimension of culture. In addition to facilitating communication, language is a window on people's value systems and living conditions. For example, Inuit (Eskimo) languages have various words for snow, whereas the South American Aztecs used the same basic word stem for snow, ice, and cold. When translating from one language to another, it is often difficult to find words that convey the same meanings. For example, a one-word equivalent to *aftertaste* does not exist in many languages. Such challenges impede effective communication and cause misunderstandings. Miscommunication due to cultural differences gives rise to inappropriate business strategies and ineffective relations with customers. Cross-cultural risk most often occurs in encounters in foreign countries. However, the risk also can occur domestically, as when management meets with customers or business associates who visit company headquarters from abroad.

Country risk (also known as *political risk*) refers to the potentially adverse effects on company operations and profitability caused by developments in the political, legal, and economic environment in a foreign country. Country risk includes the possibility of foreign government intervention in firms' business activities. For example, governments may restrict access to markets, impose bureaucratic procedures on business transactions, and limit the amount of income that firms can take home from foreign operations. The degree of government intervention in commercial activities varies from country to country. Singapore and Ireland are characterized by substantial economic freedom—that is, a fairly liberal economic environment. By contrast, the Chinese and Russian governments regularly intervene in business affairs.[7] Country risk also includes laws and regulations that potentially hinder company operations and performance. Critical legal dimensions include intellectual property protection, product liability, and taxation policies. Nations also experience potentially harmful economic conditions, often due to high inflation, national debt, and unbalanced international trade.

Cross-cultural risk
A situation or event in which a cultural misunderstanding puts some human value at stake.

Country risk
Potentially adverse effects on company operations and profitability caused by developments in the political, legal, and economic environment in a foreign country.

Currency risk
Risk of adverse fluctuations in exchange rates.

Currency risk (also known as *financial risk*) refers to the risk of adverse fluctuations in exchange rates. Fluctuation is common for *exchange rates*—the value of one currency in terms of another. Currency risk arises because international transactions are often conducted in more than one national currency. For example, when U.S. fruit processor Graceland Fruit Inc. exports dried cherries to Japan, it is normally paid in Japanese yen.

When currencies fluctuate significantly, the value of the firm's earnings can be reduced. The cost of importing parts or components used in manufacturing finished products can increase dramatically if the value of the currency in which the imports are denominated rises sharply. Inflation and other harmful economic conditions experienced in one country may have immediate consequences for exchange rates due to the interconnectedness of national economies.

Rising value of the U.S. dollar during 2014 and 2015 relative to most currencies has cut into revenues of U.S. multinational firms such as Apple, Caterpillar, and Pfizer. Procter and Gamble's Duracell battery business experienced a 31 percent decline in profits due to weaker currencies in its foreign markets.[8]

Commercial risk
Firms' potential loss or failure from poorly developed or executed business strategies, tactics, or procedures.

Commercial risk refers to the firm's potential loss or failure from poorly developed or executed business strategies, tactics, or procedures. Managers may make poor choices in such areas as the selection of business partners, timing of market entry, pricing, creation of product features, and promotional themes. Although such failures also exist in domestic business, the consequences are usually more costly when committed abroad. For example, in domestic business, a company might terminate a poorly performing distributor simply with advance notice. In foreign markets, however, terminating business partners can be costly due to regulations that protect local firms. Marketing inferior or harmful products, falling short of customer expectations, or failing to provide adequate customer service can also damage the firm's reputation and profitability. Furthermore, commercial risk is often affected by currency risk because fluctuating exchange rates can affect various types of business deals.

Focal firm
The initiator of an international business transaction, which conceives, designs, and produces offerings intended for consumption by customers worldwide. Focal firms are primarily MNEs and SMEs.

The four types of international business risks are omnipresent; the firm may encounter them around every corner. Some international risks, such as global financial disruptions, are extremely challenging. The Greek debt crisis has now lingered on for several years and affects not only the European Union but creditors elsewhere.[9]

Although risk cannot be avoided, it can be anticipated and managed. Experienced international firms constantly assess their environments and conduct research to anticipate potential risks, understand their implications, and take proactive action to reduce their effects. This book is dedicated to providing you, the future manager, with a solid understanding of these risks as well as managerial skills and strategies to counter them effectively.

1.3 Identify major participants in international business

Who Participates in International Business?

International business requires numerous organizations, with varying motives, to work together as a coordinated team, contributing different types of expertise and inputs. There are four major categories of participants.

Distribution channel intermediary
A specialist firm that provides various logistics and marketing services for focal firms as part of international supply chains, both in the home country and abroad.

- A **focal firm** is the initiator of an international business transaction; it conceives, designs, and produces offerings intended for consumption by customers worldwide. Focal firms take center stage in international business. They are primarily large multinational enterprises (MNEs; also known as multinational corporations, or MNCs) and small and medium-sized enterprises (SMEs). Some are privately owned companies, others are public, stock-held firms, and still others are state enterprises owned by governments. Some focal firms are manufacturing businesses; others are in the service sector.
- A **distribution channel intermediary** is a specialist firm that provides various logistics and marketing services for focal firms as part of international supply chains, both in the focal firm's home country and abroad. Typical intermediaries include independent distributors and sales representatives, usually located in foreign markets where they provide distribution and marketing services to focal firms on a contractual basis.

Facilitator
A firm or an individual with special expertise in banking, legal advice, customs clearance, or related support services that assists focal firms in the performance of international business transactions.

- A **facilitator** is a firm or an individual with special expertise in banking, legal advice, customs clearance, or related support services that helps focal firms perform international business transactions. Facilitators include logistics service providers, freight forwarders, banks, and other support firms that assist focal firms in performing specific functions. A **freight forwarder** is a specialized logistics service provider that arranges international shipping on behalf of exporting firms, much like a travel agent for cargo. Facilitators are found in both the home country and abroad.

- *Governments*, or the public sector, are also active in international business as suppliers, buyers, and regulators. State-owned enterprises account for a substantial portion of economic value added in many countries, even rapidly liberalizing emerging markets such as Russia, China, and Brazil. Governments in advanced economies such as France, Australia, and Sweden have significant ownership of companies in telecommunications, banking, and natural resources. The recent global financial crisis led governments to step up their involvement in business, especially as regulators.

The activities of firms, intermediaries, and facilitators in international business overlap to some degree. The focal firm performs certain activities internally and delegates other functions to intermediaries and facilitators when their special expertise is needed. In other words, the focal firm becomes a client of intermediaries and facilitators who provide services on a contractual basis.

Whereas focal firms, intermediaries, and facilitators represent the supply side of international business transactions, customers or buyers make up the demand side. Customers consist of:

- Individual *consumers and households*.
- *Retailers*—businesses that purchase finished goods for the purpose of resale.
- *Organizational buyers*—businesses, institutions, and governments that purchase goods and services as inputs to a production process or as supplies needed to run a business or organization. Governments and nonprofit organizations such as CARE (www.care.org) and UNICEF (www.unicef.org) also often constitute important customers around the world.

Focal Firms in International Business

Imagine a typical theatrical production. It has script writers, stage managers, lighting technicians, musicians, set directors, business managers, and publicity staff in addition to performing actors. Each participant contributes in different ways, and much coordination is required among them. Advanced planning, preparation, timeliness, and synchronization are critical to ultimate success. In the same way, international business transactions require the participation of many specialist organizations, exact timing, and precision.

Focal firms are the most prominent international players. They include well-known multinational enterprises and small and medium-sized exporting firms as well as contemporary organizations such as the born global firms. Let's learn more about each of these key actors in international business.

A **multinational enterprise (MNE)** is a large company with substantial resources that performs various business activities through a network of subsidiaries and affiliates located in multiple countries. Leading MNEs are listed in the *Fortune Global 500* (www.fortune.com). Examples include well-known companies such as Nestlé, Sony, Citibank, Unilever, Nokia, Ford, Barclays, DHL, Four Seasons Hotels, and Shell Oil. In recent years, the largest MNEs have been firms in the oil industry (such as Exxon-Mobil and Royal Dutch Shell) and the automotive industry (General Motors and Honda) as well as in retailing (Walmart).

Although MNEs employ a range of foreign market entry strategies, they are best known for their foreign direct investment (FDI) activities. They operate in multiple countries, especially in Asia, Europe, and North

Freight forwarder
A specialized logistics service provider that arranges international shipping on behalf of exporting firms.

Multinational enterprise (MNE)
A large company with substantial resources that performs various business activities through a network of subsidiaries and affiliates located in multiple countries.

Source: Used with permission from The Coca Cola Company

The Coca-Cola Company is a leading example of a multinational company. Today, about 80 percent of Coca-Cola's revenues are generated outside of the United States. As a billion people rise into the middle class in the next decade, the company expects an even greater share of sales to come from emerging and developing markets around the world. Management expects more revenue from sales of juice, tea, coffee, value-added dairy and other beverages that make up its vast portfolio. Pictured is the President of Coca-Cola International, Ahmet Bozer.

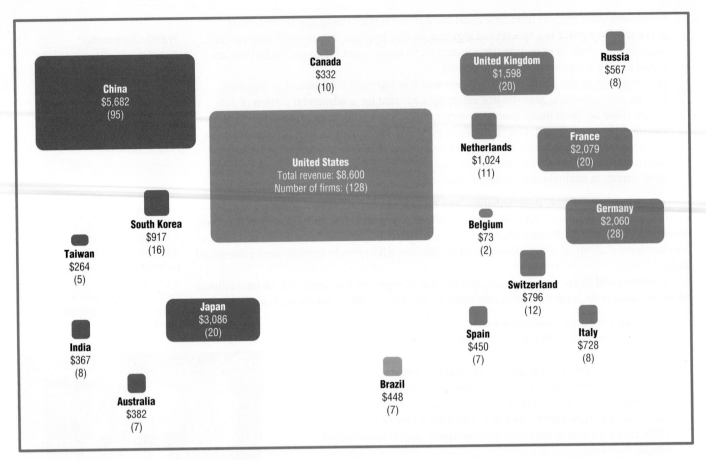

EXHIBIT 1.8

Geographic Distribution of the Headquarters of the World's 500 Largest MNEs (Exhibit shows country name, total revenues of Global 500 firms in U.S. dollars, and total number of Global 500 firms)

Sources: Scott Decarlo, "Global 500: A New World Order," *Fortune*, February 1, 2015, pp. 18–19; *Fortune*, "Global 500," Special Section, July 21, 2014, pp. F1–F8.

America, by setting up production plants, marketing subsidiaries, and regional headquarters. MNEs such as Exxon, Honda, and Coca-Cola derive much of their total sales and profits, often more than half, from cross-border operations. Although there were fewer than 7,500 MNEs worldwide in 1970, today the total count stands at roughly 80,000.[10]

Exhibit 1.8 displays the geographic distribution of the world's largest MNEs, drawn from *Fortune*'s Global 500 list. These firms are concentrated in the advanced economies. The United States was home to 128 of the top 500 MNEs in 2014, a number that has declined over time as other countries' firms increase in size. China has the second-most MNEs (95 firms), and Europe is home to many top MNEs: Germany (28 firms), France (20 firms), and the United Kingdom (20 firms).[11]

In recent years, large MNEs have begun to appear in emerging market countries, such as China, Mexico, and Russia. China currently hosts 95 of the top 500 MNEs, a number that has increased from only 15 countries in the past 10 years. Nearly all of China's top firms are state enterprises—owned by the Chinese government, which provides them substantial advantages.[12]

The new global challenge firms from emerging markets are fast becoming key contenders in world markets. For example, the Mexican firm Cemex is one of the world's largest cement producers; in Russia, Lukoil has big ambitions in the global energy sector; and China Mobile dominates the cell phone industry in Asia. These companies make best use of home–country natural resources and low-cost labor to succeed in world markets. Thousands of firms from emerging markets have big global dreams and pose competitive challenges to companies from the advanced economies.[13]

Small- and Medium-Sized Enterprises

Another type of focal firm that initiates cross-border business transactions is the SME. As defined in Canada and the United States, **small- and medium-sized enterprises (SMEs)** are manufacturers or service providers with fewer than 500 employees. (In the European Union and numerous other countries, they are defined as having fewer than 250 employees.) SMEs now make up the majority of companies active in international business. Nearly all firms, including large MNEs, started out small. Compared to large multinationals, SMEs can be more flexible and quicker to respond to global business opportunities. They are usually less bureaucratic, more adaptable, and more entrepreneurial and often sustain entrepreneurship and innovation in national economies.

Being smaller organizations, SMEs are constrained by limited financial and human resources. This explains why they usually choose exporting as their main strategy for entering foreign markets. Their limited resources prevent them from undertaking FDI, an expensive entry mode. As their operations grow, some gradually establish company-owned sales offices or subsidiaries in key target markets.

Due to their smaller size, SMEs often target specialized products to market niches too small to interest large MNEs. SMEs owe much of their international success to support provided by intermediaries and facilitators in foreign markets and to globe-spanning logistics specialists such as FedEx and DHL. Smaller firms also rely on information and communications technologies that allow them to identify global market niches and efficiently serve specialized buyer needs. SMEs are gaining equal footing with large multinationals in marketing sophisticated products around the world.

Small and medium-sized enterprise (SME) A company with 500 or fewer employees (as defined in Canada and the United States).

Born Global Firms

One type of contemporary international SME is the **born global firm**, a young entrepreneurial company that initiates international business activity very early in its evolution, moving rapidly into foreign markets. Despite the scarce resources typical of most small businesses, born globals usually internationalize within three years of their founding and may export to twenty or more countries, generating over 25 percent of their sales from abroad.

One example is History and Heraldry (www.historyandheraldry.com), a born global in the United Kingdom specializing in gifts for history buffs and those with English ancestry. In its first five years, the firm expanded its sales to sixty countries, exporting about 70 percent of its total production. History and Heraldry's biggest markets are France, Germany, Italy, Spain, and the Americas. It recently opened a subsidiary in North America.[14]

Born global firm A young entrepreneurial company that initiates international business activity early in its evolution, moving rapidly into foreign markets.

The born global phenomenon represents a new reality in international business. In countries like Australia, Denmark, Ireland, and the United States, born globals account for a substantial proportion of national exports. They use the Internet and communications technologies to facilitate early and efficient international operations. In many cases, born globals offer leading-edge products with strong potential to generate international sales.

The emergence of born globals is associated with *international entrepreneurship*, in which innovative, smaller firms pursue business opportunities everywhere, regardless of national borders. Communications and transportation technologies, falling trade barriers, and the emergence of niche markets worldwide have increased the ability of contemporary firms to view the whole world as their marketplace. Entrepreneurial managers are creative, proactive, and comfortable dealing with risk. They are usually quick to adapt company strategies as circumstances evolve. The widespread emergence of born globals implies that any firm, regardless of size or experience, can succeed in international business.[15]

Source: gyn9037/Shutterstock

Born global firms are international from their founding. Vix Technology is an Australian born global that makes fare management equipment for public transit systems worldwide.

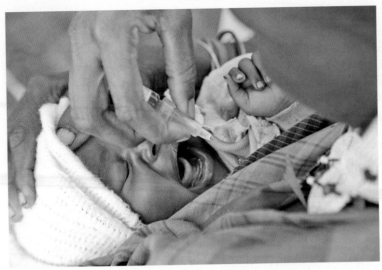

Source: Maciej Dakowicz/Alamy

The British Wellcome Trust funds nongovernmental organizations (NGOs) and research initiatives to work in collaboration with private businesses to develop remedies for diseases in Africa and other less developed areas.

Governments and Nongovernmental Organizations

In addition to profit-seeking focal firms, governments are central participants in international trade and investment. Their role is so important that we devote later chapters to government intervention, political systems, and other government-related topics. In addition, numerous *nonprofit organizations* conduct cross-border activities, including charitable groups and *nongovernmental organizations (NGOs)*. They work on behalf of special causes, such as education, research, health care, human development, and the natural environment, operating internationally either to conduct their activities or to raise funds. Examples of nonprofit organizations include the Bill and Melinda Gates Foundation and the British Wellcome Trust, both of which support health and educational initiatives. CARE is an international nonprofit organization dedicated to reducing poverty. Many MNEs operate charitable foundations that support various initiatives. GlaxoSmithKline (GSK), the giant pharmaceutical firm, operates a number of small, country-based foundations in Canada, France, Italy, Romania, Spain, and the United States.

1.4 Describe why firms internationalize

Why do Firms Internationalize?

There are multiple motives for international expansion, some strategic in nature, others reactive. An example of a strategic, or proactive, motive is to tap foreign market opportunities or to acquire new knowledge. An example of a reactive motive is the need to serve a key customer that has expanded abroad. Specific motivations include the following:

- *Seek opportunities for growth through market diversification.* Substantial market potential exists abroad. Many firms—for example, Gillette, Siemens, Sony, and Biogen—derive more than half of their sales from international markets.[16] In addition to offering sales opportunities that often cannot be matched at home, foreign markets can extend the marketable life of products or services that have reached maturity in the home market. One example is the internationalization of automatic teller machines (ATMs). The first ATMs were installed in London by Barclays Bank. The machines were adopted next in the United States and Japan. As growth of ATMs began to slow in these countries, they were marketed throughout the rest of the world. There were more than three million ATMs worldwide in 2015; a new one is installed somewhere every few minutes.
- *Earn higher margins and profits.* For many types of products and services, market growth in mature economies is sluggish or flat. Competition is often intense, forcing firms to get by on slim profit margins. By contrast, most foreign markets may be underserved (typical of high-growth emerging markets) or not served at all (typical of developing economies). Less intense competition, combined with strong market demand, implies that companies can command higher margins for their offerings. For example, compared to their home markets, bathroom fixture manufacturers American Standard and Toto (of Japan) have found more favorable competitive environments in rapidly industrializing countries such as Indonesia, Mexico, and Vietnam. Just imagine the demand for bathroom fixtures in the thousands of office buildings and residential complexes going up from Taiwan to Turkey!
- *Gain new ideas about products, services, and business methods.* International markets are characterized by tough competitors and demanding customers with various needs. Unique foreign environments expose firms to new ideas for products, processes, and business

methods. The experience of doing business abroad helps firms acquire new knowledge for improving organizational effectiveness and efficiency. For example, Japan's Toyota refined just-in-time inventory techniques, which other manufacturers and foreign suppliers around the world then applied to manufacturing in their own countries.

- *Serve key customers better that have relocated abroad.* In a global economy, many firms internationalize to better serve clients that have moved into foreign markets. For example, when Nissan opened its first factory in the United Kingdom, many Japanese auto parts suppliers followed, establishing their own operations there.

- *Be closer to supply sources, benefit from global sourcing advantages, or gain flexibility in product sourcing.* Companies in extractive industries such as petroleum, mining, and forestry establish international operations where raw materials are located. One example is the aluminum producer Alcoa, which established operations in Brazil, Guinea, Jamaica, and elsewhere to extract aluminum's base mineral bauxite from local mines. Some firms internationalize to gain flexibility from a greater variety of supply bases. Dell Computer has assembly facilities in Asia, Europe, and the Americas that allow management to shift production quickly from one region to another. This flexibility provides Dell with competitive advantages over less agile rivals—a distinctive capability that allows Dell to outperform competitors and skillfully manage fluctuations in currency exchange rates.

- *Gain access to lower-cost or better-value factors of production.* Internationalization enables the firm to access capital, technology, managerial talent, and labor at lower costs, higher quality, or better value. For example, some Taiwanese computer manufacturers established subsidiaries in the United States to access low-cost capital. The United States is home to numerous capital sources in the high-tech sector, such as stock exchanges and venture capitalists, which have attracted many firms from abroad seeking funds. More commonly, firms venture abroad in search of skilled or low-cost labor. For example, the Japanese firm Canon relocated much of its production to China to profit from that country's inexpensive and productive workforce.

- *Develop economies of scale in sourcing, production, marketing, and R&D.* Economies of scale reduce the per-unit cost of manufacturing by operating at high volume. For example, the per-unit cost of manufacturing 100,000 cameras is much cheaper than the per-unit cost of making just 100 cameras. By expanding internationally, the firm greatly increases the size of its customer base, thereby increasing the volume of goods it produces. On a per-unit-of-output basis, the greater the volume of production, the lower the total cost. Economies of scale are also present in R&D, sourcing, marketing, distribution, and after-sales service.

- *Confront international competitors more effectively or thwart the growth of competition in the home market.* International competition is substantial and increasing, with multinational competitors invading markets worldwide. The firm can enhance its competitive positioning by confronting competitors in international markets or preemptively entering a competitor's home market to destabilize and curb its growth. One example is Caterpillar's entry in Japan to confront its main rival in the earthmoving equipment industry, Komatsu. Caterpillar's preemptive move hindered Komatsu's international expansion for at least a decade. Had it not acted proactively to stifle Komatsu's growth in Japan, Komatsu's home market, Caterpillar would certainly have had to face a more potent rival sooner.

- *Invest in a potentially rewarding relationship with a foreign partner.* Firms often have long-term strategic reasons for venturing abroad. Joint ventures or project-based alliances with key foreign players can lead to the development of new products, early positioning in future key markets, or other long-term, profit-making opportunities. For example, Black and Decker

Source: Tim Drape/Dorling Kindersley Limited

A vibrant workforce is driving economic development and buying power in emerging markets. Here consumers flock to a popular shopping street in Beijing, China.

entered a joint venture with Bajaj, an Indian retailer, to position itself for expected long-term sales in the huge Indian market. The French computer firm Groupe Bull partnered with Toshiba in Japan to gain insights for developing the next generation of information technology.

At the broadest level, companies internationalize to enhance competitive advantage and find growth and profit opportunities. Throughout this book, we explore the environment within which firms seek these opportunities, and we discuss the strategies and managerial skills necessary for achieving international business success.

 MyManagementLab   **Watch It!**

If your professor has assigned this, go to the Assignments section of **mymanagementlab.com** to complete the video exercise titled MINI: Globalization

1.5 Appreciate why you should study international business

Why Study International Business?

There are many reasons to study international business. We examine them from the perspectives of the global economy, the national economy, the firm, and you as a future manager.

Facilitator of the Global Economy and Interconnectedness

International business is transforming the world as never before. In the past 50 years, international trade and investment have experienced unprecedented growth. Since the 1980s, *emerging markets* have provided new impetus to worldwide economic interconnectedness. These fast-growth developing economies—some thirty countries, including Brazil, Russia, India, and China, the so-called BRICs—are experiencing substantial market liberalization, privatization, and industrialization, which are fueling global economic transformation.

Contributor to National Economic Well-Being

International business contributes to economic prosperity, helps countries use their resources more efficiently, and provides interconnectedness to the world economy and access to a range of products and services. Consequently, governments have become more willing to open their borders to foreign trade and investment.

International trade is a critical engine for job creation. It is estimated that every $1 billion increase in exports creates more than 20,000 new jobs. In the United States, cross-border trade directly supports at least 12 million jobs. One of every seven dollars of U.S. sales is made abroad. One of every three U.S. farm acres and one of every six U.S. jobs is producing for export markets. On average, exporting firms create jobs faster and provide better pay than nonexporting firms.[17]

A Competitive Advantage for the Firm

To sustain a competitive advantage in the global economy, firms must readily participate in cross-border business and acquire the necessary skills, knowledge, and competence. Procter & Gamble sells shampoo, disposable diapers, and other consumer products in more than 150 countries. MTV broadcasts its programming in some 140 countries. Nestlé sells its food and beverage products worldwide, obtaining nearly all its revenue from foreign operations. As these examples imply, going international offers countless opportunities for firms to grow and earn additional profits.

Source: Dmitriy Shironosov/123RF

International trade is encouraging faster diffusion of consumer products and brands around the world.

ASHLEY LUMB

Ashley's Majors: Finance and International Business
Objectives: Adventure, international perspective, self-understanding, career growth, and the opportunity to learn foreign languages
Internships during college: Merrill Lynch
Jobs held since graduating:
- Junior Analyst, KPMG, London, England
- Marketing Representative, Vins Sans Frontieres, Nice, France
- Account Representative, The Ultimate Living Group, Monte Carlo, Monaco
- Marketing Associate, Made in Museum, Rome, Italy
- Advertising/Marketing Coordinator, Vogue Italia, New York, United States

In Ashley Lumb's senior year in college, a six-week study abroad program to Europe sparked a desire for an international career. Following graduation, Ashley interned as a Junior Analyst at KPMG in London, where she gained technical training and analytical skills. She took a six-month contract job at Vins Sans Frontieres (VSF), where she enrolled in its wine courses at the company headquarters in the south of France. VSF imports wine from around the world and sells it exclusively to private yachts along the French Riviera. Ashley gained experience in various marketing methods. For example, VSF attends yacht trade fairs and hosts wine tastings. Its marketing reps like Ashley scour the ports from San Remo, Italy, to St. Tropez, France, daily, speaking with yacht chefs, stewards, or captains about wine and distributing wine catalogs.

Ashley then took up a position as a marketing associate at Made in Museum (MIM) in Rome, Italy. MIM specializes in the design, production, and delivery of authorized museum reproductions and markets jewelry, sculptures, mosaics, and Etruscan pottery. Ashley organized the products into groups and restructured the inventory and website.

While in Italy, Ashley developed a passion for the fashion industry, so she decided to move to New York. Before leaving Italy, Ashley took a course entitled "Business and Marketing in the Fashion Industry" at the prestigious Polimoda International Institute of Design and Marketing in Florence. In New York, Ashley worked at the headquarters of fashion houses Hermès and J. Crew. Subsequently, she used the services of a bilingual recruiting agency, Euromonde Inc., to land a job at Vogue Italia magazine in Times Square to work as the U.S. advertising/marketing coordinator. Ashley also worked at Vogue India in Mumbai and Vogue Turkey in Istanbul. In 2014, Ashley held a position in the Middle East Department of the British Museum in London.

Ashley's Advice for an International Career

"Working abroad helped me sort through my career goals, as Europe offered a view into other industries that the U.S. lacked. I was able to experience different cultures and work environments and, although they might seem far apart, I saw a shared passion for exceptional products and dynamism. Back in the U.S., my international experience was an impressive asset to prospective employers; it is valued as proof of one's ability to handle challenging assignments and work with people from diverse cultures and backgrounds."

Success Factors

"The two most important factors in working abroad were hard work and networking. I cast a wide net and met many people, sent a lot of résumés, asked many questions, and researched the market. To keep myself afloat between assignments, I took some unglamorous jobs. Some days I wanted to give up and go home, but instead I just kept going.... Hard work and persistence are crucial."

Challenges

"The decision to work abroad carries some risks. After all, you're leaving much of what you know behind and stepping outside a clearly defined career path. The language barrier is always present. The work was usually in English, though I did pick up Italian and a bit of French through classes and immersing myself in the culture."

Source: Courtesy of Ashley Lumb.

A Competitive Advantage for You

Although most international careers are based in one's home country, managers travel the world and meet people from various cultures and backgrounds. Traveling abroad leads to exciting challenges and learning experiences. Managers rising to the top of most of the world's leading corporations honed their managerial skills in international business. In this text, you will learn about the merits of gaining international business proficiency, through the experiences of people like you, in a special feature called *You Can Do It: Recent Grad in IB*. Read about Ashley Lumb, a recent graduate who is enjoying her early experiences in international business.

An Opportunity to Support Sustainability and Corporate Citizenship

As the world's population grows, so do pressures to meet consumer demand in a sustainable way. Increasingly, companies operate in environments characterized by limited resources, vulnerable human conditions, and stakeholder consciousness on issues that affect all society. In response to this trend, companies are expanding their awareness about the social and environmental implications of their actions. Rather than being caught off guard, firms increasingly develop socially responsible policies and practices. For example, Starbucks began selling coffee only from growers certified by the Rain Forest Alliance (www.rainforest-alliance.org), a nonprofit organization that promotes the interests of coffee growers and the environment. Such multinational enterprises as Philips, Unilever, and Walmart follow business practices that promote sustainable development. McDonald's buys beef from farmers who meet special standards on animal welfare and environmental practices. Its outlets in Austria, Germany, Sweden, and the United Kingdom sell only organic milk.[18] Internationally active firms must embed corporate citizenship in their strategic decisions as well as their ongoing processes and practices. Ethics and responsible behavior in firms' international activities are of such importance that we devote Chapter 4 to this topic.

CLOSING CASE   Internationalization at Vodafone

Vodafone, a British company headquartered in Newbury, Berkshire, England, is the world's second largest mobile communications operator, with networks in 64 countries in five continents, serving 458 million customers. Its annual revenues in 2015 were UK £ 42.2 billion and its EBIDTA £ 11.9 billion. (1 £ = $ 1.51 or € 1.40).

About 90% of Vodafone's revenues come from voice communications. But data over mobile devices is gaining momentum. More than 20 million of its customers were already using 4G services in 2015. Industry forecasts predict a total of 7 billion mobile phone subscribers by 2016, with 2 billion using smartphones.

The company's business is organized in four major product units:

- *Consumer Services, Europe:* 41% of the company's service revenues in 2015. This segment is sensitive to availability of 4G networks.
- *Unified Communications:* 20% of revenues. It aims at satisfying increasing customer demand for bundling multiple technologies: 3G, 4G, WiFi, cable, and fibre.
- *Consumer Services, Emerging Markets:* 23% of revenues. Mobile banking and data are core activities of this business unit, with sales doubling annually since 2011.
- *Enterprise Services:* 27% of revenues. High growth potential, as ubiquitous round-the-clock customer and employee relations are becoming a standard enterprise practice

Regulatory and Technology Challenges, and Opportunities

Vodafone began its activities in 1982 as Racal Electronics, a manufacturer of military communications equipment, and entered the civil cellular sector in 1985, at a time when telecommunications was a highly regulated industry in most of the world. Deregulation in Europe began in mid-1980s, first in Britain and later in Continental Europe. This development was followed in the 1990s by the introduction of a pan-European technological standard, the Global System for Mobiles ('GSM'), which is now used in 219 countries on harmonized frequencies that enable seamless roaming. Vodafone was one of the very first telecommunications services providers to convert its network to the new technology.

Threat of Foreign Competitors

The advent of GSM and the abolition of state monopolies in EU mobile telephony stimulated speculative investors to get into the industry. By 1998 there were in the average three mobile operators per country. The more ambitious ones, from France and Germany, quickly saw opportunities for expansion in the Continent and Britain. Vodafone came under attack, through alliances built by competitors wanting to exploit the UK market.

International Expansion

In a defensive reaction, Vodafone's management began contemplating overseas expansion. It considered that confronting its major Continental competitors head-on was risky. Its first internationalization moves were towards former British colonies and protectorates, such as Gulf States and Malta, where cultural differences were low. The business potential of these markets was, however, limited. In a bold move, the company decided to sail across the Atlantic, where cellular telephony was still fragmented with scores of small operators jockeying for limited geographical territories. The British company was in June 1999 successful in acquiring 45% stake in AirTouch Cellular, a Californian corporation using AMPS technology standard. It was a year later renamed to Verizon Wireless.

Confident after this strategic move, Vodafone made an offer to buy controlling interest in Germany's second largest mobile operator, Mannesmann, which was already in partnership negotiations with two heavyweights of the industry, Hong Kong's Hutchinson Whampoa and France's Vivendi. But quickly Mannesmann's CEO and Board replied they were not interested to sell. Vodafone swiftly made a hostile take-over bid directly to the German company's shareholders. In spite of resistance from the German government and general public, Vodafone in February 2000 succeeded to strike a friendly merger, paying $180.95 billion for the control of 50.5% of the new company. This transaction, the largest cross-border merger ever, did not involve any cash: Mannesmann's shareholders received Vodafone shares in lieu of payment.

This company's global expansion followed rapidly, and the stock-swap payment method has been enshrined in Vodafone's financial strategy. Its strategic goal has also remained steady: to invest in the number two operator in the target country. Vodafone's network is today composed of 24 wholly- or majority-owned subsidiaries and 40 associated, partnership and joint venture operations. Customer billing is done in local currencies. Through interconnection agreements, Vodafone also offers its users roaming to practically any country on the globe. Its submarine cable infrastructure reaches 100 countries.

Vodafone is a truly multicultural organization. It employs 101,443 persons from two-dozen different nationalities. Its CEO is an Italian, while his predecessor was Indian. Women occupy 24% of senior management positions.

The Emerging Markets have taken prominence in the company's internationalization strategy, with emphasis on Asia and Sub-Saharan Africa. Vodafone is organized in two geographical divisions: Europe and AMAP (Africa, Middle East, Asia-Pacific), which contribute at 66% and 32% respectively to total revenues. Vodafone failed to enter the Chinese market with an acquisition, but it broke-through in India, where today it serves 142 million customers.

Expansion Hurdles and the Future

Vodafone's internationalization has not always been smooth. Technology incompatibility with national standards in Japan and America, shareholders' appetite for dividends, and cross-cultural issues in certain markets have forced the management to divest from its ventures in Japan, France, and USA, thus reducing the company's market value. It has now become a target of take-over bids by China Mobile, world's largest mobile operator, and AT&T of Dallas, Texas. In Europe, where mobile telephony revenues have fallen 11% between 2009 and 2015, industry consolidation is in the air, with Orange, Telefonica, Hatchinson Whampoa, Liberty, new-entrant Altice, and corporate raiders looking for acquisitions. Vodafone may benefit from this race, or become its victim.

Case Questions

1-4. What is the nature of the international business environments Vodafone faces? What types of risk does the firm face?

1-5. How has Vodafone benefited from expanding abroad? What types of advantages has the company obtained from its international expansion? What advantages acquired overseas can help Vodafone maintain its leadership in Europe?

1-6. What is the underlying rationale for Vodafone's expansion strategy to invest in the number two operator of a target country, instead of the incumbent number one?

1-7. Why did Vodafone expand first towards the U.S., through the acquisition of 45% of AirTouch's share, although there was no technology compatibility between North America and Europe, making roaming and other synergies between the UK and U.S. networks impossible? What competences did the company have that it could use in this venture?

1-8. Why did the German government and public resist the acquisition of Mannesmann by Vodafone in late 1999? Are there any similarities with the lack of success of the company to acquire a local Chinese operator, or a stake in China Mobile in recent years?

Sources: Ruth Bender and Shayndi Raice "European Telecom Companies Race to Merge", Wall Street Journal, June 1, 2015, retrieved from http://www.wjs.com; J. Couvas, *Vodafone: An English Saga* (Mumbai, Schroff, 2008); GSM Association, *The Mobile Economy 2015*, retrieved from http://www.gsmaintelligence.com; S. Kedia, *Vodafone AirTouch's Bid for Mannesmann* (Boston, HBSP, 2003); Gautam Naik and Anita Raghavan, "Vodafone, Mannesmann Set Takeover at $180.95 Billion After Long Struggle", *Wall Street Journal*, February 4, 2000, retrieved from http://www.wsj.com; Markus Walker, "The bid that couldn't fail", *Euromoney*, March 2000, retrieved from http://www.euromoney.com; "Mobile subscriptions near the 7-billion mark", *ITU News*, September 2015, retrieved from http://www.itu.int; Vodafone Group Plc Annual Report 2015, retrieved from http://www.vodafone.com.

END OF CHAPTER REVIEW

 MyManagementLab

Go to **mymanagementlab.com** to complete the problems marked with this icon .

Key Terms

born global firm   45
commercial risk   42
country risk   41
cross-cultural risk   41
currency risk   42
distribution channel intermediary   42
exporting   35

facilitator   42
focal firm   42
foreign direct investment (FDI)   36
freight forwarder   43
globalization of markets   35
importing or global sourcing   35
international business   45

international investment   36
international portfolio investment   36
international trade   35
internationalization   35
multinational enterprise (MNE)   43
small and medium-sized enterprises
   (SMEs)   35

Summary

In this chapter, you learned about:

- **Key concepts in international business**

  International business refers to the performance of trade and investment activities by firms across national borders. **Globalization of markets** is the ongoing economic integration and growing interdependency of countries worldwide. International business is characterized by international trade and investment. **International trade** refers to exchange of products and services across national borders, typically through exporting and importing. **Exporting** is the sale of products or services to customers located abroad from a base in the home country or a third country. **Importing** or **global sourcing** refers to procurement of products or services from foreign suppliers for consumption in the home country or a third country. **International investment** refers to international transfer or acquisition of ownership in assets. **International portfolio investment** is passive ownership of foreign securities such as stocks and bonds to generate financial returns. Using **foreign direct investment**, the firm establishes a physical presence abroad through acquisition of productive assets such as capital, technology, labor, land, plant, and equipment.

- **How international business differs from domestic business**

  International firms are constantly exposed to four major categories of risk that must be managed. **Cross-cultural risk** refers to a situation or event when some human value has been put at stake due to a cultural misunderstanding. **Country risk** refers to the potentially adverse effects on company operations and profitability caused

by developments in the political, legal, and economic environment in a foreign country. **Currency risk** refers to the risk of adverse fluctuations in exchange rates. **Commercial risk** arises from the possibility of a firm's loss or failure from poorly developed or executed business strategies, tactics, or procedures. The risks are ever-present in international business, and firms take proactive steps to reduce their effects.

- **Who participates in international business**

  A key participant in international business is the **multinational enterprise (MNE)**, a large company with many resources whose business activities are performed by a network of subsidiaries located in multiple countries. Also active in international business are **small and medium-sized enterprises (SMEs)**, companies with 500 or fewer employees. **Born global firms** are entrepreneurial firms that initiate international business from or near their founding. Nongovernmental organizations (NGOs) are nonprofit organizations that pursue special causes and serve as an advocate for the arts, education, politics, religion, and research.

- **Why firms internationalize**

  Companies internationalize for various reasons. These include the ability to increase sales and profits, serve customers better, access lower-cost or superior production factors, optimize sourcing activities, develop economies of scale, confront competitors more effectively, develop rewarding relationships with foreign partners, and gain access to new ideas for creating or improving products and services.

- **Why you should study international business**

  There are many reasons to study international business. It enhances a firm's competitive positioning in the global market, facilitates development of the global economy and of the interconnectedness among nations, and contributes to national economic well-being. From a career standpoint, learning about international business will provide you with a competitive edge and enhance your ability to thrive in the job market. Firms have various opportunities for ethical corporate citizenship abroad.

Test Your Comprehension   AACSB: Reflective Thinking

1-9. What is involved in the process of internationalization?

1-10. What is the difference between exporting and foreign direct investment?

⭐ **1-11.** What makes international business different from domestic business?

1-12. What are the various types of risks that firms face when they conduct international business?

1-13. Who are the major participants in international business?

1-14. What is the difference between a multinational enterprise (MNE) and a small and medium-sized enterprise (SME)?

1-15. What are some of the key motivations for firms to engage in international business?

1-16. Why should you care about international business?

Apply Your Understanding   AACSB: Communication, Reflective Thinking, Ethical Reasoning

⭐ **1-17.** In the role of financial advisor MaggieCercado, a client has approached you for guidance. The client is convinced that there is no immediate advantage in investing in domestic businesses or markets and wants to invest abroad. He wants advice regarding the transfer of his substantial assets to make a series of international investments in promising emerging markets. He wants you to explain the key elements and differences between international portfolio investment and foreign direct investment. In your view which is the safer option?

⭐ **1-18.** Your CEO has long been frustrated by poor communications, reliability and quality from overseas suppliers. He is convinced that the acquisition of assets in the supply chain will make it more efficient, reliable and responsive to the needs of the corporation. He has asked you to outline the contents of a presentation he intends to make to the stock holders in order to gain their backing and additional investment to make it happen.

1-19. You have become the president of the International Business Club at your school. You are trying to recruit new members and find that many students do not recognize the importance of international business or the career opportunities available to them. You decide to give a presentation on this theme. Prepare an outline of a presentation in which you explain what types of companies participate in international business, why students should study international business, and what career opportunities they might find.

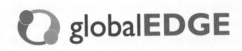 **globalEDGE** | **INTERNET EXERCISES**
(www.globalEDGE.msu.edu)

AACSB: Communication, Use of Information Technology, Analytical Skills

Knowledge Portal

globalEDGE™ is a leading knowledge portal for professionals in international business. It is a gateway to specialized knowledge on countries, international business transactions, culture, and firm practice. globalEDGE™ was developed at Michigan State University under the direction of Professor S. Tamer Cavusgil. Consult the globalEDGE™ portal to complete the Internet exercises at the end of each chapter.

1-20. You can gain valuable insights into international business by examining how countries compare to each other. Various research groups and international agencies systematically examine economic, political, and other features of nations. Visit globalEDGE™ Tools and Data, scroll down and click Interactive Rankings. Select Countries. You will find dozens of criteria ranking countries based on GDP per capita; Education—literacy rate; People—population total; People—population density; Health—mortality rate; Energy—electricity production; Infrastructure—mobile cellular subscriptions; Infrastructure—roads, total network; Trade and Investment—foreign direct investment net inflows; and many other factors. Choose the ranking criteria that interest you most and then examine the following three countries: Germany, India, and South Africa. Based on your analysis,

explain why they rank where they do. Do their relative positions make sense to you? Does each country seem like a good place to do business? Why or why not? *Hint:* Evaluate countries on a per-capita basis by dividing each criterion by the country's population.

1-21. In this chapter, we reviewed the four major risks that firms face in international business: cross-cultural risk, country risk, currency risk, and commercial risk. Identify one or more countries that interest you and then visit globalEDGE™ and research the countries to uncover examples of each of the four types of risks. For example, China is characterized by various cultural differences and a national government that tends to intervene in business. Research by entering the country name in the search engine. Visit Global Insights and Market Potential Index. Illustrate each risk with examples.

1-22. You have recently been hired by a smaller firm that is beginning to expand internationally. When first starting out, most firms choose exporting as their main foreign market entry strategy. However, no one in your firm knows how to conduct exporting. Therefore, your boss has given you an assignment: Prepare a presentation for your coworkers on how to engage in exporting. Using globalEDGE™, find and review Guide to Exporting, which you can use to create your presentation.

 MyManagementLab **Try It!**

The simulation Globalization accompanies this exercise.

 MyManagementLab

Go to **mymanagementlab.com** for Auto-graded writing questions as well as the following Assisted-graded writing questions:

⭐ **1-23.** What role do distribution channel intermediaries fulfill?

⭐ **1-24.** What risks do companies typically engage in with international business?

⭐ **1-25.** MyManagementLab Only—comprehensive writing assignment for this chapter.

Endnotes

1. We use the term *international business* to refer to the cross-border business activities of individual firms, whereas economists use *international trade* to refer to aggregate cross-border flows of products and services between nations. Although international business describes an enterprise-level phenomenon, international trade describes the macrophenomenon of aggregate flows between nations.

2. "Numbers: International Trade Hits a Wall," *BusinessWeek*, January 26–February 2, 2009, p. 15; WTO, 2011.

3. *BBC News*, "United Biscuits Sold to Turkey's Yildiz for £2bn," November 3, 2014, retrieved from www.bbc.com.

4. Lawrence Crosby, "What a Riot," *Marketing News*, February 2015, pp. 32–33; Paul Tassi, "Riot Combines 'League of Legends' with 'Super Smash Bros'" *Forbes*, March 21, 2015, retrieved from http://www.forbes.com/sites/insertcoin/2015/03/21/riot-combines-league-of-legends-with-super-smash-bros-and-the-result-needs-to-be-a-reality/.

5. Danielle Kucera, "eBay's Adventures in Brick and Mortar," *Bloomberg Businessweek*, November 11, 2011, pp. 46–48; eBay corporate profile at http://www.hoovers.com; Nick Wingfield, "eBay Sets Sights on Indian Market with Acquisition," *Wall Street Journal*, June 23, 2004, p. A3.

6. "Desert Song," *The Economist*, October 7, 2004, p. 88; Stephen Timewell, "Another Saudi Success Story," *Banker*, May 2014, pp. 106–108.

7. Marc A. Miles et al., *2008 Index of Economic Freedom* (Washington, DC: The Heritage Foundation).

8. "Strong Dollar Squeezes U.S. Firms: Rising Currency Takes a Toll on Sales and Profits; Stocks Drop as Capital Spending Slows, Too," *Wall Street Journal*, January 27, 2015.

9. Katherine Dunn, "No Country for Young People," *Maclean's*, March 9, 2015, pp. 34–35; Nektaria Stamouli and Stelios Bouras, "Greek Economy Risks Slipping Back into Recession, Say Analysts," *Wall Street Journal*, April 7, 2015, p. 1.

10. UNCTAD, *World Investment Report 2011*, New York: United Nations (2011); UNCTAD, *World Investment Report 2015*, New York: United Nations (2015).

11. Scott Decarlo, "Global 500: A New World Order," *Fortune*, February 1, 2015, pp. 18–19; "Global 500," *Fortune*, July 21, 2014, pp. F1–F8 Special Section.

12. Bob Davis and Jason Dean, "State-Run Firms Are the Giants of China's Economy," *Wall Street Journal*, February 23, 2012, p. A12; Scott Decarlo, "Global 500: A New World Order," *Fortune*, February 1, 2015, pp. 18–19.

13. Boston Consulting Group, *2014 BCG Global Challengers: Redefining Global Competitive Dynamics* (Boston: Boston Consulting Group, 2014).

14. Alison Coleman, "How to Be an Expert at Export," *Financial Times*, October 26, 2005, p. 9.

15. S. Tamer Cavusgil and Gary Knight, *Born Global Firms: The New International Enterprise* (New York: Business Expert Press, 2009); D. De Clercq, R. Yavuz, and L. Zhou, "Learning and Knowledge in Early Internationalization Research: Past Accomplishments and Future Directions," *Journal of Business Venturing* 27, No. 1 (2012), pp. 143–165; Daekwan Kim, Choton Basu, GM Naidu, and Erin Cavusgil, "The Innovativeness of Born-Globals and Customer Orientation: Learning from Indian Born-Globals," *Journal of Business Research* 64, No. 8 (2011), pp. 879–886.

16. UNCTAD, *World Investment Report 2014*, New York: United Nations (2014).

17. Jeffrey Hall and Chris Rasmussen, *Jobs Supported by State Exports 2014* (Washington DC: International Trade Administration, U.S. Department of Commerce, 2015).

18. Kerry Capell, "McDonald's Offers Ethics with Those Fries," *BusinessWeek*, January 9, 2007, retrieved from http://www.businessweek.com.

Chapter 2

Globalization of Markets and the Internationalization of the Firm

Learning Objectives *After studying this chapter, you should be able to:*

2.1 Understand market globalization as an organizing framework.

2.2 Know the drivers of globalization.

2.3 Understand technological advances and globalization.

2.4 Comprehend the dimensions of globalization.

2.5 Appreciate firm-level consequences of market globalization.

2.6 Understand the societal consequences of globalization.

The Emergence of Born Global Firms

Instagram is an online photo-sharing service founded in 2010 for use with smartphones. Instagram's strategy was to enter many international markets quickly. Today, although it has only a few dozen employees, Instagram boasts millions of consumers and businesses worldwide as its customers—constituting one of the largest social networks on the Internet. Only about 12 percent of those users live in North America; the rest are scattered around the world. Virtual InstaMeets allow users from Mumbai to Munich to take photos and share them. People want to share photos to depict their life experiences. Instagram's social feed, paired with easy-to-use editing tools, allows anyone to create and share their distinctive pictures. Its advanced technology coincides with a global shift to a more visual style of communication.

Instagram is one of a growing number of small and medium-sized enterprises (SMEs) active in international business. SMEs make up the majority of all firms in a typical country and often account for more than 50 percent of national economic activity. In contrast to large multinational enterprises (MNEs) that historically have dominated cross-border business, most SMEs have far fewer financial and human resources. International business was often beyond their reach. Globalization and recent technological advances have now made venturing abroad much less expensive. This has created a commercial environment in which many more small firms can participate in international business. Born global firms target a dozen or more countries within the first few years

Source: Steve Raymer/Corbis

of launching the firm. Their agility and flexibility help them serve both foreign and domestic customers better.

Born globals internationalize early for various reasons, some specializing in a product category for which demand is universal. Geo Search (www.geosearch.co.jp) is a Japanese company that develops high-technology equipment to help engineers survey ground surfaces for cavities and build safe roads, airports, and underground utility lines. The firm developed a land-mine detector to find buried bombs and discovered a ready market in countries such as Afghanistan, Cambodia, and Libya.

Smaller companies such as Instagram and Geo Search demonstrate that any firm of any size and resource base can participate actively in cross-border trade and investment. More companies undertake international business today than ever before.

Questions

2-1. What are the main characteristics of born global firms?

2-2. What drivers and causes of globalization have allowed born global firms such as Instagram to internationalize at or near their founding?

2-3. What advantages do you think a young company can gain by entering international markets soon after its founding?

SOURCES: S. Tamer Cavusgil and Gary Knight, "The Born-Global Firm: An Entrepreneurial and Capabilities Perspective on Early and Rapid Internationalization," *Journal of International Business Studies*, 46, No. 1 (2015), pp. 3–16; Jessi Hempel, "Instagram is Ready to Take Its Shot," *Fortune*, July 21, 2014, pp. 72–78; Lauren Johnson, "Instagram Will Hit 100 Million U.S. Users by 2018," *Adweek*, March 6, 2015, p. 1; Daekwan Kim, Choton Basu, GM Naidu, and Erin Cavusgil, "The Innovativeness of Born-Globals and Customer Orientation: Learning from Indian Born-Globals," *Journal of Business Research* 64, No. 8 (2011), pp. 879–886; G. Knight and S. Tamer Cavusgil, "Innovation, Organizational Capabilities, and the Born-Global Firm," *Journal of International Business Studies* 35, No. 2 (2004), pp. 124–141; Ingrid Lunden, "Instagram Is the Fastest-Growing Social Site Globally," *TechCrunch*, January 21, 2014; retrieved 3/15/15 from http://techcrunch.com/2014/01/21/instagram-is-the-fastest-growing-social-site-globally-mobile-devices-rule-over-pcs-for-social-access; B. Oviatt and P. McDougall, "Toward a Theory of International New Ventures," *Journal of International Business Studies* 25, No. 1 (1994). pp. 45–64.

The opening case highlights important drivers and causes of market globalization. These include worldwide reduction of barriers to trade and investment, market liberalization and adoption of free markets, and advances in technology.

Globalization of markets refers to the gradual integration and growing interdependence of national economies. Declining trade barriers and rapid changes in communications, manufacturing, and transportation technologies are enabling firms to internationalize much more rapidly and easily than ever before.

Globalization allows companies to outsource value-chain activities to the most favorable locations worldwide. Firms source raw materials, parts, components, and service inputs from suppliers around the globe. Globalization has also made it easier for companies to sell their offerings worldwide. These trends are transforming national economies. Growing world trade and foreign direct investment (FDI) provide buyers with a wider choice of products than ever before. Global competition and innovation frequently help to lower consumer prices. Firms with cross-border business create millions of jobs that raise living standards around the world.

Globalization is not new. In early history, civilizations in the Mediterranean, Middle East, Asia, Africa, and Europe all contributed to the growth of cross-border trade. Globalization evolved out of a common desire of civilizations to reach out and touch one another.[1] It is a culmination of people's recognition, thousands of years ago, of the wonders of difference and discovery. Cross-border trading opened the world to innovations and progress by giving societies the opportunity to expand and grow. Trade through the ages fostered civilization; without it, the world would consist of warring tribes bent on getting what they need through combat.[2]

> **Globalization of markets**
> Ongoing economic integration and growing interdependency of national economies.

Phases of Globalization

We can identify four distinct phases in the evolution of globalization since the 1800s. Each phase, as illustrated in Exhibit 2.1, was accompanied by revolutionary technological developments and internationalization trends.

- *The first phase of globalization* began in about 1830 and peaked around 1880.[3] International business became widespread due to the growth of railroads, efficient ocean transport, and the rise of large manufacturing and trading firms. Invention of the telegraph and telephone in the late 1800s enabled information flows between and within nations and aided early efforts to manage companies' supply chains.

- *The second phase of globalization* began around 1900 and was associated with the rise of electricity and steel production. This phase reached its height just before the Great Depression, a worldwide economic downturn that began in 1929. In 1900, Western Europe

EXHIBIT 2.1 **Phases of Globalization Since the Early 1800s**

Phase of Globalization	Approximate Period	Triggers	Key Characteristics
First phase	1830 to late 1800s, peaking in 1880	Introduction of railroads and ocean transport	Rise of manufacturing: cross-border trade of commodities, largely by trading companies
Second phase	1900 to 1930	Rise of electricity and steel production	Emergence and dominance of early MNEs (mainly from Europe and North America) in manufacturing, extractive, and agricultural industries
Third phase	1948 to 1970s	Formation of General Agreement on Tariff and Trade (GATT); conclusion of World War II; Marshall Plan to reconstruct Europe	Focus by industrializing Western countries to reduce trade barriers; rise of MNEs from Japan; development of global capital markets; rise of global trade names
Fourth phase	1980s to present	Privatization of state enterprises in transition economies; revolution in information, communication, and transportation technologies; remarkable growth of emerging markets	Rapid growth in cross-border trade of products, services, and capital; rise of internationally active SMEs and services firms; rising prosperity of emerging markets

was the most industrialized world region. Europe's colonization of countries in Asia, Africa, and the Middle East led to the establishment of some of the earliest subsidiaries of multinational enterprises (MNEs). European companies such as BASF, Nestlé, Shell, Siemens, and British Petroleum established foreign manufacturing plants by 1900.[4] In the years before World War I (pre-1914), many firms operated globally. The Italian manufacturer Fiat supplied vehicles to nations on both sides of the war.

- *The third phase of globalization* began after World War II. By the war's end in 1945, a substantial pent-up demand was created for consumer as well as industrial products to rebuild Europe and Japan. Leading industrialized countries, including Australia, the United Kingdom, and the United States, sought to reduce international trade barriers to supply goods to meet this demand.

In 1947, the Bretton Woods Conference of twenty-three nations created the *General Agreement on Tariffs and Trade (GATT)*, which reduced barriers to international trade and investment. Participating governments recognized that liberalized trade would stimulate industrialization, modernization, and better living standards. In turn, the GATT led to the formation of the **World Trade Organization** (**WTO**; www.wto.org), which grew to include about 150 member nations. The WTO aims to regulate and ensure fairness and efficiency in global trade and investment. Global cooperation in the post-war era also gave birth to the International Monetary Fund and the World Bank.

Early multinationals from the third phase of globalization originated in the United States, Western Europe, and Japan. European firms such as Unilever, Philips, Royal Dutch-Shell, and Bayer organized their businesses by establishing subsidiaries around the world.

World Trade Organization (WTO)

A multilateral governing body empowered to regulate international trade and investment.

Many companies developed internationally recognized trade names, including Nestlé, Kraft, Lockheed, Caterpillar, Coca-Cola, and Levi's. Foreign subsidiaries of such companies operated as miniature versions of the parent firm, marketing their products around the world. MNEs began to seek cost advantages by locating factories in developing countries with low labor costs. International trade and investment expanded significantly in the 1960s. Recovered from World War II, MNEs in Europe and Japan began to challenge the dominance of U.S. multinationals. Growing international trade coincided with increased cross-national flows of capital, leading to integration of global financial markets.[5]

- *The fourth phase of globalization* began in the early 1980s and featured enormous growth in cross-border trade and investment. It was triggered by the development of personal computers, the Internet, and web browsers. It was also characterized by the collapse of the Soviet Union and the market liberalization of Central and Eastern Europe. Impressive industrialization and modernization in East Asian economies followed. International prosperity began to develop in the emerging markets, including Brazil, India, and Mexico. The 1980s witnessed huge increases in FDI, especially in capital- and technology-intensive sectors. Technological advances in information, communications, and transportation supported the rise of internationally active small and medium-sized enterprises. These advances increased the ability to organize and manage exports more efficiently and at lower cost. Modern technologies also enabled the globalization of the service sector in such areas as banking, entertainment, tourism, insurance, and retailing.

Market Globalization: Organizing Framework

2.1 Understand market globalization as an organizing framework.

Firms expand abroad proactively to increase sales and profit through new markets, find lower-cost inputs, or obtain other advantages. Firms may also internationalize reactively because of unfavorable conditions in the home market such as regulation or declining local industry sales. Exhibit 2.2 presents an organizing framework for examining market globalization. The exhibit makes a distinction among:

- *drivers* or causes of globalization.
- *dimensions* or manifestations of globalization.
- *firm-level consequences* of globalization.
- *societal consequences* of globalization.

In the exhibit, the double arrows illustrate the interactive nature of the relationship between globalization and its consequences. As globalization intensifies, individual firms respond to the challenges and new advantages that it brings.

America Movil (www.americamovil.com) is a leading wireless phone service provider, with more than 225 million subscribers in 18 countries, that has pursued internationalization as a growth strategy. Based in Mexico, America Movil internationalized mainly through foreign direct investment (FDI) with initial operations in Brazil and Colombia. It then expanded to Ecuador, Chile, the Netherlands, and numerous other foreign markets. The firm entered into a joint venture with Citigroup to fund expansion in South America. It acquired Verizon's telephone operations in Puerto Rico. In each case, America Movil took advantage of such globalization trends as harmonizing communications technologies, converging buyer characteristics, and reduced trade and investment barriers. As emerging markets transform into sophisticated economies, they leapfrog older telecom technologies and embrace contemporary mobile phone technology—a boon to America Movil.

To minimize costs, many of the firm's cell phones are essentially identical worldwide. They are adapted only to accommodate for local languages, regulations, and telephone standards. America Movil's advertising emphasizes a global brand that is recognized everywhere. Worldwide convergence of buyer lifestyles and incomes help facilitate this transnational approach. Management coordinates operations on a global scale and applies common business processes in procurement and quality control. The strategies of product standardization, global branding, and selling to customers worldwide owe much of their success to the globalization of markets.[6]

1 DRIVERS OF MARKET GLOBALIZATION

- Worldwide reduction of barriers to trade and investment
- Market liberalization and adoption of free markets
- Industrialization, economic development, and modernization
- Integration of world financial markets
- Advances in technology

2 DIMENSIONS OF MARKET GLOBALIZATION

- Integration and interdependence of national economies
- Rise of regional economic integration blocs
- Growth of global investment and financial flows
- Convergence of buyer lifestyles and preferences
- Globalization of production activities
- Globalization of services

3a FIRM-LEVEL CONSEQUENCES OF MARKET GLOBALIZATION: INTERNATIONALIZATION OF THE FIRM'S VALUE CHAIN

- Countless new business opportunities for internationalizing firms
- New risks and intense rivalry from foreign competitors
- More demanding buyers who source from suppliers worldwide
- Greater emphasis on proactive internationalization
- Internationalization of firm's value chain

3b SOCIETAL CONSEQUENCES OF MARKET GLOBALIZATION

- Contagion: Rapid spread of financial or monetary crises from one country to another
- Loss of national sovereignty
- Offshoring and the flight of jobs
- Effect on the poor
- Effect on the natural environment
- Effect on national culture

EXHIBIT 2.2

The Drivers, Dimensions, and Consequences of Globalization

 MyManagementLab   **Watch It! I**
If your professor has assigned this, go to the Assignments section of **mymanagementlab.com** to complete the video exercise titled Born Global.

Drivers of Globalization

Various trends have converged in recent years as causes of globalization. The following are particularly notable:

- *Worldwide reduction in barriers to trade and investment.* The tendency of national governments to reduce trade and investment barriers has accelerated global economic integration. For example, tariffs on the import of industrial and medical equipment and countless other products have declined nearly to zero in many countries, encouraging freer international exchange of goods and services. Falling trade barriers are facilitated by the WTO. After joining the WTO in 2001, China has made its market increasingly more accessible

2.2 Know the drivers of globalization.

to foreign firms. The decrease in trade barriers is also associated with the emergence of regional economic integration blocs.

- *Market liberalization and adoption of free markets.* In the past three decades, free-market reforms in China and the former Soviet Union smoothed the integration of former command economies into the global economy. Numerous Asian economies—for example, India, Indonesia, Malaysia, and South Korea—embraced free market norms. These events opened roughly one-third of the world to freer international trade and investment. China, India, and Eastern Europe have become some of the most cost-effective locations for producing goods and services worldwide. Privatization of previously state-owned industries in these countries has encouraged economic efficiency and attracted massive foreign capital to their national economies.

- *Industrialization, economic development, and modernization.* Many emerging markets—rapidly developing economies in Asia, Latin America, and Eastern Europe—have now moved from being low value-adding commodity producers to sophisticated, competitive producers and exporters of premium products such as electronics, computers, and aircraft.[7] For example, Brazil is now a leading manufacturer of Embraer commercial aircraft. The Czech Republic excels in producing automobiles. India is a leading supplier of software.

  Economic development results in increased incomes and living standards, an important measurement of which is *gross national income (GNI)* per person.[8] Exhibit 2.3 maps the levels of GNI worldwide. It reveals that Africa and several countries in Asia and Latin America are the lowest-income countries. These areas are also characterized by lower levels of globalization.

- *Integration of world financial markets.* Financial market integration makes it possible for internationally active firms to raise capital, borrow funds, and engage in foreign currency transactions. Financial services firms follow their customers to foreign markets. Cross-border transactions are made easier because of the ease with which funds can be transferred between buyers and sellers. This takes place through networks of international commercial banks. For instance, the SWIFT network connects more than 9,000 financial institutions in some 200 countries. This global financial connectivity assists firms in developing and operating world-scale production and marketing operations. It enables companies to pay suppliers and collect payments from customers worldwide.

- *Advances in technology.* Technological advances are a remarkable facilitator of cross-border trade and investment. This is an important megatrend that requires greater elaboration.

Technological Advances and Globalization

2.3 Understand technological advances and globalization.

Perhaps the most important driver of market globalization has been technological advances in information, communications, manufacturing, and transportation. Technological advances provide the *means* for market globalization to happen.

Information Technology

Information technology (IT) is the science and process of creating and using information resources. Its effect on business has been revolutionary. The cost of computer processing fell by more than 30 percent per year during the past three decades and continues to fall. IT creates competitive advantages by giving companies new ways to outperform rivals.[9] Geographically distant subsidiaries of a multinational firm are now interconnected by intranets that facilitate instant sharing of data, information, and experience across company operations worldwide. MNEs use collaboration software to connect distant product development teams.

IT benefits smaller firms, too, allowing them to design and produce customized products they can target to narrow, cross-national market niches. Online search engines provide easy access to unlimited data for researching markets, competitors, and other key information. At a higher level, IT supports managerial decision making, such as the selection of qualified foreign business partners, by allowing firms to access key information and intelligence quickly.

Technology enables firms to interact with foreign partners and value-chain members in a more timely and cost-effective way. Such productivity advances provide substantial competitive advantages for the firm.[10] One result is the increased early internationalization by SMEs. Emerging markets and developing economies benefit from technological leapfrogging. For example, numerous African countries are adopting cell phone technology directly, bypassing the landline technology common to some advanced economies.

Panel (a) of Exhibit 2.4 shows the dramatic decrease in the cost of international communications, expressed as the cost of a 3-minute telephone call from London to New York. Panel (b) reveals the growth in Internet users in various regions since 2000. Africa has the fewest Internet users, whereas Europe and North America have the most, reflecting the level of economic and infrastructural development in each region.

Communications

The Internet, and Internet-dependent systems such as intranets, extranets, social media, and e-mail, connect billions of people and companies. Marketers use the Internet to promote the widest range of products and services to customers worldwide. Transmitting voice, data, and images is essentially costless, making Seoul, Stockholm, and San Jose next-door neighbors. South Korea has nearly 100 percent Internet access and is among the fastest broadband networks worldwide. Koreans use their phones to pay bills, do banking, and watch news programs.

The Internet opens the global marketplace to SMEs and other firms that would normally lack the resources to do international business. By establishing a presence on the web, even tiny enterprises can take the first step to become multinational firms. Services as diverse as designing an engine, monitoring a security camera, selling insurance, and doing secretarial work are easier to export than car parts or refrigerators. In China, thousands of rural farmers use Internet sites such as www.taobao.com to market their produce to urban consumers.[11]

Source: © Gilles Paire/Fotolia

Increasing availability of cell phones in Africa has helped spur economic growth there.

Ethical Connections

In six years, Nigeria increased its telecom infrastructure from just 500,000 phone lines to more than 30 million cellular subscribers. The result has been a dramatic rise in productivity and commerce, which has helped improve living standards. Greater access to cell phones saves wasted trips, provides access to education and health care services, and facilitates communication between suppliers and customers. MNE telecom investment in Africa allows firms to fulfill social responsibilities and improve the lives of millions of poor people.

Countries need modern infrastructure in communications, such as reliable telephone systems, to support economic development. Mobile phones are the most transformative technology in developing economies. Fortunately, cell phone infrastructure is inexpensive and relatively easy to install.

The *Internet of things* refers to machine-to-machine connectivity online. Worldwide, mobile telephony and app development have grown enormously, creating millions of jobs, increasing productivity, and producing big GDP gains. The number of smartphone users was expected to reach 3 billion by 2017, double the figure in 2013. People everywhere are online.[12]

Social media such as Facebook and Instagram facilitate the free flow of information, deepening the pace and impact of globalization. Global communities created by platforms such as YouTube and Twitter help mobilize audiences that transcend borders and geographic distance. The 2011 "Arab Spring" in the Middle East was facilitated in large part by social media. In view of this, in some authoritarian countries, national governments restrict access to social media, fearing the role it can play in accelerating social movements. Many companies and other organizations leverage social media to communicate with their publics through direct sales, advertising, and public relations. Social media provide the means to communicate directly with millions of connected individuals in new markets. Puma used Twitter and other platforms to market sportswear to customers in Europe and Latin America ahead of the 2014 World Cup games.

EXHIBIT 2.3

Gross National Income, in U.S. Dollars

Source: Based on World Bank (2015); World Bank Development Indicator database, http://www.data.worldbank.org.

Gross National Income Per Capita, in U.S. Dollars, 2014

- 20,000 or more
- 8,000 – 19,999
- 4,000 – 7,999
- 1,500 – 3,999
- less than 1,500
- No data

EXHIBIT 2.4

Declining Cost of Global Communication and Growing Internet Penetration Rate (as a % of the region's population)

Sources: IMF, *World Economic Outlook* (Washington, DC: International Monetary Fund, 2015); United Nations International Telecommunications Union, *Statistics Database*, (2015) at www.itu.int; Internet World Stats, *Internet Usage Statistics*, (2015) at www.internetworldstats.com.

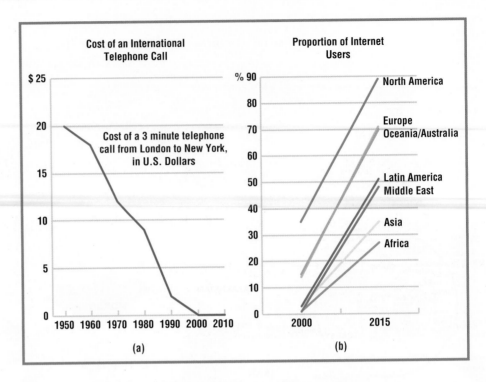

McDonald's used the social media site Renren.com to market burgers and sundaes to customers in China. Social media provide various means to reach important audiences in markets around the world.[13]

Manufacturing

Computer-aided design (CAD) of products, robotics, and production lines have transformed manufacturing, mainly by reducing production costs. Revolutionary developments facilitate low-scale and low-cost manufacturing; firms can make products cost effectively even in short production runs. Such developments benefit international business by allowing firms to adapt products more efficiently to individual foreign markets, profitably target small national markets, and compete more effectively with foreign competitors that enjoy cost advantages.

Transportation

Firms consider the cost of transporting raw materials, components, and finished products when deciding either to export or manufacture abroad. If transport costs to an important market are high, management may decide to manufacture merchandise in that market. The development of fuel-efficient jumbo jets, giant ocean-going freighters, and new transportation technology have greatly reduced shipping times and costs. Exhibit 2.5 reveals the progression of this trend. It shows world road sector diesel fuel consumption per capita in kilograms of oil; world container port traffic in TEUs, 20-foot equivalent units of transportation containers, in millions of units; and world air transport carrier departures worldwide in millions of departures. These statistics suggest how transportation of products has been revolutionized over time. They also imply that growing transportation poses an increasing threat to the natural environment in terms of the usage of energy and other resources.

In the 20-year period through 2012, the number of containers transported internationally increased by nearly five times; more than 175 million 20-foot equivalent units are shipped each year. Containers are the big boxes, usually

Source: urbans/Shutterstock

Advances in transportation and low freight costs have helped spur market globalization. Triple E class ships can carry thousands of shipping containers.

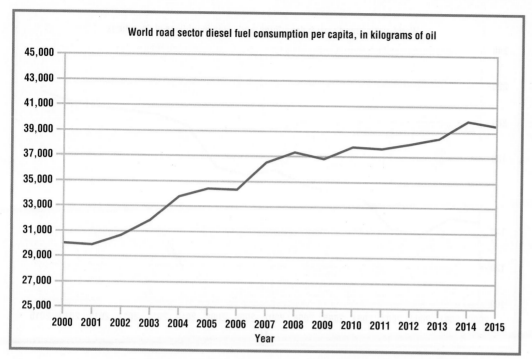

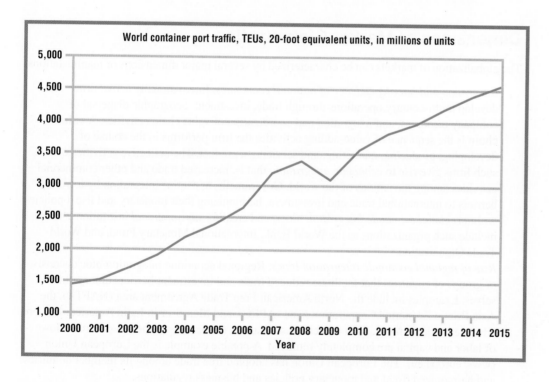

EXHIBIT 2.5

Rising Transportation Infrastructure Usage Over Time

Source: World Bank data (data.worldbank.org) and authors' analysis

40 feet long (about 12 meters), loaded on top of ships, trucks, and rail cars that carry the world's cargo. Today's ocean-going container ships hold more than 2500 containers.[14]

Shipbuilders, such as Maersk, have recently introduced container ships that can carry upward of 9,000 40-foot shipping containers. The vessels are so massive that only a handful of international ports can handle them, including Shanghai in China and Rotterdam in the Netherlands. These ships are used mainly to transport goods between Europe and Asia because they are too wide to pass through the Panama Canal. Technological advances in these Triple E vessels provide economies of scale that reduce the cost of transportation dramatically. They are energy efficient and environmentally friendly.[15]

EXHIBIT 2.5
(Continued)

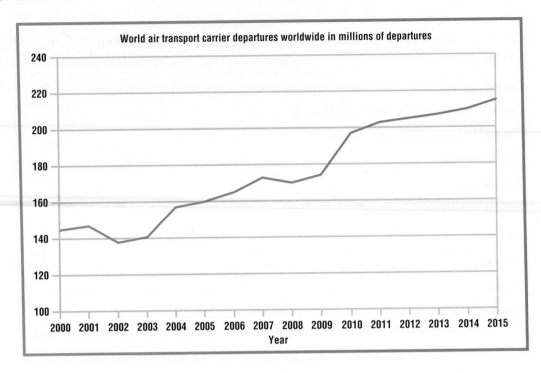

2.4 Comprehend the dimensions of globalization.

Value chain
The sequence of value-adding activities the firm performs in the course of developing, producing, marketing, and servicing a product.

Dimensions of Market Globalization

The globalization of markets can be characterized by several major dimensions or manifestations.

- *Integration and interdependence of national economies.* Internationally active firms develop multi-country operations through trade, investment, geographic dispersal of company resources, and integration and coordination of value chain activities. A **value chain** is the sequence of value-adding activities the firm performs in the course of developing, producing, marketing, and servicing a product. The collective activities of such firms give rise to *economic integration,* that is, increased trade and other commercial activities among the nations of the world. Governments assist this integration by lowering barriers to international trade and investment, harmonizing their monetary and fiscal policies within *regional economic integration* blocs, and creating *supranational* institutions. These include such organizations as the World Bank, International Monetary Fund, and World Trade Organization.

- *Rise of regional economic integration blocs.* Regional economic integration blocks consist of groups of countries that facilitate reduced trade and investment barriers among themselves. Examples include the North American Free Trade Agreement area (NAFTA), the Asia Pacific Economic Cooperation zone (APEC), and Mercosur in Latin America. In more advanced arrangements, such as a common market, the barriers to the cross-border flow of labor and capital are completely removed. A notable example is the European Union (www.europa.eu). The European Union has adopted free trade among its member countries and harmonized fiscal and monetary policies and business regulations.

- *Growth of global investment and financial flows.* In the process of conducting international transactions, firms and governments buy and sell large volumes of national currencies (such as dollars, euros, and yen). The free movement of capital around the world—the globalization of capital—extends economic activities across the globe. It further increases interconnectedness among world economies. The bond market has gained worldwide scope, with foreign bonds representing a major source of debt financing for governments and firms.

- *Convergence of consumer lifestyles and preferences.* Consumers around the world increasingly spend their money and time in similar ways. Many aspects of lifestyles and preferences are converging. Shoppers in New York, Paris, and Shanghai increasingly demand similar household goods, clothing, automobiles, and electronics. Teenagers everywhere are attracted to iPods, Levi's jeans, and Hollywood movies. Major brands enjoy a global following encouraged by movies, global media, and the Internet. Movies such as *Transformers* and *The Hunger Games* have developed global audiences of fans. Convergence of preferences is also occurring in industrial markets, where professional buyers source raw materials, parts, and components that are increasingly *standardized*—that is, similar or identical in design and structure.

- *Globalization of production.* Intense global competition is forcing firms to reduce their costs of production. Companies cut their costs and selling prices through economies of scale, standardization of finished products, and shifting manufacturing and procurement to foreign locations with less expensive labor. For example, firms in the auto and textile industries have relocated their manufacturing to low labor-cost locations such as China, Mexico, and Poland.

- *Globalization of services.* The services sector—banking, hospitality, retailing, and other service industries—is undergoing widespread internationalization. The real estate firm REMAX has established more than 5,000 offices in some 50 countries. Firms increasingly outsource business processes and other services in the value chain to vendors located abroad. In a relatively new trend, many people go abroad to undergo medical procedures, such as cataract and knee surgeries, to save money.[16]

Firm-Level Consequences of Market Globalization: Internationalization of The Firm's Value Chain

Source: Robert Harding Picture Library Ltd/Alamy

Google is one of many multinational enterprises that contribute to convergence of consumer lifestyles and preferences.

The most direct consequence of market globalization is on the firm's value chain. Globalization compels firms to organize their sourcing, manufacturing, marketing, and other value-adding activities on a global scale to achieve cost advantages and time efficiencies. In a typical value chain, the firm conducts research and product development (R&D), purchases production inputs, and assembles or manufactures a product or service. Next, the firm performs marketing activities such as pricing, promotion, and selling, followed by distribution of the product in targeted markets and after-sales service. The value-chain concept is useful in international business because it helps clarify *what* activities are performed *where* in the world. For example, exporting firms perform most upstream value-chain activities (R&D and production) in the home market and most downstream activities (marketing and after-sales service) abroad.

2.5 Appreciate firm-level consequences of market globalization.

Each value-adding activity in the firm's value chain is subject to internationalization; that is, it can be performed in locations outside the home country. Exhibit 2.6 illustrates a value chain in a typical international firm. As examples in the exhibit suggest, companies have considerable latitude regarding where in the world they can locate or configure key value-adding activities. The most typical reasons for locating value-chain activities in particular countries are to reduce the costs of R&D and production or to gain closer access to customers. Through offshoring, the firm relocates a major value-chain activity by establishing a factory or other subsidiary abroad. A related trend is global outsourcing, in which the firm delegates performance of a value-adding activity to an external supplier or contractor located abroad.

In the same month that German carmaker BMW launched a new factory in South Carolina, an aging textile plant a few miles away, Jackson Mills, closed its doors and shed thousands of

EXHIBIT 2.6

Examples of How Firms' Value-Chain Activities Can Be Internationalized

workers. Globalization created a new reality for both these firms. By establishing operations in the U.S., BMW found it could manufacture cars cost effectively while more readily accessing the huge U.S. market. In the process, BMW created thousands of high-paying, better-quality jobs for U.S. workers. Simultaneously, Jackson Mills had discovered it could source textiles of comparable quality more cost effectively from suppliers in Asia. Globalization drove these firms to relocate key value-adding activities to the most advantageous locations around the world.

Without a doubt, globalization has created a crowded and intensely competitive global marketplace. As illustrated in Exhibit 2.7, globalization has meant that firms face intense rivalry from foreign competitors. This exhibit shows that in 1989 General Motors, Ford, and Chrysler together held nearly three-quarters of the market share in light vehicle sales in the United States. By 2015, the percentage had fallen to 46 percent. The market shares of competitors such as Toyota, Hyundai, and others rose dramatically. Over time, the services sector also has been internationalizing at a fast pace. See the *You Can Do It: Recent Grad in IB* below, which features Terrance Rogers who is working in the global banking industry.

MyManagementLab   **Watch It! 2**

If your professor has assigned this, go to the Assignments section of **mymanagementlab.com** to complete the video exercise titled Rudi's Bakery: Management in the Global Environment.

EXHIBIT 2.7

Market Shares of Automakers in Light-Vehicle Sales in the U.S. 1989 and 2015

Sources: Based on Craig Trudell, "U.S. Automakers Seen Losing Market Share Amid 2012 Growth: Cars," *Bloomberg BusinessWeek*, February 8, 2012, retrieved from www.businessweek. com; J. Muller, "Automakers Gold Rush," *Forbes*, June 8, 2009, pp. 70–77; *Wall Street Journal*, "Sales and Share of Total Market by Manufacturer," March 3, 2015, retrieved from http://online.wsj.com/ mdc/public/page/2_3022-autosales. html#autosalesE, March 16, 2015.

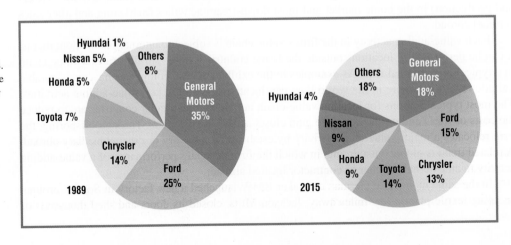

You Can Do It | RECENT GRADS IN IB

TERRANCE ROGERS

Terrance's majors: Finance and International Business
Objectives: Exploration, international perspective, self-awareness, career growth, and learning about foreign markets
Internships during college: Deutsche Bank
Jobs held since graduating:
• Business Analyst at Deutsche Bank, New York
• Management Associate at Deutsche Bank, New York
• Executive Management Rotation at Deutsche Bank, New York
• Executive Management Associate at Deutsche Bank, London and New York

After taking his first international business course, Terrance became fascinated with the idea of working abroad. As a university student, he enrolled in his college's International Business Certificate program. The program allowed Terrance to combine his passion for finance with his appetite for learning about culture and doing business abroad. Terrance took his first international trip through a short study abroad course. The course, "Financial and Managerial Issues in the EU", brought him to Paris and Brussels. Terrance and his classmates visited prominent businesses and the European Union offices to hear from leaders across multiple sectors. The experience allowed Terrance to believe that working abroad could be a real possibility.

After graduation, Terrance started his career as a business analyst with Deutsche Bank in New York. The position gave him experience in regulatory change, process improvement, and crisis management. Terrance got the opportunity to work on several global projects. After being promoted to management associate, Terrance worked directly with the Chief Operations Officer of the Americas for his division.

After spending four years gaining experience in various areas of the bank, Terrance took a position with numerous international responsibilities. Today, Terrance is an Executive Management Associate, leading business strategy, finance analysis, and communications for the United Kingdom Executive Team. In this role, he splits his time between London and New York. He is responsible for interpreting financial drivers, product strategy, and operational issues that shape each business line in the region. He works directly with the Head of Marketing and Communications to craft and execute communication strategy for the Chief Executive Officer.

Terrance's Advice for an International Career

Terrance owes his success to early exposure at his university to international business and study abroad. Terrance says that "international careers are a requirement for today's business leaders. Major clients don't just reside in the U.S. anymore, so if you want to have a long impactful career, you must find a way to gain some international exposure. Your boss will rely on you to be able to work with business associates from different cultures. Your clients will expect you to understand issues with a global perspective, and if you don't have any global experience, your competitors (for jobs and clients) will be one step ahead of you."

Success Factors

"If you want to work abroad, do the following things to increase your chances at securing an international role: (a) work on projects that expose you to people in different regions across the globe; (b) mention your interest in working abroad early and bring it up in your annual review; and (c) find a way to impress the people who can make the decision. It becomes easier to make the move when the 'right people' know that you can deliver."

Challenges

"Challenges like language barriers and cultural differences are things that should be faced as soon as you can in your career. Don't be afraid to make a mistake. It's much better to learn from cultural missteps now, so that you can be a better business leader tomorrow." Globalization is a major dimension of business today.

Source: Courtesy of Terrance Rogers.

Societal Consequences of Globalization

2.6 Understand the societal consequences of globalization.

Our discussion so far has highlighted the far-reaching, positive outcomes of globalization. Major advances in living standards have been achieved in virtually all countries that have opened their borders to increased trade and investment.[17] Yet the transition to a global marketplace also poses challenges to individuals, organizations, and governments. Low-income countries have not been able to integrate with the global economy as rapidly as others have. Poverty remains a major problem in Africa and in populous nations such as Brazil, China, and India.[18] Let's consider some of the unintended consequences of globalization.

Contagion: Rapid Spread of Monetary or Financial Crises

Starting in 2008, the world economy experienced a severe financial crisis and global recession that was triggered by unsustainably high prices in housing and commodities. As real estate prices tumbled, it left many owners with mortgage debts greater than the value of their homes. Tens of thousands of those mortgages had been bundled and sold as investments on stock markets worldwide. As the value of these homes and securities plunged or became uncertain, stock markets also plunged.[19]

Contagion
The tendency of a financial or monetary crisis in one country to spread rapidly to other countries due to the ongoing integration of national economies.

The crisis began in the United States and, like a contagious disease, spread around the world. In international economics, **contagion** refers to the tendency for a financial or monetary crisis in one country to spread rapidly to other countries due to integrated national economies.[20] Widespread borrowing by consumers to purchase homes and durable goods led to unsustainable overheating of the U.S. economy. Another cause of the financial crisis was inadequate regulation of the financial and banking sector in the United States. As we will see later in this text, having a strong legal and regulatory framework is critical to national economic well-being.[21]

Consumer confidence dwindled, triggering substantial declines in spending on cars, consumer electronics, home appliances, luxury goods, gasoline, bank loans, and new homes. Decreased spending, in turn, has been a drag on global commerce.[22] Trade has especially slowed or flattened in consumer durables, energy, financial services, new construction, and related industries. During 2009 and 2010, global growth declined sharply to levels not seen since World War II.

Canada and Mexico slipped into recession partly due to their heavy reliance on trade and investment with the United States. Japan, New Zealand, Turkey, the United States, and most countries in Europe experienced significant recessions. Living standards were severely affected, and millions of people worldwide fell into deeper poverty. This occurred partly because developing economies depend on exports to, and direct investments from, the advanced economies that were hurt by the crisis. Economic recovery beginning in 2012 helped drive economic growth in much of the world. However, numerous economies remain sluggish.[23]

Exhibit 2.8 shows how GDP growth in advanced, developing, and emerging economies varies over time. GDP in all three types of economies declined substantially during the global recession and financial crisis. One lesson the exhibit shows is that, even following deep recessions, the global economy has always rebounded, and countries' GDPs have returned to growth.

Loss of National Sovereignty

Sovereignty is defined as the ability of a nation to govern its own affairs; normally one country's laws cannot be applied or enforced in another country. Globalization, however, can threaten national sovereignty in various ways. MNE activities can interfere with a government's ability to control its own economy, social structure, and political system. Some corporations are bigger than the economies of small nations; Walmart's internal economy—its total revenues—is larger than the GDP of many of the world's nations, including Israel, Greece, and Poland. Large multinational firms can apply a lot of pressure on governments through lobbying or campaign contributions and can frequently influence the legislative process.

EXHIBIT 2.8

Percentage of Change in Annual GDP Growth

Sources: World Bank, Data, GDP Growth (Annual %), data.worldbank. org; IMF, *World Economic Outlook* (Washington, DC: International Monetary Fund, September 2011); IMF, World Economic Outlook Database, 2015, www.imf.org; United Nations, UNData, "GDP growth (annual %)," data.un.org.

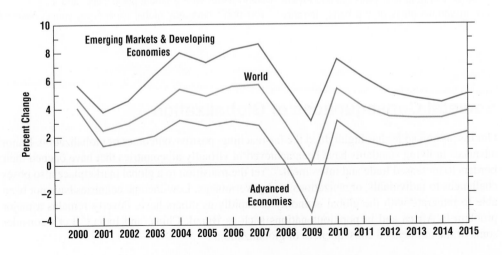

The largest firms are constrained by market forces. In countries with many competing firms, one company cannot force customers to buy its products or force suppliers to supply it with raw materials and inputs. Resources that customers and suppliers use are made through free choice. Company performance depends on the firm's skill at winning customers, working with suppliers, and dealing with competitors. Corporate dominance of individual markets is rare. In reality, market forces generally dominate companies. For example, Ford, Chrysler, and General Motors once dominated the U.S. auto market. Today, General Electric has returned washer many more automotive firms—Toyota, Honda, Hyundai, Nissan, and BMW—compete in the United States. Toyota now leads the global market in annual sales. Home-country market shares of domestic U.S. automakers have tumbled.[24]

To minimize globalization's harm and reap its benefits, governments should ensure the freedom to enter and compete in markets, protect private property, enforce the law, and support voluntary exchange through markets rather than through political processes. Banks and financial institutions should be regulated appropriately. Transparency in the affairs of business and regulatory agencies is critical.

Offshoring

Globalization has created countless new jobs and opportunities worldwide, but it also has cost many people their jobs. Ford and General Motors have laid off thousands of workers in the United States, partly the result of competitive pressures posed by carmakers from Europe, Japan, and South Korea. Ford, GM, and Volkswagen all have transferred thousands of jobs from their factories in Germany to countries in Eastern Europe.[25] *Offshoring* is the relocation of manufacturing and other value-chain activities to cost-effective locations abroad. For example, the global accounting firm Ernst & Young relocated much of its accounting support work to the Philippines. Massachusetts General Hospital has its CT scans and X-rays interpreted by radiologists in India. Many IT support services for customers in Germany are based in the Czech Republic and Romania.[26]

The first wave of offshoring began in the 1960s and 1970s with the shift of U.S. and European manufacturing of cars, shoes, electronics, and textiles to cheap-labor locations such as Mexico and Southeast Asia. The next wave began in the 1990s with the exodus of service-sector jobs in credit card processing, software code writing, and accounting services.

High-profile plant closures and manufacturing relocation have received much media attention. For example, Polaris, the U.S. manufacturer of all-terrain vehicles, moved its Wisconsin factory to Mexico to reduce production costs. Closing the plant devastated the local community.[27]

Simultaneously, however, MNEs create millions of jobs abroad, which help raise living standards. For example, U.S. MNEs now employ about one million workers in each of Canada, China, Mexico, and the United Kingdom.[28] In developing economies and emerging markets, such positions help raise living standards.

Reshoring

MNEs sometimes engage in *reshoring*—the return of manufacturing and services back to the home country. For example, Apple has returned some computer manufacturing, and General Electric has returned washer and dryer production, to the United States. Reshoring arises for various reasons, including the rise of wages and other costs in emerging markets and the desire to locate closer to key customers in the advanced economies.[29]

Effect on the Poor

Some MNEs have been criticized for paying low wages, exploiting workers, and employing child labor. Child labor is particularly troubling because it denies children educational opportunities. It is estimated that there are more than 200 million children aged 5 to 14 at work around the world.[30]

Source: Peter Cook/Dorling Kindersley

Media attention and consumer concern are helping to improve wages and sweatshop conditions slowly in developing economies, such as those in south Asia.

EXHIBIT 2.9

The Growth of World GDP, Average Annual GDP Growth Rate, 2006–2015 (%)

Source: Based on International Monetary Fund, World Economic Outlook Database, http://www.imf.org/external/pubs/ft/weo/2015/01/weodata/index.aspx.

Nike was criticized for paying low wages to shoe factory workers in Asia, some of whom worked in sweatshop conditions. Critics complained that, although founder Phil Knight is a billionaire and Nike shoes sell for $100 or more, some of Nike's suppliers paid their workers only a few dollars per day.

 MyManagementLab **Watch It! 3**

If your professor has assigned this, go to the Assignments section of **mymanagementlab.com** to complete the video exercise titled Save the Children: Social Networking.

Labor exploitation and sweatshop conditions are major concerns in many developing economies.[31] What other employment choices are available to these poorly educated people? A low-paying job is usually better than no job at all. Studies suggest that banning products made using child labor may produce negative unintended consequences such as reduced living standards.[32] Legislation passed to reduce child labor in the formal economic sector (the sector regulated and monitored by public authorities) may have little effect on jobs in the informal economic sector, sometimes called the *underground economy*. In the face of persistent poverty, abolishing formal sector jobs does not ensure that children leave the workforce and go to school.

Work conditions and salaries tend to improve, over time, in many developing countries. The growth of the footwear industry in Vietnam translated into a fivefold increase in wages. While still low by advanced economy standards, those growing wages are improving the lives of millions of workers and their families. Globalization tends to support a growing economy. Countries that liberalize international trade and investment enjoy faster per-capita economic growth. Developing economies that seek to integrate with the rest of the world tend to have faster per-capita GDP growth than those that fail to participate in the world economy.[33]

Exhibit 2.9 shows the global GDP growth rate from 2003 to 2012. Note that most nations experienced positive growth. The world's fastest-growing large economies are China and India. However, although some African countries are growing well, most continue to experience significant poverty and suffer low or negative GDP growth.

Exhibit 2.10 reveals how global poverty is declining over time.[34] This exhibit illustrates the income status of people in developing economies, especially in East and South Asia and sub-Saharan Africa (that part of Africa below the Saharan Desert). It also shows the number of people living on $2.00 or $1.25 per day, which the World Bank considers the thresholds for poverty and extreme poverty, respectively. The number of people living in poverty in these areas has declined consistently for the past few decades. Much of these improvements are due to international trade and investment activities.[35] Only sub-Saharan Africa has shown little improvement in income status during this time.

Effect on Sustainability and the Natural Environment

Globalization promotes manufacturing and economic activity that results in increased pollution, habitat destruction, and deterioration of the ozone layer. In China, for example, economic development is attracting much inward FDI and stimulating the growth of numerous industries. The construction of factories, infrastructure, and modern housing can spoil previously pristine environments. In Eastern China, growing industrial demand for electricity led to construction of the Three Gorges Dam, which flooded agricultural lands and permanently altered the natural landscape. See the *Apply Your Understanding* exercise at the end of this chapter, which presents an Ethical Dilemma problem on the environmental damage done by a large oil company in Nigeria.

It is therefore no surprise that as globalization stimulates rising living standards, concerned citizens focus on improving their environment. Over time, governments pass legislation that promotes improved environmental conditions. For example, Japan endured polluted rivers and smoggy cities in the early decades of its economic development following World War II. As its economy grew, however, the Japanese passed tougher environmental standards to restore their natural environment.

Evolving company values and concern for corporate reputations have led many firms to reduce or eliminate practices that harm the environment.[36] In Mexico, for example, big automakers

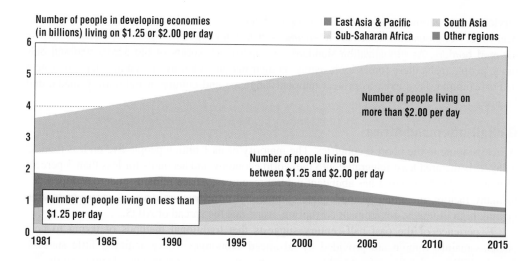

Number of people in developing economies (in billions) living on $1.25 or $2.00 per day

■ East Asia & Pacific □ South Asia
□ Sub-Saharan Africa ■ Other regions

Number of people living on more than $2.00 per day

Number of people living on between $1.25 and $2.00 per day

Number of people living on less than $1.25 per day

1981 1985 1990 1995 2000 2005 2010 2015

EXHIBIT 2.10

Number of People (in Billions) Living in Poverty

Sources: L. Chandy, N. Ledlie, and V. Penciakova, *The Final Countdown: Prospects for Ending Extreme Poverty by 2030,* Policy Paper 2013–14 (Washington DC: Brookings Institution); *Economist*, "Poverty's Long Farewell," February 28, 2015, p. 68; World Bank, *World Development Indicators* (Washington, DC: World Bank, 2015).

such as Ford and General Motors have gradually improved their environmental standards. Benetton in Italy (clothing), Alcan in Canada (aluminum), and Kirin in Japan (beverages) are examples of firms that embrace practices that protect the environment, often at the expense of profits.[37] The Conservation Coffee Alliance has committed approximately $2 million to environmentally friendly coffee cultivation in Central America, Peru, and Colombia.

Effect on National Culture

Globalization exerts strong pressures on national culture because market liberalization exposes local consumers to global brands, unfamiliar products, and different values. People worldwide are exposed to movies, television, the Internet, and other information sources that promote lifestyles of people in the United States and other advanced economies. Appetites grow for Western products and services, which are seen to signal higher living standards. For example, despite low per-capita income, many Chinese buy consumer electronics such as cell phones and TV sets. Advertising disseminates societal values modeled on Western countries. Hollywood dominates the global entertainment industry.

The flow of cultural influence often goes both ways, too. Cafe Spice is an Indian food company whose founder hails from Mumbai. The firm is transforming American tastes by selling curry dishes and other Indian favorites in cafeterias and supermarkets. Cafe Spice is helping to make Indian cuisine mainstream in the United States.[38] As the influence of the Chinese economy grows over time, Western countries will likely adopt some of China's cultural attitudes and behaviors. Chinese restaurants and some Chinese traditions are already a way of life in much of the world. Similar influences are evident from Latin America and other areas in the developing world.

Cultural imperialism is offset by the countertrend of local nationalism. Although many products and

Source: Martin Richardson/Dorling Kindersley, Limited

Western companies can influence food preferences, but cultural values tend to remain stable over time. This Burger King is in Bangkok, Thailand.

services have become largely universal, people's behaviors and attitudes remain relatively stable over time. Religious differences are as strong as ever. Language differences are steadfast across national borders. As globalization standardizes superficial aspects of life across national cultures, people resist these forces by insisting on their national identity and taking steps to protect it. For example, laws exist to protect national language and culture in Belgium, Canada, and France.

Globalization and Africa

Africa is home to the poorest countries. The majority of its 1 billion people live on less than $2 a day. It is the area least integrated into the world economy and accounts for less than 3 percent of world trade. Although it has abundant natural resources, Africa remains underdeveloped due to many factors, including an inadequate commercial infrastructure, lack of access to foreign capital, high illiteracy, government corruption, wars, and the spread of AIDS.

Experience of the past half-century suggests that traditional methods of trying to help Africa—mainly foreign aid provided by advanced economies—have achieved little success. Despite billions of dollars of aid to Africa, per-capita income has not increased significantly.[39]

One of the most effective ways to alleviate African poverty is to develop more business-based models of development.[40] Several sub-Saharan African countries have recently experienced significant economic growth by increasing international trade in commodities. Africa is a major supplier of petroleum to Europe and the United States. Angola is among the top oil suppliers to China. This activity has developed a ripple effect of economic development. Because of the boom of certain sectors in Africa, there has been an increase in foreign banks, retailers, and MNE operations in the continent.[41]

Rwanda had developed business opportunities in sectors as diverse as mining, tourism, telecommunications, and real estate. China and India are beating out U.S. firms and quickly increasing their business dealings in Africa. Chinese companies are investing billions of dollars in the continent. All this international trade and investment are helping to address many of Africa's most pressing development needs.[42] Samsung has set a goal of $10 billion in African sales and is committed to training 10,000 African engineers and technicians to develop the capabilities needed for success. Even so, it will take many more years for Africa to achieve a critical mass of infrastructure and business culture sufficient to raise average incomes substantially across the continent.

CLOSING CASE   Debating the Good and Harm of Globalization

Recently, a university sponsored a roundtable on the broader implications of international business. The participants were an anti-international business activist, a business executive with extensive international dealings, and a government trade official. Excerpts from the exchange present the diverse perspectives of globalization which different interest groups hold.

Activist

"One problem with international business is that it often ignores human rights and basic labor standards. Low-wage factories abroad create substandard working conditions. The activities of multinational companies not only result in job losses here at home, but also in low wages and exploited workers around the world. Just think of the sweatshops in Asia that make imported clothing. Think of the autoworkers in Mexico who live in horrible conditions and make only a few dollars a day. Also consider the poverty caused worldwide by the recent global financial and economic crisis."

Business Executive

"Our country needs to participate in the global economy. Companies that export provide better-paying jobs, have more profits, pay higher taxes, and stimulate purchases from local suppliers. Foreign companies that invest here create new jobs, enhance local living standards, and pressure our firms to stay competitive in a challenging global marketplace. Exporters pay higher wages and provide better benefits than non-exporting firms do. Many companies need access to foreign markets because of the huge, upfront research and development costs they accumulate. One more pill is cheap; it's the cost of research to find a cure for AIDS that is prohibitive. Pharmaceutical firms can't do the necessary R&D unless they can amortize those costs over a huge, global marketplace. In the long run, uninterrupted international commerce is good."

Trade Official

"The current administration believes in the value of free trade. The government strongly supported NAFTA, and this has already had a positive effect on the economy through increasing exports to Mexico, creating jobs, and leading to improved investment opportunities. Countries are forging ahead with international trade ties. Canada has completed a free trade agreement with Chile. Economic ties lead to cultural ties and more peaceful relations. Also, it is hard for our government to promote freedom and democracy around the world if we are not promoting free trade."

Activist

"We cannot overlook the detrimental effects of globalization on the natural environment. The more we trade internationally, the more irreparable harm will be done to the environment. International business means more environmentally damaging development. Companies internationalize so they can become more efficient. But if countries have weak environmental standards, then factories will be built with minimal environmental standards."

Business Executive

"If we trade internationally, then living standards will increase everywhere. As living standards rise, awareness of and care for the environment will also increase. International business is good for the world because it creates wealth. The more affluent the people, the more they will care about their environment and pass laws to protect it. We are also becoming more responsive to concerns over social responsibility and environmental degradation. We have shown that a good economy and a clean environment are not mutually exclusive. We can have it both ways: a clean planet and a better economic quality of life."

Trade Official

"I think part of the solution is to negotiate trade agreements that take environmental factors into account. International trade that runs roughshod over legitimate environmental concerns is counterproductive and defeats the political agendas of most governments around the world. It is clear that international trade must take environmental concerns into account."

Activist

"International trade interferes with the sovereignty of national governments. When Exxon Mobil is bigger than most countries in Europe, it is harder for governments to manage policies regarding taxes, monetary policy, social issues, and exchange rates. And who are we, trying to impose our own cultural standards on the world? When I travel in Asia or Latin America, I see McDonald's all over the place. They see Western powers exploiting globalization, harming the economic, cultural, and environmental interests of the rest of the world.

"Global corporations claim they spread modern technologies around the world. But technology is good only if you have access to it. In most of Africa, you have no on-ramp to the Internet. You need access to a computer, which is awfully difficult or impossible in countries where people make only a few dollars a day. When you're paid such a low wage, how can you afford technology? How can you afford to see a doctor? Globalization is widening the gap between rich and poor. As inequality grows, people have less and less in common. Multinational companies exploit poor countries and expose their people to harmful competition. Infant industries in developing economies can't make it when they're confronted with the power of giant multinational firms."

Business Executive

"Companies increasingly recognize the importance of being good global citizens. Motorola has profited from its business in China, but it also contributes to developing educational systems in that country. There are more literate people, especially literate women, in China than ever before. Japanese MNEs invest in the communities where they do business. Companies are not all evil; they do a lot of good for the world, too. Bill Gates is going to do more than any government to get people computers and get them hooked up on the Internet. He has created the world's biggest fund to combat diseases of the poor. He and Warren Buffett are tackling many of these diseases. GlaxoSmithKline is working with the World Health Organization to find a cure for elephantiasis, a terrible disease that ravages people in Africa."

Trade Official

"Globalization is complex and it's hard to tease out what is bad and what is good. Globalization has made rapid progress; global poverty has declined. Social indicators for many poor countries show improvement over several decades. It's true that income disparities have increased over the last 50 years while international trade has integrated the world economy. The world has experienced a generally rising tide in terms of people's standard of living. People everywhere are better off than they were 50 years ago. There are some exceptions to this, especially during recessions, but it's better to live in a world where 20 percent of the people are affluent and 80 percent are poor than a world in which nearly 100 percent of the people are poor, as was the case throughout most of history. There is a strong role for government in all this. Countries benefit from trade, but governments are responsible for protecting citizens from the negative or unintended consequences that trade may bring."

Activist

"Governments have not done enough to regulate the excesses of capitalism. We saw this clearly in the global financial and economic crises, from which the world is still recovering."

AACSB: Reflective Thinking Skills, Ethical Understanding and Reasoning Abilities

Case Questions

2-4. Do you think globalization and MNE activity are creating problems for the world? What kinds of problems can you identify? What are the unintended consequences of international business?

2-5. Summarize the arguments in favor of globalization that the business executive made. What is the role of technology in supporting company performance in a globalizing business environment?

2-6. What are the roles of state and federal governments in dealing with globalization? What is government's role in protecting citizens from the potential negative effects of foreign MNEs conducting business in your country? What kinds of government actions would you recommend?

2-7. What is the role of education in (i) addressing the problems raised in the roundtable; (ii) creating societies in which people can deal effectively with public policy issues; and (iii) creating citizens who can compete effectively in the global marketplace?

Sources: Jacques Bughin, Susan Lund, and James Manyika, "Harnessing the Power of Shifting Global Flows," *McKinsey Quarterly*, February 2015, pp. 1–13; Uri Dadush and William Shaw, *Juggernaut: How Emerging Powers Are Reshaping Globalization* (Washington, DC: Carnegie Endowment for International Peace, 2010); Luke Martell, *The Sociology of Globalization* (Malden, MA: Polity Press, 2010); OECD, statistics on globalization, retrieved from http://www.stats.oecd.org; "The Globalization Website," retrieved from Emory University Globalization website, http://www.sociology.emory.edu/globalization/index.html; Matthew Sparke, *Introducing Globalization: Ties, Tensions, and Integration in a Divided World* (Hoboken, NJ: Wiley-Blackwell, 2012).

END OF CHAPTER REVIEW

MyManagementLab

Go to **mymanagementlab.com** to complete the problems marked with this icon .

Key Terms

contagion   72
globalization of markets   58

value chain   68
World Trade Organization (WTO)   59

Summary

In this chapter, you learned about:

- **Market globalization as an organizing framework**

  Globalization of markets refers to the gradual integration and growing interdependence of national economies. Early civilizations in the Mediterranean, Middle East, Asia, Africa, and Europe all contributed to the growth of cross-border trade. Today's international trade was triggered by world events and technological discoveries and has progressed in phases, particularly since the early 1800s. The current phase was stimulated particularly by the rise of IT, the Internet, and other advanced technologies. The **World Trade Organization** is a multilateral governing body empowered to regulate international trade and investment.

- **The drivers of globalization**

  Globalization is driven by several factors, including falling trade and investment barriers; market liberalization and adoption of free market economics in formerly closed economies; industrialization and economic development, especially among emerging markets; integration of world financial markets; and technological advances.

- **Technological advances and globalization**

  Advances in technology, the most important of which have occurred in information technology, communications, the Internet, manufacturing, and transportation, are particularly important in driving globalization. These systems help create an interconnected network of customers, suppliers, and intermediaries worldwide and have made the cost of international business affordable for all types of firms.

- **The dimensions of globalization**

  Globalization can be modeled in terms of its drivers, dimensions, societal consequences, and firm-level consequences. Globalization refers to the growing integration of the world

economy from the international business activities of countless firms. It represents a growing global interconnectedness of buyers, producers, suppliers, and governments and has fostered a new dynamism in the world economy, the emergence of regional economic integration blocs, growth of global investment and financial flows, the convergence of buyer lifestyles and needs, and the globalization of both production and services. At the business enterprise level, globalization amounts to reconfiguration of company **value chains**—the sequence of value-adding activities, including sourcing, manufacturing, marketing, and distribution—on a global scale.

- **Firm-level consequences of market globalization**

  Globalization compels firms to organize their sourcing, manufacturing, marketing, and other value-adding activities on a global scale. Each value-adding activity can be performed in the home country or abroad. Firms choose where in the world they locate or configure key value-adding activities and internationalize value-chain activities to reduce the costs of R&D and production or gain closer access to customers.

- **Societal consequences of globalization**

  There is much debate about globalization's benefits and harm. Globalization was a major factor in the recent global recession and financial crisis. Critics complain that globalization interferes with national sovereignty, the ability of a state to govern itself without external intervention. Globalization is associated with *offshoring*, the relocation of value-chain activities to foreign locations where they can be performed at less cost by subsidiaries or independent suppliers. Globalization tends to decrease poverty, but it may also widen the gap between the rich and the poor. Furthermore, unrestricted industrialization may harm the natural environment. Globalization is also associated with the loss of cultural values unique to each nation. Nevertheless, trade and investment can help address many needs of developing countries, especially those of Africa.

Test Your Comprehension

2-8. What was the precursor to globalization and why was it important?

2-9. What important changes happened in the second phase of globalization?

2-10. Summarize the six dimensions of globalization. Which of these do you think is the most visible manifestation of globalization?

2-11. Describe the five drivers of globalization.

2-12. What is the role of the World Trade Organization?

2-13. In what areas have technological advances had their greatest effect on facilitating world trade and investment?

2-14. What are the pros and cons of globalization?

2-15. How has market globalization encouraged integration and interdependence and what have these countries had to do about it?

2-16. It is possible for an organization to add value by overseas operations?

Apply Your Understanding AACSB: Communication Abilities, Reflective Thinking Skills, Ethical Understanding and Reasoning Abilities, Use of Information Technology, Analytic Skills

2-17. Imagine you are studying for your international business class at a local coffee shop. The manager notices your textbook and remarks, "I don't get all that foreign business stuff. I don't pay much attention to it. I'm a local guy running a small business. Thank goodness I don't have to worry about any of that." The manager's comments make you realize there is much more to business than just local concerns. What is the likely value chain of a coffee shop? For example, how did the varieties of coffee beans get there? What is the likely effect of globalization on coffee shops? Do technological advances play any role in the shop's value chain? Does globalization imply any negative consequences for the worldwide coffee industry? Justify your answer.

2-18. Globalization provides numerous advantages to businesses and consumers around the world. At the same time, some critics believe globalization is harming various aspects of life and commerce. In what ways is globalization good for firms and consumers? In what ways is globalization harmful to firms and consumers?

2-19. *Ethical Dilemma:* Northern Energy, Inc. (Northern) is a large oil company with production and marketing operations worldwide. You are a recently hired manager at Northern's subsidiary in Nigeria, which provides jobs to hundreds of Nigerians and supports many local merchants and suppliers. Suppose Northern's drilling and refining practices have severely damaged the natural environment in Nigeria, polluting the air, land, and water. As a result, Northern has faced violent protests and much negative publicity in Nigeria. Develop suggestions for how Northern should address these issues. Keep in mind that top management is reluctant to invest significant new resources in Nigeria, given the firm's weakening business performance there.

 **INTERNET EXERCISES**
(www.globalEDGE.msu.edu)

AACSB: Reflective Thinking Skills, Ethical Understanding and Reasoning Abilities, Use of Information Technology, Analytic Skills

Refer to Chapter 1, page 54, for instructions on how to access and use globalEDGE™.

2-20. The KOF Swiss Economic Institute prepares the annual *KOF Index of Globalization*, which ranks the most globalized countries (enter "KOF Index of Globalization" at globalEDGE™ or other search engine). The index uses three dimensions to measure globalization: *economic globalization, political globalization*, and *social globalization*. Visit the index and explain what each dimension represents and why each is important for a nation to achieve a substantial presence in the global economy.

2-21. Service-sector jobs are increasingly outsourced to lower-cost locations abroad. The globalEDGE™ website has various resources that detail the nature and location of jobs that have been transferred abroad. Some experts believe the resulting foreign investment and increased demand in lower-cost countries will cause wages to rise in those countries, eliminating cost advantages from offshoring and narrowing the income gap between developed economies and low-cost countries. In other words, offshoring will help to reduce global poverty. Others believe that manufacturing jobs will be consistently moved to low-cost countries, making China and India the world's center of innovation and production. What do you think? Find three articles about outsourcing at globalEDGE™ by doing a search using the keywords "global outsourcing" or "offshoring" and write a report on the most likely consequences of these trends for your country, its workers, and consumers.

2-22. A key characteristic of globalization is the increasingly integrated world economy. MNEs and many nations have a stake in maintaining the globalization trend. If the trend were somehow reversed, participants in international business, such as exporters, would likely suffer big economic losses. In many ways, globalization's role in the world economy is critical. But just how big is the global economy? What is the extent of international trade relative to the size of the global economy? What is the proportion of international trade in the GDPs of each of the following

countries: Australia, Canada, Sweden, United Kingdom, and the United States? Consult globalEDGE™ to address these questions.

2-23. Globalization refers to the reduction of barriers to trade and investment, which is facilitating the internationalization of countless firms. Globalization is quickening and affecting firms around the world. However, it's also associated with various issues and challenges that confront firms as they undertake international business. Among the major issues are the condition of the global economy; indebtedness of national governments; power shifts to emerging markets; and country risk in the developing economies. Visit globalEDGE™ and enter the key word "globalization." Explore the information and websites that emerge from your search. Write a report on the most important contemporary issues that firms are facing as they undertake international business.

 MyManagementLab   **Try It!**

The simulation Globalization accompanies this exercise.

 MyManagementLab

Go to **mymanagementlab.com** for Auto-graded writing questions as well as the following Assisted-graded writing questions:

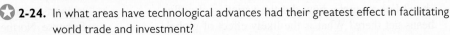

⭐ **2-24.** In what areas have technological advances had their greatest effect in facilitating world trade and investment?

⭐ **2-25.** What are the pros and cons of globalization?

⭐ **2-26.** MyManagementLab Only—comprehensive writing assignment for this chapter.

Endnotes

1. This discussion is based on Lawrence Beer, *Tracing the Roots of Globalization and Business Principles* (New York: Business Expert Press, 2011).

2. The word *trade* comes from the Anglo-Saxon term *trata*, which means to walk in the footsteps of others. Ancient trade routes were the foundation for a high level of cross-cultural exchange of ideas that led to the development of religion, science, economic activity, and government. The phrase "all roads lead to Rome" is not so much a metaphorical reference to Rome's dominance of the world 2,000 years ago, but to the fact that Rome's territorial colonies were constructed as commercial resource centers to serve the needs of the Roman Empire and increase its wealth. In an empire that stretched from England to Israel and from Germany to Africa, the Romans created more than 300,000 kilometers of roads. Roman roads were the lifeblood of the state that allowed trade to flourish. The Roman Empire was so concerned about the interruption of its shipping lanes for imported goods that it dispatched army legions to protect those lanes.

In the Middle Ages, the Knights Templar acted as guardians for pilgrims making the hazardous journey to pay homage to the birthplace of the Christian religion. In addition to protecting tourists, this warrior order created the first international banking system with the use of rudimentary traveler's checks, eliminating the need for travelers to carry valuables on their person.

In 1100, Genghis Khan not only united the Mongols but created an empire beyond the Chinese border that included Korea and Japan in the east, Mesopotamia (modern-day Iraq and Syria), Russia, Poland, and Hungary. He instituted common laws and regulations over his domain, most notably for the preservation of private property, to enhance and protect international trade.

Arab merchants traded in spices along land routes reaching from northern Arabia across modern-day Turkey, through Asia Minor, and finally reaching China. By concealing the origins of cinnamon, pepper, cloves, and nutmeg, traders gained a monopoly and controlled prices. Europeans came to believe that the spices came from Africa, when in fact they had merely changed hands in the region. Under the traditional trading system, spices, linen, silk, diamonds, pearls, and opium-based medicines reached Europe by indirect routes over land and sea. Representing one of the earliest systems of international distribution, the products passed through many hands on their long voyage. At every juncture, prices increased several fold. (This discussion is based on Lawrence Beer, 2011.)

3. C. Chase-Dunn, Yukio Kawano, and Benjamin D. Brewer, "World Globalization since 1795: Waves of Integration in the World-System," *American Sociological Review* 65, No. 1 (2000), pp. 77–95.

4. Lawrence Franko, *The European Multinationals* (Stamford, CN: Greylock Publishers, 1976).

5. Louis Emmerij, "Globalization, Regionalization, and World Trade," *Columbia Journal of World Business* 27, No. 2 (1992). pp. 6–13.

6. Company profile of America Movil, 2015, at http://www.hoovers .com/; Kyle Stock, "América Móvil Slims Down," *Bloomberg Businessweek*, July 14, 2014, p. 23; S.A.B. DE C.V., America Movil, *MarketLine Company Profile*, September 20, 2014, pp. 1–31.

7. Marcos Aguiar et al., *The New Global Challengers: How Top 100 Rapidly Developing Economies Are Changing the World*, Boston Consulting Group, May 25, 2006.

8. GNI refers to the total value of goods and services produced within a country after taking into account payments made to, and income received from, other countries.

9. Bughin et al., 2015; Michael E. Porter and Victor E. Millar, "How Information Gives You Competitive Advantage," *Harvard Business Review* 63 (July–August 1985), pp. 149–160; S. Tamer Cavusgil, "Extending the Reach of E-Business," *Marketing Management* 11, No. 2 (2002), pp. 24–29; Janice Burn and Karen Loch, "The Societal Impact of the World Wide Web— Key Challenges for the 21st Century," *Information Resources Management Journal* 14, No. 4 (2001), pp. 4–12.

10. Jacques Bughin, Susan Lund, and James Manyika, "Harnessing the Power of Shifting Global Flows," *McKinsey Quarterly* (February 2015), pp. 1–13.

11. Christina Larson, "In Rural China, You Don't Have to Read to Buy and Sell Online," *Bloomberg Businessweek*, February 13, 2014, pp. 17–18.

12. Boston Consulting Group, "The Mobile Internet Takes Off Everywhere," *BCG Perspectives*, March 20, 2015, retrieved from www.bcgperspectives.com; International Telecommunications Union, *Measuring the Information Society 2011* (Geneva, Switzerland: International Telecommunications Union).

13. "The China Puzzle," *Journal of Advertising Research* 51, No. 4 (2011), pp. 634-642; Nicola Smith, "How to Get Fans to Cheer Your Brand On," *Marketing Week*, October 9, 2014, pp. 29–32.

14. United Nations, *Regional Shipping and Port Development* (Bangkok, Thailand: Economic and Social Commission for Asia and the Pacific 2011).

15. Reynolds Hutchins, "Joining the Big-Ship Party," *Journal of Commerce*, March 9, 2015, pp. 40–42.

16. "Operating Profit," *The Economist*, August 16, 2008, pp. 74–76.

17. Stephen Fidler, "Globalization: Battered but Not Beaten," *Wall Street Journal,* January 21, 2015, p. A6.

18. Deloitte Consulting LLP, *Deloitte's Globalization Survey: Preparing for the Next Wave of Globalization,* 2014. Retrieved from www.deloitte.com, March 16, 2015.

19. F. Norris, "Crisis Is Over, but Where's the Fix?" *New York Times*, March 10, 2011, at www.nytimes.com; Gabriele Parussini, "World News: Euro-Zone Economic Outlook Darkens," *Wall Street Journal*, January 17, 2009, p. A7; Dave Shellock, "Signs of Deepening Recession Dent Confidence," *Financial Times*, February 14, 2009, p. 14; "When Fortune Frowned," *The Economist*, October 11, 2008, pp. 3–5.

20. "A Monetary Malaise," *The Economist*, October 11, 2008, pp. 20–25.

21. Shellock (2009); Norris (2011); Parussini (2009).

22. Bin Jiang, Timothy Koller, and Zane Williams, "Mapping Decline and Recovery across Sectors," *McKinsey on Finance*, Winter 2009, pp. 21–25.

23. "When Fortune Frowned," pp. 3–5; International Monetary Fund, http://www.imf.org; Shellock (2009); Rich Miller and Simon Kennedy, "The U.S. Shops and the World Applauds," *Bloomberg Businessweek*, April 9–15, 2012, pp. 22–24.

24. Liyan Chen and Andrea Murphy, "The World's Largest Public Companies," *Forbes Asia*, June 2014, pp. 50–80; Hans Greimel, "Assault on Fortress Detroit," *Automotive News*, January 19, 2015, p. 3; "When Fortune Frowned," pp. 3–5; International Monetary Fund, http://www.imf.org; Shellock (2009).

25. "The Day the Factories Stopped," *The Economist*, October 23, 2004, p. 70.

26. Pete Engrail et al., "The New Global Job Shift," *BusinessWeek*, February 3, 2003, p. 50.

27. J. Newman, "Polaris Plant Closure to Begin in March; 484 Jobs to Be Lost," *Wisconsin State Journal*, December 23, 2010, at http://www.host.madison.com/wsj.

28. David Wessel, "U.S. Firms Eager to Add Foreign Jobs," *Wall Street Journal*, November 22, 2011, p. B1.

29. Katy George, Sree Ramaswamy, and Lou Rassey, "Next-shoring: A CEO's Guide," *McKinsey Quarterly*, January 2014; Anne Smith, "Foreign Factories Come Back Home," *Kiplinger's Personal Finance,* March 2013, pp. 11–12.

30. International Labour Organization, *Children in Hazardous Work* (Geneva: International Labour Organization, 2011).

31. Tara Radon and Martin Calkins, "The Struggle Against Sweatshops: Moving Toward Responsible Global Business," *Journal of Business Ethics* 66, No. 2–3 (2006), pp. 261–269.

32. S. L. Bachman, "The Political Economy of Child Labor and Its Impacts on International Business," *Business Economics*, July 2000, pp. 30–41.

33. D. Dollar, "Globalization, Poverty, and Inequality Since 1980," *World Bank Policy Research Working Paper 3333*, June 2004, Washington, DC: World Bank.

34. UNCTAD, *World Investment Report 2011* (New York: United Nations Conference on Trade And Development, 2012); World Bank, *World Bank Development Indicators 2012* (Washington DC: World Bank, 2012).

35. Surjit Bhalla, *Imagine There's No Country: Poverty Inequality and Growth in the Era of Globalization*, (Washington DC: Peterson Institute, 2002).

36. Wolf (2004).

37. Michael Smith, "Trade and the Environment," *International Business* 5, No. 8 (1992), pp. 74.

38. "Main Street Masala," *Bloomberg BusinessWeek*, February 6–12, 2012, pp. 69–71.

39. "A Glimmer of Light at Last? Africa's Economy," *The Economist*, June 24, 2006, p. 71; World Bank, 2012.

40. Dambisa Moyo, *Dead Aid* (New York: Farrar, Straus and Giroux, 2009).

41. Patrick Dupoux, Tenbite Ermias, Stéphane Heuzé, Stefano Niavas, and Mia von Koschitzky Kimani, "Winning in Africa: From Trading Posts to Ecosystems," *bcg.perspectives*, January 9, 2014, pp. 1–24.

42. Moyo (2009); Robert Farzad, "Can Greed Save Africa?" *BusinessWeek*, December 10, 2007, pp. 446–554; C. K. Prahalad, *The Fortune at the Bottom of the Pyramid* (Upper Saddle River, NJ: Wharton School Publishing, 2004); Robert Farzad (2007); Organisation for Economic Co-operation and Development and African Development Bank.

Chapter 3

The Cultural Environment of International Business

Learning Objectives *After studying this chapter, you should be able to:*

3.1 Understand culture and cross-cultural risk

3.2 Learn the dimensions of culture

3.3 Appreciate the role of language and religion in culture

3.4 Appreciate culture's effect in international business

3.5 Learn models and explanations of culture

3.6 Understand managerial implications of culture

Baidu: Culture and Social Media in China

China has the world's largest number of Internet users. But China has banned Western social media sites—for example, Facebook and YouTube—over concerns that they facilitate access to material critical of the Chinese government. Instead, Chinese citizens flock to local social sites, such as *Baidu*, which features a search engine and numerous social sites. Founded in 2000, Baidu has more than 500 million users, almost all of them in China. The word *baidu* refers to "persistent search for the ideal" and derives from a Chinese poem written more than 800 years ago. Other popular Chinese portals are Alibaba (similar to Amazon.com), Renren (similar to Facebook), and WeChat (similar to WhatsApp).

Statistics show that Chinese Internet users are about twice as likely as U.S. nationals to post to online forums, publish blogs, or use social sites to obtain information on products and brands. This explains why successful multinational firms such as BMW, Estée Lauder, and Starbucks use social media extensively to market their products in China.

Anthropologist Geert Hofstede notes that China is a *collectivistic* society in which individuals view themselves as part of a social context that emphasizes tradition, interdependence, and harmony. The Chinese think of themselves in terms of their group memberships and societal connections and focus on social norms and family integrity. Edward Hall defined China as a "high-context, relationship-oriented" culture. Communication is subtle and characterized by emotional appeals. With its emphasis on family, relationships, and social harmony, the Chinese culture reflects values handed down from Confucius, an ancient Chinese philosopher. In various ways, social media represent manifestations of the complex dimensions of Chinese culture.

Social media allow Chinese to stay in close touch with family members. Kids love playing online games such as Happy Garden, a farming game, with their parents. Social relationships also play a big role in consumer behavior because the Chinese often look to peers for information and advice

Source: elwynn/123RF

about what product brands and services are socially acceptable to buy. Chinese use social media to express similarity to members of their social groups.

China's family-planning policy restricted many Chinese couples to having just one child. The "little emperors" born into such a system have no siblings, and they feel enormous pressure to perform—for their parents and the nation. Such pressures have increased the popularity of social media, where lonely youngsters can express themselves and find friends. In a society that emphasizes collectivism, first thanks to Confucian values and later because of communism, social media offer platforms for self-expression. It provides opportunities for nonconformity and free speech that are mostly unattainable offline.

Social media also provide the means to build *Guanxi* by fostering relationships with others. Guanxi refers to informal personal relationships that emphasize reciprocal obligations and the exchange of favors. In China, guanxi strongly influences business, organizational behavior, and human relations in general. Chinese firms and institutions tend to be very hierarchical. Confucian philosophy teaches that people play different roles in society. Unlike in many Western cultures, casual or candid exchange between colleagues of different ages and ranks is discouraged. In China, social media allows people to express their views without causing others to lose face, *mianzi,* which refers to a person's reputation and social standing.

When Baidu and Renren were first launched, they bore a strong resemblance to their Western counterparts, Amazon and Facebook. This can occur because China has a collectivist and "public interest" approach to property rights, including intellectual property such as patents and copyrights. Copying others' know-how and technology is often acceptable. Copying usually is not considered wrong as long as you're making something better or cheaper.

Questions

3-1. Why are the Chinese such heavy users of the Internet?

3-2. What are the characteristics of a collectivistic society such as China?

3-3. In what ways does social media reflect cultural values in China?

SOURCES: H. Chen, A. Ellinger, and Y. Tian, "Manufacturer–Supplier Guanxi Strategy," *Industrial Marketing Management* 40, No. 4 (2011), pp. 550–560; E. Fyrwald, "Five Keys to Profiting in China," *Bloomberg BusinessWeek*, March 16, 2011, accessed from www.Businessweek.com; Xia He and Rafael Pedraza-Jiménez, "Chinese Social Media Strategies: Communication Key Features from a Business Perspective," *El Profesional de la Información*, 24, No. 2 (2015), pp. 200–209; Li Hong. "Marketing to China's Middle Class," *China Business Review*, January 2014, pp. 11–15; *New York Times*, "China and Intellectual Property," Dec. 23, 2010, accessed at www.nytimes.com; A. Rabkin, "The Social(ist) Networks," *Fast Company*, February 2011, pp. 68–75; April Rabkin. "The Tao of the Sea Turtle," *Fast Company*, February 2012, pp. 78–99.

The opening case on Baidu highlights the challenges of operating in diverse national cultures. In international business, success requires sensitivity to national interests and cultural expectations. The framework in Exhibit 3.1 identifies the essential concepts for understanding culture and its importance in international business. In this chapter, we will examine these concepts in detail.

3.1 Understand culture and cross-cultural risk

Culture
The values, beliefs, customs, arts, and other products of human thought and work that characterize the people of a given society.

Culture and Cross-Cultural Risk

As reflected in the opening case, **culture** refers to the values, beliefs, customs, arts, and other products of human thought and work that characterize the people of a given society. Culture shapes our behavior. Although as human beings we share many similarities, as groups of people or societies, we exhibit many differences. Culture even affects the common rituals of daily life. Greeting ceremonies are a deeply embedded cultural marker and have evolved over many centuries. They specify such behaviors as whether to shake hands, what to say, and how far apart to stand. These cultural conventions may vary as a function of the age, gender, or status of the greeters. In China, friends express thoughtfulness by asking each other whether they have had their meal yet. In Turkey, a typical greeting is "What is new with you?" In Japan, elaborate greeting and parting rituals are the norm, and individuals routinely apologize to the other party just before ending a telephone conversation.

Culture captures how the members of the society live—for instance, how we feed, clothe, and shelter ourselves. Culture explains how we behave toward each other and with other groups. Culture defines our values and attitudes and the way we perceive the meaning of life.

EXHIBIT 3.1

Framework on the Essential Elements of Culture

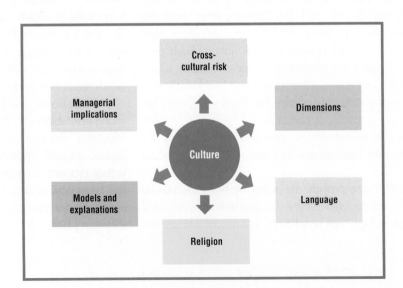

Japan:
Ebi Burger–made of shrimp

Canada:
My Poutine–French fries topped with gravy and cheese curds

Morocco:
Recette Moutarde–burger in ciabatta bread, slathered in mustard

Germany:
Beer is a beverage choice

Hong Kong:
Rice Burger–two patties of sticky rice of instead of buns

Norway:
McLaks–sandwich made of grilled salmon and sour cream dill sauce

Saudi Arabia:
McArabia – grilled beef with spices, lettuce, tomato, onion, garlic sauce, in a pita wrap

Japan:
McHotdog Mega Breakfast–hotdog with scrambled eggs and ketchup

France:
Wine is a menu favorite

Philippines:
McSpaghetti–spaghetti noodles in a sweet tomato–based sauce

India:
Paneer Salsa Wrap–cottage cheese wrap, cabbage, celery, with mayonnaise and salsa

Malaysia:
Bubur Ayam–chicken porridge, a local favorite

Food is among the most interesting aspects of national culture. In Japan, pizza is often topped with fish and seaweed. In the United States, pizza can be piled high with meat. In France, it often comes with various cheeses. Take a look at Exhibit 3.2, which depicts numerous menu items at McDonald's fast-food restaurants around the world. McDonald's attempts to offer a relatively standardized menu worldwide but often varies offerings to suit tastes in individual countries. Some cultures are very complex. As reflected in the opening case, some are relatively individualistic, whereas others are more collectivist. Some impose many norms and rules on social behavior; others are less imposing.[1]

Why should we concern ourselves with culture in cross-border business? The answer is that culture introduces new risks. Recall the four risks of international business we introduced in Chapter 1. We highlight these risks in Exhibit 3.3. **Cross-cultural risk** is a situation or event in which a cultural misunderstanding puts some human value at stake. Misunderstanding and miscommunication arise because people have differing values and expectations. They do not always communicate (verbally or nonverbally) what the other party is anticipating or may have different ways of communicating. For example, a head nod has different meanings in India and the United Kingdom. Cross-cultural misunderstandings can ruin business deals, hurt sales, or harm the corporate image. Today, developing an appreciation of, and sensitivity for, cultural differences is an imperative. Managers who are well informed about cross-cultural differences have advantages in managing employees, marketing products, and interaction with customers and business partners.

Today, firms conduct business in environments characterized by unfamiliar languages as well as unique beliefs, norms, and behaviors. Managers need to be able to reconcile these differences to create profitable ventures. They must not only understand cultural differences—they must also develop international cultural competence.

Cross-cultural risk
A situation or event in which a cultural misunderstanding puts some human value at stake.

What Culture Is *Not*

Now that you have an idea of what culture is, let us define what it is *not*. Culture is:

- *Not right or wrong*. Culture is relative. People of different nationalities simply perceive the world differently. Each culture has its own notions of acceptable and unacceptable behavior. For example, in some Islamic cultures, a wife cannot divorce her husband. In many

EXHIBIT 3.3

The Four Major Risks in International Business

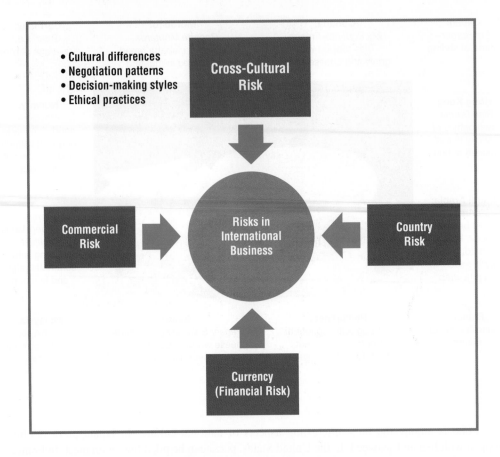

- Cultural differences
- Negotiation patterns
- Decision-making styles
- Ethical practices

Cross-Cultural Risk

Commercial Risk

Risks in International Business

Country Risk

Currency (Financial Risk)

Source: Eric Reisenberger/123RF

Turcana woman wearing beads around neck and hoop earrings.

countries, nudity is entirely acceptable on TV. In Japan and Turkey, wearing shoes in the home is taboo.

- ***Not about individual behavior***. Culture is about groups. It refers to a collective phenomenon of shared values and meanings. Thus, whereas culture defines the collective behavior of each society, individuals often behave differently.
- ***Not inherited***. Culture comes from people's social environment. No one is born with a shared set of values and attitudes. Rather, children gradually acquire specific ways of thinking and behaving as they are raised in a society. In the United States, for example, children usually learn to value individualism. In China, children learn to depend on family members and acquire values based on Confucianism. Culture is passed from generation to generation by parents, teachers, mentors, peers, and leaders. Modern methods of communication, including the media, play an enormous role in transmitting culture.

Socialization and Acculturation

This process of learning the rules and behavioral patterns appropriate to one's society is called **socialization**. Each society has rules—do's, don'ts, expectations, and preferences that guide behavior particularly of children as they the mature.[2] Such rules may be explicitly stated—for example, "We don't do things that way around here"; or they may be implicit, that is, everyone is expected to know how to function at work, at school, with friends, and so forth. Breaking a rule amounts to a failure to conform. As each of us matures, failing to follow society's rules provides opportunities for learning what the rules are. Socialization is cultural learning and provides the means to acquire cultural understandings and orientations that a particular society shares. It is a subtle process; we often adapt our behavior unconsciously and unwittingly.

Acculturation is the process of adjusting and adapting to a culture other than one's own. It is commonly experienced by people who live in other countries for extended periods, such as expatriate workers. In many ways, acculturation is challenging because adults are often less flexible than children.[3]

Socialization

The process of learning the rules and behavioral patterns appropriate for living in one's own society.

Acculturation

The process of adjusting and adapting to a culture other than one's own.

3.2 Learn the dimensions of culture

Dimensions of Culture

More than any other feature of human civilization, culture illustrates the differences among societies based on language, habits, customs, and modes of thought. Yet most of us are not completely aware of how culture affects our behavior until we encounter people from other cultures.

Anthropologists use the iceberg metaphor to call attention to the many dimensions of culture, some obvious and some not so obvious. Above the surface, certain characteristics are visible, but below, invisible to the observer, is a massive base of assumptions, attitudes, and values. These invisible characteristics strongly influence decision making, relationships, conflict, and other dimensions of international business. We are usually unaware of the nine-tenths of our cultural makeup that exists below the surface. In fact, we are often not aware of our own culture unless we meet another one. Exhibit 3.4 illustrates the *iceberg concept of culture*, using three layers of awareness: high culture, folk culture, and deep culture.

Culture emerges through the integration of our values and attitudes; manners and customs; time and space perceptions; symbolic, material, and creative expressions; education; social structure; language; and religion. Let's examine these in more detail.

Values and Attitudes

Values represent a person's judgments about what is good or bad, acceptable or unacceptable, important or unimportant, and normal or abnormal.[4] Values are the basis for our motivation and behavior. Our values guide the development of our attitudes and preferences. They guide us in the decisions we make and in how we lead our lives. Typical values in North America and northern Europe include work, or output orientation, being on time, and the acquisition of wealth. People from such countries may misjudge those from, say, Latin America, who may not hold such values. *Attitudes* are similar to opinions but are often unconsciously held and may not be based on logical facts. Prejudices are rigidly held attitudes, usually unfavorable and usually aimed at particular groups of people.

Manners and Customs

Manners and customs are ways of behaving and conducting oneself in public and business situations. Some countries are characterized by informal cultures; people treat each other as equals and work together cooperatively. In other countries, people tend to be more formal; status, power, and respect are relatively more important.

Although you may see more people around the world developing a taste for sushi and tacos, preferences for food, eating habits, and mealtimes are still varied. Customs that vary most worldwide relate to work hours and holidays, drinking and toasting, appropriate behavior at social gatherings, gift giving, and women in the workforce. Gift giving is complex in much of the world. In Japan, it is usually a mistake not to offer a gift in initial meetings. The Middle East is characterized by generous gift giving.

Handshaking varies across the world: limp handshakes, firm handshakes, elbow-grasping handshakes,

Source: Stephen Coburn/Fotolia

Cross-cultural encounters are increasingly common.

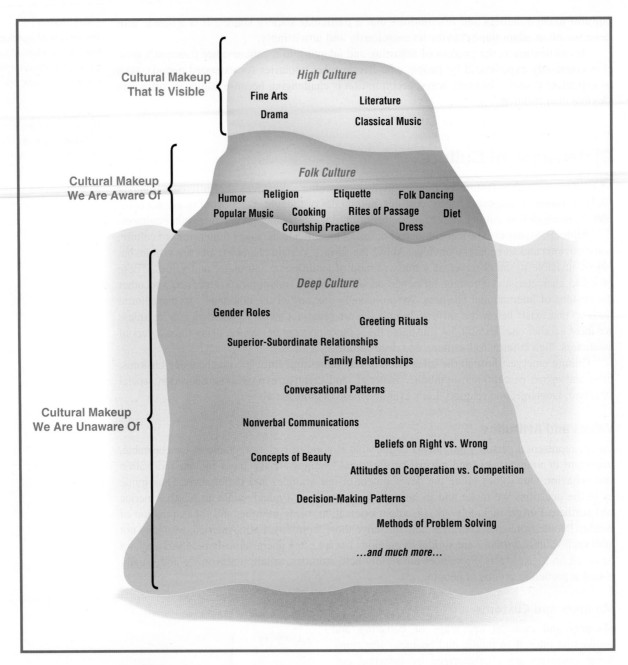

EXHIBIT 3.4

Culture as an Iceberg

and no handshake at all. In some parts of the world, people greet by kissing each other on both cheeks. In Southeast Asia, greeting involves placing the palms together in front of the chest, as in praying. In Japan, bowing is the norm.[5]

Perceptions of Time

Time has a strong influence on business. It affects people's expectations about planning, scheduling, profit flows, and promptness in arriving for work and meetings. Japanese managers tend to prepare strategic plans for long periods, such as a decade. The planning horizon for Western companies is much shorter, typically a few years. Some societies are more oriented to the past, others to the present, and still others to the future.

People in past-oriented cultures believe plans should be evaluated in terms of their fit with established traditions, customs, and wisdom. Innovation and change do not occur very often and are justified to the extent they fit with experience. Europeans are relatively past-oriented and prefer to conserve traditional ways of doing things.

Young countries such as Australia, Canada, and the United States are relatively focused on the present. They tend to have a **monochronic** orientation to time—a rigid orientation in which people are focused on schedules, punctuality, and time as a resource. They view time as *linear*, like a river flowing into the future, carrying workers from one activity to the next.

In such cultures, where people are highly focused on the clock, managers make commitments, set deadlines, and follow a strict schedule in meetings. Punctuality is a virtue and time is money. Throughout the day, workers glance at their watches, their computer's clock, or the clock on the wall. Investors are impatient and want quick returns. Managers have a relatively short-term perspective when it comes to investments and making money. Company profitability is measured on a quarterly basis. In this way, people in the United States have acquired a reputation for being hurried and impatient. Indeed, the word business was originally spelled busyness.

Some cultures have a **polychronic** perspective on time. In such societies, instead of performing single tasks serially, people are inclined to do many things at once. In this way, members of polychronic cultures are easily distracted. They can change plans often and easily, and long delays are sometimes needed before taking action. Punctuality per se is relatively unimportant, and managers consider time commitments flexible. They do not strictly follow the clock and schedules. They put more value on relationships and spending time with people.[6]

Chinese and Japanese firms typically are future-oriented. They focus not on how the firm will perform next quarter but on how it will perform a decade from now. Many large Japanese firms offer lifetime employment and invest heavily in employee training. They expect workers to remain with the firm for decades. Latin Americans have a flexible perception of time and may not arrive exactly at the predetermined time for appointments. In the Middle East, strict Muslims view destiny as the will of God ("Inshallah" or "God willing" is a frequently used phrase). They tend to downplay the importance of future planning. They perceive appointments as relatively vague future obligations.

Monochronic
A rigid orientation to time, in which the individual is focused on schedules, punctuality, and time as a resource.

Polychronic
A flexible, nonlinear orientation to time, in which the individual takes a long-term perspective and emphasizes human relationships.

Perceptions of Space

Cultures also differ in their perceptions of physical space. We have our own sense of personal space and feel uncomfortable if others violate it. Conversational distance is closer in Latin America than in northern Europe or the United States. When a North American talks to a Latin American, he or she may unconsciously back up to maintain personal space. Those who live in crowded Japan or Belgium have smaller personal space requirements than those who live in land-rich Russia or the United States. In Japan, it is common for employee workspaces to be crowded together in the same room, desks pushed against each other. One large office space might contain desks for fifty employees. U.S. firms partition individual workspaces and provide private offices for more important employees. In Islamic countries close interaction between men and women is not encouraged in public places.

Symbolic Productions

A *symbol* can be letters, figures, colors, or other characters that communicate a meaning. For example, the cross is the main symbol of Christianity. The red star was the symbol of the former Soviet Union. National symbols include flags, anthems, seals, monuments, and historical myths. Symbols can represent nations, religions, or corporations, and they can help to unite people. Mathematicians and scientists use symbols as their language. Businesses have many types of symbols, in the form of trademarks, logos, and brands. Think how easy it is to identify popular company logos such as Nike's swoosh, Apple's apple, and Cadbury's unique lettering.

Material Productions and Creative Expressions

Material productions are artifacts, objects, and technological systems that people construct to function within their environments. They are integral to human life and provide the means to accomplish objectives as well as communicate and conduct exchanges within and between societies. The most important technology-based material productions are the infrastructures that supply energy, transportation, and communications. Others include social infrastructure (systems that provide housing, education, and health care), financial infrastructure (systems for managing means of exchange in banks and other financial institutions), and marketing infrastructure (systems that support marketing-related activities such as ad agencies). Creative expressions of culture include arts, folklore, music, dance, theater, and high cuisine. Education is an especially important system that emerges within cultures.

Education

Cultural values, ideas, beliefs, traditions, and attitudes are passed from one generation to the next through education. Education takes place in various ways, especially through lessons and behavior acquired from parents, family, and peers; participation in groups (social, business, and religious); and formal schooling. In most countries, academic education usually occurs through schooling. Available talent and skill base of a region or country influences where corporations will locate international ventures such as factories or call centers. Better-educated locations tend to attract higher paying and higher skilled positions such as outsourced call centers and accounting functions. Literacy, the ability to read, is an important indicator of education level and varies substantially around the world. Exhibit 3.5 shows literacy rates in selected countries.

Social Structure

Social structure refers to the pattern of social arrangements and organized relationships that characterize a society. It refers to how a society is organized in terms of individuals, families, groups, and socioeconomic strata. All cultures have a social structure that influences our status or class in society. Understanding the social structure of international employees, clients, and suppliers is vital for avoiding cultural misunderstandings and optimizing business transactions.

Individuals. Because Western cultures emphasize individualism and individual success, social status often is determined by individual performance. This helps explain the high degree of worker mobility and entrepreneurial activity typical in Western societies. Excessive individualism, however, can reduce the effectiveness of teams, particularly in collectivist cultures typical of Asia.

Family. In many cultures, immediate and extended family holds particular importance in the nation's social structure. In such cultures, the family often plays a substantial role in

EXHIBIT 3.5

Literacy Rates in Selected Countries (% of those who can read)

Source: Central Intelligence Agency, The World Factbook 2015 (Washington DC: Central Intelligence Agency, 2015)

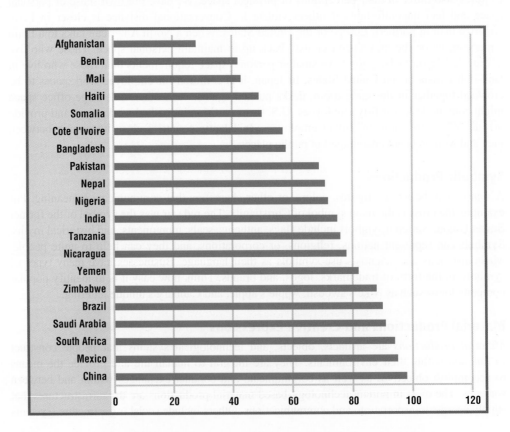

the formation and structure of business activities. In China, for example, family-owned and family-run businesses are relatively common, and ownership often passes on to successive generations.

Reference groups. In some societies, people's social status is defined by group or employer affiliation rather than by individual performance. When meeting business people in Tokyo, for instance, they typically will identify themselves in terms of the companies where they work rather than by their function or job title at that firm. In Japanese firms, objectives and strategies are typically decided by groups, rather than by individual managers.

Social stratification. In most cultures, individuals are classified within classes or social layers depending on their occupation, income level, or family history. However, societies differ in the importance they place on social strata and on the ease with which people can advance to higher strata. In most countries, senior business and government leaders typically occupy the highest social strata. The middle strata usually consist of business managers and medical or scientific professionals. Those in the lowest strata typically work in manual labor, basic services such as retailing, or lower-level administrative positions.

Social mobility. Social mobility refers to the ease with which a person can move up within social strata. The most rigid type of social mobility operates in a *caste system*, countries such as India. In a caste system, a person's social status is determined by birth, and he or she has little opportunity for social mobility. Individuals are often restricted to working in a specific occupation, such as a farmer or factory worker, depending on the caste they were born into. Understanding social norms in caste system countries is necessary to successfully manage employees who work at different levels of the social strata. Advanced economies are characterized by the *class system*, a more flexible form of social stratification within which people usually have greater mobility to move to a higher strata and change their social status. Social mobility in caste and class systems alike influences people's attitude toward work, entrepreneurship, and labor relations.

Role of Language and Religion in Culture

3.3 Appreciate the role of language and religion in culture

Language and religion are among the most important manifestations of culture. Often described as the expression or *mirror* of culture, verbal language is not only essential for communications, it also provides insights into culture. It's a major differentiator between cultural groups and castes and provides an essential means for business leaders to communicate effectively with employees, suppliers, and customers. Language can be classified as verbal and nonverbal.

Verbal Language

The world has nearly 7,000 active languages, including more than 2,000 in each of Africa and Asia. Most of these languages have only a few thousand speakers.[7] Exhibit 3.6 shows the world's major languages.

National languages, dialects, and translation tend to complicate verbal communication. It is sometimes difficult to find words to convey the same meaning in a different language. For example, a one-word equivalent to "aftertaste" does not exist in many languages. Even when a word can be translated well into other languages, its concept and meaning may not be universal. For example, the Japanese word *muzukashii* can be variously translated as "difficult," "delicate," or "I don't want to discuss it," but in business negotiations it usually means "out of the question." Advertising themes often lose their original meaning in translation or give the wrong impression.

Exhibit 3.7 shows how the popular slogans of some languages translate into unintended phrases in other languages. Pepsi's mistranslation in Taiwan is an example. Taiwanese people knew Pepsi could not bring their ancestors back from the grave, but many were surprised at Pepsi's apparent carelessness in rendering a poor translation. Even people from different countries who speak the same language may experience communication problems because some words are unique to international languages. Exhibit 3.8 shows how two English-speaking countries interpret the same word in very different ways and how misinterpretations can hamper intended meaning.[8]

EXHIBIT 3.6

The Most Common Primary Languages in the World

Sources: Based on M. Paul Lewis et al. (ed.), *Ethnologue: Languages of the World*, 18th ed. (Dallas, TX: SIL International, 2015) at http://www.ethnologue.com; and CIA World Factbook, 2015, at http://www.cia.gov.

World Rank	Language	Approximate Number of Native Speakers (Millions)	Countries with Substantial Number of Native Speakers
1	Chinese	960	China, Singapore
2	Spanish	380	Argentina, Mexico, Spain
3	English	340	Australia, Canada, United Kingdom, United States
4	Hindi	310	India
5	Arabic	305	Egypt, Saudi Arabia, United Arab Emirates
6	Portuguese	210	Brazil, Portugal
7	Bengali	200	Bangladesh, India
8	Russian	150	Russia, Kazakhstan, Ukraine
9	Japanese	125	Japan
10	Punjabi	100	India, Pakistan
11	German	90	Germany, Austria
12	Javanese	80	Indonesia
13	Korean	75	South Korea
14	French	74	France, Canada, Belgium, Algeria
15	Tamil	70	India, Sri Lanka

Sometimes business jargon—vocabulary unique to a particular country—can cause communication problems. Examples of English jargon that puzzle nonnative speakers include: "the bottom line," "to beat around the bush," "shooting from the hip," "feather in your cap," and "get down to brass tacks." Imagine the difficulty that professional interpreters encounter in translating such phrases!

An **idiom** is an expression whose symbolic meaning is different from its actual or literal meaning. It is a phrase you cannot understand by knowing only what the individual words in the phrase mean. For example, to "roll out the red carpet" is to welcome a guest extravagantly—no

Idiom
An expression whose symbolic meaning is different from its literal meaning.

Company and Location	Intended Ad Slogan	Literal Translation
Parker Pen Company in Latin America	"Use Parker Pen, avoid embarrassment!"	"Use Parker Pen, avoid pregnancy!"
Pepsi in Germany	"Come Alive with Pepsi"	"Come out of the grave with Pepsi."
Pepsi in Taiwan	"Come Alive with Pepsi"	"Pepsi brings your ancestors back from the dead."
Fisher Body (car exteriors) in Belgium	"Body by Fisher"	"Corpse by Fisher"
Salem cigarettes in Japan	"Salem—Feeling Free"	"Smoking Salem makes your mind feel free and empty."

EXHIBIT 3.7

Blunders in International Advertising

EXHIBIT 3.8

Differences in Meaning Between American and British English

Word	Meaning in U.S. English	Meaning in British English
Scheme	A somewhat devious plan	A plan
Redundant	Repetitive	Fired or laid off
Sharp	Smart	Conniving, unethical
To table	To put as issue on hold	To take up an issue
To bomb	To fail miserably	To succeed grandly
Windscreen	A screen that protects against wind	Automobile windshield

red carpet is actually used. The phrase is misunderstood when interpreted in a literal way. In Spanish, the idiom "no está el horno para bolos" literally means "the oven isn't ready for bread rolls," but the phrase is understood as "the time isn't right." In Japanese, the phrase "uma ga au" literally means "our horses meet," but the everyday meaning is "we get along with each other."

Idioms exist in virtually every culture, and people often use them as a short way to express a larger concept. Managers should study national idioms to gain a better understanding of cultural values. Exhibit 3.9 offers several expressions that reveal cultural traits of different societies.

Nonverbal Communication

Nonverbal communication is unspoken and includes facial expressions and gestures.[9] In fact, nonverbal messages accompany most verbal ones. These include facial expressions, body movements, eye contact, physical distance, posture, and other nonverbal signals. Exhibit 3.10 lists various types of nonverbal communication.

Nonverbal communications frequently can lead to confusion and misunderstandings because of cultural differences. Certain facial expressions and hand gestures have different meanings in different cultures, and a lack of awareness of the meanings of these gestures in the local culture can lead to negative consequences. For example, standing side by side with someone can indicate cooperation, whereas a face-to-face posture might indicate competition or opposition. Touching tends to indicate levels of intimacy, from shaking hands, to patting the back, to hugging.

Religion

Religion is a system of common beliefs or attitudes concerning a being or a system of thought that people consider sacred, divine, or the highest truth and includes the moral codes, values, institutions, traditions, and rituals associated with this system. Religious concepts of right and

EXHIBIT 3.9 Idioms That Symbolize Cultural Values

Country	Expression	Underlying Value
Japan	"The nail that sticks out gets hammered down."	Group conformity
Australia and New Zealand	"The tall poppy gets cut down." (Criticism of a person who is perceived as presumptuous, attention-seeking, or without merit.)	Egalitarianism
Sweden and other Scandinavian countries	"*Janteloven*" or "Jante Law." "Don't think you're anyone special or that you're better than us."	Modesty
Korea	"A tiger dies leaving its leather, a man dies leaving his name."	Honor
Turkey	"Steel that works, does not rust."	Hard work
United States	"Necessity is the mother of invention."	Resourcefulness
Thailand	"If you follow older people, dogs won't bite you."	Wisdom

EXHIBIT 3.10

Nonverbal Communication

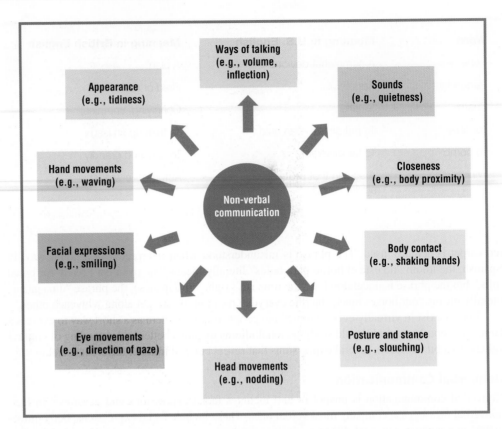

wrong have played a major role in the development of ethical values and social responsibility. Almost every culture is underpinned by religious beliefs.[10] Religion influences culture and, therefore, managerial and customer behavior in various ways. Exhibit 3.11 shows the dominant religions worldwide but only the most common religion in each location; most countries are home to people of various faiths.

Although there are thousands of distinct faith groups worldwide, four major religions dominate: *Christianity* with roughly 2 billion adherents, *Islam* with about 1.5 billion followers, and *Hinduism* and *Buddhism*, each with around 1 billion adherents. Other belief systems include *Confucianism* and *Judaism*.

Religion appears to have a positive effect on economic activity.[11] Religious affiliations help create bonds of trust and shared commitment, which facilitate lending and trade. Furthermore, religion can boost GDP in a country by reducing corruption and increasing respect for law and order. Religion that promotes moral values should help foster successful economic systems. Conversely, a lack of ethical values tends to coincide with economic decay; a lawless society cannot sustain normal business activities for long. It is noteworthy, however, that some societies with strong religious values—for example, most Middle Eastern countries and their embrace of Islam, or southern Africa and its many Christian devotees—have not produced high living standards for their citizens. This implies religion alone is insufficient to support economic development. Other factors, such as strong private property rights, political and economic freedom, and an entrepreneurial spirit, are also important. Let's review each of the four major religions.

Christianity. Followers of Jesus Christ, Christians are concentrated in the Americas, Europe, Australia, South Korea, and southern Africa. Christianity is divided into three major groups: Catholic, Protestant, and Eastern Orthodox. Catholics account for more than half of all Christians; Protestants encompass numerous denominations, including Baptists and Methodists; and Eastern Orthodox Christianity is practiced mainly in Greece and Russia.

Although the number of adherents has declined over time, particularly in Europe and North America, the cultural effects of Christianity have largely endured. For one, Sunday is still regarded as a day of rest when most people do not work. German sociologist Max Weber and other scholars have suggested a relationship between Protestantism and capitalism.

Protestantism long emphasized individual effort, orderliness, and hard work to achieve worldly success and as a duty that benefits both the individual and society. As a revolutionary movement that broke with the Catholic Church, Protestantism also long emphasized religious freedom and independent thinking. Such views are consistent with the political and economic freedoms that encouraged the rise of capitalism in the advanced economies, especially in Northern Europe and North America. Eventually, capitalism's accumulation of wealth came to be viewed as an outward symbol of the individual's hard and God-given work during his or her earthly life.[12] The Catholic notion of "good works" also contributes to hard work and economic development, especially when adherents believe their labor contributes to a greater good.

Islam. Islam is based on the *Qur'an*, the religion's holy book, which Muslims believe was revealed by God to the prophet Muhammed in the 7th century. The majority of Muslims belong to one of two denominations: Sunni and Shia. Although most Muslims live in the Middle East, North Africa, and South Asia, the most populous Muslim country is Indonesia. Adherents engage in daily ritual prayers and fasting during the month of Ramadan. The *Qur'an* strongly encourages charitable giving. Strict Muslims believe the purpose of life is to worship God (known as Allah). In most Middle East countries, Islam is the basis for government and legal systems as well as the social and cultural order; however, globalization has exposed the Islamic world to outside cultural influences. Strict Islamists tend to view Western ideals as a threat to their values, whereas liberal Muslims seek to reconcile religious tradition with Western values and secular governance. Muslim immigrants have established communities in Europe and the United States, importing values and customs rooted in Islamic faith.

Sharia, the Islamic law based on the *Qur'an*, influences the legal code to varying degrees in Muslim countries. Its influence in secular states such as Turkey is much less than in orthodox Islamic countries such as Saudi Arabia. Sharia law covers all aspects of daily life, economic activity, and public governance. Non-secular societies do not distinguish between church and state. Family is at the center of Muslim life, and Islam specifies obligations and legal rights of family members.

Islam encourages free trade through rules that prohibit restraints on market-based exchange such as monopolies and price fixing. Islam encourages the free flow of information that facilitates efficient demand and supply. The *Qur'an* condemns charging interest for money loaned. Thus, banks in Islamic countries have devised methods for financing debt without violating Sharia law.

The *Qur'an* prohibits drinking alcohol, gambling, and showing too much skin. These restrictions affect firms that deal in alcoholic beverages, resorts, entertainment, and women's clothing. Many multinational firms are reaching out to Muslim communities. Nokia launched a mobile phone application that shows Muslims the direction toward Mecca, Islam's holiest site, when they pray. Heineken, the Dutch brewing giant, rolled out the nonalcoholic malt drink *Fayrouz* for the Islamic market. In general, MNEs are allowed to operate as long as they abide by Sharia law, do not exploit people, and earn profits fairly.[13]

Hinduism. A unique faith practiced in South Asia, especially India, Hinduism emerged from various ancient traditions. Unlike Christianity and Islam, Hinduism is not connected to any one prophet and lacks a unified belief system. To its adherents, it is a traditional way of life and an open-hearted faith that fully accepts other faiths. *Dharma* is a central concept that encourages behavior that is just, harmonious, and promotes joyful living. Hindus believe in reincarnation, a cycle of birth, life, death, and rebirth. The nature of actions taken during one's lifetime, *karma*, determines future destiny. In this life and the next, evil actions lead to future suffering; good deeds bring about *nirvana* (paradise). Hindus believe that kindness in action fosters a better world. The religion values spiritual rather than material achievements.

Karma implies that people are born into a social level, or *caste*, through their good or bad deeds in earlier lives. Critics argue that the caste system promotes slower economic growth because it hinders advancement from one social level to another in organizational settings;[14] thus company advancement can be based on a person's social level rather than on merit or potential. Ambition is dampened if followers believe they are destined to remain at a particular level at work. The caste system can also promote disharmony because followers may discriminate against employees whom they perceive to fit different social levels. In Hofstede's typology, India is characterized by high power distance because a sharp distinction is often drawn between upper and lower caste workers.

Hinduism's focus on spiritual enlightenment and selfless working for the greater good of society can influence the conduct of business. A devotion to positive karma and ascetic lifestyle

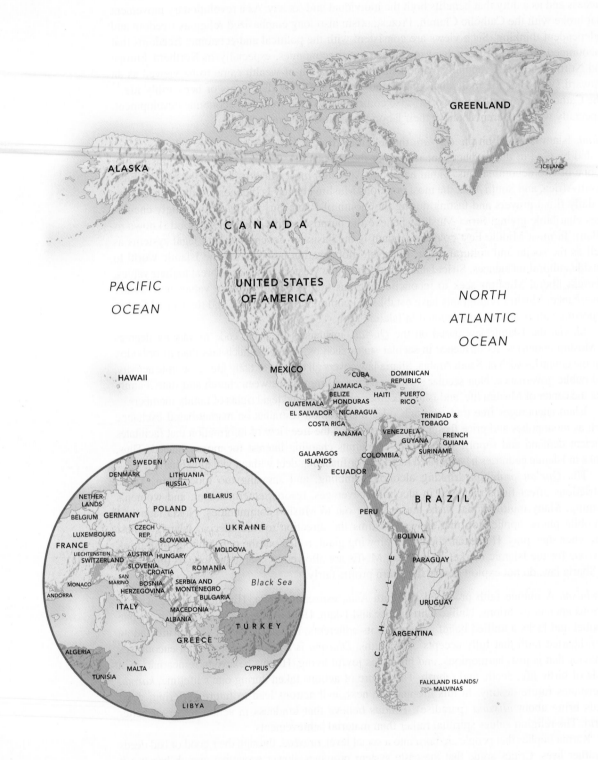

EXHIBIT 3.11

World Religions

Sources: Based on http://www.godweb.org/religionsofworld.htm and http://www.mapsofworld.com/religion-map.htm.

are potentially at odds with the relatively materialistic pursuits of business.[15] However, some argue that business performance can be enhanced by embracing Hinduism's teachings in areas such as self-control, discipline, and devotion to duty.[16]

Buddhism. Buddhism is a belief system that encompasses various traditions and practices, based on the teachings of the prophet Buddha. It is common in Asia, especially China and Japan. Buddhists subscribe to Four Noble Truths: Life is beset by suffering and pain; desire and greed are the root of all human suffering; personal suffering can be reduced by controlling desire and greed; and the way to end suffering is through righteous living, which includes good conduct, wisdom, and mental development.

Buddhism promotes harmony to achieve inner happiness and peaceful relations with others. In this way, it supports harmony and stability in commercial relations. Buddhism also encourages cooperation and tolerance for others, which are good for business. It is permissible in Buddhism to pray for security and good fortune. In this way, followers are comfortable with acquiring wealth as long as it is done with patience and harmony. Buddhism promotes a life centered on spiritual rather than worldly matters. Accordingly, it is seen to support ethical and responsible behavior in business. However, as in Hinduism, Buddhism's focus on spirituality and moderation might restrain entrepreneurial action.

Confucianism. Confucianism is a way of life taught by the philosopher Confucius, who lived about 2,500 years ago in present-day China. More a philosophy than a religion, Confucianism does not prescribe any specific rituals or practices. The main belief system of the Chinese people, it has influenced culture in China and other parts of Asia, especially Korea, Japan, and Vietnam, for thousands of years. Although East Asians profess various faiths, especially Shintoism, Taoism, and Buddhism, most also embrace some aspects of Confucianism.

Confucianism has an optimistic view of human nature and a strong emphasis on ethical behavior. Adherents believe that people are teachable, improvable, and perfectible through personal and communal efforts that emphasize learning and self-renewal. They believe it is best to behave with fairness, humanity, and charity toward others. *Ren* is a Confucian virtue that refers to doing good deeds and being kind to others. Other important qualities include loyalty, social harmony, and respect for one's parents and ancestors.

Judaism. Judaism was founded more than 3,000 years ago in the Middle East. Today the world's 14 million Jews primarily reside in Israel, Europe, and North America. Many migrated around the world in the wake of persecution or the pursuit of business opportunities. [17] Judaism strongly influenced early Christianity and Islam. Jews believe in one God and that that God is concerned with the actions of humankind. Jews attempt to conduct themselves accordingly. Strict adherents aim to apply their faith in every aspect of their lives.

The Jewish attitude toward business is positive, and much business conduct is rooted in Jewish law, which prohibits dishonest behavior. The accumulation of wealth is acceptable and even encouraged. Simultaneously, Jews are expected to be generous and charitable. Businesses should operate responsibly, emphasizing ethics and fair play beyond that required by local law.

3.4 Appreciate culture's effect in international business

Culture's Effect In International Business

Culture can differ sharply, even between neighboring countries. Exhibit 3.12 examines cultural differences between Mexico and the United States. Effective handling of the cross-cultural interface is a critical source of firms' competitive advantage. Managers not only need to develop empathy and tolerance toward cultural differences but also must acquire a sufficient degree of factual knowledge about the beliefs and values of foreign counterparts. Cross-cultural proficiency is paramount in many managerial tasks, including:

- Managing employees
- Communicating and interacting with foreign business partners
- Negotiating and structuring international business ventures
- Developing products and services
- Preparing advertising and promotional materials

EXHIBIT 3.12 Perceived Cultural Attributes of Mexico and the United States

Dimension	Mexico	United States
Role of context	High-context culture that values social trust, personal goodwill, and ritualized business	Low-context culture that emphasizes efficiency, explicit communications, and "getting down to business"
Individualism versus collectivism	Relatively group oriented. Extended families, teamwork, and group loyalty are valued.	Relatively individualistic. Emphasis on personal freedom and working alone. Group loyalty is less valued.
Time orientation	Fluid and polychronic. Long-term relationships are valued. Mexicans emphasize the past and believe they have little control over the future.	Rigid and monochronic. Business is short-term oriented and values profit above all else. Americans believe they can control the future.
Space perceptions	Conversational distance is close. Personal space is less valued.	Conversational distance is ample. Personal space is highly valued.
Religion	Christianity is very influential in daily life, and often in business.	Americans' religious orientation is diverse and declining.
Language	Spanish dominates, with little linguistic diversity.	While English dominates, there is much linguistic diversity.
Negotiations	Tend to progress slowly. Decisions take time. Legalism is avoided in agreements.	Emphasis on efficiency and quick decision making. Agreements are often legalistic.
Business relations	Relationship-oriented. Mexicans are easy-going, valuing personal bonds.	Deal-oriented. Business performance takes precedence over relationships.
Business meetings	Arriving late is acceptable. Meetings are informal and usually don't follow a strict agenda.	Americans are time-oriented, arriving promptly to meetings, which often follow a formal agenda.
Superior–subordinate relations	Firms are hierarchical, with much power distance. Senior managers are relatively authoritarian.	Lower power distance. Firms are "flatter," with less hierarchy. Relations with superiors are informal and easy-going.
Style of dress in business	Conservative, emphasizing dark suits. High-status personnel are expected to dress the part.	Business casual is widely accepted. "Dressing the part" is less important.

Sources: Based on Geert Hofstede, *Culture's Consequences* (Beverly Hills, CA: Sage, 1980); Boye De Mente, *The Mexican Mind* (Beverly Hills, CA: Phoenix Books, 2011); Lucila Ortiz, *A Primer for Spanish Language, Culture and Economics* (Bloomington, IN: Xlibris, 2011).

- Preparing for international trade fairs and exhibitions
- Screening and selecting foreign distributors and other partners
- Interacting with current and potential customers from abroad

Let's consider specific examples of how cross-cultural differences may complicate company activities.

Developing products and services. Cultural differences necessitate adapting marketing activities to suit the specific needs of target markets. Johnson & Johnson developed different varieties of its mouthwash, Listerine, for foreign markets. For instance, it created alcohol-free Listerine Zero for Muslim countries where spirits are forbidden. For Asian markets, it launched Green Tea Listerine. In Europe, consumers want their mouthwash to solve more complex problems than just bad breath, so the firm developed an advanced gum treatment rinse.[18]

Providing services. Firms that engage in services such as lodging and retailing substantially interact with customers, implying greater cultural interaction and the potential for cognitive and communication gaps. Imagine a Western lawyer who tries to establish a law office in China or a Western restaurant chain operating in Russia. Both firms will encounter substantial cultural challenges. Differences in language and national character have the same effect as trade barriers.[19]

Organizational structure. Some companies prefer to delegate authority to country managers, which results in a decentralized organizational structure. Other firms have centralized structures, in which power is concentrated at regional or corporate headquarters. Firms may be bureaucratic or entrepreneurial. How do you deal with a bureaucratic partner or manage distantly located, decentralized subsidiaries?

Teamwork. Cooperating with partners and host-country nationals to achieve common organizational goals is critical to business success. But what should managers do if foreign and domestic nationals don't get along? The Chinese home appliance manufacturer Haier (www.haier.com) delayed acquiring overseas firms because management felt it lacked the ability to manage foreign nationals and integrate differing cultural systems.

Pay-for-performance system. In some countries, merit is not the main basis for promoting employees. In China and Japan, a person's age is the most important determinant, but how do such workers perform when Western firms evaluate them using performance-based measures?

Lifetime employment. In some Asian countries, firms are very protective of their employees, who may work for the same company all their lives. The expectations that arise from such devoted relationships can complicate dealings with outside firms. Western managers may struggle to motivate employees who expect they will always have the same job.

Union–management relationships. In Germany, union bosses hold the same status as top-level managers and are allowed to sit on corporate boards. Many European firms have a business culture in which workers are relatively equal to managers. This approach can reduce the flexibility of company operations because it makes it harder to lay off workers.

Attitudes toward ambiguity. In some countries, people have a hard time tolerating *ambiguity*, which refers to situations in which information can be understood in more than one way. For example, some bosses give exact and detailed instructions, whereas others give vague and incomplete instructions. If you're not comfortable working with minimum guidance or taking independent action, you may not fit well into some cultures.

Negotiations. Negotiations arise in virtually all aspects of business, as when the firm takes on a partner or a supplier–buyer relationship. Goals, interests, ethics, and cultural assumptions vary cross-culturally, which can complicate forming and maintaining business relationships. In most of Northern Europe, negotiations are relatively efficient, impersonal, and unsociable; negotiators get down to business quickly.

Technology. In the past, distinctive cultures developed because regions had limited contact with each other. Today, various information, communications, and transportation technologies bring people into close contact. The Internet and other communications technologies imply greater likelihood of cross-cultural miscommunications and blunder. To help reduce problems, managers use software that instantly converts messages into any of dozens of languages.[20]

3.5 Learn models and explanations of culture

Models and Explanations of Culture

Scholars have developed numerous models and explanations for gaining deeper insights into the role of culture. In this section, we review cultural metaphors, idioms, Hall's high and low context cultures, and Hofstede's dimensions of culture.

Cultural Metaphors

Cultural metaphor
A distinctive tradition or institution strongly associated with a particular society.

Martin Gannon offered an insightful analysis of cultural orientations.[21] In his view, a **cultural metaphor** refers to a distinctive tradition or institution that is strongly associated with a particular society. It is a guide to deciphering people's attitudes, values, and behavior.

For example, American football is a cultural metaphor for traditions in the United States, such as being a team player and having a strong leader who moves an organization aggressively toward a desired goal. The Swedish *stuga* (cottage or summer home) is a cultural metaphor for Swedes' love of nature and desire for individualism through self-development. The Brazilian concept of *jeitinho Brasileiro* refers to an ability to cope with the challenges of daily life through creative problem solving or navigating the country's demanding bureaucracy. In the Brazilian context, manipulation and smooth talking are not necessarily viewed negatively, because individuals may need to resort to these methods to conduct business.

Low-context culture
A culture that relies on elaborate verbal explanations, putting much emphasis on spoken words.

Anthropologists and other social scientists have studied culture for centuries. Two leading interpretations of national culture are those of E. T. Hall and Geert Hofstede. Hall's contribution was to make a distinction between high- and low-context cultures. Hofstede's influential research led him to distinguish important dimensions of culture.

High- and Low-Context Cultures

Anthropologist Edward T. Hall classified cultures as low context and high context.[22] When communicating, people in **low-context cultures** rely heavily on spoken words and detailed verbal explanations. As Exhibit 3.13 shows, Europeans and North Americans tend to be low-context with long traditions of writing and speech making. In such cultures, the main function of speech is to express ideas and thoughts clearly, logically, and convincingly; communication is direct, and meaning is straightforward. In negotiations, for example, Americans typically come to the point quickly. Low-context cultures tend to value expertise and performance. Managers conduct negotiations as efficiently as possible. These cultures use specific, legalistic contracts to conclude agreements.

By contrast, **high-context cultures**, such as China and Japan, emphasize nonverbal messages and view communication as a means to promote smooth, harmonious relationships. They prefer an indirect and polite style that emphasizes mutual respect and care for others. They are on guard not to embarrass or offend others.

This helps explain why Japanese people hesitate to say *no* even when they disagree with what someone is saying. They are more likely to say "it is different," a softer response. In East Asian cultures, showing impatience, frustration, irritation, or anger disrupts harmony and is considered rude and offensive. Asians tend to be soft-spoken, and people typically are sensitive to context and body language. At a business luncheon in Tokyo, for example, the boss is almost always the senior-looking individual seated farthest from the entrance to the room. In Japan, superiors are given such favored seating to show respect. Negotiations tend to be slow and ritualistic, and agreement is founded on trust. To succeed in Asian cultures, it is critical to have a keen eye for nonverbal signs and body language.

The notion of high- and low-context cultures also plays a role in communications between people who speak the same language. British managers sometimes complain that presentations by their U.S. counterparts are too detailed. Everything is spelled out, even when meanings seem perfectly obvious.

Source: Daily Mail/Rex/Alamy

The edgy, risk-taking culture of companies under the Virgin brand owes much to the independent and flamboyant spirit of company founder Richard Branson and contrasts sharply with the conservative cultures of other British firms, despite sharing the same national culture.

High-context culture
A culture that emphasizes nonverbal messages and views communication as a means to promote smooth, harmonious relationships.

High Context
- Establish social trust first
- Personal relations and goodwill are valued
- Agreements emphasize trust
- Negotiations are slow and ritualistic

Chinese
Korean
Japanese
Vietnamese
Arab
Spanish
Italian
English
North American
Scandinavian
Swiss
German

Low Context
- Get down to business first
- Expertise and performance are valued
- Agreements emphasize specific, legalistic contract
- Negotiations are as efficient as possible

EXHIBIT 3.13

Hall's High- and Low-Context Typology of Cultures

Source: Based on *Beyond Culture* by Edward T. Hall, copyright © 1976, 1981 by Edward T. Hall. Used by permission of Doubleday, a division of Random House, Inc. For online information about other Random House, Inc. books and authors, see the Internet Web Site at http://www.randomhouse. com Mark Cleveland, Michel Laroche, and Nicolas Papadopoulos, "You are what you speak? Globalization, multilingualism, consumer dispositions and consumption," Journal of Business Research, 68 No. 3 (2015), pp. 542–552.

Donghoon Kim, Yigang Pan, and Heung Soo Park, "High- Versus Low-Context Culture: A Comparison of Chinese, Korean and American Cultures," Psychology & Marketin, 15 No. 6 (1998), pp. 507–521.

Hofstede's Research on National Culture

Dutch anthropologist Geert Hofstede conducted one of the early studies of national cultural traits. He collected data on the values and attitudes of 116,000 employees at IBM, a diverse company in terms of nationality, age, and gender. Based on this research, Hofstede identified six independent dimensions of national culture, described next.[23]

Individualism versus collectivism

Describes whether a person functions primarily as an individual or as part of a group.

Individualism versus collectivism refers to whether a person functions primarily as an individual or as part of a group. In individualistic societies, each person tends to focus on his or her own self-interest, and ties among people are relatively loose. These societies prefer individualism over agreement within the group. Competition for resources is the norm, and those who compete best are rewarded financially. Australia, Canada, the United Kingdom, and the United States tend to be strongly individualistic societies.

By contrast, in collectivist societies, ties among individuals are highly valued. Business is conducted in the context of a group in which others' views are strongly considered. The group is all-important because life is a cooperative experience. Conformity and compromise help maintain group harmony. China, Panama, and South Korea are examples of strongly collectivist societies.

Power distance

Describes how a society deals with the inequalities in power that exist among people.

Power distance describes how a society deals with the inequalities in power that exist among people. In societies with *low* power distance, the gaps between the powerful and weak are small. In Denmark and Sweden, for example, governments have set up tax and social welfare systems that ensure their citizens are relatively equal in terms of income and power. The United States also scores relatively low on power distance.

Societies characterized by *high* power distance do not care very much about inequalities and allow them to grow over time. There are substantial gaps between the powerful and the weak. Guatemala, Malaysia, the Philippines, and several Middle East countries are examples of countries with high power distance. In high power-distance firms, autocratic management styles focus power at the top and grant little self-rule to lower-level employees. In low power-distance firms, managers and subordinates are relatively equal and cooperate to achieve organizational goals.

Uncertainty avoidance

The extent to which people can tolerate risk and uncertainty in their lives.

Uncertainty avoidance refers to the extent to which individuals can tolerate risk and uncertainty in their lives. People in societies with high uncertainty avoidance create institutions that minimize risk and ensure financial security. Companies emphasize stable careers and produce many rules to regulate worker actions and minimize uncertainty. Managers may be slow to make decisions as they investigate the nature and potential outcomes of several options. Belgium, France, and Japan are countries that score high on uncertainty avoidance.

Societies that score low on uncertainty avoidance socialize their members to accept and become accustomed to uncertainty. Managers are entrepreneurial and relatively comfortable taking risks, and they make decisions relatively quickly. People accept each day as it comes and take their jobs in stride because they are less concerned about ensuring their future. They tend to tolerate behavior and opinions different from their own because they do not feel threatened by them. India, Ireland, Jamaica, and the United States are leading examples of countries with low uncertainty avoidance.

Masculinity versus femininity

Refers to a society's orientation based on traditional male and female values. Masculine cultures tend to value competitiveness, assertiveness, ambition, and the accumulation of wealth. Feminine cultures emphasize nurturing roles, interdependence among people, and taking care of less fortunate people.

Masculinity versus femininity refers to a society's orientation based on traditional male and female values. In masculine cultures, both men and women put high priority on achievement, ambition, and economic growth. Society values competitiveness and boldness. In the workplace, men and women alike are assertive and focused on career and earning money. Typical examples include Australia and Italy. The United States is a moderately masculine society. Hispanic cultures are relatively masculine and display a zest for action, daring, and competitiveness. In business, the masculinity dimension reveals itself as self-confidence and leadership.

In feminine cultures, such as the Scandinavian countries, gender roles overlap. Both men and women emphasize nurturing roles, interdependence among people, and caring for less fortunate people. Welfare systems are highly developed and education is highly supported. Men and women alike are relationship oriented, minimizing conflict, and putting emphasis on the quality of life. In business as well as in private life, they strive for consensus. Work is viewed as necessary to earn money, which is needed to enjoy life.

Long-term versus short-term orientation

Refers to the degree to which people and organizations defer pleasure and gratification to achieve long-term success.

Long-term versus short-term orientation[24] refers to the degree to which people and organizations defer pleasure or gratification to achieve long-term success. Firms and people in cultures with a long-term orientation tend to take the long view to planning and living. They focus on years and decades. The long-term dimension is best illustrated by the so-called Asian values—traditional cultural orientations of several Asian societies, including China, Japan, and Singapore. These values are partly based on the teachings of the Chinese philosopher

Confucius. They include discipline, loyalty, hard work, regard for education, respect for family, focus on group harmony, and control over one's desires. Scholars credit these values for the *East Asian miracle*, the remarkable economic growth and modernization of East Asian nations during the past several decades.[25] By contrast, the United States and most other Western countries emphasize a short-term orientation.

Indulgence versus restraint is the extent to which people try to control their desires and impulses. Indulgent cultures focus on individual happiness, having fun, and enjoying life. People feel greater freedom to express their own emotions and desires. In the workplace, people feel freer to express their opinions, give feedback, and even change jobs. They aim to be happy on the job and project a positive attitude. Mexico, Sweden, and the United States are examples of indulgent societies.

By contrast, restrained societies try to suppress needs gratification. Happiness of the individual is less valued, and people are reluctant to express their own emotions and needs. People avoid expressing personal opinions, and job mobility is often limited. Basic drives are often controlled by strict social norms. China, Egypt, and Russia exemplify restrained countries.

Source: Wavebreak Media Ltd/123RF

Mexico emphasizes collectivism and loyalty to the group. Business is characterized by long-term, easy-going relationships. Substantial power distance is the norm in larger companies, where the dress code is typically conservative.

Indulgence versus restraint

The extent to which people try to control their desires and impulses.

Although useful, the Hofstede framework has its weaknesses. The original research was based on data collected around 1970. Much has changed since then, including successive phases of globalization, widespread exposure to global media, technological advances, and changes in the role of women in the workforce. In addition, Hofstede's findings are based on the employees of a single company—IBM—in a single industry, making it difficult to generalize. Hofstede's data were collected using questionnaires, which is not effective for probing some of the deep issues that surround culture. Finally, Hofstede did not capture all potential dimensions of culture. Nevertheless, Hofstede's framework is useful as a general guide and for gaining deeper understanding in cross-national interactions with business partners, customers, and value-chain members.[26]

Deal versus Relationship Orientation

Another important dimension of culture concerns the nature of business relationships. In deal-oriented cultures, managers focus on the task at hand and prefer getting down to business. At the extreme, such managers may even avoid small talk and other preliminaries. They prefer to seal agreements with a legalistic contract and take an impersonal approach to settling disputes. Leading examples of deal-oriented cultures include those of Australia, northern Europe, and North America.

In relationship-oriented cultures, managers put more value on relationships with people. To these managers, it is important to build trust and understanding and get to know the other party in business interactions.

For example, it took nine years for Volkswagen to negotiate the opening of a car factory in China, a strong relationship-oriented society. For the Chinese, Japanese, and many in Latin America, relationships are more important than the deal.[27] In China, the concept of *guanxi* (literally, "connections") is deeply rooted in ancient Confucian philosophy, which values a social chain of command and people's responsibilities to each other. It stresses the importance of relationships within the family and between superiors and subordinates.

Managerial Implications of Culture

3.6 Understand managerial implications of culture

Although culture shapes behavior generally, it also plays a major role in cross-border business. Let's consider the nature of culture at three distinct levels. Exhibit 3.14 suggests that company employees are socialized by three cultures: *national culture, professional culture,* and *corporate culture.*[28] Working effectively within these overlapping cultures is challenging. The influence of professional and corporate culture tends to grow as people are socialized into a profession and workplace.

EXHIBIT 3.14
National, Professional, and Corporate Culture

Source: Based on V. Terpstra and K. David, *Cultural Environment of International Business*, 3rd ed. (Cincinnati, OH: South-Western, 1991).

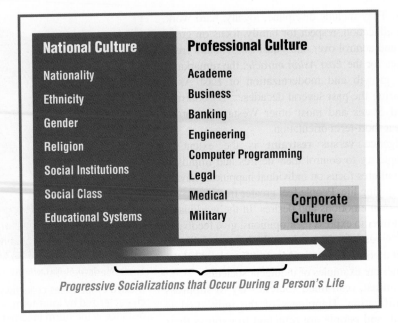

National Culture	Professional Culture
Nationality	Academe
Ethnicity	Business
Gender	Banking
Religion	Engineering
Social Institutions	Computer Programming
Social Class	Legal
Educational Systems	Medical
	Military

Corporate Culture

Progressive Socializations that Occur During a Person's Life

Most companies have a distinctive set of norms, values, and modes of behavior that distinguish them from other organizations. Such differences are often as distinctive as national culture, so that two firms from the same country can have vastly different organizational cultures. For example, Standard Chartered (www.standardchartered.com), a time-honored British bank, has a conservative culture that may be slow to change. By contrast, Virgin (www.virgin.com), the much younger British music and travel provider, has an experimental, risk-taking culture.

These cultural layers present yet another challenge for the manager: To what extent is a particular behavior caused by national culture? In companies with a strong organizational culture, it is hard to determine where the corporate influence begins and the national influence ends.

In the French cosmetics firm L'Oreal (www.loreal.com), the distinction between national and corporate cultures is not always clear. The French have a great deal of experience in the cosmetics and fashion industries, but L'Oreal is a global firm staffed by managers from around the world. Their influence, combined with management's receptiveness to world culture, has shaped L'Oreal into a unique organization, distinctive within French culture.

Cultural Orientations

Ethnocentric orientation
Using our own culture as the standard for judging other cultures.

One aspect of cross-cultural risk is **ethnocentric orientation**—using our own culture as the standard for judging other cultures. It is also known as home-country orientation.[29] Most managers are raised in a single culture and tend to view the world mainly from their own perspective. Ethnocentric managers usually believe their own race, religion, or ethnic group is somehow superior to others. Although the tendency to be ethnocentric is widespread, the most effective international managers avoid it; instead, they adopt a polycentric or geocentric orientation. A **polycentric orientation** refers to a host-country mindset in which the manager develops a strong attachment to the country in which she or he conducts business. **Geocentric orientation** refers to a global mindset through which the manager can understand a business or market without regard to country boundaries. A geocentric orientation implies an openness to, and awareness of, diversity across cultures.[30] Managers with a geocentric orientation possess a cosmopolitan view and acquire skills for successful social behavior in cross-cultural encounters.[31] They adopt new ways of thinking and learn to analyze cultures. They avoid the temptation to judge different behavior as somehow inferior.[32]

Polycentric orientation
A host-country mindset in which the manager develops a strong attachment to the country in which she or he conducts business.

Geocentric orientation
A global mindset by which the manager can understand a business or market without regard to country boundaries.

 MyManagementLab **Watch It!**

If your professor has assigned this, go to the Assignments section of **mymanagementlab.com** to complete the video exercise titled Impact of Culture on Business: Spotlight on China.

How to Acquire Cross-Cultural Competence

Managers are more effective in cross-cultural encounters when they keep an open mind, are inquisitive, and don't jump to conclusions about others' behaviors. Even experienced managers undergo cultural training that emphasizes people-watching skills and human relations techniques. Skills are more important than pure information because skills can be transferred across countries, whereas information is often country-specific. Planning that combines informal mentoring from experienced managers and formal training through seminars, courses, and simulations abroad and at home can go far in helping managers meet cross-cultural challenges.

Although every culture is unique, certain basic guidelines are appropriate for gaining cross-cultural competence. Let's review three guidelines managers can follow to prepare for successful cross-cultural encounters.

GUIDELINE 1: Acquire factual knowledge about the other culture and try to speak the language. Successful managers acquire a base of knowledge about the values, attitudes, and lifestyles of the cultures that they encounter. Managers study the political and economic background of target countries—their history, current national affairs, and perceptions about other cultures. Such knowledge increases understanding about the partner's mindset, organization, and objectives. Decisions and events become easier to interpret. Sincere interest in the target culture helps establish trust and respect. It helps lay the foundation for open and productive relationships. Even modest attempts to speak the local language are welcome. Superior language skills help ensure international business success. In the long run, managers who can converse in multiple languages are more likely to negotiate successfully and have positive business meetings.

GUIDELINE 2: Avoid cultural bias. Problems arise when managers simply assume that foreigners think and behave just like the folks back home. Such ethnocentric assumptions lead to poor business strategies in both planning and execution. Managers new to international business can find the behavior of a foreigner odd and perhaps improper. For example, it is easy to be offended when a foreigner does not appreciate our food, history, entertainment, or everyday traditions. In this way, cultural bias can be a significant barrier to successful interpersonal communication.

A person's own culture conditions how he or she reacts to different values, behavior, or systems, so most people unconsciously assume that people in other countries experience the world as they do. They view their own culture as the norm; everything else may seem strange. This is known as the **self-reference criterion**—the tendency to view other cultures through the lens of our own culture. Understanding the self-reference criterion is a critical first step to avoiding cultural bias and ethnocentric mistakes.

To compete effectively, companies must continually improve ways to communicate with and manage customers and partners around the world. Global teams with members from various cultural backgrounds enable firms to profit from knowledge amassed across the organization's worldwide operations. Such teams function best when the members engage in high-quality communications, minimizing miscommunications caused by differences in language and culture. Nevertheless, inexperienced managers often misunderstand the behavior of foreign counterparts, which hinders the effectiveness of cross-cultural meetings. One way to minimize such problems is critical incident analysis.

Critical incident analysis is a very useful technique that managers use to analyze awkward situations in cross-cultural encounters. It encourages a more effective approach to cultural differences by helping managers become more objective and develop empathy for other points of view. Critical incident analysis involves the following steps:

- Identify the situations where you need to be culturally aware to interact effectively with people

Self-reference criterion
The tendency to view other cultures through the lens of our own culture.

Critical incident analysis
A method for analyzing awkward situations in cross-cultural encounters by becoming more objective and developing empathy for other points of view.

Source: Robert Churchill/123RF

In Japan and South Korea, bowing is common in business and personal settings.

Source: Steve Mason/Photodisc/Getty Images

Cross-cultural proficiency increases the effectiveness of meetings and other encounters in international business.

from another culture, including socializing, working in groups, and negotiating.

- When confronted with seemingly strange behavior, discipline yourself to avoid making hasty judgments. Instead, try to view the situation or the problem in terms of the unfamiliar culture. Make observations and gather objective information from native citizens or secondary sources.
- Learn to make a variety of interpretations of others' behavior, to select the most likely one in the cultural context, and only then to formulate your own response.
- Learn from this process and improve continually.

GUIDELINE 3: Develop cross-cultural skills.
Working effectively with counterparts from other cultures requires you to make an investment in your professional development. Each culture has its own ways of conducting business and negotiations and solving disputes. You're exposed to high levels of uncertainty. Concepts and relationships can be understood in a variety of ways.[33] To be successful in international business, you should strive for cross-cultural proficiency. Cross-cultural proficiency is characterized by four key personality traits:

- *Tolerance for ambiguity*: The ability to tolerate uncertainty and apparent lack of clarity in the thinking and actions of others.
- *Perceptiveness*: The ability to observe closely and appreciate hard-to-see information in the speech and behavior of others.
- *Valuing personal relationships*: The ability to recognize the importance of interpersonal relationships, which is often much more important than achieving one-time goals or winning arguments.
- *Flexibility and adaptability*: The ability to be creative in finding innovative solutions, to be open-minded about outcomes, and to show grace and kindness under pressure.

Managers with a geocentric or cosmopolitan view of the world are generally better at understanding and dealing with similarities and differences among cultures. Successful multinational firms seek to instill a geocentric cultural mindset in their employees and use a geocentric staffing policy to hire the best people for each position, regardless of national origin. Over time, such firms develop a core group of managers who are comfortable in any cultural context.

One way for managers to determine the skills they need to approach cultural issues is to measure their cultural intelligence.[34] *Cultural intelligence (CQ)* is a person's capacity to function effectively in situations characterized by cultural diversity. It focuses on specific capabilities important for high-quality personal relationships and effectiveness in culturally diverse settings and work groups.

Ethical Connections

Ethical values vary by culture. Consider two scenarios given to students. In scenario one, a car salesman failed to inform his superiors about a serious engine problem of a car he had received as a trade-in on a new car sale. In scenario two, a dealership neglected to fully repair a car transmission under warranty in the hope of securing lucrative repair work after the warranty expired. Students from China and Russia felt relatively little harm had been done in these scenarios, while students from Finland and South Korea judged the scenarios unethical.

Source: M. Ahmed, Y. Kung, J. Eichenseher, "Business Students' Perception of Ethics and Moral Judgment," *Journal of Business Ethics*, 43 (2003) pp. 89–102.

CLOSING CASE   Hollywood and Global Culture

The most commercially successful filmmaker of all time, Steven Spielberg, is synonymous with U.S. cinema. He has directed and produced international blockbusters such as *Jurassic Park, Transformers*, and the Indiana Jones movies. But his movies have been criticized because of the values represented in his films, which are often viewed as part of the larger trend of the Americanization of global values and beliefs.

Jurassic Park ignited a storm of protest. Film critics and cultural ministries around the globe found it to be a brainless film, lacking plot and succeeding wholly through special effects and big-budget bells and whistles. French officials labeled the film a threat to their national identity.

Hollywood movies—for example, *Hotel Rwanda* and *Blood Diamond*—consistently portray Africa as scenically beautiful but terrible in every other way. Other films, for example, *Independence Day*, depict Africa as a land of backward villagers and tribal warriors. The popular movie *Lost in Translation* came under fire for portraying Japanese people as robotic characters who mix up their Ls and Rs. The image-conscious Japanese were disappointed by their depiction as comic relief. In a scene in which Bill Murray's character is taking a shower in a five-star hotel, he has to bend and contort to get his head under the showerhead. Another scene, in which Murray is shown towering at least a foot above an elevator full of local businessmen, mocks the smaller physique of the Japanese. The film was seen to reinforce negative stereotypes about the Japanese.

Today, American studios produce 80 percent of the films viewed internationally; after aerospace, Hollywood is often the United States' largest net export. In contrast, the European film industry is now about one-ninth the size it was in 1945, and today, foreign films hold less than 1 percent of the U.S. market. The copyright-based industries, which also include software, books, music, and TV, contributed more to the U.S. economy in the 2000s than any single manufacturing sector. Although the United States imports few foreign films, Hollywood's output remains in high demand worldwide.

Stereotypes and Religious Values

Under attack since their origin, Hollywood war films are widely accused of presenting biased accounts of history. According to *The*

Last Samurai and the *Kill Bill* movies, Westerners are better at martial arts than Asians are. Nations with deep religious values were offended by *Brokeback Mountain*, which portrayed a homosexual relationship between two cowboys in the United States. Crucial to U.S. dominance of world cinema is widespread acceptance of the cultural associations inherent in Hollywood films, an obstacle competitors must overcome. U.S. stars and Hollywood directors are well established in the international movie scene, with worldwide drawing power.

Movies and Comparative Advantage

According to the theory of comparative advantage, countries should specialize in producing what they do best and import the rest. Economists argue this theory applies to films as much as to any industry. As a former Canadian prime minister remarked, "Movies are culture incarnate. It is mistaken to view culture as a commodity.... Cultural industries, aside from their economic impact, create products that are fundamental to the survival of Canada as a society." Thus, some countries attempt to block imports of movies from the United States in an effort to protect their own film industries.

A Cultural Dilemma

Despite plenty of arguments on both sides of this ongoing debate, many big-budget Hollywood movies these days are in fact multinational creations. The James Bond thriller *Quantum of Solace*, with its German-Swiss director and stars hailing from Britain, Ukraine, and France, was filmed in Britain, Panama, Chile, Italy, and Austria. Russell Crowe, Charlize Theron, Penelope Cruz, Nicole Kidman, and Daniel Craig are just a few of the many global stars not from the United States. Two of the seven major film companies collectively known as Hollywood aren't even U.S. firms. Hollywood is not as American as it once was.

As the lines connecting Hollywood with the United States are increasingly blurred, protectionists should not abandon their quest to save the intellectual and artistic quality of films. In an interview with the *New York Times*, French director Eric Rohmer stated that his countrymen should fight back with high-quality movies, not protection. "I am a commercial film maker. I am for free competition and am not supported by the state."

AACSB: Reflective Thinking

Case Questions

3-4. Most aspects of foreign culture, such as language, religion, gender roles, and problem-solving strategies, are hard for the casual observer to understand. In what ways do Hollywood movies affect national culture outside the United States? What aspects of U.S. culture do Hollywood films promote around the world? Can you observe any positive effects of Hollywood movies on world cultures?

3-5. Culture plays a key role in business. In what ways have movies influenced managerial tasks, company activities, and other ways of doing business around the world? Can watching foreign films be an effective way of learning how to do business abroad? Justify your answer.

3-6. Hollywood movies are very popular abroad, but foreign films are not viewed much in the United States. What factors determine the high demand for Hollywood films? Why are they so popular in Europe, Japan, Latin America, and elsewhere? Why

are foreign films demanded so little in the United States? What can foreign filmmakers do to increase demand for their movies in the United States?

Sources: Hillary Busis, "Blame Canada: The 5 Greatest Pop Culture Insults to America's Hat," *Entertainment Weekly*, January 18, 2015, retrieved from http://www.ew.com/article/2012/10/12/canada-jokes; Hyun-key Kim Hogarth, "The Korean Wave: An Asian Reaction to Western-Dominated Globalization," *Perspectives on Global Development & Technology* 12, No. 1/2 (2013), pp. 135–151; K. Lee, "The Little State Department: Hollywood and the MPAA's Influence," *Northwestern Journal of International Law & Business* 28, No. 2 (2008), pp. 371–383; "Moreover: Culture Wars," *Economist*, September 12, 1998, pp. 97–100; K. Day, "Totally Lost in Translation," *The Guardian*, January 24, 2004; A. Marvasti and E. Canterbery, "Cultural and Other Barriers to Motion Picture Trade," *Economic Inquiry*, January 2005, pp. 39–55. This case was written by Sonia Prusaitis, under the supervision of Dr. Gary Knight.

END OF CHAPTER REVIEW

MyManagementLab

Go to **mymanagementlab.com** to complete the problems marked with this icon ⭐.

Key Terms

acculturation   89
critical incident analysis (CIA)   107
cross-cultural risk   87
cultural metaphor   102
culture   86
ethnocentric orientation   106
geocentric orientation   106
high-context culture   103

idiom   94
individualism versus
    collectivism   104
Indulgence versus restraint   105
long-term versus short-term
    orientation   104
low-context culture   102
masculinity versus femininity   104

monochronic   91
polycentric orientation   106
polychronic orientation   91
power distance   104
self-reference criterion   107
socialization   89
uncertainty avoidance   104

Summary

In this chapter, you learned about:

- **Culture and Cross-Cultural Risk**

   Culture is the values, beliefs, customs, arts, and other products of human thought and work that characterize the people of a given society. **Cross-cultural risk** arises from a situation or event in which a cultural misunderstanding puts some human value at stake. Values and attitudes are shared beliefs or norms that individuals have internalized.

- **Dimensions of Culture**

   Culture is reflected by various dimensions, including our values and attitudes; manners and customs; time and space perceptions; symbolic, material, and creative expressions; education; and social structure. Social structure is characterized by individuals, family, and groups as well as by social stratification and mobility. **Monochronic** cultures exhibit a rigid orientation to time in which the individual is focused on schedules, punctuality, and time as a resource. **Polychronic** cultures have a flexible, nonlinear orientation to time in which the individual takes a long-term perspective.

- **Role of Language and Religion in Culture**

   There are nearly 7000 active languages in the world, of which Mandarin Chinese, Hindi, English, Spanish, and Arabic are among the most common. Language has both verbal and non-verbal characteristics and is conditioned by our environment. Sometimes it is hard to find words to convey the same meaning in different languages. Religion provides meaning and motivation that define people's ideals and values and affects culture and international business deeply. The four main religions are Christianity, Islam, Hinduism, and Buddhism.

- **Culture's Effect in International Business**

   In international business, culture affects management of employees, marketing activities, and interaction with customers and partners. Culture influences the design of products and services. It affects the firm's internal environment and how managers perceive and deal with business tasks.

- **Models and Explanations of Culture**

   Culture can be interpreted through **cultural metaphors**, distinctive traditions or institutions that serve as a guide or map for deciphering attitudes, values, and behavior. An **idiom** is an expression whose symbolic meaning is different from its literal meaning. **Low-context cultures** rely on elaborated verbal explanations, putting much emphasis on spoken words. **High-context cultures** emphasize nonverbal communications and a more holistic approach to communication that promotes harmonious relationships. Hofstede's typology of cultural dimensions consists of **individualism versus collectivism, power distance, uncertainty avoidance, masculinity versus femininity, long-term versus short-term orientation**, and **indulgence versus restraint**.

- **Managerial Implications of Culture**

   Most corporations exhibit a distinctive set of norms, values, and beliefs that distinguish them from other organizations. Managers can misinterpret the extent to which a counterpart's behavior is attributable to national, professional, or corporate culture. **Ethnocentric orientation** refers to using one's own culture as the standard for judging other cultures. **Polycentric orientation** refers to a host country mindset that gives the manager greater affinity with the country in which she or he conducts business. **Geocentric orientation** refers to a global mindset by which the manager can understand a business or market without regard to country boundaries. National culture influences consumer behavior, managerial effectiveness, and the range of value-chain operations such as product and service design and marketing activities. Managers need to develop understanding and skills in dealing with other cultures and should avoid cultural bias and engage in **critical incident analysis** to avoid the **self-reference criterion**.

Test Your Comprehension

3-7. Describe culture and cross-cultural risk.

3-8. Describe the characteristics of high- and low-context cultures.

3-9. What are cultural metaphors and why are they significant?

3-10. What are the two major perceptions of time and how does each affect international business?

⭐ **3-11.** How are values and attitudes internalized?

3-12. What are the major religions and how do they affect international business?

⭐ **3-13.** What are the elements of language?

3-14. Distinguish the three layers of culture. What are the major elements of country-level and professional culture?

3-15. How can a manager use critical incident analysis in order to avoid the self-reference criterion? Why is this an important factor?

3-16. How does a manager with a deal orientation differ from a manager with a relationship orientation?

3-17. Summarize the three major guidelines for success in cross-cultural settings.

Apply Your Understanding AACSB: Communication, Reflective Thinking, Ethical Reasoning, Multiculturalism and Diversity

3-18. Suppose you get a job at Kismet Indemnity, a life insurance company. In its 45-year history, Kismet has never done any international business. Now its president, Randall Fraser, wants to expand abroad. You have noted in meetings that he seems to lack much awareness of the role of culture. Write a memo to him in which you explain why culture matters in international business. Be sure to speculate on the effects of various dimensions of culture on sales of life insurance.

3-19. People tend to see other cultures from their own point of view. They accept their own culture and its ways as the norm—everything else seems foreign or even mysterious. This chapter described a technique called critical incident analysis (CIA) that encourages an objective reaction to cultural differences by helping managers develop empathy for other points of view. Using the CIA approach, define a situation that you or someone else has experienced that led to a cross-cultural misunderstanding—perhaps an interaction with a fellow student, a visit to a store in your town, or an experience you had while traveling abroad. Explain what actually happened and how a more culturally sensitive response might have been possible if you or your fellow student had used CIA.

3-20. *Ethical Dilemma*: Suppose you work for a multinational firm and are posted to Bogota, Colombia. After renting a house in a posh neighborhood, you hire a full-time housekeeper to perform household chores, a common practice among wealthy Colombians. A colleague at work tells you that local housekeepers are typically poor women who live in Bogota's slums and earn about $200 a month. As an executive, you feel guilty about paying such a cheap wage when you can afford much more, but for cultural and socioeconomic reasons, your colleague insists you cannot pay more than the going rate. Doing so might embarrass your housekeeper and risk upsetting the economic balance in her community. Analyze this dilemma. Do you pay your housekeeper the customary local rate or a higher wage? Justify your decision. Can you think of any creative solutions to this dilemma?

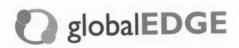 **globalEDGE** | **INTERNET EXERCISES**
(globalEDGE.msu.edu)

AACSB: Reflective Thinking

Refer to Chapter 1, page 54, for instructions on how to access and use globalEDGE™.

3-21. Ethnologue (www.ethnologue.com/web.asp) is a site that lists the world's known languages. It is an excellent resource for scholars and others with language interests and contains statistical summaries of the number of language speakers by language size, family, and country. Using Ethnologue, try the following:

  a. Visit the China page. What is the population of China? Of the country's nearly 300 languages, which has the largest number of speakers? Which has the second-most speakers? How do these figures compare to the total number of English speakers in the English-speaking countries of Australia, Britain, Canada, New Zealand, and the United States?

  b. Visit the Spain page. How many people live in Spain? How many native Spanish speakers are in Spain? How many languages altogether are spoken in Spain?

  c. Switzerland is one of the smallest European countries. What are the major languages of Switzerland, and how many speakers does each have?

  d. Ethnologue's Statistics section shows the distribution of living languages as a percent of world population. Which world region has the most languages? Which region has the fewest? Why do you suppose those regions evolved in such a way?

3-22. Cultural intelligence is a person's ability to function effectively in situations characterized by cultural diversity. globalEDGE™ and other online resources feature cultural intelligence scales. What are the components of cultural intelligence? Answer the questions on this scale and calculate your score on cultural intelligence. Compare your score to those of your classmates.

3-23. Various websites list cultural blunders or faux pas (false steps) people make in their international interactions. Neglecting to develop relationships (as in "Just sign the contract, I'm in a hurry!") and making too-casual use of first names (as in "Just call me Bill!") are examples of such blunders. Research online sources such as Kwintessential (http://www.kwintessential.co.uk/) or simply enter "cultural blunders" in an Internet search engine to identify examples of improper cultural behaviors. How can managers avoid these errors?

 MyManagementLab   **Try It!**

The simulation Global Culture and Diversity accompanies this exercise.

 MyManagementLab

Go to **mymanagementlab.com** for Auto-graded writing questions as well as the following Assisted-graded writing question:

⭐ **3-24.** Explain why culture matters in international business. In what types of contexts can cross-cultural differences cause concerns for managers?

⭐ **3-25.** Explain the major dimensions of culture.

⭐ **3-26.** MyManagementLab Only—comprehensive writing assignment for this chapter.

Endnotes

1. Yoree Koh and Daisuke Wakabayashi, "The Land of the Rising Crust," *Wall Street Journal,* September 20, 2014, p. D8; Rana, Preetika, "In India, Forget Doughnuts, It's Time to Make the Tough Guy Chicken Burger," *Wall Street Journal,* November 29, 2014, pp. A1 and A4; Harry C. Triandis, *Culture and Social Behavior* (New York: McGraw-Hill, 1994).

2. F. Kluckhohn and F. Strodbeck, *Variations in Value Orientations* (Evanston, IL: Row Peterson, 1961).

3. James Neuliep, *Intercultural Communication*, 6th ed. (Thousand Oaks, CA: Sage, 2015).

4. Alice Eagly and Shelly Chaiken, *The Psychology of Attitudes* (New York: Harcourt Brace Jovanovich, 1993); Geert Hofstede, "Attitudes, Values and Organizational Culture: Disentangling the Concepts," *Organization Studies* 19, No. 3 (1998), pp. 477–493.

5. Roger Axtell, *The Do's and Taboos of International Trade* (New York: Wiley, 1994).

6. Edward T. Hall, *The Silent Language* (Garden City, NY: Anchor, 1981); Neuliep, 2015.

7. "Babel Runs Backwards," *The Economist,* January 1, 2005, pp. 58–60; M. Paul Lewis et al. (ed.), *Ethnologue: Languages of the World*, 18th ed. (Dallas, TX: SIL International, 2015), http://www.ethnologue.com.

8. Erin Moore and Lynne Truss, *That's Not English: Britishisms, Americanisms, and What Our English Says About Us* (New York: Gotham, 2015).

9. Hall, 1981; Neuliep, 2015.

10. John Esposito, Darrell Fasching, and Todd Lewis, *World Religions* (New York: Oxford University Press, 2014).

11. Robert Grier, "The Effect of Religion on Economic Development," *Kyklos* 50, No. 1 (1997). pp. 47–62; Rachel McCleary, "Religion and Economic Development," *Policy Review* (April/May 2008), pp. 45–57; Rachel McCleary and Robert Barro, "Religion and Economy," *Journal of Economic Perspectives* 20, No. 2 (2006), pp. 49–72.

12. Adrian Furnham, *The Protestant Work Ethic* (London: Routledge, 1990); Max Weber, *The Protestant Ethic and the Spirit of Capitalism* (New York: Charles Scribner's Sons, 1959).

13. Meg Carter, "Muslims Offer a New Mecca for Marketers," *Financial Times,* August 11, 2005, p. 13.

14. *Economist*, "Untouchable and Unthinkable," October 6, 2007, pp. 15–16.

15. Esposito et al., 2014; Furnham (1990); Sethi S. Prakash and P. Steidlmeier, "Hinduism and Business Ethics," *Wiley Encyclopedia of Management*, vol. 2 (2015), pp. 1–5; Weber (1959).

16. Esposito et al., 2014; Charles Hee, "A Holistic Approach to Business Management: Perspectives from the Bhagavad Gita," *Singapore Management Review* 29, No. 1 (2007), pp. 73–84; Sethi and Steidlmeier (2015).

17. Esposito, Fasching, and Lewis, 2014; Hershey Friedman, "The Impact of Jewish Values on Marketing and Business Practices," *Journal of Macromarketing*, 21, June (2001), pp. 74–80.

18. Rachel Abrams, "Adapting Listerine to a Global Market," *New York Times*, September 12, 2014, retrieved March 28, 2015 from http://www.nytimes.com/2014/09/13/business/adapting-listerine-to-a-global-market.html?_r=0.

19. James Agarwal, Naresh Malhotra, and Ruth Bolton, "A Cross-National and Cross-Cultural Approach to Global Market Segmentation: An Application Using Consumers' Perceived Service Quality," *Journal of International Marketing* 18, no. 3 (2010), pp. 18–40; J. Andrew Petersen, Tarun Kushwaha, and V. Kumar, "Marketing Communication Strategies and Consumer Financial Decision Making: The Role of National Culture," *Journal of Marketing* 79, (2015), pp. 44–63.

20. Bangaly Kaba and K. Osei-Bryson, "Examining Influence of National Culture on Individuals' Attitude and Use of Information and Communication Technology: Assessment of Moderating Effect of Culture Through Cross Countries Study," *International Journal of Information Management* 33, no. 3 (2013), pp. 441–452; R. Rosmarin, "Text Messaging Gets a Translator," *Business 2.0* (March 2005), p. 32; Nitish Singh, Vikas Kumar, and Daniel Baack, "Adaptation of Cultural Content: Evidence from B2C E-Commerce Firms," *European Journal of Marketing* 39, Nos. 1/2 (2005), pp. 71–86; Sengun Yeniyurt and Janell Townsend, "Does Culture Explain Acceptance of New Products in a Country? An Empirical Investigation," *International Marketing Review* 20, No. 4 (2003), pp. 377–396; Yong Zhang and James Neelankavil, "The Influence of Culture on Advertising Effectiveness in China and the USA: A Cross-Cultural Study," *European Journal of Marketing* 31, No. 2 (1997), pp. 134–342.

21. Martin Gannon and Raj Pillai, *Understanding Global Cultures: Metaphorical Journeys Through 34 Nations*, 6th ed. (Thousand Oaks, CA: Sage, 2015).

22. Edward T. Hall, *Beyond Culture* (New York: Anchor, 1976); Edward T. Hall and Mildred Reed Hall, *Understanding Cultural Differences* (Boston: Intercultural Press, 1990).

23. Geert Hofstede, *Culture's Consequences* (Beverly Hills, CA: Sage, 1980); Geert Hofstede, Gert Jan Hofstede, and Michael Minkov, *Cultures and Organizations: Software of the Mind*, 3rd ed. (New York: McGraw-Hill, 2010).

24. *Ibid.*

25. Richard Priem, Leonard Love, and Margaret Shaffer, "Industrialization and Values Evolution: The Case of Hong Kong and Guangzhou, China," *Asia Pacific Journal of Management* 17, No. 3 (2000), pp. 473–482.

26. Hofstede (1980); Hofstede, Hofstede, and Minkov (2010).

27. Joyce Osland, Silvio De Franco, and Asbjorn Osland, "Organizational Implications of Latin American Culture: Lessons for the Expatriate Manager," *Journal of Management Inquiry* 8, No. 2 (1999), pp. 219–238.

28. Hofstede, 1998; Vern Terpstra and Kenneth David, *The Cultural Environment of International Business,* 3rd ed. (Cincinnati, OH: Southwestern, 1991).

29. Howard Perlmutter, "The Tortuous Evolution of the Multinational Corporation," *Columbia Journal of World Business* 4, No. 1 (1969), pp. 9–18.

30. V. Govindarajan and A. Gupta, *The Quest for Global Dominance* (San Francisco: Jossey-Bass/Wiley, 2001).

31. Robert Boyd and Peter Richerson, *Culture and Evolutionary Process* (Chicago: University of Chicago Press, 1985).

32. Harry C. Triandis, *Culture and Social Behavior* (New York: McGraw-Hill, 1994).

33. Tomasz Lenartowicz and James P. Johnson, "A Cross-National Assessment of the Values of Latin America Managers: Contrasting Hues or Shades of Gray?" *Journal of International Business Studies* 34, No. 3 (2003), pp. 266–281.

34. Kevin Groves, Ann Feyerherm, and Minhua Gu, "Examining Cultural Intelligence and Cross-Cultural Negotiation Effectiveness," *Journal of Management Education* 39, No. 2 (2015), pp. 209–243; James Johnson, Tomasz Lenartowicz, and Salvador Apud, "Cross-Cultural Competence in International Business: Toward a Definition and a Model," *Journal of International Business Studies* 37, No. 4 (2006), pp. 525–535; Soon Ang, Linn Van Dyne, and Christine Koh, "Personality Correlates of the Four-Factor Model of Cultural Intelligence," *Group & Organization Management* 31, No. 1 (2006), pp. 100–123.

Chapter 4

Ethics, Corporate Social Responsibility, Sustainability, and Governance in International Business

Learning Objectives *After studying this chapter, you should be able to:*

4.1 Appreciate ethical behavior and its importance in international business.

4.2 Recognize ethical challenges in international business.

4.3 Understand corporate social responsibility.

4.4 Understand sustainability.

4.5 Know the role of corporate governance.

4.6 Learn about a framework for making ethical decisions.

Improving the lives of Bangladeshi Garments factory workers

Bangladesh is one of the top exporters of garments with a 4.8% export market share. It is the most significant industry for the country as it accounts for around 75% of the total export revenue and employs nearly 4 million people. The biggest export destinations are the EU and the USA. New export markets are opening up in emerging economies of Russia, Brazil and China. Beside trade revenue and employment creation, this industry is very important for Bangladesh due to its contribution to social mobility, urbanisation and above all to empowerment of women. Most of the workers are female and from rural areas where agriculture is the only source of employment. The remarkable improvement Bangladesh has achieved over the last 25 years in public health, primary education, and poverty alleviation are the fruits of the success of its garment industry. However, working conditions and pay in this industry have not met the expectations.

The garment industry value chain is very much buyer driven and suppliers have very limited bargaining power. Buyer-driven value chains are usually noticed in industries where production is labor intensive, non-specialized and requires low fixed cost. Entry barriers are high in designing, distribution, branding, advertising and market intelligence but low in the production stage. Hence, maximum bargaining power rests in the hands of large brand owners, distributors and retailers which endow them with price determining powers. Suppliers are simply required to

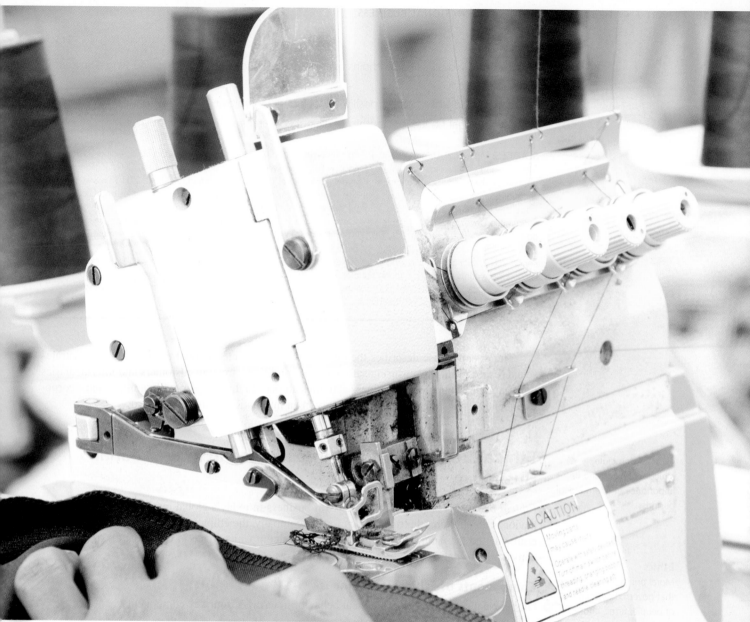

Source: Belinda Pretorius/Shutterstock

match the offered prices. This price elasticity also offers limited switching costs for buyers. Therefore, major buyers are able to significantly control their value chain without much involvement in the manufacturing process. Manufacturers are in constant pressure to gain production efficiency and achieve low cost advantages. In many cases, the health and safety issues are being overlooked to save cost. As a result several accidents took place with high number of causalities and subsequent labor unrest halts production efficiency. Many large importers also have cancelled purchase orders.

Responding to the working conditions and compliance issues the International Labor Organization, consumers, stake holders and fare trade agencies are working together with the Bangladeshi government, garments manufacturers, industrial associations and trade unions to raise working conditions and pay. The minimum wage has seen a 77% increase and rigorous inspections are in place for safety and environmental regulation compliances. Also, works are in progress in areas of job security, more value adding, productivity increase through better training and distribution of control power across the value chain etc. Consumers also need to consider the effect of fast fashion on sustainability and well-being. Now, it is ever more pressing to think of ethical consumerism for a better world.

Questions

4-1. How do industries value chains effect working conditions and determine wages in certain industries?

4-2. How could stake holders positively contribute in improving working conditions?

4-3. What might be the relationship of ethical consumption and sustainability?

SOURCES: Mariani, R.-D. and Valenti, F. (n.d.) 'Working Conditions in Th Bangladeshi Garment Sector: Social Dialouge and Compliance' Fair Wear Foundation [www.fairwear.org] last accessed [09/10/2015]; 'Bangladesh garment workers suffer poor conditions two years after reform vows' *The Guardian*, 22 April, 2015 [www .theguardian.com]; Naumann, E. (2006) 'The Multifibre Agreement – WTO Agreement on Textiles and Clothing' Trade Law Centre for Southern Africa (Tralac) Working Paper No 4/2006. International Centre for Trade and Sustainable Development. Available from <http://www.fibre2fashion.com/industry-article/pdffiles/the-multifibre-agreement.pdf> [last accessed 12/08/2014]; Naomi, H. (2011) 'Exports, Equity, And Empowerment: The Effects Of Readymade Garments Manufacturing Employment On Gender Equality In Bangladesh'., *World Development Report 2012, Gender Equality And Development*. Background Paper [online] available from <https://open-knowledge.worldbank.org/bitstream/handle/10986/9100/WDR2012-0012.pdf?sequence=1 [31 January, 2014]; BGMEA (2014) *BGMEA publications* [online] available from http://www.bgmea.com.bd/home/pages/ BGMEA_Publications#.UvkUofl_t6s 10 Feb, 2014].

The opening case describes the ethical approach to international business. It demonstrates social responsibility by ensuring safe working conditions, treating customers and intermediaries fairly, and preventing illicit business activities abroad. In this chapter, we examine ethics, corporate social responsibility, and sustainability in an international business context.

4.1 Appreciate ethical behavior and its importance in international business.

Ethical Behavior and Its Importance in International Business

Ethical behavior is essential for successful business in today's global marketplace.[1] Ethical behavior is about doing the right things for the company, the employees, the community, the government, and the natural environment. It requires companies to act in ways that all stakeholders consider honest and fair.

Components of Ethical Behavior

Global business leaders define ethical behavior in terms of four key components:

- Ethics
- Corporate social responsibility
- Sustainability
- Corporate governance

Ethics
Moral principles and values that govern the behavior of people, firms, and governments, regarding right and wrong.

Corporate social responsibility (CSR)
A manner of operating a business that meets or exceeds the ethical, legal, commercial, and public expectations of customers, shareholders, employees, and communities.

Sustainability
Meeting humanity's needs without harming future generations.

Corporate governance
The system of procedures and processes by which corporations are managed, directed, and controlled.

Ethics are moral principles and values that govern the behavior of people, firms, and governments, regarding right and wrong.[2] **Corporate social responsibility (CSR)** refers to operating a business in a manner that meets or exceeds the ethical, legal, and commercial expectations of customers, shareholders, employees, and the communities where the firm does business. **Sustainability** means meeting humanity's needs today without harming the ability of future generations to meet their needs. **Corporate governance** is the system of procedures and processes by which corporations are managed, directed, and controlled. Corporate governance provides the means through which the organization's directors and managers undertake ethical behavior, corporate social responsibility, and sustainability.

Leading corporations ensure that ethical behavior transcends all international business activities and figures prominently in management decisions about financial performance and competitive advantage. An integrated, strategic approach to ethical, sustainable, and socially responsible behavior provides the firm with competitive advantages, including stronger relationships with customers, employees, shareholders, customers, suppliers, local governments, and the communities where they do business. Exhibit 4.1 provides a framework for the key managerial approaches to ethical behavior addressed in this chapter.

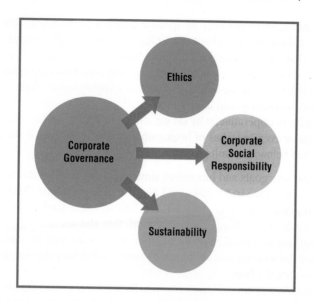

EXHIBIT 4.1

Organizing Framework for Ethical Behavior in International Business

Experienced executives understand that incorporating a culture of ethical behavior is essential to achieving their profit objectives. Just as reputation affects the success of individuals, it is critical for companies as well. Failure to protect and nurture the corporate image translates into poor performance and potential ruin. This is even more critical in cross-border business where the firm is constantly under the scrutiny of stakeholders in multiple countries. Let's examine ethics in terms of its value to firms.

Value of Ethical Behavior

Why is it imperative for firms that conduct international business to behave ethically? Here are key reasons.

- It is simply the **right thing to do**.
- It is **often prescribed within laws and regulations**. Violating laws and regulations has obvious legal consequences.
- Customers, governments, and the news media demand ethical behavior. Firms that commit ethical blunders attract unwanted attention from opinion leaders.
- Ethical behavior is **good business, leading to enhanced corporate image and selling prospects**.[3]

The firm with a reputation for high ethical standards gains advantages in hiring, motivating employees, partnering, and dealing with foreign governments. Firms that behave unethically run the risk of criminal or civil prosecution, damage to their own reputations, harm to employee morale and recruitment efforts, and exposure to blackmailers or other unscrupulous parties.[4] For all these reasons, companies need to incorporate ethical considerations into their international activities.

In host countries, firms with iconic global brands, such as Volkswagen, are especially conspicuous to consumers and can become targets of public protest. Increasingly, governments insist that firms behave in ways that serve the public interest. The European Union restricts the use of lead, mercury, and other harmful substances in manufacturing and requires firms to collect and recycle unwanted electronic products. Canada has well-developed complaint procedures for dealing with bribery, including liaison officers in 25 countries and a website (www.recol.ca) for filing complaints about possible corruption.[5]

Unethical Behavior

Before entering a country and throughout the life of the firm's operations there, management must be alert to the various ethical challenges that may confront the firm and should scan the country and potential partners for the possibility of ethical abuses and regard such scanning as an ongoing process. Managers must be constantly vigilant about their current and potential activities. With enough practice, management can develop a systematic approach to scanning and create a culture within the firm that supports alertness and ongoing analysis of potential ethical concerns.

Management should focus not only on specific national environments but also on proposed and existing value-chain activities, which often take place in multiple countries. In each country and venture, areas that merit particular attention encompass commercial environments, labor conditions, partners, customers, accounting practices, and conditions regarding the natural environment as well as the range of the firm's potential or existing value-chain activities, including sourcing, production, marketing, and distribution.

If ethical behavior is imperative, why do we still encounter abundant examples of questionable ethical practices or even breaches of responsible conduct? A study in the *Harvard Business Review* found that bad behavior results when:

- Top management sets goals and incentives aimed at promoting good outcomes (e.g., profits) that instead encourage bad behaviors. Law firms and accounting firms often encourage employees to maximize the hours they bill for their services. Under pressure, some employees pad their hours or charge clients for work they did not do.
- Employees overlook unethical behavior in others because of peer pressure or self-interest. A manager may fail to complain about toxic waste a subsidiary discharges because he doesn't want to rock the boat.
- Managers tolerate lower ethical standards in value-chain activities suppliers or third-party firms perform. Coffee producers sometimes ignore the poor working conditions of supplier farmers in Africa and Latin America.
- Unethical practices are allowed to accumulate in the firm slowly over time. When a firm is awash in bad behavior, smaller infractions seem less noticeable. A corrupt environment tends to foster further corruption.
- Bad means are justified by good ends. Pharmaceutical firms sometimes use unethical testing procedures in poor countries to validate of the effectiveness of new medications for disorders such as cancer and AIDS. The drugs help people but were developed through bad practice.[6]

Examples of Unethical Behavior

Firms may:

- *Falsify or misrepresent contracts* or financial statements.
- *Pay or accept bribes*, kickbacks, or inappropriate gifts.
- *Tolerate sweatshop conditions* or otherwise abuse employees.
- *Undertake false advertising* and other deceptive marketing practices.
- *Engage in pricing that is deceptive*, discriminatory, or predatory.
- *Deceive or abuse intermediaries* in international channels.
- *Engage in activities that harm the natural environment.*

After management possesses ongoing awareness of questionable ethical behavior, the next step is systematically to explore the ethical aspects of each decision the firm may make regarding its current and potential activities.[7]

Ethical Standards and Dilemmas Around the World

Are ethical standards uniform around the world? Not really. Each society develops its own traditions, values, attitudes, norms, customs, and laws. Each culture develops its own ethical values and understanding of ethical principles. There is no global standard of ethical behavior. Appropriate behavior in one culture may be viewed as inappropriate or unethical elsewhere.[8] Let's review some examples.

- In China, **counterfeiters** frequently publish translated versions of imported books without compensating the original publisher or authors, an illegal practice in most of the world.
- In parts of Africa, **accepting expensive gifts** from suppliers is acceptable, even if inappropriate elsewhere.

- In the United States, **CEOs receive compensation** often a hundred times greater than that of low-ranking subordinates, a practice widely considered unacceptable in other parts of the world.
- Finland and Sweden ban **advertising directed at children**, whereas the practice is well accepted in other parts of Europe.

Ethical standards often vary by levels of economic development. For example, Africa is beset by widespread hunger. Some restaurant workers steal food on the job to take home to their families. Is this equivalent to restaurant workers stealing food in rich countries? Standards also change over time. Although slavery is no longer tolerated, some multinational firms today tolerate working conditions that are akin to it. In China, many MNEs operate factories that pollute local water supplies, a practice once also commonplace in the United States and other advanced economies.

Deciding what is right and wrong is not always clear. Ethical problems arise when requirements are ambiguous, inconsistent, or based on multiple legal or cultural norms. The firm may be faced with multiple and sometimes conflicting laws and regulations. In the United States, for example, the Occupational Safety and Health Administration (OSHA) specifies numerous regulations regarding labor and employment conditions, but U.S. companies often do not need to follow OSHA regulations in their foreign operations.[9]

In many countries, legal systems are weak or laws are poorly enforced. What should the firm do? Should it follow weak local laws or should it follow the laws of the home country? Even when a country has a sound legal system, or even when the firm has a strong code of ethics, managers regularly face the challenge of determining appropriate behavior.

An *ethical dilemma* is a predicament concerning major conflicts among different interests when determining the most appropriate course of action is confounded by a set of solutions that are equally justifiable and often equally imperfect. Possible actions may be mutually exclusive; the choice of one automatically negates the other(s).[10] An example of such a dilemma is presented in the *Ethical Connections* box. It is typical of the type of ethical dilemmas that employees often encounter in international business. Managers working abroad may be most exposed because they are caught between home country ethical norms and those encountered the foreign country.

In a world of seemingly endless ethical challenges, how should managers and companies respond? Consider the framework in Exhibit 4.2. After complying with local law (the bottom of the pyramid), management should ensure that company activities follow high ethical standards (the middle). Finally, once the firm has fulfilled both its legal and ethical obligations, it should emphasize socially responsible behavior (the top of the pyramid).

Ethical Connections

Imagine you are a manager and visit a factory an affiliate owns in Colombia, only to discover the use of child labor in the plant. Upon studying the problem, you learn that child labor is accepted in many developing economies even though girls are vulnerable and may be abused or exploited, and work prevents children from attending school, which would improve their prospects for a better life. There are more than 50 million children working in India alone. However, you also learn that without their children's income, families often go hungry. If the kids are dismissed from the plant, many will turn to other income sources, including prostitution and street crime. The age at which children are deemed adults varies worldwide, sometimes as young as 15 years. What should you do? Do you make a fuss about the immorality of child labor, or do you look the other way?

Relativism and Normativism

Relativism is the belief that ethical truths are not absolute but differ from group to group. According to this perspective, a good rule is, "When in Rome, do as the Romans do." Thus, a Japanese multinational firm adhering to the position that bribery is wrong might nevertheless pay bribes in countries where the practice is customary and culturally acceptable. Relativists opt for passive acceptance of the values, behaviors, and practices that prevail in each of the countries where they do business.

Normativism is the belief that ethical behavioral standards are universal, and firms and individuals should seek to uphold them consistently around the world. According to this view, managers of the Japanese multinational firm who believe bribery is wrong will enforce this standard

Relativism
The belief that ethical truths are not absolute but differ from group to group.

Normativism
The belief that ethical behavioral standards are universal, and firms and individuals should seek to uphold them around the world.

EXHIBIT 4.2

The Pyramid of Ethical Behavior

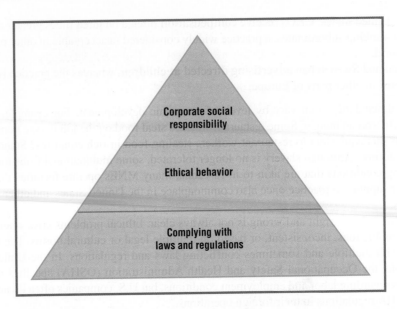

Corporate social responsibility

Ethical behavior

Complying with laws and regulations

everywhere in the world. The United Nations and other ethics proponents encourage companies to follow a normative approach in their international dealings. Responsible firms attempt to correct unethical practices that arise in their ongoing business dealings around the world.[11]

In reality, most firms apply a combination of relativism and normativism abroad. Most corporations strike a balance between corporate values developed in the home country and local ethical values. In countries with questionable ethical norms, it is usually best to maintain ethical standards *superior* to what is required by local laws and values. This strategy helps win goodwill in the local market and prevents potentially damaging publicity in the firm's other markets.

To make ethical practices, CSR, and sustainability succeed in the firm, it is important for corporate directors and executives to undertake systematic and ongoing education of employees, suppliers, and intermediaries. As the firm builds a track record of positive ethical behavioral changes and successes, it will begin to build a culture of appropriate behavior in its operations worldwide. As they ply the waters of international business, addressing the moral integrity of strategic and daily operational decisions is a prime consideration for companies today.[12]

Ethical Challenges in International Business

4.2 Recognize ethical challenges in international business.

Companies encounter ethical challenges in a range of international activities. Ethical challenges include corruption, bribery, unethical management practices, harmful global sourcing, illicit products and marketing, and intellectual property infringement. Let's examine these challenges in more detail.

Corruption

Corruption is an extreme form of unethical behavior.[13] It is the practice of obtaining power, personal gain, or influence through illegitimate means and usually occurs at others' expense. Why is corruption bad? Corruption influences our political, social, and economic environments. It diminishes trust in public institutions, undermines the rule of law, and challenges democratic principles. It stunts economic development by discouraging foreign direct investment and hurts small businesses that lack the means to pay up.

More than 30 percent of MNEs believe corruption is a major concern in their activities worldwide. Recent data suggest that the cost of corruption amounts to more than five percent of global GDP annually (more than $2.6 trillion) and increases global business costs by up to 10 percent.[14]

How is corruption encountered in international business? Mainly in the following ways:

- *Bribery* occurs when a person offers or gives another person a gift, cash, or favor to act dishonestly in exchange for personal gain.

- *Embezzlement* is the theft or misuse of funds typically placed in one's care or belonging to one's employer.
- *Fraud* involves wrongfully deceiving a person or other party to give up assets or cash.
- *Extortion and blackmail* involve threats of harm against another person or party unless payment is received or some other demand is met. Threats can include physical harm, false imprisonment, exposure of an individual's secrets or past, or other harmful outcomes.
- *Money laundering* is the concealment of the origins of funds obtained through illegal means, typically by transferring the funds illicitly through banks or other legitimate businesses.

Corruption may appear as political corruption, in which officials abuse public power or profit improperly from government resources. It may arise as police corruption, in which law enforcement officials obtain financial or other benefits in exchange for granting favors such as not pursuing crimes. In firms, corruption occurs across the range of value chain activities.

To assess corruption worldwide, *Transparency International* (www.transparency.org) surveys business executives every year regarding their perceptions of bribery, embezzlement, and other illicit behavior in the public sector in 180 countries. The result is the *Corruption Perceptions Index*, presented in Exhibit 4.3, which ranks countries on a scale from 1 to 100.[15]

Singapore, the Netherlands, and other nations that score well on the Corruption Perceptions Index attract much direct investment partly because managers know business in such countries is conducted fairly. Commercial laws are fair and adequately enforced, and financial and accounting information is transparent, reliable, and easily accessed. By contrast, foreign firms are reluctant to invest in countries such as Somalia and Russia, due to rampant corruption. In Russia, for example, entrepreneurs typically are required to pay thousands of dollars in bribes to officials to gain the right to launch their businesses and run them smoothly.

Widespread corruption hinders economic development. This relationship points to an important dilemma—trade and investment help reduce poverty, but MNEs avoid doing business with corrupt countries. Corruption harms the poorest in societies, those forced to pay bribes to gain access to needed products and services, such as water, electricity, and phone service. Various bodies have issued international conventions against corruption. The United Nations issued a declaration against corruption in international transactions.

Bribery

Bribery, widely practiced around the world, is the most notable form of corruption in international business. It is estimated that more than $1 trillion in bribes are paid worldwide every year to gain access to important markets and achieve other business goals. One study found that 40 percent of business executives have been asked to pay a bribe when dealing with public institutions. Twenty percent claimed to have lost business because of bribes paid by a competitor. Recently, Brazil's largest company, Petrobras, was caught in a major bribery scandal.[16] Numerous countries have signed the anti-bribery convention developed by the Organisation for Economic Co-operation and Development (OECD). In the United States, the Foreign Corrupt Practices Act (FCPA) makes it illegal for U.S. firms to offer bribes to foreign parties to secure or retain business. Firms can be fined $2 million and managers can be imprisoned for up to five years. The FCPA excludes *grease payments,* small payments made to low-level government officials to perform routine duties more efficiently.

Bribery is especially common in developing economies such as Egypt, Indonesia, Nigeria, and Pakistan, where it can be nearly impossible to achieve important business objectives without paying bribes to public officials and other individuals. The problem is especially common in the global energy, mining, and telecommunications industries. This helps explain why firms from these industries, such as Halliburton and Siemens, have been implicated in major bribery scandals.

Bribery has led to countless negative consequences, such as illegal logging in Indonesia, terrible work conditions in China, and poorly constructed buildings that collapsed in Turkey. Paying bribes increases the risks and costs of doing business. It promotes a culture and practice of dishonesty and immorality that opens the door to other types of wrongdoing. Bribery threatens fundamental business principles of fair competition and merit-based selection, and even the essential functioning of market economies.

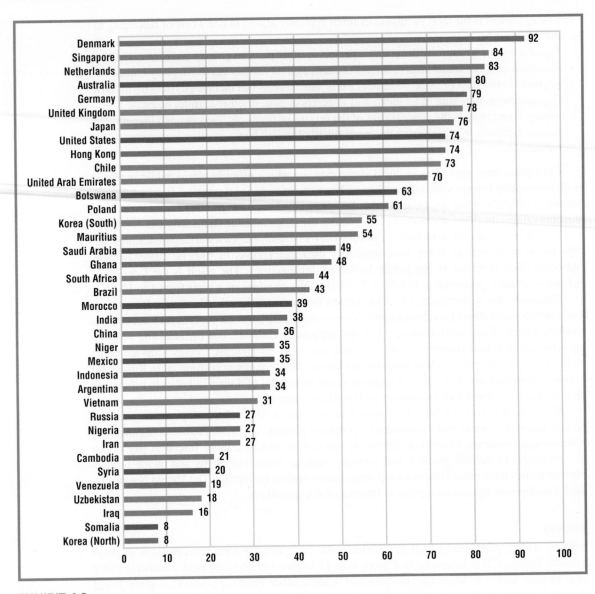

EXHIBIT 4.3

Corruption Perceptions Index 2014

Note: Countries with the highest scores have the lowest levels of corruption.

Sources: Based on *Corruption Perceptions Index*. Copyright © 2014 Transparency International: The Global Coalition Against Corruption, www.transparency.org.

Executives of Walmart's Mexico subsidiary allegedly paid millions of dollars in bribes to Mexican officials in the late 1990s and early 2000s. The bribes were paid to expedite permits for construction and operation of hundreds of its retail stores in Mexico. Walmart headquarters' own investigation revealed that its subsidiary indeed had paid millions of dollars in bribes to local politicians and their organizations, actions that appeared to violate both Mexican and United States law. Ultimately, no executives in the firm's Mexican operations were disciplined, but in the wake of the scandal, Walmart exposed itself to substantial class-action lawsuits.[17]

MyManagementLab **Watch It! I**

If your professor has assigned this, go to the Assignments section of **mymanagementlab.com** to complete the video exercise titled Global Ethics and Siemens.

Unethical Management Practices

Unethical management practices are a significant factor at the level of individual firms, especially in countries that lack adequate regulation and professional standards. A corporate culture that advocates profit over sustainability and human welfare can lead to employee abuse, harmful procedures, and other unsustainable practices. The recent global financial crisis resulted in part because top management in banks and financial firms neglected to devise safeguards against making bad loans or offering high-risk securities. Lax management standards also give rise to dishonest accounting practices, in which companies provide deceptive information to investors, customers, and government authorities. In much of the world, managers may unduly favor certain suppliers or colleagues over others, leading to lost productivity and demoralized employees. Managers may harass employees over issues of sex, race, religion, or political affiliation.

Source: epa european pressphoto agency b.v./Alamy

Workers at a Foxconn factory in China, a leading supplier to Apple. Following charges about poor working conditions at Foxconn plants, Apple and Foxconn took steps to improve the work environment.

Harmful Global Sourcing

Global sourcing is the procurement of products or services from suppliers located abroad. In a typical scenario, the focal firm buys parts and components from foreign companies that manufacture such goods, or the firm may establish its own factories abroad. However, global sourcing raises concerns about ensuring human rights and protecting the environment. Some companies operate illicit sweatshop factories in which employees are children or work long hours for very low wages, often in harsh conditions.[18] Suppliers might operate factories that generate much pollution. The use of third-party suppliers is challenging for firms such as Nike and Philips with thousands of partners that operate in a range of cultures and belief systems worldwide.

Illicit Products and Marketing

Firms might market defective or harmful products or engage in unethical marketing practices. Flawed products or packaging can lead to disastrous outcomes for public health and safety or for natural environments. For example, millions of electronic products from cell phones to computers are discarded every year. Products that could be recycled instead end up in landfills. Excessive product packaging generates pollution and consumes energy and natural resources. Excessive use of plastic packaging is wasteful and, because plastic does not easily decompose, the amount of plastic waste is steadily increasing on land and in the oceans.

Intellectual property
Ideas or works that individuals or firms create, including discoveries and inventions; artistic, musical, and literary works; and words, phrases, symbols, and designs.

Some companies use deceptive means to induce consumers to buy their products. Marketers may make false claims about the qualities or effectiveness of a product. Advances in communications technologies allow fraudulent marketers to easily target victims in foreign countries. The transnational nature of such scams makes it difficult for law enforcers to catch and prosecute perpetrators. International marketing provides many benefits but also presents challenges for protecting consumers worldwide.

Intellectual Property Infringement

Intellectual property refers to ideas or works that individuals or firms create and includes a variety of proprietary, intangible assets: discoveries and inventions;

Source: Pongtorn Hiranlikit/123RF

Global companies with well-known brands are especially conspicuous to consumers and need strong ethical values to thrive under public scrutiny. This Louis Vuitton store is in Singapore.

artistic, musical, and literary works; and words, phrases, symbols, and designs. Illicit use of intellectual property is common worldwide, typically through outright theft or illegal copying.

Intellectual property rights
The legal claim through which the proprietary assets of firms and individuals are protected from unauthorized use by other parties.

Trademarks, copyrights, and *patents* are examples of **intellectual property rights**, the legal claim through which proprietary assets are protected from unauthorized use by other parties. *Trademarks* are distinctive signs and indicators that firms use to identify their products and services. *Copyrights* grant protections to the creators of art, music, books, software, movies, and TV shows. *Patents* confer the exclusive right to manufacture, use, and sell products or processes. Intellectual property rights are not guaranteed in much of the world. Laws enacted in one country are enforceable only in that country and offer no protection abroad.[19]

Intellectual property infringement arises in the form of *piracy* and *counterfeiting*, the unauthorized reproduction or use of copyrighted or patented work, for financial gain. Pirated goods typically are sold at low prices in illicit markets, in person, or through the Internet. The total value of internationally traded counterfeit and pirated products exceeded $1 trillion annually in 2015.[20] In Russia, software and movies produced by such firms as Microsoft and Disney often fall prey to counterfeiting. Global brands—Rolex, Louis Vuitton, and Tommy Hilfiger, among others—are frequently pirated, eroding firms' competitive advantages and brand equity.

Piracy and counterfeiting hurt the world economy in various ways, especially regarding:

- *International trade* – exports of legitimate products must compete with trade in counterfeit goods.
- *Direct investment* – firms avoid investing in countries known for widespread intellectual property violations.
- *Company performance* – piracy and counterfeiting undermine the sales, profits, and strategies of firms that produce legitimate products. Business costs rise because the brand value of pirated goods can fall over time and companies must invest more to market their products and combat illicit competitors.
- *Innovation* – companies avoid doing research and development in countries beset by illegal copying of intellectual property.
- *Tax revenues* – pirates usually don't pay taxes, which, together with reduced legitimate business activity, hurts government tax revenues.
- *Criminal activity* – piracy and counterfeiting often encourage, or are supported by, organized crime.
- *The natural environment* – intellectual property violators disregard environmental standards when producing illicit goods.
- *National prosperity and wellbeing* – in the long run, widespread piracy and counterfeiting harm job prospects, prosperity, and moral standards in affected nations.

Pirated and counterfeit products are usually of inferior quality. They can be used unknowingly in the manufacture of military hardware, infrastructure, and consumer products. In Kenya, counterfeit batches of the medicine Zidolam were distributed to patients receiving treatment for HIV/AIDS. Nearly 3,000 people failed to receive appropriate therapy, resulting in increased illness in life-threatening conditions. In the United States, dozens of patients were affected when they received fake doses of Avastin, a drug used to treat cancer. Many people have died due to consumption of counterfeit goods.

In 2014, U.S. Department of Homeland Security agents seized pirated and counterfeit products at U.S. borders with an estimated retail value of more than $1.2 billion. Exhibit 4.4 highlights the categories of seized illicit commodities.[21] Among the most counterfeited goods are jewelry, consumer electronics, and pharmaceuticals. In 2014, by far the largest single source of counterfeit products was China, which accounted for 63 percent of Homeland Security seizures, followed by Hong Kong, an administrative region of China, amounting to 25 percent of seizures. All other countries accounted for the remaining 12 percent.[22] MNEs seeking to do business

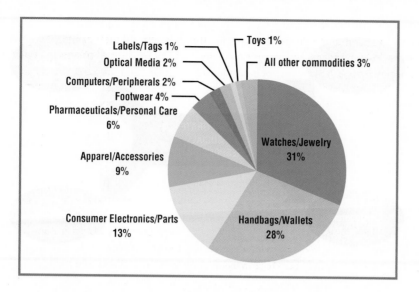

Labels/Tags 1%
Optical Media 2%
Computers/Peripherals 2%
Footwear 4%
Pharmaceuticals/Personal Care 6%
Apparel/Accessories 9%
Consumer Electronics/Parts 13%
Toys 1%
All other commodities 3%
Watches/Jewelry 31%
Handbags/Wallets 28%

EXHIBIT 4.4

Top Counterfeit Commodities Seized, United States, 2014

Source: "Intellectual Property Rights Seizure Statistics Fiscal Year 2014," Washington, DC: Homeland Security, U.S. Customs and Border Protection and U.S. Immigration and Customs Enforcement (2015), at www.cbp.gov/sites/default/files/documents/2014%20IPR%20Stats.pdf.

within China may become victims of domestic counterfeiting activities. For example, Disney has struggled to launch its DVD movie business in China, due to rampant local piracy. Legitimate Disney DVDs of films such as *Finding Nemo* and *The Lion King* cost up to ten times as much as knockoffs, restricting sales to a trickle.[23] In Russia, illicit websites sell popular music downloads for as little as five cents apiece or less than one U.S. dollar for an entire CD. Russia's laws regarding counterfeiting are often insufficient to thwart such crimes, and enforcement is weak.[24]

Suppose you work for a small online retailer that decides to offer pirated music through the company website to potential buyers in Russia and other emerging markets with weak intellectual property laws. How should you respond to this dilemma? Later in this chapter, we present a framework for ethical conduct that you can use to analyze this problem and identify an appropriate way forward.

Corporate Social Responsibility

4.3 Understand corporate social responsibility.

Corporate social responsibility (CSR) refers to operating a business in a manner that meets or exceeds the ethical, legal, and commercial expectations of customers, shareholders, employees, and the communities where the firm does business. Companies that practice CSR aim to do more for the betterment of others than is required by laws, regulations, or special interest groups. Sometimes called corporate citizenship, CSR emphasizes the development of *shared value* for both shareholders and stakeholders, creating a double-win scenario.

Firms that practice CSR behave ethically and support a voluntary, self-regulated business model. Managers develop strategies that thoughtfully considers the social, economic, and environmental impact of company actions and aims to improve the life quality of employees, the community, and society.

Settings of Corporate Social Responsibility

CSR is a broad concept and applicable to various settings, as illustrated in Exhibit 4.5. Workplace CSR focuses on the firm's employees and implies a thoughtful approach to diversity, recruitment, salary, safety, health, and working conditions. Marketplace CSR emphasizes company interactions with customers,

Source: bright/123RF

Environmentally friendly policies are an important part of most corporate social responsibility programs. Accepting computers and parts for recycling is an example of CSR initiatives at companies such as Acer and Apple.

EXHIBIT 4.5

Settings for Corporate Social Responsibility

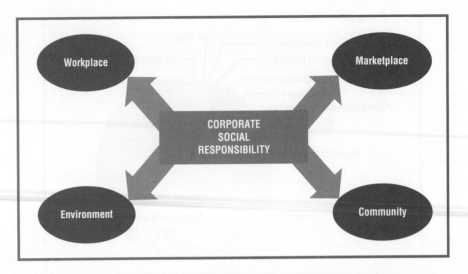

competitors, suppliers, and distributors. It implies appropriate behavior regarding product development, marketing, and advertising as well as approaches that suppliers and distributors follow. Environmental CSR refers to the firm's activities to minimize or eliminate the creation of pollutants as well as efforts to improve the natural environment. Community CSR accounts for the firm's activities aimed at benefiting the community and society. It includes employee volunteering programs and philanthropy.[25]

Adhering to CSR principles implies a *proactive* approach to ethical behavior in which firms not only seek to maximize profits but also to benefit society and the environment. Examples of CSR values include:

- Avoiding human rights abuses.
- Upholding the right to join or form labor unions.
- Eliminating child labor.
- Avoiding workplace discrimination.
- Protecting the natural environment.
- Guarding against corruption.
- Undertaking philanthropic efforts.[26]

Successes and Failures of CSR

Failure to adopt CSR behaviors can have adverse, even ruinous, consequences. Efforts by the China National Petroleum Company (CNPC) to raise money on the New York Stock Exchange in 2000 were partly depressed by the firm's activities in Sudan, which human rights groups had criticized. The Shell Oil Company has faced protests and lost revenues due to its oil-drilling activities in Nigeria, which were seen as harming community interests and generating excessive pollution. In India, Walmart faced lost sales and massive protests because of concerns the firm's market entry would hurt small retailers. Following the massive BP oil spill in the Gulf of Mexico, BP gas stations in the United States reported that sales fell between 10 and 40 percent due to backlash against the firm. BP lost billions of dollars in federal penalties, state-mandated grants, and enormous claims. Damage to BP's reputation and sales were enormous.[27]

In contrast, countless firms have improved their performance by adopting CSR. The most successful companies focus on maximizing the value of key intangible assets such as reputation and a trustworthy brand name. The African MNE Celtel is a leading exemplar. Africa is one of the world's most underserved telecommunications markets. To address pent-up demand, African native Mo Ibrahim launched Celtel, a mobile communications company. To do so, he had to design, build, and operate phone systems in countries with antiquated or nonexistent infrastructure, including poor roads as well as scarce electricity, water, and other utilities. Celtel developed a plan to deal with corruption. It built schools and clinics, trained local staff, and provided health insurance to employees. Because customers lacked access to modern payment methods, Celtel developed a system of cheap, prepaid phone cards. Today, Celtel provides mobile phone services in more than 15 African countries, including Uganda, Malawi, Gabon, and Sierra Leone.

EXHIBIT 4.6 **Corporate Social Responsibility: A Sampling of MNE Accomplishments**

Company	Industry	Sample Accomplishments
ABN AMRO (Netherlands)	Financial services	Finances various socially responsible projects, including biomass fuels and micro enterprises
SC Johnson (United States)	Consumer products	Shifted packaging to lightweight bottles, saving millions of kilograms of consumer waste annually
GlaxoSmithKline (United Kingdom)	Pharmaceuticals	Devotes substantial R&D to poor-country ailments, such as malaria and tuberculosis; was first to offer AIDS medication at cost
Hindustan Unilever (India)	Consumer products	Provided microfinance and training to 65,000 poor women to start their own wholesale firms, doubling their incomes
Nokia (Finland)	Telecommunications	Makes telephones for low-income consumers; has been a leader in environmental practices such as phasing out toxic materials
Norsk Hydro (Norway)	Oil and gas	Cut greenhouse gas emissions by 32 percent; consistently measures the social and environmental impact of its projects
Philips Electronics (Netherlands)	Consumer electronics	Top innovator of energy-saving appliances and lighting products as well as medical devices for developing economies
Toyota (Japan)	Automobiles	The world leader in developing efficient gas-electric vehicles such as the top-selling Prius

Sources: Pete Engardio, "Beyond the Green Corporation," *Business Week*, January 29, 2007, pp. 50–64; Fisk Johnson, "How I Did It: SC Johnson's CEO on Doing the Right Thing, Even When It Hurts Business," *Harvard Business Review*, April, 2015, pp. 33–36; Kasturi Rangan, Lisa Chase, and Sohel Karim, "The Truth about CSR," *Harvard Business Review*, January/February, 2015, pp. 40–49.

Ibrahim's firm has proven enormously profitable and, while enjoying huge success, has dramatically improved conditions for millions of people and businesses around Africa.[28]

Exhibit 4.6 summarizes additional CSR initiatives firms have undertaken worldwide. For example, Africa accounts for the most deaths from AIDS, but few Africans can afford to pay the high cost of medications to treat the terrible disease. GlaxoSmithKline (GSK) offers its AIDS medications to Africans at or below its production costs. Indeed, GSK sells 90 percent of its vaccines, in volume terms, at not-for-profit prices to customers in the developing economies.[29] In Scotland, the large utility firm Scottish and Southern Energy (SSE) emphasizes sustainability in providing energy to its customers. In Ireland, the firm provides electricity through numerous wind farms. Only two of SSE's power plants are fueled by coal, which is more polluting than other energy sources.[30]

In 2009, Denmark enacted laws that require firms to incorporate CSR activities and report on them in their financial reports.[31] Communications technology allows it to learn quickly about the misdeeds of any firm with which it does business. Over time, many consumers tend to choose products made by firms with strong CSR.

In addition to profit-seeking focal firms, more nongovernmental organizations (NGOs) are undertaking international CSR initiatives, often in conjunction with multinational firms. For example, such NGOs as CARE, Médecins Sans Frontières, and the Bangladesh Rural Advancement Committee work to reduce global poverty and frequently partner with private companies to provide vital products and services.[32] Read the *You Can Do It Recent Grad in IB* feature, which profiles Javier Estrada, who has gained much experience working on poverty and sustainability issues in various emerging markets and developing economies.

Sustainability

4.4 Understand sustainability.

Sustainability implies the development and execution of company practices that avoid harming the ability of future generations to meet their needs. It is endorsed by economic development experts, environmentalists, and human rights activists. The sustainable firm carries out value

EXHIBIT 4.7

Air Pollution in Selected Cities (Particulate matter concentration in micrograms per cubic meter)

Source: World Bank, *World Bank Development Indicators 2014*, Washington DC: World Bank; World Bank, *Clean Air and Healthy Lungs: Enhancing the World Bank's Approach to Air Quality Management* (Washington DC: World Bank, February 2015).

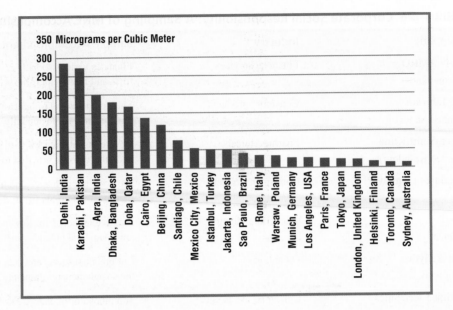

chain activities in ways that protect and preserve economic, social, and natural environments. For example, sustainable firms pay fair wages, ensure worker safety, and avoid emitting toxic waste. Examples of sustainable practices include:

- *Beneficial agricultural practices.* The appropriate use of crop rotation and natural pesticides improves the quality of crops grown and preserves land for use by future farmers.
- *Water conservation.* Clean water is an increasingly scarce resource worldwide. Companies that depend heavily on water, seek ways to recycle used water and minimize waste.
- *Air quality protection.* As shown in Exhibit 4.7, industrialization generates much air pollution. Industrial practices to reduce air pollution improve life quality and enhance competitive advantages.
- *Reduced energy and fuel consumption.* Efforts to support the natural environment include regulation of fossil fuel usage and government incentives to use renewable energy sources.
- *Increased use of solar and wind energy.* Cost-effective solar and wind energy can contribute enormously to reducing dependence on nonrenewable and polluting power sources.
- *Improved work processes.* Modifying work processes to improve sustainability reduces corporate costs and supports the natural environment.

A Sustainable Business Simultaneously Pursues Three Types of Interests

- *Economic interests* refer to the firm's economic impact on the localities where it does business. Management considers the effect of the firm's activities on such local concerns as job creation, wages, tax flows, disadvantaged communities, public works, and other areas where the firm can contribute positively to local economic interests.

- *Social interests* refer to how the firm performs relative to societies and social justice, often termed *social impact*. The firm with a strong social interest optimizes work conditions and diversity in hiring. It avoids using sweatshops, child labor, and other practices that harm workers. Instead, the sustainable firm provides safe work environments, health insurance, retirement benefits, and educational opportunities for employees.

- *Environmental interests* refer to the extent of the firm's contribution to preserving environmental quality, commonly known as *environmental impact*. This concept refers to reducing the effect of the firm's value-chain activities on the natural environment. The sustainable firm maximizes its use of recycled or renewable raw materials and environmentally friendly energy. It minimizes pollutants, designs production lines to use water and energy efficiently, and constantly seeks ways to reduce waste. Many firms establish a green purchasing policy, through which they procure inputs that support environmental interests.

- *Sources:* John Blewitt, *Understanding Sustainable Development* (London: Earthscan, 2008); F. Reimann Kaufmann, M. Ehrgott, and J. Rauer, "Sustainable Success," *Wall Street Journal*, June 22, 2009, retrieved from www.wsj.com; Nancy Landrum and Sandra Edwards, *Sustainable Business: An Executive's Primer* (New York: Business Expert Press, 2009).

MNE Role in Sustainability

Leading firms view sustainability as an opportunity for resource efficiency, cost effectiveness, reduced waste, and increased competitive advantage.[33] Businesses function by employing resources and raw materials derived from the natural environment. Industrial activities can produce smog, acid rain, and other toxins that harm the atmosphere. Many industrial firms use or produce synthetic chemicals and materials that contain hazardous substances. Consumer and industrial products are themselves a major source of toxic waste.[34]

Firms consume vast quantities of water resources, contributing to the creation or expansion of deserts (desertification) and loss of important ecosystems around the world. For example, Brazil recently has endured a drought of historic proportions, and some experts believe loss of Amazon rain forest is an important cause.[35] Many countries endure chronic water shortages, and industrial activity pollutes clean water supplies. Residential and industrial activity results in land loss and the destruction of ecosystems needed for healthy natural environments. Long-term, successful business performance necessitates healthy ecosystems.

Businesses are major consumers of all the natural environment offers and, hence, must take pains to ensure ecological sustainability. Reversing environmental damage requires industrialized countries to reduce their emissions of pollutants substantially. The pace with which resources and raw materials are depleted should not exceed their rate of regeneration. The rate of waste production should not exceed the environment's ability to absorb it. Thus, firms increasingly seek ways to employ renewable resources and minimize pollutants in their operations. Because of their size, MNEs are among the most important stewards of the environment through skillful use of innovative technologies, improved water productivity, management of shortages in vulnerable areas, and planning that incorporates sustainability practices.

The most advanced companies monitor suppliers to ensure that they use sustainable practices. For example, following charges that some of its Indian subcontractors were using forced child labor, GAP withdrew a line of children's wear from its clothing stores worldwide. Sustainable firms usually opt for local suppliers to reduce the pollution that transporting goods long distances causes.[36]

At the consumer products company Unilever, management has committed to tackling big social and environmental problems such as pollution, disease, and poverty. The firm aims to halve its environmental footprint and ensure that sourced foods are grown using sustainable farming practices. Unilever's global handwashing campaign aims to reduce diarrhea and other noxious diseases in Africa and Asia. The firm is also developing a laundry detergent that can clean clothes in a few minutes at any water temperature, thereby saving

Source: Tim Gainey/Alamy

As water becomes scarce in much of the world, some multinational firms are conserving their use of this critical resource. Coca-Cola, a major water consumer, conducts a water sustainability program to address shortages in India.

energy and water. Unilever's plan includes 60 targets, such as sourcing "75% of the paper and board for our packaging from certified sustainably managed forests or recycled material." CEO Paul Polman ensures that CSR and sustainability are incorporated into all of the firm's strategy making.[37]

BMW is introducing a series of electric cars to serve the firm's sustainability goals. The cars will have carbon-fiber bodies to reduce weight and save fuel. Recycled aluminum is used in the chassis, and interior panels and seats are made of hemp fibers and recycled water bottles. Lithium-ion batteries allow users to drive for up to 100 miles before charging. Smartphone apps show the way to charging stations and smart parking spots. BMW hopes to make such features standard on a wide range of vehicles.[38]

Like CSR, sustainable practices pay off in various ways such as promoting a strong corporate reputation, the ability to hire and retain superior employees, cost savings from more efficient production, better linkages with suppliers, and smoother relations with foreign governments.

Achieving sustainability often requires the firm to be flexible and creative. A good example is Coca-Cola, which had to deal with water sustainability challenges. As water resources dwindled in some countries, Coke began to experience conflicts with communities and other water users, especially in India. To address such challenges, Coke developed a water sustainability program that goes well beyond efficiency and legal compliance needs alone. Management devised global projects that protect water resources and ensure access to clean drinking water. Coke mobilized the international community to anticipate and deal with ever-severe water crises worldwide.[39]

 MyManagementLab   Watch It! 2

If your professor has assigned this, go to the Assignments section of **mymanagementlab.com** to complete the video exercise titled Root Capital: International Strategy.

4.5 Know the role of corporate governance.

The Role of Corporate Governance

Implementing ethical conduct, CSR, and sustainability is challenging for most firms, especially those with extensive operations across many countries. Corporate governance provides the means through which the firm's directors and managers undertake such behaviors. Leading companies implement corporate governance by creating (a) a *set of values* that serve as a guide for employees; and (b) a *set of ground rules* for guiding behavior, which include criteria for acceptable decision-making, used by all employees. The values and ground rules should be established in the firm's Code of Ethics and Code of Conduct documents.

Code of ethics
A document that describes the values and expectations that guide decision making by all employees in the firm.

A **code of ethics** is a document that describes the *values and expectations* that guide decision-making by all employees in the firm. The code aims to function like a moral compass for the firm's operations worldwide. It should be designed to ensure that any employee can identify ethical problems and distinguish between right and wrong actions. The code should be general enough to apply to any ethical challenge that confronts the firm. It should list the general principles that guide daily decisions and interactions with customers, employees, and partners. The code should be created by senior management and disseminated throughout the firm. It should be translated into all languages the firm uses in its international operations.[40]

Code of conduct
A document that translates the code of ethics into specific rules regarding behaviors and practices that are prohibited or required.

The **code of conduct** translates the code of ethics into specific rules regarding behaviors and practices that are prohibited or required. It identifies the consequences for specific violations and the conditions for continued employment. Inappropriate behaviors the Code of Conduct addresses might include sexual harassment, conflicts of interest, racial discrimination, and acceptance of gifts. Due to differing cross-national laws and practices, developing a single Code to cover the firm's operations worldwide is often impractical. Many companies develop codes of conduct for individual countries or regions to address local conditions. In numerous Asian countries, for example, gift giving is relatively acceptable and even expected. In some Muslim countries, interaction between male and female employees is discouraged.

Integrating local codes with the firm's global standards is challenging. One approach is to have such codes developed broadly by cross-functional and cross-national teams that represent the interests of headquarters and subsidiaries as well as specific functional areas. Managers native to specific countries are positioned best to identify and clarify approaches in those countries. Senior management commitment to appropriate behavior is critical to fostering ethics and CSR in international operations and should regularly communicate the importance of ethical and conduct codes. The firm should devise continuing education programs to ensure that employees understand and practice ethical and conduct codes. In addition to helping ensure ethical conduct, CSR, and sustainable practices, implementing a code of ethics and a code of conduct also foster trust with customers, employees, and partners.[41]

Embracing Ethical Behavior

In a world ever sensitive to social and environmental issues, managers increasingly undertake the following types of practices.

- Build internal and external capabilities to enhance the firm's contribution to the local community and global environment
- Ensure that diverse voices are heard by creating organizational structures that employ managers and workers from around the world
- Develop global ethical standards and objectives that are communicated and implemented across the firm worldwide
- Train managers in global ethical principles and integrate these into managerial responsibilities.
- Develop closer relations with foreign stakeholders to understand their needs better and jointly work toward solutions.

Ethical Standard Approaches for Corporate Governance

Scholars have devised five ethical standards approaches that managers can use to examine ethical dilemmas. These are summarized in the following box.[42]

Utilitarian Approach	Rights Approach	Fairness Approach	Common Good Approach	Virtue Approach
The best ethical action is the one that provides the most good or the least harm. It produces the greatest balance of good over harm to customers, employees, shareholders, the community, and the natural environment.	The best action protects and respects the moral rights of everyone involved. It is based on the belief that, regardless of how you deal with an ethical dilemma, human dignity must be preserved.	The best action treats everyone equally and fairly. Workers should be paid a fair wage that provides a decent standard of living, and colleagues and customers should be treated as we would like to be treated.	The best action emphasizes the welfare of the entire community or nation. It asks what action contributes most to the quality of life of all affected people. Respect and compassion for all, especially the vulnerable, are the basis for decision making.	The best action emphasizes virtues that provide for the full development of our humanity. The most important virtues are truth, courage, compassion, generosity, tolerance, love, integrity, and prudence.

Using these approaches to analyze ethical dilemmas can be challenging because they occasionally conflict with each other. Not everyone agrees on which standard to use in all situations. Different cultures adhere to differing norms of morality and human rights and basic standards or norms of right and wrong. Many ethical dilemmas are complex, and proposed approaches may not provide adequate guidance in determining the best course of action. Nevertheless, each standard is useful because it helps guide ethical behavior in almost any predicament. In most cases, they lead to similar solutions.

A Global Consensus

Incorporating ethics, CSR, and sustainability into global operations is a path to long-term superior performance. Various resources are available to assist managers. International organizations such as the United Nations, the World Bank, and the International Monetary Fund have launched programs to combat international corruption.

The **International Chamber of Commerce** has adopted Rules of Conduct to Combat Extortion and Bribery, and the **United Nations** issued a Declaration against Corruption and Bribery in International Commercial Transactions.

The **Organisation for Economic Co-operation and Development (OECD)** has developed an anti-bribery agreement, which was signed by its 30 member nations (essentially, all the advanced economies) plus several Latin American countries.[43]

The **United Nations Global Compact** (see www.unglobalcompact.org) is a policy platform and practical framework for companies committed to sustainability and responsible business practices. It seeks to align business operations and strategies with universally accepted principles in the areas of human rights, labor, corruption, and the natural environment. It is the world's largest voluntary corporate citizenship initiative, representing thousands of businesses in more than 135 countries.

The **Global Reporting Initiative** (www.globalreporting.org) pioneered the development of the most widely used sustainability reporting framework. It sets out the principles and indicators that organizations can use to measure and report their economic, environmental, and social performance. Today, most large MNEs produce sustainability reports, many following the GRI guidelines.

Going Deep, Wide, and Local

Ultimately, pursuing a culture of ethical behavior requires the firm to go deep, wide, and local. *Going deep* means institutionalizing appropriate behavior in the organization's culture so it becomes part and parcel of strategy. *Going wide* implies a continuous effort to understand how CSR and sustainability affect every aspect of the firm's operations worldwide. *Going local* goes hand in hand with globalization. It requires the firm to examine its global operations to identify and improve specific local issues that affect customers, competitive position, reputation, and any other dimension that affects the firm's operations worldwide.[44]

Benefits of Corporate Governance

Corporate governance that ensures ethical practices, CSR, and sustainability provides numerous benefits to the firm.[45] These benefits include:

- *Increased employee commitment.* Firms that practice ethics, CSR, and sustainability find it easier to attract and retain employees. When workers are proud of their employer, they tend to work more diligently and increase productivity.
- *Increased customer loyalty and sales.* Many customers prefer to patronize businesses that emphasize ethical practices. Best practices that benefit society enhance sales prospects.
- *Improved reputation and brand image.* Operating ethically and responsibly enhances the firm's public image, customer preference, and the ability to attract capital. Firms with a strong image are less likely to conflict with value-chain members and government authorities.
- *Reduced likelihood of government intervention.* The increased trust, transparency, and accountability that follow from applying superior corporate governance can reduce the likelihood of governments imposing burdensome regulations and other forms of government intervention.
- *Reduced business costs.* Various efficiencies arise from CSR and sustainable practices, including the ability to hire quality employees, reduced employee turnover, and decreased regulatory scrutiny. Sustainability efforts such as recycling and using alternative energy help reduce waste and the cost of inputs.
- *Improved financial performance.* Several recent studies have shown that companies with sound values, strong ethical behavior, and strong social and environmental practices have significantly greater rates of growth than those firms focused only on company profits.

Read the *You Can Do It: Recent Grad in IB* feature, which profiles Javier Estrada. Javier found exciting opportunities in social enterprise and the charity sector in emerging markets.

JAVIER ESTRADA

Javier's major: Business

Objectives: Integrating business skills with social planning in a public agency and pursuing a career in politics

Jobs held since graduating:

- United Nations World Food Programme in Guatemala and Honduras
- Director of Research, Bates Advertising, Dominican Republic
- Manager in a major charity in Mexico

Javier Estrada graduated from a state university several years ago with a bachelor's degree in business. He moved to the Dominican Republic, where he took a research position in the local office of Bates Advertising, a global ad agency that handled accounts such as Wendy's, Purina, and Bell South. Along the way, Javier also worked in the social sector. He served as a coordinator in the United Nations World Food Programme in Guatemala and Honduras. He also became the manager of a charity in Mexico.

Success Factors

"My parents felt strongly that our lives should be influenced not only by the quality of our education, but also by our travels . . . . In school we were among the most traveled kids." Javier was lucky enough to visit several countries during his teens and twenties. He comments: "You get to know yourself when you're completely alone in a new culture and establishing a network of friends and work contacts." International experience contributed to Javier's independent spirit and his ability to function successfully around the world.

Javier enjoyed going to other countries and meeting different people. "My job provided the chance to help companies and customers. I would not have gotten the job if I had not worked hard in school. Management training provided me with the skills to perform effectively. Sensitivity is important, since you need to be able to communicate with people who are culturally different from you. You need a strong empathy for your customers. You need to identify which research questions are best."

What's Ahead?

Javier has ever-higher goals for his career. He has been long concerned about poverty issues in Latin America, and his experiences with the United Nations affected him profoundly. Javier earned a master's degree in social policy and planning from the London School of Economics. Having worked in both business and development, Javier found his passion in integrating his business skills with social planning at the governmental level. Recently, Javier worked for a major charity organization in Mexico. He says, "I need to dream big."

Source: Photo courtesy of Javier Estrada

A Framework for Making Ethical Decisions

Scholars suggest that managers follow a systematic approach to resolving ethical dilemmas. Exhibit 4.8 presents a five-step framework for arriving at ethical decisions that will help you arrive at appropriate solutions to ethical dilemmas.[46] With practice, it can become second nature. The steps in the framework follow:

4.6 Learn about a framework for making ethical decisions.

- *Identify the problem.* The first step is to acknowledge the presence of an ethical problem. Ask questions such as: Is something wrong? Is an ethical dilemma present? Is there a situation that might harm personnel, customers, the community, or the nation? In international business, recognizing the issue can be tricky because subtleties of the situation may be outside your knowledge or experience. Often, it is best to rely on your instincts. If some action feels wrong, it probably is.
- *Examine the facts.* Determine the nature and dimensions of the situation. Have all the relevant persons and groups been consulted? What individuals or groups have a stake in the outcome? How much weight should be given to the interests of each? Do some parties have a greater stake because they are disadvantaged or have a special need? This stage is often

EXHIBIT 4.8

Framework for Arriving at Ethical Decisions

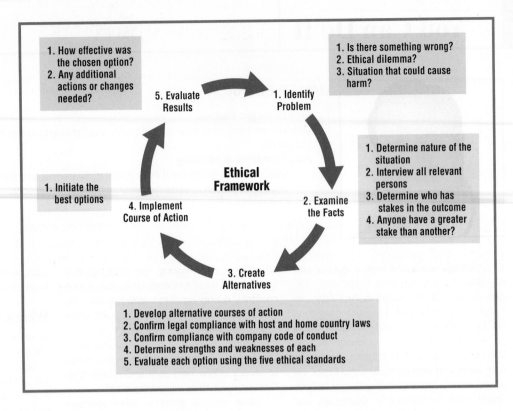

challenging because determining specific details and distinguishing facts from irrelevant information is challenging. The process often involves interviewing personnel and stakeholders who may offer differing versions or opinions about the issue at hand. The manager's task is to identify and validate the most useful, valid information that makes the true nature of the problem clear.

- *Create alternatives.* Identify potential courses of action and evaluate each. Initially, consistent with the pyramid of ethical behavior, review any proposed action to ensure that it is legal. If it violates host or home country laws or international treaties, it should be rejected. Next, review any proposed action to ensure that it is acceptable according to company policy, the firm's code of conduct, and its code of ethics. If discrepancies are found, the action should be rejected. Finally, evaluate each proposed action to assess its consistency with accepted ethical standards, using the approaches described earlier:

  - Utilitarian—which action results in the most good and least harm?
  - Rights—which action respects the rights of everyone involved?
  - Fairness—which action treats people most fairly?
  - Common good—which action contributes most to the overall quality of life of the people affected?
  - Virtue—which action embodies the character strengths you value?

  The goal is to arrive at the best decision or most appropriate course of action. It might be useful to enlist the aid of local colleagues familiar with the situation to provide insights and help generate options. Assess the consequences of each action from the perspective of all parties who will be affected by it. Any decision should be tested by asking whether you would feel comfortable explaining it to your mother, a colleague you respect, or a valued mentor. If you had to defend the decision on television, would you be comfortable doing so?

- *Implement the course of action.* Put the chosen plan into action. This implies making new rules, processes, or procedures and putting these into effect. Implementation is critical because it determines the success or failure of the chosen action. Managers need to be particularly diligent at this stage to ensure that the action is carried out according to plan.

* *Evaluate results.* After the decision is implemented, management will need to evaluate it to see how effective it was. How did it turn out? If you had it to do again, would you do anything differently? Results evaluation may require collecting, analyzing, and using information to answer questions about the chosen course of action. The goal is to ensure that the action achieves its intended effect and discover whether the firm should modify the approach or pursue a different one.

To illustrate briefly, let's revisit the example of you as a manager visiting a company factory in Colombia, where you discover child labor. Without the children's income, their families might go hungry, or the children could turn to illicit activity such as street crime. Having identified the problem, you examine facts by consulting colleagues at both the plant and the headquarters. You seek information about the status of the employed children as well as local law and customs on child labor. You then create alternative possible solutions, ensuring that they are legal and consistent with company policy. Keeping the five ethical standards in mind, you evaluate each proposed action. Finally, you choose and implement the best course of action and evaluate its effectiveness.

Managers must make ethical behavior, CSR, and sustainability part of company activities and operations. MNE pursuits generate environmental harm and bring firms into contact with various activities—from R&D to manufacturing to marketing—that can pose various ethical dilemmas. Business executives should balance their obligation to shareholders with explicit contributions to the broader public good. Most executives agree that generating high returns for investors should be accompanied by a focus on providing good jobs, supporting social causes in local communities, and going beyond legal requirements to minimize pollution and other negative effects of business.

CLOSING CASE   Bribery and Corruption at Siemens

One day in 2004, a senior executive at Siemens Company said he received a disturbing phone call from a Saudi Arabian businessman. The caller said he represented a Saudi consulting firm that had been a business partner of Siemens. He wanted $910 million in U.S. currency in payments and, if Siemens didn't pay up, he would forward documents to government authorities detailing bribes paid on Siemens' behalf to win telecommunications contracts in Saudi Arabia. The incident was the beginning of a series of events—police raids, forensic investigations, and arrests of top executives—that became one of the biggest corruption cases in corporate history.

Based in Germany, Siemens is one of the world's largest electronics and industrial engineering firms. It produces industrial controls, lighting products, power generation equipment, and transportation systems. Siemens operates in 190 countries, with recent annual revenues exceeding $100 billion.

A Culture of Corruption?

Since the 1970s, a series of scandals have stung Siemens, including accusations of bribery brought by governments in numerous countries, the European Union, and the United Nations. One former executive was accused of handling $77 million in bribes. Another admitted to bribing a labor union. A court found that Siemens had paid millions in 2007 to bribe government officials in Libya, Nigeria, and Russia.

Investigators alleged that there was a culture at Siemens, endorsed by senior managers, to use bribes and slush funds to win contracts, especially in its communications and power-generation divisions. Millions of dollars were regularly dispensed, the money carted off to foreign destinations in suitcases by managers who often felt confident they were doing business as usual.

Reckoning and Deliverance

In the end, bribery caught up with Siemens. In a ruling under the Foreign Corrupt Practices Act, U.S. authorities ordered the company to pay $800 million in fines. The United States found that, to win infrastructure contracts, Siemens allegedly spent more than $1 billion bribing government officials around the world, including the former president of Argentina. The U.S. Securities and Exchange Commission (SEC) claimed that Siemens made more than 4,000 bribe payments, intended to obtain contracts to supply medical devices in Russia, transmission lines in China, transit systems in Venezuela, medical equipment in Vietnam, power equipment in Iraq, and telecommunications equipment in Bangladesh, over seven years. A U.S. grand jury indicted Siemens and two of its employees in a fraud scheme to pay $500,000 to win a $49 million contract. Two former Siemens officials were convicted of bribery for their involvement in multimillion-dollar payments to officials of a power utility in Italy.

In response to the scandals, some Siemens customers indicated they would delay ordering telecommunications equipment from the firm, and Nokia Corporation announced it would postpone a planned joint venture. In the wake of the crisis, Siemens' profits declined, partly due to the creation of a fund for expenses related to bribery investigations. The World Bank required Siemens to pay $100 million to help global anticorruption efforts and to forgo bidding on World Bank development projects for two years. In the end, Siemens' two top executives, the chairman and the CEO, were forced to resign.

In Germany, Siemens executives indicted in the scandal received only suspended prison sentences. A German court ordered Siemens to pay $284 million, a modest fine for a firm that usually generates billions in annual net profits. Germany is the world's leading exporter, and bribery cases often include efforts to generate foreign business, especially in developing economies. Until 1999, German firms were permitted to write off such bribes as business expenses. Many European countries did not outlaw paying bribes overseas until the late 1990s.

Remedial Actions

Following the scandal, Siemens management took steps to prevent further bribery. The company appointed a law firm to conduct an independent review of its compliance system and uncover possible improprieties. Sixty-five countries were flagged for scrutiny. Siemens' own internal investigation identified more than $1.5 billion in suspicious transactions worldwide between 2000 and 2006. Management remarked on the difficulty of closely monitoring activities of the firm's 430,000 employees in 190 countries and bank accounts that once numbered 5,000 and handled up to 50 million transactions a day. International subsidiaries were free to act with substantial autonomy.

Siemens hired an independent ombudsman, strengthened its business-conduct code, and established a task force to improve internal controls over international funds transfers, reduce the number of bank accounts, and supervise the opening and maintenance of bank accounts. Subsidiaries were required to provide comprehensive details of all transactions. The German government tightened standards for managers, seeking to ensure that those at all large firms report regularly to supervisory boards regarding compliance with ethics codes.

Conclusion

In the United States, the number of companies reporting foreign corruption investigations into their activities abroad is up sharply; foreign companies that do business in the United States are attracting greater scrutiny as well. In most countries, however, antibribery laws are weak or poorly enforced. Bribery is difficult to detect when funds are channeled through consultants and other intermediaries or when company operations are widely dispersed and decentralized.

Why should firms care about bribery? For one thing, it is bad business. Bribery distorts legitimate efforts to sustain and enhance company performance. Where corruption becomes a pattern, the firm is eventually caught and its reputation tarnished. Corruption also inhibits development in poor countries and is at the root of persistent poverty in many. It sustains repressive governments and can lead to the failure of societies and national economies.

The best firms create a culture in which ethical conduct is valued as highly as efforts to maximize sales and profits. It is insufficient merely to publicize the need for integrity; managers must lead through ongoing actions that demonstrate adherence to ethical standards. They must establish transparency and compliance processes that ensure that senior executives know what is going on throughout the firm.

AACSB: Reflective Thinking Skills, Multicultural and Diversity Understanding, Ethical Understanding and Reasoning Abilities

Case Questions

4-4. What does the case suggest is the value of ethical behavior? What did Siemens gain by introducing controls to minimize the likelihood of corruption?

4-5. Most countries lack adequate laws or enforcement to deal with bribery and other forms of corruption. Why is this? How do countries benefit from a strong rule of law that minimizes corruption?

4-6. Do you think Siemens was penalized enough for its corruption? Why or why not? What can governments or other organizations do to discourage firms and others from engaging in corrupt behavior?

4-7. Some argue that because ethical standards are lax in many countries, Siemens and other firms must pay bribes to obtain new business. Do you agree with this view? Stated differently, when doing business around the world, is it generally better to emphasize normativism or relativism? Justify your answer.

Sources: C. Bray, J. Palazzolo, S. Romig, and P. Grontzki, "Former Siemens Executives Facing U.S. Bribery Charges," *Wall Street Journal*, December 14, 2011, p. B3; A. Choudhary, "Anatomy and Impact of Bribery on Siemens AG," *Journal of Legal, Ethical & Regulatory Issues* 16, No. 2 (2013), pp. 131–142; M. Esterl and D. Crawford, "Siemens to Pay Huge Fine in Bribery Inquiry," *Wall Street Journal*, December 15, 2008, p. B1; "Siemens to Tighten Controls on Money," *Financial Times*, April 18, 2007, p. 16; "Action Against Bribery Requires Political Will," *Financial Times*, April 10, 2007, p. 14; V. Fuhrmans, "Siemens Settles with World Bank on Bribes," *Wall Street Journal*, July 3, 2009, p. B1; A. Preuschat, "Siemens Posts Loss Due to Charges But Says Its Orders Remain Strong," *Wall Street Journal*, November 14, 2008, p. B3; C. Verschoor, "Siemens AG Is Latest Fallen Ethics Idol," *Strategic Finance* 89, No. 5 (2007), pp. 11–13; "Two Siemens Ex-Officials Convicted in Bribery Case," *Wall Street Journal*, May 15, 2007, p. C6; D. Crawford and M. Esterl, "Siemens Fine Ends a Bribery Probe," *Wall Street Journal*, October 5, 2007, p. A2; D. Crawford and M. Esterl, "Widening Scandal: At Siemens, Witnesses Cite Pattern of Bribery," *Wall Street Journal*, January 31, 2007, p. A1; R. Milne, "Siemens 'Had a System for Paying Bribes'," *Financial Times*, March 14, 2007, p. 27; R. Milne and M. Scheele, "Probe Finds 'General Practice' of Alleged Bribery at Siemens," *Financial Times*, May 7, 2007, p. 1; D. Crawford and M. Esterl, "Siemens Ruling Details Bribery Across the Globe," *Wall Street Journal*, November 16, 2007, p. A1; D. Crawford and M. Esterl, "Inside Bribery Probe of Siemens," *Wall Street Journal*, December 28, 2007, p. A4; M. Esterl and D. Crawford, "Ex-Siemens Manager Sentenced," *Wall Street Journal*, November 25, 2008, p. B2; M. Esterl and D. Crawford, "At Siemens, a Conviction Could Trigger More Cases," *Wall Street Journal*, July 29, 2008, p. B1; "Stopping the Rot; Face Value," *The Economist*, March 8, 2008, p. 89; "Bavarian Baksheesh; The Siemens Scandal," *The Economist*, December 20, 2008, p. 112; *US News & World Report*, "Greek Authorities Say 64 to Stand Trial over Allegedly Corrupt Siemens Telecom Deal," March 9, 2015, retrieved from www.usnews.com, April 9, 2015.

END OF CHAPTER REVIEW

 MyManagementLab

Go to **mymanagementlab.com** to complete the problems marked with this icon .

Key Terms

code of conduct   130
code of ethics   130
corporate governance   116
corporate social responsibility (CSR)   116

ethics   116
intellectual property   123
intellectual property rights   124
normativism   119

relativism   119
sustainability   116

Summary

In this chapter, you learned about:

- **Ethical behavior and its importance in international business.**

  Ethics are the moral principles and values that govern the behavior of people, firms, and governments. Ethical standards vary around the world. **Relativism** is the belief that ethical truths are not absolute but differ from group to group. **Normativism** holds that ethical standards are universal, and firms and individuals should uphold them consistently around the world. An ethical dilemma is a predicament involving major conflicts among different interests. Determining the best course of action is confounded by several possible solutions that may be equally justifiable.

- **Ethical challenges in international business.**

  Companies encounter various ethical challenges, including violations of intellectual property, corruption, bribery, and unethical management practices. Corruption implies obtaining power, personal gain, or influence through illegitimate means. **Intellectual property** refers to ideas or works created by individuals or firms. Governments aim to protect intellectual property, but protection is not guaranteed in much of the world.

- **Corporate social responsibility.**

  Maintaining **corporate social responsibility (CSR)** means operating a business in a manner that meets or exceeds the ethical, legal, commercial, and public expectations of stakeholders. **Sustainability** refers to meeting humanity's needs without harming future generations. In addition to complying with laws, regulations, and basic ethical standards, prudent MNEs emphasize corporate social responsibility in their activities. A strong business rationale for CSR includes the firm's ability to motivate employees and develop superior strategy. Failure to develop a CSR has important negative consequences for the firm.

- **Sustainability.**

  Sustainable businesses simultaneously pursue three types of interests: economic, social, and environmental. They maximize the use of recycled or renewable materials and environmentally friendly energy; reduce waste in manufacturing and minimize harmful air and water pollution; provide health insurance, training, and care for employees in various other ways. They are active in the local community with initiatives in education, health care, and environmental protection. Sustainable firms choose and work with suppliers that adhere to high social and environmental standards.

- **Corporate governance.**

  Corporate governance is the system of procedures and processes by which corporations are managed, directed, and controlled. Management utilizes corporate governance to implement ethics, CSR, and sustainability, which support the firm's best interests. Scholars have devised five standards managers can use to examine ethical dilemmas, based on utilitarianism, rights, fairness, common good, and virtue. Senior managers should develop a code of ethics that describes what the firm expects of its employees when facing ethical dilemmas.

- **A framework for making ethical decisions.**

  Scholars have devised a five-step framework for making ethical decisions. Initially, the manager should recognize the existence of an ethical problem. The next steps are to get the facts, evaluate alternative courses of action, implement the decisions, and evaluate the results. Ethical behavior and CSR must be part of managers' day-to-day pursuits. Various resources from organizations such as the United Nations and the World Bank are available to assist managers.

Test Your Comprehension AACSB: Reflective Thinking, Analytical Skills, Ethical Reasoning

4-8. Distinguish between ethics and corruption in international business.

4-9. Describe typical ethical problems that firms encounter in international business.

4-10. What is the Corruption Perceptions Index and how can a manager use it to assess international risk?

4-11. What is intellectual property? What industries are most affected by threats to intellectual property?

4-12. How can the most justifiable solution to a dilemma be identified?

4-13. What is an ethical dilemma? Give an example of an ethical dilemma that MNEs encounter abroad.

4-14. Distinguish relativism and normativism. Which one should the firm apply in its activities?

4-15. What is corporate social responsibility (CSR)? How does it differ from general ethical behavior?

4-16. Why is CSR important to the internationalizing firm?

4-17. What are the three key areas that a sustainable businesses tries to address?

4-18. How does an organization's management use corporate governance to implement ethics and CRS?

4-19. Why should ethical behavior be a part of a manager's everyday activities?

4-20. Describe the steps in the framework for ethical conduct.

Apply Your Understanding
AACSB: Reflective Thinking, Analytical Skills, Communication, Ethical Reasoning

4-21. *Ethical Dilemma:* You were recently hired by ThunderCat Corporation, a major aircraft producer with a manufacturing presence in numerous countries. ThunderCat's sales personnel constantly travel the world, selling fighter jets and commercial aircraft to airlines and foreign governments. You are keenly aware that countries vary enormously in terms of culture, laws, and political systems. Top management has asked you to develop a code of ethics to guide ThunderCat employees in their interactions anywhere in the world. Given the diversity of countries where ThunderCat operates, what sort of code will you develop? What issues should you consider? Given the diversity of countries around the world, is it possible to develop a code that guides ethical behavior everywhere?

4-22. *Ethical Dilemma:* Royal Dutch Shell has been doing business in Nigeria since the 1920s and has announced new plans to develop oil and gas projects there. However, over the years, Shell has experienced a series of complex issues. Its operations are centered in Nigeria's Ogoni region, where the local citizens have protested Shell's drilling and refining activities, which harm the natural environment and reduce the amount of available farmland. Protestors also accuse Shell of extracting wealth from the region without adequately compensating local residents. Following sabotage of its facilities, the firm suspended some of its Nigerian operations and then came under pressure to divest its operations and pay reparations to the local people. Despite these problems, Shell has persisted in Nigeria. Management instituted various community development programs in the region, budgeted at $50 million per year. Using the ethical framework in this chapter, identify steps Shell can take to be a better corporate citizen in Nigeria.

4-23. *Ethical Dilemma:* American International Group (AIG) is the largest insurance company in the United States. When AIG faced financial ruin in 2008, the U.S. government used taxpayer money to loan AIG more than $170 billion in exchange for an 80 percent stake in the firm. A few months later, it was revealed that AIG had used part of the money (at least $30 billion) to pay off banks in Europe, largely for debt obligations it incurred in foreign transactions. U.S. government officials were furious. The furor intensified when AIG tried to renegotiate loans with some of its U.S. creditors, implying they were less important than the European banks. Suppose you were the chief financial officer at AIG. What would you have done? How would you handle this predicament? Use the ethical framework in this chapter to analyze how AIG might have handled the situation better.

 **globalEDGE** | **INTERNET EXERCISES**
(globaledge.msu.edu)

AACSB: Analytical Skills, Use of Information Technology, Ethical Reasoning

Refer to Chapter 1, page 54, for instructions on how to access and use globalEDGE™.

4-24. Various organizations have devised international standards for ethical corporate behavior. These include the United Nations' Universal Declaration for Human Rights (available at www.un.org), the OECD's Guidelines for Multinational Enterprises (www.oecd.org), the International Labour Organization's International Labour Standards (www.ilo.org), and the U.S. Department of Commerce's Model Business Principles (www.commerce.gov). Visit these online portals and prepare a set of guidelines firms can follow in pursuing acceptable ethical standards in international business.

4-25. Transparency International (www.transparency.org) publishes information about the nature of corruption around the world. Suppose you worked at a firm that makes computer software and wanted to begin doing business in Brazil and Russia. Your task is to examine reports and indices about these countries at the Transparency International site and write a brief report explaining how your firm should conduct business in these countries, with a view to avoiding problems associated with corruption. Key issues to consider include bribery and threats to intellectual property.

4-26. The websites for Lenovo (China, www.lenovo.com), Nokia (Finland, www.nokia.com), and Banco do Brasil (Brazil, www.bb.com.br, click English) contain substantial information about how these firms undertake corporate social responsibility (CSR). Visit each website and write a report in which you compare and contrast each firm's CSR. Which firm appears most effective in CSR? How does the CSR of a bank differ from that of manufacturing firms such as Lenovo and Nokia? Lenovo and Banco do Brasil are based in emerging markets, whereas Nokia is in an advanced economy. What differences in the firms' CSR orientations can you detect based on this distinction? Justify your answer.

 MyManagementLab **Try It!**

The simulation International Ethics accompanies this exercise.

 MyManagementLab

Go to **mymanagementlab.com** for Auto-graded writing questions as well as the following Assisted-graded writing question:

⭐ **4-27.** What advantages do firms gain from behaving according to high ethical standards?

⭐ **4-28.** Why is CSR important to the internationalizing firm?

⭐ **4-29.** MyManagementLab Only—comprehensive writing assignment for this chapter.

Endnotes

1. We are grateful to Professor Larry Beer, Arizona State University Emeritus, for his helpful comments regarding this chapter.

2. O. C. Ferrell and L. Gresham, "A Contingency Framework for Understanding Ethical Decision Making in Marketing," *Journal of Marketing* 49, No. 3 (1985), pp. 87–96; Naresh Malhotra and G. Miller, "An Integrated Model for Ethical Decisions," *Journal of Business Ethics* 17, No. 3 (1998), pp. 263–280; D. McAlister, O. C. Ferrell, and L. Ferrell, *Business and Society* (Boston: Houghton Mifflin, 2003).

3. Marco Celentani, Juan-Jose Ganuza, and Jose-Luis Peydros, "Combating Corruption in International Business Transactions," *Economica* 71, No. 283 (2004), pp. 417–449; McAlister, Ferrell, and Ferrell, 2003; David Zussman, "Fighting Corruption Is a Global Concern," *Ottawa Citizen*, October 11, 2005, p. A15.

4. Larry Beer, *Business Ethics for the Global Business and the Global Manager: A Strategic Approach* (New York: Business Expert Press, 2010); United Nations Conference on Trade and

Development (UNCTAD), *World Investment Report 2009* (New York: UNCTAD, 2009).

5. Larry Beer, 2010; Lutz Kaufmann, Felix Reimann, Matthias Ehrgott, and Johan Rauer, "Sustainable Success," *Wall Street Journal*, June 22, 2009, http://www.wsj.com; Malhotra and Miller (1998); Alan Muller and Ans Kolk, "Extrinsic and Intrinsic Drivers of Corporate Social Performance: Evidence from Foreign and Domestic Firms in Mexico," *Journal of Management Studies* 47, No. 1 (2010), pp. 1–26.

6. Max Bazerman and Ann Tenbrunsel, "Ethical Breakdowns," *Harvard Business Review*, April 2011, pp. 58–65.

7. John Sullivan, *The Moral Compass of Companies: Business Ethics and Corporate Governance as Anti-Corruption Tools* (Washington, DC: International Finance Corporation, World Bank, 2009).

8. Sullivan (2009); Muller and Kolk (2010); Transparency International, *Progress Report: OECD Anti-Bribery Convention 2009*, http://www.transparency.org.

9. Ferrell and Gresham (1985); McAlister, Ferrell, and Ferrell (2003).

10. Beer (2010); Kaufmann, Reimann, Ehrgott, and Rauer (2009); Muller and Kolk (2010).

11. Transparency International, *Progress Report: OECD Anti-Bribery Convention 2009*, http://www.transparency.org.

12. Beer (2010).

13. Beer (2010).

14. Celentani, Ganuza, and Peydros (2004); International Chamber of Commerce, Transparency International, the United Nations Global Compact, and World Economic Forum, *Clean Business Is Good Business: The Business Case Against Corruption*, retrieved from http://www.weforum.org/pdf/paci/BusinessCaseAgainstCorruption.pdf on April 5, 2015; Zussman (2005).

15. Transparency International, *Corruption Perceptions Index 2014* (Berlin: Transparency International, 2014), accessed at www.transparency.org.

16. Will Connors and Luciana Magalhaes, "Brazil Cracks Open Vast Bribery Scandal," *Wall Street Journal,* April 7, 2015, pp. A1, A10; Transparency International, *Global Corruption Report 2009* (Cambridge, UK: Cambridge University Press, 2009).

17. David Barstow, "The Bribery Aisle: How Wal-Mart Used Payoffs to Get Its Way in Mexico," *New York Times*, December 18, 2012, pp. A1, A3; Beer (2010); James Detar, "Wal-Mart Loses Round In Alleged Mexico Bribery Action," *Investor's Business Daily*, May 9, 2014, p. 01; Russell Gold, "Halliburton Ex-Official Pleads Guilty in Bribe Case," *Wall Street Journal*, September 4, 2008, p. A1; Russell Gold, "Halliburton to Pay $559 Million to Settle Bribery Investigation," *Wall Street Journal*, January 27, 2009, p. B3; Sullivan (2009); Transparency International, *Progress Report: OECD Anti-Bribery Convention 2009*, http://www.transparency.org; Transparency International, "Promoting Good Governance in Africa," March 5, 2009, http://www.transparency.org; N. Watson, "Bribery Charge Hits Halliburton Profits," *Petroleum Economist*, May 2009, p. 2; John Zhao, Seung Kim, and Jianjun Du, "The Impact of Corruption and Transparency on Foreign Direct Investment: An Empirical Analysis," *Management International Review* 43, No. 1 (2003), pp. 41–62; Zussman (2005).

18. Tara Radin and Martin Calkins, "The Struggle Against Sweatshops: Moving toward Responsible Global Business," *Journal of Business Ethics* 66 (2006), pp. 261–268.

19. Transparency International, *Progress Report: OECD Anti-Bribery Convention 2009*, http://www.transparency.org.

20. Frontier Economics, *Estimating the Global Economic and Social Impacts of Counterfeiting and Piracy* (London: Frontier Economics, Ltd., 2011), accessed at The International Chamber of Commerce, www.iccwbo.org; International Chamber of Commerce (2015).

21. CBP Office of International Trade, *Intellectual Property Rights: Fiscal Year 2014 Seizure Statistics* (Washington DC: U.S. Immigration and Customs Enforcement, 2015) at http://www.cbp.gov/sites/default/files/documents/2014%20IPR%20Stats.pdf; International Chamber of Commerce, *Roles and Responsibilities of Intermediaries: Fighting Counterfeiting and Piracy in the Supply Chain* (Paris: International Chamber of Commerce, April 2015); U.S. Customs and Border Protection, "CBP, ICE HSI Report $1.2 Billion in Counterfeit Seizures in 2014," April 2, 2015, retrieved from http://www.cbp.gov/newsroom/national-media-release/2015-04-02-000000/cbp-ice-hsi-report-12-billion-counterfeit-seizures, April 7, 2015.

22. CBP Office of International Trade (2015).

23. Sarah McBride and Loretta Chao, "Disney Fights Pirates at China Affiliate," *Wall Street Journal*, November 21, 2008, p. B1; Michael Schuman and Jeffrey Ressner, "Disney's Great Leap into China," *Time*, July 18, 2005. pp. 52–54.

24. "Business: The Reluctant Briber," *Economist,* November 4, 2006, p. 79; Carter Dougherty, "One Hot List You Don't Want to Be On," *BloombergBusiness*, March 5, 2015, http://www.bloomberg.com/news/articles/2015-03-05/counterfeiters-named-shamed-on-notorious-markets-list; Vara Vauhini, "Russian Websites Offer Cheap Songs, But Piracy Is Issue," *Wall Street Journal,* January 26, 2005, p. D10.

25. European Commission, *European Competitiveness Report 2008* (Luxembourg: Office for Official Publications of the European Communities, 2009).

26. Alan Muller and Gail Whiteman, "Exploring the Geography of Corporate Philanthropic Disaster Response: A Study of Fortune Global 500 Firms," *Journal of Business Ethics* 84, No. 4 (2009), pp. 589–603; UNCTAD (2009); N. Isdell, *21st Century Capitalism*, speech to Council on Foreign Relations, New York, 2009, http://fora.tv/2009/03/06/Neville_Isdell_21st_Century_Capitalism; K. Rehbein, S. Waddock, and S. Graves, "Understanding Shareholder Activism: Which Corporations Are Targeted?" *Business and Society* 43, No. 3, (2004), pp. 239–267.

27. V. Agarwal and Krishna Pokharel, "India's Populists Resist Big Retail," *Wall Street Journal,* October 9, 2007, p. A6; Chip Cummins, "Shell, Chevron to Cut Deliveries of Oil amid Protests in Nigeria," *Wall Street Journal*, December 23, 2004, p. A2; Stephen Fidler and John Labate, "Sudan Ties Jeopardize Chinese Oil Listing," *Financial Times*, October 6, 1999, p. 8; U. Idemudia, "Oil Extraction and Poverty Reduction in the Niger Delta: A Critical Examination of Partnership Initiatives," *Journal of Business Ethics* 90 (May 2009), pp. 91–116; Kris Maher, "Wal-Mart Tops Global Agenda for Labor Leaders," *Wall Street Journal*, August 18, 2005, p. A2. Harry Weber, "Time to Scrap BP Brand? Gas-Station Owners Divided," *USA Today,* July 31, 2010,

retrieved April 4, 2015, from http://usatoday30.usatoday.com/money/industries/energy/2010-07-31-bp-amoco-rebrand_N.htm.

28. *Foreign Affairs*, "Africa Calling," 94, No. 1 (January/February 2015), pp. 24–30; Mo Ibrahim, "Celtel's Founder on Building a Business on the World's Poorest Continent," *Harvard Business Review*, October 2012, pp. 41–44; Ricardo Geromel, "Can We Use Corporate Social Responsibility to Evaluate Companies?" *Forbes*, May 21, 2012, retrieved March 14, 2015 from http://www.forbes.com/sites/ricardogeromel/2012/05/21/csr-corporate-social-responsibility.

29. Andrew Witty, "New Strategies For Innovation In Global Health: A Pharmaceutical Industry Perspective," *Health Affairs* 30, No. 1 (2011), pp. 118–126.

30. Ilana Polyak, "Greener Approach," *Financial Planning* 40, No. 8 (2010), accessed at www.financial-planning.com.

31. C. Bhattacharya, Daniel Korschun, and Sankar Sen, "What Really Drives Value in Corporate Responsibility?" *McKinsey Quarterly*, December 2011, accessed at www.mckinseyquarterly.com; C. Bhattacharya, S. Sen, and D. Korschun, "Using Corporate Social Responsibility to Win the War for Talent," *MIT Sloan Management Review* 49, No. 2 (2008), pp. 37–44; M. Orlitzky, F. Schmidt, and S. Rynes, "Corporate Social and Financial Performance: A Meta-analysis," *Organization Studies* 24, No. 3 (2003), pp. 403–441; Porter and Kramer (2006); Transparency International (2009); R. Trudel and J. Cotte, "Does Being Ethical Pay?" *Wall Street Journal*, May 12, 2008, p. R4; World Economic Forum, *More with Less: Scaling Sustainable Consumption and Resource Efficiency*, Geneva: World Economic Forum, accessed at www.weforum.org.

32. Beer (2010); Philip Kotler and Nancy Lee, *Up and Out of Poverty: The Social Marketing Solution* (Upper Saddle River, NJ: Wharton School Publishing, 2009); Hildy Teegen, Jonathan Doh, and Sushil Vachani, "The Importance of Nongovernmental Organizations (NGOs) in Global Governance and Value Creation: An International Business Research Agenda," *Journal of International Business Studies* 35, No. 4 (2004), pp, 463–483.

33. Beer, 2010; Sheila Bonini, Lenny Lendonca, and Jeremy Oppenheim, "When Social Issues Become Strategic," *McKinsey Quarterly* 2 (2006), http://www.mckinseyquarterly.com; Erin Cavusgil, "Merck and Vioxx: An Examination of an Ethical Decision-Making Model," *Journal of Business Ethics* 76, No. 4 (2007), pp. 451–461; Kaufmann, Reimann, Ehrgott, and Rauer (2009); Malhotra and Miller (1998); McAlister, Ferrell, and Ferrell (2003); MIT Sloan Management Review and Boston Consulting Group, *Sustainability: The 'Embracers' Seize Advantage*, research report (Cambridge, MA: Massachusetts Institute of Technology, 2011); Michael Porter and Mark Kramer,

"Strategy & Society: The Link Between Competitive Advantage and Corporate Social Responsibility," *Harvard Business Review*, December 2006, pp. 178–192.

34. Emmanuelle Bournay, *Vital Waste Graphics 2* (New York: United Nations, 2007).

35. BBC, "Brazil's Most Populous Region Faces Worst Drought in 80 Years," January 24, 2015, www.bbc.com.

36. Jo Johnson and Aline van Duyn, "Forced Child Labour Claims Hit Clothes Retailers," *Financial Times,* October 29, 2007, p. 3; Landrum and Edwards (2009); Masha Zager, "Doing Well by Doing Good: Gap Inc.'s Social Responsibility Program," *Apparel*, August 2009, p. 10.

37. Marc Gunther, "Unilever's CEO Has a Green Thumb," *Fortune*, June 10, 2013, pp. 124–128.

38. Alex Taylor, "BMW Gets Plugged In," *Fortune*, March 18, 2013, pp. 150–155.

39. Andrew Batson, "Coke Aims to Improve Water Recycling," *Wall Street Journal,* June 6, 2007, p. A10; Jenny Wiggins, "Coke Develops Thirst for Sustainability," *Financial Times,* July 2, 2007, p. 26; Daniel Vermeer and Robert Clemen, "Why Sustainability Is Still Going Strong," *Financial Times,* February 19, 2015, http://www.ft.com.

40. Sullivan (2009).

41. Bonini, Lendonca, and Oppenheim (2006); Muller and Kolk (2010).

42. Ferrell and Gresham (1985); T. Low, L. Ferrell, and P. Mansfield, "A Review of Empirical Studies Assessing Ethical Decision Making in Business," *Journal of Business Ethics* 25, No. 3 (2000), pp. 185–204; Malhotra and Miller (1998); McAlister, Ferrell, and Ferrell (2003).

43. Transparency International, *Progress Report: OECD Anti-Bribery Convention 2009*, http://www.transparency.org.

44. Vermeer and Clemen (2009).

45. Bonini, Lendonca, and Jeremy Oppenheim (2006); Cavusgil (2007); Malhotra and Miller (1998); McAlister, Ferrell, and Ferrell (2003); MIT Sloan Management Review and Boston Consulting Group (2011); Michael Porter and Mark Kramer (December 2006).

46. A version of this framework appeared originally in *Issues in Ethics* 1, No. 2 (1988). It was developed at the Markkula Center for Applied Ethics at Santa Clara University, California. See also Bonini, Lendonca, and Oppenheim (2006); Cavusgil (2007); Ferrell and Gresham (1985); Low, Ferrell, and Mansfield (2000); Malhotra and Miller (1998); McAlister, Ferrell, and Ferrell (2003); UNCTAD, *World Investment Report* 2006 (New York: UNCTAD, 2006); and Sullivan (2009).

Theories of International Trade and Investment

Learning Objectives *After studying this chapter, you should be able to:*

5.1 Appreciate why nations trade.

5.2 Learn about how nations can enhance their competitive advantage.

5.3 Understand why and how firms internationalize.

5.4 Explain the strategies internationalizing firms use to gain and sustain competitive advantage.

Taobao's Rise

2014 has been touted as the Year of Internalisation of the Chinese Technology. China has formally joined the World Trade Organisation in 2000. Ever since then, the Chinese government has promoted the "Go Global Policy". In 2013, Taobao became of the world's top 10 most visited websites, the combined gross merchandise of Taobao Marketplace and Tmail.com exceeded 1 trillion yuan. Ma Yun or better known as Jack Ma created the business-to-business e-commerce platform Alibaba in 1999. In May 2003, he founded retail website Taobao.com. Taobao comprises of a C2C (consumer to consumer) company and a B2C (business to consumer) business called Tmall. Taobao is similar as Ebay and Amazon. But Taoabo has more members than them.

Taobao has 500 million members and the daily consumers are 60 million. Taobao was founded by the Alibaba Group on May 10, 2003. The rise of Taobao metaphors the "ants and the elephants" and Taobao has fought its way through to reach the current situation.

Gaining competitive advantage in technology in China is very difficult. The industry is fast changing. Taobao's competitive advantage is linked to the Dunning's Eclectic Theory. The first advantage is location–China. With 560 million Internet users spending 20 hours a week online, China is by far the largest Internet market in the world. And notably, China is skipping traditional retailing in favour of e-tailing. The second advantage is the economies of scope; the cost savings associated with the

Source: Giles Robberts/Alamy

offering for sale of different products by a single corporation through the same sales channels. In this case, sites. Alibaba has two retail sites – Taobao, which features thousands of non-brand name products sold by smaller-unknown merchants; and Tmall, for brand name products. The variety of products offered on each side, especially Taobao is astonishing. The third advantage is scale, the cost savings associated with a larger volume of sales As argued by Juro Osawa, Alibaba through Taobao and Tmall accounts has controlled more than half of the market in China. Also, in 2012, the total volume of transactions by Taobao and Tmall has topped one million yuan

(US$163 billion). The total volume is greater than the volume transacted by Amazon and eBay. The fourth advantage, and perhaps the most important, is networking, the benefits arising from an expanding network of users of a product or service. The larger the network, the more valuable the product becomes to each user. The fifth advantage is Alibaba's good relations with the Chinese government. To ensure that Taobao is able to have a good relationship with the Chinese government, they need to develop more markets to strengthen its competitive advantage.

Questions

5-1. What is competitive advantage?

5-2. Using Dunning's theory, explain the advantage of Taobao.

5-3. Can Taobao sustain its competitive advantage? Discuss.

SOURCES: Beijing Review (2014) E-Commerce pioneer goes global. September 25, 2014. Isenberg Marketing (2014) The rise of Taobao, September 29, 2014. Mourdoukoutas, P. (2014) Alibaba's Five Advantages. *Forbes.* April 15, 2014. Si, S. (2014) 2014: The internalization of Chinese Tech. *L'Telier.* January 14, 2014. Wang, X. & Ren. J. (2013) A Tale of Two Games: Global Strategies of Multinational Companies in China's E-commerce Market. *The World Financial Review.* March 14, 2013.

The opening story illustrates the benefits of global free trade. International trade enables Taobao to keep its manufacturing costs low and sell its desired products at competitive global prices.

Imagine a scenario in which countries did not trade with each other. What would we be missing? At a minimum, we would not have access to products and services made elsewhere. We would end up paying higher prices for offerings that other nations can produce more economically. We would waste scarce resources making some products that other countries could produce more efficiently, using fewer resources.

Similarly, try to imagine a scenario in which firms could only do business within their national borders. What would be the consequences? Paying higher prices for some domestic inputs they could have imported from other nations? What would they lose if they could not sell their products to foreign customers or gain competitive advantage by learning from foreign partners or acquiring ideas, capital, or expertise? Numerous other undesirable outcomes would follow.

Fortunately, nations and firms are generally free to do business outside of their national borders. Free trade allows consumers to access the products they want at lower costs, which helps increase living standards worldwide. Although the rationale for trading and investing beyond national borders is intuitive, economists have grappled with thoughtful explanations of cross-border trade and investment.

In this chapter, we review these formal explanations or theories, many of which have been developed over time, some becoming ever more sophisticated. They address the underlying economic rationale for international business and why firms and nations trade and invest internationally. We consider questions such as:

Comparative advantage
Superior features of a nation that provide unique benefits in global competition. These features typically are derived from either natural endowments or deliberate national policies.

- What is the underlying economic rationale for international business activity?
- Why does trade take place?
- What are the gains to nations and firms from international trade and investment?

Central to understanding trade among nations are concepts of comparative advantage and competitive advantage, so let's explore these concepts next.

Comparative advantage describes superior features of a *nation* that provide unique benefits in global competition. These features typically are derived from either natural endowments or deliberate national policies. Also known as *country-specific advantage*, comparative advantage includes inherited resources, such as labor, climate, arable land, and petroleum reserves, such as those enjoyed by countries in the Middle East. Other types of comparative advantages are acquired over time, such as entrepreneurial orientation, availability of venture capital, and innovative capacity.

Competitive advantage
Assets or capabilities of a firm that are difficult for competitors to imitate. They are typically derived from specific knowledge, competencies, skills, or superior strategies.

Competitive advantage refers to assets and capabilities of a *company* that are difficult for competitors to imitate. Such advantages help the firm enter and succeed in foreign markets.

These capabilities take various forms such as specific knowledge, competencies, innovativeness, superior strategies, or close relationships with suppliers. Competitive advantage is also known as *firm-specific advantage*.

In recent years, business executives and scholars have used *competitive advantage* to refer to the advantages possessed by nations *and* individual firms in international trade and investment. To be consistent with the recent literature, we adopt this convention as well.

Exhibit 5.1 arranges leading theories of international trade and investment into two broad groups. The first group includes *nation-level* theories. These are classical theories, widely accepted since the eighteenth century. They address two questions.

- *Why* do nations trade?
- *How* can nations enhance their competitive advantage?

The second group includes *firm-level* theories. These are more contemporary theories of how firms can create and sustain superior organizational performance. Firm-level explanations address two additional questions.

- *Why* and *how* do firms internationalize?
- *How* can internationalizing firms gain and sustain competitive advantage?

We organize the remainder of our discussion according to these four fundamental questions.

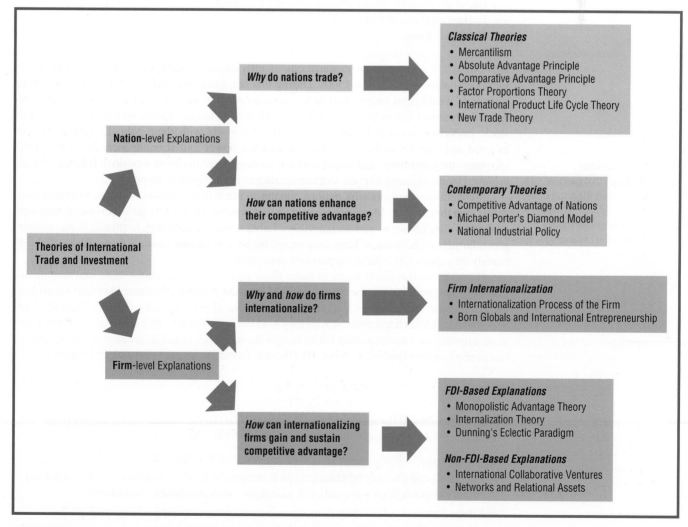

EXHIBIT 5.1

Theories of International Trade and Investment

5.1 Appreciate why nations trade.

Why Do Nations Trade?

Why do nations trade with one another? The short answer is that trade enables countries to use their national resources more efficiently through specialization and thus enables industries and workers to be more productive. These outcomes help keep the cost of many everyday products low, which translates into higher living standards. Without international trade, most nations would be unable to feed, clothe, and house their citizens at current levels. Even resource-rich countries such as the United States would suffer greatly without trade. Some types of food would become unavailable or very expensive. Coffee and sugar would be luxury items. Petroleum-based energy sources would dwindle. Vehicles would stop running, freight would go undelivered, and people would not be able to heat their homes in winter. In short, not only do nations, companies, and citizens benefit from international trade, modern life would be nearly impossible without it.

Classical Theories

Six classical perspectives help explain the underlying rationale for trade among nations.

- Mercantilism
- Absolute advantage principle
- Comparative advantage principle
- Factor proportions theory and the Leontief Paradox
- International product life cycle theory
- New trade theory

MERCANTILISM   The earliest explanations of international business emerged with the rise of European nation–states in the 1500s. During this era, gold and silver were the most important sources of wealth, and nations sought to amass as much of these treasures as possible. Nations typically received payment for exports in gold, but although exports increased nations' gold stock, imports reduced it because they paid for imports with their gold. Exports were seen as good and imports as bad. Because the nation's power and strength increase as its wealth increases, **mercantilism** argues that national prosperity results from a positive balance of trade achieved by maximizing exports and minimizing or even impeding imports.

Mercantilism
The belief that national prosperity is the result of a positive balance of trade, achieved by maximizing exports and minimizing imports.

Mercantilism explains why nations attempt to run a *trade surplus*—that is, to export more goods than they import. Many people believe that running a trade surplus is beneficial; they subscribe to a view known as *neo-mercantilism*. Labor unions (which seek to protect home–country jobs), farmers (who want to keep crop prices high), and certain manufacturers (those that rely heavily on exports) all tend to support neo-mercantilism.

However, mercantilism tends to harm firms that import, especially those that import raw materials and parts used in the manufacture of finished products. Mercantilism also harms consumers because restricting imports reduces the choice of products they can buy. Product shortages that result from import restrictions may lead to higher prices—that is, inflation. When taken to an extreme, mercantilism may invite beggar-thy-neighbor policies, promoting the benefits of one country at the expense of others. By contrast, free trade is a generally superior approach.

Free trade
Relative absence of restrictions to the flow of goods and services between nations.

Free trade refers to the relative absence of restrictions to the flow of goods and services between nations. Free trade typically produces the following outcomes:

- Consumers and firms can more readily buy the products they want.
- Imported products may be cheaper than domestically produced products (if the exporting country benefits from some national advantages such as abundant resources).
- Lower-cost imports can help reduce company expenses, thereby raising their profits (which may be passed on to workers in the form of higher wages).
- Lower-cost imports help consumers save money, thereby increasing their living standards.
- Unrestricted international trade generally increases the overall prosperity of poor countries.

ABSOLUTE ADVANTAGE PRINCIPLE   Have you ever thought about why your iPhone or iPad is not assembled in the United States even though it is designed in California? If you answer it is because labor cost is lower in China, you already know something about the absolute advantage principle. Because countries differ in national endowments (e.g., land, labor, technological capabilities), they are better off to specialize in the production of certain products and services and import others.

In 1776, Scottish political economist Adam Smith published *An Inquiry into the Nature and Causes of the Wealth of Nations*, a groundbreaking book. Smith attacked the mercantilist view by suggesting that nations have much to benefit from free trade. Smith argued that mercantilism deprives individuals of the ability to trade freely and to benefit from voluntary exchange. By minimizing imports and maximizing exports, a country wastes much of its national resources by having to produce products it is not suited to produce efficiently. The inefficiencies of mercantilism end up reducing the wealth of the nation as a whole while enriching a limited number of individuals and interest groups. Relative to others, each country is more efficient in the production of some products and less efficient in the production of other products. This simple idea that nations differ in their ability to produce a product efficiently is a well-accepted premise and is known as the absolute advantage principle.

Smith's **absolute advantage principle** states that a country benefits by producing primarily those products in which it has an absolute advantage—those that it can produce using fewer resources than any other country. (By "resources," early writers referred to tangible assets such as land and labor. Today, resources include intangibles such as knowledge and work ethic and capabilities such as design or zero defect production.) Each country can increase its wealth by specializing in the production of goods in which it has unique advantages, exporting those goods, and then importing other goods in which it has no particular advantage. If every nation follows this practice, each can consume more than it otherwise could, generally at lower cost.

Source: creativehearts/123RF

Scottish political economist Adam Smith was among the first to articulate the advantages of international trade.

Absolute advantage principle
The idea that a country benefits by producing only those products it can produce using fewer resources.

The absolute advantage principle applies to our daily choices as well. Consider the following scenario. Suppose you are employed as a corporate financial analyst. Imagine your car breaks down and you know nothing about repairing cars. You have the opportunity to take a leave from your job, enroll in a crash course in auto mechanics, and try to fix the car over several days. Alternatively, you can take your car to a professional mechanic. Which option would you choose? Most people will likely choose paying a professional mechanic since the alternative— forgoing wages you would have earned during the duration of the crash course—is less desirable. The professional mechanic has an absolute advantage in car repair. You have an absolute advantage in doing your financial analyst job. Using the services of a professional mechanic saves you both time and wages.

Now let's carry the absolute advantage principle to the country level. Imagine that there are only two nations: the Dairycountry, which produces and consumes only milk, and the Cattlecountry, which produces and consumes only beef. In this simplistic scenario, we ignore the cost of shipping products. Exhibit 5.2 presents the productivity of each nation. One unit of resources (labor) in Dairycountry can produce 10 gallons of milk or 8 pounds of beef. The Cattlecountry's efficiency is lower; one unit of resource produces only 2 gallons of milk or 4 pounds of beef.

We note that one unit of resources in the Dairycountry creates more of both products (10 gallons of milk or 8 pounds of beef) than the Cattlecountry (2 gallons of milk or 4 pounds of beef). Therefore, we conclude that the Dairycountry has an absolute advantage in both products; it is more efficient in the production of both milk and beef.

In the preceding example, keep in mind that we made a simplistic assumption by using a single resource: labor. Of course, in a real-world scenario, producing milk or beef requires

	Quantity of products produced by one unit of resources (*labor*)	
	Milk (gallons)	*Beef (pounds)*
Dairycountry	10	8
Cattlecountry	2	4

EXHIBIT 5.2

Productivity of the Dairycountry and the Cattlecountry in Producing Milk and Beef

multiple resources, labor, land, capital, appropriate climate, technical knowledge, and so on. The quantity and quality of these productive resources vary from country to country.

Even if the Dairycountry has absolute advantage in the production of both milk and beef, does it still make sense for the two nations to trade with each other? Are there benefits from trade for each nation? For the answers to these questions, we turn to the comparative advantage principle.

COMPARATIVE ADVANTAGE PRINCIPLE In his 1817 book *The Principles of Political Economy and Taxation*, British political economist David Ricardo explained why it is beneficial for two countries to trade even though one of them may have an absolute advantage in the production of all products. Ricardo demonstrated that what matters is not the absolute cost of production, but rather the *relative efficiency* with which the two countries can produce the products. Thus, the **comparative advantage principle** states that it will be beneficial for two countries to trade with each other as long as one is *relatively* more efficient at producing goods or services needed by the other. The principle of comparative advantage is the foundational logic for free trade among nations today.

To illustrate, let's recall the Dairycountry and the Cattlecountry scenario. Dairycountry has an absolute advantage in the production of both milk and beef. Therefore, you might initially conclude that Dairycountry should produce all the milk and beef it needs and not trade with Cattlecountry. However, it is still beneficial for Dairycountry to trade with Cattlecountry.

How can this be true? The answer is that rather than absolute efficiency, it is the *relative efficiency* between the two countries that matters. As we see in Exhibit 5.2, Dairycountry is five times (10/2) more efficient at producing milk, but only twice (8/4) as efficient than Cattlecountry at producing beef. Although Cattlecountry is unable to produce either milk or beef more efficiently than Dairycountry, it produces beef more efficiently than it produces milk.

Conversely, Dairycountry is relatively more efficient at producing milk than beef (10/2 versus 8/4). Thus, Dairycountry should devote all its resources to producing milk and import all the beef it needs from Cattlecountry. Cattlecountry should specialize in producing beef and import its milk from Dairycountry. Each country can then produce and consume relatively more of the goods it desires for a given level of resource.

Recall the car repair example. Let's assume you are a mechanically inclined do-it-yourselfer and can fix your car faster than the professional auto mechanic. You hold absolute advantages both in car repair *and* in financial analysis. The auto mechanic, although not as efficient as you in either financial analysis or car repair, is still pretty good at repairing cars. Therefore, he should specialize in auto repair. By the same argument, you are better off focusing on your financial analyst job, no matter how talented you are at auto repair. In other words, although the car mechanic lacks absolute advantage in both tasks, he has comparative advantage in automotive repair.

Whereas a nation might conceivably have a sufficient variety of resources to provide every kind of product and service, it cannot produce all with equal proficiency. The United States could produce all the shoes its citizens need, but only at high cost. This occurs because shoes require much labor to produce, and manufacturing wages in the United States are relatively high. By contrast, producing shoes is a reasonable activity in China, where labor is abundant and wages are relatively low. It is advantageous, therefore, for the United States to specialize in a product such as patented pharmaceuticals. The production of pharmaceuticals more efficiently employs the United States' abundant supply of knowledge workers and technology in the pharmaceutical industry. The United States is better off exporting medications and importing shoes from China. (In fact, footwear marketers such as Nike and Reebok design their own shoes but source the finished product from China and other low labor cost countries.)

The comparative advantage view is optimistic because it implies that a nation need not be the first-, second-, or even third-best producer of a particular product to benefit from international trade. A country needs to be only *relatively* capable in producing various types of goods. In this way, the comparative advantage view implies that it is generally advantageous for *all* countries to participate in international trade.

Now, you might ask what accounts for national differences in efficiency. Initially, scholars focused on the importance of *inherited* or *natural resource advantages*, such as fertile land, abundant minerals, and favorable climate. Because South Africa has extensive mineral deposits,

Comparative advantage principle
It may be beneficial for two countries to trade with each other as long as one is relatively more efficient at producing a product needed by the other.

it produces and exports diamonds. Because Brazil has abundant fertile land and a suitable climate, it produces and exports wheat and beef.

In addition to naturally occurring advantages such as these, it has become clear that countries can also *create* or *acquire* comparative advantages. Consider the case of Japan—in the years following World War II, Japan intentionally acquired many advantages (e.g., capital, specialized knowledge, and capabilities in quality assurance) that benefited its consumer electronics industry. The investments the Japanese government, banks, and manufacturing firms made paid off enormously. Companies such as Hitachi, Panasonic, and Sony invested massive resources to acquire the knowledge and skills needed to become world leaders in consumer electronics. Today, Japan accounts for a huge proportion of the industry's total world production, including digital cameras, flat panel TVs, and personal computers. More recently, South Korea has made similar investments, giving rise to such leading-edge firms as LG and Samsung.

 MyManagementLab   Watch It!

If your professor has assigned this, go to the Assignments section of **mymanagementlab.com** to complete the video exercise titled Comparative and Competitive Advantages in Global Competition: Spotlight on InfoSys.

Limitations of Absolute and Comparative Advantage Theories

Although the concepts of absolute advantage and comparative advantage provide the rationale for international trade, they overlook factors that make contemporary trade complex, such as the following:

- Government restrictions such as tariffs (taxes on imports), import barriers, and regulations can hamper international trade.

- Just as Japan did after World War II, governments may target and invest in certain industries, build infrastructure, or provide subsidies, all to boost the competitive advantages of home–country firms.

- Large-scale production in certain industries may provide *economies of scale* and, therefore, lower prices. Economies of scale tend to compensate for weak national comparative advantages. Similarly, modern communications and the Internet tend to reduce the cost and complexity of cross-border trade.

- The main participants in international trade are individual firms that differ in significant ways. Far from being homogeneous enterprises, many are highly entrepreneurial and innovative or have access to exceptional human talent, all of which support international business success.

- International shipping and insurance, critical for cross-border trade to take place, are relatively costly and make imported goods more expensive.

- Traded products are not just commodities anymore, such as milk and beef. Today, most traded goods are relatively complex. They are characterized by strong branding and differentiated features.

- Many services, such as banking and retailing, cannot be exported in the usual sense and must be internationalized through foreign direct investment.

In light of such limitations, scholars have introduced additional explanations of international trade, which we review next.

FACTOR PROPORTIONS THEORY   A significant contribution to explaining international trade was developed in the 1920s. Two Swedish economists, Eli Heckscher and his student, Bertil

Ohlin, proposed the *factor proportions theory*, sometimes called the factor endowments theory.[1] This view rests on two premises:

- Products differ in the types and quantities of factors (labor, natural resources, and capital) required for their production.
- Countries differ in the type and quantity of production factors that they possess.

The theory suggests that each country should export products that intensively use relatively abundant factors of production and import goods that intensively use relatively scarce factors of production. For example, the United States produces and exports capital-intensive products, such as pharmaceuticals and commercial aircraft. Argentina produces land-intensive products, such as wine and sunflower seeds.

Factor proportions theory differs somewhat from earlier theories by emphasizing the importance of each nation's factors of production. The theory states that, in addition to differences in the *efficiency* of production, differences in the *quantity* of production factors countries hold also determine international trade patterns. In this way, a country that possesses an abundance of a given production factor (e.g., labor, land) obtains a *per-unit-cost advantage* in the production of goods that use that factor intensively.

In the 1950s, research by Russian economist Wassily Leontief seemed to contradict the factor proportions theory. His *Leontief Paradox* suggests that, because the United States has abundant capital, it should be an exporter of capital-intensive products. However, Leontief's analysis revealed that the United States often exported labor-intensive goods and imported more capital-intensive goods than the theory would ordinarily predict. What accounts for the inconsistency? One explanation is that numerous factors determine the composition of a country's exports and imports. Another is that, in Leontief's time, U.S. labor was relatively more productive than labor elsewhere in the world.

Perhaps the main contribution of the Leontief paradox is its suggestion that international trade is complex and cannot be fully explained by a single theory. Subsequent refinements of factor proportions theory suggested that other country-level assets—knowledge, technology, and capital—are instrumental in explaining each nation's international trade prowess. Taiwan, for example, is very strong in electronics technology and is home to a sizable population of knowledge workers in this sector.

INTERNATIONAL PRODUCT LIFE CYCLE THEORY In a 1966 article, Raymond Vernon sought to explain international trade based on the evolutionary process that occurs in the development and diffusion of products to markets around the world.[2] In his *International Product Life Cycle (IPLC) Theory*, Vernon observed that each product and its manufacturing technologies go through three stages of evolution: introduction, maturity, and standardization. This is illustrated in Exhibit 5.3.

Historically, in the introduction stage, a new product typically originated in an advanced economy, such as Germany or the United States. Such countries possess abundant capital and research and development (R&D) capabilities, providing key advantages in the invention of new goods. Advanced economies also have abundant, high-income consumers who are willing to try new products, which are often expensive. During the introduction stage, the new product is produced in the inventing country, which enjoys a temporary monopoly.

As the product enters the maturity phase, the product's inventors mass-produce it and seek to export it to other advanced economies. Gradually, however, the product's manufacturing becomes more routine, and foreign firms begin producing alternative versions, ending the inventor's monopoly power. At this stage, as competition intensifies and export orders begin to come from lower-income countries, the inventor may earn only a narrow profit margin.

Source: Khrushchev Georgy/Shutterstock

Factor proportions theory describes how abundant production factors give rise to national advantages. Russia, for example, has a very large workforce in numerous industries.

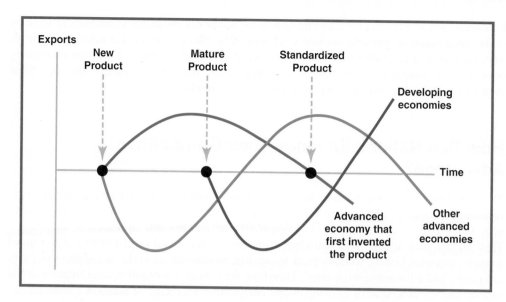

EXHIBIT 5.3

Illustration of Vernon's International Product Life Cycle

Source: Adapted from Raymond Vernon, "International Investment and International Trade in the Product Cycle," *Quarterly Journal of Economics* 80 (May 1966), pp. 190–207 and http://www.provenmodels.com/583/international-product-life-cycle/raymond-vernon.

In the standardization phase, knowledge about how to produce the product is widespread and manufacturing has become straightforward. Early in the product's evolution, production had required specialized workers skilled in R&D and manufacturing. Once standardized, however, mass production becomes the dominant activity and can be accomplished using cheaper inputs and lower-cost labor. Production shifts to low-income countries where competitors enjoy low-cost advantages and can economically serve export markets worldwide. The country that invented the product eventually becomes a net importer. It and other advanced economies become saturated with imports of the good from developing economies. In effect, exporting the product has caused its underlying technology to become widely known and standardized around the world.

As an example, consider the evolution of television sets. The base technology was invented in the United States. U.S. firms began domestic production of TV sets in the 1940s. U.S. sales grew rapidly for many years. However, once TVs became a standardized product, production shifted to China, Mexico, and other countries that offered lower-cost production. Today the United States imports nearly all its television sets.

The IPLC illustrates that national advantages do not last forever. Firms worldwide are continuously creating new products, and others are constantly imitating them. The product cycle is continually beginning and ending. Vernon assumed the product diffusion process occurs slowly enough to generate temporary differences between countries in their access and use of new technologies. This assumption is no longer valid today—the IPLC has become much shorter as new products diffuse much more quickly around the world. Buyers in emerging markets are particularly eager to adopt new technologies as soon as they become available. This trend explains the rapid spread of new consumer electronics such as smartphones and tablets around the world.

NEW TRADE THEORY In the 1970s, economists, including Paul Krugman, observed that trade was growing fastest among industrialized countries with similar factors of production. In some new industries, there appeared to be no clear comparative advantage. The solution to this puzzle became known as the *new trade theory*. It argues that increasing returns to scale, especially *economies of scale*, are important for superior international performance in industries that succeed best as their production volume increases. For example, the commercial aircraft industry has high fixed costs that necessitate high-volume sales to achieve profitability. As a nation specializes in the production of such goods, productivity increases and unit costs fall, providing significant benefits to the local economy.

Many national markets are small, and the domestic producer may not achieve economies of scale because it cannot sell products in large volume. New trade theory implies that firms can solve this problem by exporting and gaining access to the much larger global marketplace.

Industries such as generic pharmaceuticals achieve minimally profitable economies of scale by selling their output in multiple markets worldwide. The effect of increasing returns to scale allows the nation to specialize in a smaller number of industries in which it may not necessarily hold factor or comparative advantages. According to new trade theory, trade is thus beneficial even for countries that produce only a limited variety of products.

How Can Nations Enhance Their Competitive Advantage?

5.2 Learn about how nations can enhance their competitive advantage.

The globalization of markets has fostered a new type of competition—a race among nations to reposition themselves as attractive for business and investment. The more competitive economies today possess a combination of comparative advantages and firm-specific advantages. They feature such strengths as abundant resources, sophisticated infrastructure, well-trained workers, powerful brands, technological leadership, worldwide networks of suppliers and collaborators, and a favorable work ethic. Therefore, we conceive national competitiveness as the sum of national comparative advantages and competitive advantage of a nation's firms collectively. This notion is illustrated in Exhibit 5.4.

Now let's explore how nations can enhance their national competitiveness.

Three contemporary perspectives help explain the development of national competitive advantage: the competitive advantage of nations, the determinants of national competitiveness, and national industrial policy. Let's explain each of these in turn.

The Competitive Advantage of Nations

How can nations position themselves in a global race for national competiveness? An important contribution came from Professor Michael Porter in his 1990 book, *The Competitive Advantage of Nations*.[3] According to Porter, the competitive advantage of a nation depends on the collective competitive advantages of the nation's firms. Over time, this relationship is reciprocal; the competitive advantages the nation holds tend to drive the development of new firms and industries with these same competitive advantages.

For example, Britain achieved a substantial national competitive advantage in the prescription drug industry due to its first-rate pharmaceutical firms, such as GlaxoSmithKline and AstraZeneca. The United States has a national competitive advantage in professional services because of such leading firms as Goldman Sachs (investment banking), Marsh & McLennan (insurance), and McKinsey (consulting). The presence of these and numerous other strong services firms, in turn, has provided the United States with overall national competencies in the global services sector.

At both the firm and national levels, competitive advantage and technological advances grow out of *innovation*.[4] Companies innovate in various ways. They develop new product designs, new production processes, new approaches to marketing, and new ways of organizing or training. Firms sustain innovation (and by extension, competitive advantage) by continually finding better products, services, and ways of doing things.[5] For example, Australia's Vix (http://www.vixtechnology.

Comparative Advantage		**Competitive Advantage**		**National Competitiveness**
Location-specific advantage arises from an abundance in a **country** of: • Valuable natural resources (e.g. Brazil) • Arable or buildable land (e.g. Canada) • Strategic location (e.g. Hong Kong) • Favorable climate (e.g. Spain) • Low-cost labor (e.g. Indonesia) • Skilled labor (e.g. Singapore) • Inexpensive capital (e.g. China)	**+**	Firm-specific advantage, or ownership-specific advantage, arises from an abundance in a **firm** of: • Specific knowledge • Specific capabilities • Certain types of skills • Superior strategies • Strong networks • Other assets	**=**	in that particular industry. For example: • Mining in Brazil • Forest products in Canada • Exporting/importing in Hong Kong • Tourism in Spain • Home appliances in Indonesia • Biotechnology in Singapore • Automobiles in China

EXHIBIT 5.4

Components of National Competiveness: Comparative Advantage and Competitive Advantage

com) is a world leader in fare collection equipment and software systems for the transit industry. The firm has installed systems in subways, bus networks, and other mass transit systems in such major cities as Melbourne, Rome, San Francisco, Stockholm, and Singapore. It has won numerous awards for its innovative products that have allowed the firm to internationalize quickly. Vix's investment in R&D has been significant, running as high as 23 percent of the firm's revenue.

Innovation results primarily from R&D. Among the industries most dependent on technological innovation are biotechnology, information technology, new materials, pharmaceuticals, robotics, medical equipment, fiber optics, and various electronics-based industries.

In a report called the *Global Innovation 1000*, the management consultancy Strategy& (www.strategyand.pwc.com) annually reports on MNEs that spend the most on R&D. Most top European, Japanese, and U.S. firms spend half or more of their total R&D in countries other than where they are headquartered. The firms do this for several reasons:

- Gain access to talent—gifted engineers and scientists reside around the world in countries such as China and India.
- To cut costs by hiring lower-paid engineers and scientists abroad to replace higher-paid personnel in the home country.
- To relocate certain R&D activities abroad where they can gain insights on specific needs of target markets.[6]

Innovation also promotes *productivity*, which is measured as output per unit of labor or capital. The more productive a firm is, the more efficiently it uses its resources. The more productive the firms in a nation are, the more efficiently the nation uses its resources.[7]

At the national level, productivity is a key determinant of the nation's long-run standard of living and a basic source of national per-capita income growth. Exhibit 5.5 depicts productivity levels in various nations over time, measured as output per hour of workers in manufacturing. Colombia and South Korea have been very successful in growing their productivity over time.

Determinants of National Competitiveness

As part of his explanation in *The Competitive Advantage of Nations*, Michael Porter described several factors that give rise to competitive advantage at both the company and national levels. Named the Porter Diamond Model, it comprises four major elements.

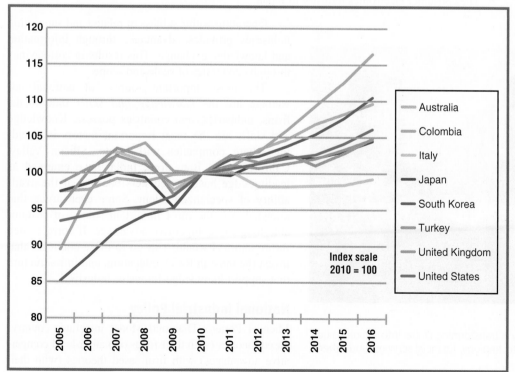

EXHIBIT 5.5

Labor Productivity Levels in Selected Countries: Output per Hour in Manufacturing, 2005–2016, Index Scale, 2010 = 100

Source: OECD, *OECD Data: Productivity* (Organisation for Economic Cooperation and Development, 2015), https://data.oecd.org/lprdty/labour-productivity-forecast.htm#indicator-chart.

- *Demand conditions* refer to the nature of home-market demand for specific products and services. The presence of demanding customers pressures firms to innovate faster and produce better products. For example, the United States has a large population of prosperous senior citizens who suffer from various health problems. These conditions have created an enormous market for quality medical equipment and cutting-edge pharmaceutical medications.

- *Firm strategy, structure, and rivalry* refer to the nature of domestic rivalry and conditions in a nation that determines how firms are created, organized, and managed. Vigorous competitive rivalry puts these firms under continual pressure to innovate and improve. They compete not only for market share but also for human talent, technical leadership, and superior product quality. The presence of strong competitors in a nation helps to create and maintain national competitive advantage. Japan has one of the world's most competitive consumer electronics industries, with major players such as Hitachi, Nintendo, Sony, and Toshiba producing semiconductors, computers, video games, and liquid crystal displays. Intense rivalry has pushed firms like Sony to a leading position in the industry worldwide and has enabled Japan to emerge as a leader in consumer electronics.

- *Factor conditions* describe the nation's resources such as labor, natural resources and advanced factors such as capital, technology, entrepreneurship, advanced work force skills, and know-how. Each nation has a relative abundance of certain factor endowments. This helps determine the nature of its national competitive advantage. For example, Germany's abundance of workers with strong engineering skills has propelled the country to commanding heights in the global engineering and design industries.

- *Related and supporting industries* refer to the presence of clusters of suppliers, competitors, and skilled workforce. An **industrial cluster** refers to a concentration of businesses, suppliers, and supporting firms in the same industry located at a particular geographic location.

Industrial cluster
A concentration of businesses, suppliers, and supporting firms in the same industry at a particular location, characterized by a critical mass of human talent, capital, or other factor endowments.

Industrial clusters are characterized by a critical mass of human talent, capital, or other factor endowments. Examples of industrial clusters include:

- The fashion industry in northern Italy.
- The pharmaceutical industry in Switzerland.
- The footwear industry in Vietnam.
- The medical technology industry in Singapore.
- Wireless Valley in Stockholm, Sweden.
- The consumer electronics industry in Japan.

Source: galina_savina/Fotolia

Visionary national industrial policy is transforming Dubai into a high value–adding economy based on IT, biotechnology, financial services, and other knowledge-intensive industries.

Operating within a mass of related and supporting industries provides advantages through information and knowledge exchange. This results in cost-savings through economies of scale and scope.

The most important sources of national advantage are the *knowledge and skills* individuals, firms, industries, and countries possess. Knowledge and skills are the most important factors in deciding where companies will locate. Silicon Valley, California, and Bangalore, India, have emerged as leading-edge business clusters because of the availability of specialized talent. Some even argue that knowledge is the most important source of sustainable long-run competitive advantage. If correct, then future national wealth will go to those countries that invest the most in R&D, education, and infrastructure that support knowledge-intensive industries.

National Industrial Policy

Michael Porter's Diamond Model integrates country-based theories (with their focus on nation-level comparative advantages) with firm-based theories (with their focus on firm-level competitive advantages) to determine national competitiveness. Many countries develop national industrial policies. A **national industrial policy** is a proactive economic development plan a government launches to build or strengthen a particular industry, often implemented in collaboration with the private sector. Usually, governments design such policies to support high value-adding industries, those that yield higher corporate profits, better wages, and tax revenues. Historically, governments favored traditional industries, including automobiles, shipbuilding, and heavy machinery—all with long value chains that produce enormous added value.

High value–adding industries typically are knowledge-intensive industries such as IT, biotechnology, medical technology, and financial services. Dubai developed a national industrial policy to become an international commercial center in the information and communications technology (ICT) sector. Singapore's Innovation Manifesto has propelled the city–state to become a world-class center of excellence in such areas as nuclear technology.

Governments play a key role in influencing each of the four components of the Porter diamond. They can do this either positively or negatively. Governments can influence *demand conditions* and *related and supporting industries* through regulations. They can influence *factor conditions* by supporting educational initiatives and capital markets. Government tax policies and regulations can influence *firm strategy, structure, and rivalry*.

> **National industrial policy**
> A proactive economic development plan a government initiates to build or strengthen a particular industry.

Features of National Industrial Policies

- *Tax incentives.* Tax incentives encourage citizens and firms to save and invest money, which can then be used as capital for public and private investment in R&D, plant, equipment, and worker skills.

- *Monetary and fiscal policies.* These include low-interest loans that provide a stable supply of capital.

- *Educational systems.* Superior educational systems ensure a steady stream of competent workers in high technology or high value-adding industries.

- *Infrastructure.* Modern national infrastructure in areas such as IT, communication systems, and transportation enhance productivity.

- *Legal and regulatory systems.* These institutions ensure the stability of national economies.

Sources: Iurii Vinslav, "National Industrial Policy," *Problems of Economic Transition* 56, No. 9 (2014), pp. 16-47; Lester Thurow, *Head to Head: The Coming Economic Battle Among Japan, Europe, and America* (New York: William Morrow, 1992).

National Industrial Policy in Practice

How well does national industrial policy work in practice? Let's examine the experience of New Zealand. For much of the early twentieth century, government policies limited New Zealand's ability to flourish and trade with the rest of the world. Living standards were low and many wondered about the nation's future. In the 1980s, the New Zealand government developed pro-trade policies in cooperation with the private sector that resulted in national advantages.

EXHIBIT 5.6 Transformation of New Zealand's Economy, 1992 to 2014

Statistic	New Zealand in 1992	New Zealand in 2003	New Zealand in 2014
GDP per capita	48% of the G7 average	65% of the G7 average	96% of the G7 average
Unemployment rate	10.6%	4.8%	5.2%
National debt	89% of the nation's GDP	26% of the nation's GDP	33% of the nation's GDP

Source: International Monetary Fund, World Economic Outlook Databases, www.imf.org.

Source: amorfati.art/Shutterstock

Following many years of poor economic performance, the government of New Zealand implemented various national industrial policies that succeeded in elevating several key economic indicators, thus raising living standards for the New Zealand people.

The government helped systematically transform the country from an agrarian, protectionist, and regulated economy to an industrialized, globally competitive, and free-market economy. New Zealand's economy grew rapidly and achieved high living standards.

These accomplishments are summarized in Exhibit 5.6. Between 1992 and 2014, New Zealand raised its per-capita GDP from 48 to 96 percent of the average of the G7 countries, the world's seven largest advanced economies. This represents a 100 percent improvement in real terms of personal income. During this period, New Zealand's unemployment rate declined by more than half to 5.2 percent. The government reduced its national debt as a proportion of GDP from 89 to 33 percent. Although New Zealand's per-capita GDP decreased during the global recession, it stabilized in 2014 to more than $40,000 per-capita GDP. This is among the highest in the world.

New Zealand Successfully Transforming Its Economy Using National Industrial Policy

- Government-controlled wages, prices, and interest rates were freed and allowed to fluctuate according to market forces.

- The banking sector was liberalized, foreign exchange controls were eliminated, and the New Zealand dollar was allowed to float according to market forces.

- Most trade barriers were removed.

- Subsidies formerly granted to agriculture and other sectors were eliminated.

- The government worked earnestly with labor unions to reduce wage inflation, helping ensure that jobs remained in New Zealand and were not outsourced to lower-wage countries.

- The government initiated programs to encourage development of a knowledge economy. New Zealanders continuously upgraded skills and knowledge, providing a supply of scientists, engineers, and trained managers.

- Personal and corporate income tax rates were reduced, and the tax base was diversified to stabilize government revenues. This move fostered entrepreneurship, boosted consumer spending, and increased the nation's attractiveness for investment from abroad.

- State-owned enterprises—such as the national airline, post office, telecom, and other utilities—were sold to the private sector.

Sources: Dean Hyslop and Dave Mar, "Skill Upgrading in New Zealand, 1986–2001," *Australian Economic Review*, 42, No. 4 (2009), pp. 422-434; Johan Christensen, "Bureaucracies, Neoliberal Ideas, and Tax Reform in New Zealand and Ireland," *Governance* 26, No. 4 (2013), pp. 563–584.

As Exhibit 5.6 reveals, dynamic growth boosted real incomes and greatly improved living standards in New Zealand. Recently, *Forbes* magazine and the World Bank ranked New Zealand as the second most business-friendly country in the world.[8]

5.3 Understand why and how firms internationalize.

Why and How Do Firms Internationalize?

Earlier theories of international trade focused on why and how cross-national business occurs. Beginning in the 1960s, scholars turned their attention to why and how individual firms pursue internationalization. Let's examine these views.

Internationalization Process of the Firm

Scholars developed the *internationalization process model* in the 1970s to describe how companies expand abroad. According to this model, internationalization takes place in incremental stages over a long period.[9] Initially and without much analysis or planning, firms begin exporting, the simplest foreign market entry strategy. As they become more knowledgeable, firms gradually progress to foreign direct investment (FDI), the most complex entry strategy. The relatively slow nature of internationalization often results from managers' uncertainty and uneasiness about how to proceed. They lack information about foreign markets and experience with cross-border transactions. The progression from exporting to FDI coincides with increasing levels of both risk and control.

This gradual, incremental model of internationalization is illustrated in Exhibit 5.7. Preoccupied with business in its home market, the firm starts out with a *domestic focus*. Management may be unable or unwilling to start doing international business because of concerns over its readiness or perceived obstacles in foreign markets. Eventually, the firm advances to the *pre-export stage*, often because it receives unsolicited product orders from abroad. In this stage, management investigates the feasibility of undertaking international business. Later, the firm advances to the *experimental involvement stage* by initiating limited international activity, typically through basic exporting. As managers begin to view foreign expansion more favorably, they undertake *active involvement* in international business. This occurs through the systematic exploration of international options and the commitment of resources and managerial time to achieve international success. Management may finally advance to the *committed involvement stage*. This stage is characterized by genuine interest and commitment of resources to making international business a key part of the firm's profit-making and value-chain activities. In this stage, the firm targets numerous foreign markets through various entry modes, especially FDI.[10]

To illustrate, let's examine the consumer electronics firm Samsung Corporation, headquartered in Seoul, South Korea (www.samsung.com). In the 1970s, Samsung began exporting televisions and other products to Europe and North America. In the 1990s, it entered joint ventures with various partners abroad to manufacture televisions, refrigerators, and video equipment. Around the same time, Samsung used FDI to establish regional headquarters in China, Europe, Singapore, and the United States. In the 1990s, the firm set up factories in China and other countries to manufacture consumer electronics and appliances. By 2005, Samsung had established 64 manufacturing and sales subsidiaries and 13 R&D centers around the world.[11]

Born Global Firms

Is the gradual, cautious internationalization process previously described still valid today? Current research suggests it is not.[12] What we see today is an increasing number of young, entrepreneurial firms that intently pursue customers in foreign markets from an early age. Scholars and management consultants alike referred to this relatively novel breed of companies as *born global firms*.[13] Born globals are innovative start-ups that initiate international business soon after their founding. Instagram is a born global. Founded in 2010, the firm soon found a ready market for its photo-sharing services in markets scattered around the world. Today, only about 12 percent of Instagram's customers are located in North America, where the company is based.[14]

Born global firms are now found in virtually all economies. This has developed despite the scarcity of financial, human, and tangible resources that characterize most new businesses. Born globals have emerged in large numbers for two main reasons.

- Globalization has made doing international business easier than ever before.
- Advances in communication and transportation technologies have reduced the costs of operating internationally.

The born global phenomenon has given rise to a new academic field, *international entrepreneurship*.[15] Current trends suggest that early internationalizing firms will become even more common in international business.

EXHIBIT 5.7

Stages in the Internationalization Process of the Firm

5.4 Explain the strategies internationalizing firms use to gain and sustain competitive advantage.

How Can Internationalizing Firms Gain and Sustain Competitive Advantage?

Since the 1950s, such MNEs as Nestlé, Unilever, Sony, Coca-Cola, and Caterpillar have all expanded abroad on a massive scale. Such MNEs have helped shape international patterns of trade, investment, and technology flows. Over time, the aggregate activities of these firms became a key driving force of globalization and ongoing integration of world economies. Let's examine how multinationals gain and sustain competitive advantage in global markets.

FDI-Based Explanations

Most explanations of international business have emphasized FDI, the preferred entry strategy of MNEs. These large, resource-rich companies conduct business through networks of production facilities, marketing subsidiaries, regional headquarters, and other operations around the world. One way to illustrate the huge volume of FDI is to examine *FDI stock*. FDI stock refers to the total value of assets that MNEs invest abroad.

Exhibit 5.8 shows the stock and growth of inward FDI for 2003 and 2013 for a group of leading FDI destination countries. The exhibit highlights three interesting points.

- Even smaller economies such as Ireland or South Africa are popular destinations for direct investment.
- Both developed and developing economies are major recipients of FDI.
- Hong Kong and Singapore receive considerable FDI as important *entrepôt* ports. In such ports, merchandise can be imported without paying import duties. The goods are then transshipped to and from China, the world's largest emerging market.

Historically, most of the world's FDI was invested both by and in Western Europe, the United States, and Japan. Today, rapidly developing economies now account for a huge proportion of global FDI. An exception is Africa. It receives relatively little FDI, which hinders its ability to raise living standards in the region.[16]

Exhibit 5.9 shows the stock and growth of outward FDI for a collection of the leading FDI-providing countries. Note that firms from both advanced economies and emerging markets invest substantial FDI abroad. Emerging markets such as China, India, and Russia have greatly increased their FDI investments in recent years. Total outward FDI stock now constitutes nearly one-third of global GDP, an impressive amount.[17]

Scholars have developed three alternative theories of how firms can use FDI to gain and sustain competitive advantage. These are the monopolistic advantage theory, internalization theory, and Dunning's eclectic paradigm. These theoretical perspectives are summarized in Exhibit 5.10.

MONOPOLISTIC ADVANTAGE THEORY   Monopolistic advantage refers to resources or capabilities a company holds that few other firms have. Monopolistic advantage theory suggests that firms that use FDI as an internationalization strategy must own or control certain resources and capabilities not easily available to competitors. This gives them a degree of monopoly power over local firms in foreign markets. This monopolistic advantage should be specific to the MNE itself, such as a proprietary technology or a brand name, rather than to the locations where it does business.

Monopolistic advantage theory argues that at least two conditions should be present for a firm to target a foreign market over its home market. First, returns accessible in the foreign market should be superior to those available in the home market. This would provide the firm with incentives to expand abroad to take advantage of its monopoly power. Second, returns achievable in the foreign market should be superior to those earned by existing domestic competitors in the foreign market. This would give the firm an opportunity to earn monopoly profits that domestic firms in the foreign market cannot imitate.

To illustrate, let's revisit Samsung Corporation. By being on the leading edge of innovation, Samsung established many pioneering standards in the consumer electronics industry. Over time, Samsung's superior R&D and internal controls allowed the firm to acquire and keep a large body of relatively unique knowledge. This unique knowledge provided the firm with various monopolistic advantages. Samsung invented many popular products that were, for a time, relatively unique. Continuous innovation within the firm allowed Samsung to keep this uniqueness for many years.

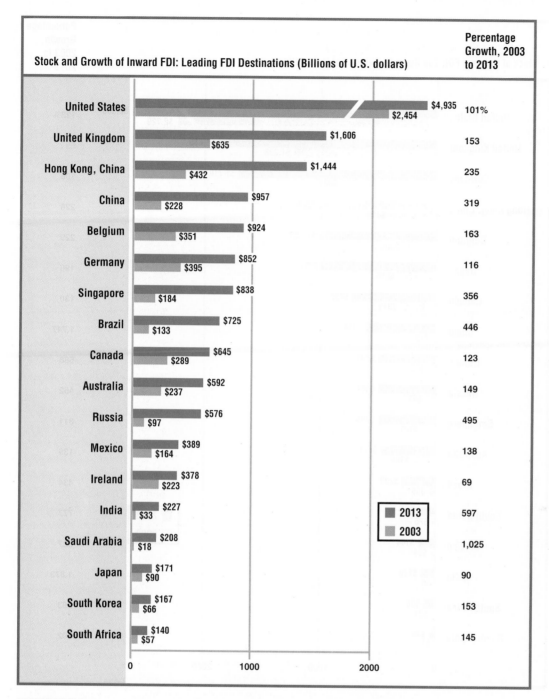

EXHIBIT 5.8

Stock and Growth of Inward FDI: Leading FDI Destinations (Billions of U.S. dollars) and Percentage Growth, 2003 and 2013

Sources: UNCTAD, *UNCTAD Stat* 2014 (New York: United Nations, 2014), retrieved May 3, 2015, at http://unctad.org/en/pages/Statistics.aspx.

Samsung used its superior innovativeness to develop monopoly power and dominate world markets in such products as LCD panels and smartphones. As the Samsung example implies, the most important monopolistic advantages are superior knowledge and intangible skills.[18]

INTERNALIZATION THEORY **Internalization theory** explains the process by which firms acquire and retain one or more value-chain activities inside the firm. Internalizing value-chain activities (instead of outsourcing them to external suppliers) reduces the disadvantages

Internalization theory
An explanation of the process by which firms acquire and retain one or more value-chain activities inside the firm. This minimizes the disadvantages of dealing with external partners and allows for greater control over foreign operations.

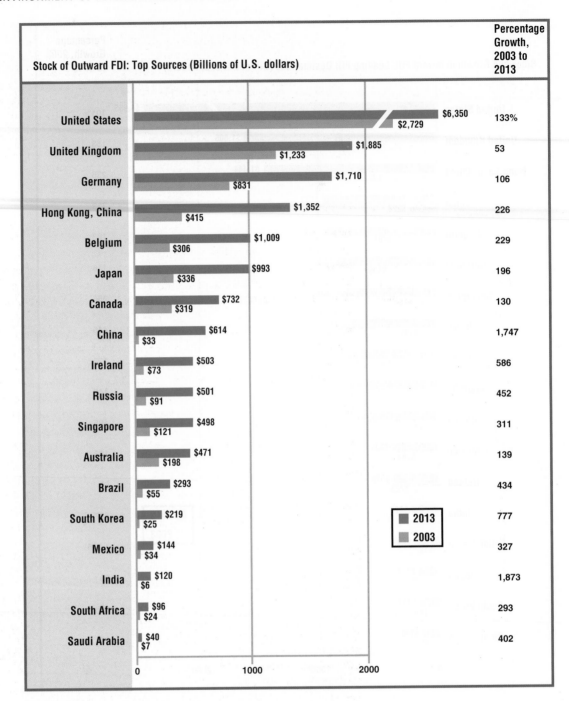

Stock of Outward FDI: Top Sources (Billions of U.S. dollars)	Percentage Growth, 2003 to 2013
United States — $6,350 / $2,729	133%
United Kingdom — $1,885 / $1,233	53
Germany — $1,710 / $831	106
Hong Kong, China — $1,352 / $415	226
Belgium — $1,009 / $306	229
Japan — $993 / $336	196
Canada — $732 / $319	130
China — $614 / $33	1,747
Ireland — $503 / $73	586
Russia — $501 / $91	452
Singapore — $498 / $121	311
Australia — $471 / $198	139
Brazil — $293 / $55	434
South Korea — $219 / $25	777
Mexico — $144 / $34	327
India — $120 / $6	1,873
South Africa — $96 / $24	293
Saudi Arabia — $40 / $7	402

■ 2013
■ 2003

EXHIBIT 5.9

Stock of and Growth of Outward FDI: Top Sources of Outward FDI (Billions of U.S. dollars) and Percentage Growth, 2003 to 2013

Sources: UNCTAD, *UNCTAD Stat 2014* (New York: United Nations, 2014), retrieved May 3, 2015, at http://unctad.org/en/pages/Statistics.aspx.

of dealing with outside partners for performing arms-length activities such as exporting and licensing. Internalization also gives the firm greater control over its foreign operations.

For example, the MNE might internalize manufacturing by acquiring or establishing its own plant in the foreign market. This enables the firm to produce needed inputs itself rather than sourcing from independent suppliers. Alternatively, it might internalize the marketing function by establishing its own distribution subsidiary abroad instead of contracting with an independent foreign distributor to handle its marketing in the foreign market. The firm replaces business

Theory	Key Characteristics	Benefits	Examples
Monopolistic Advantage Theory	The firm controls one or more resources, or offers relatively unique products and services that provide it a degree of monopoly power relative to foreign markets and competitors.	The firm can operate foreign subsidiaries more profitably than the local firms that compete in their own markets.	The European pharmaceutical Novartis earns substantial profits by marketing various patent medications through its subsidiaries worldwide.
Internalization Theory	The firm acquires and retains one or more value-chain activities within the firm.	• Minimizes the disadvantages of relying on intermediaries, collaborators, or other external partners. • Ensures greater control over foreign operations, helping to maximize product quality, reliable manufacturing processes, and sound marketing practices. • Reduces the risk that knowledge and proprietary assets will be lost to competitors.	The Japanese MNE Toshiba: • Owns and operates factories in dozens of countries to manufacture laptop computers. • Controls its own manufacturing processes, ensuring quality output. • Ensures its marketing activities are carried out per headquarters' plan. • Retains key assets within the firm, such as leading-edge knowledge for producing the next generation of laptops.
Dunning's Eclectic Paradigm	• *Ownership-specific advantages*: The firm owns knowledge, skills, capabilities, processes, or physical assets. • *Location-specific advantages*: Factors in individual countries provide specific benefits, such as natural resources, skilled labor, low-cost labor, and inexpensive capital. • *Internalization advantages*: The firm benefits from internalizing foreign manufacturing, distribution, or other value-chain activities.	Provides various advantages relative to competitors, including the ability to own, control, and optimize value-chain activities—R&D, production, marketing, sales distribution, after-sales service, as well as relationships with customers and key contacts—performed at the most beneficial locations worldwide.	The German MNE Siemens: • Owns factories at locations worldwide that provide optimal access to natural resources, as well as skilled and low-cost labor. • Leverages the knowledge base of its employees in 190 countries. • Internalizes a wide range of manufacturing activities in categories such as lighting, medical equipment, and transportation machinery.

EXHIBIT 5.10

Theoretical Perspectives on Why Firms Choose FDI

activities performed by independent suppliers in external markets with business activities it performs itself.

Another key reason companies internalize certain value-chain functions is to control proprietary knowledge critical to the development, production, and sale of their products and services. Because independent foreign companies are outside the MNE's direct control, they can acquire and exploit proprietary knowledge to their own advantage. They might even use the acquired knowledge to become competitors.[19]

Procter & Gamble initially considered exporting when it entered Japan. With exporting, P&G would have had to contract with an independent Japanese distributor to handle warehousing and marketing of its soap, diapers, and other products. Instead, P&G chose to enter Japan through FDI for three reasons: (1) trade barriers imposed by the Japanese government, (2) the strong market power of local Japanese firms, and (3) the risk of losing control over its proprietary knowledge. It established its own marketing subsidiary and national headquarters in Tokyo.

In the 1980s, Samsung followed a policy of exporting its products to Europe and North America. Management realized it could improve and speed up international operations by creating its own sales and production facilities in strategic markets. In the 1990s, Samsung internalized much of its production and distribution channels in Brazil, China, Mexico, and the United Kingdom. To ensure product quality, Samsung internalized production of semiconductors and circuit boards for use in making telecommunications equipment. The firm gradually transferred its manufacturing operations from Western to Eastern Europe to profit from lower-cost labor in the East. Samsung also produces various software through its subsidiary, Samsung R&D Institute in India.

Dunning's Eclectic Paradigm

Professor John Dunning proposed the eclectic paradigm as a framework to explain the extent and pattern of the value chain operations that companies should own abroad. He drew from various theories, including comparative advantage, factor proportions, monopolistic advantage, and internalization theory. The eclectic paradigm is often viewed as the most comprehensive of FDI theories.

The eclectic paradigm specifies three conditions that determine whether a company will internationalize through FDI:

- Ownership-specific advantages,
- Location-specific advantages, and
- Internalization advantages.

Let's explain each condition in turn.

Ownership-specific advantages An MNE should hold knowledge, skills, capabilities, key relationships, and other advantages that it owns and that allow it to compete effectively in foreign markets. To ensure international success, the firm's competitive advantage must be substantial enough to offset the costs that it incurs in establishing and operating foreign operations. It should also be specific to its own organization and not readily transferable to other firms. Competitive advantage may incorporate proprietary technology, managerial skills, trademarks or brand names, economies of scale, or access to substantial financial resources. The more valuable the firm's ownership-specific advantages, the more likely it is to internationalize by FDI.

Alcoa has 60,000 employees in 35 countries. The company's integrated operations include bauxite mining and aluminum refining. Its products include primary aluminum (which it refines from bauxite), automotive components, and sheet aluminum for beverage cans and Reynolds Wrap®. One of Alcoa's most important ownership-specific advantages is the proprietary technology it has acquired through its R&D activities. It has also acquired special managerial and marketing skills in the production and marketing of refined aluminum. The firm has a well-known brand name that facilitates sales. As a large firm, Alcoa also profits from economies of scale and the ability to finance expensive projects. These advantages have allowed Alcoa to generate maximal profits from its international operations.

Location-specific advantages The second condition that determines whether a firm will internationalize by FDI is the presence of location-specific advantages. These are the comparative advantages available in individual foreign countries that may be translated into firm competitive advantages. These may include natural resources, skilled labor, low-cost labor, or inexpensive capital. Alcoa located refineries in Brazil because of Brazil's huge deposits of bauxite, a mineral found in relatively few other locations. The Amazon and other major rivers in Brazil generate huge amounts of hydroelectric power, which is a critical ingredient in electricity-intensive aluminum refining. Alcoa also benefits from Brazil's low-cost, relatively well-educated laborers who work in the firm's refineries. The presence of these location-specific advantages helped persuade Alcoa to locate in Brazil through FDI.

Internalization advantages The third condition that determines FDI-based internalization is the presence of internalization advantages. The firm gains these benefits from internalizing foreign-based manufacturing, distribution, or other value chain activities. When profitable, the firm will transfer its ownership-specific advantages across national borders within its own organization rather than dissipating them to independent, foreign entities. The FDI decision depends on which is the best option—internalization versus using external partners and whether they are licensees, distributors, or suppliers. Internalization advantages include the ability to control how the firm's products are produced or marketed, greater control of its proprietary knowledge, and greater buyer certainty about product value.[20]

With Alcoa, the firm had five reasons to internalize many of its operations instead of letting external suppliers handle them. First, management was concerned about minimizing the dissemination of proprietary knowledge, specifically its aluminum-refining operations—knowledge the firm acquired at great expense. Second, internalization provides the best net return, allowing Alcoa to minimize the cost of operations. Third, Alcoa needs to control sales of its aluminum products to avoid depressing world aluminum prices through oversupply. Fourth, the firm wants to be able to apply a differential pricing strategy, charging different prices to different customers, a strategy it could not implement without controlling distribution. Finally, aluminum refining is complex, and Alcoa wants to maintain control of it to ensure product quality.

Non-FDI-Based Explanations

FDI became a popular entry mode with the rise of the MNE in the 1960s and 1970s. In the 1980s, firms began to recognize the importance of collaborative ventures and other flexible entry strategies.

INTERNATIONAL COLLABORATIVE VENTURES   A collaborative venture is a form of cooperation between two or more firms. There are two major types: equity-based *joint ventures* that result in a new legal entity and non-equity-based (project-based) strategic alliances in which the firms' partner, for a finite duration, to collaborate on projects related to R&D, design, manufacturing, or any other value-adding activity. In both cases, collaborating firms pool resources and capabilities and generate synergy. In other words, collaboration allows the partners to carry out activities that each might be unable to perform on its own. Collaborating firms share the risk of their joint efforts, which reduces vulnerability for any one partner.

Collaboration is critical in international business. A firm sometimes has no choice but to partner with other companies to gain access to resources and capabilities unavailable within its own organization. In addition, occasionally a government will restrict companies from entering its national market through wholly owned FDI. For example, the Mexican government prohibits foreign firms from attaining full ownership of ventures in its domestic oil industry because oil is critical to Mexico's economy. Where such restrictions exist, the firm may have no choice but to collaborate with a foreign partner to enter the market.[21]

A collaborative venture can give a company access to foreign partners' expertise, capital, distribution channels, marketing assets, or the ability to overcome government-imposed obstacles. By collaborating, the firm can position itself better to create new products and enter new markets. For example, Starbucks now boasts more than 1,000 coffee shops in Japan, thanks to a joint venture with its local partner, Sazaby League, Ltd. The venture allowed Starbucks to internationalize and navigate the marketplace with the help of a knowledgeable local partner.[22]

NETWORKS AND RELATIONAL ASSETS   Networks and relational assets represent the economically beneficial long-term *relationships* the firm undertakes with other business entities. These include manufacturers, distributors, suppliers, retailers, consultants, banks, transportation suppliers, governments, and any other organization that can provide needed capabilities. Firm-level relational assets represent a distinct competitive advantage in international business. Japanese keiretsu, complex groupings of firms with interlinked ownership and trading relationships that foster inter-firm organizational learning, are their predecessors.[23] Like the keiretsu, networks are neither formal organizations with clearly defined hierarchical structures nor impersonal, decentralized markets.

The International Marketing and Purchasing (IMP) research consortium in Europe (www.impgroup.org) has driven much of the theory development on networks.[24] Network theory was proposed to compensate for the inability of traditional organizational theories to account for much that goes on in business markets.[25] In networks, buyers and sellers become bound to one another through continuous exchanges and linkages of products, services, finance, technology, and knowledge. Continued interaction among the partners results in stable relationships based on cooperation and creates value and competitive advantage even among competitors. Network linkages represent a key route by which many companies expand their business abroad, develop new markets, and develop new products. In international business, mutually beneficial and enduring strategic relationships provide real advantages to partners and reduce uncertainty and transaction costs.

Samsung Corporation has many network connections that provide substantial benefits. The firm produces cell phones and telecommunications equipment with various partners in China. It is also well connected in the Korean financial sector. Network relationships with the Korean Industrial Bank and Korea Commercial Bank have provided Samsung with much of the financing it needs to conduct R&D and perform other key value-chain activities. In short, Samsung's network and relational assets have been critical to its success.

As we'll see later in this book, in the contemporary global economy, many firms have shied away from making permanent, direct investments in host countries. Instead, many firms now opt for more-flexible collaborative ventures or other relationships with independent business partners abroad.

CLOSING CASE   Hyundai: Leading the Way in the Global Auto Industry

The automotive industry is one of the largest and most internationalized business sectors. Some 20 major global automotive companies produce more than one million cars a year. Hyundai Motor Company is South Korea's leading automotive manufacturer and, based on the number of cars sold, the fifth largest in the world after Toyota, Volkswagen, GM, and Renault-Nissan. In 2014, the company sold about eight million vehicles globally. Its global market share was about 10 percent based on the number of vehicles manufactured in 2013. It sells vehicles in 187 countries, producing about a dozen car and minivan models, plus trucks, buses, and other commercial vehicles. Popular models in the United States are the Accent and Sonata, whereas exports to Europe and Asia include the GRD and Equus.

The Industry

During the recent global recession, global automotive sales declined to near-record lows. Automotive industry profits suffered due to significant excess production capacity. Although there is capacity to produce 80 million cars worldwide, total global demand fell to only about 60 million. Global automobile production reached to 90 million cars and commercial vehicles in 2014. A wave of consolidations followed across the globe in light of the excess capacity. Hyundai acquired a 34 percent interest in Kia Motors, then Korea's second largest automaker. Indian Tata Motors acquired Jaguar and Land Rover from Ford Company for $2.3 billion. In 2010, Ford Motor sold its Volvo brand to a Chinese automobile company, Zhejiang Geely Holding Group.

Consistent with the new trade theory, the required scale compels automakers to target world markets also, where they can achieve economies of scale and maximize sales. In 2015, for example, Ford announced it is building two new production facilities in Mexico. Beginning in 2016, Hyundai will expand production in China by building two additional plants there.

The Industry in South Korea

Despite its large size, the motor vehicle market in South Korea (Korea) is insufficient to sustain indigenous automakers such as

Hyundai. Korea holds numerous competitive advantages in the car industry. The country is a world center of new technology development. It has many cost-effective knowledge workers who drive innovations in design, features, production, and product quality. The country also has a high savings rate, with massive inward FDI, which ensures a ready supply of capital for carmakers to fund R&D and other ventures. Collectively, Korea's abundance of production factors in cost-effective labor, knowledge workers, high technology, and capital represent key location-specific advantages.

Korean consumers are demanding, so carmakers take great pains to produce high-quality automobiles. Intense rivalry in the domestic auto industry ensures that carmakers and auto parts producers improve products continuously.

The Korean economy is dominated by several conglomerates, called *chaebols*. They include Hyundai, Samsung, LG, and SK, of which Samsung Group and the Hyundai Motor Group accounted for more than 33 percent of South Korea's GDP in 2012. The Korean government has imposed stringent accounting controls on many of these firms. The government cooperates closely with the business sector, protecting some industries, ensuring funds for others, and sponsoring still others. The government promoted imports of raw materials and technology at the expense of consumer goods and encouraged savings and investment over consumption. Partly due to these efforts, Korea is home to a substantial industrial cluster for the production of cars and car parts. The nation benefits from the presence of numerous suppliers and manufacturers in the global automotive industry.

Background on Hyundai

Chung Ju-yung, a visionary entrepreneur from a peasant background, founded the Hyundai Engineering and Construction Company in 1947 and, 20 years later, Hyundai Motor Company. By the 1970s, the firm had begun an aggressive effort to develop engineering capabilities and new designs in the auto industry. In 1986, Hyundai began exporting the Excel, an economy car priced at $4,995, to the United States. An instant success, the car model sold more than one million units globally. However, the Excel suffered from quality issues and a weak dealer network. Buyer confidence waned in the late 1990s. In response, Hyundai initiated intensive quality improvement programs and introduced a 10-year warranty feature to its customers. This was unprecedented in the auto industry at the time. It was a major turning point for the firm.

Geographic Diversification

In 1997, Hyundai built a car factory in Turkey, giving the firm convenient access to key markets in the Middle East and Europe. Next, Hyundai opened a plant each in China and India. The firm also established a plant for commercial vehicles through a 50–50 joint venture with Guangzhou Motor Group in China. In addition to gaining access to low-cost, high-quality labor in emerging markets, Hyundai hopes its presence in local showrooms will improve consumer awareness and drive new sales.

Hyundai uses FDI to cultivate markets around the world. Management chooses locations based on the advantages they bring to the firm and has substantial production facilities in Brazil, China, the Czech Republic, India, Russia, Turkey, and the United States. Hyundai also has R&D centers in Europe, Japan, and North America. It has distribution centers and marketing subsidiaries at various locations that deliver parts to its expanding base of car dealers worldwide. Hyundai also has regional headquarters in Asia, Europe, and North America. To guarantee control over production and marketing, the firm has internalized many of its operations.

To remain competitive, Hyundai employs inexpensive, high-quality labor. Engines, tires, and other key inputs are sourced from low-cost suppliers. The firm has entered various collaborative ventures to cooperate in R&D, design, manufacturing, and other value-adding activities. These allow Hyundai access to foreign partners' expertise, capital, distribution channels, marketing assets, and the ability to overcome government-imposed obstacles. For example, Hyundai enjoys a partnership with Shell to improve supply chain management. Compared to Japanese or Western rivals, Hyundai has superior cost advantages in the acquisition of high-quality inputs.

Although Japanese auto giants such as Toyota and Honda rely heavily on U.S. sales for their profits, Hyundai is more diversified. In 2014, North America accounted for 36 percent of Hyundai's exports, followed by the Middle East and Africa markets. Total global sales increased about 5.8 percent, and Kia, the affiliate of Hyundai Motor Group, increased its presence in China and North America. Europe accounted for only 9 percent of Hyundai's sales in 2014.

Recent Events

Hyundai continues to launch new marketing campaigns and replaced General Motors as the official automotive sponsor of the Academy Awards. Hyundai's Elantra model was named the North American Car of the Year at the 2012 Detroit Auto Show, and the Hyundai Genesis was a finalist for the award in 2015. To boost sales in Canada, the company launched an advertising campaign in 2015 called The H-Factor as part of its new brand positioning strategy. The company's Assurance Program, by which buyers can return their recently purchased cars if they lose their job within one year of purchase, also appeals to buyers.

Hyundai has pursued internationalization aggressively, and whereas many global firms struggle to stay afloat, Hyundai is seeking to expand. Hyundai saw the global recession as an opportunity. It improved quality and increased sales against all odds. Given its focus on quality, energy efficiency, cost control, and customer satisfaction, perhaps Hyundai is the new standard-bearer in the global auto industry.

AACSB: Reflective Thinking Skills, Analytic Skills, Multiculturalism, and Diversity

Case Questions

5-4. What are the roles of comparative and competitive advantages in Hyundai's success? Illustrate your answers by providing specific examples of natural and acquired advantages that Hyundai employs to succeed in the global automotive industry.

5-5. In terms of factor proportions theory, what abundant factors does Hyundai leverage in its worldwide operations? Provide examples and explain how Hyundai exemplifies the theory. In what ways does Hyundai's success contradict the theory? Justify your answer.

5-6. Discuss Hyundai and its position in the global car industry in terms of the determinants of national competitiveness. What are the relationships of the roles of demand conditions; factor conditions; related and supporting industries; and firm strategy, structure, and rivalry to Hyundai's international success?

5-7. The Korean government has been instrumental to Hyundai's success. In terms of national industrial policy, what has the government done to support Hyundai? What can the government do to encourage future success at Hyundai? What can the government in your country do to support development or maintenance of a strong auto industry?

5-8. Consistent with Dunning's eclectic paradigm, describe the ownership-specific advantages, location-specific advantages, and internalization advantages Hyundai holds. Which of these advantages do you believe has been most instrumental to the firm's success? Justify your answer.

Sources: "Hyundai to Build Fourth & Fifth Chinese Plants," *Automotive Manufacturing Solutions*, March/April 2015, p. 11; "2012 Hyundai Elantra: Why it Won Car of the Year Award," *International Business Times*, January 9, 2012, www.ibtimes.com; "Hyundai Motor Company," *Hoover's Company Records*, 2015, http://www.hoovers.com; "2014 Production Statistics," OICA, 2015, http://oica.net; Chris Reiter, "The Contender," *Bloomberg Businessweek*, January 30, 2012, pp. 21–22; In-Soo Nam, "Hyundai Plans to Expand in China," *Wall Street Journal*, December 31, 2014, p. B3; Gabe Nelson, "New Product, New Marketing Are Key for Hyundai," *Automotive News*, January 25, 2015, p. S006; *New York Times*, "Tata Motors Finds Success in Jaguar Land Rover," August 30, 2012, http://www.nytimes.com/2012/08/31/business/global/tata-motors-finds-success-in-jaguar-land-rover.html; Reuters, "Peugeot Citroen CEO Says Will Build Minicar with Toyota," September 19, 2013, http://www.reuters.com/article/2013/09/19/us-toyota-peugeot-idUSBRE98I0U220130919; Hyundai Motor Company, worldwide.hyundai.com/WW/Corporate/CorporateInformation/History, retrieved May 3, 2015.

Note: This case initially was written by Nukhet Vardar, Yeditepe University, Turkey, and updated by Carol Sánchez, Grand Valley State University, Michigan, and by Ilke Kardes, Georgia State University.

END OF CHAPTER REVIEW

MyManagementLab

Go to **mymanagementlab.com** to complete the problems marked with this icon .

Key Terms

Summary

In this chapter, you learned about:

- **Why nations trade.**

  Each nation specializes in producing certain goods and services and then trades with other nations to acquire those goods and services in which it is not specialized. Classic explanations of international trade began with **mercantilism**, which argued that nations should seek to maximize their wealth by exporting more than they import. The **absolute advantage principle** argues that a country benefits by producing only those products in which it has absolute advantage or can produce using fewer resources than another country. The principle of **comparative advantage** contends that countries should specialize and export those goods in which they have a relative advantage compared to other countries. Comparative advantage is based on *natural advantages* and *acquired advantages*. **Competitive advantage** derives from distinctive assets or competencies of a firm, such as cost, size, or innovation strengths, which are difficult for competitors to replicate or imitate. *Factor proportions theory* holds that nations specialize in the production of goods and services whose factors of production they hold in abundance. *International product life cycle theory* describes how a product can be invented in one country and eventually mass-produced in other countries, with the innovating country losing its initial competitive advantage.

- **How nations enhance their competitive advantage.**

  A major recent contribution to trade theory is Porter's determinants of national competitive advantage, which specify the four conditions in each nation that give rise to national competitive advantages: *demand conditions; firm strategy, structure, and rivalry; factor conditions;* and *related and supporting industries*. An **industrial cluster** is a concentration of companies in the same industry in a given location that interact closely with one another, gaining mutual competitive advantage. Competitive advantage of nations describes how nations acquire international trade advantages by developing specific skills, technologies, and industries. **National industrial policy** refers to governments' efforts to direct national resources to developing expertise in specific industries.

- **Why and how firms internationalize.**

  The *internationalization process model* describes how companies expand into international business gradually, usually progressing from simple exporting to the most committed stage, FDI. Born global firms internationalize at or near their founding and are part of the emergent field of international entrepreneurship.

- **How internationalizing firms can gain and sustain competitive advantage.**

  MNEs have value chains that span geographic locations worldwide. Foreign direct investment means that firms invest at various locations to establish factories, marketing subsidiaries, or regional headquarters. *Monopolistic advantage theory* describes how companies succeed internationally by developing resources and capabilities that few other firms possess. Internalization is the process of acquiring and maintaining one or more value-chain activities inside the firm to minimize the disadvantages of subcontracting these activities to external firms. **Internalization theory** explains the tendency of MNEs to internalize value-chain stages when it is to their advantage. The *eclectic paradigm* specifies that the international firm should possess certain internal competitive advantages, called *ownership-specific advantages, location-specific advantages*, and *internalization advantages*. Many companies engage in international *collaborative ventures*, inter-firm partnerships that give them access to assets and other advantages foreign partners hold.

Test Your Comprehension AACSB: Reflective Thinking Skills, Analytic Skills

5-9. Describe the classic theories of international trade. Which theories do you believe are relevant today?

5-10. How does factor proportions theory compare to international product life cycle theory?

5-11. Summarize factor proportions theory. What factors are most abundant in China, Japan, Germany, Saudi Arabia, and the United States? Visit globalEDGE™ for helpful information.

5-12. What are the main sources of national competitive advantage? Think about a successful product in your country; what are the sources of competitive advantage that explain its success?

5-13. Do you believe your country should adopt a national industrial policy? Why or why not?

5-14. There is a tendency for organizations to move from simple exporting operations to FDI over a period of time. Why is this often the case? What might slow or stop the process?

⭐ **5-15.** Industrial clusters can be valuable tools for a country's economy. Identify three global examples and describe their development. Do not choose your own country.

⭐ **5-16.** Are collaborative ventures the best option when a business has little knowledge of the market?

Apply Your Understanding AACSB: Reflective Thinking Skills, Analytic Skills, Communication Abilities, Ethical Understanding and Reasoning Abilities

5-17. South Africa is home to huge reserves of coal, gold, diamonds, and natural gas. In addition to their intrinsic value, gold and diamonds have many industrial uses, and precious-mineral mining has transformed South Africa into a major emerging market economy. To handle international shipping, the government developed major ports that connect South Africa to markets worldwide. South Africa is also home to a large pool of low-wage workers in mining and related industries. The government has devised a collection of plans that support specific industries, especially mining. These developments support a cluster of highly specialized firms in the mining and extractive industries. Some of the world's most knowledgeable firms in these industries are concentrated in South Africa, especially De Beers SA (www.debeers.com), which has substantial capabilities in marketing and international strategy and a near-monopoly in the global diamond industry. The firm collaborates with MNEs that hold major financial resources. Use the theories discussed in this chapter to explain the advantages South Africa and De Beers hold. What insights emerge from these theories that shed light on South Africa and De Beers?

5-18. Economist Lester Thurow once posed the question, "If you were the president of your own country and could specialize in one of two industries, computer chips or potato chips, which would you choose?" When faced with this question, many people choose potato chips, because "everybody can use potato chips, but not everybody can use computer chips." However, the answer is much more complex. Whether to choose computer chips or potato chips depends on such factors as the relationship between national wealth and the amount of value added in manufacturing products, the possibility that the country can benefit from monopoly power (few countries can make computer chips), and the likelihood of spin-off industries (computer chip technology gives rise to other technologies, such as computers). In light of these and other possible considerations, which would you choose, computer chips or potato chips? Justify your answer.

5-19. *Ethical Dilemma:* To reduce poverty in Africa, government officials want to increase African exports to Europe. Africa's top exports include agricultural products, such as meat, coffee, peanuts, and fruit, and many Africans depend on food exports for their livelihood. However, the European Union (EU) imposes high trade barriers on the import of agricultural products. Among various reasons, Europeans are concerned about food quality, and the EU has adopted rigorous agricultural safety standards. However, the tough regulations hurt African countries, which have experienced problems with food toxins and bovine diseases in the past. In addition, the agricultural lobby in Europe is powerful, and the EU subsidizes farmers heavily. Many European politicians do not want to risk angering Europe's farm lobby by supporting free international trade in agricultural products. Suppose you are part of an EU government task force investigating trade barriers on African agricultural imports. Using the ethical framework in Chapter 4, analyze the arguments for and against agricultural trade with Africa. What should the EU do? Justify your answer.

globalEDGE | INTERNET EXERCISES
(www.globalEDGE.msu.edu)

AACSB: Analytic Skills, Use of Information Technology

Refer to Chapter 1, page 54, for instructions on how to access and use globalEDGE™.

5-20. Suppose your company is interested in importing wines from Argentina. In analyzing this opportunity, you want to identify the strengths and weaknesses of the Argentine wine industry. What are the conditions that make Argentina a favorable location for wine cultivation? Provide a short description of the status of Argentina's wine exports and a list of the top importing countries of Argentine wines. In addition to globalEDGE™, some useful websites for this research include www.winesofargentina.org and www.ita.doc.gov.

5-21. Volvo (www.volvo.com) and Pilkington (www.pilkington.com) are major multinational firms with operations that span the globe. Investigate these firms by visiting their websites as well as www.hoovers.com (a site that provides specific company information) and globalEDGE™. For each company, describe its ownership-specific advantages, location-specific advantages, and internalization advantages.

5-22. The World Bank works to alleviate world poverty and provides information about conditions in developing countries, which it uses to measure progress in economic and social development. World Development Indicators (www.worldbank.org/data) is the Bank's premier source for data on international development. The Bank measures more than 800 indicators of national conditions regarding people, environment, and economy. Consult the website, click World Development Indicators or Indicators, and answer the following questions: (a) In countries with developing economies, what indicators are most associated with poverty? (b) What types of industries are most typically found in poor countries? (c) Based on comparing development indicators in poor and affluent countries, speculate on what types of actions governments in developing countries can take to help spur economic development and alleviate poverty.

CAREER TOOLBOX

What is a CKR Career Skills Toolbox exercise?

Career Skills Toolbox is a practical exercise designed to familiarize you with key managerial challenges and decisions that professionals typically encounter in international business. Completing Career Skills Toolbox exercises in this text enables you to acquire practical, real-world skills that will help you perform well in your career. Each exercise presents a managerial challenge presented as a real-world scenario, the skills you will acquire in solving the exercise, and a methodology and the resources to use in solving it. The second half of the exercise is provided at the Pearson MyManagementLab website (mymanagementlab.com).

Career Toolbox Porter's Diamond Model and Manufacturing

The principle of comparative advantage suggests that every country possesses distinctive resources that give it advantages in the production of specific products. Michael Porter's diamond model in his book, *Competitive Advantage of Nations*, argues that nations become adept at certain industries due to the presence of certain resources and four conditions: demand conditions; firm strategy, structure, and rivalry; factor conditions; and related and supporting industries. Firms establish production facilities in those countries where they can obtain the most favorable resources and advantages.

When locating value-chain activities abroad, management should try to ascertain the best location for each activity. A good approach is to identify the factors that most influence company success (which tends to vary by industry) and then conduct research to find countries that offer the best combination of these factors.

In this exercise, you will gain an understanding of the factors to consider when locating company operations, learn how these factors relate to maximizing the firm's competitive advantage, and gain research skills for acquiring knowledge for planning company operations.

Background

Choosing the best foreign location for manufacturing provides numerous advantages, including the ability to minimize manufacturing costs, maximize the quality of produced goods, and access the best factors of production and technological resources. For example, Hoya Company, which makes eyeglass lenses, established its main factory in the Netherlands to be close to Europe's superior technology in the lens-making industry. Intel established an R&D center in Taiwan to access Taiwan's engineers and other superior knowledge in the microprocessor industry.

In this exercise, you will use the elements in Porter's diamond model to conduct research online to identify the best countries to establish a manufacturing plant in each of the following industries: dress shoes, flat-screen televisions, and pharmaceutical drugs. The diamond model states that competitive advantage results from the existence and quality in a country of four major elements.

- *Demand conditions* refer to the nature of home-market demand for specific products and services. The presence of highly demanding buyers pressures firms to innovate faster and produce better products. For example, U.S. consumers have strong spending power and suffer from various health conditions. This situation has led the United States to become one of the leading producers of patent medications and medical technology. Canadians have much experience driving in the snow in rugged conditions, which makes them demanding consumers of four-wheel-drive trucks and sport utility vehicles. Hence, Canada is a superior location for producing such products.

- *Firm strategy, structure, and rivalry* refer to the nature of domestic rivalry and conditions in a nation that govern how companies are created, organized, and managed. Here the focus is on the presence of strong competitors in the nation. When a country has numerous competitors in the same industry, the level of technology, resources, and factors of production in the nation will be relatively advanced. For example, Japan is home to some of the world's leading firms in the air conditioning industry. Constant competitive rivalry continuously pressures these firms to innovate and improve. The firms in Japan's air conditioning industry compete for managerial talent, technical leadership, and superior product quality, factors that have reached a high level in the industry in Japan.

- *Factor conditions* describe the nation's position in factors of production, such as labor, capital, infrastructure, science, and IT. Every country has more of certain factor endowments and less of others, a situation that determines the nature of national competitive advantages. For example, Germany's numerous workers with strong engineering skills have propelled the country to leadership in the global scientific instruments industry. Mexico's millions of low-wage workers have allowed the country to develop competitive advantage in the manufacture of labor-intensive industrial products, such as car parts.

- *Related and supporting industries* reflect the presence in the nation of clusters of suppliers, competitors, and complementary firms that excel in particular industries. The resulting business environment is highly supportive for the founding of particular types of firms. Operating within a mass of related and supporting industries provides advantages through information and knowledge synergies, economies of scale and scope, and access to appropriate or superior inputs. For example, Silicon Valley in California is home to hundreds of successful software companies, which collectively create synergies that make for a strong base in the industry. The southeastern part of China is a good place to locate a factory to manufacture office furniture because of the presence there of thousands of very knowledgeable firms and workers in that industry. One city in the region is the world capital of chair manufacturing with 210,000 chair workers. The firms in this industry exchange much useful knowledge about furniture manufacturing that accelerates new product development and innovations.

To complete this exercise in your MyLab, go to the Career Toolbox.

Note: Some material in this exercise is based on Michael Porter, *The Competitive Advantage of Nations* (New York: Free Press, 1990).

MyManagementLab

Go to **mymanagementlab.com** for Auto-graded writing questions as well as the following Assisted-graded writing questions.

⭐ **5-23.** Why do nations engage in international business? That is, what are the benefits of international trade and investment?

⭐ **5-24.** Summarize the international product life cycle theory. Use the theory to explain the international evolution of automobiles and laptop computers.

⭐ **5-25.** MyManagementLab Only—comprehensive writing assignment for this chapter.

Endnotes

1. John Romalis, "Factor Proportions and the Structure of Commodity Trade," *The American Economic Review* 94, No. 1 (2004), pp. 67–97; Robert Zymek, "Factor Proportions and the Growth of World Trade," *Journal of International Economics* 95, No.1 (2015), pp. 42–53.

2. Raymond Vernon, "International Investment and International Trade in the Product Cycle," *Quarterly Journal of Economics* 80 (May 1966), pp. 190–207.

3. Michael Porter, *The Competitive Advantage of Nations* (New York: Free Press, 1990).

4. Mourad Dakhli and Dirk De Clercq, "Human Capital, Social Capital, and Innovation: A Multi-Country Study," *Entrepreneurship and Regional Development* 16, No. 2 (2004), pp. 107–128; Jože Damijan and Crt Kostevc, "Learning from Trade Through Innovation," *Oxford Bulletin of Economics & Statistics* 77, No. 3 (2015), pp. 408-436.

5. Richard Nelson and Sidney Winter, *An Evolutionary Theory of Economic Change* (Cambridge, MA: Belknap Press, 1982).

6. Barry Jaruzelski and Kevin Dehoff, "Beyond Borders: The Global Innovation 1000," *Strategy Business* 53 (2008), pp. 52–67.

7. Richard Dobbs, Jeremy Oppenheim, and Fraser Thompson, "Mobilizing for a Resource Revolution," *McKinsey Quarterly*, January 2012, www.mckinseyquarterly.com.

8. Kurt Badenhausen, "Best Countries for Business," *Forbes*, October 3, 2011, www.forbes.com; *Country Reports: New Zealand: New Zealand Country Monitor* (Lexington, MA: HIS Global, 2014).

9. Warren Bilkey, "An Attempted Integration of the Literature on the Export Behavior of Firms," *Journal of International Business Studies* 9 (Summer 1978), pp. 3–46; S. Tamer Cavusgil, "On the Internationalization Process of Firms," *European Research* 8, No. 6 (1980), pp. 27–81; Jan Johanson and Jan-Erik Vahlne, "The Internationalization Process of the Firm—A Model of Knowledge Development and Increasing Foreign Commitments," *Journal of International Business Studies* 8 (Spring/Summer 1977), pp. 2–32.

10. Ibid.

11. Samsung, *Samsung History*, 2014, http://www.samsung.com/us/aboutsamsung/corporateprofile/history04.html; Dae-Oup Chang, "Samsung," (2014) http://www.amrc.org.hk/system/files/Labour%20in%20Globalising%20Asian%20Corps%20-20 Chap%201-2.pdf.

12. G. Knight and S. T. Cavusgil, "The Born Global Firm: A Challenge to Traditional Internationalization Theory," in *Advances in International Marketing*, vol. 8, ed. S. T. Cavusgil and T. Madsen (Greenwich, CT: JAI Press, 1996), pp. 11–26.

13. S. Tamer Cavusgil and Gary Knight, "The Born-Global Firm: An Entrepreneurial and Capabilities Perspective on Early and Rapid Internationalization," *Journal of International Business Studies* 46, No. 1 (2015), pp. 3–16; S. T. Cavusgil and Gary Knight, *Born Global Firms: A New International Enterprise* (New York: Business Expert Press, 2009); Gary Knight and S. T. Cavusgil, "Innovation, Organizational Capabilities, and the Born-Global Firm," *Journal of International Business Studies* 35, No. 2 (2004), pp. 12–41; Benjamin Oviatt and Patricia McDougall, "Toward a Theory of International New Ventures," *Journal of International Business Studies* 25, No. 1 (1994), pp. 4–64; Michael Rennie, "Born Global," *McKinsey Quarterly* No. 4 (1993), pp. 4–52.

14. Jessi Hempel, "Instagram Is Ready to Take Its Shot," *Fortune*, July 21, 2014, pp. 72–78; Lauren Johnson, "Instagram Will Hit 100 Million U.S. Users by 2018," *Adweek*, March 6, 2015, p. 1; Ingrid Lunden, "Instagram Is the Fastest-Growing Social Site Globally," *TechCrunch*, January 21, 2014, retrieved 4/28/15 at http://techcrunch.com/2014/01/21/instagram-is-the-fastest-growing-social-site-globally-mobile-devices-rule-over-pcs-for-social-access.

15. Marian Jones, Nicole Coviello, and Yee Kwan Tang, "International Entrepreneurship Research (1989–2009): A Domain Ontology and Thematic Analysis," *Journal of Business Venturing*, 26 No. 6, (2011), pp. 632–659; Patricia McDougall and Benjamin Oviatt, "International Entrepreneurship: The Intersection of Two Research Paths," *Academy of Management Journal*, 43 No. 5 (2000), pp. 902–906.

16. UNCTAD, *World Investment Report 2011* (New York: United Nations, 2011), accessed January 29, 2012 at http://www.unctad.org/templates/WebFlyer.asp? intItemID=6018&lang=1.

17. Ibid.

18. Dae-Oup Chang (2014); Samsung (2014); Stephen Hymer, *The International Operations of National Firms* (Cambridge, MA: MIT Press, 1976).

19. Peter Buckley and Mark Casson, *The Future of the Multinational Enterprise* (London: MacMillan, 1976); John Dunning, "The Eclectic Paradigm of International Production: A Restatement and Some Possible Extensions," *Journal of International Business Studies*, 19 (1988), pp. 1–31.

20. John Dunning, "The Eclectic Paradigm of International Production: A Restatement and Some Possible Extensions," *Journal of International Business Studies*, 19 (1988), pp. 1–31.

21. John Dunning, *International Production and the Multinational Enterprise* (London: Allen and Unwin, 1981); Bruce Kogut, "Joint Ventures: Theoretical and Empirical Perspectives," *Strategic Management Journal* 9 (1988), pp. 319–332; P. Rajan Varadarajan and Margaret H. Cunningham, "Strategic Alliances: A Synthesis of Conceptual Foundations," *Journal of the Academy of Marketing Science* 23 (1995), pp. 282–296.

22. "For Starbucks, There's No Place Like Home," *BusinessWeek*, June 9, 2003, p. 48; Lauren Gensler, "Piping Hot: Starbucks Sales Rise 18%," *Forbes.com*, April 23, 2015, p. 13.

23. James Lincoln, Christina Ahmadjian, and Eliot Mason, "Organizational Learning and Purchase-Supply Relations in Japan," *California Management Review* 40, No. 3 (1998), pp. 244–264.

24. Hakan Hakansson, *International Marketing and Purchasing of Industrial Goods: An Interaction Approach* (New York: Wiley, 1982).

25. Ibid.

Chapter 6

Political and Legal Systems in National Environments

Learning Objectives *After studying this chapter, you should be able to:*

6.1 Distinguish political and legal environments in international business.

6.2 Understand political systems.

6.3 Understand legal systems.

6.4 Know the participants in political and legal systems.

6.5 Identify the types of country risk produced by political systems.

6.6 Identify the types of country risk produced by legal systems.

6.7 Know about managing country risk.

Risks in Russia's Political and Legal Systems

Paying bribes to gain favors, whether small or large amounts, is commonplace in many countries. In Russia, it is not unusual for business people to make payments to facilitate business, and some bribes exceed U.S. $100,000, enough to buy a small flat in Moscow. Survey data suggests that most Russians consider paying bribes a normal cost of doing business.

Counterfeiting is also a problem. Take a walk through the open-air markets in Moscow, and you will likely find vendors selling pirated software, music, and movies. Russian police are aware of these products but usually do not issue fines or arrest the sellers. Some corrupt officers even get a cut of the vendors' total sales.

Country risk and a confusing legal system are serious business impediments in Russia. President Vladimir Putin even remarked that anyone who successfully registers a business in Russia deserves a medal. Vague and overlapping regulations enrich a host of public officials. Any new venture may necessitate dozens of government licenses, and each license may require paying a bribe.

Russia's political system remains volatile. There are countless incidents of strong-handed government interference in the private sector. Criminal raiders, sometimes in collaboration with government officials, have seized independently operating businesses. One example is Yukos, an oil company once controlled by the Russian industrialist Mikhail Khodorkovsky, whom the government imprisoned for alleged tax evasion. Claiming that Yukos owed back taxes, Russia's government sold part of the firm and kept the $9.3 billion in proceeds.

Organized crime is also part of the difficult landscape. The deputy chairman of Russia's central bank was shot dead in Moscow. He was trying to reform a corrupt banking

Source: filtv/Fotolia

system and had closed dozens of banks linked to organized crime. Other contract killings have occurred as criminal organizations have attempted to maintain their stronghold on much of Russia's economy. Criminal groups are believed to control some large Russian firms. Foreign MNEs routinely perform background checks on employees and contractors to identify people linked to organized crime. Foreign companies provide for the security of staff and facilities.

Many direct investors hesitate to do business in Russia. Instability in Russia's legal environment has triggered much capital flight. Corruption and crime have raised doubts about Russia's evolving legal system and its commitment to market economics. Ambiguous regulations, inadequate laws, and capricious enforcement pose important challenges. Numerous firms, from Boeing to IKEA, have invested billions in Russia. Potential rewards are promising for firms that plan ahead and protect their assets.

Questions

6-1. What is the nature of country and political risk in Russia?

6-2. How does country risk and corruption affect starting a business in Russia?

6-3. Why do foreign businesses hesitate to invest in Russia?

SOURCES: Andrew Barber, "Wealthy Russians Seek New Havens amid Sanctions, Legal Pressure," *Institutional Investor*, April 6, 2015, p. 1; "Emerging Europe Monitor," *Russia & CIS* (Business Monitor International, May 2015); "Russia Economy: Grease My Palm," *EIU ViewsWire*, November 28, 2008, p. 1; Luminita Ionescu, "Contemporary Economic Crime and Corruption in Russia," *Economics, Management & Financial Markets* 6, No. 2 (2011), pp. 137–142; "Russia: Corporate Raiding Challenges Investors," *Oxford Analytica Daily Brief Service*, August 21, 2008, p. 1; A. Kouznetsov and M. Dass, "Areas of Corruption in the Distribution of Foreign-Made Goods Where a Firm's Size and Origin Play a Role: The Russian Experience," *Journal of East-West Business* 16, No. 1 (2010), pp. 24–44; C. Matlack and M. Elder, "The Peril and Promise of Investing in Russia," *BusinessWeek*, October 5, 2009, pp. 48–52.

Most of us expect a familiar business landscape when we conduct business at home. Yet foreign markets differ in terms of political and legal systems as well as business norms. As illustrated by the opening case, foreign markets often pose major challenges and create vulnerabilities for the firm. Managers must be able to navigate difficult regulations and practices and avoid unethical or questionable conduct.

At the same time, the political and legal context may also present opportunities for companies. Preferential subsidies, government incentives, and protection from competition reduce business costs and influence strategic decision making. Many governments encourage domestic investment from foreign MNEs by offering tax holidays and cash incentives to employ local workers.

Country risk

Exposure to potential loss or adverse effects on company operations and profitability caused by developments in a country's political and/or legal environments.

Country risk is defined as exposure to potential loss or adverse effects on company operations and profitability caused by developments in a country's political and/or legal environments. Sometimes termed *political risk*, it is one of four major types of international business risks introduced in Chapter 1. Although the immediate cause of country risk is a political or legal factor, underlying such factors may be economic, social, or technological developments. Exhibit 6.1 identifies dimensions of country risk prevalent in international business. We address them in this chapter. Government intervention, protectionism, and barriers to trade and investment are particularly notable in international business. Mismanagement or failure of the national economy can lead to financial crises, recessions, market downturns, currency crises, and inflation. Such events usually arise from business cycles, poor monetary or fiscal policies, a defective regulatory environment, or imbalances in the underlying economic fundamentals of the host country.

Political or legislative actions can harm business interests, such as laws that are unexpectedly strict or result in unintended consequences. Many laws favor host-country interests—that is, interests in foreign countries where the firm has direct operations. For example, Coca-Cola's business suffered in Germany after the German government enacted a recycling plan that required consumers to return nonreusable soda containers to stores for a refund of 0.25 euros. Rather than coping with unwanted returns, big supermarket chains responded by yanking Coke from their shelves and pushing their own store brands instead. In China, the government censors

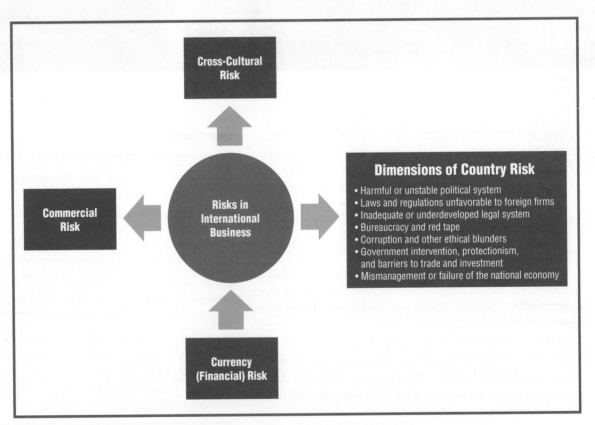

EXHIBIT 6.1

Country Risk as One of Four Major Risks in International Business

TV programs such as *Downton Abbey, House of Cards*, and *The Walking Dead*, whose content is considered inappropriate for Chinese citizens. Chinese authorities forbid the broadcast of Western shows that feature sex, violence, extramarital affairs, and content critical of the Chinese government.[1]

How Prevalent Is Country Risk?

Exhibit 6.2 presents the level of country risk in selected countries, measured as political stability, legal environment, economic indicators, and tax policy. Venezuela is dominated by an unpredictable, dictatorial government. Zimbabwe remains under the dictatorial rule of President Robert Mugabe. Afghanistan is risky in the wake of war and political instability. Such countries suffer from unstable governments, underdeveloped legal systems, or biased law enforcement. Conversely, countries such as Canada, Japan, and Singapore are characterized by stable, transparent, and well-founded political and legal systems. Exhibit 6.2 indicates that risk tends to be lower in countries with a favorable legal climate and political stability and higher in countries with political instability and substantial government intervention. Many of the riskiest states are poor countries that would benefit enormously from direct investment and integration into the world economy.[2] For the complete list of countries ranked by risk, visit the Risk Briefing site at the Economist Intelligence Unit (www.viewswire.eiu.com).

Country risk may affect all firms in a country equally or only a subset. Unrest in Egypt in 2011 tended to affect all firms. By contrast, the Russian government targeted only Yukos with politically motivated persecution, despite the presence of several competitors in Russia such as ConocoPhillips and Royal Dutch Shell.[3]

When they held power in India's government, Hindu nationalists openly opposed foreign investment and influence on Indian society and enacted laws that targeted foreign firms for harassment. The KFC restaurant chain stepped up security after local political groups threatened to destroy the firm's fast-food outlets. About one hundred farmers ransacked a KFC restaurant in Bangalore. ArcelorMittal, Nissan, and numerous other firms have faced delays in establishing operations in India due to government bureaucracy and Indian activist groups, which often oppose industrial development.[4]

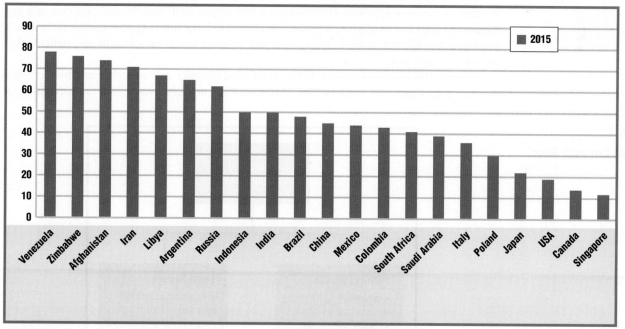

EXHIBIT 6.2

Country Risk in Selected Countries, 2015 (ranked 0 to 10; a high number indicates greater risk)

Source: Based on *Economist Intelligence Unit* (2015), "Risk Briefing," www.viewswire.eiu.com, and Euler Hermes Country Risk Ratings (2015), http://www.eulerhermes.com.

Political system
A set of formal institutions that constitute a government.

Legal system
A system for interpreting and enforcing laws.

Political and Legal Environments in International Business

A **political system** is a set of formal institutions that constitute a government. It includes legislative bodies, political parties, lobbying groups, and trade unions. The principal functions of a political system are to:

- Provide protection from external threats.
- Ensure stability based on laws.
- Govern the allocation of valued resources among the members of a society
- Define how a society's members interact with each other.

Each country's political system is unique, having evolved within a particular historical, economic, and cultural context. Political systems are also constantly evolving in response to constituent demands and the evolution of the national and international environments. *Constituents* are the people and organizations that support the political system and receive government resources.

A **legal system** is a system for interpreting and enforcing laws. Laws, regulations, and rules establish norms for conduct. A legal system includes institutions and procedures that:

- Ensure order,
- Resolve disputes in civil and commercial activities,
- Tax economic output.
- Provide protections for private property, including intellectual property and other company assets.

Exhibit 6.3 identifies the aspects of political and legal systems that contribute to country risk. Political and legal systems are dynamic and constantly changing. The two systems are interdependent—changes in one affect the other. Adverse developments in political and legal systems give rise to country risk. They can result from installation of a new government, shifting values or priorities in political parties, initiatives special interest groups develop, and the creation of new laws or regulations. Gradual change is easier for the firm to accommodate; sudden change is harder to deal with and poses greater risk to the firm.

Unfavorable developments give rise to new conditions that may threaten the firm's products, services, or business activities. For example, a new import tariff may increase the cost of a key component used to manufacture a product. A change in labor law may alter the hours the firm's employees are allowed to work. Installing a new political leader may lead to government takeover of corporate assets.

Country risk is *always* present, but its nature and intensity vary over time and from country to country. In China, for example, the government is currently overhauling the national legal

EXHIBIT 6.3
Sources of Country Risk

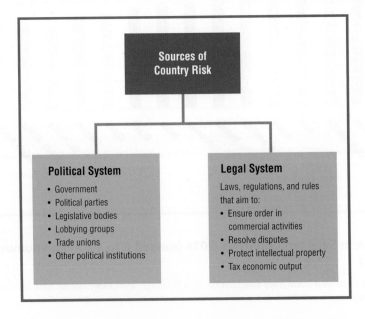

system, making it more harmonious with Western systems. Some new regulations have been poorly formulated or are confusing or contradictory. For example, at one point, the Beijing government announced that foreign investments in China's Internet industry were illegal. By this time, Western firms had already invested millions in the Chinese dot-com sector without knowing the investments were inappropriate. In disputes between local and foreign firms, governments are often inclined to protect local interests. Even where Western firms obtain favorable judgments in the courts, they may not be enforced. Let's delve into political and legal systems in more detail.

Political Systems

6.2 Understand political systems.

The world is characterized by three major types of political systems: totalitarianism, socialism, and democracy. Exhibit 6.4 highlights countries that exemplify these systems. These categories are not mutually exclusive. Most democracies also include some elements of socialism. Most former totalitarian regimes now embrace a mix of socialism and democracy. To address sluggish economic conditions, governments in Europe have implemented relatively socialistic policies such as nationalizing firms in the banking industry. China has applied some democratic approaches, such as land reforms and open markets, to stimulate commercial activity.

Totalitarianism

Well-known totalitarian states from the past include Nazi Germany (1933–1945), Spain (1939–1975), China (1949–1980s), and the Soviet Union (1918–1991). Under totalitarianism, the state attempts to regulate most aspects of public and private behavior. A totalitarian government seeks to control not only all economic and political matters but also the attitudes, values, and beliefs of the citizenry. Often, the entire population is mobilized in support of the state and a political or religious ideology. Totalitarian states are generally either theocratic (religion-based) or secular (non–religion-based). Usually there is a state party led by a dictator, such as Kim Jong-un in North Korea. Party membership is mandatory for those seeking to advance within the social and economic hierarchy. Power is maintained by means of secret police, propaganda disseminated through state-controlled mass media, regulation of free discussion and criticism, and the use of terror tactics. Totalitarian states usually do not tolerate activities by individuals or groups such as churches, labor unions, or political parties that are not directed toward the state's goals.[5]

Many totalitarian states have either disappeared or evolved toward democracy and capitalism. China initiated major reforms in the 1980s, and the Soviet Union collapsed in 1991. Agricultural land and state enterprises were sold to private interests, and entrepreneurs gained the right to establish their own businesses. The transition has not been easy, and former totalitarian states continue to maintain political control, including government intervention in business (as in Russia in the opening case). Former Soviet Union states and China are still characterized by substantial red tape and bureaucracy that hinder economic activity (for examples, see the World Bank's www.doingbusiness.org). Today, numerous states exhibit elements of totalitarianism, particularly in Africa, Asia, and the Middle East. Several countries are controlled by heads of state with substantial dictatorial powers, such as Omar al-Bashir in Sudan, Emomali Rahmon in Tajikistan, and Nicolas Maduro in Venezuela.

EXHIBIT 6.4

Examples of Countries Under Various Political Systems

Elements of Totalitarianism Found in	Elements of Socialism Found in	Largely Democratic
Cuba	Bolivia	Australia
North Korea	China	Canada
Several countries in Africa (such as Eritrea, Sudan, Equatorial Guinea, Zimbabwe)	Egypt	Japan
	India	New Zealand
	Romania	United States
	Russia	Most European countries
	Venezuela	Most Latin American countries

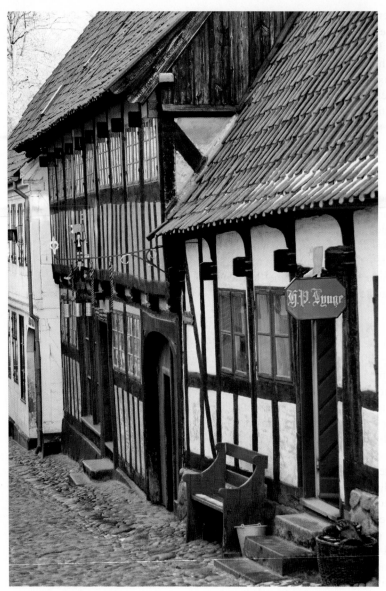

Source: Dhoxax/Shutterstock

By protecting private property rights, democracies promote entrepreneurship. The proprietors of these shops in Denmark enjoy the profits of their ownership.

Socialism

Socialism's fundamental principle is that capital and wealth should be vested in the state and used primarily as a means of production rather than for profit. Socialism is based on a collectivist ideology. Collective welfare of people is seen to outweigh the welfare of the individual. Socialists argue that capitalists receive a disproportionate amount of society's wealth relative to workers. They believe that in a capitalist society, the pay of workers does not represent the full value of their labor. They argue government should control the basic means of production, distribution, and commercial activity.

Socialism has manifested itself in much of the world as *social democracy* and has been most successful in Western Europe. It has also played a major role in the political systems of large countries such as Brazil and India. It remains a viable system in much of the world. Social democratic governments frequently intervene in the private sector and in business activities, as in Italy and Norway. Corporate income tax rates are often relatively high, as in France and Sweden. Even robust economies such as Germany have experienced net outflows of FDI as businesses seek to escape extensive regulation.

Democracy

Democracy is characterized by two major features:

- *Private property rights* Individuals can own property and assets and increase one's asset base by accumulating private wealth. Property includes tangibles, such as land and buildings, as well as intangibles, such as stocks, contracts, patent rights, and intellectual assets. Democratic governments devise laws that protect property rights. People and firms can acquire property, use it, buy or sell it, and bequeath it to whomever they want. These rights are important because they encourage individual initiative, ambition, and innovation as well as thrift and the desire to accumulate wealth. People are less likely to have these qualities if there is uncertainty about whether they can control their property or profit from it.

- *Limited government* The government performs essential functions that serve all citizens. These include national defense; maintenance of law and order and diplomatic relations; and constructing and maintaining infrastructure such as roads, schools, and public works. State control and intervention in the economic activities of private individuals or firms is minimal. By allowing market forces to determine economic activity, the government ensures that resources are allocated with maximal efficiency.[6]

Under democracy, the individual pursuits of people and firms are sometimes at odds with equality and justice. Because people have differing levels of personal and financial resources, each performs with varying degrees of success, leading to inequalities. Critics of pure democracy argue that when these inequalities become excessive, government should step in to correct them. Each society balances individual freedom with broader social goals. In democracies such as Japan and Sweden, the democracy's rights and freedoms are construed in larger societal terms rather than on behalf of individuals.

Virtually all democracies include elements of socialism, such as government intervention in the affairs of individuals and firms. Socialism emerges because of abuses or negative externalities that occur in purely democratic or capitalistic systems. For the past two decades, Japan has been striving to achieve the right balance between democracy and socialism. Poor management practices and an economic recession led to the bankruptcy of thousands of Japanese firms. To maintain jobs and economic stability, the Japanese government intervened to support numerous large firms and banks that, under pure capitalism, would have failed. However, such policies led to inflexibility in the Japanese economy and a delay of needed structural improvements.

Many countries, including Australia, Canada, the United States, and those in Europe, are best described as having a mixed political system—characterized by a strong private sector and a strong public sector, with considerable government regulation and control.

Democracy's Link to Economic Freedom and Transparency

Compared to totalitarianism and socialism, democracy is associated with greater economic freedom and higher living standards. Economic freedom flourishes when governments support the institutions necessary for that freedom, such as freely operating markets and the rule of law.[7] Exhibit 6.5 reveals that political freedom and economic freedom are closely related. As countries develop economic ties with foreign trading partners and integrate themselves with the global economy, they tend to liberalize their markets and reduce restrictions on foreign business. This has happened, for example, with the introduction of economic reforms and open markets in India since the 1990s.[8] The exhibit also reveals how countries with the highest living standards—for example, Australia, France, Germany, Japan, United States—also tend to have the most political and economic freedoms. By contrast, countries with the lowest living standards—for example, Libya, North Korea, Pakistan—tend to score lowest on political and economic freedoms.

Political freedom is characterized by:

- Free and fair elections,
- The right to form political parties,
- Fair electoral laws,
- Existence of a parliament or other legislative body,
- Freedom from domination by the military, foreign powers, or religious hierarchies.
- Self-determination for cultural, ethnic, and religious minorities.

EXHIBIT 6.5

Relationship Between Political Freedom and Economic Freedom for a Sample of Countries

Sources: James Gwartney, Robert Lawson, and Joshua Hall, *Economic Freedom of the World: 2014 Annual Report* (Vancouver, Canada: Fraser Institute, 2014); Freedom House, *Freedom in the World 2015* (Washington DC: Freedom House, 2015).

Economic freedom is related to:

- The extent of government interference in business,
- The strictness of the regulatory environment.
- The ease with which commercial activity is carried out according to market forces.

Visit Freedom House (www.freedomhouse.org) to view the latest information on political and economic freedom around the world.

Democracy is closely associated with *openness*, or lack of regulation or barriers to the entry of firms in foreign markets. The greater the openness, the fewer the constraints placed on foreign firms. Absence of excessive regulations also benefits buyers because openness increases the quantity and variety of products available. Competition pressures firms to improve product quality continually. Increased efficiency and lower prices may follow. After India's government lowered entry barriers in the Indian automobile market, foreign automakers steadily entered the market. Their presence increased the number of models available for sale, raised the quality of available cars, and lowered prices. A similar response occurred in the mobile telephone market in China.[9]

The Relationship Between Political Systems and Economic Systems

Each political system tends to be associated with a particular type of economic system. Generally speaking, totalitarianism is associated with command economies, democracy with market economies, and socialism with mixed economies. Let's review these economic systems.

COMMAND ECONOMY   Also known as a centrally planned economy, a command economy makes the state a dominant force in the production and distribution of goods and services. Central planners make resource allocation decisions, and the state owns major sectors of the economy. In command economies, sizable bureaucracy thrives, and central planning tends to be less efficient than market forces in synchronizing supply and demand. For example, goods shortages were so common in the Soviet Union that people often waited in lines for hours to buy basic necessities such as sugar and bread. Today, countries such as China and Russia still exhibit some characteristics of command economies. However, the system is gradually dying out and being replaced by market economies and mixed economies.

MARKET ECONOMY   Market forces—the interaction of supply and demand—determine prices in a market economy. Government intervention in the marketplace is limited, and economic decisions are left to individuals and firms. Market economies are closely associated with capitalism, in which the means of production are privately owned and operated. Participants typically exhibit a market-oriented mentality and entrepreneurial spirit. The task of the state is to establish a legal system that protects private property and contractual agreements. However, the government may also intervene to address the inequalities that market economies sometimes produce.

MIXED ECONOMY   A mixed economy exhibits the features of both a market economy and a command economy. It combines state intervention and market mechanisms for organizing production and distribution. Most industries are under private ownership, and entrepreneurs freely establish, own, and operate corporations. But the government also controls certain functions, such as pension programs, labor regulation, minimum wage levels, and environmental regulation. State-owned enterprises operate in key sectors such as transportation, telecommunications, and energy. In France, for example, the government partly owns dozens of companies, mainly in the transportation, communication, and energy industries. Peugeot and Renault are partially state owned. In Germany, Japan, Norway, Singapore, and Sweden, the government often works closely with business and labor groups to determine industrial policy, regulate wage rates, and/or provide subsidies to support specific industries.[10]

The past century saw a large increase in the number of mixed economies and a concurrent rise in government involvement in economic matters. For example, in the United States, combined government spending increased from about 27 percent of GDP in 1960 to roughly 40 percent today and is expected to attain 50 percent by 2038. In Belgium, Denmark, France, Sweden, and several other countries in Europe, annual government spending now exceeds 50 percent of GDP. In recent years, governments in Europe, Japan, and North America have imposed many new regulations on private firms.[11] Regulations were adopted that covered workplace safety, minimum wages, pension benefits, and environmental protection.

Legal Systems

6.3 Understand legal systems.

Legal systems provide a framework of rules and norms of conduct that mandate, limit, or permit specified relationships among people and organizations and provide punishments for those who violate these rules and norms. Laws require or limit specific actions while empowering citizens to engage in others, such as entering into contracts and seeking remedies for contract violations. Legal systems are dynamic—they evolve over time to represent each nation's changing social values and the evolution of their social, political, economic, and technological environments.

Political systems—totalitarianism, socialism, and democracy—tend to influence their respective legal systems. Democracies tend to encourage market forces and free trade. In countries with well-developed legal systems, such as Australia, Canada, Japan, the United States, and most European countries, laws are widely known and understood. In such countries, laws are effective and legitimate because they are:

- Applied to all citizens equally.
- Issued through formal procedures by recognized government authorities.
- Enforced systematically and fairly by police forces and formally organized judicial bodies.

In these countries, a tradition of law exists in which citizens consistently respect and follow the rule of law. **Rule of law** refers to a legal system in which rules are clear, publicly disclosed, fairly enforced, and widely respected by individuals, organizations, and the government. International business flourishes in societies where the rule of law prevails. In the United States, for example, the Securities and Exchange Act encourages confidence in business transactions by requiring public companies to disclose their financial indicators to investors frequently. Legal systems can be eroded by declining respect for the law, weak government authority, or burdensome restrictions that attempt to forbid behavior prevalent in the society. In the absence of the rule of law, firms must contend with great uncertainty, and economic activity can be impeded.

Nations are primarily governed by one of four basic legal systems: common law, civil law, religious law, or mixed. These legal systems are the foundation for laws and regulations. Exhibit 6.6 provides examples of countries where these legal systems are dominant.

Rule of law
A legal system in which rules are clear, publicly disclosed, fairly enforced, and widely respected by individuals, organizations, and the government.

Common Law

Also known as case law, common law is a legal system that originated in England and spread to Australia, Canada, the United States, and former members of the British Commonwealth. The basis of common law is tradition, previous cases, and legal precedents set by the nation's courts through interpretation of statutes, legislation, and past rulings. The national legislature in common-law countries (such as Parliament in Britain and Congress in the United States) holds ultimate power to pass or amend laws. In the United States, because the constitution is difficult to amend, the Supreme Court and even lower courts have much flexibility to interpret the law. Common law is more flexible than other legal systems because it is more open to interpretation by courts. Judges in a common-law system have substantial power to interpret laws based on the unique circumstances of individual cases.

Civil Law

Also known as code law, civil law is found in France, Germany, Italy, Japan, Turkey, and Latin America. Its origins go back to Roman law and the Napoleonic Code. Civil law is based on an

EXHIBIT 6.6

Dominant Legal Systems in Selected Countries

Source: Based on World Legal Systems at www.juriglobe.ca.

Primarily Common Law	Primarily Civil Law	Primarily Religious Law	Mixed Systems
Australia	Much of western	Much of the	Bangladesh
Canada	Europe and Latin	Middle East and	India
Ireland	America	North Africa	Indonesia
New Zealand	Japan	Afghanistan	Israel
United Kingdom	Russia	Mauritania	Kenya
United States	South Korea	Pakistan	Malaysia
		Sudan	Philippines

all-inclusive system of laws that have been codified; the laws are clearly written and accessible. It is divided into three codes: commercial, civil, and criminal. Civil law is considered complete as a result of catchall provisions found within the law. Rules and principles form the starting point for legal reasoning and administering justice. The codified rules emerge as specific laws and codes of conduct produced by a legislative body or some other supreme authority.

Both common law and civil law systems originated in Western Europe and represent the common values of western Europeans. A key difference between the two systems is that common law is primarily judicial in origin and based on court decisions, whereas civil law is primarily legislative in origin and based on laws passed by national and local legislatures. Differences in common and civil law give rise to differing business approaches in different countries. These are highlighted in Exhibit 6.7. In reality, common-law systems generally contain elements of civil law and vice versa. The two systems complement each other, and countries that employ one also tend to employ some elements of the other.

Religious Law

This legal system is strongly influenced by religious beliefs, ethical codes, and moral values viewed as mandated by a supreme being. The most important religious legal systems are based on Hindu, Jewish, and Islamic law. Among these, the most widespread is Islamic law, found mainly in the Middle East and North Africa. In addition to these areas, other countries with substantial populations of Muslims (followers of Islam) include India (about 175 million Muslims), Indonesia (205 million), Nigeria (75 million), and Pakistan (180 million).

Islamic law, also known as the *shariah*, is based on the Qur'an, the holy book of Muslims, and the teachings of the Prophet Mohammed. Adherents generally do not differentiate between religious and secular life. Islamic law governs relationships among people, between people and the state, and between people and a supreme being. It spells out norms of behavior regarding politics, economics, banking, contracts, marriage, and many other social issues. Thus, Islamic law might be said to encompass all possible human relationships. Because it is seen as divinely ordained, it is relatively static and absolute. Unlike other legal systems, it evolves very little over time.[12]

Most Muslim countries currently maintain a dual system, in which both religious and secular courts coexist. Other countries with large Muslim populations, such as Indonesia, Bangladesh, and Pakistan, have secular constitutions and laws. Turkey, another country with a majority Muslim population, has a strongly secular constitution. Saudi Arabia and Iran are unusual in that religious courts have authority over all aspects of jurisprudence.

Contemporary liberal movements within Islam oppose traditional views of religious law. For example, strict interpretation of Islamic law prohibits the giving and receiving of interest on loans

Legal Issues	Civil Law	Common Law
Ownership of intellectual property	Determined by registration.	Determined by prior use.
Enforcing agreements	Commercial agreements become enforceable only if properly notarized or registered.	Proof of agreement is sufficient for enforcing contracts.
Specificity of contracts	Contracts tend to be brief because many potential problems are already covered in the civil code.	Contracts tend to be very detailed, with all possible contingencies spelled out. Usually more costly to draft a contract.
Compliance with contracts	Noncompliance is extended to include unforeseeable human acts such as labor strikes and riots.	Acts of God (floods, lightning, hurricanes, etc.) are the only justifiable excuses for noncompliance with the provisions of contracts.

EXHIBIT 6.7

Examples of Differences Between Common Law and Civil Law

or investments. To comply with Islamic law, financial institutions employ a variant of international banking known as Islamic finance, based on the principles of shariah law. Many Western banks—for example, JP Morgan and Deutsche Bank—have subsidiaries in Islamic countries that comply with shariah laws. Instead of requiring interest payments, they charge administrative fees or take equity positions in the projects they finance. Many issue *sukuks*, Islamic-compliant bonds that offer revenue from an asset, such as a rental property, rather than interest. The global market for shariah-compliant financial instruments now exceeds one trillion U.S. dollars.[13]

Mixed Systems

Mixed systems consist of two or more legal systems operating together. In most countries, legal systems evolve over time, adopting elements of one system or another that reflect their unique needs. The contrast between civil law and common law has become blurred as many countries combine them. For example, legal systems in South Africa and the Philippines mix elements of civil law and common law. Legal systems in Indonesia and most Middle Eastern countries share elements of civil law and Islamic law.

Source: Ahmad Faizal Yahya/Shutterstock

Islamic law specifies norms of behavior regarding commercial relations, contracts, banking, and other areas. This man is washing himself in preparation for prayers at a mosque in Brunei Darussalam, in south Asia.

Historically, socialist law was a legal system found in the former Soviet Union, China, and a few states in Africa. It was based on civil law, with elements of socialist principles that emphasized state ownership of property. The rights of the state dominated those of the individual. When the Soviet Union collapsed and China began transitioning to capitalism, socialist law gave way to other legal systems, especially civil law.

MyManagementLab   **Watch It!**

If your professor has assigned this, go to the Assignments section of **mymanagementlab.com** to complete the video exercise titled Anthony Shadid: Unrest in the Middle East and North Africa.

Participants in Political and Legal Systems

6.4 Know the participants in political and legal systems.

Political and legal systems evolve from the interplay among various societal institutions at both the national and international levels. Five types of participants are active in transforming political and legal systems.

Government

The government, or the public sector, is the most important participant, operating at national, state, and local levels. Governments have the power to enact and enforce laws. They strongly influence how firms enter host countries and how they conduct business there. Governments regulate international business activity through a complex system of institutions, agencies, and public officials. Agencies that possess such powers in the United States include the U.S. Trade Representative and the International Trade Administration (www.ita.doc.gov). In Canada, such functions are handled by the Ministry of Foreign Affairs (www.international.gc.ca), the Ministry of Finance, and the Export and Import Controls Bureau. Similar agencies operate in Australia, Britain, and virtually all other countries.

International Organizations

Supranational agencies such as the World Trade Organization (www.wto.org), the United Nations (www.un.org), and the World Bank (www.worldbank.org) strongly influence international business. For example, the United Nations Conference on Trade and Development (UNCTAD, www.unctad.org) helps oversee international trade and development in the areas of investment, finance, technology, and enterprise development. Such organizations facilitate free and fair trade by providing administrative guidance, governing frameworks, and, occasionally, giving financial support.

Regional Trade Organizations

Regional economic integration refers to the growing economic interdependence that results when two or more countries within a geographic region form an alliance whose goal is to reduce barriers to trade and investment. Regional trade organizations, such as the European Union (EU), the North American Free Trade Agreement (NAFTA), and the Association of Southeast Asian Nations (ASEAN), aim to advance the economic and political interests of their members. The EU is especially well developed, with its own executive, legislative, and bureaucratic bodies. It enacts and enforces laws and regulations that directly affect business. For example, following new regulations forced by Lithuania's entry into the EU, the supermarket chain IKI had to spend millions to build separate entrances for fresh meat delivery in each of its 136 stores.[14]

Special Interest Groups

Special interest groups operate to advance the goals of a particular community. Numerous special interest groups serve the interests of specific countries, industries, or causes. For example, the Organisation for Economic Co-operation and Development (OECD, www.oecd.org) supports the economic developmental and business goals of advanced economies. The Organization of Petroleum Exporting Countries (OPEC, www.opec.org) is a powerful cartel that controls global oil prices, which, in turn, affect consumer prices and the cost of doing business. OPEC emerged as a powerful voice for oil-producing countries, including Saudi Arabia, Iran, Venezuela, Nigeria, and Indonesia. Other groups exercise similar control over the production and allocation of commodities such as sugar, coffee, and iron ore.

Special interest groups engage in political activity to advance specific causes, ranging from labor rights to environmental protection. They often influence national political processes and produce outcomes with far-reaching consequences for business. Many target industries and affect individual firms. In China, activists are pressuring the government to reduce pollution. Industrialization and a sharp rise in the use of fossil fuels are contaminating China's air, water, and soil.[15] In the United States, Greenpeace and other environmentalist groups opposed construction of the Keystone pipeline, fearing it would produce oil spills, polluting ground water and killing wildlife. Environmentalist groups were instrumental in halting construction of the pipeline in 2015.[16] Exhibit 6.8 provides a sample of interest groups and their likely stance toward various business issues.

Competing Firms

Rival domestic firms with a strong presence in the host country naturally have an interest in opposing the entry of foreign firms into the local market and may lobby their government for protection. For example, host-country competitors often complain when foreign firms receive financial support from the parent or host-country governments. Asterix, a French theme park, opposed French government support for U.S.-based Disney when the latter established Disneyland Paris. Similarly, U.S. automakers in Detroit opposed BMW's construction of a factory in South Carolina. However, the state government of South Carolina supported the BMW facility on the grounds that it would generate jobs and increase tax revenues.

EXHIBIT 6.8 Issues of Concern to Special Interest Groups

Group	Typical Issue	Example
Labor unions	Oppose imported goods and global sourcing	U.S. united steelworkers union opposed imports of steel from China
Competing businesses	Dislike competition from foreign firms	Japanese rice producers opposed imports of rice from the United States
Customers	May avoid foreign-made products. Dislike improper marketing practices.	Motorists in Australia accused BP of unfair pricing of petroleum products
Conservationists	Fight against wildlife loss and destruction of the natural environment	Environmentalists oppose lumber imports from countries with tropical rain forests

Types of Country Risk Produced by Political Systems

6.5 Identify the types of country risk produced by political systems.

How do political systems create challenges for firms engaged in international business? Let's examine the specific risks produced by political systems.

Government Takeover of Corporate Assets

Governments occasionally seize the assets of corporations. The industry sectors most often targeted by government seizure are natural resources (for example, mining and petroleum), utilities, and manufacturing. Fortunately, aggressive seizure is less common these days as governments in many developing countries have adopted institutional reforms that aim to attract FDI from abroad and foster economic growth.

Government seizure takes on various forms

- *Confiscation* is the seizure of corporate assets without compensation. Beginning in the 1980s, for example, Zimbabwe's dictator Robert Mugabe systematically seized more than 5,000 farms that farmers of mostly European descent owned, and redistributed the land to native Zimbabweans. Recently, Mugabe announced plans to confiscate mines that foreign mining companies owned.

- *Expropriation* is seizure with compensation. In Venezuela, ExxonMobil and ConocoPhillips were forced to abandon multibillion-dollar investments in the local oil industry. Recently, Bolivia's President Evo Morales ordered his government to seize Sabsa, a Spanish airline operating in his country. Gradual yet persistent pressure from the Russian government led TNK-BP, a Russian subsidiary of British energy giant BP, to sell a major stake in its oil business to the national gas monopoly Gazprom.

- *Nationalization* describes government seizure of an entire industry, with or without compensation. For example, the government of Bolivia nationalized much of the oil and gas industry in that country. President Hugo Chavez nationalized the cement industry in Venezuela. Nationalization occurs in advanced economies as well. Following the global financial crisis, the federal government of Iceland nationalized most of the country's banking industry.

Sources: Economist, "Your Mine is Mine," September 3, 2011, www.economist.com; Sergio Manaut, "The Pain in Spain," *Latin Trade*, May/June, 2013, pp. 30–31; Robert Wade and Silla Sigurgeirsdottir, "Iceland's Rise, Fall, Stabilisation and Beyond," *Cambridge Journal of Economics* 36, No. 1 (2012), pp. 127–144.

"Creeping expropriation" is a subtle form of country risk in which governments modify laws and regulations after foreign MNEs have made substantial local investments in property and plants.[17] Examples include abrupt termination of contracts and the creation of new laws that favor local firms. As reported in the opening case, corporate raiders and government officials in Russia occasionally raid the offices of competitors and subject them to questionable criminal investigations. Such tactics occasionally force foreign MNEs to cede control of their operations to local interests.[18] Governments in Bolivia, Kazakhstan, Russia, and Venezuela have modified tax regimes to extract revenues from foreign coal, oil, and gas companies. Troops stormed the Kazakhstan offices of U.S. mining company AES to enforce an alleged tax fine amounting to some $200 million. One of the country's largest providers of electricity, AES reduced its operations in Kazakhstan in the wake of persistent abuse by the Kazakh government.[19] Subtle or devious approaches to government takeover make country risk harder to predict.

Embargoes and Sanctions

Most countries are signatories to international treaties and agreements that specify rules, principles, and standards of behavior in international business. Nevertheless, governments may unilaterally resort to sanctions and embargoes to respond to offensive activities of foreign countries. A *sanction* is a type of trade penalty imposed on one or more countries by one or more other countries. Sanctions typically take the form of tariffs, trade barriers, import duties, and import or export quotas. They generally arise in the context of an unresolved trade or policy dispute, such as a disagreement about the fairness of some international trade practice. There is much evidence suggesting

Source: E. O./123RF

Activists called for a boycott of Russian products and the 2014 Sochi Winter Olympics over charges that Russia's government discriminates against gays and lesbians. Pictured is the Kremlin in Moscow, site of the official residence of Russia's President.

that sanctions often do not achieve desired outcomes. For example, the United States has imposed trade sanctions on Iran and Syria. However, goods continue to flow in and out of both countries from China, Germany, Japan, and numerous other trading partners.[20]

An *embargo* is an official ban on exports to or imports from a particular country to isolate it and punish its government. It is generally more serious than a sanction and is used as a political punishment for some disapproved policies or acts. For example, the United States has enforced embargoes against Iran and North Korea, at times labeled as state sponsors of terrorism. The European Union has enacted embargoes against Belarus, Sudan, and China in certain areas, such as foreign travel, to protest human rights and weapon-trading violations.

Boycotts Against Firms or Nations

Consumers and special interest groups occasionally target particular firms perceived to have harmed local interests. Consumers may refuse to patronize firms that behave inappropriately. A *boycott* is a voluntary refusal to engage in commercial dealings with a nation or a company. Boycotts and public protests result in lost sales and increased costs (for public relations activities needed to restore the firm's image). Disneyland Paris and McDonald's have been the targets of boycotts by French farmers, who believe these firms represent U.S. agricultural policies and globalization, which many French citizens despise. Activists in numerous countries organized a boycott of petroleum company BP following its oil spill in the Gulf of Mexico.[21] In 2013, activist groups advocated boycotting Russian products and the Sochi Winter Olympics over concerns that Russia's government discriminates against gays and lesbians.[22]

Terrorism

Terrorism is the threat or actual use of force or violence to attain a political goal through fear, coercion, or intimidation.[23] It is sometimes sponsored by national governments. Terrorism has escalated in much of the world, as exemplified by attacks in France, India, the Philippines, Spain, the United Kingdom, and the United States, as well as various countries in the Middle East. In India, more than 30,000 people have died in terrorist attacks in the past two decades.[24] Most recent terrorist attacks have occurred in Afghanistan, Iraq, Nigeria, Pakistan, and Syria. In addition to causing loss of life, terrorism can severely damage commercial infrastructure and disrupt business activities. It induces fear in consumers, who reduce their purchasing, potentially leading to economic recession. The transportation and retailing industries are particularly affected. Terrorism also affects financial markets. In the days following the September 11, 2001, attacks in New York, the value of the U.S. stock market dropped some 14 percent.[25]

War, Insurrection, and Violence

War, insurrection, and other forms of violence pose significant problems for business operations. Although such events usually do not affect companies directly, their indirect effects can be disastrous. Violent conflict among drug cartels and security services along the U.S.–Mexico border has led some firms and financiers to withdraw investments from Mexico because of perceived heightened risks and political instability. In India, Tata Motors (www.tatamotors.com) shifted the location of a major new factory due to violent protests by local farmers who feared the loss of their livelihood.[26] To minimize losses from violent acts, firms can purchase risk insurance.

Types of Country Risk Produced by Legal Systems

6.6 Identify the types of country risk produced by legal systems.

In addition to political concerns, country risk also arises due to peculiarities of national legal systems. Especially relevant to international business are *commercial law*, which specifically covers business transactions, and *private law*, which regulates relationships between persons and organizations, including contracts and liabilities that may arise due to negligent behavior. In many countries, the legal system favors home-country nationals. Laws are designed to promote the interests of local businesses and the local economy.

Legal systems in both the host country and the home country pose various challenges to firms, which we review next.

Country Risk Arising from the Host-Country Legal Environment

Governments in host countries impose various laws and regulations on foreign companies doing business there.

FOREIGN INVESTMENT LAWS These laws affect the type of entry strategy firms choose as well as their operations and performance. Many nations impose restrictions on inward FDI. For example, Indonesia restricts foreign investment in certain industries, such as tourism, alcoholic beverages, and some chemical manufactures, to protect the country's security or cultural assets. Investment in several other industries requires obtaining special permission from Indonesia's central government.[27] The United States restricts foreign investments that might affect national security. Proposed investments can be reviewed by the U.S. Committee on Investments. In 2006, the U.S. Congress opposed a management contract that would have granted control of several U.S. ports to Dubai Ports World, a firm based in the United Arab Emirates. Under opposition from the U.S. public and Congress, the firm abandoned its investment plans.

CONTROLS ON OPERATING FORMS AND PRACTICES Governments impose laws and regulations on how firms can conduct production, marketing, and distribution activities within their borders. Such restrictions can hinder company performance abroad. For example, host countries may require companies to obtain permits to import or export. They may devise complex regulations that complicate transportation and logistical activities or limit the options for entry strategies. In China's huge telecommunications market, the government requires foreign investors to seek joint ventures with local firms; local operations cannot be wholly owned by foreigners. The government's goal is to ensure that China maintains control of its telecommunications industry but obtains inward transfer of technology, knowledge, and capital. In 2014, United States authorities banned Huawei, a giant Chinese telecommunications company, from bidding on U.S. government contracts because of concerns over the possibility of espionage.[28]

MARKETING AND DISTRIBUTION LAWS These laws determine which practices are allowed in advertising, promotion, and distribution. For example, Finland, France, and Norway prohibit cigarette advertising on television. Germany largely prohibits comparative advertising, in which a product is promoted as superior to a competing brand. Many countries cap the prices of critical goods and services, such as food and health care. Such constraints affect firms' marketing and profitability. Product safety and liability laws hold manufacturers and sellers responsible for damage, injury, or death defective products cause. In the case of violations, firms and company executives are subject to legal penalties, such as fines or imprisonment, as well as civil lawsuits. Product liability laws in developing countries are generally weak. Some firms take advantage of these weaknesses. For example, as litigants pursued tobacco companies in Europe and the United States, these companies shifted much of their marketing of cigarettes to developing countries.

Source: Peter Wilson/Dorling Kindersley, Ltd.

In Japan, foreign-owned large stores such as Carrefour and Walmart have faced restrictive laws designed to protect local retailers.

LAWS ON INCOME REPATRIATION   MNEs earn profits in various countries and typically seek ways to transfer these funds back to their home country. However, in some countries, governments devise laws that restrict such transfers. The action is often taken to preserve hard currencies, such as euros, U.S. dollars, or Japanese yen. Repatriation restrictions limit the amount of net income or dividends that firms can remit to their home–country headquarters. Although such constraints often discourage inward FDI, they are common in countries experiencing a shortage of hard currencies.

ENVIRONMENTAL LAWS   Governments enact laws to preserve natural resources; to combat pollution and the abuse of air, earth, and water resources; and to ensure health and safety. In Germany, for example, companies must follow strict recycling regulations. Manufacturers and distributors bear the burden of recycling product packaging. Governments usually try to balance environmental laws against the impact such regulations may have on employment, entrepreneurship, and economic development. For example, environmental standards in Mexico are looser or less well enforced than in some other countries, but the Mexican government is reluctant to strengthen them for fear that foreign MNEs may reduce their investments there.

CONTRACT LAWS   International contracts attach rights, duties, and obligations to the contracting parties. Contracts are used in five main types of business transactions:

- Sale of goods or services, especially large sales.
- Distribution of the firm's products through foreign distributors.
- Licensing and franchising—that is, a contractual relationship that allows a firm to use another company's intellectual property, marketing tools, or other assets for a fee.
- FDI, especially in collaboration with a foreign entity, to create and operate a foreign subsidiary.
- Joint ventures and other types of cross-border collaborations.

Source: Demetrio Carrasco/Dorling Kindersley, Ltd.

Governments around the world are contemplating ways to tax and regulate e-commerce and the Internet. Pictured is an Internet café in Budapest, Hungary.

Numerous countries are attempting to develop an international standard for international sales contracts. The United Nations Convention on Contracts for the International Sale of Goods (CISG) is a uniform text of law for international sales contracts. More than 75 countries are now party to the CISG, covering about three-quarters of all world trade. Unless excluded by the express terms of a contract, the CISG is deemed to supersede any otherwise applicable domestic law(s) regarding an international sales transaction.

INTERNET AND E-COMMERCE REGULATIONS   Internet and e-commerce regulations are the new frontier in legal systems and continue to evolve.[29] Firms that undertake e-commerce in countries with weak laws face considerable risk. In China, for example, the government has developed legislation to ensure security and privacy due to the rapid spread of the Internet and e-commerce. Many consumer-privacy laws have yet to be enacted, and progress has been delayed on the development of methods to protect private data from criminal or competitive eyes. Protections for online contracting methods have been implemented with the recent adoption of e-signature laws. Emergent e-signature laws offer protections for online contracting.

INADEQUATE OR UNDERDEVELOPED LEGAL SYSTEMS   Just as laws and regulations can lead to country risk, an underdeveloped regulatory environment or poor enforcement of existing laws can also pose challenges for the firm. Worldwide, safeguards for intellectual property are often inadequate. Regulations to protect intellectual property may exist on paper but not be adequately enforced. When an innovator invents a new product, develops new computer software, or produces some other type of intellectual property, another party may copy and sell the innovation without paying the inventor. As reported in the opening case, Russia's legal framework is relatively weak and inconsistent. Russian courts lack substantial experience ruling on business matters. Due to the unpredictable and potentially harmful legal environment, Western firms frequently abandon joint ventures and other business initiatives in Russia.[30]

Inadequate legal protection is most common in developing economies but can be a factor in developed economies as well. The most recent global

CHRISTOPHER JOHNSON

Christopher' Majors: Accounting
Objectives: Become an expert and develop innovative strategies for taxation
Internships during college: State of Georgia; Georgia Lottery; Deloitte, Chicago
Jobs held since graduating: Deloitte Tax LLP in Chicago, Illinois and Atlanta, Georgia

During his junior year, Christopher participated in a two-week study abroad program in Istanbul, Turkey. The program gave Chris a global business perspective and inspired a passion to work for a multinational organization in the financial industry. Meetings with business executives and with students from a local university proved invaluable. The experience whetted Chris' desire to learn as much as possible about global business. Chris learned about various aspects of the political and legal environment in international business.

After graduation, Chris interned with Deloitte Tax. There he gained technical, analytical, and enhanced communication skills. Following his internship, Chris entered graduate school and earned a Master's in Accountancy. Upon graduation, he took a full-time position with Deloitte in their tax division. Initially he worked in domestic compliance and global jurisdictional exposure. After two

years with the firm, Chris began consulting with multiple clients.

Christopher's Advice for International Exposure

"Capitalizing on an opportunity to broaden your educational and professional horizon is not only enjoyable, but essential in an ever-changing global society. Understanding the role that international business plays across cultural variations will allow for a well-developed global commerce perspective. Such exposure will also assist with determining your specific career path of choice."

Professional Success Factors

"The transition from college to corporate America has the potential to be extremely difficult. My advice to those that are approaching this milestone is to *have a strong sense of*

self. Knowing your strengths and limitations will allow you to succeed anywhere your career takes you, domestically or abroad. Don't hesitate to step into unfamiliar situations, countries, or cultures. This experience will only give you more self-confidence. I believe exposing myself to a remarkably different country such as Turkey turned out to be more instructive than studying in London or Rome."

Challenges

"The biggest challenge I faced in my early professional career was to learn how to take time for personal interests such as family, friends, and the study of cultures. Often, young professionals who are new to the corporate setting view themselves as working machines rather than actual human beings that require more than their employer's support. I have learned to enjoy the journey of success."

Source: Courtesy of Christopher Johnson.

financial crisis was precipitated, in part, by insufficient regulation in the financial and banking sectors of the United States, Europe, and other regions. Government authorities have been considering how regulatory structures can be revamped to provide a sounder footing for connecting global savers and investors, as well as reliable methods for managing financial instability. Governments seek to expand regulation, provide new means to increase transparency and information flows, and find ways to harmonize regulatory policies and legal frameworks across national borders. Banks and other financial institutions are revising disclosure rules to make information more specific and consistent. Some experts believe the financial crisis does not imply that more regulation is needed. Rather, they argue for more intelligent regulation, better enforcement of existing regulation, and better supervision of financial institutions.[31]

Read the *You Can Do It: Recent Grad in IB*, which features Christopher Johnson. Chris enhanced his knowledge about the international regulatory and taxation environment through study abroad.

Country Risk Arising from the Home–Country Legal Environment

Does country risk arise only due to the host country's legal environment? No, home–country legal systems also play a role. **Extraterritoriality** refers to the application of home–country laws to persons or conduct outside national borders. In most cases, such laws are intended to prosecute individuals or firms located abroad for some type of wrongdoing.

Examples of extraterritoriality in international business abound. A French court ordered Yahoo! to bar access to Nazi-related items on its website in France and to remove related messages

Extraterritoriality
Application of home-country laws to persons or conduct outside national borders.

and images from its sites accessible in the United States. In 2015, the European Union charged Google with monopolistic practices in the promotion of its web search services. Monopolies are considered harmful because they can unfairly restrain trade. Businesses generally oppose extraterritoriality because it tends to increase the costs and uncertainty of operating abroad.[32]

THE FOREIGN CORRUPT PRACTICES ACT (FCPA)   Passed by the U.S. government in 1977, the Foreign Corrupt Practices Act (FCPA) banned firms from offering bribes to foreign parties to secure or retain business. The FCPA was enacted after more than 400 U.S. companies admitted paying bribes to foreign government officials and politicians. The Act was strengthened in 1998 to cover foreign firms and managers who act in furtherance of corrupt payments while in the United States. The FCPA also requires companies with securities listed in the United States to meet U.S. accounting provisions. Such firms must devise and maintain accounting systems that control and record all company expenditures.[33] One problem with the FCPA is that *bribe* is not clearly defined. For example, the Act draws a distinction between bribery and facilitation payments; the latter may be permissible if making such payments does not violate local laws.[34]

Some U.S. managers argue the FCPA harms their interests because foreign competitors often are not constrained by such laws. FCPA criminal and civil penalties are increasingly harsh. Firms can be fined up to $2 million, and individuals can be fined up to $100,000 and face imprisonment. In 2014, the French engineering giant Alstom SA pleaded guilty to charges it had violated the FCPA by paying huge bribes in various countries to secure energy contracts. Avon was similarly charged with large-scale bribery in China. However, recent U.S. Justice Department FCPA prosecutions have slowed amid bureaucracy and potential political considerations.[35]

ACCOUNTING AND REPORTING LAWS   Accounting practices and standards differ greatly around the world, posing difficulties for firms. For example, when assigning value to stocks and other securities, most countries use the lower of cost or market value. Brazil, however, encourages firms to adjust portfolio valuations because of historically high inflation. When valuing physical assets such as plant and equipment, Canada uses historical costs. Some Latin American countries use inflation-adjusted market value. Although firms can write off uncollectible accounts in the United States, the allowance is not permitted in France, Spain, and South Africa. Research and development costs are expensed as incurred in most of the world but capitalized in South Korea and Spain. Belgium, Malaysia, and Italy use both conventions.

Transparency
The degree to which companies regularly reveal substantial information about their financial condition and accounting practices.

TRANSPARENCY IN FINANCIAL REPORTING   The timing and transparency of financial reporting vary widely around the world. **Transparency** is the degree to which firms regularly reveal substantial information about their financial condition and accounting practices. In the United States, public firms are required to report financial results to stockholders and to the Securities and Exchange Commission each quarter. In much of the world, however, financial statements are prepared annually or less often, and they often lack transparency. Transparency improves business decision making and the ability of citizens to hold companies accountable.

Recently, the U.S. Congress passed the Dodd–Frank Wall Street Reform and Consumer Protection Act, which aims to increase transparency in the United States financial sector. Passed in response to the late-2000s recession, the Act created an oversight board that monitors banking activities. It aims to reduce financial risk-taking by restricting certain banking activities and requiring bank executives to be responsible for compliance. Running to more than 2,000 pages of new regulations, banks have condemned the Act for imposing too many regulatory costs. U.S. affiliates of foreign multinational banks must comply with the Act's provisions. In an effort to avoid rigid financial requirements, some European banks are reducing their banking activities in the United States. Recently, the European Union introduced the Basel III global regulatory standard, which aims to increase the quality and transparency of the capital base of European banks. U.S. banks will be required to comply with the new Basel III rules.[36]

Ethical Connections

Many countries lack antibribery laws for international transactions. The *Organisation for Economic Cooperation and Development* recently called for a ban on grease payments, small-scale bribes intended to speed up telephone hookups, government paperwork, and other everyday matters in international commerce. A culture of grease payments and other corruption is corrosive, harming the rule of law and sustainable economic development.

Managing Country Risk

6.7 Know about managing country risk.

How should managers respond to country risk? In the discussion that follows, we highlight several specific strategies managers can employ to manage country risk.

Proactive Environmental Scanning

Anticipating country risk requires advance research. Initially, managers develop a comprehensive understanding of the political and legal environment in target countries. They then engage in *scanning* to assess potential risks and threats to the firm. Scanning allows the firm to improve practices in ways that conform to local laws and political realities and to create a positive environment for business success.[37]

One of the best sources of intelligence in the scanning process is employees working in the host country. They are knowledgeable about evolving events and can evaluate them in the context of local history, culture, and politics. Embassy and trade association officials regularly develop and analyze intelligence on the local political scene. Some consulting firms, such as Verisk Maplecroft (www.maplecroft.com) and Business Entrepreneurial Risk Intelligence (www.beri.com), specialize in country-risk assessment and provide guidelines for appropriate strategic responses. Once the firm has researched the political climate and contingencies of the target environment, it develops and implements strategies to facilitate effective management of relations with policymakers and other helpful contacts in the host country. The firm then takes steps to minimize its exposure to country risks that threaten its performance.

Strict Adherence to Ethical Standards

Ethical behavior is important not only for its own sake but also because it helps insulate the firm from some country risks that less-conscientious firms encounter. Those companies that engage in questionable practices or operate outside the law naturally invite redress from the governments of the host countries where they do business.

Alliances with Qualified Local Partners

A practical approach to reducing country risk is to enter target markets in collaboration with a knowledgeable and reliable local partner. Qualified local partners are better informed about local conditions and better situated to establish stable relations with the local government. Western firms often enter China and Russia by partnering with local firms that assist in navigating complex legal and political landscapes.

Protection Through Legal Contracts

A legal contract spells out the rights and obligations of each party. Contract law varies widely from country to country, and firms must adhere to local standards. For example, a Canadian firm doing business in Belgium generally must comply with the laws of both Belgium and Canada as well as with the evolving laws of the European Union.

Firms generally employ any of three approaches for resolving international disputes.

- *Conciliation* is the least adversarial method. It is a formal process of negotiation with the objective to resolve differences in a friendly manner. The parties in a dispute employ a conciliator, who meets separately with each in an attempt to resolve their differences. Parties can also employ mediation committees—groups of informed citizens—to resolve civil disputes.

- *Arbitration* is a process in which a neutral third party hears both sides of a case and decides in favor of one party or the other, based on an objective assessment of the facts. Compared to litigation, arbitration saves time and expense while maintaining the confidentiality of proceedings. Arbitration is often handled by supranational organizations such as the International Chamber of Commerce in Paris or the Stockholm Chamber of Commerce.

- *Litigation* is the most adversarial approach and occurs when one party files a lawsuit against another to achieve desired ends. Litigation is most common in the United States; most other countries favor arbitration or conciliation.

CLOSING CASE	Political Legal, and Ethical Dilemmas in the Global Pharmaceutical Industry

The global pharmaceutical industry is dominated by a dozen firms, with about half headquartered in the United States, two in Switzerland, two in the United Kingdom, and one in each of France, Germany, and Israel. Examples include GlaxoSmithKline (United Kingdom, www.gsk.com), Novartis AG (Switzerland, www.novartis.com), Teva (Israel, www.tevapharm.com), Merck (United States, www.merck.com), and Pfizer (United States, www.pfizer.com). North America accounts for about 40 percent, and each of Europe and emerging market countries (e.g., Brazil, China) account for roughly 25 percent, of worldwide pharmaceutical sales, respectively. The industry is confronted with several challenges.

High Cost of Research and Development

Among all industries, the pharmaceutical industry invests the most in R&D, creating and marketing drugs meant to treat everything from cancer to hair loss. Thousands of pharmaceutical medications allow people to live longer and healthier lives. Europe and the United States benefit from strong patent protection laws and abundant investment capital. A pharmaceutical compound is a substance formed from two or more chemical elements to produce a drug. According to industry statistics, it takes 12 to 15 years, and more than $1 billion in R&D expense, to bring new pharmaceutical compounds to market successfully. Only three out of every ten new, approved compounds are successful enough to recover their R&D costs. For their successful products, pharmaceutical firms must charge prices high enough to recover not only the high costs of product development but also to recover the cost of products that never achieve profitability.

Limited Protection for Intellectual Property

Protecting property rights is a key objective of legal systems. Governments grant patents and provide other types of protections for intellectual property. In practice, such protection is often inadequate, especially in developing countries, where pharmaceutical firms encounter substantial country risk. India has a history of weak intellectual property protection, which has discouraged R&D and innovation. India is a poor country, and few of its citizens can afford medications. India has a long history of producing counterfeit and pirated medications, often by violating the drug patents of foreign pharmaceutical firms. Illicit laboratories in India have freely infringed on drug patents and engaged in a selling free-for-all in the huge Indian pharmaceutical market. They reverse-engineered patented compounds developed by European and U.S. companies and began selling the pirated generics at drastically lower prices. The foreign pharmaceuticals routinely pursue legal action against these violations but, given limited patent protection, India's generic drug manufacturers have flourished.

The Challenge from Generic Brands

Under World Trade Organization (WTO) rules, a patent protects a drug inventor from competition for up to 20 years. In reality, when the lengthy testing and approval phase is factored in, the effective life of a drug patent is often less than 12 years. The manufacturer typically has only 5 to 8 years of patent protection in which to recover its investment before generic manufacturers can legally enter the market. Once a patent expires, generic manufacturers have the right to produce medications originally invented by major pharmaceuticals. Generic manufacturers typically sell the medications that they produce at very low prices. Patent protections are important because they encourage innovation by allowing inventors a limited opportunity to recover their R&D investments. However, patent protection laws governing pharmaceuticals differ substantially around the world.

Each year pharmaceutical firms invest some 20 percent of revenues in R&D to invent new compounds, used to develop pharmaceutical drugs. The main reason that generic manufacturers can charge lower prices is that they do not incur the high costs of R&D to develop new drugs. Because the medications are already established in the marketplace, generic manufacturers also incur substantially lower marketing and sales expenses.

In the world of generic drugs, Israel-based Teva is the largest manufacturer with global sales of more than $20 billion. In the United States, generic medications account for over half of all dispensed prescriptions. Once a branded compound's patent expires, generic manufacturers begin producing generic versions. Retail prices for the compound can fall by as much as 90 percent within 12 to 18 months.

Counterfeit Drugs

Worldwide, enforcement of intellectual property law varies. Many governments fail to ensure the quality of imported medicines. As a result, a growing industry of counterfeit and bio-inequivalent medications has emerged worldwide. A counterfeit ring from China supplied 1 million fake OneTouch Test Strips (used to treat diabetes) to hundreds of pharmacies in Canada, India, the United States, and numerous other countries. A healthy 22-year-old woman in Argentina died from liver failure after receiving iron injections to treat mild anemia. The medicine she received was a highly toxic counterfeit. In Niger, some 2,500 people died after receiving fake vaccines for meningitis. Recently, European Union officials seized more than 35 million fake pills at ports around Europe, including drugs intended to treat malaria, cancer, cholesterol, and pain.

The United Nations estimates that sales of counterfeit pharmaceuticals exceeds $500 billion annually. Counterfeiting is greatest in countries where regulatory oversight is weakest. The WHO estimates that up to 30 percent of medicines sold in developing countries may be counterfeit. It is estimated that between 200,000 and 300,000 people die each year in China due to counterfeit or substandard medicine.

Internet-based pharmacies are especially dubious. MarkMonitor, an industry watchdog, found that only a fraction of several thousand online pharmacies it examined were legitimate. Many of the pharmacies claiming to be based in Canada and the United States were in fact traced to China, Russia, and India. It is estimated that more than 50 percent of medicines sold through the Internet are fake—often containing no or too little of the active ingredient.

Because of the threats counterfeit manufacturers pose, branded pharmaceutical firms spend significant resources to protect their patents and intellectual property around the world. Branded pharmaceutical manufacturers have pursued legal actions at the WTO and against individual nations. The WTO's agreement on Trade-Related Aspects of Intellectual Property Rights (TRIPS) was approved by approximately 150 WTO member countries.

Neglected Therapeutic Areas

A large portion of pharmaceutical research is focused on developing treatments for diseases that can return the cost of capital and generate profits. For these reasons, pharmaceutical firms tend to target the most attractive markets. For example, these firms are more likely to develop a drug for cancer and cardiovascular diseases than for ailments common to poor countries such as tuberculosis. R&D to develop drugs common in poor countries is often perceived as too costly and risky.

At the same time, governmental and private initiatives have begun to address these market realities by providing incentive packages and public–private partnerships. For example, the Bill and Melinda Gates Foundation (www.gatesfoundation.org) is investing billions of dollars to fight AIDS, tuberculosis, and various infectious diseases that affect developing countries.

Public Scrutiny

The pharmaceutical industry's actions are often subject to public scrutiny within national political and legal systems. For example, the government of South Africa got into a tussle with several manufacturers of branded AIDS drugs. Because of high prices, the government sanctioned the importation of nonapproved generics. The reaction from branded pharmaceutical manufacturers was to sue South Africa, which created an international backlash against the firms. Not only did the episode generate much negative publicity for the branded pharmaceutical firms, it made people more aware of the generic drug industry and its potential for helping those the AIDS pandemic affects. In the wake of the South African debacle, Brazil and several other countries threatened to break patents if pharmaceutical firms did not make their drugs more affordable. In the interest of good public relations, several branded pharmaceutical firms began to offer their AIDS drugs at lower prices in Africa. The United States and various European governments have provided billions of dollars in subsidies to support AIDS treatment in Africa.

The Future

Without adequate intellectual property protection, the pharmaceutical industry has fewer incentives to invent new drugs. At the same time, consumers in poor countries need access to drugs but can't afford them. Lax intellectual property laws facilitate the production of cheap generic drugs, but without these protections, major pharmaceutical firms have fewer incentives to fund the R&D that results in new treatments for the diseases that plague the world. As selling prospects in Brazil, China, and other emerging markets develop over time, pharmaceutical firms increasingly target those markets but face enormous challenges.

Case Questions

5-4. Specify the types of country risks that pharmaceutical firms face in international business. How do the political and legal systems of countries affect the global pharmaceutical industry?

5-5. People need medications, but the poor often cannot afford them. Governments may not provide subsidies for health care and medications. Meanwhile, pharmaceutical firms focus their R&D on compounds likely to provide the best returns. What is the proper role of the following groups in addressing these dilemmas: national governments, branded pharmaceutical firms, and generic manufacturers?

5-6. Consult www.phrma.org, the Pharmaceutical Research and Manufacturers of America. What steps is the branded industry taking to address the various ethical issues it faces, such as providing affordable drugs to poor countries?

5-7. Consult the TRIPS agreement at the WTO portal (www.wto.org). What are the latest developments regarding this treaty? What types of protection does this treaty provide to pharmaceutical firms? What enforcement mechanisms does TRIPS provide for ensuring that these protections will be carried out?

5-8. Recommend a strategy that management at a large pharmaceutical firm should employ to reduce the likelihood of political and legal risks that such firms face. What steps should management take to minimize its exposure to such risks?

Sources: Barnes Reports, *Pharmaceutical Preparation Mfg. Industry (NAICS 325412) 2015 World Industry & Market Outlook* (C. Barnes & Co., www.cbarnes.com, 2015); Robert Coopman, "The Road Ahead for Research-Based Drug Companies," *Chain Drug Review*, January 2, 2012, p. 71; Chris Enyinda, Chris Mbah, and Alphonso Ogbuehi, "An Empirical Analysis of Risk Mitigation in the Pharmaceutical Industry Supply Chain: A Developing-Country Perspective," *Thunderbird International Business Review* 52, No. 1 (2010), pp. 54–69; IFPMA, *The Pharmaceutical Industry and Global Health* (Geneva: International Federation of Pharmaceutical Manufacturers & Associations, 2014); IMAP, *Pharmaceuticals & Biotech Industry Global Report—2011*, http://www.imap.com; P. Jayakumar, "Patently Justified," *Business Today*, March 15, 2015, pp. 58–64; PhRMA, *2015 Profile: Biopharmaceutical Research Industry* (Washington DC: Pharmaceutical Research and Manufacturers of America, 2015), www.phrma.org; Dennis Ostwald, Katharina Zubrzycki, and Julian Knippel, *The Economic Footprint of the Pharmaceutical Industry* (Darmstadt, Germany: WiFOR, 2015); Peter Pitts, "Counterfeit Drugs and China," 2009, the Center for Medicine in the Public Interest website, http://www.cmpi.org; Nancy Shute, "Fake Medications Are a Growing Threat," *US News and World Report*, August 21, 2007, http://www.health.usnews.com; U.S. Food and Drug Administration, "Counterfeit Drugs," 2009, http://www.fda.gov/counterfeit/; Leonora Walet, "Fighting Fake Drugs," *Chemical & Engineering News*, February 23, 2015, p. 28–29; World Health Organization, "Counterfeit Medicines," Fact Sheet No. 275, May 2012, http://www.wto.int.

Note: Kevin McGarry assisted in the development of this case.

END OF CHAPTER REVIEW

MyManagementLab

Go to **mymanagementlab.com** to complete the problems marked with this icon .

Key Terms

country risk   174
extraterritoriality   189

legal system   176
political system   176

rule of law   181
transparency   190

Summary

In this chapter, you learned about:

- **Political and legal environments in international business**

  International business is influenced by political and legal systems. **Country risk** refers to exposure to potential loss or to adverse effects on company operations and profitability caused by developments in national political and legal environments. A political system is a set of formal institutions that constitute a government. A legal system is a system for interpreting and enforcing laws. Adverse developments in political and legal systems increase country risk. These can result from events such as a change in government or the creation of new laws or regulations.

- **Political systems**

  The three major political systems are totalitarianism, socialism, and democracy. They provide frameworks within which laws are established and nations are governed. Democracy is characterized by private property rights and limited government. Socialism occurs mainly as social democracy. Today, most governments combine elements of socialism and democracy. Totalitarianism is associated with command economies, socialism with mixed economies, and democracy with market economies.

- **Legal systems**

  There are four major legal systems: common law, civil law, religious law, and mixed systems. The **rule of law** implies a legal system in which laws are clear, understood, respected, and fairly enforced.

- **Participants in political and legal systems**

  Actors include government, which exists at the national, state, and municipal levels. The World Trade Organization and the United Nations are typical of international organizations that influence international business. Special interest

  groups serve specific industries or country groupings and include labor unions, environmental organizations, and consumers that promote particular viewpoints. Companies deal with competing firms in foreign markets, which may undertake political activities aimed at influencing market entry and firm performance.

- **Types of country risk produced by political systems**

  Governments impose constraints on corporate operating methods in areas such as production, marketing, and distribution. Governments may expropriate or confiscate the assets of foreign firms. Governments or groups of countries also impose embargoes and sanctions that restrict trade with certain countries. Boycotts are an attempt to halt trade or prevent business activities and are usually pursued for political reasons. War and revolution have serious consequences for international firms. Terrorism has become more salient recently.

- **Types of country risk produced by legal systems**

  Foreign investment laws restrict FDI in various ways. Such laws include controls on operating forms and practices, regulations affecting marketing and distribution, restrictions on income repatriation, environmental laws, and Internet and e-commerce regulations. **Extraterritoriality** is the application of home–country laws to conduct outside of national borders. Accounting and reporting laws vary around the world. **Transparency** is the degree to which firms reveal substantial and regular information about their financial condition and accounting practices.

- **Managing country risk**

  Successful management requires developing an understanding of the political and legal context abroad. The firm should scan the environment proactively and strictly adhere to ethical standards. Country risk is also managed by allying with qualified local partners abroad. The firm should seek protection through legal contracts.

Test Your Comprehension AACSB: Reflective Thinking Skills

6-9. Adverse and sudden developments in political and legal systems can create country risk. Suggest three examples of such adverse developments.

6-10. Distinguish among totalitarianism, socialism, and democracy. What are the implications of each for internationalizing firms?

6-11. What are the specific characteristics of democracy? How do these characteristics facilitate international business?

6-12. What are the pillars upon which effective and legitimate laws are based?

⭐ **6-13.** Special interest groups operate in most countries. They tend to have distinctive agendas. What is their role in the political and legal system?

⭐ **6-14.** Why should an organization strictly adhere to ethical standards wherever it operates?

Apply Your Understanding
AACSB: Reflective Thinking Skills, Communication Abilities, Ethical Understanding and Reasoning Abilities

6-15. Country risk refers to the ways governments restrict, or fail to restrict, business activities. The nature of such restrictions varies around the world. In each country, national economic success substantially depends on the quality of laws and regulations. Government must strike the right balance—too little regulation promotes uncertainty; too much causes hardship. Country risk is revealed in various ways.

- Foreign investment laws
- Controls on operating forms and practices
- Environmental laws
- Contract laws
- E-commerce laws
- Underdeveloped legal systems
- Accounting and reporting laws

Conduct research online and give specific examples of each type of country risk. Describe how each might help or hinder company activities.

6-16. Suppose you get a job at Aoki Corporation, a firm that manufactures glass for industrial and consumer markets. Aoki is a large firm but has little international experience. Senior managers are considering a plan to move Aoki's manufacturing to China, Mexico, or Eastern Europe and to begin selling its glass in Latin America and Europe. However, they know little about the country risks that Aoki may encounter. Describe how each of the following factors might contribute to country risk as Aoki ventures abroad: foreign investment laws, controls on operating forms and practices, and laws regarding repatriation of income, environment, and contracts.

6-17. *Ethical Dilemma*: The United States imposed a trade and investment embargo on Iran. U.S. citizens were barred from doing business with Iran. Proponents argued the embargo was justified because Iran has supported terrorism, is developing nuclear weapons, and is a disruptive force in the Middle East. However, critics condemned the trade sanctions for several reasons. First, they argued the sanctions represented a double standard because the United States supports other countries that have engaged in terrorism and other bad behaviors. Second, the best way to nurture healthy dissent and civil society in Iran may be to engage the country rather than restrict economic relationships. Third, the sanctions harmed the Iranian people, who were deprived of the benefits of trade with the United States. Fourth, the sanctions were largely ineffective because other countries supply Iran with products it needs. Finally, the sanctions harmed U.S. companies, especially oil and gas firms, which were prevented from doing business with Iran. What is your view? Using the Ethical Framework in Chapter 4, analyze the arguments for and against trade with Iran. Can the United States, acting alone, compel desired changes in Iran by imposing sanctions? Justify your answer.

globalEDGE | INTERNET EXERCISES

(www.globaledge.msu.edu)

AACSB: Reflective Thinking Skills, Communication Abilities, Use of Information Technology, Ethical Understanding and Reasoning Abilities

Refer to Chapter 1, page 54, for instructions on how to access and use globalEDGE™.

6-18. Supranational organizations such as the World Bank (www.worldbank.org) and the World Trade Organization (www.wto.org) oversee much of the legal framework within which the world trading system operates. Political frameworks for industries or country groupings are influenced by organizations such as the Organization of Petroleum Exporting Countries (www.opec.org) and the Organisation for Economic Co-operation and Development (www.oecd.org). Using globalEDGE™ and the online portals cited here, address the following question: What is the goal of each organization, and how does it go about achieving its goal? By viewing the news and press releases at each website, summarize the latest initiatives of each organization.

6-19. When companies venture abroad, managers seek information on the legal and political environments in each country. This information is available from various web sources, as illustrated in the following exercises. (a) Suppose you want to sign up distributors in the European Union and want to learn about EU contract law. What should you do? Consult the globalEDGE™ portal to learn about EU trade and contract laws. Try the following: At globalEDGE™, click Reference Desk, Global Resource Directory, and then Trade Law. Describe the resources there for learning about contract law in Europe. (b) The Central Intelligence Agency's portal provides up-to-date information about national governments and political environments. Go to www.cia.gov, click World Factbook, and summarize the political environment in each of China, Colombia, France, and Russia.

6-20. Freedom House is a nonprofit organization that monitors the state of freedom worldwide. It conducts an annual Freedom in the World Survey, which you can view at www.freedomhouse.org. The survey compares the state of political rights and civil liberties in nearly 200 countries over time. Visit the site and answer the following questions. (a) What is the role of political rights and civil liberties in the Freedom House rankings? (b) What can governments in these countries do to facilitate more rapid social and political development? (c) What are the implications of the rankings for companies doing international business?

MyManagementLab   **Try It!**

The simulation Legal Differences accompanies this exercise.

MyManagementLab

Go to **mymanagementlab.com** for Auto-graded writing questions as well as the following Assisted-graded writing questions:

⭐ **6-21.** What is the relationship between political freedom and economic freedom?

⭐ **6-22.** Summarize the various participants that operate in political systems.

⭐ **6-23.** MyManagementLab Only—comprehensive writing assignment for this chapter.

Endnotes

1. Scott Cendrowski, "China's Censors Target Streaming," *Fortune*, March 1, 2015, pp. 18–20; Jack Ewing, "Germany: A Cold Shoulder for Coca-Cola," *BusinessWeek*, May 2, 2005, p. 52.

2. "Country Risk," *The Economist*, February 26, 2005, p. 102.

3. "Getting Past Yukos," *BusinessWeek*, September 13, 2004, p. 52; "Yukos 2.0?" *Economist*, September 9, 2014, p. 50.

4. S. Tamer Cavusgil, Pervez Ghauri, and Milind Agarwal, *Doing Business in Emerging Markets* (Thousand Oaks, CA: Sage, 2002); Mehul Srivastava, "What's Holding India Back," *Business Week*, October 19, 2009, pp. 38–44.

5. Steven Soper, *Totalitarianism: A Conceptual Approach* (Lanham, MD: University Press of America, 1985); Carl J. Friedrich and Zbigniew Brzezinski, *Totalitarian Dictatorship and Autocracy*, 2nd ed. (Cambridge, MA: Harvard University Press, 1965).

6. Milton Friedman and Rose Friedman, *Free to Choose* (New York: Harcourt Brace Jovanovich, 1980).

7. Amartya Sen, *Development as Freedom* (New York: Alfred Knopf, 2001).

8. Dolly Daftary, "Development in an Era of Economic Reform in India," *Development & Change* 45, No. 4 (2014), pp. 710–731; S. Maendra Dev, *India Development Report 2015* (New York: Oxford University Press, 2015).

9. Joseph Johnson and Gerald Tellis, "Drivers of Success for Market Entry into China and India," *Journal of Marketing* 72 (May 2008), pp. 1–13.

10. *Economist*, "Setting Out the Store," January 11, 2014, pp. 18–21.

11. Arthur Brooks, "The Debt Ceiling and the Pursuit of Happiness," *Wall Street Journal*, July 25, 2011, accessed at www.wsj.com; Statistical Abstract of the United States, Economics and Statistics Administration (Washington, DC: U.S. Bureau of the Census, 2004).

12. Lewis Hopfe and Brett Hendrickson, *Religions of the World*, 13th ed. (New York: Pearson, 2015).

13. Ken Owens and Yvonne Thompson, "Sovereign Sukuk a Way to Revive the Celtic Tiger?" *Accountancy Ireland*, April (2011), pp. 34–36; Maha Khan Phillips, "Doing God's Work; Islamic Finance Is Meant to Reconcile Both Commercial and Religious Ideals," *Wall Street Journal*, March 1, 2010, http://www.wsj.com; The Pew Forum, "Mapping the Global Muslim Population," 2009, http://www.pewforum.org.

14. Phyllis Berman, "The Three Marketeers," *Forbes*, July 25, 2005, p. 78.

15. *Bloomberg Business*, "China's Pollution Assault Boosting Solar, Electric Vehicles," April 7, 2015, http://www.bloomberg.com/news/articles/2015-04-08/china-s-pollution-assault-boosting-solar-electric-vehicles; Lei Xie, *Environmental Activism in China* (New York: Routledge, 2009).

16. Sarah Chacko, "XL Pipeline Clogged by Politics," *CQ Weekly*, December 8, 2014, p. 1462; Kirstin Gibbs, Tyler Johnson, Catherine McCarthy, "Energy Infrastructure Development Faces Impediments," *Natural Gas & Electricity*, April 2015, pp. 1–8.

17. David Wernick and Sumit Kundu, "Terrorism, Political Risk and International Business: Conceptual Considerations," in *Proceedings: 2008 Annual Conference, Academy of International Business* (East Lansing, MI: Academy of International Business, 2008).

18. Ibid.

19. Jason Bush, "Russia's Raiders," *BusinessWeek*, June 16, 2008, pp. 67–71; N. Vardi, "Power Putsch," *Forbes*, June 2, 2008, pp. 84–92.

20. Matthew Philips, "What Trade Sanctions?" *Bloomberg BusinessWeek*, January 30–February 5, 2012, p. 16.

21. Nicola Clark, "BP Hit by Boycott Threat Amid US Oil-Spill Crisis," *Marketing*, May 12, 2010, p. 1.

22. Michele Rivkin-Fish and Cassandra Hartblay, "When Global LGBTQ Advocacy Became Entangled with New Cold War Sentiment," *Brown Journal of World Affairs* 21, No. 1 (2014), pp. 95–111.

23. Yonah Alexander, David Valton, and Paul Wilkinson, *Terrorism: Theory and Practice* (Boulder, CO: Westview, 1979).

24. Institute for Economics & Peace, *Global Terrorism Index 2014* (Sydney, Australia: Institute for Economics & Peace, 2015); U.S. Department of State, *Country Reports on Terrorism*, April, 2014, http://www.state.gov/j/ct/rls/crt/2013/index.htm; M. Srivastava and N. Lakshman, "How Risky Is India?" *BusinessWeek*, December 4, 2008, http://www.businessweek.com.

25. Institute for Economics & Peace (2015); Jonathan Laing, "Aftershock," *Barron's*, September 9, 2002, p. 23.

26. V. Nair, "Tata Nano, World's Cheapest Car, Won't Help Pay Debt," *Bloomberg*, 2009, http://www.bloomberg.com; Srivastava (2009).

27. V. Sreeja, "Indonesia's Government to Relax Foreign Direct Investment Norms to Boost Economy as Growth Sputters," *International Business Times*, April 19, 2015, http://www.ibtimes.com/indonesias-government-relax-foreign-direct-investment-norms-boost-economy-growth-sputters-1519258.

28. Linda Yueh, "Huawei Boss Says U.S. Ban 'Not Very Important'," BBC, October 16, 2014, http://www.bbc.com/news/business-29620442; United States Trade Representative, *2011 National Trade Estimate Report on Foreign Trade Barriers*, Washington DC, March 2011, http://www.ustr.gov.

29. Tom Fairless and Stephan Fidler, "Europe Wants the World to Embrace Its Internet Rules," *Wall Street Journal*, February 25, 2015, http://www.wsj.com/articles/europe-wants-the-world-to-embrace-its-data-privacy-rules-1424821453.

30. Cavusgil, Ghauri, and Agarwal (2002).

31. J. Fox, "New World Order," *Time*, February 16, 2009, p. 29; "Krise des Bankensystems: Zu viel Finanzinnovationen, zu wenig Regulierung?" *Ifo Schnelldienst*, November 14, 2008, pp. 3–15; Laura Kodres, "What Is to Be Done," *Finance & Development*, March 2009, pp. 23–27.

32. International Chamber of Commerce, "Policy Statement: Extraterritoriality and Business," July 13, 2006; James Kanter and Mark Scott, "Challenge to Google," *New York Times*, April 15, 2015, p. B1.

33. Kurt Stanberry, Barbara C. George, and Maria Ross, "Securities Fraud in the International Arena," *Business and Society* 30, No. 1 (1991), pp. 27–36.

34. Randall Hess and Edgar Kossack, "Bribery as an Organizational Response to Conflicting Environmental Expectations," *Academy of Marketing Science* 9, No. 3 (1981), pp. 206–226; Judith Scott, Debora Gilliard, and Richard Scott, "Eliminating Bribery as a Transnational Marketing Strategy," *International Journal of Commerce & Management* 12, No. 1 (2002), pp. 1–17.

35. R. Edmonson, "Cracking Down on Corruption," *Journal of Commerce*, December 5, 2011, p. 17; *Investor's Business Daily*, "Alstom Settles Bribery Charge," December 23, 2014, p. A02; Paul Pelletier, "The Foreign-Bribery Sinkhole at Justice," *Wall Street Journal*, April 21, 2015, p. A17; *Soap, Perfumery & Cosmetics*, "Avon to Shell Out $135m Fine in China Bribery Case," January 2015, p. 11.

36. Barry Gunderson, "How Recent Banking Regulations Affect Lenders," July/August 2011, pp. 28–31; John Heltman, "Volcker, Inc.: How One Rule Became a Cottage Industry," *American Banker*, March 30, 2015, p. 1; Charles Wallace, "Foreign Banks More Worried About Volcker Rule," *Institutional Investor*, November 2011, p. 70.

37. Joe Mullich, "Risk Management: Most Overlooked Risks," *Wall Street Journal*, January 17, 2012, p. B5.

Chapter 7

Government Intervention and Regional Economic Integration

Learning Objectives *After studying this chapter, you should be able to:*

7.1 Understand the nature of government intervention.

7.2 Know the instruments of government intervention.

7.3 Explain the evolution and consequences of government trade intervention.

7.4 Describe how firms can respond to government trade intervention.

7.5 Understand regional integration and economic blocs.

7.6 Identify the leading economic blocs.

7.7 Understand the advantages and implications of regional integration.

Qatar Welcomes New Foreign Investment

Qatar, looking forward to speed up its economic growth and improve its external competitiveness, has identified the importance of trade and investment liberalization economic growth. It has been implementing development strategy to reduce the high dependence on crude oil since the mid-1990s by "raising the production and exports of liquefied natural gas, as well as promoting gas-intensive industries, such as petrochemicals and fertilizers, and, more recently, tourism; creating more job opportunities for all Qatari nationals; improving education, health services, and modernizing the infrastructure; and addressing some of the deep-rooted structural problems built over the previous decades, including that key industries, such as transport, energy, and telecommunications, remain dominated by a public company." The gradual structural reforms helped create an environmentally friendly business environment and aim to increase the role of the private sector in the economy.

Authorities have been implementing these strategies to improve the investment environment in the country. New laws have been issued or replaced [Investment Law No. 13 of 2000, and Commercial Companies Law No. 5 of 2002 replacing the Commercial Companies Law No. 11 of 1981, as amended; and the Commercial Agency Law (Law No. 8 of 2002)] to help attract foreign investment inflows. Incentive opportunities for investors have been enhanced after the 2000 investment law: "A one-stop window for investment procedures has been established to increase transparency, reduce red tape, and ease the approval process for land and industrial licenses." Under the new laws, the majority of foreign firms operating in Qatar are required to import certain products through local agents. Only firms granted 100 percent foreign ownership are excluded from the local agent requirement with distributor rights. Foreign Direct Investment helps advance Qatar's technology infrastructure, R&D, programmers, technical or marketing assistance, and education or training of the local labor force. Qatar strongly favors trade liberalization through the multilateral framework; the rules-based multilateral

Source: Makushin Alexey/Shutterstock

system should contribute to the further integration of least-developed and developing countries into the world economy.

Creating a business in Qatar requires eight procedures. The minimum capital needed is half the average annual income in Qatar. It is still relatively time-consuming to obtain the necessary permits to trade. In the majority of cases, foreign investment in businesses is capped at 49 per cent.

Qatar is now considered to be the richest country in the world. Its 2m population has a GDP Per Capita of $100,889. In the period up to 2015 there was a 10.7 per cent 5-year compound annual growth.

Questions

7-1. Outline Qatar's trade liberalization. Is the Qatari government likely to continue this process?

7-2. What are the major exports into Qatar and are these likely to change?

7-3. Identify and assess the main investment opportunities in Qatar for overseas investors?

SOURCES: "Further reforms would help sustain already impressive economic growth." February 21, 23, 2005. Accessed October 23, 2012. http://www.wto.org/english/tratop_e/tpr_e/tp244_e.htm Wallace, Douglas. "Consider Qatar." Accessed October 22, 2012. http://export.gov/middleeast/country_information/qatar/ConsiderQatarGuide.pdf.

Governments intervene in trade and investment to achieve political, social, or economic objectives. They often create trade barriers that benefit specific interest groups, such as domestic firms, industries, and labor unions. A key rationale is to create jobs by protecting industries from foreign competition. Governments also intervene to support homegrown industries or firms.

Government intervention is at odds with *free trade*, the unrestricted flow of products, services, and capital across national borders. Market liberalization and free trade are best for supporting economic growth and national living standards.[1] Many studies have found a strong association between market openness—that is, unimpeded free trade—and economic growth. Emerging markets and developing economies that emphasize openness typically enjoy average annual per-capita GDP growth in excess of 4 percent, whereas relatively closed countries—those that significantly restrict international trade and investment—grow at rates close to zero.[2]

Take the case of Poland. Over time, Poland lowered trade barriers and participated more freely in international trade, adopting the principle of comparative advantage.[3] Poland began to use its resources more efficiently. It generated more overall profits for firms and workers. It acquired more resources with which to import the goods that Polish consumers desire. As it gradually embraced free trade, Poland's average annual income rose from about $1,625 in 1990 to more than $14,000 by 2015. These gains did not occur without some turmoil. Unemployment in Poland increased in some industries as jobs producing certain goods shifted to other countries better suited to make those goods. However, free trade's positive effects substantially outweighed the negative ones.[4] Free trade provides enormous benefits for economic growth and the welfare of nations worldwide.

In reality, however, governments intervene in business and the international marketplace in ways that obstruct the free flow of trade and investment. Intervention alters the competitive position of companies and industries and the status of citizens. As highlighted in Exhibit 7.1, intervention is an important dimension of country risk. In this chapter, we examine the nature, rationale, and consequences of government intervention. We also describe what companies can do to enhance international performance in the face of government intervention worldwide. Finally, we discuss regional economic blocs and their role in international business.

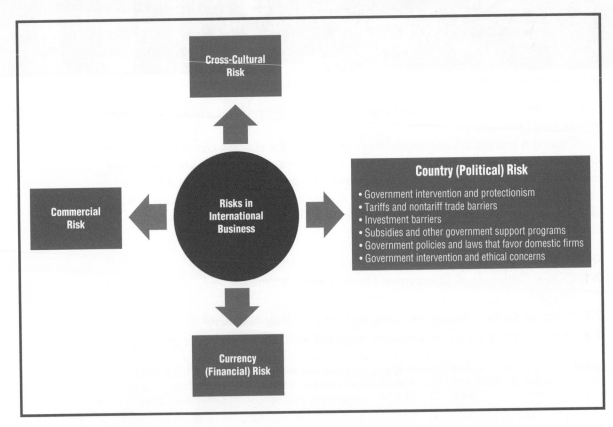

EXHIBIT 7.1

Government Intervention as a Component of Country Risk

The Nature of Government Intervention

7.1 Understand the nature of government intervention.

Protectionism is perhaps the leading manifestation of government intervention in international business. **Protectionism** refers to national economic policies designed to restrict free trade and protect domestic industries from foreign competition. Protectionism typically arises in the form of tariffs, nontariff barriers such as quotas, and administrative rules designed to discourage imports. A **tariff** (also known as a *duty*) is a tax a government imposes on imported products, effectively increasing the cost of acquisition for the customer. A **nontariff trade barrier** is a government policy, regulation, or procedure that impedes trade through means other than explicit tariffs. Trade barriers are enforced as products pass through **customs**, the checkpoints at the ports of entry in each country where government officials inspect imported products and levy tariffs. An often-used form of nontariff trade barrier is a **quota**, a quantitative restriction placed on imports of a specific product over a specified period. Government intervention may also target foreign direct investment (FDI) flows via investment barriers that restrict the operations of foreign firms.

Government intervention affects economic activity in a nation by hindering or helping the ability of its homegrown firms to compete internationally. Often companies, labor unions, and other special interest groups convince governments to adopt policies that benefit them. For example, in the 2000s, the Bush administration imposed tariffs on the import of foreign steel into the United States. The rationale was to give the U.S. steel industry time to restructure and revive itself following years of decline due to tough competition from foreign steel producers. Although the action probably saved hundreds of U.S. jobs, the tariffs increased production costs for firms that use steel, such as Ford and Whirlpool. Higher material costs made them less competitive and reduced prospects for selling their products in world markets.[5] Eventually the steel tariffs were removed but only after causing significant harm.

Another example of intervention was U.S. government–imposed voluntary export restraints on Japanese vehicles imported into the United States in the 1980s. This move helped insulate the U.S. auto industry from foreign competition. In a protected environment, however, Detroit automakers had less incentive to improve quality and design. In this way, protectionism contributed to weakening Detroit's ability to compete in the global auto industry.

Protectionist policies may also lead to price inflation because tariffs can restrict the supply of a particular product. Tariffs may also reduce the choices available to buyers by restricting the variety of products available for sale.

These examples illustrate that government intervention can lead to harmful *unintended consequences*—unfavorable outcomes of policies or laws. In a complex world, legislators and policymakers cannot foresee all possible outcomes. Government intervention should be planned and implemented with great care.

Special interest groups often advocate trade and investment barriers that protect their interests. Consider the recent trade dispute between Mexico and the United States over Mexican cement. The U.S. government imposed duties of about $50 per ton on the import of

---

Protectionism
National economic policies designed to restrict free trade and protect domestic industries from foreign competition.

Tariff
A tax imposed on imported products, effectively increasing the cost of acquisition for the customer.

Nontariff trade barrier
A government policy, regulation, or procedure that impedes trade through means other than explicit tariffs.

Customs
Checkpoints at the ports of entry in each country where government officials inspect imported products and levy tariffs.

Quota
A quantitative restriction placed on imports of a specific product over a specified period.

Four main reasons governments impose tariffs, nontariff trade barriers, and other forms of intervention.

- *To generate revenue* For example, the Hamilton Tariff, enacted July 4, 1789, was the second statute the newly founded United States passed, providing revenue for the federal government. Today, Ghana and Sierra Leone generate more than 25 percent of their total government revenue from tariffs.

- *To ensure citizen safety, security, and welfare* For example, governments pass laws to prevent importation of harmful products such as contaminated food.

- *To pursue economic, political, or social objectives* In most cases, tariffs and similar forms of intervention are intended to promote job growth and economic development.

- *To serve company and industrial interests* Governments may devise regulations to stimulate development of homegrown industries.

Mexican cement after U.S. cement makers lobbied Congress. The stakes were huge. Mexican imports can reach 10 percent of U.S. domestic cement consumption. Mexico proposed substituting import quotas in place of the tariffs. The two governments have negotiated for years to resolve the dispute.[6]

Trade and investment barriers can be considered either defensive or offensive. Governments impose defensive barriers to safeguard industries, workers, and special interest groups and to promote national security. Governments impose offensive barriers to pursue strategic or public policy objectives such as increasing employment or generating tax revenues. Let's review the specific rationale for government intervention.

Defensive Rationale

Four major defensive motives are particularly relevant: protection of the nation's economy, protection of an infant industry, national security, and national culture and identity.

PROTECTION OF THE NATIONAL ECONOMY   Proponents argue that firms in advanced economies cannot compete with those in developing countries that employ low-cost labor. Protectionists demand trade barriers to curtail the import of low-priced products. The action is intended to protect jobs and ensure higher wages for workers in advanced economies.

However, protectionism defies the principle of comparative advantage, which implies that nations should engage in more international trade, not less. Trade barriers interfere with country-specific specialization of labor. When countries specialize in the products they can produce best and then trade for the rest, they perform better. They deliver superior living standards to their citizens. Blocking imports can reduce the availability and increase the cost of products sold in the home market. Protectionism can trigger retaliation. This results in foreign governments imposing their own trade barriers, which reduces sales prospects for exporters.

PROTECTION OF AN INFANT INDUSTRY   In an emerging industry, companies are often inexperienced and lack the latest technologies and know-how. They also may lack the large size typical of competitors in established industries abroad. A very young industry may need temporary protection from foreign competitors. A government may impose temporary trade barriers on foreign imports to ensure that young firms gain a large share of the domestic market. Protecting infant industries has allowed some countries to develop a modern industrial sector. For example, government intervention allowed Japan and South Korea to become dominant players in the global automobile and consumer electronics industries. The U.S. government imposed tariffs on the import of inexpensive Chinese-made solar cells to protect the emerging U.S. solar power industry.[7]

Once in place, however, such protection may be hard to remove. Industry owners and workers tend to lobby to preserve government protection. Infant industries in many countries (especially in Latin America, South Asia, and Eastern Europe) have shown a tendency to remain dependent on government protection for many years. Protected companies are often less efficient than unprotected firms that compete in free markets. Faced with few or no competitors, protected companies may produce lower quality products or charge higher prices for them, which can harm domestic consumers.[8]

NATIONAL SECURITY   Countries impose trade restrictions on products viewed as critical to national defense and security. These include military technology and computers that help maintain domestic production in security-related products. For example, Russia blocked a bid by German engineering giant Siemens to purchase the Russian turbine manufacturer OAO Power Machines, on grounds of national security. The Russian government has strict legislation that limits foreign investment in sectors considered vital to Russia's national interests.[9] Countries may also impose **export controls**, government measures intended to manage or prevent the export of certain products or trade with certain countries. For example, many countries prohibit exports of plutonium to North Korea because it can be used to make nuclear weapons. The United States generally blocks exports of nuclear and military technology to countries it deems state sponsors of terrorism, such as Iran and Syria.

NATIONAL CULTURE AND IDENTITY   Should foreign entities, say the Japanese or the Saudis, be allowed to purchase national landmarks such as the Eiffel Tower or Rockefeller Center? In

Export control
A government measure intended to manage or prevent the export of certain products or trade with certain countries.

most countries, certain occupations, industries, and public assets are seen as central to national culture and identity. Governments may impose trade barriers to restrict imports of products or services seen to threaten such national assets. In the United States, authorities opposed Japanese investors' purchase of the Seattle Mariners baseball team because it is viewed as part of the national heritage. France does not allow significant foreign ownership of its TV stations because of concerns about foreign influence on French culture.

Offensive Rationale

Offensive rationales for government intervention fall into two categories: national strategic priorities and increasing employment.

NATIONAL STRATEGIC PRIORITIES   Government intervention sometimes aims to encourage the development of industries that bolster the nation's economy. It is a *proactive* variation of the infant industry rationale and related to national industrial policy. Countries with many high-tech or high value-adding industries, such as information technology, pharmaceuticals, car manufacturing, or financial services, create better jobs and higher tax revenue. Countries with low-tech or low value-adding industries, such as agriculture, textile manufacturing, or discount retailing create lower value jobs and less tax revenue. Governments in Germany, South Korea, and numerous other countries have devised policies that promote the development of relatively desirable industries. Such governments may provide financing for investment in high-tech or high value–adding industries. They may encourage citizens to save money to ensure a steady supply of loanable funds for industrial investment. These loans enable funding for public education to provide citizens the skills and flexibility they need to perform in key industries.[10]

INCREASING EMPLOYMENT   Governments often impose import barriers to protect employment in designated industries. Insulating domestic firms from foreign competition stimulates national output, leading to more jobs in the protected industries. The effect is usually strongest in import-intensive industries that employ much labor. For example, the Chinese government has traditionally required foreign companies to enter its huge markets through joint ventures with local Chinese firms. This policy creates jobs for Chinese workers. A joint venture between Shanghai Automotive Industry Corporation (SAIC) and Volkswagen created jobs in China.

Source: Alex Tihonov/Fotolia

To safeguard its national culture, the French government prevents foreign companies from owning television and movie companies in France. Shown here is Cannes, the site of France's popular film festival.

Instruments of Government Intervention

The main instruments of trade intervention and the traditional forms of protectionism are tariffs and nontariff trade barriers. Individual countries or groups of countries, such as the European Union (europa.eu), can impose these barriers. However, barriers can be a serious impediment to cross-border business. The United Nations estimated that trade barriers alone cost developing countries more than $500 billion in lost trading opportunities with developed countries every year.[11] Exhibit 7.2 highlights the most common forms of government intervention and their effects.

7.2 Know the instruments of government intervention.

Tariffs

The most common type of tariff is the *import tariff*, a tax levied on imported products. Import tariffs are usually *ad valorem*. They are assessed as a percentage of the value of the imported product. In other cases, a government may impose a *specific tariff*, a flat fee or fixed amount per

EXHIBIT 7.2 Types and Effects of Government Intervention

Intervention Type	Definition	Practical Effect on Customers, Firms, or Government	Contemporary Examples
Tariff	Tax imposed on imported products.	Increases cost to the importer, exporter, and usually the buyer of the product; discourages product imports; generates government revenue	Switzerland charges a 37% tariff on imported agricultural products. Bolivia charges a 35% tariff on most apparel and textiles.
Quota	Quantitative restriction on imports of a product during a specified period of time.	Gives early importers monopoly power and the ability to charge higher prices; harms late importers; usually results in higher prices to the buyer	Japan maintains strict quotas on the import of leather shoes and various types of seafood.
Local content requirements	Requirement that firms include a minimum percentage of locally sourced inputs in the production of given products or services.	Discourages imports of raw materials, parts, and supplies, which harms manufacturers' sourcing options; may result in higher costs and lower product quality for buyers	At least 50% of the value of all cars assembled in Venezuela must be from parts or other inputs produced in Venezuela.
Regulations and technical standards	Safety, health, or technical regulations; labeling requirements.	May hinder the entry of imported products and reduce the quantity of available products, resulting in higher costs to importers and buyers	Saudi Arabia bans imports of firearms and used clothing. The EU requires extensive testing on thousands of imported chemicals.
Administrative and bureaucratic procedures	Complex procedures or requirements imposed on importers or foreign investors that hinder trade and investment.	Slows the import of products or services; hinders or delays firms' investment activities	Russia imposes extensive inspections and bureaucratic procedures on the import of alcoholic beverages.
FDI and ownership restrictions	Rules that limit the ability of foreign firms to invest in certain industries or acquire local firms.	Limits how much foreigners can invest in a country, and/or the proportion of ownership that foreigners can hold in firms in the country	In Switzerland, foreign-owned insurance companies must be managed by a Swiss national, and most board members must be European citizens.
Subsidy	Financing or other resources that a government grants to a firm or group of firms, to ensure their survival or success.	Increases the competitive advantage of the grantee while diminishing the competitive advantages of those that do not receive the subsidy	Turkey gives export subsidies of up to 20% to local, Turkish producers of wheat and sugar.

Source: Adapted from the Office of the United States Trade Representative, retrieved from http://www.ustr.gov.

unit of the imported product. It is based on weight, volume, or surface area, such as barrels of oil or square meters of fabric. A *revenue tariff* is intended to raise money for the government. A tariff on cigarette imports, for example, produces a steady flow of revenue. A *protective tariff* aims to protect domestic industries from foreign competition. A *prohibitive tariff* is one so high that no one can import any of the items.

The amount of a tariff is determined by examining a product's harmonized code. Products are classified under about 8,000 unique codes in the *harmonized tariff* or *harmonized code* schedule. The harmonized code is standardized worldwide. Without it, firms and governments might have differing opinions on product definitions and the tariffs charged.

Import tariffs can generate substantial revenue for national governments. This helps explain why they are common in developing economies. The United States charges tariffs on many consumer, agricultural, and labor-intensive products. The U.S. typically collects high tariffs (often 48 percent) on imports of basic, low-quality shoes, and low tariffs (just 9 percent) on luxury shoes. Low-income shoe buyers end up paying the highest tariffs. The European Union applies tariffs of up to 191 percent on meat, 118 percent on cereals, and 106 percent on sugar and confectionary products.[12]

Exhibit 7.3 provides a sample of import tariffs in selected countries. Under the North American Free Trade Agreement (NAFTA), Canada, Mexico, and the United States have

EXHIBIT 7.3 A Sampling of Import Tariffs, Percentages

Country	Average Import Tariff	
	Agricultural Products	Nonagricultural Products
Australia	1.2%	3.0%
Canada	15.9	2.3
China	15.6	9.0
European Union	13.2	4.2
India	33.5	10.2
Japan	19.0	2.6
Mexico	19.7	5.9
United States	5.3	3.1

Note: Exhibit shows the average, most favored nation-applied tariff.

Source: Based on *World Tariff Profiles 2014*, World Trade Organization, www.wto.org.

eliminated nearly all tariffs on product imports from each other. However, Mexico maintains significant tariffs with the rest of the world—19.7 percent for agricultural products and 5.9 percent for nonagricultural goods. India's tariffs are relatively high, especially in agriculture, where the average rate is 33.5 percent. China has reduced its tariffs since joining the World Trade Organization (WTO, www.wto.org), but trade barriers remain high in some areas.

Half of all workers in Africa are employed in agriculture. Significant tariffs and other trade barriers in the advanced economies hinder imports of agricultural goods from Africa. This worsens already severe poverty in many African countries.

Because high tariffs inhibit free trade and economic growth, governments have tended to reduce them over time. This was the primary goal of the General Agreement on Tariffs and Trade (GATT; now the WTO). Countries as diverse as Chile, Hungary, Turkey, and South Korea have liberalized their previously protected markets, lowering trade barriers and subjecting themselves to greater competition from abroad. Exhibit 7.4 illustrates trends in average world tariff rates over time. Notice that developing economies have been lowering their tariff rates since the early 1980s. Continued reductions represent a major driver of market globalization.

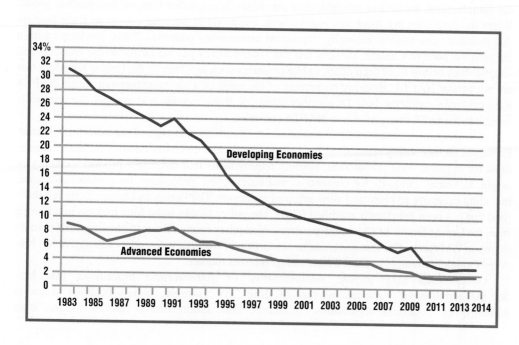

EXHIBIT 7.4

Trends in Average Tariff Rates, Percentages

Source: Based on the World Bank, http://data.worldbank.org.

Nontariff Trade Barriers

Nontariff trade barriers are government policies or measures that restrict trade without imposing a direct tax or duty. They include quotas, import licenses, local content requirements, government regulations, and administrative or bureaucratic procedures. The use of nontariff barriers has grown substantially in recent decades. Governments sometimes prefer them because they are easier to hide from the WTO and other organizations that monitor international trade.

Quotas restrict the physical volume or value of products that firms can import into a country. In a classic type of quota, the U.S. government imposed an upper limit of roughly 2 million pounds on the total amount of sugar that can be imported into the United States each year. Sugar imports that exceed this level face a tariff of several cents per pound. U.S. sugar producers are protected from cheaper imports, giving them a competitive edge over foreign sugar producers. However, U.S. consumers and producers of certain types of products, such as Hershey's and Coca-Cola, pay more for sugar. Companies that manufacture products containing sugar may save money by moving production to countries that do not impose quotas or tariffs on sugar.

Governments can impose voluntary quotas, under which firms agree to limit exports of certain products. These are also known as *voluntary export restraints*. For example, import quotas in the European Union led to an impasse in which millions of Chinese-made garments piled up at ports and borders in Europe. The EU impounded the clothing because China had exceeded the voluntary import quotas it had negotiated with the EU.[13]

Import license
Government authorization granted to a firm for importing a product.

Governments occasionally require importing firms to obtain an **import license**, a formal permission to import, which restricts imports in a way that is similar to quotas. (Do not confuse import licenses with licens*ing*, a strategy for entering foreign markets in which one firm allows another the right to use its intellectual property in return for a fee.) Governments sell import licenses to companies on a competitive basis or grant the licenses on a first-come, first-served basis. This tends to discriminate against smaller firms, which typically lack the resources to purchase them. Obtaining a license can be costly and complicated. In some countries, importers must pay hefty fees to government authorities. In other countries, they must deal with bureaucratic red tape. In Russia, a complex web of licensing requirements limits imports of alcoholic beverages.

Local content requirements require manufacturers to include a minimum of local value added—that is, production that takes place locally. Local content requirements are usually imposed in countries that are members of an economic bloc, such as the EU and NAFTA. The so-called *rules of origin requirement* specifies that a certain proportion of products and supplies, or of intermediate goods used in local manufacturing, must be produced within the bloc. For a car manufacturer, the tires or windshields it purchases from another firm are intermediate goods. When the firm does not meet this requirement, the products become subject to trade barriers that member governments normally impose on nonmember countries. Thus, producers within the NAFTA zone of Canada, Mexico, and the United States pay no tariffs on the products and supplies they obtain from each other, unlike countries such as China or the United Kingdom that are not part of NAFTA. Roughly 60 percent of the value of a car manufactured within NAFTA must originate within the NAFTA member countries. If this condition is not met, the product is subject to the tariffs charged to non-NAFTA countries.

Government regulations and technical standards are another type of nontariff trade barrier. Examples include safety regulations for motor vehicles and electrical equipment, health regulations for hygienic food preparation, labeling requirements that indicate a product's country of origin, technical standards for computers, and bureaucratic procedures for customs clearance, including excessive red tape and slow approval processes. The European Union strictly regulates food that has been genetically modified (GM). The policy blocks some food imports into Europe from the United States. In China, the government requires foreign firms to obtain special permits to import GM foods. Chinese government censorship of material it considers subversive has hindered Google's attempts to enter China's huge Internet market.[14]

Governments may impose *administrative or bureaucratic procedures* that hinder the activities of importers or foreign firms. For example, India's business sector is burdened by countless regulations, standards, and administrative hurdles at the state and federal levels. In Mexico, government-imposed bureaucratic procedures led United Parcel Service to suspend its ground delivery service temporarily across the U.S.–Mexican border. Similarly, the United States barred Mexican trucks from entering the United States on the grounds that they were unsafe.[15]

Saudi Arabia is home to various restrictive practices that hinder international trade. Every foreign business traveler to the Arab kingdom must hold an entry visa that can be obtained only by securing the support of a sponsor. A sponsor can be a Saudi citizen or organization who vouches for the visitor's actions. Because few Saudis are willing to assume such responsibility, foreigners who want to do business in Saudi Arabia face difficulty.[16]

Investment Barriers

As we saw in the opening case, countries also impose restrictions on FDI and ownership. These restrictions hinder the ability of foreign firms to invest in some industry sectors or acquire local firms. Excessive restrictions in India prevent the approval of many investment proposals that could produce billions of dollars in revenue to the local economy and government. Worldwide, FDI and ownership restrictions are particularly common in industries such as broadcasting, utilities, air transportation, military technology, and financial services. The restrictions are also present in industries in which the government has major holdings, such as oil and key minerals. The Mexican government restricts FDI by foreign investors to protect its oil industry, which is deemed critical to the nation's security. The Canadian government restricts foreign ownership of local movie studios and TV networks to protect its indigenous film and TV industries from excessive foreign influence. FDI and ownership restrictions are particularly burdensome in the services sector because services usually cannot be exported and providers must establish a physical presence in target markets to conduct business there.

Currency controls restrict the outflow of widely used currencies, such as the dollar, euro, and yen, and occasionally the inflow of foreign currencies. Controls can help conserve especially valuable currency or reduce the risk of capital flight. They are particularly common in developing economies. Some countries employ a system of dual official exchange rates, offering exporters a relatively favorable rate to encourage exports, while importers receive a relatively unfavorable rate to discourage imports.

Currency controls both help and harm firms that establish foreign subsidiaries through FDI. They favor companies when they export their products from the host country but harm those that rely heavily on imported parts and components. Controls also restrict the ability of MNEs to *repatriate* their profits—that is, transfer revenues from profitable operations back to the home country.

As an example, Venezuela's currency controls have led to a shortage of dollars and other hard currencies. Multinational firms avoid doing business in Venezuela because strict currency rules limit the amount of profit they can take out of the country or limit their ability to receive payment for imports at reasonable prices. Venezuela imposed the controls to keep imports inexpensive and maintain a base of hard currencies in the country.[17]

Subsidies and Other Government Support Programs

Subsidies are monetary or other resources that a government grants to a firm or group of firms, intended either to encourage exports or simply to facilitate the production and marketing of products at reduced prices, to help ensure that the involved companies prosper. Subsidies come in the form of outright cash disbursements, material inputs, services, tax breaks,

Currency control
Restrictions on the outflow of hard currency from a country or on the inflow of foreign currencies.

Subsidy
Monetary or other resources that a government grants to a firm or group of firms, usually intended to encourage exports or facilitate the production and marketing of products at reduced prices, to ensure that the favored firms prosper.

Source: Keith Dannemiller/Alamy

State-owned oil company PEMEX (Petroleos de Mexico) benefits from investment barriers in Mexico that prevent foreign firms from gaining control of Mexican oil companies.

the construction of infrastructure, and government contracts at inflated prices. For example, the French government has provided large subsidies to Air France, the national airline.

In China, several leading corporations such as China Minmetals and Shanghai Automotive, are state enterprises wholly or partly owned by the Chinese government, which provides them with huge financial resources. State-owned enterprises account for more than 40 percent of China's economic output.[18]

Critics argue that subsidies give unfair advantages to recipients by reducing their cost of doing business. In India, the government provides massive subsidies to state-owned oil companies, which allow them to offer gasoline at very low prices. Foreign MNEs such as Royal Dutch Shell cannot compete profitably against rivals that offer such prices and consequently avoid doing business in the market.[19] The WTO prohibits subsidies when it can be proven that they hinder free trade. Subsidies, however, are hard to define. For example, when a government provides land, infrastructure, telecommunications systems, or utilities to the firms in a corporate park, this is technically a subsidy. Yet many view this type of support as an appropriate public function.

In Europe and the United States, governments frequently provide agricultural subsidies to supplement the income of farmers and help manage the supply of agricultural commodities. The U.S. government grants subsidies for more than two dozen commodities, including corn, soybeans, wheat, cotton, and rice.[20]

Countervailing duty

Tariff imposed on products imported into a country to offset subsidies given to producers or exporters in the exporting country.

Governments sometimes retaliate against subsidies by imposing **countervailing duties**, tariffs on products imported into a country to offset subsidies given to producers or exporters in the exporting country. In this way, the duty serves to cancel out the effect of the subsidy, eliminating the price advantage the exporters would otherwise obtain.

Dumping

Pricing exported products at less than their normal value, generally less than their price in the domestic or third-country markets, or at less than production cost.

Subsidies may allow a manufacturer to practice **dumping**—that is, to charge an unusually low price for exported products, typically lower than that for domestic or third-country customers, or even lower than the cost to manufacture the good.[21] The European Union has provided billions of euros in subsidies every year to EU sugar producers, which allowed Europe to become one of the world's largest sugar exporters at artificially low prices. Without the subsidies, Europe would be one of the world's biggest sugar importers.

Dumping violates WTO rules because it amounts to unfair competition, but dumping is hard to prove because firms usually do not reveal data on their cost structures. A large MNE that charges very low prices could conceivably drive competitors out of a foreign market, achieve a monopoly, and then raise prices later.[22]

Investment incentive

Transfer payment or tax concession made directly to foreign firms to entice them to invest in the country.

Related to subsidies are governmental **investment incentives**, transfer payments or tax concessions made directly to individual foreign firms to entice them to invest in the country. Hong Kong's government put up most of the cash to build Hong Kong Disneyland (www.hongkongdisneyland.com). Although the park and facilities cost about $1.81 billion, the government provided Disney an investment of $1.74 billion to develop the site.

Recently, Austin, Texas, and Albany, New York, competed for the chance to have the Korean manufacturer Samsung Electronics (www.samsung.com) build a semiconductor plant in their regions. Austin offered $225 million worth of tax relief and other concessions in its successful bid to attract Samsung's $300 million plant, estimated to create nearly 1,000 new jobs locally. To entice MNEs to establish local production facilities, the country of Macedonia offers such incentives as low corporate taxes, immediate access to utilities and transportation, and financial support for training workers (see www.investinmacedonia.com).

Governments also support domestic industries by adopting *procurement policies* that restrict purchases to home–country suppliers. Several governments require air travel purchased with government funds to be booked with home–country carriers. Such policies are especially common in countries with large public

Source: Sean Pavone/Shutterstock

The Ministry of Economy, Trade, and Industry in Japan is typical of national federal agencies that promote international trade and investment.

sectors, such as China and Russia. In the United States, government agencies favor domestic suppliers unless their prices are high compared to foreign suppliers. In Japan, government agencies often do not even consider foreign bids, regardless of pricing. Public procurement agencies often impose requirements that effectively exclude foreign suppliers.

Evolution and Consequences of Government Intervention

7.3 Explain the evolution and consequences of government trade intervention.

A century ago, trade barriers worldwide were relatively high. The trading environment worsened through two world wars and the Great Depression. The United States passed the Smoot-Hawley Tariff Act in 1930. It raised U.S. tariffs to near-record highs of more than 50 percent, compared to only about 4 percent today. Tariffs that other countries imposed to retaliate against Smoot-Hawley choked off foreign markets for U.S. agricultural products. This resulted in falling farm prices and many bank failures. In an effort to revive trade, many governments began to reduce tariffs in the late 1940s.

However, governments in Latin America and other developing nations gradually adopted protectionist policies aimed at supporting domestic industrialization. The approach did not succeed. Domestic firms that enjoyed government subsidies and the protection of high tariffs never became competitive in world markets. Living standards remained relatively low.

By contrast, from the 1970s onward, Singapore, Hong Kong, Taiwan, and South Korea achieved rapid economic growth by encouraging the development of export-intensive industries. Their model, known as *export-led development*, proved highly successful. These countries, along with Thailand, Indonesia, and others in East Asia, substantially increased international trade and raised living standards. A rising middle class helped transform these countries into competitive economies.

Japan launched an ambitious program of industrialization and export-led development. The country's rise from poverty in the 1940s to become one of the world's wealthiest countries by the 1980s has been called the *Japanese miracle*. The feat was achieved with the help of national strategic policies. The policies included tariffs that fostered and protected Japan's infant industries such as automobiles, shipbuilding, and consumer electronics.

China and India long sheltered themselves through protectionism and government intervention. Both countries relied on centralized economic planning in which agriculture and manufacturing were controlled by state-run industries. Around 1990, China and India began to liberalize their economies. In 2001, China joined the WTO and committed to reducing trade barriers. Trade became an enormous factor stimulating the Chinese economy. By 2015, its GDP was more than ten times the 1998 level. The value of China's exports reached $2.2 trillion. In India, trade liberalization and privatization of state enterprises helped fuel economic progress. Between 2000 and 2015, India's average annual income rose from about $470 in real terms to more than $1,800 in 2015, an impressive achievement.

In 1947, 23 nations signed the **General Agreement on Tariffs and Trade (GATT)**, the first major effort to reduce trade barriers systematically worldwide. The GATT created a process to reduce tariffs through continuous negotiations among member nations, an agency to serve as watchdog over world trade, and a forum for resolving trade disputes.

The GATT introduced the concept of *normal trade relations* in which each nation agreed to extend the tariff reductions covered in a trade agreement with a trading partner to all other countries. A concession to one country became a concession to all. In 1995,

Source: Dmitry Kalinovsky/Shutterstock

India is a major clothing exporter that faces high tariffs, especially in markets in advanced economies. Here, an Indian textile merchant shows his samples.

the WTO succeeded the GATT and grew to include more than 150 member nations. The organization proved extremely effective and resulted in the greatest global decline in trade barriers in history.

The global recession and financial crisis that began in 2008 have raised new questions about government's role in national economies. The crisis arose from inadequate regulation in the banking and finance sectors. In response, governments worldwide increased regulation.[23]

Some governments increased protectionism in an effort to safeguard jobs and wage levels. Argentina and Brazil, for example, increased import tariffs on numerous products. Russia raised tariffs on dozens of goods, including cars and combine harvesters.[24] The United Kingdom provided substantial subsidies to U.K. banks and financial institutions. China pumped hundreds of billions of dollars into its own economy.[25] The new round of protectionism has had an impact on international commerce, extending beyond the banking and financial areas.[26]

In general, however, as illustrated in Exhibit 7.4, average tariffs have declined over time. Simultaneously, as shown in Exhibit 7.5, world trade and GDP have flourished. Decreasing trade barriers are a major factor in the growth of global commerce and consequently in rising incomes around the world. Firms that participate actively in international trade and investment not only improve their performance but also contribute to reducing global poverty.[27]

Ease of Doing Business is an index the World Bank develops annually. It ranks 189 countries and is useful for evaluating the effects of government intervention. A high ease of doing business ranking means a country's regulatory environment is conducive to starting and operating a company there. The index obtains a total ranking by rating each country in terms of ten variables: starting a business, dealing with construction permits, getting electricity, registering property, getting credit, protecting minority investors, paying taxes, trading across borders, enforcing contracts, and resolving insolvency.[28]

Exhibit 7.6 shows the ease of doing business for each country. Most of the easiest countries are advanced economies that enjoy high living standards. The easiest group also includes numerous emerging markets that have simplified their regulatory environment in an effort to encourage

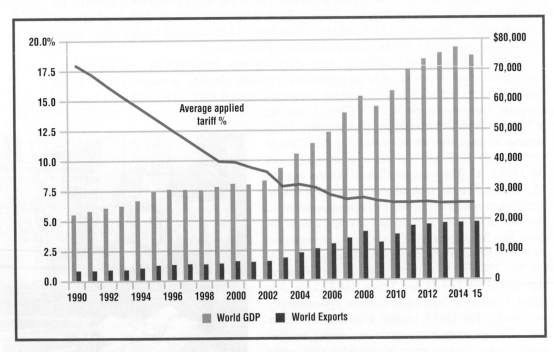

EXHIBIT 7.5

Relationship Among Tariffs, World GDP, and the Volume of World Trade

Note: Tariffs given as average percent (red line), World GDP given in billions of U.S. $ (blue column), and Volume of World Exports given in billions of U.S. $ (purple column). Left axis measures tariffs. Right axis measures world GDP and volume of world exports.

Sources: Based on International Monetary Fund World Economic Outlook Database, at www.imf.org; UNCTAD, at http://unctadstat.unctad.org; World Bank, http://data.worldbank.org.

entrepreneurship and investment. The exhibit's moderately hard and hardest countries are relatively difficult places to do business and are characterized by severe poverty and other hardships.

Government intervention and trade barriers raise ethical concerns for developing economies. For example, United States import tariffs on clothing and shoes often exceed 20 percent. The tariffs hurt poor countries such as Bangladesh, Pakistan, India, and several nations in Africa, where clothing and shoe exporters are concentrated. United States tariffs on imports from Cambodia are far higher than on imports from the United Kingdom. The tariffs that confront less-developed economies are often several times those faced by the richest countries.[29]

Government intervention can also offset harmful effects. For example, trade barriers can create or protect jobs. Subsidies can help counterbalance harmful consequences that disproportionately affect the poor. In Europe, for example, globalization has affected thousands of workers whose jobs have been shifted to other countries with lower labor costs. Governments in Europe provide subsidies for the unemployed, aimed at retraining workers to upgrade their job skills or find work in other fields.[30]

How Firms Can Respond to Government Intervention

7.4 Describe how firms can respond to government trade intervention.

Firms generally must cope with protectionism and other forms of intervention. In extractive industries such as aluminum and petroleum, for example, companies may have little choice but to operate in nations that impose formidable barriers. The food-processing, biotechnology, and pharmaceutical industries also encounter countless laws and regulations abroad.

Strategies for Managers

China, India, and numerous other countries in Africa, Asia, and Latin America feature extensive trade barriers and government involvement. Yet many firms target emerging markets and developing economies because of the huge long-term potential they offer.[31] Firms devise various strategies to manage harmful government intervention.

RESEARCH TO GATHER KNOWLEDGE AND INTELLIGENCE Experienced managers continually scan the business environment to identify the nature of government intervention and to plan market-entry strategies and host-country operations. They review their return-on-investment criteria to account for the increased cost and risk of trade and investment barriers. For example, the EU is devising new guidelines that affect company operations in areas ranging from product liability laws to standards for investment in European industries.

CHOOSE THE MOST APPROPRIATE ENTRY STRATEGIES Tariffs and most nontariff trade barriers apply to exporting, whereas investment barriers apply to FDI. If high tariffs are present, managers may consider FDI, licensing, and joint ventures that allow the firm to operate directly in the target market and avoid import barriers. For example, Taiwan's Foxconn, a contract manufacturer for Apple and other electronics firms, built a factory in Brazil partly to avoid the country's high tariffs on imported goods.

Tariffs usually vary with the *form* of an imported product. To minimize the impact of tariffs, many firms ship manufactured products knocked-down (as parts and components) and then assemble them in the target market. For example, Eastman Kodak imports parts into the United States and uses them to manufacture photographic equipment. Kodak could produce the finished equipment abroad, but the tariff on parts and components is lower. By manufacturing in the United States, Kodak avoids paying higher tariffs.[32]

Source: Bernd Kröger/Fotolia

Many firms lobby national governments, such as Germany's parliament in Berlin, for lower barriers to trade and investment.

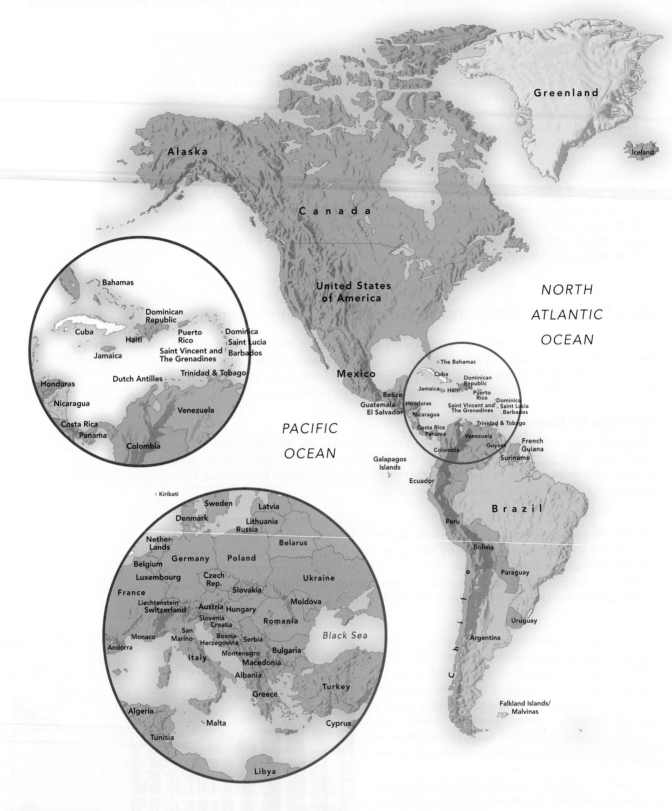

EXHIBIT 7.6

Countries Ranked by Ease of Doing Business, 2015

Sources: Based on *Doing Business: Economy Rankings* and *Doing Business 2015*, World Bank Group, Washington, DC, http://www.doingbusiness.org/rankings.

ARCTIC OCEAN

Norway

Sweden

Finland

United
Kingdom

Ireland

Denmark

Netherlands
Belgium
Luxembourg
France
Switz.
San Marino
Monaco
Andorra

Germany

Czech
Rep.
Liech. Austria
Slovenia
Croatia
Bosnia-
Herzegovina
Montenegro
Italy Albania

Estonia

Latvia
Lithuania
Russia

Poland

Slovakia
Hungary

Serbia

Macedonia

Greece

Belarus

Ukraine

Moldova

Romania

Bulgaria

Russia

Kazakhstan

Mongolia

Georgia
Armenia

Azerbaijan

Uzbekistan

Kyrgyzstan

Turkmenistan

Tajikistan

North
Korea

South
Korea

Japan

Portugal

Spain

Tunisia

Malta

Cyprus
Syria
Lebanon
Israel
Jordan

Iraq

Iran

Afghanistan

China

Turkey

Morocco

Algeria

Libya

Egypt

West Bank
and Gaza

Kuwait

Bahrain

Qatar

United
Arab
Emirates

Saudi
Arabia

Oman

Pakistan

India

Nepal

Bhutan

Bangladesh

Myanmar
(Burma)

Macau

Hong
Kong

Taiwan

Laos

Western
Sahara

Cape Verde

Mauritania

Mali

Niger

Chad

Sudan

Eritrea

Yemen

Djibouti

Somalia

Sri
Lanka

Maldives

Thailand

Vietnam

Cambodia

Philippines

Senegal
Gambia
Guinea-bissau
Guinea
Sierra Leone
Liberia
Côte d'Ivoire

Ivory
Coast

Ghana
Togo
Benin

Nigeria

Burkina
Faso

Central
African
Republic

Ethiopia

Micronesia

Cameroon

Equatorial
Guinea
São Tomé
Gabon

Congo
Republic

Congo
Democratic
Republic
(Zaire)

Uganda

Rwanda
Burundi

Kenya

Tanzania

Seychelles

INDIAN

OCEAN

Brunei

Malaysia

Singapore

Indonesia

Papua
New
Guinea

Timor-leste

Solomon
Islands

SOUTH

ATLANTIC

OCEAN

Angola

Namibia

Zambia

Zimbabwe

Botswana

Malawi

Mozambique

Madagascar

Comoros

Mauritius

Réunion

Samoa

Vanuatu

Fiji

New
Caledonia

Tonga

Swaziland

South
Africa

Lesotho

Australia

PACIFIC

OCEAN

New
Zealand

Level of economic freedom

- Easiest – 80–100%
- Moderately Easy – 60–79.9%
- Average – 40–59.9%
- Moderately Hard – 20–39.9%
- Hardest – 0–19.9%
- Not Ranked

Foreign trade zone (FTZ)

An area within a country that receives imported goods for assembly or other processing and re-export. For customs purposes, the FTZ is treated as if it is outside the country's borders.

TAKE ADVANTAGE OF FOREIGN TRADE ZONES In an effort to create jobs and stimulate local economic development, governments establish foreign trade zones (also known as *free trade zones* or *free ports*). A **foreign trade zone (FTZ)** is an area within a country that receives imported goods for assembly or other processing and subsequent re-export.[33] Products brought into an FTZ are not subject to duties, taxes, or quotas until they, or the products made from them, enter the non-FTZ commercial territory of the country where the FTZ is. Firms use FTZs to assemble foreign dutiable materials and components into finished products, which are then re-exported. Firms may use FTZs to manage inventory of parts, components, or finished products that eventually will be needed at some other location. In the United States, for example, Japanese carmakers store vehicles at the port of Jacksonville, Florida, without having to pay duties until the cars are shipped to U.S. dealerships.

FTZs exist in more than 75 countries, usually near seaports or airports. In Panama, the Colon Free Zone (www.colonfreezone.com) is an enormous FTZ where products are imported, stored, modified, repacked, and re-exported without being subject to tariffs or customs regulations. The many private firms and wholesalers that set up shop inside the huge zone transship their merchandise from Panama to other parts of the Western Hemisphere and Europe. Some firms obtain FTZ status within their own physical facilities.

Maquiladoras

Export-assembly plants in northern Mexico along the U.S. border that produce components and typically finished products destined for the United States on a tariff-free basis.

Maquiladoras are one example of FTZs. Maquiladoras are export-assembly plants in northern Mexico along the U.S. border. They produce components and finished products typically destined for the United States. Since the 1960s, maquiladoras have imported materials and equipment on a tariff-free basis for assembly or manufacturing and then re-exported the assembled products. Today under NAFTA, maquiladoras employ millions of Mexicans who assemble clothing, furniture, car parts, electronics, and other goods. The arrangement enables firms from the United States, Asia, and Europe to tap low-cost labor, favorable duties, and government incentives while serving the U.S. market. Maquiladoras account for about half of Mexico's exports.

SEEK FAVORABLE CUSTOMS CLASSIFICATIONS FOR EXPORTED PRODUCTS One approach for reducing exposure to trade barriers is to have exported products classified in the appropriate harmonized product code. Many products can be classified within two or more categories, each of which may imply a different tariff. For example, some telecommunications equipment can be classified as electric machinery, electronics, or measuring devices. The manufacturer should analyze the trade barriers on differing categories to ensure that exported products are classified under the lowest tariff code. Alternatively, the manufacturer may be able to modify the exported product in a way that helps minimize trade barriers. South Korea faced a quota on the export of nonrubber footwear to the United States. By shifting manufacturing to rubber-soled shoes, Korean firms increased footwear exports.

TAKE ADVANTAGE OF INVESTMENT INCENTIVES AND OTHER GOVERNMENT SUPPORT PROGRAMS Obtaining economic development incentives from host- or home–country governments is another strategy to reduce the cost of trade and investment barriers. When Mercedes built a factory in Alabama, it benefitted from reduced taxes and direct subsidies the Alabama state government provided. When Siemens built a semiconductor plant in Portugal, it received subsidies from the Portuguese government and the EU. Incentives cover nearly 40 percent of Siemens's investment and training costs. In Europe, Japan, and the United States, governments increasingly provide incentives to entice firms to set up shop within their borders. In addition to cash outlays, incentives also include reduced utility rates, employee training programs, tax holidays, and construction of new roads and other infrastructure.

LOBBY FOR FREER TRADE AND INVESTMENT More nations are liberalizing markets to create jobs and increase tax revenues. The trend results partly from the efforts of firms to lobby domestic and foreign governments to lower their trade and investment barriers. The Japanese have achieved much success in reducing trade barriers by lobbying U.S. and European governments. In China, domestic and foreign firms often lobby the government to relax protectionist policies and regulations that make China a difficult place to do business. Foreign firms often hire former Chinese government officials to help lobby their former colleagues.[34] The private sector lobbies federal authorities to undertake government-to-government trade negotiations aimed at lowering barriers.

MyManagementLab Watch It! I

If your professor has assigned this, go to the Assignments section of **mymanagementlab.com** to complete the video exercise titled Government Intervention: Spotlight on China and Germany.

Regional Integration and Economic Blocs

Related to government intervention is the worldwide trend toward **regional economic integration**. Also known as *regional integration*, regional economic integration refers to the growing economic interdependence that results when two or more countries within a geographic region form an alliance aimed at reducing barriers to trade and investment. As happened following formation of the European Union (EU), regional integration increases economic activity and makes doing business easier among nations within the alliance. At a minimum, the countries in an economic bloc become parties to a **free trade agreement**, a formal arrangement between two or more countries to reduce or eliminate tariffs, quotas, and other barriers to trade in products and services. The member nations also undertake cross-border investments within the bloc.

In the past half-century, most countries have sought to cooperate with others, aiming for some degree of regional integration. Today, more than 50 percent of world trade occurs as part of a preferential trade agreement signed by groups of countries. The trend is based on the premise that, by cooperating, nations within a common geographic region connected by historical, cultural, linguistic, economic, or political factors can gain mutual advantages.[35]

Regional integration results from the formation of a *regional economic integration bloc* or, simply, an *economic bloc*. This refers to a geographic area that consists of two or more countries that agree to pursue economic integration by reducing tariffs and other restrictions to the cross-border flow of products, services, capital, and, in more advanced stages, labor. (In this text, following convention, we use the French term *bloc* instead of *block*.) Two of the best-known examples are the European Union (EU) and the North American Free Trade Agreement (NAFTA). NAFTA consists of Canada, Mexico, and the United States.

More advanced economic blocs, such as the EU, permit the free flow of capital, labor, and technology among their member countries. The EU is also harmonizing monetary policy (to manage the money supply and currency values) and fiscal policy (to manage government finances, especially tax revenues) and gradually integrating the economies of its member nations. However, recent crises in Greece, Italy, Spain, and Portugal, and general discord among EU members, are challenging the progress of regional integration in Europe.

Why would a nation opt to be a member of an economic bloc instead of working toward a system of worldwide free trade? The main reason is that it is much easier to reach agreement on free trade with a handful of countries than with all the nations in the world. This helps explain why there are hundreds of regional trade integration blocs around the world today. They present both opportunities and challenges to internationalizing firms.[36]

Levels of Regional Integration

Exhibit 7.7 identifies five possible levels of regional integration. We can think of these levels as a continuum, with economic interconnectedness progressing from a low level of integration—the free trade area—through higher levels to the most advanced form of integration—the *political union*. The political union represents the ultimate degree of integration among countries, which no countries have yet achieved.

The **free trade area** is the simplest and most common arrangement, in which member countries agree to eliminate formal barriers gradually to trade in products and services within the bloc. Each member country maintains an independent international trade policy with countries outside the bloc. NAFTA is an example. The free trade area emphasizes the pursuit of comparative advantage for a group of countries rather than for individual states. Governments may impose *local content requirements*. They specify that locally produced products must contain a minimum proportion of locally manufactured parts and components. If the content requirement is not met, the product becomes subject to the tariffs that member governments normally impose on nonmember countries.

7.5 Understand regional integration and economic blocs.

Regional economic integration
The growing economic interdependence that results when two or more countries within a geographic region form an alliance aimed at reducing barriers to trade and investment.

Free trade agreement
A formal arrangement between two or more countries to reduce or eliminate tariffs, quotas, and barriers to trade in products and services.

Free trade area
A stage of regional integration in which member countries agree to eliminate tariffs and other barriers to trade in products and services within the bloc.

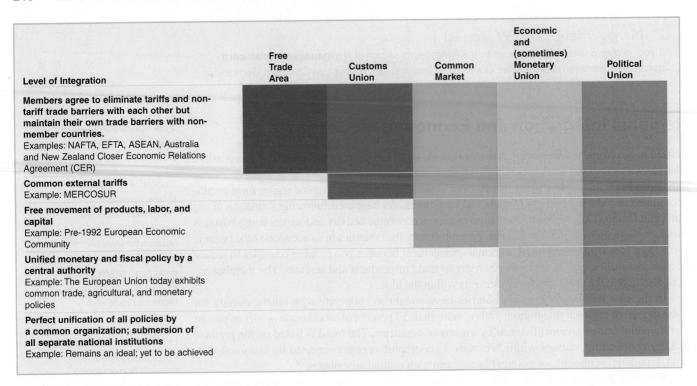

Level of Integration	Free Trade Area	Customs Union	Common Market	Economic and (sometimes) Monetary Union	Political Union
Members agree to eliminate tariffs and non-tariff trade barriers with each other but maintain their own trade barriers with nonmember countries. Examples: NAFTA, EFTA, ASEAN, Australia and New Zealand Closer Economic Relations Agreement (CER)					
Common external tariffs Example: MERCOSUR					
Free movement of products, labor, and capital Example: Pre-1992 European Economic Community					
Unified monetary and fiscal policy by a central authority Example: The European Union today exhibits common trade, agricultural, and monetary policies					
Perfect unification of all policies by a common organization; submersion of all separate national institutions Example: Remains an ideal; yet to be achieved					

EXHIBIT 7.7

Five Potential Levels of Regional Integration Among Nations (For example, a *customs union* has the features of a free trade area plus common external tariffs.)

Source: Based on Bela Balassa, *The Theory of Economic Integration* (Milton Park, Oxford, UK: Routledge Revivals, 2012).

Customs union

A stage of regional integration in which the member countries agree to adopt common tariff and nontariff barriers on imports from nonmember countries.

Common market

A stage of regional integration in which trade barriers are reduced or removed; common external barriers are established; and products, services, and factors of production are allowed to move freely among the member countries.

Economic union

A stage of regional integration in which member countries enjoy all the advantages of early stages but also strive to have common fiscal and monetary policies.

The second level of regional integration is the **customs union**. It is similar to a free trade area except that member states harmonize their external trade policies and adopt *common* tariff and nontariff barriers on imports from nonmember countries. MERCOSUR, an economic bloc in Latin America, is an example of this type of arrangement. The adoption of a common tariff system means that an exporter outside MERCOSUR faces the *same* tariffs and nontariff barriers when trading with *any* MERCOSUR member country. Determining the most appropriate common external tariff is challenging because member countries must agree on the percentage level of the tariff and on how to distribute proceeds from the tariff among the member countries.

In the third stage of regional integration, member countries establish a **common market** (also known as a single market), in which trade barriers are reduced or removed, common external barriers are established, and products, services, and *factors of production* such as capital, labor, and technology are allowed to move freely among the member countries. Like a customs union, a common market also establishes a common trade policy with nonmember countries. The EU is a common market. It has gradually reduced or eliminated restrictions on immigration and the cross-border flow of capital. A worker from an EU country has the right to work in other EU countries, and EU firms can freely transfer funds among their subsidiaries within the bloc. In the EU, Germany has seen an influx of workers from Poland and the Czech Republic because these workers can earn much higher wages in Germany than they can in their home countries.

An **economic union** is the fourth stage of regional integration, in which member countries enjoy all the advantages of early stages but also strive to have common fiscal and monetary policies. At the extreme, each member country adopts identical tax rates. The bloc aims for standardized monetary policy, which requires establishing fixed exchange rates and free convertibility of currencies among the member states, in addition to allowing the free movement of capital. This standardization helps eliminate discriminatory practices that might favor one member state over another. Through greater mobility of products, services, and production factors, an economic union enables firms within the bloc to locate productive activities in member states with the most favorable economic policies.

The EU has made great strides toward achieving an economic union. For example, 19 EU countries have established a *monetary union* in which a single currency, the euro, is now in circulation. Monetary union and the euro have greatly increased the ease with which European financial institutions establish branches across the EU and offer banking services, insurance, and savings products. The single currency also makes trading and investment easier for European firms doing business within the union.

The United States provides a good analogy for an economic union. Imagine each state is like an individual country, but all are joined in a union. The members have a common currency and a single central bank with a uniform monetary policy. Trade among the members takes place unobstructed, and both labor and capital move freely among them. The federal government applies a uniform tax and fiscal policy. Just as would occur in an economic union, the individual U.S. states also govern themselves in such areas as education, police protection, and local taxes. This analogy only goes so far, of course. The United States is a country and, unlike members of a real economic union, the states cannot withdraw.

Leading Economic Blocs

The leading economic blocs are illustrated in Exhibit 7.8. Europe has the longest experience with regional integration and is home to several economic blocs. The most important of these are the EU and the European Free Trade Association.

7.6 Identify the leading economic blocs.

The European Union

In 1957, six countries—Belgium, France, Italy, Luxembourg, the Netherlands, and West Germany—formed an alliance called the European Economic Community (EEC). Its successor is today's European Union (EU), established in 1992. The EU features 28 countries from both Eastern and Western Europe. It is the world's most advanced and largest regional economic bloc. Home to a half billion people, the EU's total annual GDP is about $18 trillion.

The EU has taken the following specific steps to become an economic union.

- *Market access* Tariffs and most nontariff barriers have been eliminated for trade in products and services. Rules of origin favor manufacturing using inputs produced in the EU.
- *Common market* Barriers to the cross-national movement of production factors—labor, capital, and technology—have been removed. For example, an Italian worker now has the right to take a job in Ireland, and a French company can invest freely in Spain.
- *Trade rules* Customs procedures and regulations have been eliminated, streamlining transportation and logistics within Europe.
- *Standards harmonization* Technical standards, regulations, and enforcement procedures related to products, services, and commercial activities are being harmonized. For example, where British firms once used imperial measures (pounds, ounces, and inches), they have converted to the metric system that all EU countries use.

In the long run, the EU is seeking to adopt common fiscal, monetary, taxation, and social welfare policies. Introduction of the euro—the EU's common currency and now one of the world's leading currencies—simplified cross-border trade and enhanced Europe's international competitiveness. The *European Central Bank* is based in Luxembourg and oversees EU monetary functions.

Other EU institutions include the *Council of the European Union,* a representative body that makes decisions on economic policy, budgets, foreign policy, and admission of new member countries. The *European Commission* proposes legislation and policies and is responsible for implementing the decisions of the European Parliament and the Council of the EU. The *European Parliament* consists of elected representatives and develops EU legislation, supervises EU institutions, and makes decisions about the EU budget. The *European Court of Justice* interprets and enforces EU laws and settles legal disputes between member states.[37]

The newest EU members are mainly in Eastern Europe. They are important, low-cost manufacturing sites for EU firms.[38] Most of the newest EU entrants are one-time satellites of the former Soviet Union and have grown rapidly. Most are poised to achieve per-capita income

EXHIBIT 7.8
The Most Active Economic Blocs

ARCTIC OCEAN

NORWAY
SWEDEN
FINLAND

RUSSIA

ESTONIA
LATVIA
LITHUANIA
RUSSIA
BELARUS

UNITED KINGDOM
IRELAND
DENMARK
NETHERLANDS
GERMANY
POLAND
BELGIUM
LUXEMBOURG
CZECH REP.
SLOVAKIA
UKRAINE
FRANCE
LIECH.
AUSTRIA
SWITZ.
SLOVENIA
HUNGARY
MOLDOVA
CROATIA
ROMANIA
MONACO
BOSNIA HERZEGOVINA
SERBIA AND MONTENEGRO
BULGARIA
ANDORRA
ITALY
MACEDONIA
ALBANIA
GREECE
TURKEY

KAZAKHSTAN

MONGOLIA

NORTH KOREA
SOUTH KOREA
JAPAN

SPAIN
PORTUGAL

TUNISIA
CYPRUS
SYRIA
LEBANON
ISRAEL
JORDAN
IRAQ
GEORGIA
ARMENIA
AZERBAIJAN
TURKMENISTAN
UZBEKISTAN
KYRGYZSTAN
TAJIKISTAN

CHINA

MOROCCO

WESTERN SAHARA

ALGERIA
LIBYA
EGYPT

SAUDI ARABIA

QATAR
UNITED ARAB EMIRATES
OMAN

IRAN

AFGHANISTAN

PAKISTAN

KUWAIT

NEPAL
BHUTAN

INDIA

BANGLADESH
MYANMAR (BURMA)
LAOS

TAIWAN

PACIFIC OCEAN

MAURITANIA
MALI
NIGER
CHAD
SUDAN
YEMEN

ENEGAL
AMBIA
JINEA-BISSAU
GUINEA
IERRA LEONE
LIBERIA
IVORY COAST
GHANA
TOGO
BENIN
BURKINA FASO
NIGERIA

ERITREA
DJIBOUTI
SOMALIA

CENTRAL AFRICAN REPUBLIC
CAMEROON
ETHIOPIA

THAILAND
CAMBODIA
VIETNAM

PHILIPPINES

SRI LANKA

EQUATORIAL GUINEA
GABON
CONGO REPUBLIC
CONGO DEMOCRATIC REPUBLIC (ZAIRE)
UGANDA
RWANDA
BURUNDI
KENYA
TANZANIA

BRUNEI
MALAYSIA
SINGAPORE

INDONESIA

PAPUA NEW GUINEA

SOLOMON ISLANDS

INDIAN OCEAN

SOUTH ATLANTIC OCEAN

ANGOLA
ZAMBIA
MALAWI
MOZAMBIQUE
ZIMBABWE
NAMIBIA
BOTSWANA
MADAGASCAR
MAURITIUS
RÉUNION

VANUATU
FIJI

AUSTRALIA

NEW CALEDONIA

SWAZILAND
SOUTH AFRICA
LESOTHO

NEW ZEALAND

The most active economic blocs

EU
EFTA
NAFTA
MERCOSUR
CARICOM
CAN
ASEAN
APEC
CER

levels similar to those of the EU's wealthier countries. However, less-developed economies such as Romania, Bulgaria, and Lithuania will require years of developmental aid to catch up. In recent years, economic crises afflicted long-standing EU members such as Greece and Spain.

The EU's Common Agricultural Policy (CAP) is a system of agricultural subsidies and programs that guarantees a minimum price to EU farmers and ranchers. The CAP consumes almost half the EU's annual budget and complicates negotiations with the WTO for reducing global trade barriers. High import tariffs on agricultural goods harm exporters from developing economies such as Africa. The EU is working to reform the CAP, but progress has been slow.

 MyManagementLab **Watch It! 2**

If your professor has assigned this, go to the Assignments section of **mymanagementlab.com** to complete the video exercise titled Regional Economic Integration: Outlook for the European Union.

North American Free Trade Agreement (NAFTA)

Launched in 1994, NAFTA consists of Canada, Mexico, and the United States. It is the most significant economic bloc in the Americas and comparable to the EU in size (see www.nafta-sec-alena.org). NAFTA's passage was smoothed by the existence, since the 1960s, of the *maquiladora* program under which U.S. firms located factories in northern Mexico to access low-cost labor and avoid tariffs.

What has NAFTA accomplished for its members? Initially, the accord increased market access between Canada, Mexico, and the United States. It eliminated tariffs and most nontariff barriers for products and services traded in the bloc and made it possible for member–country firms to bid for government contracts in all three countries. NAFTA also established trade rules and uniform customs procedures and regulations. The members agreed to rules for investment and intellectual property rights. NAFTA also provides for dispute settlement in such areas as investment, unfair pricing, labor issues, and the environment.

Since the bloc's inception, Canada and Mexico have become the most important export markets of the United States, accounting for about one third of U.S. exports. In the three-year period through 2012, the largest increase in U.S. export growth stemmed from exports to Canada and Mexico. In the 1980s, Mexico's tariffs averaged 100 percent and gradually decreased over time, eventually disappearing under NAFTA. Annual NAFTA foreign investment in Mexico rose dramatically as U.S. and Canadian firms invested in their southern neighbor. Following NAFTA's passage, Mexico's per-capita income has risen substantially. Mexico is now Latin America's wealthiest country in per-capita income terms.[39]

Source: Shaen Adey/Dorling Kindersley, Ltd.

These workers harvest wheat in Africa, used to make bread. External tariffs of NAFTA and the EU hinder African agricultural exports to Europe and North America.

Other economic blocs are found worldwide. They include:

- The *European Free Trade Association* includes Iceland, Liechtenstein, Norway, and Switzerland. It is linked to the European Union. It has free trade agreements with many countries worldwide.

- *MERCOSUR*, or the *El Mercado Comun del Sur* (the Southern Common Market), the strongest bloc in South America, established in 1991 (see www.mercosur.int).

- The *Association of Southeast Asian Nations* (*ASEAN*) was created in 1967 with the goal of maintaining political stability and promoting regional economic and social development among its members (see www.aseansec.org).

- *Asia Pacific Economic Cooperation* (*APEC*) aims for greater free trade and economic integration of the Pacific Rim countries. It incorporates 21 nations on both sides of the Pacific, including Australia, Canada, Chile, China, Japan, Mexico, Russia, and the United States (see www.apec.org).

- The *Australia and New Zealand Closer Economic Relations Agreement* (*CER*) was founded in 1983 and promotes free trade between the two nations.

- The *Gulf Cooperation Council* (*GCC*; see www.gcc-sg.org/eng) aims to coordinate economic, social, and cultural affairs among its members: Bahrain, Kuwait, Oman, Qatar, Saudi Arabia, and the United Arab Emirates.

Sources: Sara Muñoz, "Latin Countries Forge Trade Accord with Eyes on Asia," *Wall Street Journal*, February 11, 2014, p. A10; H. Vinayak, Fraser Thompson, and Oliver Tonby, "Understanding ASEAN," *McKinsey & Company*, May 2014, www.mckinsey.com/insights.

Advantages and Implications of Regional Integration

7.7 Understand the advantages and implications of regional integration.

Regional integration is the most popular form of reciprocal trade liberalization. In pursuing regional integration, nations seek at least four advantages:[40]

Expand Market Size

Regional integration greatly increases the scale of the marketplace for firms inside the economic bloc. For example, although Belgium has a population of just 10 million, membership in the EU gives Belgian firms free access to a total market of nearly 500 million EU buyers.

Achieve Scale Economies and Enhanced Productivity

Expansion of market size within an economic bloc gives member–country firms the opportunity to increase the scale of operations in both production and marketing, gaining greater concentration and increased efficiency. Although a German firm may be only moderately efficient when producing 10,000 units of product for Germany, it greatly increases its efficiency by producing 50,000 units for the much larger EU market. Internationalization inside the bloc helps firms learn to compete outside the bloc as well. More efficient resource usage can lead to greater productivity and lower prices for consumers.

Attract Direct Investment From Outside the Bloc

Foreign firms prefer to invest in countries that are part of an economic bloc because factories they build there receive preferential treatment for exports to all member countries within the bloc. Many non-European firms—for example, General Mills, Samsung, and Tata—invested heavily in the EU to take advantage of Europe's economic integration. By establishing operations in a single EU country, these firms gain free trade access to the entire EU market.

Source: Dario Ricardo/Fotolia

Mercosur building at dusk. Former "Parque Hotel". Montevideo Uruguay.

Acquire Stronger Defensive and Political Posture

Regional integration helps strengthen member–countries relative to other nations and world regions. This was one of the motives for creating the European Community (the precursor to the EU), whose members sought to fortify their mutual defense against the former Soviet Union. Today, the EU is one way Europe counterbalances the power and international influence of the United States. Broadly speaking, countries are more powerful when they cooperate than when they operate alone.

In 1990, there were approximately 50 regional economic integration agreements worldwide. Today, some 400 are in various stages of development. Many nations belong to more than one. Regional economic integration is not slowing the progress of global free trade. Rather, global free trade will tend to emerge as economic blocs link with each other over time. The evidence suggests regional economic integration is gradually giving way to a system of free trade worldwide.

Managerial implications of regional integration include:

- *Internationalization inside the bloc.* The elimination of trade and investment barriers presents new opportunities. Regional integration pressures or encourages member–companies to internationalize into neighboring countries within the bloc.

- *Restructuring operations.* In the early stages of regional integration, firms begin to view the bloc as a unified whole. Managers develop strategies suited to the region as a whole rather than to individual countries. For example, a firm might combine multiple plants into a single factory.

- *Regional products and marketing.* As firms increasingly view the bloc as one large market, they tend to standardize their products and marketing. They start selling much the same products, using similar marketing approaches, to all countries inside the bloc.

- *Internationalization from outside the bloc.* Emergence of an economic bloc makes a region more attractive to companies based outside the bloc. Many will use FDI to establish a physical presence inside the bloc to access better all the benefits the bloc can offer.

CLOSING CASE Government Intervention at Airbus and Boeing

Historically, United States companies such as Boeing (www.boeing.com) and McDonnell Douglas were the dominant players in the global aircraft industry. Founded in 1916 in Seattle, Boeing had many years to develop the critical mass necessary to become the world's leading aerospace manufacturer. During World War II and the subsequent Cold War years, Boeing received many lucrative contracts from the U.S. Department of Defense.

No single country in Europe possessed the means to launch an aerospace company capable of challenging Boeing. Manufacturing commercial aircraft is complex and capital-intensive and requires a highly skilled workforce. In the 1970s, the governments of France, Germany, Spain, and the United Kingdom formed an alliance, supported with massive government subsidies, to create Airbus S.A.S. (www.airbus.com). By 1981, the four-country alliance succeeded in becoming the world's number-two civil aircraft manufacturer. Airbus launched the A300, among the best-selling commercial aircraft of all time. The Airbus A320 received more than 400 orders before its first flight, becoming the fastest-selling large passenger jet in aviation history. By 1992, Airbus captured roughly one-third of the global commercial aircraft market. Airbus surpassed Boeing in orders for new aircraft in most of the 15 years through 2015.

Government Support for Airbus

Since the 1940s, European governments have pursued public policies based on democratic socialism. Under this system, Europeans became accustomed to government playing a significant role in guiding economic affairs.

Airbus has benefitted enormously from government support. The firm has received tens of billions of euros of subsidies and soft loans from the four founding country governments and the European Union (EU). Airbus must repay the loans only if it achieves profitability. Government aid has financed, in whole or part, every major Airbus aircraft model. European governments have forgiven Airbus's debt, financed R&D for civil aircraft projects, and provided infrastructure and huge equity infusions.

Airbus is currently a stock-held company jointly owned by the British, Germans, French, and Spanish. It is based in Toulouse, France, but has R&D and production operations scattered throughout Europe. European governments justify their financial aid to Airbus on several grounds. First, Airbus R&D activities result in the development of valuable new technologies. Second, Airbus provides jobs to some 55,000 skilled and semiskilled Europeans. Third, its value-chain activities attract massive amounts of capital into Europe. Finally, Airbus generates enormous tax revenues.

Complaints about Unfair Government Intervention

Boeing and the U.S. government have long complained about the massive subsidies and soft loans that were responsible not only for Airbus's birth, but also for its ongoing success. The outcry became louder in the 2000s, when Airbus surpassed Boeing in annual sales, becoming the world's leading commercial aircraft manufacturer. Boeing has argued that Airbus never would have gotten this far without government support.

The U.S. government has brought several complaints to the World Trade Organization (WTO). Among these are charges that EU member states have approved billions of dollars in subsidies and soft loans to Airbus. The U.S. alleged that financial aid for the A350, A380, and earlier Airbus aircraft qualified as subsidies under the WTO's Agreement on Subsidies and Countervailing Measures (ASCM) and that the subsidies constitute unfair international trade. Under the ASCM, subsidies to specific firms or industries from a government or other public bodies are prohibited. Airbus had applied to the governments of France, Germany, Spain, and the United Kingdom for aid to launch its model A350.

In 2012, the WTO ruled that EU aid to Airbus had caused Boeing to lose market share in Asia and other markets. EU officials argued that government subsidies to Airbus were permissible and that it was up to individual EU countries to decide whether to provide them. However, the WTO also ruled that Boeing received more than $5 billion in U.S. government subsidies in the development of the 787 Dreamliner.

Government Support for Boeing

The EU argues the United States government has indirectly subsidized Boeing through massive defense contracts paid by tax dollars. The U.S. government gave Boeing more than $23 billion in indirect government subsidies by means of R&D funding and other indirect support from the Pentagon and NASA, the nation's space agency. Boeing is at liberty to use the knowledge acquired from such projects to produce civilian aircraft. The state of Washington, Boeing's primary manufacturing and assembly location, has provided the firm with tax breaks, infrastructure support, and other incentives totaling billions of dollars.

The EU also has a case at the WTO regarding Boeing's relations with Japanese business partners. Boeing entered an alliance with Japan's Mitsubishi, Kawasaki, and Fuji to build the 787 Dreamliner. The Japanese firms provided billions in soft loans, repayable only if the aircraft is commercially successful.

Recent Aircraft from Airbus and Boeing

In 2011, Boeing successfully launched the 787 Dreamliner and is ahead of Airbus in launching innovative and fuel-efficient aircraft. About the same time, Airbus launched the A380, an innovative airplane with an upper deck extending the entire length of the fuselage and a cabin that provides 50 percent more floor space than Boeing's largest aircraft. The A380 can seat between 555 and 853 passengers, depending on the seating configuration. It has a maximum range of 15,000 kilometers (8,000 nautical miles). The total cost to develop and launch the A380 reached 15 billion euros (U.S. $21 billion), partly supported by funding from European governments.

The government of China is developing its capacity to produce jumbo jets, part of its quest to challenge Boeing and Airbus in the global aircraft industry. China Commercial Aircraft Company was established in Shanghai amid forecasts that China's domestic market for commercial aircraft will increase fivefold by 2026.

AACSB: Reflective Thinking Skills, Ethical Understanding and Reasoning Abilities

Case Questions

7-4. Where do you stand? Do you think EU subsidies and soft loans to Airbus are fair? Why or why not? What advantages are gained by Airbus from free financial support from the EU governments? Are complaints about EU subsidies fair in light of Europe's history of democratic socialism?

7-5. Do you believe U.S. military contracts with Boeing amount to subsidies? Have these types of payments provided Boeing with unfair advantages? Justify your answer.

7-6. Assuming that Airbus cannot compete without subsidies and loans, is it likely that the EU will discontinue its financial support of Airbus? Is it in the EU's interests to continue supporting Airbus? Justify your answer.

7-7. If the WTO rules against Airbus and tells it to stop accepting subsidies and soft loans, how should Airbus management respond? What new approaches can management pursue to maintain Airbus's lead in the global commercial aircraft industry?

Sources: Doug Cameron and David Kesmodel, "Warning Is Issued About Plane Glut," *Wall Street Journal*, February 23, 2012, pp. B6–B6; Corporate profiles of Airbus and Boeing at www.hoovers.com; Deloitte, *2015 Global Aerospace and Defense Industry Outlook*, www.deloitte.com; Matthew Dalton, "EU Files Complaint with WTO About Boeing," *Wall Street Journal*, December 22, 2014, retrieved from www.wsj.com; K. Epstein & J. Crown, "Globalization Bites Boeing," *BusinessWeek*, March 24, 2008, p. 32; D. Gauthier-Villars and D. Michaels, "Airbus Buyers Get French Aid," *Wall Street Journal*, January 27, 2009, p. B4; Max Kingsley-Jones, "Throwing Down the Gauntlet," *Airline Business*, October 2011, pp. 28–30; Pilita Clark, Joshua Chaffin, and James Politi, "WTO Rules that Boeing Received $5.3bn in Aid," *Financial Times*, April 1, 2011, p. 19; "China to Make Jumbo Jetliners, Trim Roles of Boeing, Airbus," *Wall Street Journal*, May 12, 2008, p. B4; "How Airbus Flew Past Its American Rival," *Financial Times*, March 17, 2005, p. 6; Mavis Toh, "Rising in the East," *Airline Business*, April 2015, pp. 32–35; Stephan Wittig, "The WTO Panel Report on Boeing Subsidies: A Critical Assessment," *Intereconomics*, May 2011, pp. 148–153.

Note: The authors acknowledge the assistance of Stephanie Regales with this case.

MyManagementLab **Watch It! 3**

If your professor has assigned this, go to the Assignments section of **mymanagementlab.com** to complete the video exercise titled Airbus versus Boeing.

END OF CHAPTER REVIEW

 MyManagementLab

Go to **mymanagementlab.com** to complete the problems marked with this icon .

Key Terms

common market   216
countervailing duty   208
currency control   207
customs   201
customs union   216
dumping   208
economic union   216
export control   202

foreign trade zone (FTZ)
  214
free trade agreement   215
free trade area   215
General Agreement on Tariffs
  and Trade (GATT)   209
import license   206
investment incentive   208

maquiladoras   214
nontariff trade barrier   201
protectionism   201
quota   201
regional economic integration
  215
subsidy   207
tariff   201

Summary

In this chapter, you learned about:

- **The nature of government intervention**

  Despite the value of free trade, governments often intervene in international business. **Protectionism** refers to national economic policies designed to restrict free trade and protect domestic industries from foreign competition. Government intervention arises typically in the form of tariffs, nontariff trade barriers, and investment barriers. **Tariffs** are taxes on imported products, imposed mainly to collect government revenue and protect domestic industries from foreign competition. **Nontariff trade barriers** consist of policies that restrict trade without directly imposing a tax. Governments impose trade and investment barriers to achieve political, social, or economic objectives. Such barriers are either defensive or offensive. A key rationale is the protection of the nation's economy, its industries, and its workers. Governments also impose barriers to protect infant industries.

- **Instruments of government intervention**

  Governments also impose regulations and technical standards as well as administrative and bureaucratic procedures.

Countries may also impose **currency controls** to minimize international withdrawal of national currency. FDI and ownership restrictions ensure that the nation maintains partial or full ownership of firms within its national borders. Governments also provide **subsidies**, a form of payment or other material support. With **dumping**, a firm charges abnormally low prices abroad. Governments support homegrown firms by providing **investment incentives** and biased government procurement policies.

- **Evolution and consequences of government intervention**

  From the 1930s onward, countries reduced trade barriers worldwide. The nature and outcomes of government intervention have varied across Latin America, Japan, India, and China. The most important development for reducing trade barriers was the General Agreement on Tariffs and Trade (GATT), replaced by the World Trade Organization (WTO). Government intervention and trade barriers can raise ethical concerns that affect developing economies and low-income consumers. However, government intervention also can be used to offset such harmful effects.

- **How firms can respond to government intervention**

  Firms should conduct research to understand the extent and nature of trade and investment barriers abroad. When trade barriers are substantial, FDI or joint ventures are often the most appropriate entry strategies. When importing is essential, the firm can take advantage of **foreign trade zones**, areas where imports receive preferential tariff treatment. Government assistance in the form of subsidies and incentives helps reduce the impact of protectionism. Firms sometimes lobby the home and foreign governments for freer trade and investment.

- **Regional integration and economic blocs**

  Under **regional economic integration**, groups of countries form alliances to promote free trade, cross-national investment, and other mutual goals. This integration results from *regional economic integration blocs* (or economic blocs), in which member countries agree to eliminate tariffs and other restrictions on cross-national commerce. At minimum, the countries in an economic bloc become parties to a **free trade agreement**, which eliminates tariffs, **quotas**, and other trade barriers. The stages of regional integration include the **free trade area**, the **customs union**, the **common market**, and the **economic union**.

- **The leading economic blocs**

  There are hundreds of economic integration agreements in the world. The European Union (EU) is the most advanced. It has increased market access, improved trade rules, and harmonized standards among its members. The North American Free Trade Agreement (NAFTA) consists of Canada, Mexico, and the United States. Other blocs are prominent worldwide and have achieved varying degrees of success.

- **Advantages and implications of regional integration**

  Regional integration contributes to corporate and industrial growth and hence to economic growth, better living standards, and higher tax revenues for the member countries. It increases market size by integrating the economies within a region. It increases economies of scale and factor productivity among firms in the member countries and attracts foreign investors to the bloc. Regional integration leads to increased internationalization by firms inside their economic bloc. Firms restructure their operations. Managers revise marketing strategies by standardizing products.

Test Your Comprehension AACSB: Reflective Thinking Skills

7-8. Explain tariffs, nontariff trade barriers, investment barriers, and government subsidies. What are their main characteristics? How do they differ?

7-9. In what ways do government subsidies amount to protectionism?

7-10. How are tariff payments physically assessed and collected by a country?

7-11. Describe various company strategies to manage government intervention.

7-12. What are the roles of FDI, licensing, and joint ventures in reducing the impact of import tariffs?

7-13. What is a regional economic integration bloc (also called an economic bloc)?

7-14. What is the difference between a free trade area and a customs union? Between a customs union and a common market?

✪ **7-15.** The United States and Russia belong to an economic bloc, how is this the case?

✪ **7-16.** What are the stages of regional integration? Why are countries likely to go beyond a free trade agreement?

7-17. Why might a corporate based outside a bloc choose FDI as their method of entry into the bloc?

Apply Your Understanding AACSB: Ethical Understanding and Reasoning Abilities, Reflective Thinking Skills, Communication Abilities

7-18. TelComm Corporation is a manufacturer of components for the cell phone industry. TelComm founder Alex Bell heard that China has the world's largest number of cell phone users and wants to begin exporting the firm's products there, but TelComm has little international experience. Mr. Bell is unaware of the various types of nontariff trade barriers that TelComm might face in China and other foreign markets. Please summarize major nontariff trade barriers to Mr. Bell.

What types of investment barriers might TelComm face if management decides to establish a factory in China to manufacture cell phone components? What can TelComm management do to minimize the threat of these nontariff trade and investment barriers?

7-19. *Ethical Dilemma*: You are Vice President for International Sales at FoodTrade, a large trading company that exports processed foods to Africa. You are often frustrated that African countries impose high tariffs (typically 75 percent) on processed food imports. These barriers raise FoodTrade's cost of doing business and make your prices less competitive in African markets. However, Africa suffers from widespread poverty, and African governments use tariffs to raise needed revenues and achieve policy objectives. Using the concepts in this chapter and the Ethical Framework in Chapter 4, analyze the arguments for and against high agricultural tariffs in Africa. How do the tariffs harm or benefit Africa? Do you perceive any ethical concerns in Africa's use of high tariffs on agricultural goods? What ethical concerns do you perceive in FoodTrade's efforts to avoid the tariffs? How should FoodTrade respond to the tariffs?

7-20. Levi Strauss & Co. (LS) makes and sells blue jeans, Dockers, and Slates brand name apparel in more than 60 countries. With the onset of regional integration in Europe and Latin America, LS management decided to revise the firm's production and marketing strategies to make them more appropriate for regional, as opposed to national, operations. Based on the regional integration changes underway in these areas, and on your understanding of the business implications of regional integration, what should LS do? In answering, think in terms of LS's major value chain activities, especially production and marketing. What are the pros and cons to LS of producing and marketing its apparel on a regional basis as opposed to a national or global basis? Justify your answer.

7-21. *Ethical Dilemma*: Suppose you are a member of a government task force evaluating the future of NAFTA between Canada, Mexico, and the United States. Proponents want to transform NAFTA into a common market by removing barriers to the movement of labor. The goal is to reduce poverty in Mexico by allowing Mexican citizens to work freely and legally in Canada and the United States. Critics oppose the common market because of the big income difference between the countries. They argue that an open border would encourage millions of Mexicans to migrate northward, seeking work, and threaten jobs in the United States and Canada. Proponents argue that, as economic integration progressed under a common market, average wages in the three countries would equalize and eliminate pressures on northern job markets. Analyze this situation using the Ethical Framework in Chapter 4. Should the task force recommend the common market? What could U.S. and Canadian firms do to maintain their competitiveness relative to Mexican firms, given Mexico's low-wage advantage?

globalEDGE | INTERNET EXERCISES

(www.globaledge.msu.edu)

AACSB: Reflective Thinking Skills, Analytic Skills, Ethical Understanding, and Reasoning Abilities

Refer to Chapter 1, page 54, for instructions on how to access and use globalEDGE™.

7-22. Your firm is considering exporting to two countries: Kenya and Vietnam. However, management's knowledge about the trade policies of these countries is limited. Conduct a search at globalEDGE™ to identify the current import policies, tariffs, and restrictions in these countries. Prepare a brief report on your findings. In addition to globalEDGE™, other useful sites include the World Trade Organization (www.wto.org; enter country name in the search engine) and the U.S. Commercial Service (www.buyusa.gov).

7-23. The United States Trade Representative (USTR) develops international trade and investment policies for the U.S. government. Visit the USTR website from globalEDGE™ or directly (www.ustr.gov). Search for "National Trade Estimate Report" for the latest year. This document summarizes trade barriers around the world. See the reports for the country of your choice. What are the country's import policies and practices? What are its nontariff trade barriers? What about barriers in the services sector? Are there any sectors that seem to be particularly protected (for example, energy, telecommunications)? What is the nature of government restrictions on e-commerce? If you worked at a firm that exported its products to the country, how would you use the USTR report to develop international business strategies?

7-24. There has been much opposition to the Trans-Pacific Partnership (TPP). For a sampling of arguments against this proposed pact, visit www.globalexchange.org, www.citizenstrade.org, and www.citizen.org. Also visit the U.S. government site promoting the TPP at http://ustr.gov/tpp or obtain information on the proposed pact from globalEDGE™. Based on your reading of this chapter, evaluate the arguments against the TPP. Do you agree with arguments the critics make? Why or why not? Would the proposed TPP harm special interest groups? Would it be a boon international trade? Justify your answers.

CAREER TOOLBOX

Performing a Preliminary Country Risk Analysis

Before venturing into most countries, managers investigate the likelihood and nature of country risk and its probable effect on company operations and performance. Country risk refers to potentially adverse effects on company operations and performance caused by changes in a country's political and legal environments. Finding out about country risks is a task performed in MNEs and other firms with substantial international operations. Smaller companies with limited resources, and thus less able to withstand failure, also perform country risk analysis when expanding abroad.

In this exercise, you will gain an understanding of the factors that determine country risk; acquire an understanding of the variables to consider when locating company operations abroad; develop market research skills for acquiring knowledge concerning country risk for planning company operations abroad; and obtain exposure to the types of country risk that firms encounter.

Assume you are an employee with a company that plans to build a factory abroad. Management is considering each of three countries as possible locations: China, Mexico, and Poland. You must decide which location is best for building the factory. Management prefers the country with the lowest risk. Your task is to conduct market research to investigate the degree of country risk in China, Mexico, and Poland. Then prepare a brief report that includes an estimate of the level of country risk in each of these countries by examining corruption, political rights, freedom status, and economic freedom.

To complete this exercise in your MyLab, go to the Career Toolbox.

Background

Country risk arises primarily from government intervention. Governments may impose laws and regulations that increase business costs, delays, or lost opportunities. Governments may restrict access to important markets, impose complex bureaucratic procedures, or limit the amount of returns that can be realized from foreign operations.

Political or legislative actions can harm business interests. Every country needs a sufficient legal and regulatory framework to support economic activity. Many governments impose too much regulation, poorly conceived regulation, or regulation that results in harmful, unintended consequences. Countries should aim for the right balance of appropriate regulation, not too much and not too little. However, finding the right balance is always challenging and evolves with time and circumstances.

Country risk affects management decision making regarding strategies for entering foreign markets. By entering a market by exporting, the firm's level of market commitment and risk are relatively low, and if substantial risk arises, the firm can rapidly withdraw or reduce its operations there. By contrast, the level of risk is relatively high for firms that internationalize by FDI, which results in establishing a physical facility in the target country, usually to perform production or marketing activities. Country risk is especially common in emerging markets and other less economically developed countries.

MyManagementLab   **Try It!**

The simulation Tariffs, Subsidies, and Quotas accompanies this exercise.

MyManagementLab

Go to **mymanagementlab.com** for Auto-graded writing questions as well as the following Assisted-graded writing questions:

⭐ **7-25.** Discuss the relationship between government intervention and protectionism.

⭐ **7-26.** How did government intervention evolve between the first and second halves of the twentieth century?

⭐ **7-27.** MyManagementLab Only—comprehensive writing assignment for this chapter.

Endnotes

1. David Dollar and Aart Kraay, "Trade, Growth, and Poverty," Policy Research Working Paper no. WPS 2615, June 2001, Washington, DC: World Bank, Development Research Group; Ailín González, "Impacto del Tratado de Libre Comercio de América Del Norte, La Unión Europea y El Tratado de Libre Comercio para República Dominicana y Centro América en las Exportaciones de Puerto Rico," *Revista Internacional Administración & Finanzas* 5, No. 4 (2012), pp. 1–12; Romain Wacziarg and Karen Welch, "Trade Liberalization and Growth: New Evidence," *World Bank Economic Review* 22, No. 2 (2008), pp. 187–231; United Nations, *World Economic and Social Survey*, 2005, http://www.un.org.

2. Kazunobu Hayakawa and Toshiyuki Matsuura, "Trade Liberalization in Asia and FDI Strategies in Heterogeneous Firms: Evidence from Japanese Firm-Level Data," *Oxford Economic Papers*, 67 No. 2 (2015), pp. 494–513; Jeffrey D. Sachs and Andrew Warner, "Economic Reform and the Process of Global Integration," *Brookings Papers on Economic Activity*, Issue no. 1 (Washington, DC: Brookings Institute, 1995); Heritage Foundation, retrieved from the Heritage Foundation website at http://www.heritage.org/research/features/index/.

3. David Ricardo, *Principles of Political Economy and Taxation* (London: Everyman Edition, 1911; first published in 1817).

4. Andrzej Cieslik and Jan Hagemejer, "The Effectiveness of Preferential Trade Liberalization in Central and Eastern Europe," *International Trade Journal* 25, No. 5 (2011), pp. 516–538; International Monetary Fund, *World Economic Outlook Databases*, www.imf.org; Delia Velculescu, "Poland: Bright Spot in Recession-Hit Europe," *IMF Survey Magazine*, August 13, 2009, International Monetary Fund, www.imf.org.

5. "Bush Move Marks U.S. Trade Policy Turning Point," *Financial Times*, March 6, 2002, p. 6.

6. Jim Carlton, "U.S. Nears Mexican Cement Pact," *Wall Street Journal*, August 29, 2005, p. A7.

7. Jean-François Tremblay, "Victims of a Trade War," *Chemical & Engineering News*, February 9, 2015, 93 No. 6, p. 19.

8. Eugen Kováč and Krešimir Žigić, "International Competition in Vertically Differentiated Markets with Innovation and Imitation," *Economica*, 81 No. 323 (2014), pp. 491–521; Stefanie Lenway, Kathleen Rehbein, and Laura Starks, "The Impact of Protectionism on Firm Wealth: The Experience of the Steel Industry," *Southern Economic Journal*, 56, No. 4 (1990), pp. 1079–1093.

9. G. Chazan and G. White, "Kremlin Weighs on Growth," *Wall Street Journal*, October 17, 2005, p. A16.

10. Robert Reich, *The Work of Nations: Preparing Ourselves for 21st Century Capitalism* (New York: Knopf, 1991); Lester Thurow, *Head to Head: The Coming Economic Battle among Japan, Europe, and America* (New York: William Morrow, 1992).

11. Kym Anderson, *Benefits and Costs of the Trade Targets for the Post-2015 Development Agenda* (Copenhagen: Copenhagen Consensus Center, 2014); UNCTAD, *Non-tariff Measures to Trade: Economic and Policy Issues for Developing Countries* (New York: United Nations, 2013); World Trade Organization, "Trade Liberalization Statistics," www.wto.org, May 7, 2015.

12. Ed Gresser, "Shoe Tariffs: America's Worst Tax," *DLC Commentary,* December 13, 2010, www.dlc.org; NPR, "Would Lower Shoe Tariffs Actually Encourage American Jobs?" *National Public Radio*, May 8, 2015, www.npr.org; World Trade Organization, *Tariff Profile on the European Union, 2013*, http://www.wto.org.

13. "Textiles: Knickers in a Twist," *The Economist*, August 27, 2005, p. 50.

14. Amir Efrati, Loretta Chao, and Kersten Zhang, "Google Softens China Stance," *Wall Street Journal*, January 12, 2012, pp. B1–B2.

15. World Bank, *Doing Business: Benchmarking Business Regulations*, 2009, http://www.doing business.org.

16. U.S. Trade Representative, "2015 National Trade Estimate Report on Foreign Trade Barriers," http://www.ustr.gov.

17. Corina Pons and Daniel Cancel, "Venezuela's Great Dollar Drought," *Bloomberg Businessweek*, February 28, 2011, pp. 15–16; Ezequiel Minaya, "Venezuela Revises Foreign Exchange Rules," *Wall Street Journal,* February 10, 2015, www.wsj.com.

18. Bob Davis and Jason Dean, "State-Run Firms Are the Giants of China's Economy," *Wall Street Journal*, February 23, 2012, p. A12.

19. M. Kripalani, "India Takes a Bath on Oil Subsidies," *BusinessWeek*, June 16, 2008, p. 36.

20. Michael Grunwald, "Down on the Farm," *Time International*, November 12, 2007, pp. 22–29.

21. World Trade Organization, Glossary, 2009, http://www.wto.org.

22. Ibid.

23. United Nations Conference on Trade and Development, *The Global Economic Crisis: Systemic Failures and Multilateral Remedies* (Geneva, Switzerland: United Nations, 2009).

24. D. Brady, "Beware Politicians Bearing Election-Year Trade Deals," *Bloomberg Businessweek*, March 19–25, 2012, pp. 41–43; G. Rachman, "When Globalisation Goes into Reverse," *Financial Times*, February 2, 2009, http://www.ft.com.

25. J. Miller, "Nations Rush to Establish New Barriers to Trade," *Wall Street Journal*, February 6, 2009, pp. A1, A6.

26. R. Wright, "Financial Crises and Reform: Looking Back for Clues to the Future," *McKinsey Quarterly*, December 2008.

27. "World Trade: Barriers to Entry," *The Economist*, December 20, 2008, p. 121.

28. *Doing Business: Economy Rankings* and *Doing Business 2015*, World Bank Group, Washington, DC, http://www.doingbusiness.org/rankings.

29. Democratic Leadership Council, "Trade Fact of the Week: U.S. Tariffs Are 23 Times Higher on Cambodian Goods than on British Goods," www.dlc.org; Smith (2002).

30. *Economist*, "Generation Jobless," April 27, 2013, www.economist.com; C. Giles, "Big Ideas Fail to Mop Up Europe's Current Mess," *Financial Times*, February 26, 2009, p. 2.

31. "In the Shadow of Prosperity," *The Economist*, January 20, 2007, pp. 32–34.

32. Belay Seyoum and Juan Ramirez, "Foreign Trade Zones in the United States: A Study with Special Emphasis on the Proposal for Trade Agreement Parity," *Journal of Economic Studies* 39, No. 1 (2012), pp. 13–30.

33. Militiades Chacholidades, *International Economics* (New York: McGraw-Hill, 1990); James Ingram, *International Economics* (New York: Wiley, 1983); William McDaniel and Edgar Kossack, "The Financial Benefits to Users of Foreign-Trade Zones," *Columbia Journal of World Business* 18, No. 3 (1983), pp. 33–41.

34. Eugene Salorio, Jean Boddewyn, and Nicolas Dahan, "Integrating Business Political Behavior with Economic and Organizational Strategies," *International Studies of Management & Organization* 35, No. 2 (2005), pp. 28–35; Scott Kennedy, "The Barbarians Learn How to Lobby at the Gates of Industry," *Financial Times*, September 28, 2005, p. 5.

35. Alessandro Antimiani and Luca Salvatici, "Regionalism versus Multilateralism: The Case of the European Union Trade Policy," *Journal of World Trade*, 49, No. 2 (2015), pp. 253–275; Bela Balassa, *The Theory of Economic Integration* (Homewood, IL: Irwin, 1961); Jacob Viner, *The Customs Union Issue* (New York: Carnegie Endowment for International Peace, 1950).

36. Antimiani and Salvatici, 2015.

37. European Union, website at http://www.europa.eu.

38. "Transformed: EU Membership Has Worked Magic in Central Europe," *The Economist*, June 25, 2005, pp. 6–8.

39. "Happy Birthday, NAFTA," *BusinessWeek*, December 22, 2003, p. 112; *Progressive Economy*, "A third of all U.S. export growth since 2009 has gone to Canada and Mexico," January 18, 2012, www.globalworksfoundation.org.

40. Viner (1950); Franklin Root, *International Trade and Investment*, 5th ed. (Cincinnati, OH: South-Western Publishing, 1984); Emile Dreuil, James Anderson, Walter Block, and Michael Saliba, "The Trade Gap: The Fallacy of Anti World-Trade Sentiment," *Journal of Business Ethics* 45, No. 3 (2003), pp. 269–278.

Chapter 8

Understanding Emerging Markets

Learning Objectives *After studying this chapter, you should be able to:*

8.1 Understand advanced economies, developing economies, and emerging markets.

8.2 Know what makes emerging markets attractive for international business.

8.3 Learn how to assess the true potential of emerging markets.

8.4 Evaluate the risks and challenges of emerging markets.

8.5 Learn the success strategies for emerging markets.

8.6 Understand corporate social responsibility, sustainability, and the crisis of global poverty.

The New Global Challengers: MNEs from Emerging Markets

Consider a company that describes itself in the following way: "Today, we are the most important baking company in the world on the basis of brand positioning, production volume, and sales.... We are also the indisputable leader in our field in Mexico, Latin America, and the United States. We are present in 22 countries in America, Asia, and Europe; we have over 10,000 products and over 100 brands of acknowledged prestige."

You probably did not guess that this is Grupo Bimbo, a leading company based in Mexico (www.grupobimbo.com). Did you know that Grupo Bimbo owns such brands as Sara Lee, Brownberry, Arnold, and Plus Vita, among others? From its humble beginnings in 1945, this privately held company is now a global player in the bread, bakery, and snack markets.

Grupo Bimbo is one of hundreds of companies from emerging markets that compete on a global scale. Emerging markets are lower-income countries that, in contrast to advanced economies, are currently experiencing rapid industrialization, modernization, and economic growth. Examples include Brazil, China, India, Russia, and Mexico. Emerging markets represent attractive markets and low-cost manufacturing bases. However, they also have high-risk business environments with evolving commercial infrastructure and legal systems. Despite their drawbacks, emerging markets have begun to produce *new global challengers*, top firms that are fast becoming key contenders in world markets. Grupo Bimbo is an example of a global challenger.

Other examples of large multinational companies originating from emerging markets include Mexico's Cemex (one of the world's largest cement producers), Russia's Lukoil (global energy), and Turkey's Yildiz Holding (a diversified conglomerate that owns Godiva Chocolatier and United Biscuits). Brasil Foods (BRF) exemplifies the challengers' international entrepreneurial savvy. The firm generated net sales of $29 billion in 2014, of which half were from international markets. It operates farms and markets processed foods and ready-to-eat meals. BRF has built world-class distribution and supply-chain management systems and exports about half its annual production.

Source: Aania/Fotolia

New global challengers leverage low-cost labor in their home countries. They also possess engineering and managerial talent often superior to that of competitors in advanced economies. Many new global challengers are family-owned or family-run businesses (family conglomerates) and enjoy numerous advantages. They often access low-interest loans from home-country, government-owned banks.

Many are expanding internationally by taking their established brands to global markets. China's Hisense operates in multimedia, household appliance, telecommunications, information technology, technology services, and real estate. The firm is known for stylish, low-priced consumer electronics. Hisense sells its products in more than 130 countries.

Some new global challengers leverage superior engineering capability. Hong Kong's Johnson Electric is the world leader in small electric motors for automotive and consumer applications. Brazil's Embraer taps the large pool of experienced, low-cost engineers in that country to build innovative small jets. It has become the world's leading producer of regional jet aircraft.

Many global challengers benefit from local bases of natural resources. Russia's Rusal is extracting the country's rich reserves of bauxite to produce aluminum for international markets. Most the world's natural resources are located in developing economies, and a growing number of new global challengers use these to their advantage. China's CNOOC (China National Offshore Oil Corporation), for example, is acquiring oil and gas reserves in Asia and Africa.

The new global challengers pose a growing competitive challenge to companies from advanced economies such as Europe, Japan, and North America.

Questions

8-1. What are emerging markets? Give examples of emerging markets.

8-2. What are new global challengers? What advantages do they typically possess?

8-3. Do new global challengers pose any threat to firms from advanced economies? Explain.

SOURCES: S. Banerjee, J. Prabhu, and R. Chandy, "Indirect Learning: How Emerging-Market Firms Grow in Developed Markets," *Journal of Marketing 79*, No. 1 (2015), pp. 10–28; *Meet the 2014 BCG Global Challengers*, Boston Consulting Group, September 10, 2014; Juichuan Chang, "The Early and Rapid Internationalization of Asian Emerging MNEs," *Competitiveness Review*, March 1, 2011, pp. 171–187; "Emerging-Market Multinationals: The Challengers," *Economist*, January 12, 2008, pp. 62–63; "Hisense a Global Leader in Smart TV Market," *China Daily Europe*, June 20, 2014, retrieved from europe.chinadaily.com.cn; "Multipolarity: The New Global Economy," *The World Bank*, 2011; Carol Liao, Christoph Nettesheim, and David Lee, "Will China's Global Challengers Be the Next Global Leaders?" *BCGPerspectives*, January 8, 2015, www.bcgperspectives.com; "'Multilatinas' on the Move," *Business Latin America*, January 9, 2012, pp. 4–5; P. Pananond, "Motives for Foreign Direct Investment: A View from Emerging Market Multinationals," *Multinational Business Review* 23, No. 1 (2015), pp. 77–86.

The opening case describes how emerging market countries are giving birth to multinational companies that are challenging their counterparts from the advanced economies. These *new global challenger* firms leverage local advantages such as low-cost labor and superior skills to compete successfully around the world. Historically, most trade and investment were conducted among the advanced economies, the world's wealthiest countries. Today, however, developing economies and especially emerging markets play important and growing roles in international business.

In this chapter, we discuss emerging market economies and contrast them with the advanced and developing economies. Each country group poses distinctive opportunities and risks. By analyzing a country in terms of its stage of economic development, the manager can gain insights into the purchasing power of its citizens, the sophistication of its business sector, the adequacy of its commercial infrastructure, and numerous other areas. Let's explore the country groups in detail.

8.1 Understand advanced economies, developing economies, and emerging markets.

Advanced economies
Post-industrial countries characterized by high per-capita income, highly competitive industries, and well-developed commercial infrastructure.

Developing economies
Low-income countries characterized by limited industrialization and stagnant economies.

Emerging markets
Former developing economies that have achieved substantial industrialization, modernization, and rapid economic growth since the 1980s.

Advanced Economies, Developing Economies, and Emerging Markets

The map in Exhibit 8.1 highlights the country groups differentiated by degree of economic development and per-capita income.

Let's define the different country groups.

Advanced economies Post-industrial countries characterized by high per-capita income, highly competitive industries, and well-developed commercial infrastructures. They are the world's richest nations and include Australia, Canada, Japan, New Zealand, the United States, and most European countries.

Developing economies Low-income countries characterized by limited industrialization and stagnant economies. They make up the largest group of countries and include Bangladesh, Nicaragua, and Zaire.

Emerging markets Also called emerging market economies, they are former developing economies that have achieved considerable industrialization, modernization, and rapid economic growth since the 1980s. Some 35 countries are considered emerging markets and are found mainly in Asia, Latin America, and Eastern Europe. The largest are Brazil, Russia, India, and China (sometimes abbreviated BRIC).

Exhibit 8.2 provides an overview of key differences among the three country groups. The group with the largest number of countries by far is the developing economies. However, they contribute least to world GDP, and their citizens have very low incomes. Their *disposable income*, the proportion of personal income they spend on purchases other than food, clothing, and housing, is very limited. More than one-third of all developing economy residents live on less than $2 per day.[1] The combination of low income and often high birth rates promotes poverty in these countries.

Exhibit 8.2 also reveals countries' technological development. The developing economies are at a very early stage, whereas the emerging markets are quickly catching up to the advanced economies. *Technology* is the knowledge and application of tools, techniques, systems, and methods of organization to serve industry, science, and the arts. Technology is vital to economic development and includes not just hardware computers, telephones, and industrial machinery; it also includes the educational systems, worker skill levels, and banking infrastructure. In the advanced economies and emerging markets, information and communications technologies have had an enormous impact on knowledge acquisition and on worker and personal productivity. Absence of such technologies in the developing economies helps explain why they are well behind the other countries in education, economic output, and future prospects.

Another way to visualize the three groups of countries is to examine a map of the world at night, shown in Exhibit 8.3. The advanced economies are the most visible areas because, with the highest levels of industrialization, they are generally the most brightly lit. The map also suggests significant economic activity in the emerging market countries. However, it reveals very low levels of industrialization across large stretches of Africa, central Asia, eastern Russia, and major parts of Latin America. These represent developing economies and other areas with little or no industrialization and limited economic development. Note how areas of advanced industrialization tend to consume the most energy. Increasingly, nations must consider how economic development can be achieved without excessive ecological harm. Let's discuss the three country categories in detail.

Advanced Economies

Having reached a mature state of industrial development, advanced economies have largely evolved from manufacturing economies into sophisticated, largely service-based economies. Home to only about 14 percent of the world's population, they have long dominated international business. They account for nearly two-thirds of world GDP, more than half of world trade in products, and three-quarters of world trade in services.

Advanced economies have democratic, multiparty systems of government. Their economic systems are usually based on capitalism. They have tremendous purchasing power, with few restrictions on international trade and investment. They host the world's largest MNEs. Advanced economies include the United States, Canada, Japan, and many in Western Europe.

Developing Economies

Developing economies are sometimes called *underdeveloped countries* or *third-world countries*. These terms are imprecise and often offensive because, despite poor economic conditions, developing economies tend to be highly developed in historical and cultural terms.

Developing economies are hindered by high infant mortality, malnutrition, short life expectancy, illiteracy, and poor education systems. For example, the proportion of children who finish primary school in most African countries is less than 50 percent.[2] Because education is strongly correlated with economic development, poverty tends to persist. Lack of adequate health care is a major concern. Some 95 percent of the world's AIDS victims are found in developing economies, an additional hardship that hampers their development. Many adults cannot work or care for their children and require significant medical care. As a result, productivity is stagnant in many areas, leading to a vicious cycle of persistent poverty.

Governments in developing economies are often severely indebted. Some countries in Africa, Latin America, and South Asia have debt levels that approach or exceed their annual gross domestic product. This means it would cost a year's worth of national productive output just to pay off the national debt. Much of Africa's poverty is the result of government policies that discourage entrepreneurship, trade, and investment. Bureaucracy and red tape in developing economies deter firms from these countries from participating in the global economy.

EXHIBIT 8.1
Advanced Economies, Developing Economies, and Emerging Markets

ARCTIC OCEAN

NORWAY
SWEDEN
FINLAND

NETHERLANDS
IRELAND
UNITED
KINGDOM
DENMARK

ESTONIA
LATVIA
LITHUANIA
RUSSIA
BELARUS

BELGIUM
GERMANY
POLAND
LUXEMBOURG
CZECH
REP.
UKRAINE
FRANCE
LIECH.
AUSTRIA
SLOVAKIA
SWITZ.
SLOVENIA
HUNGARY
MOLDOVA
CROATIA
BOSNIA
ROMANIA
HERZEGOVINA
MONACO
YUGOSLAVIA
BULGARIA
ANDORRA
ITALY
MACEDONIA
ALBANIA
GREECE
TURKEY

RUSSIA

KAZAKHSTAN

MONGOLIA

SPAIN
PORTUGAL

GEORGIA
ARMENIA
AZERBAIJAN
UZBEKISTAN
KYRGYZSTAN
TURKMENISTAN
TAJIKISTAN

CYPRUS
LEBANON
SYRIA
IRAQ
ISRAEL
JORDAN
KUWAIT
TUNISIA

MOROCCO

WESTERN
SAHARA

ALGERIA
LIBYA
EGYPT

AFGHANISTAN

IRAN
PAKISTAN

NEPAL
BHUTAN
QATAR
UNITED ARAB
EMIRATES
SAUDI
ARABIA
OMAN

BANGLADESH

INDIA

MYANMAR
(BURMA)
LAOS

CHINA

NORTH
KOREA
SOUTH
KOREA

JAPAN

PACIFIC
OCEAN

TAIWAN

MAURITANIA

MALI
NIGER
CHAD

SENEGAL
GAMBIA
GUINEA-BISSAU
BURKINA
FASO
GUINEA
NIGERIA
SIERRA LEONE
IVORY
COAST
BENIN
TOGO
GHANA
LIBERIA

SUDAN

ERITREA
YEMEN

DJIBOUTI

THAILAND
CAMBODIA
VIETNAM

PHILIPPINES

CENTRAL AFRICAN
REPUBLIC
ETHIOPIA
SOMALIA

SRI
LANKA

BRUNEI
MALAYSIA
SINGAPORE

CAMEROON

EQUATORIAL
GUINEA
GABON
CONGO
REPUBLIC
CONGO
DEMOCRATIC
REPUBLIC
(ZAIRE)

UGANDA
KENYA
RWANDA
BURUNDI
TANZANIA

INDIAN
OCEAN

INDONESIA

PAPUA
NEW
GUINEA

SOLOMON
ISLANDS

SOUTH
ATLANTIC
OCEAN

ANGOLA
ZAMBIA
MALAWI
MOZAMBIQUE
NAMIBIA
ZIMBABWE
BOTSWANA
MADAGASCAR
MAURITIUS
RÉUNION

VANUATU
FIJI

SWAZILAND
SOUTH
AFRICA
LESOTHO

NEW
CALEDONIA

AUSTRALIA

NEW
ZEALAND

Advanced Economies - Post-industrial countries characterized by high per-capita income, highly competitive industries, and well-developed commercial infrastructure.

Emerging Markets - Former developing economies that have achieved substantial industrialization, modernization, and rapid economic growth since the 1980s.

Developing Economies - Low-income countries characterized by limited industrialization and stagnant economies.

EXHIBIT 8.2 Key Differences Among the Three Major Country Groups

Dimension	Advanced Economies	Developing Economies	Emerging Markets
Representative Countries	Canada, France, Japan, United Kingdom, United States	Angola, Bolivia, Nigeria, Bangladesh	Brazil, China, India, Indonesia, Turkey
Approximate Number of Countries	35	120	40
Population (% of world)	14%	25%	61%
Approximate Average Per-Capita Income (U.S. dollars; PPP basis)	$44,155	$3,618	$11,050
Approximate Share of World GDP (PPP basis)	65%	4%	31%
Population (millions)	979	1,706	4,155
Telephone Lines per 1,000 People (fixed and mobile)	803	442	694
Personal Computers per 1,000 People	517	39	191
Internet Users per 1,000 People	751	165	422
Motor Vehicles per 1,000 People	537	65	236

Sources: Based on World Bank at http://www.worldbank.org and International Monetary Fund at http://www.imf.org.

EXHIBIT 8.3

The World at Night, Showing Varying Areas of Industrialization

Source: C. Mayhew and R. Simmon (NASA/GSFC), NOAA/NGDC, DMSP Digital Archive.

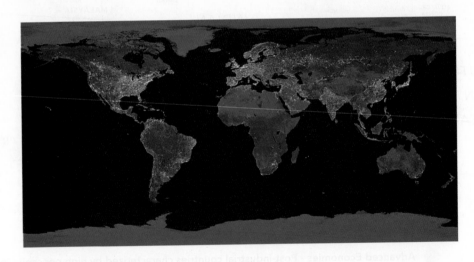

As illustrated in Exhibit 8.4, there are substantial differences in the economic profiles of the three country groups. In particular, the exhibit reveals that developing economies lack numerous conditions needed for successful economic development, including low trade barriers and substantial international trade and investment. Advanced economies rank well in these areas, and emerging markets are showing consistent improvement.

Emerging Market Economies

Emerging markets are found in East and South Asia, Eastern Europe, Latin America, and a few in Africa and the Middle East. Their most distinguishing characteristic is rapidly improving living standards and a growing middle class with rising economic aspirations.[3] As a result, they have become very attractive destinations for exports, FDI, and global sourcing.

Because their economies have transformed so dynamically, Hong Kong, Israel, Singapore, South Korea, and Taiwan have moved beyond the emerging-market stage. Several emerging

EXHIBIT 8.4 Trade Conditions in the Major Country Groups

Trade Condition	Advanced Economies	Developing Economies	Emerging Markets
Industry	Highly developed	Poor	Rapidly improving
Competition	Substantial	Limited	Moderate, but increasing
Trade Barriers	Minimal	Moderate to high	Rapidly liberalizing
Trade Volume	High	Low	High
Inward FDI	High	Low	Moderate to High

Sources: Based on International Monetary Fund at http://www.imf.org; World Bank, 2015, at http://www.worldbank.org; and Central Intelligence Agency, *World Factbook*, 2015, https://www.cia.gov/library/publications/the-world-factbook/.

markets are likely to join the group of wealthy nations in the not-too-distant future. For example, the Czech Republic and Poland have now matured into dynamic and competitive economies. Similarly, some countries currently classified as developing economies have the potential to become emerging markets in the near future. These frontier economies include the European countries of Estonia, Latvia, Lithuania, Slovakia; and the Latin American countries of Costa Rica, Panama, and Uruguay. In the Middle East, the United Arab Emirates has also transformed itself into a dynamic economy with a sophisticated commercial infrastructure.

Finally, you should know that economic prosperity often varies *within* a particular emerging market. There are usually two parallel economies in these countries—the urban areas and the rural sector. Compared to rural areas, urban areas tend to have more developed economic infrastructure and more middle-class consumers with greater disposable income, which then facilitates discretionary consumption.[4]

Certain emerging markets that have evolved from centrally planned economies to liberalized markets—specifically China, Russia, and several Eastern European countries—are called **transition economies**. These countries were once socialist states but have been largely transformed into capitalism-based systems, partly through a process of **privatization**—the transfer of state-owned industries to private concerns. Privatization and the promotion of new, privately owned businesses have allowed the transition economies to attract substantial direct investment from abroad. Long burdened by excessive regulation and entrenched government bureaucracy, they are gradually introducing legal frameworks to protect business and consumer interests and ensure intellectual property rights. They hold much potential.[5]

Exhibit 8.5 contrasts the national characteristics of emerging markets with the other two country groups. Developing economies tend to be rooted in the agriculture and commodities sectors, which provide little basis for creating wealth. By contrast, emerging markets and advanced economies specialize in knowledge- and capital-intensive manufacturing and services sectors. These sectors provide ample added value and create superior living standards.

In purchasing-power terms, emerging markets now account for more than half of world GDP.[6] Exhibit 8.6 shows the total, incremental contribution to world GDP of the leading economies from 2000 through 2020. Emerging markets, especially China, India, and Brazil, have contributed enormously to world growth in GDP and will continue to do so in the future. Although advanced economies such as the United States and Europe will remain relatively robust, the emerging markets hold the most promise as target markets and engines of global commerce in the future. In coming decades, it is estimated that the majority of growth in world GDP will come from emerging markets, especially Brazil, Russia, India and China, the BRIC countries. Presently, emerging markets represent more than one-third of world exports and receive more than one-third of world FDI.

In addition to proactive market liberalization, several factors contributed to the rise of emerging markets. The presence of low-cost labor; knowledge workers; government support; low-cost capital; and powerful, highly networked conglomerates also helped make these countries formidable players in the global economy. As highlighted in the opening case,

Transition economies
A subset of emerging markets that evolved from centrally planned economies into liberalized markets.

Privatization
Transfer of state-owned industries to private concerns.

EXHIBIT 8.5 **National Characteristics of Major Country Groups**

Characteristic	Advanced Economies	Developing Economies	Emerging Markets
Median Age of Citizens	39 years	24 years	32 years
Major Sector Focus	Services, branded products	Agriculture, commodities	Manufacturing, some services
Economic and Political Freedom	Free or mostly free	Mostly repressed	Moderately free or mostly not free
Economic/Political System	Market	Command or Mixed	Mixed
Regulatory Environment	Minimal regulations	Highly regulated, burdensome	Achieved much economic liberalization
Country Risk	Low	moderate to high	Variable
Intellectual Property Protection	Strong	Weak	Moderate and improving
Infrastructure	Well-developed	Inadequate	Moderate but improving

Sources: Based on International Monetary Fund at http://www.imf.org. and Central Intelligence Agency, *World Factbook*, 2015, https://www.cia.gov/library/publications/the-world-factbook/.

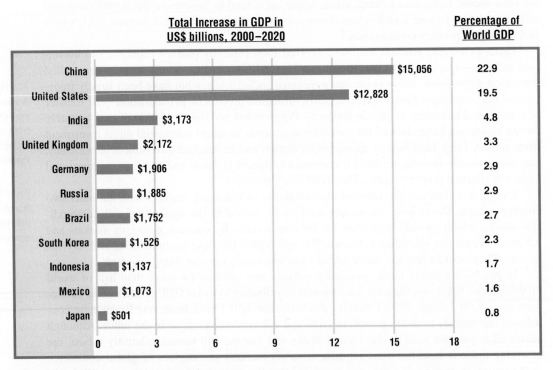

EXHIBIT 8.6

Estimated Total Contribution to World GDP, 2000 through 2020, in Billions of U.S. Dollars and as a Percentage of World GDP

Source: Based on International Monetary Fund, World Economic Outlook Database, 2015.

EXHIBIT 8.7 Emerging Market Global Challengers

Country	Example Multinational Firms	Representative Industries
Brazil	Brasil Foods Embraer Natura Cosmeticos	Food processor Aerospace Cosmetics
China	Alibaba Group Huawei Technologies Lenovo Group	E-commerce Information and communications technology Computer technology
India	Bharti Airtel Infosys Tata Motors	Telecommunications services Technology consulting Automotive
Mexico	America Movil Cemex Grupo Bimbo	Telecommunication Building materials Baking, snacks
Russia	Gazprom Lukoil Severstal	Natural gas Oil Steel and mining
Turkey	Koc Holding Sabanci Holding Yildiz Holding	Industrial Industrial and financial Confectionary, biscuits, snacks

Source: Based on Boston Consulting Group 2014, September 10, "Meet the 2014 BCG Global Challengers."

new global challengers are leading firms from emerging markets that are fast becoming key contenders in world markets. Exhibit 8.7 provides a sample of these firms. Most are highly diversified, operating in sectors from manufacturing, services, trade, and even education.

An example from Egypt is Global Telecom Holding, formerly Orascom Telecom Holding (www.gtelecom.com). This mobile telecommunications provider has become an industry leader in Africa and the Middle East. As the world's sixth-largest mobile telecommunications provider, it has strung together a telecom empire of more than 86 million subscribers in Africa, Asia, Europe, North America, and the Middle East.

Emerging market multinationals have also been on a shopping spree, acquiring companies in the advanced economies. In the auto industry, for example, Zhejiang Geely Holdings of China now owns Volvo. Tata of India acquired Jaguar and Land Rover. Emerging market multinationals have acquired numerous former United States brands. Examples include Godiva (owned by Turkish Yildiz) and AMC Theaters (owned by Dalian Wanda group of China),

Each year, *Forbes* magazine catalogs the leading 2,000 global firms. The number of companies from emerging markets in the list now exceeds 500. Over the past several years, some firms from advanced economies have fallen off the Forbes list. For example, eight Japanese companies were removed in 2015. These statistics reveal how fast new global challengers are displacing traditional MNEs from the advanced economies and becoming key competitors in world markets. Managers need to devise innovative strategies to compete skillfully with them. [7]

China is the largest emerging market. Its population of 1.3 billion people represents one-fifth of the world's total, and its economy has been growing at an impressive rate. The country's role in international business is expanding rapidly. China already has produced numerous new global challengers, such as Shanghai Automotive (China's top automaker), Sinopec (a large oil company), and Shanghai Baosteel (a steel manufacturer). Chinese exports now account for about 12 percent of total world merchandise exports.[8] The figure is impressive given that most of the world's 200 or so countries export. [9]

New global challengers
Leading firms from emerging markets that are fast becoming key contenders in world markets.

MyManagementLab **Watch It! I**

If your professor has assigned this, go to the Assignments section of **mymanagementlab.com** to complete the video exercise titled The New Global Challengers.

8.2 Know what makes emerging markets attractive for international business.

What Makes Emerging Markets Attractive for International Business?

Emerging markets are attractive to internationalizing firms as target markets, manufacturing bases, and sourcing destinations.

Emerging Markets as Target Markets

Emerging markets have become important target markets for a wide variety of products and services. The largest emerging markets have doubled their share of world imports in the past few years. The growing middle class in emerging markets implies rising demand for various consumer products, such as electronics and automobiles, and services such as health care.[10] Roughly one-quarter of Mexico's 122 million people enjoy affluence equivalent to that of the middle class in the advanced economies. In some product categories, demand is growing fastest in emerging markets. For example, the fastest-growing markets for power tool companies such as Black & Decker and Robert Bosch are in Asia, Latin America, Africa, and the Middle East.[11] Even during the recent global recession, technology firms such as Cisco, Hewlett-Packard, and Intel generated a large and growing proportion of their revenues from sales to such countries.[12]

Source: Keith Dannemiller/Alamy

Workers at the Hawker Beechcraft aerospace plant in Chihuahua, Mexico construct jet airplane parts for export to the USA.

Global pharmaceutical companies such as Pfizer and GlaxoSmithKline, have increased their emphasis on developing and marketing drugs in emerging markets. This change in strategy has resulted from a rapidly expanding middle class whose members can pay for quality medications. Industry forecasts indicate that the global pharmaceutical market will reach nearly $1.3 trillion by 2018, with emerging markets accounting for about half of total global growth and nearly half of total sales. For example, Merck and Pfizer have launched popular drugs in India, using innovative pricing strategies that make once-expensive medications affordable for millions of low-income consumers.[13]

Businesses in emerging markets are important targets for machinery, equipment, and technology sales. For example, demand is huge for textile machinery in India, for agricultural equipment in China, and for oil and gas exploration technology in Russia. In a similar way, governments and state enterprises in emerging markets are major targets for sales of infrastructure-related products and services such as machinery, power transmission equipment, transportation equipment, high-technology products, and other products that countries in the middle stage of development typically need.

Emerging Markets as Manufacturing Bases

Firms from Japan, Europe, the United States, and other advanced economies have invested vast sums to develop manufacturing facilities in emerging markets. These markets are home to low-wage, high-quality labor for manufacturing and assembly operations. In addition, some emerging markets have large reserves of raw materials and natural resources. For example, Mexico, India, and China are important production platforms for manufacturing cars and consumer electronics. South Africa is a key source for industrial diamonds. Brazil is a center for mining bauxite, the main ingredient in aluminum. Thailand has become an important manufacturing location for Japanese MNEs such as Sony and Sharp. Motorola, Intel, and Philips manufacture semiconductors in Malaysia and Taiwan.

Emerging markets enjoy considerable success in certain industries. Examples include Brazil in iron ore and processed foods, Taiwan and Malaysia in personal computers, and South Africa in mining. Two of the world's top-selling beer brands are new global challengers based in China (Snow, made by China Resources Snow Breweries) and Brazil (Skol, made by ABInBev). Together, these firms produce more than 50 million barrels of beer annually.[14] South Korea's Samsung is the world's largest electronics company and the leading producer of semiconductors and flat-screen TVs. It has displaced Sony (Japan) and Motorola (United States) in these industries.

Emerging Markets as Sourcing Destinations

Many companies subcontract their noncore business activities to specialized suppliers, a trend known as **outsourcing**, the procurement of selected value-chain activities, including production of intermediate goods or finished products, from independent suppliers or company-owned subsidiaries. Outsourcing helps firms become more efficient, concentrate on their core competencies, and obtain competitive advantages. When outsourcing relies on suppliers or production bases located abroad, it is known as **global sourcing** or *offshoring*.

Emerging markets serve as excellent platforms for sourcing. Numerous MNEs have established call centers in Eastern Europe, India, and the Philippines. Firms in the IT industry such as Dell and IBM reap big benefits from the ability to outsource certain technological functions to knowledge workers in India. Many Intel and Microsoft programming activities are performed in Bangalore, India. Investments from abroad benefit emerging markets because they lead to new jobs and production capacity, transfer of technology and expertise, and linkages to the global marketplace.

Assessing the True Potential of Emerging Markets

Firms targeting emerging markets for sales, manufacturing, or sourcing, must seek reliable information to support managerial decision-making. However, emerging markets are characterized by unique circumstances that usually hinder managers' ability to acquire needed facts and figures. Limited data, unreliable information, or the high cost of conducting market research pose formidable challenges for estimating the true potential of emerging markets. In such cases, MNEs may need to improvise and use creative methods to generate needed findings.[15]

In the early stages of market research, managers examine three important statistics to estimate market potential: per capita income, size of the middle class, and market potential indicators. Let's examine each in turn.

Per Capita Income as an Indicator of Market Potential

When evaluating the potential of individual markets, managers often start by examining aggregate country data, such as gross national income (GNI) or per-capita GDP, expressed in terms of a reference currency such as the U.S. dollar. For comparison, the second column in Exhibit 8.8 provides per-capita GDP for a sample of emerging markets and for the United States. For example, China's per capita GDP converted at market exchange rates was $7,589, whereas that of the United States was $54,597 in 2014.

However, per-capita GDP converted at market exchange rates paints an inaccurate picture of market potential because it overlooks the substantial price differences between advanced economies and emerging markets. Prices are usually lower for most products and services in emerging markets. For example, a U.S. dollar exchanged and spent in China will buy much more than a dollar spent in the United States.

What should managers do to estimate market potential accurately? The answer lies in using per capita GDP figures adjusted for price differences. Economists estimate real buying power by calculating GDP statistics based on **purchasing power parity (PPP)**. The PPP concept suggests that, in the long run, exchange rates should move toward levels that would equalize the prices of an identical basket of goods and services in any two countries. Since prices vary greatly among countries, economists adjust ordinary GDP figures for differences in purchasing power. Adjusted per-capita GDP more accurately represents the number of products consumers can buy in a given country, using *their own currency* and consistent with *their own standard of living*.

Outsourcing
The procurement of selected value-chain activities, including production of intermediate goods or finished products, from independent suppliers.

Global sourcing
The procurement of products or services from independent suppliers or company-owned subsidiaries located abroad for consumption in the home country or a third country.

8.3 Learn how to assess the true potential of emerging markets.

Purchasing power parity (PPP)
An adjustment for prices that reflects the number of goods that consumers can buy in their home country, using their own currency and consistent with their own standard of living.

EXHIBIT 8.8 Difference in Per Capita GDP, in Conventional and Purchasing Power Parity (PPP) Terms, U.S. Dollars, 2014

Country	Per-Capita GDP, Converted Using Market Exchange Rates	Per Capita GDP, Converted Using PPP Exchange Rates
Argentina	$12,873	$22,582
Brazil	11,604	16,096
China	7,589	12,880
Hungary	13,881	24,942
India	1,627	5,855
South Korea	28,101	35,277
Mexico	10,715	17,881
Russia	12,926	24,805
Turkey	10,482	19,610
Vietnam	2, 053	5,635
United States	54,597	54,597

Source: Based on data from International Monetary Fund, *World Economic Outlook Database, April 2015* (www.imf.org).

Now examine per capita GDP, adjusted for purchasing power parity, for the same sample of countries in the third column in Exhibit 8.8. Note that a more accurate estimate of China's per-capita GDP is $12,880, stated in PPP terms—considerably higher than per capita GDP at market exchange rates suggests. Compare the two figures for other countries as well. These adjusted estimates help explain why firms target emerging markets despite the seemingly low income levels in conventional income statistics.

Another way to illustrate the PPP concept is to examine the Big Mac Index developed by *The Economist* newsmagazine (www.economist.com). The Index first gathers information about the price of hamburgers at McDonald's restaurants worldwide. It then compares the prices based on actual exchange rates to those based on the PPP price of Big Macs to assess whether a nation's currency is under- or over-valued. Exhibit 8.9 presents the Big Mac Index for the most recent year. It reveals that most European currencies are overvalued, whereas those of most developing economies or emerging markets are undervalued. The Big Mac Index also implies that the Chinese yuan is undervalued. [16]

Even when per capita income is adjusted for purchasing power parity, managers should exercise care in relying on it as an indicator of market potential in an emerging or developing economy. There are four reasons for this caution.

- Official data do not account for the informal economy, where economic transactions are not officially recorded and are therefore left out of national GDP calculations. In developing economies, the informal economy is often as large as the formal economy. Countries usually lack sophisticated taxation systems, and individuals and businesses often underreport income to minimize tax obligations. Also not normally captured by national GDP estimates are barter exchanges in which no money changes hands.
- Most people in emerging markets and developing economies are on the low end of the income scale. As you may recall from your statistics training, mean or average does not always represent a normal distribution; often, median income more accurately depicts purchasing power.
- *Household income* is substantially larger than per capita income in these countries due to the presence of multiple wage earners in individual households. Multiple-income households have much greater spending power than individuals, a fact overlooked by statistics that emphasize per-capita GDP.
- Governments in these countries may underreport national income so they can qualify for low-interest loans and grants from international aid agencies and development banks.

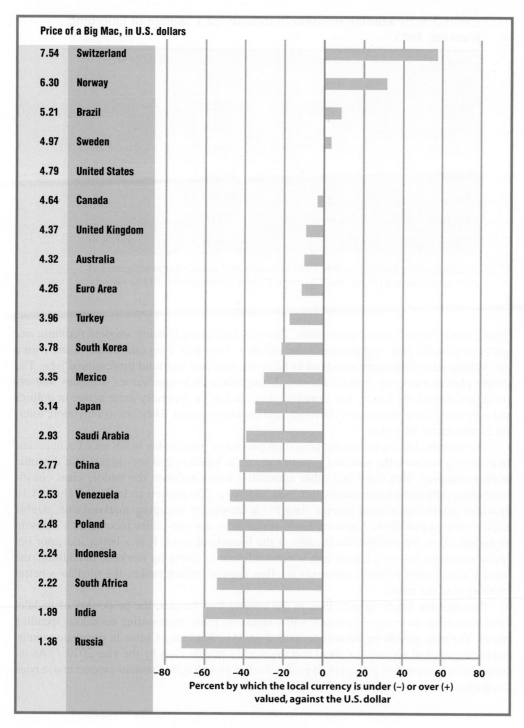

EXHIBIT 8.9

The Big Mac Index 2015

Source: Based on "The Big
Mac Index," January 22, 2015,
www.economist.com/content/
big-mac-index.

In addition to per-capita GDP, managers should examine other market potential indicators, including GDP growth rate, income distribution, commercial infrastructure, the rate of urbanization, consumer expenditures for discretionary items, and unemployment rate. Managers will also find the size and growth rate of the middle class to be revealing. Let's explore this next.

Middle Class as an Indicator of Market Potential

In every country, the middle class represents the segment of people between wealthy and poor. Middle class households in the emerging markets now have access to substantial disposable income. This allows them to engage in discretionary consumption, which means

EXHIBIT 8.10 Median Household Income for a Sample of Emerging Markets, 2015

Country	Median Income per Household (U.S. $)
Brazil	15,372
China	9,721
India	4,965
Indonesia	5,919
Mexico	20,960
Russia	14,487
Thailand	7,113
Turkey	21,966

Sources: Based on Euromonitor International January 2015 (www.euromonitor.com) and International Monetary Fund, *World Economic Outlook Database April 2015* (www.imf.org).

buying goods beyond simple necessities. These include better housing, modern furniture and appliances, health care, and education for children. They may even take holidays and own a car. Middle class consumers also tend to be better educated and hold professional jobs. The middle class in emerging markets are also distinguished by unique values, attitudes, and expectations toward the future. For example, they tend to be generally more active in politics and concerned about democracy, freedom, and the environment. They are usually more tolerant of alternative lifestyles.

The middle class makes up the largest proportion of households in advanced economies. In emerging markets, the size and growth rate of the middle class are signals of a dynamic market economy. McKinsey and other consulting forms estimate the middle class constitutes some 300 million consumers in China and some 250 million in India.[17] Exhibit 8.10 provides median household income data for a sample of emerging markets with sizable middle-class populations. Although some researchers use per-capita income as a measure of middle class, we use median income at the household level. It is a better indicator because pooled income of a family unit is more relevant in emerging markets. In addition, the income distribution in these countries is often skewed, which makes the median a better measure than the mean.

Demographic trends suggest that, in the coming two decades, the proportion of middle-class households in emerging markets will continue to grow, representing enormous spending power. The most growth by far will occur in East Asia, especially China. In population terms, Asia is expected to account for about half the world's middle class by the year 2020.[18] As incomes increase, spending patterns will evolve, fueling growth across various product and service categories.

 MyManagementLab **Watch It! 2**

If your professor has assigned this, go to the Assignments section of **mymanagementlab.com** to complete the video exercise titled Made in America: Mexico.

8.4 Evaluate the risks and challenges of emerging markets.

Risks and Challenges of Emerging Markets

Country risk takes on growing importance in an increasingly interdependent world. More MNEs are doing business in emerging markets, which are beset by various challenges.[19] National and regional crises have global implications, even for firms very remote from crisis locations.

Political Instability

The absence of reliable or consistent governance from recognized government authorities adds to business costs, increases risks, and reduces managers' ability to forecast business conditions. Political instability is associated with corruption and weak legal frameworks that discourage inward investment and the development of a reliable business environment. In Russia, for example, evolving political conditions threaten the business activities of foreign firms. Bureaucratic practices favor well-connected, home-grown firms. Western oil companies have been denied access to Russia's energy resources. In the 2015 *Ease of Doing Business* rankings of the World Bank, Brazil received an overall ranking of 120 out of 189 countries. It ranked 167th in starting a business; 174th in dealing with construction permits; and 123rd in trading across borders. Such conditions tend to discourage firms from entering the Brazilian market. [20]

Weak Intellectual Property Protection

Many countries lack strong laws that protect intellectual property. Even when such laws are present, they may not be enforced, or the judicial process may be painfully slow. In Argentina, for example, enforcement of copyrights on recorded music, videos, books, and computer software is inconsistent. Authorities attempt to stop shipments of pirated merchandise, but inadequate resources and slow court procedures hamper enforcement. Laws against Internet piracy are weak and ineffective. [21] Counterfeiting—unauthorized copying and production of a product—is common in China, Indonesia, and Russia, especially of software, DVDs, and CDs. In India, weak patent laws often discourage investment by foreign firms. In China, counterfeiting extends even to creating fake retail stores, imitating trademark retail outlets of top brands such as Apple and Ikea. [22]

Bureaucracy, Red Tape, and Lack of Transparency

Burdensome administrative rules and excessive requirements for licenses, approvals, and paperwork all delay business activities.[23] Excessive bureaucracy is usually associated with a lack of transparency, suggesting that legal and political systems may not be open and accountable to the public. Bribery, kickbacks, and extortion, especially in the public sector, cause difficulty for managers. Where anticorruption laws are weak, managers may be tempted to offer bribes to ensure the success of business deals. In the *Transparency International* ranking of the most corrupt countries (www.transparency.org), emerging markets such as Russia, Venezuela, and the Philippines are among those with substantial corruption. [24]

Poor Physical Infrastructure

In advanced economies, high-quality roads, drainage systems, sewers, and electrical utilities are taken for granted. In emerging markets, such basic infrastructure is still in development. Many people in rural India do not have access to toilets and sewage treatment systems. Poor sanitation gives rise to illness, and thousands of Indian children die every week from diarrheal illness. India's ports, roads, railways, and airports are insufficient to handle the massive volumes of cargo that enter and leave the country every day. Industrial cities such as Bangalore and Pune periodically experience power outages that can last 24 hours or more. [25] The government is working to improve infrastructure, but MNEs often must build their own systems and find creative solutions to support value-chain activities. In much of the world, firms find themselves building roads, installing localized energy sources, and developing other such systems to conduct business. A subsidiary of Tata Chemicals, part of India's giant Tata conglomerate, had to build its own road and railway infrastructure in Africa to support the firm's operations there. [26]

Partner Availability and Qualifications

Multinational firms often seek alliances with well-qualified local companies in countries characterized by inadequate legal and political frameworks. Through such partners, foreign firms can access local market knowledge, establish supplier and distributor networks, and develop key government contacts. However, well-qualified partners that can provide these advantages are not always readily available in emerging markets, especially smaller ones.

Likely Resistance from Family Conglomerates

Family conglomerate
A large, highly diversified company that is privately owned.

Many emerging market economies are dominated by large, family-owned rather than publicly owned businesses. A **family conglomerate (FC)** is a large, highly diversified company that is privately owned. FCs operate in industries ranging from banking to construction to manufacturing. They control the majority of economic activity and employment in emerging markets such as South Korea, where they are called *chaebols*; in India, where they are called *business houses*; in Latin America, where they are called *grupos*; and in Turkey, where they are called *holding companies*. Exhibit 8.11 illustrates some of the world's leading FCs.

A typical FC may hold the largest market share in each of several industries in its home country. In South Korea, the top 30 FCs account for nearly half the economy's assets and industry revenues. Samsung is perhaps the most famous Korean FC. In Turkey, the Koc Group accounts for about 20 percent of trading on the Istanbul Stock Exchange, and Sabanci provides more than 5 percent of Turkey's national tax revenue. FCs enjoy various competitive advantages in their home countries, including government protection and support, extensive networks in various industries, superior market knowledge, and access to capital. Hyundai Group was an early mover in South Korea's auto industry and now holds the largest share of that country's car market. When foreign automakers tried to enter the market, they found Hyundai's advantages overwhelming.

EXHIBIT 8.11 A Sample of Leading Family Conglomerates

Family Conglomerate	Home Country	Primary sectors	Distinction
ALFA	Mexico	Petrochemicals, machinery, foods, electronics, telecommunications	One of the world's largest producers of engine blocks and petrochemicals
Astra	Indonesia	Motor vehicles, financial services, heavy equipment, agribusiness, information technology	Largest distributor of automobiles and motorcycles in Indonesia
Ayala	Philippines	Real estate, financial services, utilities, telecommunications, electronics	Oldest and largest conglomerate in the Philippines
Hyundai	South Korea	Automobiles, shipbuilding	Truly global car company, selling Sonatas, Elantras, and other models in nearly 200 countries
Reliance Industries	India	Petroleum products, retailing, chemicals, textiles, solar energy systems	Named by *Forbes* one of the "world's 100 most respected companies"
Russian Standard	Russia	Alcoholic beverages, banking, life insurance	The leading premium producer of vodka in Russia
Sabanci Holding	Turkey	Cars, cement, energy, retailing, insurance, telecom, tires, plastic, hotels, paper, tobacco	Controls about 70 companies, including Turkey's largest bank, Akbank
Tatung	Taiwan	Computers, liquid crystal display televisions, network devices, media players, home appliances	OEM manufacturer for HP, Acer and Dell; world's largest producer of flat panels for the TV industry
Votorantim Group	Brazil	Finance, energy, agribusiness, mining, steel, paper	One of the largest industrial conglomerates in Latin America

An FC's origins and growth often derive from a special relationship with the government. The government may protect the FC by providing it with subsidies, loans, and tax incentives. The government may set up market-entry barriers to competitors. In some cases, the government may even launch the FC. The government of Thailand launched the Siam Cement Group. One of the largest FCs in Indonesia, the Bimantara Citra Group, got its start by selling its foreign oil allocations to the state-owned oil monopoly. The Group has long enjoyed a close relationship with the Indonesian government and secured numerous lucrative contracts. When the Hyundai Group in South Korea experienced a financial crisis, the Korean government and Hyundai's major creditors provided more than $300 million in assistance.[27]

Family conglomerates provide huge tax revenues and facilitate national economic development. This helps explain why governments eagerly support them. The fact that they dominate the commercial landscape in many emerging markets suggests they will be either formidable competitors or capable partners, possibly with much bargaining power. We return to this issue in the next section.

Success Strategies for Emerging Markets

8.5 Learn the success strategies for emerging markets.

The strategies that MNEs developed decades ago and refined in mature advanced-economy markets are often inappropriate for the unique circumstances in emerging markets. Foreign firms must devise creative strategies to succeed.[28] For example, Toyota developed a line of inexpensive cars, costing about $7,000, for low-income countries. In India, it built a large factory to boost its share of the Indian car market to 10 percent.[29] Renault and Volkswagen are building low-cost cars targeted to emerging markets such as China, India, and Russia.[30] In this section, we discuss strategies that firms employ to succeed in emerging markets.

Customize Offerings to Unique Emerging Market Needs

Successful firms develop a deep understanding of the distinctive characteristics of buyers, local suppliers, and distribution channels in emerging markets. They build constructive relationships with the communities where they operate, partly to understand local conditions better and partly to earn customer respect and loyalty. The ability to customize offerings and devise innovative business models depends largely on the firm's *flexibility* and entrepreneurial orientation. In emerging markets, many people are illiterate, and fewer than one in four has regular access to the Internet and other computer-based systems.[31] Consequently, MNEs employ creative approaches to promote their offerings in local markets. Where suppliers and distribution channels are lacking, they develop their own infrastructure to obtain needed raw materials and components or move finished goods to local buyers.[32]

MNEs must set prices appropriate for local conditions. Many firms devise innovative products and packaging to keep prices low. In India, for example, General Electric developed a lightweight electrocardiograph machine that sells for just $1,500, far cheaper than similar machines in advanced economies. Low pricing means that doctors and clinics in poor areas can purchase the machine and offer health care for a fraction of the cost required by earlier technologies. The Chinese Internet company Tencent developed a free messaging service that captured the local market for mobile phone communications. Chinese consumers prefer text messaging over voice communications because pricing is cheaper.

Source: Konstantin/Fotolia

Emerging market governments are important potential customers for various products and services. Pictured here is a government ministry in Russia.

Partner with Family Conglomerates

Family conglomerates are formidable players in their respective economies and have much capital to invest in new ventures. For example, most major FCs in Korea, as well as Koc and Sabanci in Turkey, Vitro in Mexico, and Astra in Indonesia, own their own financing operations in the form of insurance companies, banks, and securities brokers. Many FCs possess extensive distribution channels throughout their home countries. They have a deep understanding of local markets and customers. In addition, they often have political clout, which enables them to navigate the complex bureaucracy.

For foreign firms wanting to do business in emerging markets, FCs can make valuable venture partners. [33] By collaborating with an FC, the foreign firm can:

- Reduce the risks, time, and capital requirements of entering the market.
- Develop helpful relationships with governments and other key local players.
- Target market opportunities more rapidly and effectively.
- Overcome infrastructure-related hurdles.
- Leverage FC resources and local contacts.

There are many examples of successful FC partnering. Ford partnered with Kia to introduce the Sable line of cars in South Korea and benefitted from Kia's strong distribution and after-service network. Digital Equipment Corporation (DEC) designated Tatung, a Taiwanese FC, as the main distributor of its workstations and client-server products in Taiwan. DEC gained access to Tatung's local experience and distribution network. In Turkey, Danone, the French yogurt producer and owner of Evian brand of bottled water, entered a joint venture with Sabanci, a large local FC. Danone brought ample technical knowledge in packaging and bottling and a reputation for health-friendly products, but it lacked information about the local market. As the Turkish market leader, Sabanci knew the market, retailers, and distributors. The collaboration helped make Danone the most popular bottled water in the first year after entry.

Target Governments in Emerging Markets

In emerging markets and developing economies, government agencies and state-owned enterprises are an important customer group for three reasons:

- Governments buy enormous quantities of products (such as computers, furniture, office supplies, and motor vehicles) and services (such as architectural, legal, and consulting services).
- State enterprises in areas such as railways, airlines, banking, oil, chemicals, and steel buy goods and services from foreign companies.
- The public sector influences the procurement activities of various private or semiprivate corporations. In India, the government works directly in planning housing projects. Construction firms lobby the government to gain access to promising deals to build apartments and houses for local dwellers.

Tenders
Formal offers a buyer makes to purchase certain products or services.

Emerging market governments regularly announce **tenders**—formal offers made by a buyer to purchase certain products or services. A tender is also known as a request for proposals (RFPs). Government agencies seek bids from suppliers to procure bulk commodities, equipment, and technology or to build power plants, highways, dams, and public housing. Vendors submit bids to the government to work on these projects.

Governments in emerging markets as well as developing countries often formulate economic development plans and annual programs to build or improve national infrastructure. To find vendors, the government follows specific buying procedures that lead to large, lucrative sales to international vendors. Securing major government contracts usually requires substantial competencies and resources. Firms competing for such projects assemble a team of managers and technical experts, especially when pursuing large deals. Governments prefer dealing with vendors that offer complete sales and service packages. The most successful vendors also offer financing for major sales, in the form of low-interest loans or grants. Governments are attracted

You Can Do It | RECENT GRADS IN IB

ANDREW & JAMIE WASKEY

Andrew's majors: Master of International Business (MIB), Bachelor's in Spanish

Jamie's majors: Master of International Business (MIB), Bachelor's in International Affairs and Modern Language

Andrew's jobs since graduation: Various positions in international logistics at DHL and other firms; marketing intern at U.S. Department of Commerce (Shanghai, China)

Jamie's jobs since graduation: Research manager at YouGov (Dubai, United Arab Emirates); market research analyst at Delta Air Lines (Atlanta, GA); market research intern at U.S. Department of Commerce (Buenos Aires, Argentina)

Objectives: Leverage and grow our international expertise while accelerating the global positioning of our firms and creating a life filled with adventure.

Andrew and Jamie Waskey met during their Masters of International Business (MIB) program at Georgia State University. As undergraduates, both majored in international studies and Spanish. They enjoy traveling and learning languages, especially in emerging markets in Latin America. After completing college, Andrew worked for DHL, the international logistics company. The MIB degree provided an internship with DHL and the U.S. Department of Commerce office in Shanghai, China.

After completing her undergrad degree, Jamie worked for a nonprofit organization. She desired a career in international market research, so she attended an MIB program. In her last semester, she completed an internship in Buenos Aires, Argentina, performing market research for the U.S. Department of Commerce there.

Andrew and Jamie married after earning their MIB degrees and quickly secured international jobs in Atlanta with Delta Airlines and BlueLinx Corporation. Networking was key to obtaining these and later jobs. Both were committed to living and working abroad. Andrew next obtained a position with MKM Holdings/The Wafi Group in Dubai, in the firm's transportation division. In his job as a marketing and sales manager, he works with multicultural teams.

Jamie leveraged her contacts to secure a position with a UK-based market research consultancy in Dubai, YouGov. Jamie's favorite part of the job is the channel it provides for learning about and understanding the region's various cultures. She travels around the Middle East to places such as Saudi Arabia.

Success Factors

- Set goals and be persistent in working toward them. If you want to work abroad, pursue your goal actively and remain fully committed.
- Know what you want to do. Develop a clear professional path.
- Leverage friends and other contacts to connect with key people in your field.

Building a personal network is key to securing an international position.

Advice for an International Career

- Adopt a patient, flexible, and light-hearted outlook. Maintaining a positive attitude and putting challenges in perspective will enrich your life abroad.
- Keep an open mind to differing conditions and attitudes in foreign environments.
- Be curious about everything. Immersing yourself in the local culture will allow you to adapt easily and acquire a different lens for viewing the world.

Challenges

- Mastering cross-cultural communication and differing management structures
- Adapting to different living situations
- Making friends
- Striking a healthy work–life balance

Source: Photo courtesy Andrew & Jamie Waskey.

by deals that create local jobs, employ local resources, reduce import dependence, and provide other country-level advantages.

Bechtel, Siemens, General Electric, Hitachi, and other major vendors regularly participate in bidding for global tenders from emerging market governments. Some of the largest construction projects include the Panama Canal expansion and the Channel tunnel between Britain and France. Another megaproject, the Three Gorges Dam on the Yangtze River in China, cost more than $37 billion. Numerous global contractors worked on the project, including ABB, Kvaerner, Voith, Siemens, and General Electric.

Skillfully Challenge Emerging Market Competitors

As the opening case shows, the new global challengers have become formidable competitors. They possess many strengths including access to low-cost labor, skilled workforces,

Source: Nightman1965/Fotolia

Investing in emerging markets helps foster economic development and modernize critical infrastructure such as this aging port in Poland.

8.6 Understand corporate social responsibility, sustainability, and the crisis of global poverty.

government support, and family conglomerates. For example, India's Mahindra & Mahindra (www.mahindra.com) is capturing market share in the global farm equipment industry, which has been long dominated by admired names such as John Deere and Komatsu. Strong brands such as the Mahindra 5500, a powerful, high-quality tractor, sell for far less than competing models. One dealership in the U.S. state of Mississippi, a market long dominated by John Deere, sold more than 300 Mahindras in just four months.[34]

Advanced-economy firms can counter in various ways. Initially, managers must conduct research to develop an understanding of the new challengers. It is vital to analyze the advantages and strategies of the emergent firms, which often enjoy superior advantages in the industry in the target market. The next step is to acquire new capabilities that improve the firm's competitive advantages. For example, many incumbents are boosting their R&D to invent new, superior products. Others are partnering with competitors to pool resources against emerging market rivals. Incumbent firms can also match global challengers at their own game by leveraging low-cost labor and skilled workers in locations such as China, Mexico, and Eastern Europe. Many advanced economy firms partner with family conglomerates and others in emerging markets on critical value-chain activities such as R&D, manufacturing, and technical support.

Corporate Social Responsibility, Sustainability, and the Crisis Of Global Poverty

Most people in emerging markets and developing economies live in relative poverty. Economic disparity and poverty are critical global challenges.[35] Poverty increases the likelihood of disease, food shortages, terrorism, illicit trade, and international migration. Despite strong growth in emerging markets, many of these nations face cyclical poverty that reduces access to basic social infrastructure such as education, health care, and sanitation. Poverty increases the fragility of national governments.[36] Let's examine how companies help address poverty around the world.

Foster Economic Development

Historically, few companies targeted poor countries because managers assumed there were few profitable opportunities. Today, firms that offer suitable products can earn substantial profits in emerging markets and developing economies. Unilever and P&G sell shampoo for 2 cents per mini-sachet in India. Such pricing, though attractive to local Indians, is actually more profitable for these firms than in the advanced economies. Narayana Hrudayalaya is an insurance company that sells health insurance for less than 20 cents per person per month and has millions of customers. Amul is an Indian company that sells various food products to millions of poor people. Micromax and Qualcomm are marketing low-cost cell phones in India. To succeed, such firms created new business models in manufacturing, packaging, and distribution.[37]

The Swedish telecommunications company Ericsson (www.ericsson.com) helped modernize the telecom infrastructure in rural parts of Tanzania by installing phone lines and cellular systems for households, companies, and aid agencies.[38] The emergence of a cell phone market in Africa led to the emergence of related industries. Local firms produce accessories, such as devices for recharging cell phone batteries. Ericsson's experience suggests that market-based solutions not only contribute to social and economic transformation but can be profitable as well.

Advanced-economy firms that invest in less-developed countries support the development of infrastructure in transportation, communications, and energy systems. Firms create jobs and contribute to regional and sector development. Investment generates local tax revenues, which can be spent to improve living standards among the poor. Many firms develop community-oriented social programs that foster economic and social development.

Source: David Dorey/The Philippines Collection/Alamy

Microfinance helps entrepreneurs in developing economies start businesses. Here a group of women attend a microfinance meeting in the Philippines.

Microfinance to Facilitate Entrepreneurship

Microfinance provides small-scale financial services, such as microcredit and microloans, that assist entrepreneurs to start businesses in poor countries. By taking small loans, often less than $100, small-scale entrepreneurs acquire enough capital to launch successful businesses. The leading advocate of microfinance is economics professor Muhammad Yunus. He founded the Grameen Bank (www.grameen-info.org) that has made small loans to millions of borrowers in South Asia. Aspiring entrepreneurs use the small loans to buy everything from cows that produce milk to sell in markets to mobile phones that villagers can rent to make calls.[39] The Grameen Bank now has more than 2,500 branches and has inspired similar poverty-reducing efforts, such as the Omidyar Network and the Bill and Melinda Gates Foundation. For his efforts, Yunus was awarded the 2006 Nobel Peace Prize.[40]

Increasingly, mainstream banks view microfinance as a source of future growth. Various institutions now offer small-scale insurance, mortgage lending, and other financial services in poor countries. In Mexico, Cemex's Patrimonio Hoy program (www.cemex.com) has widened access to cement and other building materials. The program helps poor families build their own homes. Thanks to microfinance, home ownership is a reality for tens of thousands of low-income Mexican families.

Ethical Connections

Africa bears the burden of about one-quarter of all disease worldwide, yet has only 3 percent of the world's health care workers. Most Africans cannot obtain adequate medical care. Every day, thousands die from treatable or preventable ailments such as malaria and AIDS. MNEs play a growing role to address such challenges. Private firms such as GlaxoSmithKline and General Electric employ innovative business approaches to provide needed medications and medical care to impoverished countries in Africa. Numerous firms have established clinics that provide low-cost health care.

The Special Case of Africa

Africa is relatively stagnant in terms of trade, investment, and per-capita income. Africa's GDP has improved little since the 1960s. The continent is afflicted by illiteracy, malnutrition, and poor sanitation and water supply. Unemployment is stubbornly high in many areas.[41]

However, several African countries are experiencing economic success, with annual GDP growth now approaching 5 percent per year. Ghana is becoming a regional hub for financial and technological services. Nigeria is enjoying a boom in oil and banking. Zambia is developing strengths in mining and agriculture. Tanzania is investing in major power generation projects. Stock markets in Botswana, Nigeria, and Zambia are enjoying record investment.[42] Botswana's diamond trade is booming, thanks to investments from South Africa's De Beers. De Beers is a mining company that is investing some of its profits in Botswana to build roads and schools and treat people with HIV/AIDS. [43]

Africa looks increasingly attractive. Coca-Cola sells over 100 brands and has more than 160 bottling and canning plants there. China's telecommunications giant Huawei has established production and sales operations throughout Africa, selling its mobile phones and network solutions. Huawei provides thousands of jobs for Africans. Chinese firms are also making huge investments in Africa installing green energy systems such as solar power. [44]

Improving conditions in Africa are supported by two major trends. First, compared to earlier times, African governments are doing a better job of managing their national economies. Policy reforms in various countries emphasize economic and political freedom. Better governance in several countries is helping drive economic success.

Parts of Africa are also receiving a steady inflow of direct investment from abroad. China, India, and other emerging market firms are investing billions in Africa to manufacture and market various products and services. Inspired by such activity, more firms from Europe, Japan, and the United States are exploring Africa for business and investment opportunities.

Although Africa long lacked substantial landline telephony, cell phones are proving vital to the continent's development. Newly installed cellular networks promote economic development by facilitating dramatic gains in worker and company productivity and banking infrastructure.[45] Global Telecom Holding, Millicom, and other telecom firms are establishing cell phone operations from Egypt to South Africa, applying business models that allow them to earn profits even in countries where people live on less than $2 per day.

Gradually, MNEs are finding various market opportunities. By using innovative business models adapted to local conditions, they play a key role in addressing the continent's medical needs and generate profits. For example, establishing chains of low-cost clinics is helping address Africa's health care needs. [46]

The application of business models such as local entrepreneurship, microfinance, targeted marketing, and MNE direct investing holds enormous potential for addressing poverty in Africa.[47] However, critics charge that MNEs do much harm in Africa, such as exploiting local resources, operating sweatshops, and generating pollution. Where do you stand? Can MNEs successfully address poverty and other problems in Africa, or do such firms do more harm than good?

CLOSING CASE Prowling for Success: The Revival of Jaguar Land Rover

Transforming TATA into an emerging market challenger amid the opening up of the Indian economy in 1991 and steering it to a $100 billion global company operating in over 80 countries is considered to be Ratan Tata's crowning success. He stepped down in 2012.

The TATA group's growth had come from spending over $20 billion in acquisitions. But it was the $2.3 billion takeover of the UK's loss-making car manufacturer, Jaguar Land Rover (JLR) Group, from Ford in 2008 that created history for the group.

Analysts had argued that TATA motors overpaid for Jaguar Land Rover in 2008. True enough, JLR needed more cash injection from the TATAs and continued to lose money for another 2 years. Sales dropped to just under 72,000 units in 2009. The company, already saddled with a $3 billion debt, suffered losses of almost $468 million in 2009, with Jaguar Land Rover contributing to over $100 million of this loss.

Newspaper reports indicated that JLR would need to close at least one of its plants in the UK. But as we saw in this chapter, challengers from emerging markets demonstrate an appetite for risk as

well as resilience. TATA motors continued to invest money in Jaguar Land Rover amid a global downturn in the sales of luxury car brands. It finally succeeded in transforming the acquisition into a business that generated over $ 5.82 billion in 2012, with profits of over $533 million.

Background of Jaguar Land Rover

Historically separate car brands, Jaguar and Land Rover were part of Ford's premier automotive group (PAG) and acquired together by TATA motors.

Jaguar was founded by William Lyons to build motorcycle sidecars in 1922 as Swallow Sidecars. The name Jaguar was created in 1935, to reflect speed, sleekness, and raw power according to Jaguar Heritage Trust. A succession of mergers followed until in 1989, the Ford Motor Company acquired Jaguar Cars for $2.5 billion. Ford was forced to sell Jaguar Land Rover in 2008 amid continued losses and to concentrate on its core U.S. business

Today, Jaguar sells over 55,000 cars across 4 models; the XF, XJ, XK, and the R series. Sixty-six percent of total sales comes from the

XF series followed by 11% from the XK series. Its main markets are in the UK, China, North America, and the rest of Europe.

The Land Rover was created in 1948 by the Rover Company. A series of takeovers and mergers followed through the next three decades, culminating in the formation of the Rover Group in 1986 and the takeover of both brands by BMW in 1984. Ford acquired Land Rover in 2000 for $2.96 billion and added both Jaguar and Land Rover Brands to its Premier Automotive Group until the 2008 sale to TATA motors.

Land Rover sells over 157,000 units across 7 models; The Range Rover Evoque is the top seller (36% of total sales), followed by Range Rover Sport (19%), Freelander 2 (17%), Discovery (15%), Range Rover (9%), and the Defender (5%). Sales are predominantly from China (22%) and Europe (21%), the UK (17%), North America (15%). Declining sales of both brands continued until the Jaguar XK coupe launched in 2006 (while still owned by Ford), began reviving interest in Jaguar cars. The model built on an aluminium chassis had a new design and styling that delivered on performance too! A two-door coupe was soon added and by 2008, the new successful XF model had arrived. The launch of the Range Rover Evoque in July 2011, a compact sport utility vehicle, redefined Jaguar Land Rover as a luxury brand that could compete with Mercedes, BMW, and Audi. The Range Rover Evoque or the "new Land Rover," as customers would now refer it, was designed to appeal to young, female, and new customers and sold 81,000 units in just 9 months contributing heavily to the profitability of JLR. Seventy-five percent of total sales are exports to 170 countries earning over $2 billion in revenue, with over 36,451 units sold in China alone.

The Lure of Emerging Markets for Automobile Manufacturers

As indicated in earlier in this chapter, one of the key advantages that emerging regions possess is access to resources including financial reserves and this was clear in the TATA group's next move. Cost competiveness was improved, production was streamlined, and over 3000 jobs were cut in the company by 2009. Over $2 billion was invested in into research and development activities and by 2010 a $12 billion investment project over the next five years was announced. One of the main issues that dogged Jaguar Land Rover was a lack of new models and new engines that could appeal to a broader segment. To solve this, it turned to low cost centers in emerging regions like India and China. These regions would provide manufacturers with a unique proposition that we see in this chapter.

Emerging Markets as *Target Markets* that *Possess Low-Cost Manufacturing Bases* and *Competitive Sourcing Destinations*

Most emerging markets have large population segments seeking luxury products, as seen in the case of China that saw a threefold growth in sales of Jaguar Cars. Linking the rise in per capita income in recent years to a greater demand, one envisages these markets as a vast opportunity for Jaguar cars to sell within a rising luxury car segment. No wonder Jaguar ropes in celebrities like Victoria Beckham to sell $128,000 limited editions of the Evoque to affluent Chinese customers. The company has also announced a joint venture agreement with the Chinese manufacturer Cherry Automobile to build vehicles for the Chinese market and an engine manufacturing plant for new models.

In India, JLR has opened an assembly plant in Pune, India where completely knocked down Freelander2 models are manufactured. This is expected to be the hub for sourcing low cost components for JLR's global supply chain. It is also an attempt to lower Indian tariffs on fully imported cars—which can be as high as 100%. In 2013, JLR India announced the opening of a production factory to make the Jaguar XF saloon at its facility in Pune. The Indian market had seen a growth of 22 per cent in 2013 with 2913 cars sold in the market.

JLR is expected to have a similar entry strategy for Brazil, where high tariffs have discouraged sales of its cars. Brazil is widely expected to surpass Japan in automobile sales.

Another success factor with firms like JLR has been in its management of the Government–Industry linkage, so vital in transition and emerging economies. The TATA group is known to have government support and has leveraged this in acquiring JLR. In its entry into China, JLR had tried several JVs before getting government approval for the JV with Cherry.

Governments in developed and emerging regions have vested interests in attracting FDI into industries to sustain a large labor force. The restructuring of the UK automobile industry with both nationalization and de-nationalization strategies at various stages of JLR's history has shown a clear intervention to boost growth in vital sectors. The success of Nissan's Sunderland plant owes as much to local government incentives as it does to manufacturing competence. In the case of JLR, a clear case of inward FDI from an emerging region (India) was used to stop decline within a region and create new jobs in an advanced economy. This we see, how globalization is at play here!

Challenges to Sustained Growth

In 2014, new models and stronger sales (particularly in emerging markets), saw JLR announce record profits of $3.855 billion. It was the newly launched two- seater Evoque and the F-Type sports car that drove sales up nearly 16 per cent to 434,311 vehicles. Revenue grew 22.8per cent to 29.9billion. The profits were up 49.4 per cent. To put this into perspective, global car sales in 2014 were 85 million. It is estimated that this figure will reach 100 million by 2018. The important US market is forecast to peak at 17 million in 2017. Most continued growth will come from emerging markets.Although Jaguar Land Rover is self-sufficient in generating cash, most of its profits are going into building of competences that are present with many its competitors. It is also a late mover into many emerging regions where competitors have entrenched positions. A possible shift of manufacturing into India and China could cause resentment and labor disruption in the UK, where most of its supply chain cluster and technology cluster are located.

Conclusions

For Jaguar Land Rover, the future looks stable if new models generate the same levels of interest as the Evoque and new XK sportster in emerging markets. . After six years of declining car sales, sales were up in 2014. The important Chinese market saw sales of 21.7 million up 13 per cent. Robust growth in China is vital for Tata and JLR. In 2015 sales grew by some 10 per cent to 23.8 million cars and light trucks. Tata motors currently depends on the company to provide more than 70 percent of its total global revenue and almost 90 percent of its profits. The continued dependence on emerging markets might turn out to be a risky proposition when these economies slow down. In addition, the continued recession in its traditional home markets of the Euro Zone and North America would dampen sales. The rising cost of rubber and steel and other critical raw materials is expected to cut into the profitability of the company as it prepares to compete on price in many segments in the market. But we may see the development of new models and entry into newer markets or segments extending Jaguar Land Rover's success for years to come. The diversification into speed boats, a recent exercise, could be an interesting proposition in this direction.

AACSB: Reflective Thinking Skills, Ethical Understanding and Reasoning Abilities

Case Questions

8-4. Describe how Jaguar Land Rover leverages the advantages of its parent company in seeking new markets. Can this be a source of disadvantages as well?

8-5. How do you think the shift of economic activity to emerging regions affects growth in advanced economies? Discuss if a reverse shift of activity is possible.

8-6. What is the role of Government Business linkages in creating emerging market challengers? Do you think that emerging and

transition economies can move to a more hands-off approach with time?

8-7. Discuss if Jaguar could be spun back into an independent brand once again. What are the limitations of such a move?

8-8. Discuss Jaguar Land Rover's shift into other developing regions in Africa. What will be the implications of these on its sourcing and supply chain economies?

END OF CHAPTER REVIEW

 MyManagementLab

Go to **mymanagementlab.com** to complete the problems marked with this icon .

Key Terms

advanced economies   232
developing economies   232
emerging markets   232
family conglomerate   246

global sourcing   241
new global challengers   239
outsourcing   241
privatization   237

purchasing power parity
(PPP)   241
tenders   248
transition economies   237

Summary

In this chapter, you learned about:

- **Advanced economies, developing economies, and emerging markets**

  Advanced economies are post-industrial countries characterized by high per-capita income, highly competitive industries, and well-developed commercial infrastructure. They consist mainly of post-industrial societies of Western Europe, Japan, the United States, Canada, Australia, and New Zealand. The **developing economies** are low-income countries that have not yet industrialized. Due to low buying power and limited resources, their participation in international business is limited. The **emerging markets** are former developing economies on their way to becoming advanced economies. They are transforming themselves into market-driven economies by liberalizing trade and investment policies, privatizing industries, and forming economic blocs. Brazil, Russia, India, and China are leading exemplars.

- **What makes emerging markets attractive for international business**

  Emerging markets represent promising export markets for products and services. They are ideal bases for manufacturing activities and popular destinations for **global sourcing**— procurement of products and services from foreign locations.

- **Assessing the true potential of emerging markets**

  In the early stages of market research, to reliably estimate demand in emerging markets, managers examine three important statistics: per-capita income, size of the middle class, and market potential indicators. Income should be adjusted for **purchasing power parity**.

- **Risks and challenges of emerging markets**

  Emerging markets pose various risks, including political instability, inadequate legal and institutional frameworks, lack of transparency, and inadequate intellectual property protection. **Family conglomerates** are large, diversified, family-owned businesses that dominate many emerging markets and represent formidable rivals and attractive choices for partnerships.

- **Success strategies for emerging markets**

  Firms should adapt strategies and tactics to suit unique, local conditions. Some firms succeed by partnering with family conglomerates. Governments are often major buyers but require specific strategies. Successful advanced-economy firms conduct research, acquire capabilities specific to target markets, and leverage advantages available in emerging markets, such as low-cost labor.

- **Corporate social responsibility, sustainability, and the crisis of global poverty**

  In emerging markets and developing economies, leading firms undertake activities that facilitate economic development. They can serve low-income countries with inexpensive, specifically designed products and services and community involvement. Such efforts should aim to ensure environmental sustainability. Microfinance, availability of small-scale loans to emerging-market entrepreneurs, is promoting entrepreneurial initiatives. Although Africa long stagnated in terms of income, trade, and investment, several African countries are beginning to experience economic success. Africa receives substantial investment from abroad and benefits from microfinance and abundant mobile telephones.

Test Your Comprehension AACSB: Reflective Thinking Skills, Ethical Understanding and Reasoning Abilities

8-9. What were developing countries called in the past? What factors are there that distinguish them from other countries?

8-10. Why are countries such as Mexico, Brazil and India often considered as ideal manufacturing bases for global corporations?

⭐ 8-11. Many emerging countries have political instability, what are the consequences of this?

⭐ 8-12. Some emerging countries suffer from very poor physical infrastructure. What are the signs of this and suggest some examples of the consequences of this problem.

8-13. Describe the process for selling to foreign governments and state enterprises.

8-14. Doing business in emerging markets involves strategies that are often distinct from those of other international venues. What types of business approaches can firms use when doing business in emerging markets?

8-15. What social and sustainability characteristics are typical of emerging markets? What can businesses do to support the development of poor countries in emerging markets?

Apply Your Understanding AACSB: Communication Abilities, Reflective Thinking Skills

8-16. Suppose you work at Microsoft in its Xbox video game console division. Microsoft has long targeted Xbox to the advanced economies, especially in North America and Europe. Management would like to sell more Xbox 360s to emerging markets. What characteristics of emerging markets might make them attractive for sales of the Xbox? Identify the major risks and challenges that Microsoft might encounter in selling the Xbox 360 to emerging markets.

8-17. CBKing has been trying to export its products to various emerging markets and has enjoyed little success so far. You know a lot about emerging markets and have been anxious to share your views with CBKing's president, Mr. Roger Wilko. What strategies would you recommend Roger pursue in doing business with emerging markets? You conclude there is substantial demand among military and government agencies. Explain how your firm should go about selling to emerging market customers.

8-18. *Ethical Dilemma*: One mission of the International Monetary Fund (IMF) is to help poor countries overcome economic crises by providing loans and policy advice. During the global financial crisis, many countries suffered corporate bankruptcies, collapsing economies, and political turmoil. These effects particularly hurt Ukraine, which requested massive loans and other financial assistance from the IMF. Note, however, that taxpayers in advanced economies generally foot the bill for IMF activities, which often run to billions of dollars. Critics argue the IMF rescues countries that fail to put in place robust regulatory systems and responsible fiscal and monetary policies. The critics assert that economic prosperity is best determined by market forces and free enterprise. They claim that reviving poor countries is too costly and discourages responsible behavior because if local officials know they can count on bailouts from wealthy countries, they are less likely to enact policies that ensure stable economic growth. Suppose you are a financial officer at the IMF. Where do you stand? Use the Ethical Framework in Chapter 4 and decide whether the IMF should bail out Ukraine.

globalEDGE | INTERNET EXERCISES
(www.globaledge.msu.edu)

AACSB: Analytic Skills, Reflective Thinking Skills, Ethical Understanding and Reasoning Abilities

Refer to Chapter 1, page 54, for instructions on how to access and use globalEDGE™.

8-19. The World Bank sponsors the Doing Business database (www.doingbusiness.org), which provides measures of business regulations and their enforcement for countries worldwide. Firms can use these measures to analyze specific regulations that enhance or constrain investment, productivity, and growth. Visit the site and choose two emerging markets. Then answer the following questions: How well does each country rank in terms of ease of starting a business, employing workers, and trading across borders? How long does it take to start a business? How much time does it take to pay taxes? Review other statistics and identify which country is most friendly for doing business.

8-20. Using globalEDGE™, find the country commercial guide for two emerging markets of your choice. Compare the two countries on the following dimensions: "leading sectors for exports and investment" and "marketing products and services." Which of the two countries is more promising for marketing laptop computers? Which of the two countries is more promising for sales of portable electrical power generators?

Which of the two countries is more promising for sales of telecommunications equipment? Justify your answers.

8-21. The three groups of countries described in this chapter can be contrasted in terms of degree of economic freedom. It refers to the extent to which economic activities in a nation can take place freely and without government restrictions. Various organizations have developed indexes of economic freedom, including the Cato Institute (www.cato.org), the Heritage Foundation (www.heritage.org), and the Fraser Institute (www.fraserinstitute.org). In measuring economic freedom, such indexes consider factors such as trade policies, extent of government intervention, monetary policies, inward foreign direct investment, property rights, and commercial infrastructure. Countries are classified into categories such as free, mostly free, mostly unfree, and repressed. Explore one of the economic freedom indexes by visiting one of the mentioned sites and entering "economic freedom" in the search engine. How are emerging market and developing economies classified? What is the relationship between market liberalization and economic development? How might market liberalization contribute to reducing poverty in developing economies?

CAREER TOOLBOX

Learning About and Assessing Emerging Markets

Emerging markets are rapidly industrializing and dynamic economies. When deciding to do business in emerging markets, the first step is to identify the most attractive countries to enter. This involves comparing numerous countries across various criteria. Because each emerging market is distinctive, the manager researches and determines which markets to enter. Such knowledge helps avoid wasting company resources and maximizes the firm's profits and competitive advantages. In this exercise, assume you are a product manager of a firm that makes and markets mobile telephones. Your task is to analyze factors in leading emerging markets and choose the best one to target with exports of your product.

Background

Emerging markets are high-growth, high-potential economies with relatively high living standards. They are industrialized, vibrant

economies with a growing middle class. They represent a middle ground between developed economies and developing economies. Emerging markets house the largest proportion of world population, and their participation in foreign trade is big and growing. They are increasingly viable markets for various products. Although the advanced economies represent the present and past of international business, emerging markets represent the future. There are numerous emerging markets, with distinctive characteristics. Dynamic changes in these societies complicate assessing their current market potential. The firm needs to investigate the most appropriate emerging markets to enter. A complete list of the emerging market countries follows.

To complete this exercise in your MyLab, go to the Career Toolbox.

MyManagementLab

Go to **mymanagementlab.com** for Auto-graded writing questions as well as the following Assisted-graded writing questions:

⭐ **8-22.** How can managers estimate the true market potential of emerging markets?

⭐ **8-23.** For entering an emerging market, what benefits can an MNE obtain by partnering with a local family conglomerate? What are the disadvantages of such a partnership?

⭐ **8-24.** MyManagementLab Only—comprehensive writing assignment for this chapter.

Endnotes

1. World Bank, *World Bank Development Indicators* (Washington, DC: World Bank, 2012).

2. World Bank (2012).

3. Fred Campano and Dominick Salvatore, *Income Distribution* (Oxford, UK: Oxford University Press, 2006); Mary Anastasia O'Grady, "The Rise of Mexico's Middle Class," *Wall Street Journal*, March 5, 2012, p. A13.

4. S. Tamer Cavusgil and Ilke Kardes, "Defining and Measuring Middle Class In Emerging Markets: The GSU-CIBER Middle Class Scorecard," *Research World (ESOMAR)*, March–April (2013), pp. 46–49.

5. Jack Behrman and Dennis Rondinelli, "The Transition to Market-Oriented Economies in Central and Eastern Europe," *European Business Journal* 12 (2000), pp. 87–99.

6. *The Economist*, "When Giants Slow Down," July 27, 2013, pp. 54–63.

7. "Forbes Global 2000" for 2005 and 2011, www.forbes.com; "Fortune Global 500" for 2005 and 2011, http://www.money. cnn.com/magazines/fortune/global500; Carol Liao, Christoph Nettesheim, and David Lee, "Will China's Global Challengers Be the Next Global Leaders?" *BCGPerspectives*, January 8, 2015, www.bcgperspectives.com.

8. "Trade Profiles," *World Trade Organization*, September 2014, http://stat.wto.org/CountryProfile.

9. "Britain's Lonely High-Flier," *The Economist*, January 10, 2009, pp. 60–61; UNCTAD, *UNCTAD Handbook of Statistics 2012* (New York: United Nations, 2012).

10. "Two Billion More Bourgeois: The Middle Class in Emerging Markets," *The Economist*, February 14, 2009, p. 18.

11. Michael Deneen and Andrew Gross, "The Global Market for Power Tools," *Business Economics*, July 2006, pp. 66–73; O'Grady (2012).

12. L. Lee, "Thank Heaven for Emerging Markets," *BusinessWeek*, January 7, 2008, pp. 62–63.

13. "Racing Down the Pyramid," *The Economist*, November 15, 2008, p. 76; IMS Institute for Healthcare Informatics, *The Global Use of Medicines: Outlook Through 2017* (Parsippany, NJ: IMS Institute, 2013); IMS Institute for Healthcare Informatics, *Global Outlook for Medicines Through 2018* (Parsippany, NJ: IMS Institute, 2014).

14. Malcolm Moore, "SABMiller's Asia Chief Ari Mervis Raises a Glass to Snow Beer," *The Telegraph*, August 22, 2011, www.telegraph.co.uk.

15. Ali Shah, "Business Strategies in the Emerging Markets," *Journal of Asia-Pacific Business* 13, No. 1 (2012), pp. 4–15.

16. "The Big Mac Index," January 22, 2015. From *The Economist* online.

17. Cavusgil and Kardes, 2013.

18. Surjit Bhalla, *Second Among Equals: The Middle Class Kingdoms of India and China* (Washington, DC: Peterson Institute for International Economics, Washington, 2007); "Burgeoning Bourgeoisie: A Special Report on the New Middle Classes in Emerging Markets," *The Economist*, February 14, 2009, Special Section; Homi Kharas, *The Emerging Middle Class in Developing Countries*, Working Paper No. 285 (Paris: OECD Development Centre, 2010).

19. Adel Al Khattab, "The Role of Corporate Risk Managers in Country Risk Management," *International Journal of Business and Management* 6, No. 1 (2011), pp. 11–20.

20. *Doing Business: Economy Rankings and Doing Business 2015*, World Bank Group, Washington, DC, http://www.doingbusiness.org/rankings.

21. United States Trade Representative, *National Trade Estimate Report on Foreign Trade Barriers*, 2012, http://www.ustr.gov.

22. Laurie Burkitt and Loretta Chao, "Made in China: Fake Stores," *Wall Street Journal*, August 3, 2011, www.wsj.com.

23. *Doing Business: Economy Rankings and Doing Business 2015*, World Bank Group, Washington, DC, http://www.doingbusiness.org/rankings.

24. Transparency International, *Corruption Perceptions Index 2011*, http://www.transparency.org.

25. "Creaking, Groaning: Infrastructure Is India's Biggest Handicap," *The Economist*, December 13, 2008, pp. 11–13.

26. M. Valente and A. Crane, "Private, but Public," *Wall Street Journal*, March 23, 2009, p. R6.

27. Daekwan Kim, Destan Kandemir, and S. Tamer Cavusgil, "The Role of Family Conglomerates in Emerging Markets: What Western Companies Should Know," *Thunderbird International Business Review*, 46 (2004), pp. 13–20.

28. A. Bhattacharya and D. Michael, "How Local Companies Keep Multinationals at Bay," *Harvard Business Review*, March 2008, pp. 85–95.

29. Hans Greimel, "Tiny Etios for India Teaches Toyota to Simplify, Cut Costs," *Automotive News*, August 1, 2011, p. 46; Peter Marsh, "Toyota Gears Up for Production Drive in India," *Financial Times*, March 5, 2007, p. 21.

30. G. Edmondson, "Renault's Race to Replace the Rickshaw," *BusinessWeek*, 2007, http://www.businessweek.com.

31. "The World of the Internet," *Business 2.0*, August 2007, pp. 20–21.

32. Ted London and Stuart Hart, "Reinventing Strategies for Emerging Markets: Beyond the Transnational Model," *Journal of International Business Studies* 35 (2004), pp. 350–363; Valente & Crane (2009).

33. Jeffrey Garten, *The Big Ten: The Big Emerging Markets and How They Will Change Our Lives* (New York: Basic Books, 1997); G. Kolodko, ed., *Emerging Market Economics: Globalization and Development* (Aldershot, Hants, England: Ashgate, 2003); Kim, Kandemir, and Cavusgil (2004).

34. Pete Engardio, "Emerging Giants," *BusinessWeek*, July 31, 2006, pp. 40–49; Kushan Mitra, "Top Gun," *Business Today*, October 2, 2011, pp. 44–52.

35. World Economic Forum, *Global Risks 2012*, 6th ed. (Geneva, Switzerland: World Economic Forum).

36. Ibid.

37. Bruce Einhorn, "Qualcomm Rewires for India," *Bloomberg BusinessWeek*, September 12–18, 2011, pp. 37–38; C. K. Prahalad, "Aid Is Not the Answer," *Wall Street Journal*, August 31, 2005, p. A8; C. K. Prahalad, *The Fortune at the Bottom of the Pyramid: Eradicating Poverty Through Profits* (Philadelphia: Wharton School Books, 2005); Jennifer Reingold, "Can P&G Make Money in Places Where People Earn $2 a Day?" *Fortune*, January 17, 2011, pp. 86–90.

38. International Telecommunications Union, "Africa Has 300 Million Mobile Phone Subscribers," 2009, press release, http://www.itu.int; "Mobile Phone Growth Biggest in Africa," *African Business*, April 2009, p. 8.

39. Brigit Helms, *Access for All: Building Inclusive Financial Systems* (Washington, DC: The World Bank, 2006).

40. "Grabbing Grameen," *Economist*, January 28, 2012, p. 67; Muhammad Yunus, *Creating a World Without Poverty* (New York: Public Affairs, 2009).

41. Christopher Beshouri, "A Grassroots Approach to Emerging-Market Consumers," *McKinsey Quarterly* 4 (2006), http://www.mckinseyquarterly.com.

42. "Opportunity Knocks," *The Economist*, October 11, 2008, pp. 33–35.

43. Farzad (2007); J. Nocera, "Diamonds Are Forever in Botswana," *New York Times*, August 9, 2008, p. C1.

44. David Doya and Mike Cohen, "Kenya, Nigeria, and Africa's New Hope for Growth," *Bloomberg Businessweek*, November 6, 2014, www.businessweek.com; Randall Hackley, "Africa's Powerful New Friends in China," *Bloomberg BusinessWeek*, September 12–18, 2011, pp. 56–57; Devon Maylie, "By Foot, by Bike, by Taxi, Nestlé Expands in Africa," *Wall Street Journal*, December 1, 2011, p. B1; Tom Nevin, "Coca-Cola: 125 Years of Making Friends," *African Business*, December 1, 2011, pp. 44–45.

45. L. Enriquez, S. Schmitgen, and G. Sun, "The True Value of Mobile Phones to Developing Markets," *McKinsey Quarterly*, February 2007, www.mckinseyquarterly.com; Han Huipers, Mikael Michiels, and Michael Seeberg, *Africa Blazes a Trail in Mobile Money* (Boston: Boston Consulting Group, February 2015).

46. M. Conway, S. Gupta, and K. Khajavi, "Addressing Africa's Health Workforce Crisis," *McKinsey Quarterly*, November 2007, http://www.mckinseyquarterly.com.

47. *Economist*, "A Fall to Cheer," March 3, 2012, pp. 81–82; Dambisa Moyo, *When Help Does Harm* (New York: Farrar, Straus and Giroux, 2009); D. Zeng, ed., *Knowledge, Technology, and Cluster-Based Growth in Africa* (Washington, DC: The World Bank Group, 2008).

Chapter 9

The International Monetary and Financial Environment

Learning Objectives *After studying this chapter, you should be able to:*

9.1 Learn about exchange rates and currencies in international business.

9.2 Explain how exchange rates are determined.

9.3 Understand the emergence of the modern exchange rate system.

9.4 Describe the monetary and financial systems.

9.5 Identify the key players in the monetary and financial systems.

9.6 Understand the global debt crisis.

The European Union and the Euro

The European Union (EU) was established in 1993. In 2015, it had 28 member countries. The EU created the European Monetary Union (EMU) and the European Central Bank (ECB) www.ecb.int) with the goal of establishing a common currency, the euro. In 2002, euro banknotes and coins were issued and replaced older, national currencies. In 2015, the euro was the sole official currency of 19 EU member states: Austria, Belgium, Cyprus, Estonia, Finland, France, Germany, Greece, Ireland, Italy, Latvia, Lithuania, Luxembourg, Malta, Netherlands, Portugal, Slovakia, Slovenia, and Spain. The remaining EU countries opted not to join the eurozone. By establishing a common currency, the EMU aims to knit the participating EU economies into a unified whole, reduce the problem of fluctuating exchange rates, and facilitate trade and price comparisons.

MNEs operating in the eurozone have reduced business costs by simplifying their accounting, financial, and marketing activities with the use of a single currency. The euro allows firms to coordinate prices across the EU.

The ECB treats the eurozone as one region rather than as separate countries with differing economic conditions. ECB monetary policy is complex because of the diverse economic and fiscal conditions that characterize each eurozone country. For example, the ECB aims to keep inflation low by carefully limiting the supply of euros, but the policy response for controlling deflation, just as harmful as inflation, is to increase the money supply. ECB policy aimed at fixing deflation in one country might trigger inflation in another. Devising monetary policy that suits economic conditions in all EMU countries is challenging.

Monetary policy is further complicated by the recent admission into the EU of lower-income countries such as Slovakia and Slovenia. As more countries join the EU, the risk of very diverse economic conditions across the union rises. Such pressures have increased in Europe's recent economic

Source: Jennifer Barrow/123RF

crisis, especially in Greece, Portugal, and Spain. The EU plan to assist Greece includes loans and surveillance from the ECB. The crisis has sparked discussion about the risks of EU monetary integration and survival of the euro.

A key goal of launching the euro was to shield EMU countries from exchange rate risk by creating a large, unified economy. Historically, the euro was relatively strong against the U.S. dollar. More recently the euro has weakened. A weak euro helps European exporters because it makes their products less expensive to foreign importers. A weak euro yields stronger earnings for European MNEs when they convert non-euro profits into euros. On the negative side, a weak euro decreases the buying power of European firms and consumers who purchase non-euro foreign goods.

The success of the euro as a unifying force in Europe has changed the international balance of power. The EU and EMU have empowered European governments to challenge U.S. policy initiatives in the wider global arena. The central banks of numerous countries—including Canada, China, and Russia—have given greater weight to the euro in their foreign currency reserves. Some governments are increasing their euro holdings, and Asia is now less dollar-centric than in the past.

Questions

9-1. What benefits does using a single currency, the euro, provide to European countries?

9-2. What challenges does the European Central Bank face in developing monetary policy for the EU?

9-3. What is the effect of a weak euro on European exporters? What is the effect on European consumers?

SOURCES: T. Catan, "Spain's Struggles Illustrate Pitfalls of Europe's Common Currency," *Wall Street Journal*, September 14, 2009, p. A2; Gianmarco Daniele and Benny Geys, "Public Support for European Fiscal Integration in Times of Crisis," *Journal of European Public Policy* 22, No. 5 (2015), pp. 650–670; *Economist*, "Don't Get Europhoric," April 11, 2015, pp. 12–14; J. Perry, "ECB Expects No Recovery Before 2010," *Wall Street Journal*, June 10, 2009, p. A7; Carla Power, "Border Control," *Time International*, March 5, 2012, pp. 40–44; "Too Long an Illness," *Economist*, February 25, 2012, p. 66; S. Zwick, "World Rattles on Wobbly Euro/Dollar Axis," *Futures*, April 2010, pp. 22–26.

International business transactions take place within the global monetary and financial systems. Fluctuating exchange rates are an important challenge and risk for international managers. The opening case explains how the European Union aimed to eliminate this problem in the EU by introducing a single currency, the euro. Before its launch, numerous national currencies—the French franc, the Spanish peso, the Italian lira, among others—were the means of exchange for doing business in Europe.

As the barriers that once restricted global trade and investment have faded, the monetary and financial activities of firms and nations have intensified. People usually think of international trade as trade in products and services. However, the markets for foreign exchange and capital are much larger. Firms regularly trade the U.S. dollar, European euro, Japanese yen, and other leading currencies to meet their international business obligations. In this chapter, we explore the monetary and financial structure that makes trade and investment possible. We explain the nature, organization, and functions of the foreign exchange market and the monetary and financial issues that confront internationalizing firms.

Exchange Rates and Currencies in International Business

9.1 Learn about exchange rates and currencies in international business.

More than 150 currencies are in use around the world today. Cross-border transactions occur through an exchange of these currencies between buyers and sellers. A currency is a form of money and a unit of exchange. Each country prefers using its own unique currency, which complicates international business transactions. When buying a product or service from a Mexican supplier, for example, you must convert your own currency to Mexican pesos to pay the supplier. The currency system is being simplified in some locations. As we saw in the opening case, many countries in Europe use the euro. Other countries, such as Ecuador, Panama, and East Timor, have adopted the U.S. dollar as their currency, a process known as dollarization.

Exchange rate

The price of one currency expressed in terms of another; the number of units of one currency that can be exchanged for another.

The **exchange rate**—the price of one currency expressed in terms of another—varies over time. It links different national currencies so that buyers and sellers can make international price and cost comparisons. Exhibit 9.1 shows the exchange rates for the U.S. dollar and a sample of other currencies. The values of these national currencies and, thus, their exchange rates, fluctuate constantly. Specifically, currencies *appreciate* (go up in value) and *depreciate* (go down in value) relative to other currencies.

Currency risk

Potential harm that arises from changes in the price of one currency relative to another.

Exchange rate fluctuations and similar complications in international business create **currency risk**, the potential harm that can arise from changes in the price of one currency relative to another. It is one of the four types of international business risk that we introduced in Chapter 1. It is also known as *financial risk*. If you buy from a supplier whose currency is appreciating against yours, you may need to pay a larger amount of your currency to complete

EXHIBIT 9.1 U.S. Dollar Exchange Rates for a Sample of Currencies on May 11, 2015

Currency	Currency per One U.S. Dollar	U.S. Dollars per Unit of Currency
Australian dollar	1.261	0.793
Brazilian real	2.975	0.336
British pound	0.647	1.546
Canadian dollar	1.208	0.828
Chinese renminbi (yuan)	6.206	0.161
Euro	0.892	1.120
Indian rupee	63.705	0.016
Japanese yen	119.780	0.008
Mexican peso	15.122	0.066
New Zealand dollar	1.334	0.749
Norwegian kroner	7.787	0.134
Saudi Arabian riyal	3.750	0.267
Singapore dollar	1.328	0.753
South African rand	11.924	0.084
Turkish lira	2.675	0.374

Source: Adapted from www.x-rates.com.

Constantly fluctuating exchange rates require international managers to keep in mind three facts:

- The prices the firm charges can be quoted in the firm's currency or in the currency of each foreign customer.
- Because several months can pass between placement and delivery of an order, fluctuations in the exchange rate during that time can cost or earn the firm money.
- The firm and its customers can use the exchange rate as it stands on the date of each transaction, or they can agree to use a specific exchange rate.

the purchase. Currency risk also arises if you expect payment from a customer whose currency is depreciating against your own. You may receive a smaller amount of your currency if the sale price was expressed in the currency of the customer. If the foreign currency fluctuates in your favor, you may gain a windfall. Exporters or importers worry constantly about *losses* that arise from currency fluctuations.

Exporters and licensors also face risk because foreign buyers must either pay in a foreign currency or convert their currency to that of the vendor. Foreign direct investors face currency risk because they both receive payments and incur obligations in foreign currencies.

Convertible and Nonconvertible Currencies

A *convertible currency* can be easily exchanged for other currencies. The most easily convertible are called *hard currencies* and include the British pound, European euro, Japanese yen, and U.S. dollar. They are strong, stable currencies that are universally accepted and used most often for international transactions. Nations prefer to hold hard currencies as reserves because of their relative strength and stability in comparison to other currencies.

A currency is *nonconvertible* when it is not acceptable for international transactions. Some governments may not allow their currency to be converted into a foreign currency. They prevent this conversion to preserve their supply of hard currencies, such as the euro or the U.S. dollar, or to avoid the problem of capital flight. **Capital flight** is the rapid sell-off by residents or foreigners of their holdings in a nation's currency or other assets. This usually occurs in response to a domestic crisis that causes them to lose confidence in the country's economy. The investors exchange their holdings in the weakening currency for those of another, often a hard currency. Capital flight from a country diminishes its ability to service debt and pay for imports.

As national economies have become more integrated in recent years, capital flight has become a relatively common occurrence. For example, investors withdrew trillions of rubles from Russia as foreign investors lost confidence in the Russian economy in 2014. After coming to power in Venezuela, President Hugo Chavez confiscated foreign company assets and made questionable financial deals. Dubious governance, depreciating currency, and other economic problems panicked foreign investors and Venezuela's wealthier citizens, and they withdrew their liquid assets from the country's economy.[1] In some developing economies, currency convertibility is so strict that firms may avoid using currencies altogether. They receive payments in goods; in other words, they engage in barter.

Foreign Exchange Markets

Money facilitates payment for the products and services that companies sell. Getting paid in your own country is straightforward; the U.S. dollar is accepted throughout the United States, the euro is widely used in Europe, and the Japanese use the yen to transact with each other. But suppose a Canadian needs to pay a Japanese, or a Japanese needs to pay an Italian, or an Italian needs to pay a Canadian. What then? The Japanese wants to be paid in yen, the Italian wants to be paid in euros, and the Canadian wants to be paid in Canadian dollars. All these currencies are known as *foreign exchange*. **Foreign exchange** represents all forms of money that are traded internationally, including foreign currencies, bank deposits, checks, and electronic transfers. Foreign exchange resolves the problem of making international payments and facilitates international investment and borrowing among firms, banks, and governments.

Currencies such as the euro, yen, and U.S. dollar are traded on the **foreign exchange market**, the global marketplace for buying and selling national currencies. The market has no fixed location. Rather, trading occurs through continuous buying and selling among banks, currency traders, governments, and other exchange agents located worldwide. International business would be impossible without foreign exchange and the foreign exchange market.

Currency Risk

In 1999, 11 EU countries switched to the euro, eliminating the problem of exchange rate fluctuations in trade and investment with each other. By 2015, 19 member states were participating in the eurozone. Other countries in Latin America, the Caribbean, and the Middle East have opted to use a regional or hard currency. The challenges posed by fluctuating exchange rates motivate countries to coordinate their monetary policies. Governments attempt to manage exchange rates by buying and selling hard currencies and by keeping inflation under control. However, the foreign exchange market is huge and it shifts very quickly. Even major governments have difficulty controlling exchange rate movements.

As illustrated in Exhibit 9.2, exchange rate fluctuations between the euro, U.S. dollar, and other currencies are sometimes dramatic. In 2012, for example, the Indian rupee was trading at 48 rupees to the U.S. dollar. By 2013, the rate had depreciated to 58 rupees—the rupee's value went down relative to the dollar by more than 20 percent. Specifically, in 2012, an Indian could buy one dollar for 48 rupees; by 2013, he had to pay 58 rupees. From a U.S. perspective, in 2012 an American could obtain 48 rupees for one dollar; by 2013 the same dollar bought 58 rupees. Implications for international business with India were substantial. In the span of only 12 months, Indian firms perceived a significant upturn in their exports because Indian products became less expensive to Americans. Meanwhile, as rupee-buying power for dollars decreased, U.S. firms experienced a decline in their exports to India.[2] Exhibit 9.2 also shows that the French franc is one of the European currencies taken out of circulation and replaced by the euro.

Capital flight
The rapid sell-off by residents or foreigners of their holdings in a nation's currency or other assets, usually in response to a domestic crisis that causes investors to lose confidence in the country's economy.

Foreign exchange
All forms of money that are traded internationally, including foreign currencies, bank deposits, checks, and electronic transfers.

Foreign exchange market
The global marketplace for buying and selling national currencies.

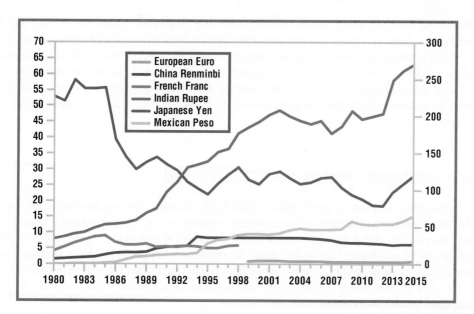

EXHIBIT 9.2

Selected Exchange Rates Against the U.S. Dollar over Time

Note: Right-hand scale is for Japanese yen; left-hand scale is for all other currencies. For example, in 2015, the Mexican peso was trading at 15 pesos per one U.S. dollar. The euro became the common currency of various European Union countries in 1999, replacing the French franc and other European currencies.

Sources: Based on data from the International Monetary Fund and World Bank.

Fluctuating exchange rates affect both firms and customers. Suppose today the euro–dollar exchange rate is €1 = $1; that is, for a European to buy one U.S. dollar, he or she must pay one euro. Next, suppose that during the coming year the exchange rate goes to €1.50 = $1. Now the dollar is much more expensive to European firms and consumers than before—it costs 50 percent more to acquire a dollar. Let's examine the effect of this change on Europeans.

Effect on European Firms

- European firms must pay more for inputs from the United States, such as raw materials, components, and support services they use to produce finished products and services.
- Higher input costs reduce profitability and may force firms to raise prices to final customers; these higher prices reduce customer demand for goods and services.
- Because the euro has become less expensive for U.S. consumers, firms can increase their exports to the United States. Firms can even raise their export prices and remain competitive in the U.S. market.
- Increased exports to the United States generate higher revenues and higher profits.

Effect on European Consumers

- Because U.S. products and services now cost more, European consumers demand fewer of them.
- The cost of living rises for those Europeans who consume many dollar-denominated imports.
- Fewer European tourists can afford to visit the United States. Fewer European students study at U.S. universities.

Now, suppose the euro–dollar exchange rate goes to €0.50 = $1. What are the effects on European firms and consumers? They are essentially the opposite of those summarized previously. European firms pay less for inputs from the United States, which means they can drop their prices on goods and services. Because U.S. products and services now cost less, consumers demand more of them.

A fluctuating exchange rate affects both sides of international transactions. Management must monitor exchange rates constantly and create strategies to maintain company performance in light of strong and weak currencies. We discuss these strategies in Chapter 10.

In 2014–2015, U.S. companies such as Caterpillar and Microsoft saw dramatic falls in their international sales due to strengthening of the U.S. dollar against world currencies. In the year through June 2015, the dollar rose in value by more than 20 percent against the EU euro and the Japanese yen. Sales at Tiffany's department store in New York fell nearly 10 percent as a strong U.S. dollar resulted in fewer European tourists visiting the United States. Tiffany's depends heavily on foreign tourists for sales at its flagship stores. Meanwhile, American tourists flocked to Europe in the summer of 2015 as the dollar hit a 12-year high against the euro. European exports to nations outside the eurozone soared. The cheaper euro made European travel and products a bargain.[3]

9.2 Explain how exchange rates are determined.

How Exchange Rates are Determined

In a free market, the price of any currency—that is, its exchange rate—is determined by supply and demand. Supply and demand adjust according to market forces. Exchange rates fluctuate constantly because the global market for most major currencies is free and active. Continuous shifts in the supply of and demand for dollars result in continuous changes in the dollar exchange rate. Some currencies are pegged to fixed exchange rates and, thus, may not respond to market forces.

In a free market, the levels of supply and demand for a currency vary inversely with its price. Thus, all else being equal,

- The greater the supply of a currency, the lower its price.
- The lower the supply of a currency, the higher its price.
- The greater the demand for a currency, the higher its price.
- The lower the demand for a currency, the lower its price.

Suppose a Canadian consumer wants to buy a BMW, sourced from Germany and priced at the nominal price of 30,000 euros. Assume further that the exchange rate of the euro to the Canadian dollar is €1 = $1.25. Now suppose the consumer delays six months, during which the exchange rate shifts, becoming €1 = $1.50. That is, due to increased demand for and/or decreased supply of euros, the euro has become more expensive to Canadian customers. Assuming the euro price of the BMW remains unchanged, the car will now cost more in Canadian dollars, making the consumer less inclined to buy the BMW. By contrast, if, during the six-month period, the euro becomes cheaper (with, say, an exchange rate of €1 = $1), the Canadian consumer will be more inclined to buy the BMW. As this example implies, the greater the demand for a country's products and services, the greater the demand for its currency.

Four main factors influence the supply and demand for a currency: economic growth, interest rates and inflation, market psychology, and government action. Let's examine these.

Economic Growth

Economic growth is the increase in value of the goods and services an economy produces. To ensure accuracy, we usually measure economic growth of a nation as the annual increase in real GDP in which the inflation rate is subtracted from the growth rate. Economic growth results from continual economic activities, especially innovation and entrepreneurship. It implies a continued increase in business activities and a corresponding increase in consumer need for money to facilitate more economic transactions.

Central bank
The monetary authority in each nation that regulates the money supply and credit, issues currency, and manages the exchange rate of the nation's currency.

To accommodate economic growth, the **central bank** increases the nation's money supply. The central bank is the monetary authority in each country that regulates the money supply, issues currency, and manages the exchange rate of the nation's currency relative to other currencies. Economic growth is associated with an increase in the supply and demand of the nation's money supply and, by extension, the nation's currency. Thus, it has a strong influence on the supply and demand for national currencies. For example, recent rapid economic growth in East Asian countries has increased demand for their currencies by firms and individuals, both domestic and foreign.[4]

Inflation and Interest Rates

Inflation is an increase in the price of goods and services. When inflation occurs, money buys less than in preceding years. Exhibit 9.3 shows that inflation rates can reach high levels. Argentina, Zimbabwe, and some other countries have had prolonged periods of *hyperinflation*—persistent

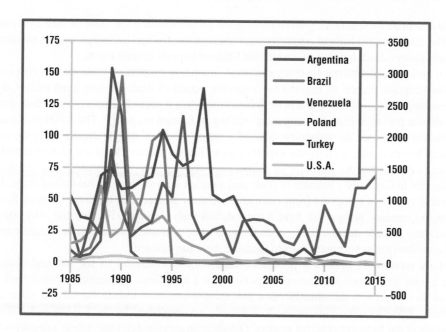

EXHIBIT 9.3

Inflation in Selected Countries, 1985–2015

Note: Chart shows annual percentage rate of inflation. Left-hand scale is for Turkey, Venezuela, and the United States; right-hand scale is for Argentina, Brazil, and Poland.

Sources: Based on International Monetary Fund, World Economic Outlook Database, 2015, at http://www.imf.org; and *CIA World Factbook*, at http://www.cia.gov.

annual double-digit and sometimes triple-digit rates of price increases. A practical effect of hyperinflation is the need for a restaurant owner to change the menu every few days to increase the prices. With high inflation, the purchasing power of the nation's currency is constantly falling.

Interest rates and inflation are closely related. In countries with high inflation, interest rates tend to be high because investors expect to be compensated for the inflation-induced decline in the value of their money. If inflation is running at 10 percent, for example, banks must pay more than 10 percent interest to attract customers to open savings accounts.

Inflation occurs when demand for money grows more rapidly than supply, or when the central bank increases the nation's money supply faster than the rise in national productive output. Inflation is often a problem for developing economies and emerging markets. When inflation occurs, the value of the nation's currency will fall relative to foreign currencies. Triggered by big increases in the national money supply, for example, annual inflation in Brazil ran to more than 1000 percent in the mid-1990s. Imagine the difficulty to both buyers and sellers of adjusting to a constant decline of the currency's value and ever-rising prices!

The link between interest rates and inflation, and between inflation and the value of currency, implies that there is a relationship between real interest rates and the value of currency. For example, when interest rates in Japan are high, foreigners seek profits by buying Japan's interest-bearing investment opportunities, such as bonds and deposit certificates. Investment from abroad will have the effect of increasing demand for the Japanese yen.

Market Psychology

Exchange rates are often affected by *market psychology*, the unpredictable behavior of investors. *Herding* is the tendency of investors to mimic others' actions. *Momentum trading* occurs when investors buy stocks whose prices have been rising and sell stocks whose prices have been falling. It is usually carried out with computers set to do massive buying or selling when asset prices reach certain levels. Herding and momentum trading tend to occur in the wake of financial crises. Recently, Brazil, Russia, and other emerging markets have experienced large-scale flight of portfolio investment amid concerns about deteriorating economic conditions. Foreign investors have panicked and many have deserted stocks in those countries.[5]

Government Action

The pricing of currencies affects company performance. When a nation's currency is expensive to foreigners, its exports are likely to fall.[6] When a nation's currency is cheap to foreigners, exports increase. When the value of a nation's currency depreciates over a prolonged period, consumer and investor confidence can be undermined. Steep currency depreciation weakens the nation's ability to pay foreign lenders, possibly leading to economic and political crisis.

Trade surplus
A condition in which a nation's exports exceed its imports for a specific period of time.

Trade deficit
A condition in which a nation's imports exceed its exports for a specific period of time.

Devaluation
Government action to reduce the official value of its currency relative to other currencies.

Balance of payments
The annual accounting of all economic transactions of a nation with all other nations.

To minimize these effects, governments often act to influence the value of their own currencies. The Chinese government regularly intervenes in the foreign exchange market to keep the renminbi undervalued, helping to ensure that Chinese exports remain strong.

An undervalued national currency can result in a **trade surplus**. A trade surplus arises when a nation's exports exceed its imports for a specific period of time, causing a net inflow of foreign exchange. By contrast, a **trade deficit** results when a nation's imports exceed its exports for a specific period of time, causing a net outflow of foreign exchange. The *balance of trade* is the difference between the monetary value of a nation's exports and its imports over the course of a year. For example, if Germany exports cars to Kenya, money flows out of Kenya and into Germany because the car importer in Kenya pays the exporter in Germany. This results in a surplus item in Germany's balance of trade and a deficit item in Kenya's balance of trade. If the total value of Kenya's imports from Germany becomes greater than the total value of Kenya's exports to Germany, Kenya will have a trade deficit with Germany. Factors that affect the balance of trade include the prices of goods manufactured at home, exchange rates, trade barriers, and the method the government uses to measure the trade balance.

Many economists believe a persistent trade deficit is harmful to the national economy. When a trade deficit becomes severe or persists for a long time, the nation's central bank may devalue its currency. A **devaluation** is a government action to reduce the official value of its currency relative to other currencies. It is usually accomplished by the buying and selling of currencies in the foreign exchange market. Devaluation aims to deter the nation's residents from importing from other countries, potentially reducing the trade deficit.[7]

At a broader level, governments must manage their **balance of payments**, the annual accounting of all economic transactions of a nation with all other nations. The balance of payments is the nation's balance sheet of trade, investment, and transfer payments with the rest of the world. It represents the difference between the total amount of money coming into and going out of a country. Consider an American MNE that builds a factory in China. In the process, money flows from the United States to China, generating a deficit item for the United States and a surplus item for China in their respective balance of payments. The balance of payments is affected by other transactions as well, as when citizens donate money to a foreign charity, when governments provide foreign aid, or when tourists spend money abroad.

9.3 Understand the emergence of the modern exchange rate system.

Emergence of the Modern Exchange Rate System

During much of the period from the late 1800s through the 1920s, global trade grew significantly. The Great Depression (1929–1939) and World War II (1939–1945) coincided with a collapse of the international trading system and relationships among nations. Following the war, several countries came together to energize international commerce and devise a framework for stability in the international monetary and financial systems. In 1944, the governments of 44 countries negotiated and signed the Bretton Woods Agreement.

The Bretton Woods Agreement

This agreement pegged the value of the U.S. dollar to an established value of gold at a rate of $35 per ounce. The U.S. government agreed to buy and sell unlimited amounts of gold to maintain this fixed rate. Each of Bretton Woods' other signatory countries agreed to establish a par value of its currency in terms of the U.S. dollar and to maintain this pegged value through central bank intervention. In this way, the Bretton Woods system kept exchange rates of major currencies fixed at a prescribed level relative to the U.S. dollar and, therefore, to each other.

In the 1960s, however, emergent global economic conditions led to high trade deficits in the United States. Gradually growing demand for U.S. dollars exceeded supply. The U.S. government could no longer maintain an adequate stock of gold. This situation put pressure on governments in Europe, Japan, and the United States to revalue their currencies. As a result, the link between the U.S. dollar and gold was suspended in 1971. The promise to exchange gold for U.S. dollars was withdrawn. This action brought an end to the Bretton Woods system.

The Bretton Woods agreement left a legacy of principles and institutions that remain in use today. Specifically, Bretton Woods established:

- The concept of international monetary cooperation, especially among the central banks of leading nations.
- The importance of currency convertibility, in which countries agree not to impose restrictions on currency trading and to avoid discriminatory currency arrangements.
- The concept of fixing exchange rates within an international regime to minimize currency risk.
- The **International Monetary Fund** (IMF; www.imf.org) and the **World Bank** (www.worldbank.org). The IMF is an international agency that attempts to stabilize currencies by monitoring the foreign exchange systems of member countries and lending money to developing economies. The World Bank is an international agency that provides loans and technical assistance to low- and middle-income countries, with the goal of reducing poverty.

International Monetary Fund (IMF)
An international agency that aims to stabilize currencies by monitoring the foreign exchange systems of member countries and lending money to developing economies.

World Bank
An international agency that provides loans and technical assistance to low- and middle-income countries with the goal of reducing poverty.

Following the 1997 Asian financial crisis, finance ministers and central bank heads from 20 advanced and emerging market economies established the Group of Twenty (G-20). The organization aims to bring greater stability to the global financial system. Representing about 90 percent of the world economy, its members have met annually to develop measures that promote economic growth and strong financial systems. They have held meetings in Canada, South Korea, the United Kingdom, and the United States. The members were instrumental in devising new policies to address the financial and economic crisis that began in 2008. Policies included increasing financial resources, coordinating expansionary macroeconomic policies, and enhancing national financial regulations. The G-20 cooperates closely with the IMF and World Bank.

The Modern Exchange Rate System

Today most major currencies are traded freely, with their value floating according to the forces of supply and demand. The official price of gold was formally abolished. Governments became free to choose the type of exchange rate system that best suited their individual needs. Fixed exchange rate systems were given equal status with floating exchange rate systems. Countries were no longer compelled to maintain specific pegged values for their currency. Instead, they were urged to pursue domestic economic policies that would support the stability of their currency relative to others. The exchange rate system today consists of two main types of foreign exchange management: the floating system and the fixed system.

THE FLOATING EXCHANGE RATE SYSTEM Most advanced economies use the floating exchange rate system. Currency values are determined by market forces. Major world currencies—including the British pound, Canadian dollar, euro, U.S. dollar, and Japanese yen—float independently on world exchange markets. Their exchange rates are determined daily by supply and demand. The floating system gives governments the flexibility to modify monetary policy to fit the circumstances they face at any time. If a country is running a trade deficit, the floating rate system allows it to be corrected more naturally than if the country uses a fixed exchange rate regime.

THE FIXED EXCHANGE RATE SYSTEM This approach is similar to the system used under the Bretton Woods

Source: Chee-Onn Leong/123RF

The Bretton Woods Agreement, which set the course for contemporary global financial relations, was conceived by 44 nations at the Mount Washington Hotel in Bretton Woods, New Hampshire, United States, in 1944.

Source: david_franklin/Fotolia

The international monetary system provides the framework within which national currencies, including the U.S. dollar, British pound, and European Euro, are exchanged for one another.

agreement and is sometimes called a *pegged exchange* rate system. Using this system, the value of a currency is set relative to the value of another (or to the value of a basket of currencies) at a specified rate. As this *reference value* rises and falls, so does the currency pegged to it. In the past, some currencies were also fixed to some set value of gold.

Many developing economies and some emerging markets use the fixed system today. China pegs its currency to the value of a basket of currencies. Belize pegs its currency to the U.S. dollar. To maintain the peg, the governments of China and Belize, for instance, will intervene in currency markets to buy and sell dollars and other currencies to maintain the exchange rate at a fixed, preset level. A fixed regime promotes greater stability and predictability of exchange rate movements and helps stabilize a nation's economy. The central bank must stand ready to fill any gaps between supply and demand for its currency.

At times, countries try to hold the value of their currency within some *range* against the U.S. dollar or other important reference currency, in a system often referred to as *dirty float*. That is, the value of the currency is determined by market forces, but the central bank intervenes occasionally in the foreign exchange market to maintain the value of its currency within acceptable limits relative to a major reference currency. Many Western countries resort to this type of intervention from time to time.

The Monetary and Financial Systems

9.4 Describe the monetary and financial systems.

We have seen how currencies facilitate international transactions and how exchange rates affect the amount of international trade. Let's now examine the two systems that determine exchange rates: the international monetary system and the global financial system.

International Monetary System

International monetary system
Institutional framework, rules, and procedures by which national currencies are exchanged for one another.

Firms seek to be paid for the products and services they sell abroad. Portfolio investors seek to invest in stocks and other liquid assets around the world. The resulting monetary flows take the form of various currencies traded among nations. Accordingly, the **international monetary system** consists of the institutional frameworks, rules, and procedures that govern how national currencies are exchanged for one another. By providing a framework for the monetary and foreign exchange activities of firms and governments worldwide, the system facilitates international trade and investment. To function well, national governments and international agencies have focused on creating a system that inspires confidence and ensures liquidity in monetary and financial holdings.

Global Financial System

Global financial system
The collective of financial institutions that facilitate and regulate investment and capital flows worldwide, such as central banks, commercial banks, and national stock exchanges.

The **global financial system** consists of the collective financial institutions that facilitate and regulate flows of investment and capital funds worldwide. Key players in the system include finance ministries, national stock exchanges, commercial banks, central banks, the Bank for International Settlements, the World Bank, and the International Monetary Fund. The system incorporates the national and international banking systems, the international bond market, the collective of national stock markets, and the market for bank deposits denominated in foreign currencies.

The global financial system is built on the activities of firms, banks, and financial institutions engaged in ongoing international financial activity. It also has many linkages with national financial markets. Since the 1960s, the global financial system has grown substantially in volume and structure, becoming increasingly more efficient, competitive, and stable.

Today, the global financial system can accommodate massive cross-national flows of money and the huge foreign exchange markets these transactions have engendered. Initially triggered by the rapid growth in world trade and investment, the globalization of finance accelerated in the 1990s with the opening of the former Soviet Union and China to international business. More recently, very large flows of capital—mostly in the form of pension funds, mutual funds, and life insurance investments—have been pouring into stock markets worldwide. Firms can increasingly access a range of capital markets and financial instruments around the world.[8]

Money flowing abroad as portfolio investments is a relatively new trend. The volume of these flows is enormous. For example, more than 25 percent of total outstanding U.S. long-term securities are typically held by people outside the United States.[9] In developing economies, inward investment increases foreign exchange reserves, reduces the cost of capital, and stimulates local development of financial markets.

> **The growing integration of financial and monetary activity worldwide has several causes, including:**
>
> - The evolution of monetary and financial regulations worldwide.
> - The development of new technologies and payment systems and the use of the Internet in global financial activities.
> - Increased global and regional interdependence of financial markets.
> - The growing role of single-currency systems, such as the euro.

Capital flows are much more volatile than FDI-type investments because it is much easier for investors to withdraw and reallocate liquid capital funds than FDI funds. FDI funds are directly tied to factories and other permanent operations that firms establish abroad.[10]

The globalization of financial flows has yielded many benefits, but it is also associated with increased risk. Economic difficulties in one country can quickly spread to other countries like a contagion. Financial instability is worsened when governments fail to regulate and monitor their banking and financial sectors adequately.[11] Let's discuss various organizations that attempt to reduce capital flight and manage other challenges in the global monetary and financial systems.

Ethical Connections

The recent global financial crisis raised various ethical issues. Globalization of the financial sector allowed the crisis to spread quickly, harming people worldwide. However, financial globalization has contributed greatly to economic development in poor countries. Critics point to self-interest in the banking sector as a basic cause of the crisis. But self-interest is a natural human condition. Pensioners and other investors happily accept rapid gains in stocks and bonds, often ignorant of how the gains are made. Some argue the real cause of the crisis was a failure of governments to regulate the financial sector adequately.

Key Players in the Monetary and Financial Systems

9.5 Identify the key players in the monetary and financial systems.

A variety of national, international, private, and government players make up the international monetary system and the global financial system. Exhibit 9.4 highlights the major players and the relationships among them. These players operate at the levels of the firm, the nation, and the world.

The Firm

As companies engage in international trade and are paid by their customers abroad, they typically acquire large quantities of foreign exchange and must convert them to the currency of the

EXHIBIT 9.4

Key Participants and Relationships in the Global Monetary and Financial Systems

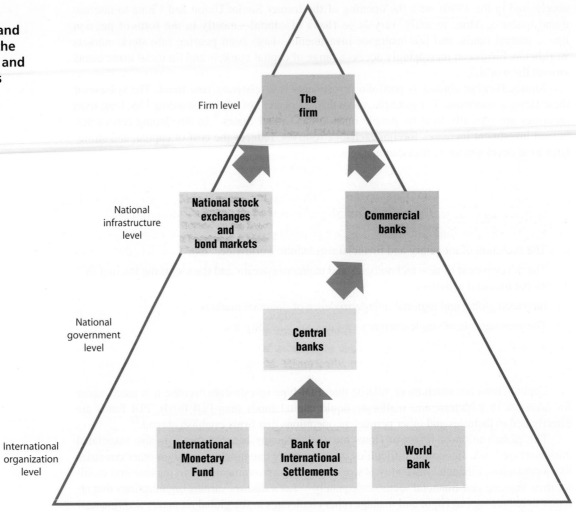

home country. Firms also engage in investment, franchising, and licensing activities abroad that generate revenues they must exchange for their home currency. For example, Jim Moran Enterprises in Florida, the largest importer of Toyota cars in the United States, imports thousands of cars every year and must ultimately pay for them in Japanese yen. Moran deals with the foreign exchange market to convert U.S. dollars to yen.

Some MNEs with spare cash acquire foreign currencies for speculative purposes. They invest in currencies with the intention of profiting from exchange rate fluctuations. Other firms may acquire foreign currency to invest in foreign stock markets and other foreign investment vehicles for short-term gains. Other private-sector players in the international monetary and financial systems include life insurance companies, savings and loan associations, and stockbrokers that manage pensions and mutual funds. Some large MNEs have in-house finance departments that manage their foreign exchange and financial transactions.

Nontraditional financial institutions play a key role in international funds transfers. Foreign residents in Australia, Canada, the United States, and countless other countries use wire-transfer technology to wire billions of dollars to family members in India, Mexico, and many other less-developed economies. These funds are then converted into local currencies. Such remittances by Africans living abroad constitute a major source of funds flowing into Africa, helping sustain the continent's poorest countries. Some nations receive more foreign income from remittances than from either foreign aid or inward FDI.[12] Read this chapter's "You Can Do It: Recent Grad in IB" feature, which highlights Maria Petit, who works in finance for a major multinational firm.

National Stock Exchanges and Bond Markets

Selling stock (shares of ownership) is an important way for firms to raise the funds they need to engage in international business. A *stock exchange* is a facility for trading securities and other financial instruments, including shares issued by companies, trust funds, pension funds, and corporate and government bonds. Information technology has revolutionized the functioning of stock markets, greatly reducing the speed and cost of transactions. Today, many exchanges are electronic networks not necessarily tied to a fixed location. Each country sets its own rules for issuing and redeeming stock.

Trade on a stock exchange is by members only. For example, the Tokyo Stock Exchange (TSE; http://www.jpx.co.jp/english/) is the home stock market to such firms as Toyota, Sony, and Canon and the major vehicle through which some 2,000 Japanese firms raise capital to fund their business activities. Several foreign companies, such as BP and Chrysler, are also listed on the TSE. Today, MNEs often list themselves on a number of exchanges worldwide to maximize their ability to raise capital.

The character of markets varies worldwide. For example, corporations hold the majority of shares in the Japanese market. In Britain and the United States, individuals hold more shares. Despite these differences, stock exchanges are increasingly integrated into the global securities market.

Bonds are another type of security sold through banks and stockbrokers. They are a form of debt that corporations and governments incur by issuing interest-bearing certificates to raise capital. Bonds enable the issuer to finance long-term investments. For example, SK Telekom, the main wireless communications provider in South Korea, financed much of its operations by selling bonds in the global market. Several European telecommunications providers, such as Telecom Italia, Deutsche Telecom, and France Telecom, issued international bonds to fund their activities.[13]

In many national stock and bond markets, the most important players today are *institutional investors*—managers of pensions and mutual funds, as well as insurance companies. They have now assumed an enormous role in driving capital markets around the world.

Commercial Banks

Banks are important players in the global financial sector. They raise funds by attracting deposits, borrowing money in the interbank market, or issuing financial instruments in the global money market or securities markets. Commercial banks—for example, Bank of America, Mizuho Bank in Japan, and BBVA in Spain—operate at the most essential level of the international monetary system. They circulate money and engage in a wide range of international financial transactions. Banks are regulated by national and local governments, which have a strong interest in ensuring the solvency of their national banking system.

The many types of banks and their primary activities include the following:

Investment banks underwrite (guarantee the sale of) stock and bond issues and advise on mergers, such as the merger of Goldman Sachs in the United States and Nomura Securities in Japan.

Merchant banks provide capital to firms in the form of shares rather than loans. They are essentially investment banks that specialize in international operations. They do not provide regular banking services to the general public. The Arab-Malaysian Merchant Bank is an example.

Private banks manage the assets of the very rich. Union Bank in Switzerland (UBS) and ABN AMRO Private Banking in Luxembourg are examples.

Offshore banks are located in jurisdictions with low taxation and regulation, such as Switzerland and Bermuda. Banco General in Panama and Bank of Nova Scotia in the British Virgin Islands are examples.

Commercial banks deal mainly with corporations or large businesses. Credit Lyonnais in France and Bank of America are examples.

For firms, the most important functions of banks are to lend money to finance business activity, exchange foreign currencies, and facilitate adjustments in national money supplies.

MARIA PETIT

Maria's majors: Finance, International Business, and Spanish
Objectives: Move into the executive suite at Motorola or other multinational firm
Maria's jobs since graduation: Various jobs at Motorola—credit analyst (U.S.); finance manager (U.K.); financial controller (Dubai, United Arab Emirates)

In college, Maria Petit spent a year in Spain and served as the president of the international business club. She majored in Finance, International Business, and Spanish. After graduation, she took a job as a credit analyst with Motorola (www.motorola.com), a leading producer of cell phones and other wireless handsets. Maria used analytical, problem-solving, and communication skills acquired in college to serve Motorola clients and subsidiaries throughout Latin America.

At Motorola, Maria analyzed risk levels of various customers and countries. She managed accounts receivable and conducted audits in Motorola's international operations. These duties required her to travel often to Latin America. She became the primary contact for financial analysis support to northern Latin America, the Caribbean, and Central America. Her tasks included the analysis, tracking, and reconciliation of Motorola's funds for regional marketing activities.

Eager to gain experience in Europe, Maria volunteered to transfer to Motorola's London office, where she served as a finance manager in the firm's $160 million mobile phone business for the Middle East, North Africa, and Turkey. She also sought her CIMA certification, the British equivalent of certified public accountant (CPA). After two years in London, Maria transferred to Dubai, the United Arab Emirates, as financial controller in Motorola's Middle East region. In this role, she coordinated the management of Motorola's financial activities in the Islamic world.

Lessons Learned

Maria commented on her experience in the world of international financial management. "One of my big challenges was increased regulations that required stricter auditing of financial records in the wake of accounting scandals. It's critical to ensure that all of Motorola's legal entities are compliant worldwide. Local regulations also must be assimilated and integrated. The time I allocated to compliance activities greatly increased. Simultaneously, competition in the mobile devices industry grew, and I had to increase support to our sales and marketing operations as well."

"The languages in my region are French (North Africa), Arabic (Middle East), and Turkish (Turkey). Although I studied Arabic, I still cannot carry a business conversation in Arabic and only manage to use my Spanish while visiting a particular distributor in Morocco that is partially owned by Telefonica (www.telefonica.com), Spain's telecom provider. Luckily, most of our business partners spoke English. There is definitely a disadvantage to not speaking the local language."

"Much of the Islamic world has specific norms for women, who usually do not participate in professional business activities. But people generally treat me with respect. I have found that if I establish myself as a knowledgeable professional, people in the Middle East generally treat me as well as they do their male colleagues. There is one last cultural difference that puts me at a disadvantage: being a nonsmoker in countries where people still smoke a lot. Most of the debriefing after a challenging meeting happens during cigarette breaks. Given the relaxed atmosphere, the parties are more likely to discuss issues in a candid manner. But I'm not willing to take up smoking to be more effective in my job. It is a cultural difference that I accept."

Maria's Advice

The qualities that contributed most to Maria's success include "hard work, having a deliberate career strategy, and cultivating relationships with helpful people both when I was in college and in the professional world. You really have to plan. Set goals for yourself and work hard to meet them." As for the future, Maria hopes to move into the executive suite at a multinational firm. But having a career, especially an international one, is still challenging these days for women who also want to start a family. Maria looks forward to fulfilling both her career and personal goals.

Source: Courtesy of Maria Petit.

The major world banking centers are London, New York, Tokyo, Frankfurt, and Singapore, with London having the world's greatest concentration of international banks. Many banks are MNEs themselves, such as Citibank, Britain's HSBC, and Spain's BBVA. Smaller banks participate in international business by interacting with larger, correspondent banks abroad. A correspondent bank is a large bank that maintains relationships with other banks worldwide to facilitate international banking transactions.

Banking practices vary widely. In some countries, banks are owned by the state and are extensions of government. In other countries, they face little regulation and may lack safety nets that might prevent their failure. In developing economies, private banks are usually subject to substantial government regulation.

The density of banks varies cross-nationally. Consider Canada, Sweden, and the Netherlands. Just five banks in each country control more than 80 percent of all banking assets. In Germany, Italy, and the United States, by contrast, the top five banks control less than 30 percent of all banking assets. Banks also charge different rates for their services. For a typical customer, the annual price of core banking services in Italy is over $300, in the United States it is $150, and in China and the Netherlands it is only $50.[14]

Source: Gang Liu/Shutterstock

Chinese banks play a growing role in global finance. China is home to four of the world's largest banks: Bank of China, ICBC, Agricultural Bank of China, and China Construction Bank. Pictured here is the Chinese central bank headquarters in Beijing.

Banking has long been problematic in Africa. Egypt and South Africa are among the few African countries that possess a thriving, homegrown banking sector. In the rest of Africa, industry and governments have tended to rely on international banks because local banks are sometimes unstable and corrupt. Heavy restrictions on foreign banks reduced competition in the past and often delayed the development of a strong indigenous banking sector. Recently, however, globalization of the financial industry has contributed substantially to the development of efficient markets and financial institutions. Foreign banks have brought technology, managerial expertise, and new product ideas to Africa. Tough foreign competition has put pressure on indigenous banks to be more innovative. In addition, some innovative banks are using widespread mobile telephone technology to offer various banking services in Africa.[15]

Central Banks

As the official national bank of each country, the central bank regulates the money supply and credit, issues currency, and manages the rate of exchange. The central bank also seeks to ensure the safety and soundness of the national financial system by supervising and regulating the nation's banking system. A key goal is to keep price inflation low. The central bank regulates the nation's money supply and credit by:

- Buying and selling money in the banking system.
- Increasing or decreasing interest rates on funds loaned to commercial banks.
- Buying and selling government securities, such as treasury bills and bonds.

Many central banks also buy and sell government securities to finance government programs and activities.

Monetary intervention describes how central banks manipulate currency rates, usually with the aim of maintaining stable or orderly exchange rates. Such intervention is achieved by buying or selling currencies in the foreign exchange market. For example, if the central bank of the United States (called the Federal Reserve Bank) wants to support the value of the U.S. dollar, it might buy dollars in the foreign exchange market. By so doing, the supply of dollars is reduced, which increases the value of dollars still in circulation.

Other central banks include the Reserve Bank of India, the Bank of England, the Banque de France, and the Bank of Japan. They work with the International Monetary Fund, the Bank for International Settlements, the Organisation for Economic Co-operation and Development (OECD), and other international agencies to ensure sound international monetary and financial policies in global markets.

Monetary intervention
The buying and selling of currencies by a central bank to maintain the exchange rate of a country's currency at some acceptable level.

Source: Perfect Illusion/Shutterstock

Banks, stock exchanges, and other participants in the global monetary and financial systems make international business possible. Shown here is the central business district in Singapore.

The Bank for International Settlements

Based in Basel, Switzerland, the Bank for International Settlements (www.bis.org) is an international organization that fosters cooperation among central banks and other governmental agencies. It provides banking services to central banks and assists them in devising sound monetary policy. It seeks to support stability in the global monetary and financial systems and help governments avoid becoming too indebted. It also attempts to ensure that central banks maintain reserve assets and capital/asset ratios above prescribed international minimums. Maintaining adequate capital is prescribed by the Basel Capital Accord, a set of recommendations on how central banks should structure their banking laws and regulations.[16]

International Monetary Fund

Headquartered in Washington, DC, the IMF provides the framework of and determines the code of behavior for the international monetary system. The agency promotes international monetary cooperation, exchange rate stability, and orderly exchange arrangements and encourages countries to adopt sound economic policies. These functions are critical because economic crises can destroy jobs, slash incomes, and cause human suffering.

Governed today by 188 countries, the IMF stands ready to provide financial assistance in the form of loans and grants to support policy programs intended to correct macroeconomic problems. During the recent global financial crisis, the IMF pledged several billion dollars to assist Romania, Hungary, Ukraine, Turkey, and Pakistan, whose economies were affected by the crisis.[17]

Special Drawing Right (SDR)

A unit of account or a reserve asset, a type of currency central banks use to supplement their existing reserves in transactions with the IMF.

To help manage currency valuation worldwide, the IMF established a type of international reserve known as the **Special Drawing Right (SDR)**. The SDR is a unit of account or a reserve asset, a type of currency central banks use to supplement their existing reserves in transactions with the IMF and manage international exchange rates. For example, a central bank might use SDRs to purchase foreign currencies to manage the value of its currency on world markets. The value of the SDR is very stable because it is based on a basket of currencies: the euro, the Japanese yen, the U.K. pound, and the U.S. dollar.

The IMF plays an important role in addressing financial and monetary crises nations face around the world. Typical crises fall into three major categories.

A *currency crisis* results when the value of a nation's currency depreciates sharply or when its central bank must expend substantial reserves to defend the value of its currency. This usually results in a rise in interest rates. Currency crises occur more commonly in smaller countries and are sometimes the result of a sudden loss of confidence in the national economy or speculative buying and selling of the nation's currency.

A *banking crisis* results when domestic and foreign investors lose confidence in a nation's banking system that leads to widespread withdrawals of funds from banks and other financial institutions. This situation arose in the United States in the 1930s during the Great Depression. Millions of people panicked about their savings and rushed to withdraw funds from their bank accounts. The crisis led to the failure of numerous banks. Banking crises tend to occur more frequently in developing economies with inadequate regulatory and institutional frameworks. These crises can lead to other problems, such as exchange rate fluctuations, inflation, abrupt withdrawal of FDI funds, and general economic instability.

A *foreign debt crisis* arises when a national government borrows an excessive amount of money, either from banks or from the sale of government bonds. For example, China's total foreign debt now exceeds $800 billion. The debt is manageable because China's economy and foreign exchange reserves are huge. By contrast, Portugal's foreign debt exceeds 150 percent of the country's GDP. In an effort to pay its debt, Portugal must use financial resources that it might invest instead in important national priorities. Indebted governments draw huge sums out of their national money supply, which reduces the availability of these funds to consumers and to firms attempting to finance business activities.[18]

The IMF assists countries in resolving crises by offering technical assistance and training. It provides assistance by setting fiscal policy, devising monetary and exchange rate policies, and supervising and regulating banking and financial systems. It also provides loans to help distressed countries in recovery. However, the agency has been criticized because its prescriptions often require national governments to undertake painful reforms. For example, the IMF may recommend that a government downsize state-owned enterprises or give up subsidies or price supports for basic commodities. Some critics charge that the IMF harms countries by imposing too much austerity in times of financial distress. The IMF argues that any country in an economic crisis usually must undergo substantial restructuring, such as the deregulation of national industries or privatization of state enterprises.

The World Bank

Originally known as the International Bank for Reconstruction and Development, the World Bank (www.worldbank.org) was founded to fund reconstruction of Japan and Europe after World War II. Today it aims to reduce world poverty and is active in various development projects to bring water, electricity, and transportation infrastructure to poor countries. Headquartered in Washington, DC, the bank is a specialized agency of the United Nations, with more than one hundred offices worldwide. It is supported by some 187 member countries that are jointly responsible for how the institution is financed and how its money is spent.

The World Bank's collection of sub-agencies oversees various international development activities. The International Development Association loans billions of dollars each year to the world's poorest countries. The International Finance Corporation works with the private sector to promote economic development. It invests in sustainable private enterprises in developing countries and provides equity, loans, loan guarantees, risk management products, and advisory services to clients in need. The Multilateral Investment Guarantee Agency aims to encourage FDI to developing countries by providing guarantees to foreign investors against losses caused by noncommercial risks.

The IMF and the World Bank often work together. Whereas the IMF focuses on countries' economic performance, the World Bank emphasizes longer-term development and the reduction of poverty. The IMF makes short-term loans to help stabilize foreign exchange, and the World Bank makes long-term loans to promote economic development.

 MyManagementLab **Watch It!**

If your professor has assigned this, go to the Assignments section of **mymanagementlab.com** to complete the video exercise titled The G20 and the Global Monetary and Financial Systems.

The Global Debt Crisis

9.6 Understand the global debt crisis.

Growing imbalances in the finances of numerous national governments is an emergent crisis in the international monetary and financial environment.[19] Exhibit 9.5 shows the amount of gross government debt as a percentage of GDP for selected countries. Debt is especially high in Japan and Greece. In these countries, as well as in Belgium, Italy, and the United States, gross government debt exceeds 100 percent of each nation's GDP. National debt in

EXHIBIT 9.5

Gross Government Debt as a Percentage of GDP

Source: Based on International Monetary Fund, *World Economic Outlook Database*, 2015.

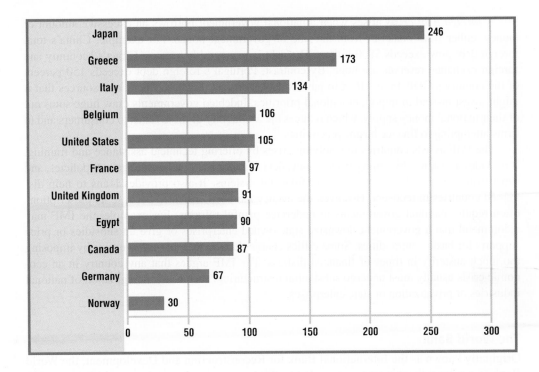

total dollar terms is highest in the United States, but the indicator is less useful than debt as a percentage of GDP. The reason is that countries can pay down their debt more easily if it is a smaller percentage of their annual GDP. For example, in 2015, the national debt of Germany was about $2 trillion, a huge amount in dollar terms. However, because it represents only 67 percent of Germany's GDP, it would take just eight months (67 percent of a year) of national productive output for Germany to pay it off. By contrast, Japan's debt is approaching 250 percent of its GDP. Japan would need to give up roughly 250 percent of its annual GDP to pay its national debt.

Fiscal imbalances are an important source of risk and uncertainty in the global business environment. Recently, debt has substantially increased in major advanced economies. This is mainly due to excessive government spending and insufficient revenues. Governments spent huge sums of borrowed money in the latest global recession to bail out financial systems and reduce recessionary pressures. Governments face unfunded liabilities of pension and health care programs. Japan, the United States, numerous countries in Europe, and others are suffering under the weight of excessive government debt.[20] Since 2012, credit rating agencies Moody's and Standard & Poor's have downgraded the sovereign debt ratings of several European countries to reflect their susceptibility to growing financial and monetary risks.[21]

Research shows that national debt that exceeds 90 percent of a nation's GDP tends to diminish GDP growth, which exacerbates government debt.[22] As the government tries to pay down its debt, money is drawn out of the national money supply. This hinders economic activity and reduces tax revenues. In the past few years, numerous countries have surpassed the 90 percent threshold, including Japan, the United States, and several countries in Europe. The International Monetary Fund and other agencies have stated that, without significant adjustments, most advanced economies face serious threats to fiscal solvency in the long-run.[23]

The largest proportion of government debt results from national pension and health care programs. In the advanced economies, pension shortfalls have emerged because birth rates have declined in the past several decades, resulting in less workforce participation. Combined with the tendency for people to live longer, advanced economies face severe challenges in generating tax revenues sufficient to fund pensions and health care programs for seniors and others. MNEs should proceed with caution when entering countries with substantial government debt because such nations tend to experience economic instability, reduced buyer purchasing power, and other challenges.

CLOSING CASE   Asian IFCs–Singapore and Hong Kong

IFCs: an overview

IFCs are nowadays one of the most dynamics realities of international finance; according to the IMF's definition, international Financial Centres (IFCs)—such as London, New York, and Tokyo—are large international full-service centres with advanced settlement and payments systems. They serve multiple purposes, first of all supporting large domestic economies with deep and liquid markets where both the sources and uses of funds are diverse, and where legal and regulatory frameworks are adequate to safeguard the integrity of principal-agent relationships and supervisory functions.

Asia, centre of the world manufacturing, is also home to a few financial hubs, or IFCs - i.e., a city or centre where financial services providers, especially banks, insurance companies and stock exchanges, concentrate. Two of them have become especially famous in the course of last century, presenting some similar characteristics but also substantial differences: Hong Kong and Singapore. More specifically,

The existence of the IFCs is not a novelty, and places like London and New York have a long tradition in this sense: Asian hubs, more recent, are assuming a more prominent character to reflect the new, dynamic role of Asia as one of the centres of world economy. Both Hong Kong and Singapore do figure prominently in the Global Financial Centres Index, compiled semiannually by the London-based British Z/Yen, a financial think-tank sponsored by the Qatar Financial Centre Authority. The tow Asian hubs represent respectively the third (Hong Kong) and fourth (Singapore) world IFCs after London and New York. "While the reputation of New York and London - the traditional financial centres- remains unchanged, Hong Kong and Singapore are narrowing the gap, and the financial centres of Korea and China are also gearing up for a new leap forward." (GFCI17, 2015, online)Both have, on top of that, a central place in the East Asian production and distribution channels, as leading RDCs (regional distribution centres) and important locations of free trade zones, that add to their attractiveness.

Hong Kong

Hong Kong SAR (Special Administrative Region) is the oldest of the two, a former British colony handed over to China in 1997 that has nonetheless preserved an autonomous and independent economy from the Mainland according to the formula "One country, two Systems". While considered here especially under its characteristics of financial hub, Hong Kong is certainly more than that, even though its financial role has strongly contributed to its success as trade and logistics hub and a leading exhibition centre of the region. The territory is the world's 10th largest trading economy, the second in Asia as recipient of FDIs after China and often the first port of call for Western companies approaching Asian markets, both to export and for sourcing. In terms of GDP composition, Hong Kong is a very sophisticated service economy, where services account for about 90% in terms of contribution. More to the point, financial services constitute the second in importance (16.1% of GDP in 2011), after trading and logistics, and before tourism and other professional services.

Hong Kong is home to the HKEx (Hong Kong Stock Exchange), the Asia's third largest in terms of market capitalisation behind the Tokyo Stock Exchange and Shanghai Stock Exchange, and the sixth largest in the world. As of 31 August 2015, the Hong Kong Stock Exchange had 1,810 listed companies, 920 of which are from Mainland China - i.e., H Shares and Red Chips - and 788 from Hong Kong itself.An important addition has been at the end of 2014 the Shanghai-Hong Kong Stock Connect, which gave for the first time the opportunity to the investors in Hong Kong (including foreign companies) to access, through Shanghai,Mainland China's stock market.

Singapore

While Hong Kong looks at the China and at the northern part of East-Asia, Singapore offers instead access to Southeast Asia, and, from its location on the tip of Peninsular Malaysia, aims at serving the fast-growing emerging markets of ASEAN. Compared to Hong Kong, Singapore is of more recent institution, having emerged as a US dollar-linked economy only in the course of the 1960s.

A veritable trade hub, Singapore, like Hong Kong, is now a key component in the Asian supply chains, and, on top of that, it presents a strong and transparent legal framework, which has proved substantial in attracting many international corporations to choose it as centre for their holdings. The fact of offering tax breaks and low rates has certainly helped in this sense.Also, it has been an early starter for what concernspreferential trade agreements, which have progressively become a fundamental tool in international trade, contributing to Singapore's success in attracting corporations.

Its share of financial services of the GDP, while inferior to Hong Kong, is still a quite impressive 12% of the total, and growing.The Singapore Stock Exchange (SGX) was formed on 1 December 1999 as a holding company, joining together the capitals of three previous exchange companies - namely Stock Exchange of Singapore (SES), Singapore International Monetary Exchange (Simex) and Securities Clearing and Computer Services Pte Ltd (SCCS). As for 31 August 2015, there were 773 listed companies, with the commodity derivatives being the fastest-growing part of the trading. Forex is another important sector, whose importance is on the rise. In 2013, Singapore overtook Tokyo as the first exchange in Asia, and world's third-largest behind London and New York.

Competition between the Asian hubs

There has always been an ongoing competition between the two hubs, with mutating fortunes over the years, which have seen one or the other taking advantages of the world's economic and financial situation.

The main point is that, being their domestic economies rather small, both hubs are affected by what happens first in the markets they serve as access point and more in general by the rest of the financial environment.

The competition between the two is evident not only in the financial sector, but in services in general, especially the ones related to international trade. Their deepwater ports are consistently among the world's most competitive and busy. Singapore leads in terms of container ports (world-second after Shanghai, while Hong Kong is currently forth) while the rival hosts the busiest airport for international cargoes.

This competition extends to other areas. There are many people, especially among expats, that prefer settling down and working in Singapore rather than in Hong Kong. The Lion City is considered a more suitable location in terms of superior living standards, quality of life, environment (more green areas in the city) and more affordable accommodation. Whereas Hong Kong is certainly superior to its southern rival is in terms of stock exchange for equities and IPOs. HKSE ranks just third after New York and London. For example, in the first 10 months of 2014 Hong Kong got 67 new listings for US $17.6 bn, while Singapore got only 8 for a total US $1.9 bn(FT, 24 October 2014). Wealth management also sees Hong Kong prevailing, with three times the number of billionaires that have chosen Hong Kong over its rival (Hong Kong counted 82 for US $ 343 bn in 2014, according the research company Wealth-X, as reported by the FT).

Scenarios

IFCs are at present ones of the most important realities of global finance, and given the present world's economy and status of financial markets, there is evidence their centrality will continue and even soar in the following years.

Hong Kong and Singapore are the two most important Asian IFCs and they have seen their relevance growing together with the others. What makes their position somehow different is that both are certainly going to be affected by the economic fortunes of China as they have been so far and even more, if possible.

In the case of Hong Kong, being China, unsurprisingly, the main supplier of imports, even if many countries take benefit of the free-trade regime, the signature of CEPA, Closer Economic Partnership Arrangement (CEPA) since 2004 will continue to foster a progressively closer integration of Hong Kong's economy with the China Mainland, not only in the traditional manufacturing and logistics sectors, but in services too, which are generally off-limits to foreign companies. Thanks to CEPA's provisions, Hong Kong suppliers are enjoying preferential treatment when entering into the Mainland market in various service areas, and can also have professional titles and qualifications recognised in China.

But Singapore too is well positioned to exploit the increasingly busy Chinese market, especially for what concerns the financial sector, and, already as East Asia's largest centre for both commodity and foreign exchange trading, Singapore has recently become also the hub of negotiation for the renminbi, China's currency yet not convertible. This opens even more opportunities for the rise of Singapore as the leading forex centre of East Asia.

In addition to that, the ongoing regional integration in Asia, starting from the free trade area of ASEAN (AFTA) to more ambitious plans to integrate also China, Japan and Australia in that framework, are going to offer even more opportunities for the two hubs to thrive.

Risks to Singapore and Hong Kong can come instead from exogenous threats (like global financial crisis or the recent downfall of the Chinese stock market in 2015) or from the rise of local competitors, like Shanghai, that, building on existing vantage points like logistics and manufacturing can threaten their supremacy.

Case Questions

9-4. Discuss the IMF definition of IFCs and explain how this applies to the two Asian territories here in exam.

9-5. Describe structural similarities and differences between Hong Kong and Singapore, and describe the two IFCs in terms of financial markets and stock capitalisation. What are the most striking differences among them? What are the respective points of strength and weakness?

9-6. Both IFCs are central not only for financial services, but also for other factors, like supply chain, exhibition business and logistics hub. Especially their deepwater container ports consistently among the world top ten. In which way this helps their status as financial centres?

9-7. Now consider the last section, what lies ahead, and research the sources provided. Which one is more promising in terms of scenarios and why? What has to happen for having Singapore to overtake Hong Kong as the most important IFC of the region? What can do Hong Kong to maintain its dominant position?

Sources: IMF, "Offshore Financial Centers: IMF Background Paper", 23 June 2000, available at: https://www.imf.org/external/np/mae/oshore/2000/eng/back.htm; Credit Suisse, Singapore As a Financial Hub, 2014, https://www.credit-suisse.com/sg/en/private-banking/bank/financialhub.html; GFCI17 - Global Financial Centres Index, March 2015, http://www.zyen.com/research/gfci.html; Singapore jostles with Hong Kong for financial crown, FT, October 24, 2014, http://www.ft.com/cms/s/0/b18372a6-5297-11e4-a236-00144feab7de.html#axzz3pIN6Gfw1; CEPA partnership Agreement, available at: http://www.tid.gov.hk/english/cepa/cepa_overview.html; World Bank Statistics on container port traffic's in TEU statistics, available at: http://data.worldbank.org/indicator/IS.SHP.GOOD.TU; Hong Kong Stock Exchange, official website http://www.hkex.com.hk/eng/listing/listhk/our_markets.htm; Singapore Stock Exchange, official website http://www.sgx.com/wps/portal/sgxweb/home/marketinfo/market_statistics; Forbes, Chinese Stock Markets Do Not Matter, OCT 1, 2015, http://www.forbes.com/sites/kennethkim/2015/10/01/chinese-stock-markets-do-not-matter/; Qz, Beijing is blaming everyone but itself for China's stock market collapse, 1 Sept 2015, http://qz.com/492115/beijing-is-blaming-everyone-but-itself-for-chinas-stock-market-collapse/

END OF CHAPTER REVIEW

 MyManagementLab

Go to **mymanagementlab.com** to complete the problems marked with this icon .

Key Terms

balance of payments   268
capital flight   264
central bank   266
currency risk   262
devaluation   268
exchange rate   262

foreign exchange   264
foreign exchange market   264
global financial system   270
International Monetary Fund
(IMF)   269
international monetary system   270

monetary intervention   275
Special Drawing Right
(SDR)   276
trade deficit   268
trade surplus   268
World Bank   269

Summary

In this chapter, you learned about:

- **Exchange rates and currencies in international business**

  Much of international trade requires the exchange of currencies such as the dollar, euro, and yen. An **exchange rate** is the price of one currency expressed in terms of another. **Currency risk** arises from changes in exchange rates and affects firms' international business prospects. A convertible currency is one that can be readily exchanged for other currencies. Some currencies are nonconvertible and not readily exchangeable. **Foreign exchange** refers to all forms of money that are traded internationally, including foreign currencies, bank deposits, checks, and electronic transfers. **Capital flight** refers to the tendency of international investors to reduce their investments drastically in a troubled currency or other assets. Currencies are exchanged in the **foreign exchange market**—the global marketplace for buying and selling currencies—mainly by banks and governments.

- **How exchange rates are determined**

  Currency values are determined by various factors, including *economic growth, inflation, market psychology*, and *government action*. As inflation rises, so do interest rates, usually accompanied by a decrease in currency value. **Trade deficit** refers to the amount by which a nation's imports exceed its exports for a specific time period. **Trade surplus** is the amount by which a nation's exports exceed its imports for a specific time period. Government action to influence exchange rates is broadly termed **monetary intervention**. When the goal is **devaluation**, the government acts to reduce

the official value of its currency relative to other currencies. The **balance of payments** is the annual accounting of *all* economic transactions of a nation with all other nations.

- **Emergence of the modern exchange rate system**

  The Bretton Woods agreement of 1944 aimed to stabilize exchange rates worldwide. But the system collapsed in 1971 as currency values began floating according to market forces. Today, currency values are determined in some countries by a *floating exchange rate system*, according to market forces, and in developing economies by a *fixed exchange rate system*, controlled by government intervention. The **International Monetary Fund (IMF)** is a key international agency that aims to stabilize currencies by monitoring the foreign exchange systems of member countries and lending money to developing economies. The **World Bank** is an international agency that provides loans and technical assistance to low- and middle-income countries with the goal of reducing poverty.

- **The monetary and financial systems**

  The **international monetary system** is the institutional framework, rules, and procedures by which national currencies are exchanged for each other. It includes institutional arrangements that countries put in place to govern exchange rates. The **global financial system** is the collective of financial institutions that facilitate and regulate investment and capital flows and make possible massive trading of currencies and financial assets. It reflects the activities of companies, banks, and financial institutions, all engaged in ongoing financial activity.

- **Key players in the monetary and financial systems**

  Key participants include firms that generate revenues and acquire foreign exchange in the course of international business, invest abroad, and inject money into the financial system. Trading of securities and bonds takes place in *national stock exchanges* and *bond markets*. Each country has a **central bank**, the monetary authority that regulates the money supply and credit, issues currency, manages the rate of exchange, and acts as lender of last resort. The IMF employs **Special Drawing Rights**, a type of international reserve, to help manage currency valuation worldwide. A *currency crisis* results when the value of the nation's currency depreciates sharply. A *banking crisis* results when investors lose confidence in a nation's banking system and massively withdraw funds. Excessive *foreign debt* can harm the stability of national financial systems.

- **The global debt crisis**

  Growing imbalance in the finances of numerous national governments is an important emergent global risk. Governments spent huge sums to bail out financial systems in the global financial crisis and face financing long-term liabilities of pension and health care programs. National debt that exceeds 90 percent of a nation's GDP diminishes GDP growth; numerous countries have surpassed this threshold. Firms doing international business must proceed with caution because massive government debt can indicate economic instability, reduced buyer purchasing power, and other challenges in national markets.

Test Your Comprehension AACSB: Reflective Thinking Skills

9-8. Distinguish between *exchange rate* and *foreign exchange*. What does each term mean?

9-9. Why might a country fear capital flight?

9-10. Distinguish between a trade surplus and a trade deficit and suggest the implications for a country's economy.

9-11. What is the role of the International Monetary Fund (IMF) and who funds its operations?

9-12. What are the reasons behind the perceived growth of financial and monetary integration?

9-13. What is the difference between the international monetary system and the global financial system?

9-14. What are the key players in the international monetary and financial systems?

9-15. What are the aims of the World Bank and the International Monetary Fund?

Apply Your Understanding AACSB: Reflective Thinking Skills, Analytic Skills and Ethical Understanding and Reasoning Abilities

9-16. Everest Company has been exporting its line of mountain-climbing equipment to buyers worldwide for 30 years. Top markets include France, Norway, Switzerland, India, and Japan. Customers in these countries always pay in their local currency. Everest's vice president for international sales often states that the firm's biggest day-to-day challenge is dealing with foreign currencies. Why does he say this? What are the consequences of fluctuating exchange rates for Everest's sales revenue and other performance indicators?

9-17. Nearly 20 European Union (EU) countries have adopted the euro as their national currency and are termed the *eurozone*. Sharing a single currency eliminates exchange fluctuations and simplifies trade. Eurozone firms had to make various operational changes, especially regarding finance and accounting, but generally prefer dealing in the euro. The ECB views the eurozone as one region and must apply the same monetary policy to all EU members, but this is problematic at times. The United Kingdom opted not to join the monetary union, keeping the British pound as its currency. What types of competitive advantages and disadvantages are associated with the implementation of the euro from the perspective of the firm? What types of changes did firms make once the euro became the new currency? Was adopting the euro worth it? Why or why not?

9-18. *Ethical Dilemma:* You are an adviser to a legislator who oversees the banking industry. During the recent global financial crisis, several banks collapsed and private citizens lost much money. Problems arose largely due to inadequate or inappropriate regulation of the banking industry. In recent decades, however, an unrestricted global banking sector has produced numerous benefits. The relative absence of restrictions on international financial flows gave firms access to low-cost capital. The free flow of capital also provided much-needed funding to governments and entrepreneurs in poor countries. A liberated world currency market greatly facilitated international trade. Nations benefit enormously from inward capital flows as portfolio investments. Given the pros and cons of a relatively unregulated global banking system, how would you advise the legislator? Are new regulations needed in the banking sector? If so, what types of regulations? Use the ethical framework in Chapter 4 to help formulate your answer.

 | INTERNET EXERCISES
(http://www.globalEDGE.msu.edu)

AACSB: Communication Abilities, Reflective Thinking Skills

Refer to Chapter 1, page 54, for instructions on how to access and use globalEDGE™.

9-19. There are numerous foreign exchange calculators on the Internet, such as www.x-rates.com. You can find them through globalEDGE™ or by entering the keywords *exchange rate* in a Google search. Visit one of these calculators and compare the exchange rates of various currencies, including the dollar, euro, yen, and renminbi. What is the rate for these currencies today? What was the euro–dollar exchange rate one year ago? What factors might have caused the fluctuation in this rate during the year? Does this website provide a way to trade foreign currencies? What is the amount of commission or other fees charged?

9-20. Assume you are a manager at a firm interested in doing business in Russia. As part of your initial analysis, top management would like to know about the level of currency and financial risks associated with the Russian market. Using resources at globalEDGE™, write a short report on the current status of these risks as well as the state of the Russian financial system and historical exchange rate stability. Based on these findings, what is your recommendation?

9-21. The International Monetary Fund (IMF) lists its purposes as follows.
- Promote international monetary cooperation through consultation and collaboration on international monetary problems.
- Facilitate the expansion and balanced growth of international trade.
- Promote exchange stability to maintain orderly exchange arrangements among members and avoid competitive exchange depreciation.
- Visit the IMF website (www.imf.org) and list several examples of how the IMF undertakes and accomplishes these goals. What kinds of specific actions has the IMF taken over the past year to address economic or financial crises of various nations?

MyManagementLab

Go to **mymanagementlab.com** for Auto-graded writing questions as well as the following Assisted-graded writing questions:

⭐ **9-22.** Summarize the four major factors that determine exchange rates.

⭐ **9-23.** What is the relationship between inflation, interest rates, and currency values?

⭐ **9-24.** MyManagementLab Only—comprehensive writing assignment for this chapter.

Endnotes

1. *The Moscow Times*, "Russian Capital Flight Slows to $32.6 Billion in First Quarter," April 10, 2015, pp. 20, 28; "Economic Structure and Context: Development and Strategy," *Venezuela Country Monitor*, January 2012, pp. 19–20; "The Weakening of the 'Strong Bolivar' Venezuela's Devaluation," *Economist*, January 16, 2010, p. 39.

2. *Federal Reserve Bulletin*, various years, at http://www.federalreserve.gov; K. Kumar and Y. Muniraju, "Exchange Rate Fluctuations and Its Impact on Foreign Trade: An Empirical Study," *Finance India* 28, No. 3 (2014), pp. 973–983.

3. Jonathan Berr, "Europe Braces for a Flood of U.S. Tourists," *CBS Moneywatch*, March 12, 2015, www.cbsnews.com; Todd Buell and Bertrand Benoit, "Germany Reached Records in Exports, Imports in 2014," *Wall Street Journal*, February 10, 2015, p. A5; Paul Ziobro, Josh Mitchell, and Theo Francis, "Strong Dollar Squeezes U.S. Firms," *Wall Street Journal*, January 28, 2015, pp. A1, A2.

4. Peter Morgan, "The Role of Macroeconomic Policy in Rebalancing Growth," *Journal of Asian Economics* 23, No. 1 (2012), pp. 13–25.

5. Landon Thomas Jr., "Skittish over Emerging Markets," *New York Times*, December 17, 2014, p. B1.

6. Abdul-Hamid Sukar and Seid Hassan, "U.S. Exports and Time-Varying Volatility of Real Exchange Rate," *Global Finance Journal* 12 (2001), pp. 109–114.

7. Josef Brada, Ali Kutan, and Su Zhou, "The Exchange Rate and the Balance of Trade: The Turkish Experience," *Journal of Development Studies* 33 (1997), pp. 675–684.

8. International Monetary Fund, *Global Financial Stability Report*, 2015, http://www.imf.org.

9. Marc Labonte and Jared Nagel, *Foreign Holdings of Federal Debt* (Congressional Research Service, Report No. 7-5700) June 16, 2014.

10. Alan Greenspan, "The Globalization of Finance," *Cato Journal* 17 (1997), http://www.cato.org.

11. International Monetary Fund, "Effects of Financial Globalization on Developing Countries: Some Empirical Evidence," 2003, http://www.imf.org.

12. Meiling Pope et al., "Mobile Payments: The Reality on the Ground in Selected Asian Countries and the United States," *International Journal of Mobile Marketing* 6, No. 2 (2011), pp. 88–104; Adam Thomson, "Families Struggle to Survive as Flow of Dollars Dries Up," *Financial Times*, August 19, 2009, p. 4.

13. "Telcos Offer Incentives to Lure Bond Investors," *Corporate Finance*, July 2000, p. 4.

14. "Open Wider: A Survey of International Banking," *Economist*, May 21, 2005, special section.

15. "AFRICA: Mobile Banking Prospects Remain Positive," *Oxford Analytica Daily Brief Service*, October 3, 2008, p. 1; Moin Siddiqi, "Banking in Africa," *African Business*, April 2000, pp. 25–27.

16. Bank for International Settlements, *Consultative Document: The New Basel Capital Accord*, 2001, http://www.bis.org.

17. International Monetary Fund, *Financial Statements*, for the years ending April 30, 2010, and April 30, 2011, http://www.imf.org.

18. Wayne Arnold, "Has China Got an External-Debt Problem? Not Likely," *Wall Street Journal*, June 13, 2014, blogs .wsj.com.

19. Mathias Dolls, Andreas Peichl, and Klaus Zimmermann, "A Challenge for the G20: Global Debt Brakes and Transnational Fiscal Supervisory Councils," *Intereconomics* 47, No. 1 (2012), pp. 31–38; World Economic Forum, *Global Risks 2011*, 6th ed. (Geneva, Switzerland, 2011).

20. Ibid.

21. Liz Alderman and Rachel Donadio, "Debt Rating Cut for 9 Countries Amid Euro Woes," *New York Times*, January 14, 2012, pp. A1 and B6; Moody's, "Moody's Adjusts Ratings of 9 European Sovereigns to Capture Downside Risks," February 13, 2012, www.moodys.com; Moody's, "Moody's Downgrades Russia's Sovereign Rating to Ba1 from Baa3, Outlook Negative," February 20, 2015, www.moodys.com.

22. World Economic Forum (2011).

23. J. Gokhale, "Measuring the Unfunded Obligations of European Countries," National Centre for Policy Analysis (NCPA) Policy Report No. 319 (Washington, DC: National Center for Policy Analysis, 2009); International Monetary Fund, *United States: Selected Issues Paper, IMF Country Report No. 10/248*, July 12, 2010 (Washington, DC: International Monetary Fund); L. Kotlikoff, "A Hidden Fiscal Crisis?" *Finance and Development*, September 2010, (Washington, DC: International Monetary Fund).

Chapter 10

Financial Management and Accounting in the Global Firm

Learning Objectives *After studying this chapter, you should be able to:*

10.1 Understand how to choose a capital structure.

10.2 Understand how to raise funds for the firm.

10.3 Explain how to manage working capital and cash flow.

10.4 Describe how to perform capital budgeting.

10.5 Explain how to manage currency risk.

10.6 Understand how to manage the diversity of international accounting and tax practices.

The Netherlands and the Euro: A Continuous Debate

Elections for the European Parliament generally arouse little controversy in the Netherlands: the percentage of people casting their vote is low. But in the run-up to the 'European' elections of 2014 an interesting development occurred. VNO, a major lobbying group of employers, took the unprecedented step of preparing commercials that were aired on Dutch television. In these commercials it was stressed how important the European Union is for the Netherlands. Special attention was given to the euro. The Netherlands is a small open economy with exports amounting to 500 billion Euros a year. Of these exports, around 75% have Europe as their destination, notably the countries participating in the common currency. Therefore, the commercial concluded, the euro is of paramount importance to the Netherlands.

The commercial was made against a strong backlash against the common currency in the country. Even before the Eurocrisis, the euro was not very popular in the Netherlands as people felt that the introduction of the currency had fueled inflation. The problems of Greece and other countries in the Eurozone after 2009 (which led to huge transfers of 'Dutch' money to these countries) made that resentment even stronger.

Many economists agreed, however, with the lobbying group of employers. They pointed to several advantages of the common currency for the Netherlands:

a. Economic stability. Germany is the most important trading partner of the Netherlands. If the Netherlands and Germany still had their own currencies and the value of the Dutch guilder would increase substantially vis-à-vis the Deutschmark, this would have disastrous consequences for the Dutch economy. As both countries share the euro, this risk does not exist.

Source: PhotographyByMK/Shutterstock

Before the euro was created, Dutch companies were sometimes confronted with major currency fluctuations in Europe. Thus, in 1992 the Italian lira devalued by some 20 percent. Dutch companies that exported to Italy were severely hit by this devaluation: many of them lost their competitiveness on the Italian market instantly.

b. Reduction of costs for companies. Dutch companies export all over the world. As currencies are volatile, they need to protect themselves against currency fluctuations. There are ways of doing that (for instance through hedging) but such hedging contracts may be expensive and in general they only provide protection for a limited amount of time. The existence of the euro abolished currency risks in the most important export markets of the Netherlands.

c. Increased competition. Having one currency in Europe, increases the transparency and competition in Europe. Dutch companies (some of which are very competitive!) profit from that transparency. For instance, French companies that want to do business with Dutch counterparts, do not need to take different currencies into account anymore – it is immediately clear which of their potential business partners is the best and the cheapest.

d. Increased rationality as regards sourcing. In the past, Dutch companies were hesitant about transferring production facilities to, for instance, Germany: wouldn't production costs (measured in guilders!) rise significantly if the Deutschmark were revaluated i.e. became more expensive? Having one common currency, abolishes this risk, allowing for more rational decisions are regards sourcing.

e. Increase of global bargaining power. The Netherlands is a small economy and the guilder used to be a minor currency. Being part of the common currency has increased the Dutch influence on the world stage as the euro is, just like the American dollar, one of the most important global currencies.

In 2011, Dutch government agency CPB tried to quantify the advantages of the adoption of the common currency for the Netherlands. According to CPB, participation in the Eurozone results in one extra weekly salary per year for Dutch citizens. For those who felt that this was not enough to warrant the adoption of the common currency, the CPB had a stark warning: leaving the Eurozone would be disastrous. The Eurozone, according to CPB, was like Hotel California, a famous song by the Eagles: you may think you can check out any time you want, but in reality you can never leave.

Questions

10-1. In 2012, a Eurosceptical political party (i.e., a political party that does not have a positive view of the European Union) commissioned a report regarding Dutch membership of the Eurozone. Go online and find out about the Lombard Street report. Do you agree with the argument?

10-2. Switzerland is not a member of the European Union. At the beginning of 2015, a major currency shock affected the Swiss franc. What happened and why? Did Dutch exporters profit from these currency developments? How could this episode be used by proponents of the euro to underline the value of the common currency?

10-3. In what way does the individual citizen of the Eurozone profit from the existence of the euro?

SOURCES: http://nos.nl/video/643404-wientjes-we-verdienen-boterham-met-export-naar-eu.html; http://www.dnhk.org/nl/niederlande/fakten/handel-met-nederland/; http://www.cbs.nl/en-GB/menu/themas/internationale-handel/publicaties/artikelen/archief/2015/forse-toename-export-naar-zwitserland-na-duurdere-frank.htm; https://www.rijksoverheid.nl/actueel/nieuws/2012/08/02/nederland-belangrijke-handelspartner-voor-alle-eu-landen; http://www.economist.com/blogs/economist-explains/2015/01/economist-explains-13; http://www.ad.nl/ad/nl/5597/Economie/article/detail/2354349/2006/12/21/Nibud-helft-Nederlanders-wil-gulden-terug.dhtml; http://www.reuters.com/article/2011/10/05/us-eurozone-germany-mark-idUSTRE7941M320111005; http://www.ft.com/intl/cms/s/0/45dc6d7e-66c1-11e1-863c-00144feabdc0.html#axzz3qt1g5Qv6.

The opening case pays close attention to *international financial management*. International financial management is the acquisition and use of funds for cross-border trade, investment, R&D, manufacturing, marketing, outsourcing, and other commercial activities. It is a complex but critical business function. Firms face various international financial challenges. These arise from globalization, integration of financial markets, rise of global e-commerce, global financial crises, and expanding opportunities to profit from financial activities.

A key job of financial managers is to obtain funds from wherever in the world capital is least costly. Sources include investors in the world stock and bond markets, banks, and venture capital firms anywhere in the world. An additional source is *intracorporate financing:* obtaining funds from within the MNE's operations worldwide. Managers' ability to minimize risk and seize opportunities depends on their financial management skills and their understanding of the regulations that govern financial systems worldwide.

Key Tasks in International Financial Management

International financial management is challenging for large MNEs. Motorola (www.motorola.com) has facilities in nearly 50 countries. Its network of subsidiaries and strategic business units raises funds in financial markets worldwide. International financial managers at firms like Markel and Motorola acquire and allocate financial resources for the firm's current and future activities to help maximize company value. In this chapter, we examine six financial management tasks that are critical to MNE success. They are highlighted in Exhibit 10.1.

- *Choosing a capital structure.* Determine the ideal long-term mix of financing for the firm's international operations.
- *Raising funds for the firm.* Obtain financing for funding value-adding activities and investment projects. Financing might come from selling stocks, borrowing money, or using internally generated funds.
- *Managing working capital and cash flow.* Administer funds passing in and out of the firm's value-adding activities.
- *Performing capital budgeting.* Assess the financial attractiveness of major investment projects such as foreign expansion.
- *Managing currency risk.* Oversee transactions in various foreign currencies and manage risk exposure resulting from exchange-rate fluctuations.
- *Managing the diversity of international accounting and tax practices.* Learn to operate in a global environment with diverse accounting practices and international tax regimes.

Such tasks become especially relevant as the firm expands the scale of its international operations. Increasing global operations gives the firm strategic flexibility. Companies with extensive international operations benefit from increased opportunities to tap lower-cost capital, minimize taxes, and increase the efficiency of their financial operations. Let's delve into each of the six tasks.

EXHIBIT 10.1

International Financial Management Tasks

Choosing a Capital Structure

A *capital structure* is the mix of long-term equity financing and debt financing that firms use to support their international activities. Capital structure affects the profitability and stability of the firm and its international operations. Companies obtain capital in two basic ways: by borrowing it or by selling shares of ownership in the firm. **Equity financing** is selling shares of stock to investors, which provides them with an ownership interest—that is, *equity*—in the firm. The firm can also retain earnings—that is, reinvest profit rather than paying it out as dividends to investors. In new companies, founders often provide equity financing from their personal savings. **Debt financing** comes from either of two sources: (a) loans from banks and other financial intermediaries or (b) the sale of corporate bonds to individuals or institutions.

Debt service payments—the periodic principal and interest payments to pay off a loan—are a fixed cost. Using debt financing can add value to the firm because some governments allow firms to deduct interest payments from their taxes. MNEs want to minimize the possibility of bankruptcy and maintain a good credit rating. Thus, most MNEs keep the debt proportion of their capital structure below a level that they can service even during tough times. Too much debt can force companies into financial distress and even bankruptcy.[1]

How much debt a firm should hold depends partly on the nature of its industry and its target markets. For example, an insurance company with relatively stable sales to wealthy foreign markets can keep a higher debt ratio than a consumer goods firm that sells mostly to poor countries with cyclical sales.

The riskiness of debt is perceived differently around the world. The average debt ratio in Germany, Italy, Japan, and numerous developing economies typically exceeds 50 percent. High reliance on debt financing can arise if a country lacks a well-developed stock market or other systems for obtaining capital from equity sources. Under such conditions, firms may have little choice but to borrow money from banks. In other nations, firms maintain close relationships with banks. In Japan, large MNEs are often part of a conglomerate or holding company that includes a bank. Sony Corporation has its own bank, Sony Bank.

10.1 Understand how to choose a capital structure.

Equity financing
The issuance of shares of stock to raise capital from investors and the use of retained earnings to reinvest in the firm.

Debt financing
The borrowing of money from banks or other financial intermediaries or the sale of corporate bonds to individuals or institutions to raise capital.

Raising Funds for the Firm

Lufthansa Airlines raised several hundred million euros by issuing stock shares to acquire A380 airplanes from Airbus. Grupo Mexico, a giant producer of copper and silver, issued millions of peso-denominated shares to pay expenses incurred by its foreign subsidiaries. Stanley Works, the U.S. toolmaker, funds part of its Japanese operations by selling shares on the Tokyo Stock Exchange.

10.2 Understand how to raise funds for the firm.

Global money market
The collective financial markets where firms and governments raise short-term financing.

Global capital market
The collective financial markets where firms and governments raise intermediate and long-term financing.

Companies can obtain financing in the **global money market**, the collective of financial markets worldwide where firms and governments raise *short-term* financing. Alternatively, companies may obtain financing from the **global capital market**, the collective of financial markets worldwide where firms and governments raise *intermediate* and *long-term* financing. Because funding for most projects comes from instruments whose maturity period is longer than one year, we refer to all such funding as *capital*. In this chapter, we focus on the global capital market.

The great advantage for international investors of participating in the global capital market is the ability to access a wide range of investment opportunities. The benefit for corporations is the ability to access funds from a large pool of sources at a competitive cost. Access to capital is one of the main criteria that businesses consider when deciding to expand abroad.[2]

Financial Centers

The global capital market is concentrated in major *financial centers*, such as New York, London, and Tokyo and, increasingly, in Hong Kong, Singapore, and Shanghai. At these locations, firms can access the major suppliers of capital through banks, stock exchanges, and venture capitalists. Exhibit 10.2 lists the proportion of major financial activity in Japan, the United States, major European countries, and the rest of the world. The United Kingdom, France, and Germany are home to the largest proportion of foreign-exchange trading (45 percent). The United States has the largest share of market capitalization of companies listed in its stock exchanges (35 percent). In the "rest of world" category, China is emerging as an important center of global finance.

The global capital market is huge and growing rapidly, despite significant shrinkage during the recent global financial crisis. In 2015:

- International issues of equity in world securities markets amounted to about $800 billion, up from $83 billion in 1996.
- The stock of cross-national bank loans and deposits exceeded $29,000 billion, up from $12,000 billion a decade earlier.
- Outstanding international bonds and notes accounted for more than $21,000 billion, up from around $4,000 billion in 1998.[3]

EXHIBIT 10.2

Share of Financial Activity in Major World Regions (percent)

Sources: Based on *BIS Quarterly Review*, March 2015; *Triennial Central Bank Survey*, 2014; and *Statistics*, all retrieved from Bank for International Settlements at www.bis.org; World Bank, "Market Capitalization of Listed Companies," 2015, data.worldbank.org.

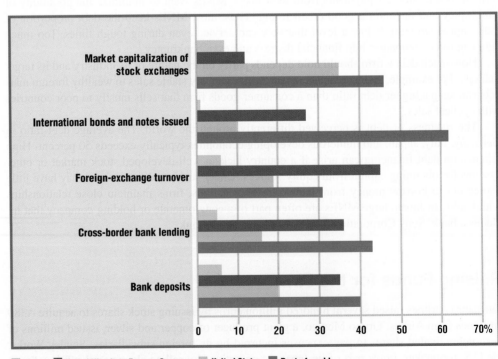

The global capital market has grown rapidly due to:

- *Government deregulation*, which has made international movement of capital easier.

- *Innovation in information and communication technologies*, which has increased the ease and speed of global financial transactions.

- *Globalization* of business and global competition, which pressures firms to seek cost-effective ways to finance international operations.

- Widespread *securitization* of financial instruments. This refers to an increased ability to convert traditional financial instruments (such as bank loans) into tradable securities (such as bonds). Such instruments have a ready market worldwide.

Some of the preceding factors contributed to the global financial crisis that began in 2008. The crisis arose partially because of the large-scale availability of credit and easy movement of capital across national borders. As investors bought commodities and real estate, the prices of such assets became unrealistically high. Eventually investors realized that valuations in credit markets were too risky, so they sold assets on a massive scale. The total world value of financial assets (stocks, bonds, and loans) declined from $194 trillion in 2007 to $178 trillion in 2008. Fortunately, robust growth returned in 2010, and the total value of financial assets now exceeds $225 trillion.[4]

The global capital market provides three key advantages to the firm:

- Broader base from which to draw funds to finance company operations.

- Ability to access funds at lower, competitive costs because of increased access to a larger pool of funding sources from around the world.

- Greater variety of investment opportunities for MNEs, professional investment firms, and individuals.

Sources of Funds for International Operations

Firms obtain funds for their activities from three primary sources: equity financing, debt financing, and intra-corporate financing.

EQUITY FINANCING   When the firm uses equity financing, it obtains capital by selling stock. Shareholders—those who buy the stock—gain a percentage of ownership in the firm and, often, a stream of dividend payments. The main advantage is that the firm obtains capital without debt. However, whenever new equity is sold, the firm's ownership is diluted. Management also risks losing control if one or more shareholders acquire a controlling interest. Internationally, companies obtain equity financing in the **global equity market**—stock exchanges worldwide where investors and firms meet to buy and sell shares of stock. Exhibit 10.3 lists the world's largest stock exchanges. Total global market capitalization now exceeds 70 trillion U.S. dollars. Historically, exchanges in Europe, Japan, and the United States dominated the list. More recently, exchanges in China have grown in size and influence. Among the roughly 2,800 firms listed on the New York Stock Exchange, about 520 are foreign-owned and represent 46 countries. Aside from the United States, countries with the most listed companies are Canada (146 firms), China, (73 firms), and the United Kingdom (34 firms).[5]

As an investor, you are not limited to buying stock on the stock exchanges of your home country. Many investors today buy stocks on foreign exchanges.[6] Investing in local stocks on foreign exchanges makes sense for two main reasons. First, it provides new opportunities for profitable investing. Second, it helps lessen losses during slumps in the home economy. For example, U.S. investors can buy stock from several hundred companies listed on the London exchange, including Kingfisher, Canon, and South African Breweries. Thanks to the Internet,

Global equity market
The worldwide market of funds for equity financing—stock exchanges around the world where investors and firms meet to buy and sell shares of stock.

EXHIBIT 10.3

Largest Stock Exchanges in the World, in Billions of U.S. Dollars

Source: Based on World Federation of Exchanges, *2015 WFE Market Highlights*, January 31, 2015, www.world-exchanges.org.

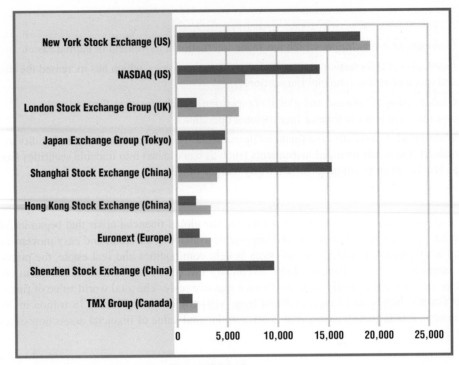

■ Total Annual Value of Share Trading (billions of US dollars)
■ Domestic Equity Market Capitalization (billions of US dollars)

investors now trade on world stock markets at low cost. Foreign investors can increasingly access stock markets in China. Even a small market such as the Cayman Islands Stock Exchange (www.csx.com.ky) offers full online investing opportunities.[7]

Pension funds, which invest employee savings for retirement, represent the largest segment of international investing. The total value of private pension funds worldwide exceeds $19 trillion, substantially more than the GDP of the United States.

DEBT FINANCING   In international business, debt financing consists mainly of international loans and the eurocurrency market as well as domestic and foreign bonds. We review these next.

International Loans   Exhibit 10.4 shows the world's primary banking centers. In the past decade, China gained much momentum as a world banking center. In general, a firm can borrow from banks in its home market or in foreign markets. Borrowing internationally is complicated. Challenges include differences in national banking regulations, poor banking infrastructure, capital shortages, economic problems, and fluctuating currency values.[8] Banks are often reluctant to extend credit to small and medium-sized enterprises (SMEs). Such firms may turn to government agencies such as the Export Import (Ex-IM) Bank (www.exim.gov) in the United States, a federal agency for loans and loan guarantees. Governments in the developing world often provide loans to promote inward direct investment projects such as the construction of dams, power plants, and airports. Many subsidiaries of large MNEs obtain loans from their parent firm or a sister subsidiary.

The Eurocurrency Market   Another key source of loanable funds is money deposited in banks outside a firm's country of origin. **Eurodollars** are U.S. dollars held in banks outside the United States, including foreign branches of U.S. banks. Thus, a U.S. dollar-denominated bank deposit in Barclays bank in London or in Mizuho Bank in Tokyo is a Eurodollar deposit. More broadly, any currency deposited in a bank outside its origin country is called **eurocurrency**. In addition to the U.S. dollar, the other main eurocurrencies are the European

Eurodollars
U.S. dollars held in banks outside the United States, including foreign branches of U.S. banks.

Eurocurrency
Any currency deposited in a bank outside its country of origin.

Bond
A debt instrument that enables the issuer (the borrower) to raise capital by promising to repay the principal on a specified date (at maturity) along with periodic interest payments.

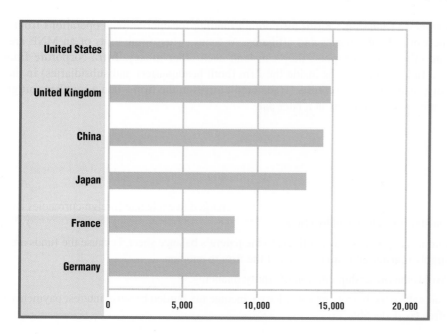

EXHIBIT 10.4
World's Primary Banking Centers, 2015 (total assets of commercial banks, in US$ billions)

Sources: Based on Bank for International Settlements, *Statistics*, 2015, www.bis.org; International Monetary Fund, *Data and Statistics*, www.imf.org; KPMG, *Mainland China Banking Survey 2014*, www.kpmg.com; Qatar Financial Centre, *The Global Financial Centres Index 17*, March 2015, www.longfinance.net.

Global bond market
The international marketplace in which bonds are bought and sold, primarily through bond brokers.

Eurobond
A bond sold outside the issuer's home country but denominated in its own currency.

Foreign bond
A bond sold outside the issuer's country and denominated in the currency of the country where issued.

euro, the British pound, and the Japanese yen. Eurodollars account for roughly two-thirds of all eurocurrencies.[9] As much as two-thirds of U.S. banknotes are held outside the United States as a reserve currency.

Hitachi, Matsushita, and many other Japanese firms borrowed eurodollars in Japan to help finance their operations worldwide. U.S. companies sometimes borrow euros or yen deposited in the United States to finance their activities. The eurocurrency market is attractive to firms because these funds are not subject to the government regulations of their home–country banking systems. U.S. dollars in French banks and euros in U.S. banks are free of the reserve requirements of their home countries. Banks typically offer higher interest rates on eurocurrency deposits and charge lower interest rates for eurocurrency loans. This has contributed to the emergence of a huge Eurocurrency market.

Bonds A major source of debt financing is bonds. A **bond** is a debt instrument that enables the issuer (the borrower) to raise capital by promising to repay the principal on a specified date (at maturity) along with periodic interest payments. Firms, governments, states, and other institutions all sell bonds. Investors buy bonds and redeem them at face value in the future. The **global bond market** is the international marketplace in which bonds are bought and sold, mainly through bond brokers.

Foreign bonds are sold outside the bond issuer's country in the currency of the country where issued. When Mexican cement giant Cemex sells dollar-denominated bonds in the United States, it is issuing foreign bonds. **Eurobonds** are sold outside the bond issuer's home country but denominated in its own currency. When Toyota sells yen-denominated bonds in the United States, it is issuing Eurobonds. The telecommunications giant AT&T has issued hundreds of millions of dollars in Eurobonds to support its international operations. Pharmaceutical firms Eli Lilly and Merck have funded much of their multinational operations with Eurobonds. Eurobonds are typically issued in denominations of $5,000 or $10,000, pay interest annually, and are sold in major financial centers, especially London.

Source: Krisztian Miklosy/123RF

Eurocurrencies are funds banked outside their country of origin and represent a key source of capital for international business. Pictured is one of the world's leading financial centers, London.

Intracorporate financing
Funds from sources inside the firm (both headquarters and subsidiaries) such as equity, loans, and trade credits.

Intracorporate Financing   Firms also obtain funding for international operations from within their network of subsidiaries and affiliates. At times, when some units of an MNE are cash-rich and others are cash-poor, they can lend each other money. **Intra-corporate financing** refers to funds from sources inside the firm (both headquarters and subsidiaries) in the form of equity, loans, and trade credits. Trade credit arises in the firm when a supplier unit grants a buyer unit the option to pay at a later date.

Loaning funds to the firm's own foreign subsidiaries provides several advantages.

- Saves bank transaction costs, such as fees charged to exchange foreign currencies and transfer funds between locations.
- Eliminates possible costly effects to the parent's balance sheet, because the funds are simply transferred from one area of the firm to another.
- Avoids the ownership dilution of equity financing.
- Can reduce the borrowing subsidiary's income tax burden because interest payments are often tax deductible.

IBM's global financing division invests in international financing assets and obtains and manages international debt to support IBM's global operations. The division provides loan financing to internal users for terms of two to five years. It provides inventory and accounts receivable financing to IBM's dealers and subsidiaries in various countries.[10]

Managing Working Capital and Cash Flow

10.3 Explain how to manage working capital and cash flow.

Working capital refers to the current assets of a company. *Net working capital* is the difference between current assets and current liabilities. As part of working capital management, firms manage all current accounts, such as cash, accounts receivable, inventory, and accounts payable. Cash comes from various sources, especially sales of goods and services. In the MNE, an important task of working capital management is ensuring that cash is available where and when needed. Cash-flow needs arise from everyday company activities, such as paying for labor and materials or paying taxes and interest on debt. To optimize global operations, international financial managers develop strategies to transfer funds among the firm's operations worldwide.

The volume and complexity of intracorporate transfers depends on the number of headquarters, subsidiaries, alliances, and business relationships the firm maintains worldwide. For companies with extensive international operations, the network of funds transfers can be vast. Roughly one-third of world trade results from collective trading activities within individual MNE networks.

Methods for Transferring Funds within the MNE

Financial managers employ various methods for transferring funds within the MNE. Funds must be moved efficiently, both to lessen transaction costs and tax liabilities and to increase returns that the funds can earn. Exhibit 10.5 depicts a typical company with subsidiaries in Mexico and Taiwan. Within its network, this firm can transfer funds through trade credit, dividend remittances, royalty payments, fronting loans, transfer pricing, and multilateral netting. Here is how each works:

- Through *trade credit*, a subsidiary can defer payment for goods and services received from the parent firm. The 30-day credit is the U.S. norm, whereas 90-day credit is typical in Europe, with longer terms elsewhere.

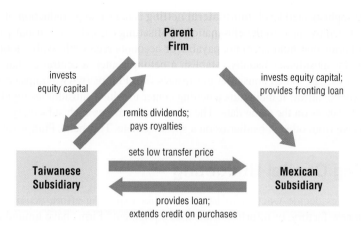

EXHIBIT 10.5

Typical Methods for Transferring Funds within the MNE

- *Dividend remittances* are common for transferring funds from foreign subsidiaries to the parent but vary depending on tax levels and currency risks. Some host governments levy high taxes on dividend payments or limit how much MNEs can remit.
- *Royalty payments* are compensation paid to owners of intellectual property. Assuming the subsidiary has licensed technology, trademarks, or other assets from the parent or other subsidiaries, royalties can be an efficient way to transfer funds and are tax deductible in many countries. A parent MNE can collect royalties from its own subsidiaries as a way of generating funds.
- In a **fronting loan**, the parent deposits a large sum in a foreign bank, which transfers it to a subsidiary as a loan. Fronting allows the parent to circumvent restrictions that foreign governments impose on direct intracorporate loans. The loan may be made through a bank in a tax haven. A **tax haven** is a country hospitable to business and inward investment because of its low corporate income taxes. The parent can minimize taxes that might be due if the loan is made directly. Although some countries restrict the amount of funds MNEs can transfer abroad, such restrictions usually do not apply to repayment of bank loans.
- *Transfer pricing* (also known as *intracorporate pricing*) is the price that subsidiaries and affiliates of the same corporate family charge each other as they buy and sell intermediate or finished products within the firm. For example, when Daimler USA sells truck parts to a Daimler plant in Germany, it charges a price, the transfer price. Firms can use transfer pricing to shift profits from high-tax to low-tax countries, improving internal cash flows.[11]

Fronting loan
A loan between the parent and its subsidiary, channeled through a large bank or other financial intermediary.

Tax haven
A country hospitable to business and inward investment because of its low corporate income taxes.

Multilateral Netting

In the past, cash was frequently held in each foreign subsidiary responsible for funding its own short-term needs. Today, MNE managers use a method known as *pooling* to bring surplus funds together in a regional or global *centralized depository*. They then direct these funds to needy subsidiaries or invest them to produce income.

Managers invest the funds from the centralized depository to produce maximal returns. If the depository is in a financial center (such as London, New York, or Sydney), management can also access various short-term investments that pay higher rates of return. Such depositories tend to centralize expertise and financial services, which benefits subsidiaries at lower cost.

Large MNEs conduct many international transactions, each of which creates transaction costs. Suppose a firm's Japanese subsidiary owes the Spanish subsidiary $8 million and the Spanish subsidiary owes the Japanese subsidiary $5 million. Although the firm could cancel these debts in separate transactions, a more intelligent solution that reduces transaction costs has the Japanese subsidiary pay the Spanish subsidiary $3 million. Transferring an amount considerably lower than either of the two original amounts reduces transactions costs such as fees and delays in funds transfers.

Multilateral netting
Strategic reduction of cash transfers within the MNE family through the elimination of offsetting cash flows.

At a more sophisticated level, **multilateral netting** is the strategic reduction of cash transfers within the MNE family through the elimination of offsetting cash flows. It usually involves three or more subsidiaries that hold accounts payable or accounts receivable with another subsidiary. MNEs with many subsidiaries usually establish a netting center, a central exchange, that headquarters supervises. The Dutch consumer electronics firm Philips (www.philips.com) has operating units in sixty countries. It maintains a netting center to which subsidiaries regularly report all intracorporate balances on the same date. The center then advises each subsidiary of the amounts to pay and receive from other subsidiaries on a specified date. This helps Philips save money.

10.4 Describe how to perform capital budgeting.

Performing Capital Budgeting

How do companies decide whether to launch a major exporting effort, acquire a distribution center, build a new factory, or refurbish industrial equipment? Firms have limited resources and cannot afford to invest in every project opportunity. The purpose of *capital budgeting* is to help managers decide which international projects provide the best financial return.

The decision depends on the project's initial investment requirement, its cost of capital, and the incremental cash flow or other advantages it can provide. Many variables affect the potential profitability of a venture. Investors in the fast-food industry consider the cost of alternate locations and the level of local competition as well as the distance to highways, availability of public transportation, and amount of traffic at each location.[12]

Net Present Value Analysis of Capital Investment Projects

Managers typically perform net present value (NPV) analysis to evaluate domestic and international capital investment projects. NPV is the difference between the present value of a project's incremental cash flows and its initial investment requirement.[13]

Managers can use NPV in two ways. One is to estimate the incremental after-tax operating cash flows in the subsidiary's local currency and then discount them at the project's cost of capital. The cost of capital is expressed as a percentage and is usually the required rate of return appropriate for the project's level of risk. If the NPV is positive, the project is expected to earn its required return and add value to the subsidiary. This approach takes the *project's perspective* in capital budgeting, and managers can use it as a first screening method.[14]

The second approach, called the *parent's perspective*, estimates future cash flows from the project in the *functional currency* of the parent—that is, the currency of the primary economic environment in which it operates. Thus, U.S.-based firms' functional currency is the U.S. dollar; for Japan-based firms, it is the yen. This approach uses forecasts of future *spot exchange rates* and converts the local currency cash flows to the functional currency at those rates. It then calculates the present value using a discount rate in line with the required return on projects of similar risk. Managers then compute the NPV in the parent's functional currency by subtracting the initial investment cash flow from the present value of the project cash flows. To be acceptable, the project must add value to the parent company. It must have positive NPV from the parent's perspective.

Estimating project cash flows is complex and requires forecasting a range of variables that contribute to anticipated revenues and

Source: rcfotostock/Fotolia

The Rheinauhafen district in Cologne, Germany, houses German subsidiaries of numerous multinational firms, including Microsoft and Electronic Arts. Managers use capital budgeting to decide which foreign locations are best for setting up operations.

costs over several years. The largest component of revenue is usually sales. Initial and ongoing costs typically include R&D, development of essential project resources, labor, factor inputs, and marketing.

> **Capital budgeting in the MNE is complicated by four factors:**
> - Project cash flows are usually in a currency other than the reporting currency of the parent firm.
> - Tax rules in the project location and the parent's country usually differ.
> - Governments may restrict the transfer of funds from the project to the parent firm.
> - The project may be exposed to country risk, such as government intervention or adverse economic conditions.

Managing Currency Risk

10.5 Explain how to manage currency risk.

Shifting currency values are among the biggest day-to-day challenges facing international firms. Foreign direct investors face currency risk because they receive payments and incur obligations in foreign currencies. Managers of foreign investment portfolios also face currency risk. A Japanese stock might gain 15 percent in value, but if the yen falls 15 percent, the stock gain is zero.[15]

Currency crises affect other local asset prices, including debt, equipment, and real estate markets. Firms face currency risk when their cash flows and the value of their assets and liabilities change due to unexpected changes in foreign-exchange rates. Exporters and licensors face currency risk—from unexpected fluctuations in exchange rates—because foreign buyers typically pay in their own currency. If the firm could quote its prices and get paid in its home–country currency, it could eliminate its currency risk, but the risk would still exist for its foreign customers. To please foreign buyers, companies frequently quote their prices in the buyer's currency. In international transactions, either the buyer or the seller incurs currency risk.

Three Types of Currency Exposure

Currency fluctuations result in three types of exposure for the firm: transaction exposure, translation exposure, and economic exposure.[16]

Transaction exposure is currency risk that firms face when outstanding accounts receivable or payable are denominated in foreign currencies. Suppose Dell imports 3 million Taiwan dollars' worth of computer keyboards and pays in the foreign currency. At the time of the purchase, suppose the exchange rate was US$1 = T$30, but Dell pays on credit terms three months after the purchase. If during the three-month period the exchange rate shifts to US$1 = T$27, Dell will have to pay an extra US$11,111 as a result of the rate change ([3,000,000/27] – [3,000,000/30]). From Dell's standpoint, the Taiwan dollar has become more expensive. Such gains or losses are real. They affect the firm's value directly by affecting its cash flows and profit.

Translation exposure results when an MNE translates financial statements denominated in a foreign currency into the functional currency of the parent firm as part of *consolidating* international financial results. **Consolidation** is the process of combining and integrating the financial results of foreign subsidiaries into the parent firm's financial records. Accounting practices usually require the firm to report consolidated financial results in the functional currency.

Translation exposure occurs because, as exchange rates fluctuate, so do the functional-currency values of exposed assets, liabilities, expenses, and revenues. Translating quarterly or annual foreign financial statements into the parent's functional currency results in gains or losses on the date financial statements are consolidated. When translated into dollars, the quarterly net income of the Japanese subsidiary of a U.S. MNE may drop if the Japanese yen depreciates

Transaction exposure
The currency risk that firms face when outstanding accounts receivable or payable are denominated in foreign currencies.

Translation exposure
The currency risk that results when a firm translates financial statements denominated in a foreign currency into the functional currency of the parent firm as part of consolidating international financial results.

Consolidation
The process of combining and integrating the financial results of foreign subsidiaries into the financial statements of the parent firm.

against the dollar during the quarter. Note that gains or losses in translation exposure are paper, or virtual, changes and do not affect cash flows directly. This contrasts with transaction exposure, in which gains and losses are real.

Economic exposure (also known as *operating exposure*) results from exchange-rate fluctuations that affect the pricing of products and inputs and the value of foreign investments. Exchange-rate fluctuations help or hurt sales by making the firm's products relatively more or less expensive for foreign buyers. If the yen appreciates against the euro, a European firm can expect to sell more goods in Japan because the Japanese have more buying power for buying euros. But if the yen weakens against the euro, the European firm's sales will likely drop in Japan unless management lowers its Japanese prices by an amount equivalent to the fall in the yen. Similarly, the firm may be harmed by currency shifts that raise the price of inputs sourced from abroad. The value of foreign investments can also fall, in home currency terms, with exchange-rate changes.

Transaction exposure affects ongoing contractual transactions. By contrast, economic exposure affects long-term profitability through changes in revenues and expenses. Such effects are reflected in the firm's financial statements. For example, strengthening of the U.S. dollar against the euro gradually increases the value of U.S. investments in Europe and decreases the cost of euro-denominated input goods. But it also weakens prospects for U.S. firms to sell their dollar-denominated products in the EU.

The three types of currency exposure can produce positive results when exchange rates fluctuate favorably for the firm. Managers are more concerned with fluctuations that harm the firm. Such problems help explain why many countries in Europe use a single currency, the euro. With a single medium of exchange, currency risk is eliminated in trade among the countries using the euro. For international firms operating outside the euro zone, however, currency risk is still a significant problem.

Foreign-Exchange Trading

A relatively small number of currencies facilitate cross-border trade and investment. Around 63 percent of allocated foreign reserves are in U.S. dollars, 22 percent are in euros, 4 percent are in British pounds, 4 percent are in Japanese yen, and 7 percent are in the world's remaining national currencies.[17] The volume of currencies exchanged is huge. The daily volume of global trading in foreign exchange amounts to more than $4 trillion. It can often exceed $5 trillion per day, depending on the level of cross-national economic activity.[18] To put this in perspective, that is more than 100 times the daily value of global trade in products and services.

Information technology is critical to currency trading. For example, the Swiss investment bank UBS (www.ubs.com) offers a range of currency-related products. Customers transact nearly all their spot, forward, and currency-swap trades online using UBS's computer platforms in dozens of countries.[19] Citibank (www.citibank.com) leverages its comprehensive customer portal, CitiFX, to provide clients a wide range of services, including library research, currency trading, and analytical tools.[20]

Large banks are the primary dealers in currency markets. They quote the prices at which they will buy or sell currencies. If an importer wants to exchange $100,000 for euros to finance a purchase from Austria, the currency exchange typically will be handled through the importer's bank. Large banks such as Citibank maintain reserves of major currencies and work with foreign *correspondent banks* to facilitate currency buying and selling. Currency transactions between banks occur in the *interbank market*.

Currency also can be bought and sold through brokers that specialize in matching up buyers and sellers. They are especially active in major financial centers such as London, New York, and Sydney. Trading can also be done through online brokers and dealers at sites such as www.forex.com and www.everbank.com.

The foreign-exchange market uses specialized terminology to describe the functions that currency dealers perform. The **spot rate** is the exchange rate applied when the current exchange rate is used for immediate receipt of a currency. The rate applies to transactions between banks for delivery within two

Economic exposure
The currency risk that results from exchange-rate fluctuations affecting the pricing of products, the cost of inputs, and the value of foreign investments.

Spot rate
The exchange rate applied when the current exchange rate is used for immediate receipt of a currency.

Source: Arto/Fotolia

Multinational firms must skillfully manage multiple-currency transactions and the risk associated with exchange rate fluctuations.

business days, or for immediate delivery for over-the-counter transactions involving nonbank customers—for example, when you buy currencies at airport kiosks.

The **forward rate** is the exchange rate applicable to the collection or delivery of foreign currencies at some future date. Dealers in the forward exchange market promise to receive or deliver foreign exchange at a specified time in the future, but at a rate determined at the time of the transaction. The primary function of the forward market is to provide protection against currency risk.

Dealers quote currency exchange rates in two ways. The **direct quote**, also known as the *normal quote*, is the number of units of domestic currency needed to acquire one unit of foreign currency. For example, on May 23, 2015, it cost $1.10 to acquire one euro (abbreviated as €). The **indirect quote** is the number of units of foreign currency obtained for one unit of domestic currency. For example, on May 23, 2015, it cost €0.91 to acquire $1.00. Please review this chapter's appendix to learn more about currency trading.

You may have observed at airports that when foreign-exchange dealers quote prices, they always quote a *bid* (buy) rate and an *offer* (sell) rate at which they will buy or sell any particular currency. The difference between the bid and offer rates—*the spread*—is the margin on which the dealer earns a profit.

Types of Currency Traders

Hedgers, speculators, and arbitragers represent the three main types of currency traders. **Hedgers**, typically MNEs and other international trade or investment firms, seek to minimize their risk of exchange-rate fluctuations, often by entering into forward contracts or similar financial instruments. They are not necessarily interested in profiting from currency trading.

Speculators are currency traders who seek profits by investing in currencies with the expectation that their value will change in the future and then sell them later at the different value. A speculator might purchase a certificate of deposit denominated in Mexican pesos or a money market account tied to the Chinese yuan, believing the value of these currencies will rise. The speculator can also bet on a currency's downturn by taking a *short position* in that currency. When investors take a short position, they sell a currency that they previously borrowed from a third party (usually a broker) with the intention of buying the identical currency back at a later date to return to the lender. In so doing, the short seller hopes to profit from a decline in the value of the currency between the sale and the repurchase because the seller will pay less to buy the currency than the seller received on selling it. Exhibit 10.6 shows a sample speculation in the foreign-exchange market through a forward contract.

Forward rate
The exchange rate applicable to the collection or delivery of a foreign currency at some future date.

Direct quote
The number of units of domestic currency needed to acquire one unit of foreign currency; also known as the normal quote.

Indirect quote
The number of units of foreign currency obtained for one unit of domestic currency.

Hedgers
Currency traders who seek to minimize their risk of exchange-rate fluctuations, often by entering into forward contracts or similar financial instruments.

Speculators
Currency traders who seek profits by investing in currencies with the expectation that their value will change in the future and then sell them at the different value.

EXHIBIT 10.6

An Example of Speculation in the Foreign-Exchange Market

Scenario: A speculator is offered a forward contract by a bank to be able to sell the bank €1 in exchange for $1.45 one year from now. Suppose that the speculator expects the spot exchange rate to be €1 = $1.40 a year from now. The speculator may try to profit from the difference between the expected spot exchange rate and the quoted forward exchange rate by entering into a forward contract with the offering bank. In this case, the speculator is taking a risk by attempting to make a profit based on an uncertain future spot exchange rate.

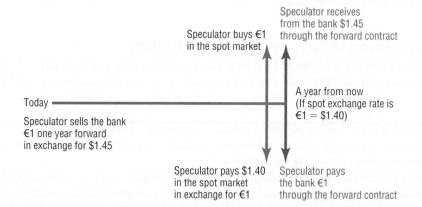

Outcome: If the spot exchange rate is actually €1 = $1.40 a year from now, the speculator earns a profit of $0.05. However, if the spot exchange rate turns out to be €1 = $1.50, the speculator will lose $0.05 as a result of having to sell the bank, through the forward contract, €1 for $1.45 instead of its actual spot value of $1.50.

Arbitragers
Currency traders who buy and sell the same currency in two or more foreign-exchange markets to profit from differences in the currency's exchange rate.

Arbitragers are currency traders who buy and sell the same currency in two or more foreign-exchange markets to profit from differences in the currency's exchange rate. But unlike the speculator who bets on the future price of a currency, the arbitrager attempts to profit from a current disequilibrium in currency markets based on known prices. If the euro-dollar exchange rate quoted in New York on Monday morning is €1 = $1.25, but the quoted exchange rate in London at that moment is €1 = $1.30, a trader could buy €1 million for $1.25 million in New York and simultaneously sell those euros in London for $1.3 million, yielding a riskless profit of $50,000 before commission and expenses. But don't get too excited! When such arbitrage opportunities exist, they quickly disappear because the very actions of the arbitragers force the exchange rates to adjust to the equilibrium level.

Exchange-Rate Forecasting

Losses due to exchange-rate risk are common in international business. Avon Products, Inc. is a United States cosmetics company that produces nearly 90 percent of its sales in foreign markets. The dollar's appreciation against the Brazilian real, the euro, and other world currencies in 2015 hurt Avon's sales. Procter & Gamble, Johnson & Johnson, and other U.S. multinationals experienced similar declines in international sales due to the stronger dollar. Such firms raise prices in global markets to offset losses caused by the dollar's rise. However, higher prices reduce the attractiveness of U.S. products to consumers outside the United States. Many U.S. firms have shifted their manufacturing to major foreign markets to avoid exporting the goods. The strategy reduces U.S. firms' vulnerability to harmful currency fluctuations.[21]

Financial managers monitor currency trading daily. They are especially alert for news and developments that affect currency values. In 2014, companies withdrew billions of dollars of investments from Russia due to concerns about political risk, economic woes, and corruption. As foreign investors sold off holdings from the stock exchange and other markets in Russia, they converted huge sums of Russian rubles into foreign currencies. The event led to substantial depreciation of the ruble.[22] In most countries, exchange rates respond immediately to economic information, such as the election of a new government and labor disputes. Major *supply shocks* also affect exchange rates, as when oil-exporting countries suddenly announce a drop in supply. In addition to forecasting such events, managers must assess the likely actions of foreign-exchange traders.

Firms with extensive international operations develop capabilities to forecast exchange rates that combine in-house forecasting with reports provided by major banks and professional forecasters. *Technical analysis* looks at recent movements in exchange rates and *fundamental analysis* studies involving macroeconomic data.

SMEs usually lack the resources to do substantial in-house forecasting and rely on forecasts from banks and business news sources. A table in each issue of the *Economist* magazine describes recent exchange-rate trends. Other useful information sources include the Bank for International Settlements (www.bis.org), the World Bank (www.worldbank.org), and the European Central Bank (www.ecb.int).

Managing Exposure to Currency Risk Through Hedging

Suppose you want to buy a Toyota and the local car dealer insists that you must pay in Japanese yen. You probably wouldn't buy the car, partly because you'd need to acquire yen and partly because other dealers let you pay in your own currency. Customers around the world prefer to deal in their own currency. If firms insist on quoting prices and getting paid in their own currency, the burden is on foreign buyers to monitor and manage foreign exchange. Even small exporters learn to operate in foreign currencies to remain competitive. In so doing, they also learn to minimize their exposure to currency risk.

Hedging
Using financial instruments and other measures to reduce or eliminate exposure to currency risk by locking in guaranteed foreign-exchange positions.

The most common method for managing exposure is **hedging**. It refers to the use of financial instruments and other measures to lock in guaranteed foreign-exchange positions. If the hedge is perfect, the firm is protected against the risk of adverse changes in the price of a currency. Banks offer forward contracts, options, and swap agreements to facilitate hedging. Banks charge fees and interest payments on amounts borrowed to carry out the transactions. The firm must balance these costs against expected benefits.

In *passive hedging*, each exposure is hedged as it occurs and the hedge stays in place until maturity. In *active hedging*, the firm frequently reviews total exposure and hedges only a subset of its total exposures, especially those that pose the greatest risk. Hedges may be withdrawn before they reach maturity. Some active hedgers seek to profit from hedging, even maintaining active in-house trading desks. However, most firms are conservative and simply try to cover all exposures—or their most important ones—and leave hedges in place until maturity.

Hedging Instruments

Having assessed its level of currency risk exposure, the firm attempts to balance exposed assets and exposed liabilities. The four most common hedging instruments are forward contracts, futures contracts, currency options, and currency swaps.

A **forward contract** is an agreement to exchange two currencies at a specified exchange rate on a set future date. No money changes hands until the delivery date of the contract. Banks quote forward prices in the same way as spot prices—with bid and ask prices at which they will buy or sell currencies. The bank's bid–ask spread is a cost for its customers.

Forward contracts are especially appropriate for hedging transaction exposure. Suppose Dow Chemical (www.dow.com) sells merchandise to a German importer for €100,000, payable in 90 days. During the 90 days, Dow has a transaction exposure to currency risk. It will receive fewer dollars if the euro depreciates during that time. To hedge against this risk, Dow executes a forward contract with a bank to sell €100,000 in 90 days at an exchange rate agreed upon today. This ensures that Dow will receive a known dollar amount in the future. Exhibit 10.7 illustrates the cash flows of Dow Chemical's forward market hedge.

Like a forward contract, a **futures contract** represents an agreement to buy or sell a currency in exchange for another at a specified price on a specified date. Unlike forward contracts, futures contracts are standardized to enable trading in organized exchanges, such as the Chicago Mercantile Exchange. Although the terms of forward contracts are negotiated between a bank and its customer, futures contracts have standard amounts and maturity periods. Futures contracts are especially useful for hedging transaction exposure.

A **currency option** gives the purchaser the right, but not the obligation, to buy (sell) a certain amount of foreign currency at a set exchange rate within a specified length of time. The seller of the option must sell (buy) the currency at a time specified by the option buyer at the price originally set. Currency options typically are traded on organized exchanges, such as the International Securities Exchange (www.ise.com) and the Philadelphia Stock Exchange (PHLX; www.nasdaqtrader.com), and only for major currencies.[23]

There are two types of options. A *call option* is the right, but not the obligation, to buy a currency at a specified price within a specific period (called an *American option*) or on a specific date (called a *European option*).[24] A *put option* is the right to sell the currency at a specified

Forward contract
A contract to exchange two currencies at a specified exchange rate on a set future date.

Futures contract
An agreement to buy or sell a currency in exchange for another at a specified price on a specified date.

Currency option
A contract that gives the purchaser the right, but not the obligation, to buy a certain amount of foreign currency at a set exchange rate within a specified length of time.

EXHIBIT 10.7

An Example of Hedging in the Foreign-Exchange Market

Scenario: Dow Chemical sells merchandise to a German importer for €100,000, payable in 90 days. Given that the U.S. dollar - euro spot exchange rate 90 days from now is not known today, Dow faces uncertainty regarding how much it will be receiving from its German customer in U.S. dollar terms. To hedge against this risk, Dow enters into a forward contract with a bank to sell €100,000 90 days from now at an exchange rate of €1 = $1.45 agreed upon today, ensuring that it receives a known dollar amount in future.

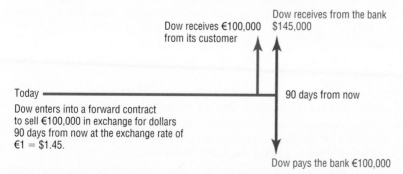

Dow receives €100,000 from its customer

Dow receives from the bank $145,000

Today

90 days from now

Dow enters into a forward contract to sell €100,000 in exchange for dollars 90 days from now at the exchange rate of €1 = $1.45.

Dow pays the bank €100,000

Outcome: Today, Dow is able to see that the €100,000 it will be receiving from its European customer will be worth $145,000 regardless of how much the actual spot price of the euro is 90 days from now.

Currency swap
An agreement to exchange one currency for another according to a specified schedule.

price. Each option is for a specific amount of currency. Options are useful as an insurance policy or disaster hedge against harmful currency movements.

In a **currency swap**, two parties agree to exchange a given amount of one currency for another and, after a specified period of time, give back the original amounts. Thus, a swap is a simultaneous spot and forward transaction. When the agreement is activated, the parties exchange the base amount (the principal) at the current spot rate. Usually, each party must pay interest on the principal too. If Party A loaned dollars and borrowed euros, it pays interest in euros and receives interest in dollars. Let's give an example. Suppose an MNE agrees to pay 4 percent compounded annually on a euro principal of €1,000,000 and receive 5 percent compounded annually on a U.S. dollar principal of $1,300,000 every year for two years. As a result, it will receive €1,000,000 and pay $1,300,000 today. It will then pay €40,000 annual interest and receive $65,000 annual interest for 2 years. At the end of the second year, the MNE will receive $1,300,000 and pay €1,000,000.

Best Practice in Minimizing Currency Exposure

Managing currency risk across many countries is challenging. Management must stay informed about the firm's evolving exposures as well as shifting laws, regulations, and market conditions. Managers need to pursue a systematic approach to minimize currency risk.

Exhibit 10.8 presents guidelines that managers can use to minimize currency risk. The last recommendation, maintaining strategic flexibility in manufacturing and sourcing, is an ultimate solution. If the firm operates in numerous markets, each with varying degrees of currency, economic, and political stability, it will be well positioned to optimize its operations. For example, Dell outsources parts and components from various countries. It can quickly shift sourcing from one country or supplier to another, depending on the favorability of exchange rates and other factors.

 MyManagementLab   Watch It! 1
If your professor has assigned this, go to the Assignments section of **mymanagementlab.com** to complete the video exercise titled Yongshua USA, LLC: Value of Yuan in China.

EXHIBIT 10.8 Managerial Guidelines for Minimizing Currency Risk

1. *Seek expert advice.* Initially, management should obtain expert help from banks and consultants to set up programs and strategies that minimize risk.
2. *Centralize currency management within the MNE.* Although some currency management activities may be delegated to local managers, company headquarters should set basic guidelines for the subsidiaries to follow.
3. *Decide on the level of risk the firm can tolerate.* The level varies, depending on the nature of the project, amount of capital at risk, and management's tolerance for risk.
4. *Devise a system to measure exchange-rate movements and currency risk.* The system should provide ongoing feedback to help management develop appropriate risk-minimizing strategies.
5. *Monitor changes in key currencies.* Exchange rates fluctuate constantly. Continuous monitoring can avert costly mistakes.
6. *Be wary of unstable currencies or those subject to exchange controls.* The manager should deal in stable, readily convertible currencies. Be wary of government restrictions that affect the ability to exchange currencies.
7. *Monitor long-term economic and regulatory trends.* Exchange-rate shifts usually follow evolving trends such as rising interest rates, inflation, labor unrest, and the installation of new governments.
8. *Distinguish economic exposure from transaction and translation exposures.* Managers often focus on reducing transaction and translation exposures. However, the long-run effects of economic exposure on company performance can produce even greater harm.
9. *Emphasize flexibility in international operations.* A flexible production and outsourcing strategy means the firm can shift production and outsourcing to various nations to benefit from favorable exchange rates.

Managing the Diversity of International Accounting and Tax Practices

Accounting systems differ around the world. There are dozens of approaches for determining company profits, R&D expenditures, and cost of goods sold.[25] Balance sheets and income statements vary internationally, not just in language, currency, and format but also in their underlying accounting principles. Financial statements prepared according to the rules of one country may be difficult to compare with those of another.

Source: Tifonimages/Fotolia

Transparency is the degree to which companies regularly reveal information about their financial condition and accounting practices. Pictured here is the stock exchange in Santiago, Chile, one of several countries attracting more inward investment by improving transparency in their business sectors.

Transparency in Financial Reporting

Local accounting practices determine the degree of transparency in the reporting of financial information. **Transparency** is the degree to which companies regularly reveal substantial information about their financial condition and accounting practices. The more transparent a nation's accounting systems, the more regularly, comprehensively, and reliably the nation's public firms report their financial results to creditors, stockholders, and the government. Transparency facilitates better managerial decision making and lets investors accurately evaluate company performance. Chile, Costa Rica, and the Czech Republic have attracted greater FDI by increasing the transparency of their regulatory systems. By contrast, most developing economies have confusing accounting systems, delayed financial reporting, and published information that is unreliable or incomplete. After the global financial crisis that began in 2008, governments and central banks in Asia, Europe, and the Americas increased the transparency and strictness of their accounting standards. They also strengthened supervision of banks and other financial institutions.[26]

10.6 Understand how to manage the diversity of international accounting and tax practices.

Transparency
The degree to which companies regularly reveal substantial information about their financial condition and accounting practices.

Trends Toward Harmonization

The growth of international business has pressured multinational firms and international organizations to harmonize world accounting systems. Organizations such as the International Accounting Standards Board (IASB), the United Nations, the European Union, and the Asociación Interamericana de Contabilidad (Interamerican Association of Accounting) have sought improvements in accounting measurement, disclosure, and auditing. The IASB is attempting to develop a single set of high-quality, understandable, and enforceable global accounting standards.

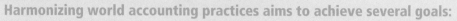

Harmonizing world accounting practices aims to achieve several goals:

- Reduce the cost of preparing financial statements.
- Increase the efficiency of consolidating financial information from various countries.
- Enhance the reliability of financial reporting by increasing comparability and transparency of accounting practices.
- Facilitate international investment in securities and ventures by helping investors and managers make better decisions.

Harmonization is particularly important to MNEs that seek foreign investors by listing on foreign stock exchanges. More than 120 countries require or allow the use of International

Financial Reporting Standards (IFRS; www.ifrs.com) in public company accounting. In the United States, firms comply with Generally Accepted Accounting Practices (GAAP). However, many large U.S. firms, such as Procter & Gamble, use IFRS standards in their foreign subsidiaries. Europe's IASB and the U.S. Financial Accounting Standards Board have worked to harmonize GAAP and IFRS. However, the effort has been delayed in light of practical and political considerations in Europe and the United States.[27]

Consolidating the Financial Statements of Subsidiaries

A critical task in international accounting is *foreign currency translation*, or translating data denominated in foreign currencies into the firm's functional currency. Each of the firm's foreign subsidiaries normally maintains its financial records in the currency of the country where it is located. When subsidiary results are consolidated into headquarters' financial statements, they must be expressed in the parent's functional currency. Consolidation also facilitates headquarters' efforts to plan, evaluate, and control the firm's activities around the world.

When headquarters consolidates financial records, foreign currencies are translated into the functional currency by using one of two methods: the current rate method or the temporal method. The **current rate method** translates foreign currency balance sheets and income statements at the current exchange rate. That is, the method uses the spot exchange rate in effect on the day (in the case of balance sheets) or for the period (in the case of income statements) the statements are prepared. This method is typically used when translating records of foreign subsidiaries that are considered separate entities rather than part of the parent firm's operations. Consider Computershare, an Australian firm that markets financial software through its network of subsidiaries worldwide. The company translates the financial statements of its subsidiaries by using the current rate method because these subsidiaries are stand-alone legal entities. Amounts payable and receivable in foreign currencies are converted to Australian dollars at the exchange rate in effect on the day of consolidation.[28]

The current rate results in gains and losses, depending on the exchange rates in effect during the translation period. For example, the value of income received in a foreign currency six months earlier may differ substantially from its value on the day it is translated. For firms with extensive international operations, the accounting translation method can strongly influence company performance and valuation.

When firms use the **temporal method**, the choice of exchange rate depends on the underlying method of valuation. If assets and liabilities are normally valued at historical cost, they are translated at historical rates. That is, they are translated at the exchange rates in effect when the assets were acquired. If assets and liabilities are normally valued at market cost, they are translated at the current rate of exchange. Thus, monetary items such as cash, receivables, and payables are translated at the current exchange rate. Nonmonetary items such as inventory, property, plant, and equipment are translated at historical rates.

According to U.S. accounting standards, if the functional currency of the subsidiary is that of the local operating environment (for example, if the yen is the main currency the Japanese subsidiary of a U.S. multinational firm uses), the company must use the current rate method. If the functional currency is the parent's currency, the MNE must use the temporal method. The choice of method results in different profitability and other performance outcomes.

International Taxation

In the countries where they operate, companies pay direct taxes, indirect taxes, sales taxes, and value-added taxes, among others. *Direct taxes* are typically imposed on income from profits, capital gains, royalties, interest, and dividends. *Indirect taxes* apply to firms that license or franchise products and services or that charge interest. In effect, the local government withholds some percentage of royalty payments or interest charges as tax. A *sales tax* is a flat percentage tax on the value of goods or services sold. It is paid by the ultimate user of the good or service. A *value-added tax* (*VAT*) is payable at each stage of processing in the value chain of a product or service. VAT is calculated as a percentage of the difference between the sale and purchase price of a product. The tax is common in Canada, Europe, and Latin America. Each business in a product's value chain is required to bill the VAT to its customers and pay the tax on its

Current rate method
Translation of foreign currency balance sheet and income statements at the current exchange rate—the spot exchange rate in effect on the day or for the period when the statements are prepared.

Temporal method
Translation of foreign currency balance sheet and income statements at an exchange rate that varies with the underlying method of valuation.

purchases, crediting the amounts it paid against the amounts due on its own activities. The net result is a tax on the added value of the good.

The most common form of direct tax is the *corporate income tax*. Exhibit 10.9 provides rates for a sample of countries. It is called *corporation tax* in some localities. It affects international planning because it encourages managers to organize business operations in ways that minimize the tax, usually by deducting business expenses from revenues. In most countries, firms reduce their tax burden substantially by taking deductions and allowances specified by national laws. MNEs employ various tax avoidance strategies; thus, the *effective* rate of taxation is often much lower than that indicated in Exhibit 10.9.

Income tax influences the timing, size, and composition of company investment in plant and equipment, R&D, inventories, and other assets. The exhibit reveals that many countries have reduced tax rates because they recognize high taxes can discourage investment.[29] In Canada, the corporate income tax was reduced from 36 percent in 2004 to 27 percent in 2014.[30] In China, the rate went from 33 to 25 percent. Ireland has the lowest income tax rate, about 13 percent. The low tax is part of Ireland's effort to attract FDI and stimulate business.

Almost since its founding in 1903, the U.S. automaker Ford sold cars in Canada, Japan, and other countries. At one time, whenever Ford sold cars in Canada, it was required to pay direct taxes on its income in both Canada and the United States.[31] Because of a lack of harmony in international tax rules, many MNEs were subject to double taxation, which reduced company

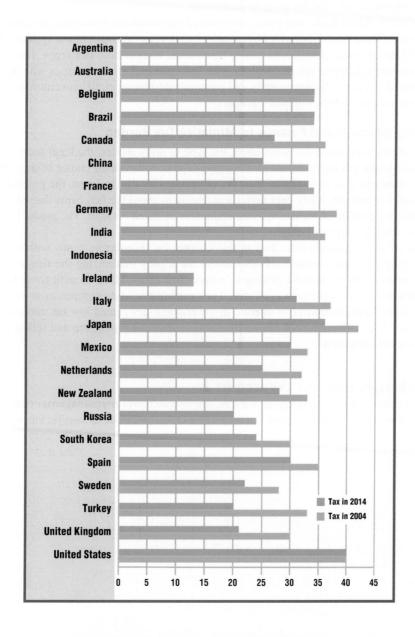

EXHIBIT 10.9

Corporate Income Tax Rates in Selected Countries (as a percent of corporate income, rounded to the nearest whole percent)

Source: Based on KPMG International, "KPMG's Corporate Tax Rates Survey 2004," www.us.kpmg.com; "Corporate & Indirect Tax Rate Survey 2014," http://www.kpmg.com.

earnings and discouraged firms from investing abroad. To resolve the problem, most countries signed tax treaties with their trading partners that help ensure that firms pay an appropriate amount of tax. A typical tax treaty between country A and country B states that, if the firm pays income tax in A, it does not pay the tax in B (or vice versa). This result is accomplished with foreign tax credits—an automatic decrease in domestic tax liability when the firm can prove it has already paid income tax abroad. Or the firm may be liable to pay tax in each country, but the amount is adjusted so the total is no more than the maximum tax in either country. Most tax treaties also obligate nations to assist each other in tax enforcement. This helps prevent tax evasion by ensuring that MNEs pay taxes in one country or the other.

Because tax systems vary around the world, MNEs have an incentive to structure their global activities in ways that minimize taxes. They take advantage of tax havens like the Bahamas, Luxembourg, Singapore, and Switzerland, either by establishing operations in them or by funneling business transactions through them. Nissan and Kraft Foods moved their European headquarters to Switzerland to take advantage of lower corporate tax rates. The Irish rock band U2 moved its music-publishing business to the Netherlands to shelter its songwriting royalties from taxation. Apple has subsidiaries in low-tax rate countries such as Ireland, the Netherlands, Luxembourg, and the British Virgin Islands.[32] The use of tax havens for tax reduction is generally legal but is restricted by some governments. The United States has limited firms' ability to move major operations to such countries.[33] Corporations sometimes use tax havens to park revenues until needed elsewhere for trade or investment.

The OECD, World Bank, and other international organizations discourage the wrongful use of tax havens. These organizations lobby countries to develop transparent tax systems. The EU and OECD also pressure countries to reduce harmful tax competition. In Europe, foreign investors tend to establish operations in countries with low taxes and avoid countries with high taxes. Because this discourages European unity and economic development, EU governments are seeking to harmonize taxation throughout Europe.

Managing International Finance to Minimize Tax Burden

Taxation affects managerial decisions about the type of entry modes, the legal form of foreign operations, transfer pricing, methods for obtaining capital, and even the choice of target markets. Financial managers seek to minimize their tax obligations legally. In Japan, the government imposes a high tax on malt, a key beer ingredient. Partly to avoid the tax, firms that brew beer in Japan employ a distillation technology that eliminates the need for malt. The product tastes like beer but is actually a type of liquor.

Many of the techniques described in this chapter for transferring funds within the MNE and managing currency exposure are also useful for legally minimizing the firm's taxes. For example, many firms use transfer pricing to reduce their taxes. MNEs benefit from differences in tax rates and systems between countries. They establish holding companies or finance corporations in particular countries or operate in government-designated low-tax zones known as *foreign trade zones*. The approach allows the firms to structure production and selling activities to minimize tax obligations.

MyManagementLab   **Watch It! 2**

If your professor has assigned this, go to the Assignments section of **mymanagementlab.com** to complete the video exercise titled Did Burger King Defect to Canada to Save Tax Money?

CLOSING CASE   International Financial Management at Tektronix

An oscilloscope is a measuring device with a display screen that checks the condition of electronic equipment. In 1946, founders of U.S.-based Tektronix, Inc. (www.tek.com) built their first oscilloscope from electronic parts purchased from government surplus sales. Those oscilloscopes and other measuring devices contributed greatly to the development of computers and communications equipment.

TEK, as the firm is known, became a public company in 1963 and employs several thousand employees in dozens of countries. The firm earns roughly half its annual sales from North America, 25 percent from Europe, 15 percent from Japan, and the rest from other countries. TEK owes part of its original success to venture capital funding. However, the majority of its capital comes from equity financing and debt sources.

International Operations

TEK launched its first foreign distributor in Sweden in 1948. In later years, the firm set up many sales subsidiaries abroad. It developed joint ventures in Japan (Sony-TEK) and China to distribute TEK products in those countries. It also established manufacturing plants in Germany, Italy, and Malaysia. TEK still manufactures most of its products in the United States, whereas competitors HP, Kodak, and Xerox have manufacturing plants in numerous countries around the world. TEK management prefers to centralize manufacturing to synchronize production with R&D, ensure quality control, and exploit economies of scale.

Because TEK manufactures in the United States and sells abroad, it has substantial foreign-exchange exposure. Most of TEK's foreign sales are invoiced in local country currencies. If the U.S. dollar strengthens against those currencies, TEK's profits are reduced when it converts local country revenues into U.S. dollars. TEK also sources many inputs from abroad, which creates currency risks in its accounts payable.

For financial accounting, many of TEK's non-U.S. subsidiaries use their local country currencies as their functional currency. Thus, assets and liabilities are translated into U.S. dollars at end-of-period exchange rates. Income and expense items are translated at the average rate during the accounting period. To minimize currency risk, management deals proactively with transaction, translation, and economic exposures.

Tax-Related Decisions

In recent years, countries such as France and Germany have increased their tax audits of foreign firms' local country subsidiaries. To help address these and other tax challenges, TEK centralized all its European treasury functions, including cash management, inventory, and receivables, to the firm's subsidiary in England. In addition, the firm sets all the pricing for its markets worldwide at company headquarters. Such approaches provide efficiencies in company financial activities, simplify tax preparation, and enhance TEK's ability to use foreign tax credits. The goal is to minimize TEK's average tax rate legally across all its markets, which had been running at 32 percent.

Currency Risk Management

TEK has employed currency hedging selectively. Not all risks can be profitably hedged because of the high cost of banking fees and interest charges. As a result, TEK has experienced foreign-exchange losses in the past. To help minimize these losses, management established a unit at headquarters responsible for assessing and managing currency risk. TEK managers obtain intelligence from online sources and the forecasting departments of large banks and regularly monitor changes in key national currencies. Among the approaches that TEK applies are multilateral netting, offsetting cash flows, a centralized depository, forward contracts, and currency options.

Multilateral Netting

TEK has many ongoing transactions with and among its subsidiaries. Its financial managers can strategically reduce cash transfers, transaction costs, and bank fees by eliminating offsetting cash flows between headquarters and the local country subsidiaries. In TEK's multilateral netting process, all subsidiaries report to headquarters what is owed in foreign currencies to other subsidiaries, customers, suppliers, and headquarters. Financial managers then advise each subsidiary how much to pay to minimize the number and amount of intersubsidiary cash transfers. Management also matches hedging instruments with the firm's most pressing currency exposures. The launch of the euro simplified international transactions and lessened the need for some netting operations in Europe.

Offsetting Cash Flows

Whenever possible, management consolidates accounts receivable and accounts payable, matching them against one another. If TEK owes a French supplier 800,000 euros, it can grant a trade credit in the amount of 800,000 euros to a German customer, making the receivable and payable offset each other in the same currency. TEK also has some flexibility to change the invoicing currency of its subsidiaries and affiliates—for example, by denominating some invoices from its Japan subsidiary in yen instead of dollars. Cash flows are also offset with counterbalanced investments in Asia and Europe and skillful transfer pricing and other intracorporate financing activities. If headquarters wants to spend $1 million to establish a new subsidiary in Europe, it will direct existing European subsidiaries to retain a similar amount of their earnings in euros. Then, instead of converting the foreign earnings into U.S. dollars, TEK uses the retained euro earnings to build the new subsidiary.

Centralized Depository

Although some currency management is delegated to local country managers, headquarters in the United States is in charge and sets guidelines for the subsidiaries to follow. Management pools funds into centralized depositories and directs them to subsidiaries where needed or invests them to generate income. Management also pools accounts receivable for some European subsidiaries into a regional depository. This approach makes receipt and dispersal of cash more manageable, creates economies of scale in the investment and other uses of excess cash, and reduces the need for local borrowing. The centralized approach also concentrates managerial expertise and financial services at one location. Finally, the firm employs an invoicing center that invoices foreign subsidiaries in the local currency but receives invoices in U.S. dollars.

Forward Contracts and Currency Options

TEK hedges against currency risk by taking positions in forward contracts. These instruments allow financial managers to buy or sell currency at a specific future date at an agreed-upon exchange rate. If there is much uncertainty about the value of a future receivable, management can guarantee a fixed exchange rate and minimize currency risk. The firm also employs currency options, contracts that grant the holder the right to buy or sell currency at a specified exchange rate during a specified period. TEK uses currency futures contracts with maturities of one to three months to mitigate currency risk. At any time, the firm's currency contracts can exceed $100 million. The downside is that TEK must pay substantial trading fees and other costs for its currency hedging activities.

Other Financial Developments

Some years ago, TEK undertook a major restructuring of company operations. The sale of a major division generated proceeds of more than $900 million. Management used the funds partly to pay down the firm's corporate debt. In comparison to its equity holdings, the firm's debt is modest and manageable. Management favors a low debt-to-equity ratio.

Although TEK regularly experiences fluctuations in sales and currency values, management has developed substantial expertise to weather difficult challenges. Careful planning and implementation of financial operations will help the firm continue to reign as the leader in oscilloscopes and other measuring equipment.

AACSB: Reflective Thinking Skills, Analytic Skills

Case Questions

10-4. What are the implications for currency risk of TEK focusing its manufacturing in the United States but generating most of its sales abroad? Competitors such as HP and Kodak are more geographically diversified in their sourcing. What advantages does this create for them?

10-5. The case lists various approaches TEK follows to minimize its exposure to currency risk. If hired by TEK, what other strategies and tactics would you recommend to reduce the firm's exposure even further? Justify your answer.

10-6. TEK management attempts to maintain a reasonable ratio of debt to equity. Most firms prefer relatively low levels of debt in their capital structures. Why? What other approaches could TEK use to generate financing for its international operations? What approaches can TEK use to transfer funds within its operations worldwide?

10-7. The case describes approaches TEK follows to minimize its international tax liability. Based on your reading of the chapter, how would you advise TEK management to reduce its taxes around the world further?

Sources: "Tektronix Finds Surprising Results from Net Promoter Scores," *B to B*, June 9, 2008, p. 14; "Danaher to Acquire Tektronix," *Canadian Electronics*, November/December 2007, p. 1; Danaher, Inc., 2013 Annual Report, Washington, DC; Joseph Epstein, "Did Rip Van Winkle Really Lift Its Head?" *Financial World*, April 8, 2006, pp. 42–45; Lori Ioannou, "Taxing Issues," *International Business*, March 1995, pp. 42–45; Marshall Lee, *Winning with People: The First 40 Years of Tektronix* (Beaverton, OR: Tektronix, Inc., 1986); Tim McElligott, "This Way Out: Rick Wills, Tektronix," *Telephony*, June 4, 2001, pp. 190–191; Arthur Stonehill, Jerry Davies, Randahl Finnessy, and Michael Moffett, "Tektronix (C)," *Thunderbird International Business Review* 46, No. 4 (July/August 2004), pp. 465–469; Tektronix, Inc., "Tektronix Named Finalist for 'Best in Test' 2010 Awards," press release, http://www.tek.com; Tektronix corporate profile http://www.hoovers.com; Tektronix corporate website, www.tek.com; Tektronix, Inc. *Marketline Company Profile*, January 29, 2015, pp. 1–21.

The case was written by Betty Feng and Lawrence Yu, under the supervision of S. Tamer Cavusgil.

END OF CHAPTER REVIEW

 MyManagementLab

Go to **mymanagementlab.com** to complete the problems marked with this icon .

Key Terms

arbitragers 300	currency swap 302	economic exposure 298
bond 293	current rate method 304	equity financing 289
consolidation 297	debt financing 289	Eurobond 293
currency option 301	direct quote 299	Eurocurrency 293

Summary

In this chapter, you learned about:

- **Choosing a capital structure.**

  International financial management involves the acquisition and use of funds for cross-border trade and investment activities. The capital structure is the mix of long-term financing—**equity financing** and **debt financing**—that the firm uses to support its international activities. Equity financing is obtained by selling shares in stock markets and by retaining earnings. Debt financing is obtained by borrowing money from banks and other financial institutions or by selling bonds.

- **Raising funds for the firm.**

  Companies can raise money in the **global capital market**. Equity financing can be obtained in the **global equity market**—the stock exchanges throughout the world where investors and firms meet to buy and sell shares of stock. In terms of debt financing, firms may borrow in the **Eurocurrency** market, which uses currency banked outside its country of origin. Firms also sell bonds—often **foreign bonds** or **Eurobonds**—in the global bond market. In addition, MNEs can support the operations of their subsidiaries through **intracorporate financing**.

- **Managing working capital and cash flow.**

  Net working capital is the difference between current assets and current liabilities. Firms often manage intracorporate funds by developing a *centralized depository*, into which funds are pooled from the firm's network of subsidiaries and affiliates to distribute to units that need funds. The various methods for transferring funds within the MNE include *dividend remittances, royalty payments, transfer pricing*, and *fronting loans*. A **fronting loan** is a loan from a parent firm to its subsidiary, channeled through a bank or other financial intermediary. **Multilateral netting** is the process of strategically reducing the number of cash transfers between the parent and subsidiaries by eliminating the offsetting cash flows between these entities. **Tax havens** are countries with low taxes that are friendly to business and inward investment.

- **Performing capital budgeting.**

  Capital budgeting rests on analyses that management undertakes to evaluate the viability of proposed international projects. Management calculates the *net present value* of a proposed project to decide whether it should be implemented.

- **Managing currency risk.**

  There are three main types of currency exposure: transaction exposure, economic exposure, and translation exposure. A firm faces **transaction exposure** when outstanding accounts receivable or payable are denominated in foreign currencies. **Economic exposure** results from exchange-rate fluctuations affecting the pricing of products, the cost of inputs, and the value of foreign investments. **Translation exposure** arises as the firm combines the financial statements of foreign subsidiaries into the parent's financial statements, a process called **consolidation**. Currency trading takes place between banks and currency brokers, often on behalf of multinational firms. Currency traders include **hedgers, speculators**, and **arbitragers**. Managers attempt to forecast exchange rates to minimize their firm's exposure to currency risk. Approaches for minimizing exposure to currency risk include centralizing currency management, measuring currency risk, monitoring long-term trends, and emphasizing flexibility in international operations. Firms also employ **hedging**, the use of specialized financial instruments to balance positions in foreign currencies. Key hedging tools include **forward contracts, futures contracts, currency options**, and **currency swaps**.

- **Managing the diversity of international accounting and tax practices.**

  Financial statements prepared in one country may be difficult to compare with those from other countries. Through **transparency**, firms regularly and comprehensively reveal reliable information about their financial condition and accounting practices. Various factors account for differences in national accounting systems. Several international organizations are aiming to harmonize cross-national accounting practices. Managers use the **current rate method** and the **temporal method** for currency translation. Internationally, firms seek to minimize taxes, which consist of direct taxes, indirect taxes, sales taxes, and value-added taxes. Governments use two major methods for eliminating multiple taxation: the foreign tax credit and tax treaties.

Test Your Comprehension AACSB Reflective Thinking Skills

⭐ **10-8.** What are the components of the capital structure in the typical MNE? What about MNEs in Japan and Germany? What about a typical firm in your country?

10-9. From a managerial perspective, what are the advantages and disadvantages of financing obtained from each of the following: equity, debt, and intracorporate sources?

10-10. Suppose you had to raise capital to fund international value-adding activities and investment projects. From what types of sources (e.g., stock markets) would you most likely obtain each type of financing? What are financial centers and where are they located?

10-11. Identify five global tax havens. Explain their purpose and their attraction for global businesses.

⭐ **10-12.** Why would an organization use net present value analysis in order to evaluate domestic and

10-13. The European market is a good for a British manufacturer. The problem is that sales are falling as Sterling strengthens against the Euro. What can the British manufacturer do to protect it sales?

⭐ **10-14** A French business needs $30,000 for an immediate transaction, what exchange rate would they pay?

10-15. What are the major methods for translating foreign–currency denominated financial statements into the financial statements of the parent firm?

Apply Your Understanding AACSB: Reflective Thinking Skills, Analytic Skills, Ethical Understanding and Reasoning Abilities

10-16. Marite Perez is CEO of Havana, Inc., a large manufacturer of high-tech medical equipment based in North Miami Beach, Florida. The firm makes vital signs monitors, MRIs, X-ray machines, and other equipment for exploratory medical diagnostics. Marite wants to expand the firm rapidly into foreign markets. To accomplish this, she plans to invest much money in developing new products and establishing production and marketing subsidiaries abroad. What can Marite do to raise capital for these projects? What are the various methods that Marite might employ to raise capital for her firm? What are the advantages and disadvantages associated with each?

10-17. Michael Norton is the president of Liberty Enterprises, a large MNE based in Singapore that makes computers and related peripherals. The firm has many subsidiaries around the world. Demand for Liberty's products has been growing in Asia and Europe, especially in Indonesia, Japan, France, and Spain. Michael has always used external sources to finance the firm's working capital needs. Currently,

with rapidly expanding business, he needs to access more working capital. What is the feasibility of raising funds through intracorporate sources? What methods can Michael use to transfer funds within the firm? What should Michael know about multilateral netting?

10-18. *Ethical Dilemma:* Suppose you are president of West Turner Bank (WTB). WTB made loans for major construction projects in countries in Eastern Europe and North Africa. However, WTB's fortunes declined in recent years, and the bank now faces financial ruin. WTB senior management decided to call in loans made to these countries to strengthen the bank's deteriorating finances. That is, management decided to force borrowers in the construction projects to repay their loans immediately. You know that calling the loans will cause thousands of workers in the affected countries to lose their jobs. What should you do? Use the ethical framework in Chapter 4 to analyze this situation. Can you find any creative solutions to the dilemma?

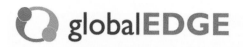 **globalEDGE** | **INTERNET EXERCISES**
(www.globalEDGE.msu.edu)

AACSB: Reflective Thinking Skills, Analytic Skills

Refer to Chapter 1, page 54, for instructions on how to access and use globalEDGE™.

10-19. The World Federation of Exchanges is the organization that represents major stock exchanges worldwide. Visit the online portal at www.world-exchanges.org and use the annual report of the Federation as well as detailed statistics available on individual exchanges to answer the following questions.

   a. What percentage of the world market capitalization is represented by the top 10 exchanges?

   b. For the most recent year, what exchanges accounted for the largest increases in market capitalization?

   c. Which exchanges have seen the greatest increase recently in the number of firms listed?

   d. Worldwide consolidation trends have also affected the stock exchanges. A good example is the merger of Paris-based Euronext with the NYSE. What are the underlying causes of these cross-border mergers?

10-20. Suppose your job is to ensure that your firm has enough foreign exchange on hand to pay outstanding accounts payable. Assume your firm owes 1 million yen to a Japanese supplier, which is due exactly 60 days from now. Your task is to exchange dollars for the right amount of yen. To do this, you can enter a contract with a bank today to buy 1 million yen 60 days forward or wait 60 days and buy 1 million yen at the then-prevailing spot exchange rate. Which alternative do you prefer, and why? If you expect the spot rate 60 days from now will be the same as it is today, what is the expected dollar cost of buying 1 million yen in the spot market 60 days from now? How many dollars will it cost you to obtain 1 million yen if you entered the forward contract? To obtain the spot exchange rates, go to www.ft.com and click Markets and then choose Currencies or go to globalEDGE™ and enter "exchange rates" in the search engine.

10-21. Many corporate websites provide financial information, including financial statements, as well as other information about companies' status and progress. As an institutional investor, you are thinking of investing in one of the following firms: Diageo (www.diageo.com), the premium drinks firm; Vivendi (www.vivendi.com), a French telecom; Grupo Carso (www.gcarso.com.mx), a major Mexican retailing conglomerate; and SK Telecom (www.sktelecom.com), the largest wireless communication services provider in South Korea. Look up each firm's corporate website. Based on the information provided, answer the following questions:

   a. How would you rate the transparency of each firm?

   b. How inclined are you to invest in each firm, based on the information provided? Justify your answer.

   c. In terms of transparency and investor-oriented information, which site is best?

   d. Based on the best site, what recommendations would you make to the firm that owns the weakest site to improve its transparency and attract investors?

CAREER TOOLBOX

Finding the Best Location for a Bank Branch Abroad

Banks are a critical participant in the world economy. They provide capital, foreign exchange, and other forms of money to national economies. Banks are expanding their operations to new markets around the world. Branch banking is a relatively cost-effective way to enter foreign markets. Under a branch banking model, the bank opens branches in target countries.

The problem of choosing the best markets for locating bank branches abroad is complex. What makes a good location? What types of indicators should be considered? Before locating new branches abroad, managers ascertain the most appropriate location to maximize bank performance. The successful international manager investigates the best locations in advance. Given the number of potential locations and the variables to consider, deciding on the best locations is challenging.

In this exercise, you will acquire skills on researching monetary and financial statistics for international markets, factors to consider when locating bank branches abroad, and understanding how these factors relate to bank performance and competitive advantages abroad.

Assume you are a manager at Barclays, Citibank, or some other large bank. Management wants to establish additional bank branches abroad. Your task is to identify the most appropriate foreign location for setting up a bank branch. Based on your analysis, make a recommendation on which country is most promising.

Background

Banking is a critical industry for various reasons. It has become truly international for various reasons. These include growing interdependence of national economies, expansion of world trade, deregulation of financial services, and advances in communications and information technologies.

Large banks often establish foreign branches. The best approach is through branch banking, that is, setting up bank branches at customers' locations abroad. Branch banks provide much the same financial services as local banks abroad. Banks that expand internationally help create jobs, supply capital to local economies, and contribute to the tax base.

However, the international environment entails various risks. When banks establish branches abroad, they want to maximize conditions for success and minimize risk. Banks seek the best markets and the most effective locations to grow and deliver services to current and new customers.

To complete this exercise in your MyLab, go to the Career Toolbox.

MyManagementLab

Go to **mymanagementlab.com** for Auto-graded writing questions as well as the following Assisted-graded writing questions:

 10-22. What are the major tasks in international financial management?

 10-23. Summarize the various markets and sources from which MNE financial managers can raise funds for the firm.

 10-24. MyManagementLab Only—comprehensive writing assignment for this chapter.

Appendix

The Math of Currency Trading

News outlets such as the *Financial Times* and the *Wall Street Journal*, as well as online sources, publish bilateral exchange-rate tables that list currency values in terms of other currencies. These tables report bid–ask midpoints and so do not represent prices that can actually be traded in the market. Here is an example:

	£	€	¥	$
U.K. pound (£)	1	0.9051	0.006865	0.6329
Euro (€)	1.1049	1	0.007585	0.6993
Japanese yen (¥)	145.68	131.85	1	92.20
U.S. dollar ($)	1.5800	1.4300	0.010846	1

The numeric cells contain the number of units of the currency in the left-most column that equal one unit of the currencies along the top row of the table (e.g., £0.9051/€1). Rather than trying to remember this convention, it is usually easier to infer the convention used in these tables from the values of your domestic currency. In the preceding example, Japanese and U.S. residents are likely to know that the dollar/yen price of 92.20 reflects a yen-per-dollar exchange rate of ¥92.20/$1, rather than a dollar-per-yen price. This is a direct price for a Japanese resident and an indirect price for a U.S. resident. The yen-per-dollar price is then simply the reciprocal of the dollar-per-yen price:

$$1/(¥92.20/\$) = \$0.010846/¥$$

Note that the values in this table are *internally consistent*. Thus, the yen-per-pound exchange rate must equal the yen-per-dollar rate times the dollar-per-pound rate:

$$¥145.68/£ = (¥92.20/\$) = (\$1.5800/£)$$

Alternatively, the yen-per-pound rate can be calculated by dividing the yen-per-dollar rate by the pound-per-dollar rate:

$$¥145.68/£ = (¥92.20/\$) / (£0.6329/\$)$$

Keeping track of the currency units ensures that the answer has the correct units.

Exchange rates that do not involve the domestic currency are called *cross rates*. Cross rates for infrequently traded currencies can be calculated by comparing them against an actively traded currency such as the dollar. For example, the cross rate between the Chilean peso (CLP) and Japanese yen can be calculated by combining the CLP-per-dollar rate with the yen-per-dollar rate. If one U.S. dollar is worth 507.75 Chilean pesos, then the CLP-per-yen rate must be:

$$(CLP\ 507.15/\$) / (¥92.20/\$) = CLP\ 5.5005/¥$$

Again, it is important to keep track of the currency units to ensure the desired result.

Endnotes

1. Peter Yeoh, "Causes of the Global Financial Crisis: Learning from the Competing Insights," *International Journal of Disclosure and Governance* 7, No. 1 (2010), pp. 42–69.

2. Ernst and Young, "Globalisation Act II: Team Europe Defends Its Goals," (results of 2006 survey on the attractiveness of Europe) (Paris: Ernst & Young, 2006).

3. Bank for International Settlements, Statistics Division, http://www.bis.org; OICU-IOSCO, *Securities Market Risk Outlook 2014–2015*, www.iosco.org.

4. Richard Dobbs, Susan Lund, Jonathan Woetzel, and Mina Mutafchieva, "Debt and (Not Much) Deleveraging," February 2015, *McKinsey Global Institute*, www.mckinsey.com/mgi; Charles Roxburgh, Susan Lund, Richard Dobbs, James Manyika, and Haihao Wu, "The Emerging Equity Gap: Growth and Stability in the New Investor Landscape," December 2011, *McKinsey Global Institute*, www.mckinsey.com/mgi; Richard Murphy, "New Global Hot Spots for Investors," *Fortune*, December 26, 2011, pp. 125–133.

5. World Federation of Exchanges, *2015 WFE Market Highlights*, January 31, 2015, www.world-exchanges.org; World Federation of Exchanges, "Strong Increase of Equity Trading Volumes (+17.4%) in 2014," January 31, 2015, www.world-exchanges.org; New York Stock Exchange, "Listings Directory" and "Current List of All Non-U.S. Issuers," www.nyse.com.

6. K. Lewis, "Trying to Explain Home Bias in Equities and Consumption," *Journal of Economic Literature* 37 (1999), pp. 571–608.

7. Robert Cottrell, "Thinking Big: A Survey of International Banking," *Economist*, May 20, 2006, survey section; Daniel Inman, Deng Chao, and Nicole Hong, "An Opening in Great Wall of Stocks," *Wall Street Journal*, September 4, 2014, p. C3.

8. Cottrell (2006).

9. Steve Hanke, "When Currencies Falter," *Forbes*, June 8, 2009, p. 106; Michael Sesit and Craig Karmin, "How One Word Haunts the Dollar," *Wall Street Journal*, March 17, 2005, p. C16; Howard Simons, "Fighting the Next War in the Eurodollar Market," *Futures: News, Analysis & Strategies for Futures, Options & Derivatives Traders*, December 2014, pp. 32–34.

10. IBM, Inc., *2014 Annual Report*, http://www.ibm.com.

11. Here is an example of how transfer pricing works: Consider an MNE with subsidiaries in three countries. Suppose that subsidiary A operates in country A with high corporate income taxes, and subsidiary B operates in country B, a tax haven. One way to minimize taxes is for subsidiary A to sell merchandise to subsidiary B for a low transfer price. Subsidiary B then resells the merchandise to subsidiary C in the third country at a high transfer price. This results in lower overall taxes for subsidiary A because of its low profits, for subsidiary B because of country B's low tax rates, and for subsidiary C because the high cost of its purchase reduces its profits. Although this approach to transferring funds within the MNE is quite common, transfer pricing has some drawbacks. First, although transfer pricing between members of the corporate family is legal when carried out within reasonable limits, governments strongly disapprove of the practice of avoiding tax obligations. Thus, many governments impose policies that restrict transfer pricing. Coca-Cola's Japan subsidiary was fined 15 billion yen for making royalty payments from trademarks and products to its U.S. parent that Japan's National Tax Administration judged as too high. Second, transfer pricing can distort the financial results of foreign subsidiaries. For instance, a subsidiary that is required to charge low prices for its exports may experience unusually low profitability, which harms its performance and can demoralize local staff. Third, some MNEs use artificial transfer prices to hide the poor results of a badly performing subsidiary or achieve other goals aimed at concealing the true performance of the firm.

12. Timor Mehpare and Seyhan Sipahi, "Fast-Food Restaurant Site Selection Factor Evaluation by the Analytic Hierarchy Process," *Business Review* 4 (2005), pp. 161–167.

13. Here is an illustration of net present value analysis: A U.S.-based MNE is considering an expansion project through its subsidiary in Mexico. The project requires an initial investment of 220 million Mexican pesos (MXP) and has an economic life of five years. The project is expected to generate annual after-tax cash flows of MXP120 million, MXP125 million, MXP150 million, MXP155 million, and MXP200 million, which will be remitted to the parent company during the next five years. The current spot exchange rate is MXP11/$1, and the spot rates are expected to be MXP11.10/$1, MXP11.25/$1, MXP11.50/$1, MXP11.55/$1, and MXP11.75/$1 for the next five years. Assuming that the appropriate discount rate for this project is 10 percent, what is the NPV of the project from the parent company's perspective? Should the MNE accept this project based on its NPV? Let's analyze. The U.S. cash flows of the project can be calculated as follows:

	0	1	2	3	4	5
Mexican peso cash flows	−MXP 220 Million	MXP 120 Million	MXP 125 Million	MXP 150 Million	MXP 155 Million	MXP 200 Million
Prevailing spot exchange rate	MXP 11/$1	MXP 11.10/$1	MXP 11.25/$1	MXP 11.50/$1	MXP 11.55/$1	MXP 11.75/$1
U.S. dollar cash flows	$20,000,000	$10,810,811	$11,111,111	$13,043,478	$13,419,913	$17,021,277

The NPV of the project can be calculated as follows:

$$NPV = -\$20,000,000 + \$10,810,811/(1+0.10)^1 + \$11,111,111/(1+0.10)^2 + \$13,043,478/(1+0.10)^3 + \$13,419,913/(1+0.10)^4 + \$17,021,277/(1+0.10)^5$$

NPV = $28,545,359

The MNE can accept the project because it has a positive NPV.

14. The discount rate used in the NPV analysis of international projects may be higher due to a premium for additional risks involved in doing business internationally. Management may insist on a higher level of required return in the net present value calculation because higher country-political and currency risks indicate a higher probability of venture failure. A firm might apply a 7 percent discount rate to potential investments in Germany and Japan because those countries enjoy political and economic stability. However, the same firm might use a 14 percent discount rate for similar potential investments in Pakistan and Russia because those countries experience political and economic turmoil. The higher the discount rate, the higher the projected net cash flows must be for the investment to have a positive net present value contribution. Occasionally, the discount rate for international projects can be lower than for domestic ones. Risk arises from various sources, and management must systematically assess the range of potentially influential factors.

15. Reshma Kapadia, "The Currency Conundrum," *SmartMoney*, April 2012, pp. 78–82.

16. Robert Aliber, *Exchange Risk and International Finance* (New York: Wiley, 1979).

17. International Monetary Fund, "Currency Composition of Official Foreign Exchange Reserves (COFER)," March 31, 2015, www.imf.org; Kapadia (2012); James Ramage, "Currency-Trading Volumes Jump," *Wall Street Journal*, January 27, 2015, www.wsj.com.

18. Morten Bech, "FX Volume During the Financial Crisis and Now," Bank for International Settlements, March 2012, http://www.bis.org; Anchalee Worrachate and David Goodman, "Currency Trading at $5 Trillion a Day Surpassed Pre-Lehman High, BIS Says," *Bloomberg*, March 12, 2012, www.bloomberg.com; World Trade Organization, *International Trade Statistics 2014* (Geneva: World Trade Organization), www.wto.org.

19. Gordon Platt, "World's Best Foreign Exchange Banks 2005," *Global Finance* 19 (2005), pp. 24–33.

20. Adam Rombel, "The World's Best Internet Banks," *Global Finance* 16 (2002), pp. 37–38.

21. David Sedgwick, Diana Kurylko, Jamie LaReau, and Rick Kranz, "As Dollar Falls, Automakers Must Adjust Plans," *Automotive News Europe*, March 17, 2008, p. 16.

22. Ira Iosebashvili, "Capital Flees Russia, Damping Official Hopes over Putin's Win," *Wall Street Journal*, April 5, 2012, p. A8; *Moscow Times*, "Russian Capital Flight Slows to $32.6 Billion in First Quarter," April 10, 2015, pp. 20, 28.

23. Ariful Hoquea, Felix Chana, and Meher Manzur, "Efficiency of the Foreign Currency Options Market," *Global Finance Journal* 19, No. 2 (2008), pp. 157–170.

24. Here is a simple example of an option transaction from a familiar context. Say you are in the market to buy a house. You find one that you like, but you are not sure whether you want to buy it. At this stage, you opt to put a deposit down to have the seller keep his for-sale house for you for two weeks. Later, if you buy the house, the deposit counts toward the purchase price. If you do not buy the house, you lose your deposit. You have the option to buy the house at an agreed-upon price but not the obligation to do so.

25. W. Wallace and J. Walsh, "Apples to Apples: Profits Abroad," *Financial Executive*, May–June, 1995, pp. 28–31.

26. Hank Boerner, "Europe Faces Eagle Eye of US Financial Regulation," *European Business Forum* 21 (2005), pp. 46–49.

27. Paul Miller and Paul Bahnson, "The Demise of the Drive to Bring International Standard-Setting to the U.S.," *Accounting Today*, February 2012, pp. 16–17.

28. Computershare, *2003 Annual Report*, http://www.computershare.com.

29. Alan J. Auerbach and Martin Feldstein, *Handbook of Public Economics*, 3rd ed. (Amsterdam: North-Holland, 2001); Peter Cohn and Matthew Caminiti, "Corporate Taxes: The Multinational Advantage," *Bloomberg Businessweek*, January 24–30, 2011, p. 31; KPMG International, "Corporate & Indirect Tax Survey 2014," http://www.kpmg.com.

30. Mark Brown, "Why Investors Love Inversions," *Canadian Business*, Fall 2014, pp. 89–90; Jason Clemens, "Canada, Land of Smaller Government," *Wall Street Journal*, August 9, 2010, pA15.

31. Joseph Froomkin and Ira Wender, "Revenue Implications of United States Income Tax Treaties," *National Tax Journal* 7, No. 2 (1954), pp. 177–181.

32. Peter Coy and Jesse Drucker, "Profits on Overseas Holiday," *Bloomberg Businessweek*, March 21–27, 2011, pp. 64–69; Charles Duhigg and David Kocieniewski, "How Apple Sidesteps Billions in Taxes," *New York Times*, April 29, 2012, p. A1; Timothy Noah, "Bono, Tax Avoider," *Slate*, October 31, 2006, http://www.slate.com.

33. Dries Lesage, David McNair, and Mattias Vermeiren, "From Monterrey to Doha: Taxation and Financing for Development," *Development Policy Review* 28, No. 2 (2010), pp. 155–162; Brody Mullins, "Accenture Lobbyists Near Big Win on Securing Tax-Haven Status," *Wall Street Journal*, July 14, 2005, p. A2; Andrea Thomas, "Germany Debates Tax Cuts amid Rapid Rise in Revenue," *Wall Street Journal*, April 26–27, 2014, p. A8.

34. The authors gratefully acknowledge Professor Hakan Saraoglu, Bryant University, for his assistance in preparing Chapter 10–Financial Management and Accounting in the Global Firm.

Chapter 11

Strategy and Organization in the International Firm

Learning Objectives *After studying this chapter, you should be able to:*

11.1 Describe strategy in international business.

11.2 Understand building the global firm.

11.3 Describe the integration-responsiveness framework.

11.4 Learn to identify strategies based on the integration-responsiveness framework.

11.5 Understand organizational structure in international business.

11.6 Understand foreign market entry strategies.

IKEA's Strategies for Global Success

IKEA evolved from a small, Swedish company to become the leading global retailer of specialty furniture. Ingvar Kamprad founded the firm in Sweden in 1943. IKEA originally sold pens, picture frames, jewelry, and nylon stockings—anything Kamprad could sell at a low price. In 1950, IKEA began selling furniture and housewares. In the 1970s, the firm expanded into Europe and North America and began to grow rapidly. Total sales in 2015 exceeded $35 billion, making IKEA the world's largest furniture retailer. Usually located in major cities, IKEA stores are huge warehouse-style outlets that stock some 9,500 items. They include everything for the home—from sofas to plants to kitchen utensils.

IKEA's philosophy is to offer high-quality, well-designed furnishings at low prices. Its functional, utilitarian, and space-saving pieces have a distinctive Scandinavian style and are knock-down furniture, which the customer assembles at home.

IKEA's corporate offices are located in the Netherlands, Sweden, and Belgium. The firm employs numerous global strategies that enable its success. Product development, purchasing, and warehousing are located in Sweden. Headquarters designs and develops IKEA's global branding and product line, often collaborating closely with external suppliers. About 30 percent of IKEA products are made in Asia and two-thirds in Europe. A few items are sourced in North America to address the specific needs of that market. Approximately 90 percent of IKEA's product line is identical worldwide. Store managers constantly report market research to headquarters on sales and customer preferences.

IKEA targets moderate-income households with limited living space. The preferred market segment is progressive, well-educated people who care little about status. Targeting a global customer segment allows IKEA to offer standardized

Source: ITAR-TASS Photo Agency/Alamy

products at uniform prices. This strategy lowers the costs of international operations. IKEA's global strategy seeks scale economies by consolidating worldwide design, purchasing, and manufacturing.

Each IKEA store follows a centrally developed advertising strategy in which the catalogue and the catalogue app are the most important marketing tools. In 2015, more than 215 million copies of the catalogue were printed in 32 languages. It represents the largest circulation of a free publication in the world. The catalog is also available online (www.ikea.com). The catalogue is prepared in Sweden to ensure conformity with IKEA's cosmopolitan style. Each product has a unique proper name. IKEA uses Scandinavian rivers or cities for sofas (Henriksberg, Falkenberg), women's names for fabric (Linne, Mimmi, Adel), and men's names for wall units (Billy, Niklas, Ivar).

IKEA employees ("coworkers") worldwide are widely acknowledged as a key contributor to the firm's success. Corporate culture is informal, and the firm uses a flat organizational structure. There are few titles, no executive parking spaces, and no corporate dining rooms. Managers fly economy class and stay in inexpensive hotels. Most initiatives are developed at headquarters in Sweden and communicated to all stores worldwide. This speeds decision making and ensures that the IKEA culture is easily globalized. Management in each store is required to speak either English or Swedish to ensure efficient communications with headquarters.

IKEA organizes an anti-bureaucratic week each year in which managers wear sales clerks' uniforms and do everything from operating cash registers to driving forklifts. The system keeps managers in touch with all IKEA operations and close to suppliers, customers, and sales staff. The firm's culture emphasizes consensus-based decision making. This lets managers share their knowledge and skills with coworkers and helps employees and suppliers feel they are important members of a global organization. The strong appeal of global culture supports IKEA's continued growth.

IKEA manages approximately 315 stores, 20 franchises, 147,000 employees, 47 distribution centers, and 1,002 suppliers in 51 countries. IKEA chooses its markets strategically. The firm suspended investment in Russia because of burdensome government intervention. It has established several stores in key cities in China. Management is expanding to India but must deal with substantial government red tape. Elsewhere, IKEA faces much complexity in adapting to national markets regarding employment, operations, supplier relationships, government regulations, and customer preferences. Among other challenges, IKEA must figure out how to:

- Incorporate customer feedback and design preferences from diverse markets into decision making at headquarters.
- Reward employees and motivate suppliers despite varying business customs and expectations from country to country.
- Achieve the real benefits of international operations—efficiency on a global scale and learning—while remaining responsive to local needs.
- Keep designs standardized across markets yet be responsive to local preferences and trends.
- Delegate adequate autonomy to local store managers while retaining central control.

IKEA fared well during the recent global recession. Its value-oriented furniture and housewares appealed to customers during tough economic times.

Questions

11-1. What strategies and other approaches does IKEA follow that have allowed the firm to become the world's leading furniture retailer?

11-2. Describe IKEA's organizational culture. How does it contribute to the firm's success?

11-3. What strategic challenges does IKEA face going forward?

SOURCES: "IKEA's Russian Saga," *Business Eastern Europe*, January 17, 2011, p. 2; IKEA, *IKEA Group FY2014 Yearly Summary*, www.ikea.com; "IKEA: How the Swedish Retailer Became a Global Cult Brand," *Business Week*, November 14, 2005, http://www.businessweek.com; Beth Kowitt, "It's IKEA's World," *Fortune*, March 15, 2015, pp. 166–175; M. Lloyd, "IKEA Sees Opportunity During Hard Times," *Wall Street Journal*, February 18, 2009, p. B1; IKEA corporate website at http://www.IKEA-group.IKEA.com; IKEA company profile at http://www.hoovers.com; Amol Sharma, "IKEA Wary of Entering India," *Wall Street Journal*, January 24, 2012, p. B4.

As the IKEA opening case shows, multinational managers strive to coordinate sourcing, manufacturing, marketing, and other value-adding activities on a worldwide basis. They often adopt organization-wide standards and common processes. They also frequently seek to develop products that appeal to the broadest base of customers worldwide. Organizing the firm on a global scale is challenging. It requires skillfully configuring activities across diverse settings, integrating and coordinating these activities, and implementing common processes to ensure that the activities are performed optimally. In addition, the firm must simultaneously respond to the specific needs and conditions that characterize the individual locations where it does business. In this chapter, we discuss the role of strategy and organization, and the various company attributes that support them, in building the successful international firm. We also discuss company foreign market entry strategies. Entry strategies range from global sourcing, exporting, and licensing, to joint ventures and foreign direct investment. Let's begin by examining the role of strategy in international business.

Strategy in International Business

Strategy is a planned set of actions that managers employ to make best use of the firm's resources and core competencies to gain competitive advantage. When developing strategies, managers start by examining the firm's specific strengths and weaknesses. They then analyze the particular opportunities and challenges that confront the firm. Once they understand the firm's strengths, weaknesses, opportunities, and threats, managers then decide:

- which customers to target.
- what product lines to offer.
- how best to deal with competitors.
- how generally to configure and coordinate the firm's activities around the world.

International strategy is strategy carried out in two or more countries. MNE managers develop international strategies to allocate scarce company resources and configure value-adding activities on a worldwide scale, participate in major markets, implement valuable partnerships abroad, and engage in competitive moves in response to foreign rivals.[1]

Managers devise strategies that develop and ensure the firm's competitive advantages. The most widely accepted approach for building sustainable, competitive advantage in international business is that of Bartlett and Ghoshal.[2] These scholars argued the firm should simultaneously strive to develop:

- Global-scale efficiency in its value-chain activities.
- Multinational flexibility to manage diverse country-level risks and opportunities.
- Learn from operating internationally and exploit that learning on a worldwide basis.[3]

Thus, firms that want to become globally competitive must seek simultaneously three strategic objectives—efficiency, flexibility, and learning.[4] Let's review these next.

Efficiency

The firm must build efficient international value chains. Efficiency refers to lowering the cost of the firm's operations and activities on a global scale. MNEs with multiple value chains must pay special attention to how they organize their R&D, manufacturing, product sourcing, marketing, and customer service. For example, automotive companies seek economies of scale by concentrating manufacturing and sourcing in a limited number of locations. For Toyota (www.toyota.com), this means manufacturing in low-cost countries such as China and in major markets like the United States. Toyota works with its suppliers to that ensure they provide low-cost parts while maintaining quality. Its logistical operations for shipping its cars around the world are efficient and cost effective.

Flexibility

The firm must develop worldwide flexibility to accommodate diverse country-specific risks and opportunities. The diversity and volatility of international environments are especially challenging for managers. Successful firms are skillful at tapping local resources and exploiting local opportunities in the markets where they do business. The firm may develop contractual relationships with independent suppliers and distributors in some countries. It may engage in foreign direct investment in others. The firm may adapt its marketing and human resource practices to suit unique country conditions. Exchange rate fluctuations may prompt managers to switch to local sourcing or to adjust prices. The firm organizes its operations to ensure that it can respond to specific customer needs in individual markets, especially those critical to company performance.[5]

Learning

The firm must create the ability to learn from operating in international environments and exploit this learning on a worldwide basis. The diversity of the international environment

11.1 Describe strategy in international business.

Strategy
A planned set of actions that managers employ to make best use of the firm's resources and core competencies to gain competitive advantage.

presents the internationalizing firm with unique learning opportunities. By operating in various countries, the MNE learns and gains various new capabilities. For example, the firm can acquire:

- New technical and managerial know-how.
- New product ideas.
- Improved R&D capabilities.
- Partnering skills.
- The ability to survive in unfamiliar environments.

The firm's partners or subsidiaries capture and disseminate this learning throughout their corporate network. For example, Procter & Gamble (www.pg.com) is headquartered in the United States. Its Belgium research center developed a special water-softening technology to deal with Europe's hard water. The firm's subsidiary in Japan formulated a laundry detergent that works well in cold water. Japanese customers prefer cold-water washing. P&G assimilated these innovations into its global knowledge base and then applied the knowledge to the development of products for other markets around the world.

International business success is ultimately determined by the degree to which the firm masters all three skills—efficiency, flexibility, and learning. It is often difficult to excel in all three simultaneously. One firm may be highly efficient, whereas another excels at flexibility and a third at learning. Many Japanese firms achieved international success by developing highly efficient manufacturing systems. Numerous European firms succeeded internationally by being locally responsive, despite sometimes failing to achieve optimal efficiency or technological leadership. Many MNEs from the United States have struggled to adapt their activities to the cultural and political diversity of national environments. Instead, they have proven skillful at achieving efficiency by economies of scale. During the recent global recession, efficiency and flexibility became particularly important to the success of multinational firms.[6]

11.2 Understand building the global firm.

Building the Global Firm

Exhibit 11.1 illustrates the dimensions of the successful international firm. Visionary leadership, strong organizational culture, and superior organizational processes characterize successful global firms. They employ an appropriate organizational structure and employ strategies that optimize international operations.[7] We examine each of these five key dimensions in detail next.

EXHIBIT 11.1

Five Key Dimensions of Successful International Firms

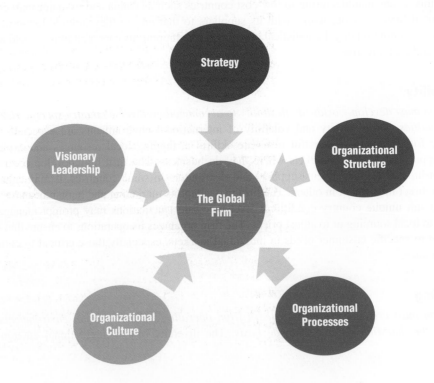

Visionary Leadership

In successful companies, senior management develops a vision of what it wants its firm to become or achieve. Such companies usually craft a *mission statement*, which expresses the firm's purpose for existence. It serves as a guide for employees to set priorities and perform in ways that advance the goals of the firm. **Visionary leadership** is a quality of senior management that provides inspirational guidance and motivation to personnel, leading the firm to a better future. Visionary leaders exhibit superior creativity, discipline, and passion in the course of leading others to realization of their vision.[8] Leadership is more complex and challenging in firms with extensive international operations. This is because it employs valuable organizational assets, such as productive capabilities, brands, and human resources, across different countries with diverse business environments. Visionary leadership is vital in firms with complex international operations.

How do leaders differ from managers? The main difference is that managers focus on directing the firm's day-to-day operations. They are responsible for administering or controlling specific activities in the firm. Alternatively, leaders are visionary and hold a long-term perspective on the challenges and opportunities that confront the firm. Leaders invest substantial energy in developing skilled managers and fostering employee engagement. Leaders are exceptionally skilled at motivating people and at setting the tone for how the firm will pursue its goals and objectives.[9]

Consider Peter Brabeck, chairman of Nestlé (www.nestle.com). From headquarters in Switzerland, Brabeck led Nestlé into the worldwide market for products that meet consumers' growing interest in health and nutrition. To pursue this market, Nestlé purchased Jenny Craig, the U.S. weight management and food-products company. In Germany, Nestlé launched an institute to advise consumers on dietary issues and provided nutritional advice to more than 300,000 customers per month. In France, Brabeck created a nutritional home-care service, supporting patients with special dietary needs. These initiatives position Nestlé in a growing global market to generate global brand loyalty for the firm's line of healthy food products.[10]

Visionary leadership
A quality of senior management that provides inspirational guidance and motivation to personnel, leading the firm to a better future.

In international business, visionary leaders are characterized by four major traits:

- *International mind-set and cosmopolitan values* Visionary leadership requires managers to acquire an international mind-set—an openness to, and awareness of, diversity across cultures. Rigid, close-minded managers who lack vision and have difficulty adapting to other cultures are likely to fail. Those who are open minded, committed to internationalization, and ready to adapt to other cultures are likely to succeed.

- *Willingness to commit resources* The complexities of foreign markets imply that international ventures take more time than domestic ones to become profitable. Visionary leaders commit to them and believe the firm will eventually succeed. Commitment drives them to develop the financial, human, and other resources their firms need to achieve their international goals. Highly committed firms engage in systematic international market expansion. They allocate necessary resources and empower structures and processes that ensure ultimate success.

- *Strategic vision* Visionary leaders communicate a strategic vision—what the firm wants to be in the future and how it will get there. As they develop strategic vision, senior managers focus on the ideal picture of what the firm should become. The picture is a central rallying point for all plans, employees, and employee actions.

- *Willingness to invest in human assets* Visionary leaders must nurture the most critical asset of any organization—human capital. In global firms, senior leaders adopt such human resource practices as hiring foreign nationals, promoting multicountry careers, and providing cross-cultural and language training to develop international super managers.

Synclayer is a Japanese SME that possesses a clear strategic vision. One in four Japanese—about 30 million people—are over age 65. Senior management at Synclayer (www.synclayer.com) anticipates a large and growing market for new products for the elderly. Its vision of achieving worldwide

Source: CTK/Alamy

Ratan Tata is chairman of India's Tata group. Tata transformed the giant Indian conglomerate into a transnational organization with operations throughout the world.

leadership in this market led Synclayer to develop various products for seniors. These include a system that allows homebound seniors to measure their blood pressure, temperature, and other vital signs. The system sends the readings to a health care service that can dispatch an ambulance if problems are detected. Synclayer's vision is to develop the products in Japan and then launch them in other countries with sizable elderly populations.[11]

Ratan Tata is chairman of the Tata Group in India and oversees a $100 billion family conglomerate. The conglomerate owns companies that market a range of products from cars to watches. His group has made numerous international acquisitions (from Tetley Tea to the Anglo-Dutch steel firm Corus), reflecting a change in strategic vision from local to global. In its latest venture, Tata developed a $2,500 car, the Nano, targeted to emerging markets worldwide. Another visionary leader is Fujio Cho, who led Toyota to record sales in the intensely competitive global car industry. His leadership style emphasized innovation, continuous improvement, and an ability to spot future-oriented opportunities, including the Prius hybrid and the youth-oriented Scion brands of Toyota cars. Toyota's main sales focus now is emerging markets, especially China and India.[12]

Organizational Culture

Organizational culture

The pattern of shared values, behavioral norms, systems, policies, and procedures that employees learn and adopt.

Organizational culture is the pattern of shared values, behavioral norms, systems, policies, and procedures that employees learn and adopt. It spells out the correct way for employees to perceive, think, and behave in relation to new problems and opportunities that confront the firm.[13] As the opening case about IKEA showed, organizational culture usually derives from the influence of founders and visionary leaders or some unique history of the firm.

At the Japanese electronics giant Canon (www.canon.com), CEO Fujio Mitarai has developed an organizational culture focused on science and technology. Canon invests billions in R&D and is the world's second-largest recipient of new U.S. patents. Its technology focus extends from product development to the way goods are made on the factory floor. This focus has allowed Canon to become the world leader in digital cameras, copiers, printers, and flat-screen TVs.[14] Recent innovations have slashed production time and costs.

Similarly, focus on product quality is a pillar of the organizational culture at the South Korean firm Hyundai. The firm's leaders have set a goal of becoming the world-quality leader in the auto industry. A stringent quality approval system is enforced at each value-chain stage, including sourcing, procurement, manufacturing, marketing, and sales. Top managers hold quality oversight meetings every two weeks. A survey of 60,000 new car buyers ranked Hyundai third in overall quality, behind only Porsche and Lexus.[15]

Today, management at firms such as Canon and Hyundai seek to build a *global* organizational culture—an organizational environment that plays a key role in the development and execution of corporate global strategy.

Companies that proactively build a global organizational culture:

- Value and promote a global perspective in all major initiatives.
- Value global competence and cross-cultural skills among their employees.
- Adopt a single corporate language for business communications.
- Promote interdependency between headquarters and subsidiaries.
- Subscribe to globally accepted ethical standards.

Firms aspiring to become truly global seek to maintain strong ethical standards in all the markets where they do business. Ultimately, management should cultivate a culture that welcomes social responsibility and is deliberate about fulfilling its role.

Ethical Connections

The annual revenue of the five largest corporations exceeds the combined GDP of the world's poorest 100 countries. MNEs can do much to help reduce poverty. Global pharmaceuticals provide AIDS medications at cost to the poor in Africa. Global retailers develop distribution systems that increase access to needed goods at lower costs. MNEs engage in large-scale charity work. Critics argue that a company's duty is to its shareholders, not to society. Many firms, however, defy such thinking. Bimbo, Pfizer, and Unilever are among many firms that support the world's poor while earning substantial profits.

Visionary leadership and organizational culture need to be supplemented with processes that define how managers will carry out day-to-day activities to achieve company goals. Let's examine these organizational processes next.

Organizational Processes

Organizational processes are the managerial routines, behaviors, and mechanisms that allow the firm to function as intended. Typical processes include mechanisms for collecting strategic information, ensuring quality control in manufacturing, and maintaining efficient payment systems for international sales. General Electric has gained much competitive advantage by developing and continuously improving the many processes that comprise its value chains. For example, GE digitizes all key documents and uses intranets and the Internet to automate many activities and reduce operating costs.

Managers attempt to achieve global coordination and integration not just by subscribing to a particular organizational design, but also by implementing common processes or *globalizing mechanisms*. These common processes provide substantial interconnectedness within the MNE network and allow for meaningful cross-fertilization and knowledge. Globalizing mechanisms include *global teams* and *global information systems*.

Global teams are charged with problem solving and best-practice development within the firm.[16] A **global team** is an internationally distributed group of employees charged with a specific problem-solving or best-practice mandate that affects company operations, or a major aspect of company operations, worldwide.[17] Team members are drawn from geographically diverse units of the MNE and may interact by in-person meetings, corporate intranets, and video conferencing. In this way, a global team brings together employees with the experience, knowledge, and skills to resolve common challenges.

Tasks of global teams vary. *Strategic global teams* identify or implement initiatives that enhance the long-term direction of the firm in its global industry. *Operational global teams* focus on the efficient and effective operation of the business across the whole network.[18] The most successful teams are flexible, responsive, and innovative. To develop global strategies, the team should include culturally diverse managers whose business activities span the globe. Culturally diverse teams have three valuable roles: to create a global view inside the firm while remaining in touch with local realities, to generate creative ideas and make fully informed decisions about the firm's global operations, and to ensure that team decisions are implemented throughout the firm's global operations.

Senior management's desire to create a globally coordinated company is motivated by the need for world-scale efficiency and minimal redundancy. In the past, geographic distance and cross-cultural differences were impediments. Today, *global information systems*—global IT infrastructure and tools such as intranets, the Internet, and electronic data interchange—ensure that distant parts of the global network share knowledge and learn from each other.

When General Motors developed the Equinox, a sport utility vehicle to compete with Toyota's RAV4 and Honda's CR-V, it leveraged global information systems to tap GM capabilities around the world. The Equinox's V6 engine was built in China with cooperation from

Organizational processes
Managerial routines, behaviors, and mechanisms that enable the firm to function as intended.

Global team
An internationally distributed group of employees charged with a specific problem-solving or best-practice mandate that affects company operations, or a major aspect of company operations, worldwide.

engineers in Canada, China, Japan, and the United States. From a room in Toronto, engineers teleconferenced almost daily with their counterparts from Shanghai, Tokyo, and the United States. They exchanged virtual-reality renderings of the vehicle and collaborated on styling of exteriors and component design.

In later sections, we explain two especially critical dimensions of internationalizing firms: strategy and organizational structure. First, however, let's lay the foundation for these key concepts by distinguishing between multidomestic and global industries and by introducing the global integration–local responsiveness framework.

The Distinction Between Multidomestic and Global Industries

Companies that specialize in particular industries, such as processed food, consumer products, fashion, retailing, and publishing, have long approached international business by catering to the specific needs and tastes of each of the countries where they do business. For example, the British publisher Bloomsbury translates each volume of its Harry Potter series into the local language in every country where the book is sold. McDonald's varies its menu to suit differing conditions in different countries. Industries such as this, in which the firm must adapt its offerings to suit the culture, laws, income level, and other specific characteristics of each country, are known as multidomestic industries. In such industries, each country tends to have a unique set of competitors. Accordingly, a **multidomestic industry** is one in which competition takes place on a *country-by-country* basis.

By contrast, in other types of industries, such as aerospace, automobiles, metals, computers, chemicals, and industrial equipment, firms generally approach international business by catering to the needs and tastes of customers on a regional or global scale. The needs for these types of products tend to be highly standardized across countries and regions. For example, DuPont sells essentially the same chemicals around the world. Subaru markets very similar cars in most of the countries where it does business. Industries such as these, in which competition takes place on a *regional or worldwide* basis, are known as **global industries**. Most global industries are characterized by a handful of major players that compete head-on in multiple markets. Kodak must contend with the same rivals—Japan's Fuji and Europe's Agfa-Gevaert—around the world. In the earth-moving equipment industry, Caterpillar and Komatsu compete head-on in all major world markets.

Multidomestic industry
An industry in which competition takes place on a country-by-country basis.

Global industry
An industry in which competition is on a regional or worldwide scale.

The Integration-Responsiveness Framework

11.3 Describe the integration-responsiveness framework.

Global integration
Coordination of the firm's value-chain activities across countries to achieve worldwide efficiency, synergy, and cross-fertilization to take maximum advantage of similarities between countries.

Global integration is the *coordination* of the firm's value-chain activities across multiple countries to achieve worldwide efficiency, synergy, and cross-fertilization to take advantage of similarities between countries. Firms that emphasize global integration are typically found in global industries. They make and sell products and services that are relatively standardized—that is, uniform or with minimal adaptation—to capitalize on converging customer needs and tastes worldwide. Such firms compete on a *regional or worldwide* basis. They seek to minimize operating costs by centralizing value-chain activities and emphasizing economies of scale.[19]

In contrast to global integration, many companies seek to respond to specific conditions in individual countries. They are typically found in multidomestic industries. They embrace **local responsiveness**, managing the firm's value-chain activities and addressing diverse opportunities and risks on a *country-by-country* basis. Local responsiveness emphasizes meeting the specific needs of customers in individual markets.

Local responsiveness
Management of the firm's value-chain activities on a country-by-country basis to address diverse opportunities and risks.

When they operate internationally, firms try to strike the right balance between the objectives of global integration and local responsiveness. Exhibit 11.2 presents the *integration-responsiveness (IR) framework*, which illustrates the pressures companies face in attempting to achieve these often conflicting objectives.[20] It was developed to help managers better understand the trade-offs common in international business.

The primary goal of firms that emphasize global integration is to maximize the efficiency of their value-chain activities on a worldwide scale. They seek to reduce redundancy in their operations. They acknowledge that designing numerous variations of the same product for

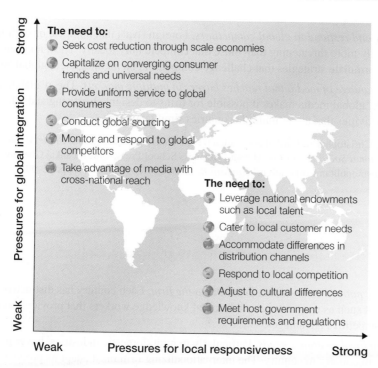

individual markets is costly, and they minimize it. They also promote learning and the transfer of knowledge within their global network to enhance innovation and gain competitive advantages. Senior management justifies global integration by citing converging buyer demand, spread of global brands, diffusion of uniform technology, availability of pan-regional media, and the need to monitor competitors on a global basis.

By contrast, companies that emphasize local responsiveness adjust the firm's practices to suit distinctive needs and conditions in each country. They adapt to local customer requirements, language, culture, regulation, the competitive environment, and the local distribution structure. For example, in Mexico, Walmart adjusts its store hours, employee training, compensation, product line, and promotional tools to suit local conditions.

Firms undertake global integration to take advantage of the following factors.

- *Seek cost reduction through scale economies.* Some industries profit from manufacturing in a few select locations, where firms can take advantage of economies of scale in production. Concentrating production also makes it easier to control the quality, speed, and cost of manufacturing.

- *Capitalize on converging consumer trends and universal needs.* Making and selling products that are standardized is more cost effective than adapting products for each market. For example, firms that make computer chips and electronic components can generally sell similar offerings worldwide. Standardization has become possible as buyer needs and tastes are increasingly similar worldwide.

- *Provide uniform service to global customers.* Services are easiest to standardize when firms can centralize their creation and delivery. MNEs with operations in numerous countries particularly value service inputs that are consistent worldwide.

- *Conduct global sourcing of raw materials, components, energy, and labor.* Firms face ongoing pressure to procure high-quality input goods cost effectively. Sourcing inputs from large-scale, centralized suppliers allows firms to obtain economies of scale, quality that is more consistent, lower costs, and generally more efficient operations.

- *Monitor and respond to global competitors.* Foreign rivals that compete on a global basis are usually more threatening than those that compete only locally. Thus, it is generally best to formulate strategies that challenge competitors on an integrated, global basis.
- *Take advantage of media that reaches buyers in multiple markets.* The availability of cost-effective, global media makes it possible for firms to design advertising and other promotional activities that target multiple countries simultaneously.

Sources: Christopher A. Bartlett and Sumantra Ghoshal, *Managing Across Borders: The Transnational Solution* (Boston: Harvard Business School Press, 1989); Pankaj Ghemawat, "The≈Cosmopolitan Corporation," *Harvard Business Review*, May 2011, pp. 92–99.

Firms undertake local responsiveness to take advantage of the following factors.

- *Leverage natural endowments available to the firm.* Each country has distinctive resources such as raw materials and skilled knowledge workers that provide foreign firms with competitive advantages.
- *Cater to local customer needs.* Particularly in multidomestic industries, buyer needs vary from country to country. The internationalizing firm must adapt its products to meet diverse cross-national needs.
- *Accommodate differences in distribution channels.* Channels can vary from market to market and may increase the need for local responsiveness. In Latin America, small stores are the most common type of retailer. Foreign firms that ordinarily distribute their goods through large stores must adapt their approach when doing business there.
- *Respond to local competition.* Foreign firms are disadvantaged in markets that have numerous local competitors. To outdo local rivals, successful MNEs must devise offerings that meet local demand best.
- *Adjust to cultural differences.* Culture's influence on business activities can be substantial, depending on the market and the product. Where cultural differences are important, such as in sales of food and clothing, the firm must adapt its products and marketing activities accordingly.
- *Meet host government requirements and regulations.* To protect local firms, governments sometimes impose trade barriers or other restrictions that hinder foreign firms. The MNE can overcome such obstacles by establishing local operations to attain the status of a local firm.

Sources: Christopher A. Bartlett and Sumantra Ghoshal, *Managing Across Borders: The Transnational Solution* (Boston: Harvard Business School Press, 1989); Pankaj Ghemawat, *Redefining Global Strategy: Crossing Borders in a World Where Differences Still Matter* (Boston: Harvard Business School Press, 2007).

11.4 Learn to identify strategies based on the integration-responsiveness framework.

Home replication strategy
An approach in which the firm views international business as separate from, and secondary to, its domestic business.

Strategies Based on the Integration-Responsiveness Framework

The integration-responsiveness framework is associated with four distinct strategies, summarized in Exhibit 11.3. Internationalizing firms pursue one or a combination of these.

In the **home replication strategy**, the firm views international business as separate from, and secondary to, its domestic business. It views expansion abroad as an opportunity to generate additional sales for domestic product lines. Thus, the firm designs products with domestic customers in mind and pursues international business to extend product life cycles and replicate home–market success. Such a firm expects little useful knowledge to flow from its foreign

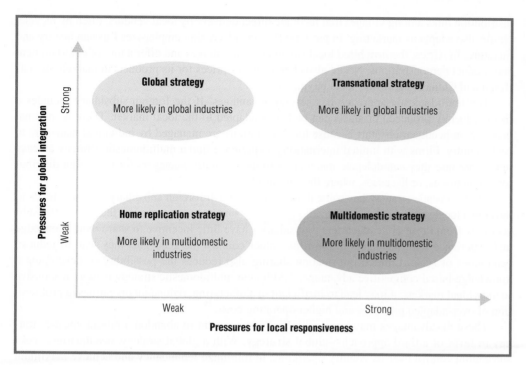

EXHIBIT 11.3

Four Distinct Strategies Emerging from the Integration-Responsiveness Framework

operations.[21] Firms that make and sell commodities (such as raw materials and basic parts) sometimes use the home replication strategy because such products often do not require a complex internationalization approach. The strategy can also succeed when the firm targets only markets that are similar to the home market.

Home replication strategy is typically employed by the smaller firm with products it wants to sell abroad to generate additional sales. It contracts with an intermediary in each of several foreign markets to import and distribute the product and generally does not adapt it for foreign customers. Because management knows little about international business and has limited human and financial resources, the firm relies heavily on its foreign intermediaries. A key consequence is that it maintains little control over how its products are marketed abroad. Replicating abroad what the firm normally does at home provides few competitive advantages in foreign markets. Consequently, for most internationalizing firms, home replication is usually an initial, temporary approach rather than a long-term strategy. It is often followed by inexperienced firms or those with limited international goals.

A second, more advanced approach is **multidomestic strategy** (sometimes called *multilocal strategy*), in which the internationalizing firm develops subsidiaries or affiliates in each of numerous foreign markets. The firm delegates autonomy to managers in each foreign unit, allowing them to operate independently and pursue local responsiveness. Using this strategy, headquarters recognizes and emphasizes differences between national markets. As a result, the firm allows subsidiaries to vary product and management practices by country. Country managers are often nationals of the host country and tend to function independently. They have little incentive to share knowledge and experience with managers in other countries. Products and services are carefully adapted to suit the unique needs of each country.[22]

The food and beverage giant Nestlé (www.nestle.com) has long applied a multidomestic strategy. In each of its country subsidiaries, the firm employs highly autonomous nationals who adapt corporate strategic guidelines to meet specific local needs and conditions. Because of this approach, Nestlé is often perceived as a local firm in each of its markets. For example, the firm varies the taste of its Nescafé brand instant coffees. In Spain, the coffee has an intense, full-bodied flavor. In Northern Europe, it is mild and aromatic. Depending on the country, Nestlé sells its products through various channels, including supermarkets, small shops, market stalls, vending machines, mobile vendors, and even door-to-door. In Nigeria, it built a network of small warehouses and ships goods by pickup trucks. In China, the firm created a system of simple

Multidomestic strategy
An approach to internationalization in which headquarters delegates considerable autonomy to each country manager, allowing him or her to operate independently and pursue local responsiveness.

distribution links among villages that facilitate direct delivery by local vendors, often by bicycle. Nestlé also adapts its marketing. In patriotic Russia, advertising emphasizes Russian history and literature. In Africa, the firm hired local singers to visit villages and offer a mix of entertainment and product demonstrations. Nestlé also charges lower prices for its products in markets such as Brazil and China to suit lower local buying power.[23]

The multidomestic approach has several advantages. If the foreign subsidiary includes a factory, locally produced products can be better adapted to the local market. There is minimal pressure on headquarters staff because local operations are managed by individual managers in each country. Firms with limited international experience find a multidomestic strategy an easy option because they can delegate many tasks to their country managers (or to foreign distributors, franchisees, or licensees, where they are used).

Multidomestic strategy has some disadvantages. Each foreign subsidiary manager tends to develop a local strategic plan, organizational culture, and business processes that may differ substantially from those of headquarters. Subsidiaries have little incentive to share their knowledge and experience with managers in the firm's other country markets. This may lead to reduced economies of scale. Limited information sharing also reduces the possibility of developing a knowledge-based competitive advantage.[24] Although multidomestic strategy is more responsive to individual markets, it may lead to inefficient manufacturing, redundant operations, a proliferation of over-adapted products, and higher operating costs.[25]

Global strategy
An approach in which headquarters seeks substantial control over its country operations to minimize redundancy and maximize efficiency, learning, and integration worldwide.

These disadvantages may eventually lead management to abandon a multidomestic strategy in favor of a third approach—**global strategy**. With a global strategy, headquarters seeks substantial control over its country operations to minimize redundancy and achieve maximum efficiency, learning, and integration worldwide. In the extreme, global strategy asks, "Why not make the same thing, the same way, everywhere?" Thus, a global strategy emphasizes central coordination and control of international operations. Headquarters managers are often largely responsible for the firm's operations worldwide. Activities such as R&D and manufacturing are centralized at headquarters, and management tends to view the world as one large marketplace.[26]

An example of global strategy is Samsung Electronics (www.samsung.com). Once a manufacturer of home appliances in South Korea, the firm now manages a wide collection of global activities from company headquarters. Its integrated value chains mean Samsung's most advanced expertise in consumer electronics, technology, production, and distribution are continuously shared among the firm's business units worldwide. Its engineers continuously seek the most cost-effective ways to produce leading-edge products based on common parts and components. Samsung R&D personnel from Asia, Europe, and the Americas work in global teams to develop semiconductors, flat-screen TVs, smartphones, and other electronics based on standardized platforms, with little cross-national variation. For example, the firm developed the Galaxy smartphone, which sold several hundred million units worldwide. In a typical Samsung smartphone, the internal electronics are identical wherever the product is sold. Internal software is varied to suit differing national preferences. The company's intranet allows R&D teams to access ideas and specifications on how to create inputs that can be integrated into Samsung products, wherever they are made.

Parts and components are sourced from a limited number of top suppliers worldwide. These suppliers operate globally to deliver to as many of Samsung's factories as possible. Samsung does much of its manufacturing in China, Brazil, and other emerging markets to keep costs low. Samsung sells its smartphones in more than 120 countries. Marketing activities are standardized and focus on making Samsung a globally recognized brand. By emphasizing a global strategy, Samsung optimizes its value chains and enjoys superior performance around the world.[27]

Source: Carabay/Fotolia LLC

Samsung is a leading manufacturer of consumer electronics, responsible for about one-fifth of South Korea's total exports. The firm's global strategy relies on first-rate suppliers worldwide and manufacturing in low-cost countries.

A global strategy offers many advantages. It provides a substantial ability to respond to worldwide opportunities. It increases opportunities for cross-national learning and cross-fertilization of the firm's knowledge among all its subsidiaries. It creates economies of scale, which result in lower operational costs. A global strategy can also improve the quality of products and processes, primarily by simplifying manufacturing and other processes. High-quality products give rise to global brand recognition, increased consumer preference, and efficient international marketing programs.

Many factors make it easier to pursue a global strategy, including converging buyer characteristics worldwide, growing acceptance of global brands, increased diffusion of uniform technology (especially in industrial markets), the spread of international collaborative ventures, and the integrating effects of globalization and advanced communications technologies.

Like other approaches, a global strategy has limitations. It is challenging for management to coordinate the activities of widely dispersed international operations closely. The firm must maintain ongoing communications between headquarters and its subsidiaries as well as between the subsidiaries. When carried to an extreme, a global strategy results in a loss of responsiveness and flexibility in local markets.

A final alternative is **transnational strategy**, a coordinated approach to internationalization in which the firm strives to be relatively responsive to local needs while retaining sufficient central control of operations to ensure efficiency and learning. A transnational strategy combines the major advantages of multidomestic and global strategies while minimizing their disadvantages.[28] It is a flexible approach: *standardize where feasible; adapt where appropriate.*

Transnational strategy
A coordinated approach to internationalization in which the firm strives to be relatively responsive to local needs while retaining sufficient central control of operations to ensure efficiency and learning.

To implement a transnational strategy, the firm should:

- Exploit scale economies by sourcing from a reduced set of global suppliers and by concentrating manufacturing in relatively few locations where competitive advantages can be maximized.
- Organize production, marketing, and other value-chain activities on a global scale.
- Optimize local responsiveness and flexibility.
- Facilitate global learning and knowledge transfer.
- Coordinate global competitive moves—that is, rather than following a country-by-country approach, deal with competitors on a global, integrated basis.

One example of transnational strategy is Lenovo (www.lenovo.com), the Chinese producer of personal computers featured in the Closing Case. Lenovo went global when it bought the PC arm of IBM, gaining a global sales force and strong global brands, such as the ThinkPad line. The firm rotates its headquarters between China and the United States; its official language is English. Planning and design are done in the United States; manufacturing is done in China (for Asian markets), Mexico (for the Americas), and Poland (for Europe). Lenovo concentrates production in these low-cost countries to maximize cost efficiencies and economies of scale.

Lenovo's basic computers are the same, but the keyboards and internal software are adapted for each market to accommodate language differences. The firm's retailing websites look identical worldwide but are adapted for language. Marketing operations, centralized to Bangalore, India, include global campaigns designed to sell computers in more than 60 countries with ads that can air in multiple regions. In short,

Source: TianYin Li/Alamy

China's Lenovo follows a transnational strategy. The firm's computers are similar worldwide except the keyboards and internal software, which are adapted for individual markets to suit language differences. Lenovo's retailing websites, which look identical across the world, are also adapted for language.

Lenovo strikes a balance between pursuing a global strategy and adapting its offerings and approaches, as needed, to suit individual markets.[29]

Given the difficulty of balancing central control and local responsiveness, most MNEs find it difficult to implement a transnational strategy. In the long run, almost all need to include some elements of localized decision making because each country has unique characteristics.

Having discussed distinct strategies that firms pursue in international expansion, let's now explore the related topic of organizational structure. Although a strategy is the blueprint for action, a firm needs a structure with people, resources, and processes to implement it.

 MyManagementLab **Watch It!**

If your professor has assigned this, go to the Assignments section of **mymanagementlab.com** to complete the video exercise titled Acer versus HP: Can Acer Surpass HP?

11.5 Understand organizational structure in international business.

Organizational structure
Reporting relationships inside the firm that specify the links between people, functions, and processes.

Organizational Structure in International Business

Organizational structure describes the reporting relationships inside the firm or the "boxes and lines" that specify the links between people, functions, and processes that allow the firm to carry out its operations. Organizational structure dictates the reporting relationships through which the firm's vision and strategies are implemented. In the large, experienced MNE, these linkages are extensive and include the firm's subsidiaries and affiliates. A fundamental issue in organizational structure is how much decision-making responsibility the firm should retain at headquarters, how much should be shared, and how much it should delegate to foreign subsidiaries and affiliates. This is the choice between *centralization* and *decentralization*. Let's examine these options in more detail.

Centralized or Decentralized Structure?

A *centralized approach* gives headquarters considerable authority and control over the firm's activities worldwide. A *decentralized approach* means that substantial autonomy and decision-making authority are delegated to the firm's subsidiaries around the world. In every company, management tends to devise a structure consistent with its vision and strategies. Thus, MNEs that emphasize global integration tend to have a centralized structure. Those that emphasize local responsiveness tend to be decentralized.

Exhibit 11.4 identifies the typical contributions of headquarters and subsidiaries. Whether headquarters or the subsidiary will make decisions about the firm's value-chain activities depends

Headquarters is the primary contributor to these activities:	**A subsidiary is the primary contributor to these activities:**	**Shared responsibility of headquarters and subsidiary:**
• Capital planning • Transfer pricing • Global profitability	• Sales • Marketing • Local market research • Human resource management • Compliance with local laws and regulations	**With the subsidiary's lead:** • Geographic strategy • Local product and service development • Technical support and customer service • Local procurement **With the headquarters' lead:** • Broad corporate strategy • Global product development • Basic research and development • Global product sourcing • Development of global managers

EXHIBIT 11.4

Headquarters and Subsidiary Contributions

on the firm's products, the size of its markets, the nature of competitor operations, and the size and strategic importance of each foreign venture. Generally, the larger the financial outlay or the riskier the anticipated result, the more headquarters will contribute to decision making. For example, decisions about developing new products or building factories abroad tend to be centralized to headquarters. Decisions that affect two or more countries are best left to headquarters managers who have a regional or global perspective.[30] Decisions about local products that will be sold in only one country, however, are typically the joint responsibility of corporate and country-level managers, with the latter taking the lead role. Decisions on day-to-day human resource issues in individual subsidiaries are generally left to local managers.

Generally, it is neither beneficial nor feasible for the firm to centralize all its operations. Retaining some local autonomy is both desirable and necessary. Companies must strike the right balance between centralization, shared decision making, and local autonomy. The challenge for managers is to achieve these goals simultaneously.[31] The phrase "Think globally, act locally" oversimplifies the true complexities of today's global competition; "Think globally and locally and act appropriately" describes better the reality MNEs face today.[32]

Source: Jenny Matthews/Alamy

A worker inspects production of Coca-Cola beverages in a plant in Africa. Although Coca-Cola headquarters provides global brand support and broad marketing guidance to its bottlers in individual countries, the local bottler assumes responsibility for local customer research, local sales promotion, retailer support, and meeting local government requirements.

Planning that managers share at headquarters and at subsidiaries, with negotiation and give-and-take on both sides, is vital to the design of effective strategies. Highly centralized, top-down decision making ignores subsidiary managers' intimate knowledge of host countries. Highly decentralized, bottom-up decision making by autonomous subsidiary managers ignores the big-picture knowledge of headquarters managers. It fails to integrate strategies across countries and regions. Ultimately, however, most decisions are subject to headquarters approval. Headquarters management should promote positive, open-minded, collaborative relationships with country managers. Specifically, they should:

- Encourage local managers to identify with broad, corporate objectives.
- Visit subsidiaries periodically to instill corporate values and priorities.
- Rotate employees within the corporate network to promote development of a global perspective.
- Encourage country managers to interact and share experiences with each other through regional and global meetings.
- Provide incentives and penalties to promote compliance with headquarters' goals.

Organizational Structures for International Operations

Generally, structure follows strategy. That is, we can think of organizational structure as a *tool* that facilitates the implementation of strategy and ultimately the firm's strategic vision.[33] Moreover, the organizational structure senior managers choose is largely the result of how important they consider international business and whether they prefer centralized, shared, or decentralized decision making. Organizational structures tend to evolve over time. As the firm's involvement in international business increases, it adopts increasingly complex organizational structures.

Exhibit 11.5 describes the advantages and disadvantages of each structure. Let's explore the major types of organizational structures.

EXPORT DEPARTMENT   For manufacturing firms, exporting is usually the first foreign market entry strategy. It rarely requires much organizational structure until export sales reach a critical point. Initially, the firm will channel exports through an outside intermediary such as a foreign distributor. When export sales reach a substantial proportion of total sales, the firm

EXHIBIT 11.5 Advantages and Disadvantages of International Organizational Structures

Structure	Advantages	Disadvantages
Export Department A unit within the firm charged with managing the firm's export operations	• Export activities unified under one department • Efficiencies in selling, distribution, and shipping • Small resource commitment	• Focus on the domestic market • Minimal learning about foreign markets • Minimal control of international operations. Potential to rely excessively on foreign intermediaries
International Division All international activities are centralized within one division in the firm, separate from domestic units	• Greater focus on internationalization • Concentration and development of international expertise • Increased commitment to, and coordination and management of, international operations	• Potential for fierce competition between domestic and international units for company resources • Limited knowledge sharing among the foreign units and with headquarters • R&D and future-oriented planning activities are separate for foreign operations and headquarters • Possibility that corporate management may favor domestic over international operations because most will have advanced through the domestic organization
Geographic Area Structure Management and control are decentralized to individual geographic regions, whose managers are responsible for operations within their region	• Greater responsiveness to customer needs and wants in each regional/local market • Better balance between global integration and local adaptation • Improved communications and coordination among the subsidiaries within each geographic region	• Geographic area managers' lack of global orientation for developing and managing products • Limited communications, coordination, and knowledge sharing with other geographic units and with headquarters • Limited economies of scale among the far-flung geographic regional units
Product Structure Management of international operations is organized by major product line	• Development of expertise with specific products, on a global basis • Individual product lines are coordinated and managed globally • Scale economies and sharing of product knowledge among units worldwide	• Duplication of corporate support functions for each product division • Possibility that headquarters may favor subsidiaries offering fastest returns • Potential for excessive focus on products and too little on developments in the firm's markets
Functional Structure Management of international operations is organized by functional activity	• Small central staff that provides strong central control and coordination • United, focused global strategy with a high degree of functional expertise	• Headquarters may lack expertise in coordinating functions in diverse geographic locations • Coordination becomes unwieldy when the firm has numerous product lines • May not respond well to specific customer needs in individual markets
Global Matrix Structure Blends product, geographic area, and functional structures to leverage the benefits of global strategy and local responsiveness	• Leverages the benefits of global strategy while responding to local needs • Aims to combine the best elements of the geographic area, product, and functional structures • Emphasizes interorganizational learning and knowledge sharing among the firm's units worldwide	• Dual reporting chain of command with risk of employees receiving contradictory instructions from multiple managers • Can result in conflicts • Difficulties managing many subsidiaries or products, or operations in many foreign markets

Export department
A unit, within the firm, charged with managing the firm's export operations.

will usually establish a separate **export department** charged with managing export operations. This approach is most closely associated with a home replication strategy. Exhibit 11.6 illustrates the export department structure.

INTERNATIONAL DIVISION STRUCTURE As the firm undertakes more advanced activities abroad, management will typically create an **international division structure**, making a

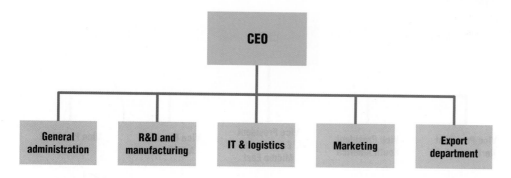

EXHIBIT 11.6

The Export Department Structure

separate unit within the firm dedicated to managing its international operations. Exhibit 11.7 illustrates this structure. The decision to create a separate division is usually accompanied by a significant shift in resource allocation and an increased focus on international business.[34] Typically, a vice president of international operations is appointed. She or he usually reports directly to the corporate CEO. Division managers oversee the development and maintenance of relationships with foreign suppliers, distributors, and other value-chain partners. Over time, the division typically undertakes more advanced internationalization options. These include licensing and small-scale foreign direct investment. In the early stages, the structure is most closely associated with a home replication strategy. However, with time, management may evolve the structure toward adopting a multidomestic or a global strategy.

The international division structure offers several advantages. It centralizes management and coordination of international operations. Its staff consists of international experts who focus on developing new business opportunities abroad and on offering assistance and training for foreign operations. Its creation signals that management is committed to international operations.

This structure can lead to a domestic-versus-international power struggle over limited corporate resources such as financial and human resources. The struggle may result in an adversarial relationship between the domestic and foreign divisions. They may see each other as competitors rather than partners. There is likely to be little sharing of knowledge between the foreign units and domestic operations or among the foreign units themselves. R&D and future-oriented planning activities tend to remain separate and may be domestically focused. Products continue to be developed for the domestic market, with international needs considered only after domestic needs have been addressed. Given these problems, many companies eventually evolve out of the international division structure.[35]

Firms at advanced stages of internationalization establish more complex organizational structures. A major rationale is to reap the benefits of economies of scale and scope—that is, high-volume manufacturing and more efficient use of marketing and other strategic resources over a wider range of products and markets. There is greater emphasis on innovative potential through learning effects, pooling of resources, and expertise.

International division structure
An organizational design in which all international activities are centralized within one division in the firm, separate from domestic units.

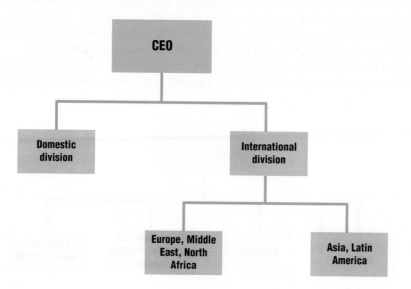

EXHIBIT 11.7

The International Division Structure

EXHIBIT 11.8

The Geographic Area Structure

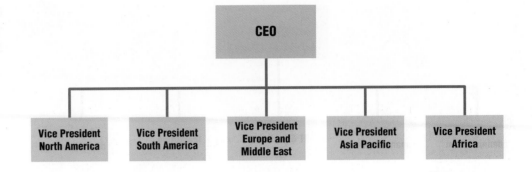

More advanced organizational structures emphasize a decentralized structure, typically organized around geographic areas, or a centralized structure organized around product or functional lines. We describe these structures next.

Geographic area structure

An organizational design in which management and control are decentralized to the level of individual geographic regions.

GEOGRAPHIC AREA STRUCTURE   A **geographic area structure** is an organizational arrangement in which management and control are highly decentralized to the level of individual geographic regions. Local managers are responsible for operations within their own regions. Exhibit 11.8 illustrates this type of organizational design. Firms that organize their operations geographically tend to market products that are relatively standardized across entire regions or groupings of countries. The structure is decentralized because headquarters management delegates operations for each locality to the respective regional managers. The structure is typically associated with a multidomestic strategy.

Firms that use the geographic area structural approach are often in mature industries with narrow product lines. These typically include the pharmaceutical, food, automotive, cosmetics, and beverage industries. For example, Nestlé organizes itself into a South America division, a North America division, an Asia division, and so forth. Nestlé treats all geographic locations, including the domestic market, as equals. All areas work in unison toward a common global strategic vision. Assets, including capital, are distributed to ensure optimal return on corporate goals, not area goals. Geographic area units usually manufacture and market locally appropriate goods within their own areas.

The main advantage of the geographic area structure is the ability to strike a balance between global integration and local adaptation on a regional basis. The area managers have the authority to modify products and strategy. Improved communications and coordination between subsidiaries are possible within each region but are often lacking with other area units and corporate headquarters. Geographic area managers typically lack a *global* orientation when it comes to developing and managing products and other issues.[36]

Product structure

An arrangement in which management of international operations is organized by major product line.

PRODUCT STRUCTURE   The **product structure** is a centralized structure in which the firm organizes its international operations by major product line. Each product division is responsible for producing and marketing a specific group of products worldwide. For example, product categories for Motorola's international operations include mobile phones and network solutions. Apple's product categories include the iPad, iPod, iPhone, and personal computers.

Exhibit 11.9 illustrates such an organization. Each product division operates as a stand-alone profit center with substantial autonomy. The goal is to achieve a high degree of worldwide

EXHIBIT 11.9

The Product Structure

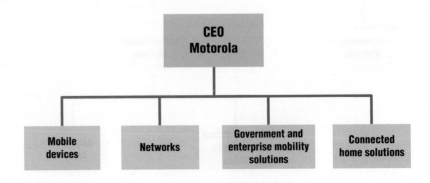

coordination within each product category. Increased coordination facilitates economies of scale and sharing of technology and product knowledge among the firm's operations worldwide. Thus, the product division structure is highly centralized and typically associated with global strategy.

The advantage of the product division structure is that all support functions, such as R&D, marketing, and manufacturing, are focused on the product. Products are easier to tailor for individual markets to meet specific buyer needs. The product division structure may lead to duplication of corporate support functions for each product division. Managers may focus their efforts on subsidiaries with the greatest potential for quick returns.[37]

Source: Martin Barlow/Alamy

Nestlé uses a geographic area structure for organizing its international operations. In Africa, Nestlé conducts advertising in local languages. Pictured is a large ad for Nido milk powder in Cameroon.

FUNCTIONAL STRUCTURE The **functional structure** is a centralized structure in which management of international operations is organized by functional activities such as production and marketing. Exhibit 11.10 illustrates such an arrangement. For example, oil companies tend to organize their worldwide operations along two major functional lines— *production* and *marketing* of petroleum products. Some cruise ship lines engage in both shipbuilding and cruise marketing, two distinctive functions that require separate departments. The advantages of functional division are a small central staff, which provides strong centralized control and coordination, and a united, focused global strategy with a high degree of functional expertise. However, the functional approach may fail if headquarters lacks expertise in coordinating manufacturing, marketing, and other functions in diverse geographic locations. When the firm deals with numerous product lines, coordination can become unwieldy.[38]

GLOBAL MATRIX STRUCTURE The experience of MNEs in the 1970s and 1980s highlighted the strengths and weaknesses of the organizational structures described previously. The geographic area structure proved effective for responding to local needs but did little to enhance worldwide economies of scale and knowledge sharing among far-flung geographic units. The product structure overcame these shortcomings but was weak in responding to local needs. In the 1980s, conditions began to evolve quickly toward a global world economy. At the same time, in some markets, customers showed a renewed preference for local brands. Gradually, MNE managers realized that such trends required them to address global and local needs simultaneously.

This new understanding led to the creation of the **global matrix structure**. The global matrix structure seeks to leverage the benefits of a global strategy and the responsiveness to local needs. Specifically, the global matrix structure is a combination of the geographic area,

Global matrix structure
An arrangement that blends the geographic area, product, and functional structures to leverage the benefits of a purely global strategy while keeping the firm responsive to local needs.

EXHIBIT 11.10
The Functional Structure

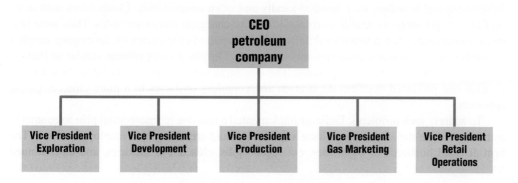

EXHIBIT 11.11

The Global Matrix Structure

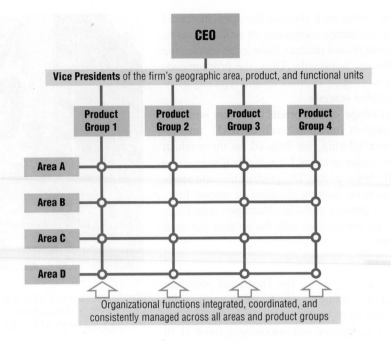

product, and functional structures. It aims to reap the advantages of each while minimizing their disadvantages. Exhibit 11.11 shows such a structure. To make it work, headquarters management should simultaneously:

- Coordinate and control international operations.
- Respond to needs in individual countries.
- Maximize interorganizational learning and knowledge sharing among the firm's units worldwide.[39]

The global matrix structure is closely associated with transnational strategy. Managerial responsibility for each product is shared by each product unit and the particular geographic areas of the firm. Firms develop a dual reporting system in which, for example, an employee in a foreign subsidiary reports to two managers, the local subsidiary general manager and the corporate product division manager. Often, the country manager is superior in authority. Global matrix structure recognizes the importance of flexible and responsive country-level operations and shows firms how to link those operations to optimize operational efficiency and competitive effectiveness. The manager working in this structure shares decision making with other managers, wherever they may be, to achieve best practice for the firm's operations worldwide.

Unilever, the $64 billion European producer of food, beverage, household, and personal care products, has successfully applied the global matrix structure. Unilever (www.unilever.com) developed out of the merger between British and Dutch firms and long pursued a multidomestic approach to international business. In the 1990s, it sourced more than 30 types of vanilla to manufacture ice cream. Its Rexona deodorant had 30 packages and 48 distinct formulations. Advertising and branding were handled locally and often amateurishly. Competitors with more centralized operations were able to respond faster to changing consumer tastes. They were better at coordinating their international units and had captured efficiencies by developing supplier channels that served many countries simultaneously. Despite a sales volume similar to P&G's, Unilever had twice as many employees. The decentralized structure of its international organization had produced needless duplication and countless obstacles to a more efficient global approach.

To address such problems, Unilever implemented a massive reorganization plan to centralize authority, reduce the autonomy of local subsidiaries, and create a global employee culture. The firm divested hundreds of businesses, cut 55,000 jobs, closed 145 factories, and discontinued

1,200 brands, retaining about 400. Today, the firm develops new products by using global teams that emphasize the *commonalities* among major-country markets. Local managers are not allowed to tinker with packaging, formulation, or advertising of global brands such as Dove soap. Unilever is well on the road to implementing a more balanced matrix approach to its global operations.[40]

Philips, the Dutch producer of electronics products, adopted a global matrix structure. Philips operates in more than 100 countries worldwide. Management has structured the firm so that its product groups are integrated across all its major country markets. Its organizational functions are integrated and coordinated across all areas and product groups. To streamline its matrix organization, Philips reorganized itself around three product core units: consumer electronics, health care, and lighting products. The matrix structure assigns various roles to regional executives. They hold responsibility for their respective regions, for the firm's core product units, and for the functions associated with the product units.[41]

Like the other organizational structures, the global matrix structure has limitations. The dual reporting relationship from superiors to subordinates can become complex. Employees may receive contradictory instructions from multiple managers who may be located far apart and come from different cultural and business backgrounds. The matrix structure can waste managerial time and result in conflicts. Potential limitations tend to emerge as the firm's international operations expand over time. For this reason, many firms that experimented with the global matrix structure eventually returned to simpler organizational arrangements.[42]

Source: Chris Jenner/Shutterstock

The multinational firm Unilever, jointly headquartered in the United Kingdom and the Netherlands, offers many global brands, such as Lipton tea, Hellman's spreads, Slimfast, and Dove personal care products. Management must balance global integration with local adaptation in product development, pricing, distribution, and marketing communications. Shown here is Unilever's British headquarters in London.

Foreign Market Entry Strategies

The choice of entry strategy is one of the key decisions that management makes in international business. Foreign market entry strategies can be classified into three distinct categories:

- *Trade of products and services* are generally *home-based* international exchange activities such as *global sourcing, exporting*, and *countertrade*. **Importing or global sourcing**, also known as *global procurement*, or global purchasing, is the strategy of buying products and services from foreign sources and bringing them into the home country or a third country. Sourcing and importing represent an inbound flow. Exporting represents *outbound* international business. Thus, **exporting** refers to the entry strategy of producing products or services in one country (often the producer's home country) and selling and distributing them to customers located in other countries. In both global sourcing and exporting, the firm manages its international operations largely from the home country. We examine exporting and global sourcing in Chapter 13.

  Countertrade refers to an international business transaction in which full or partial payments are made in kind rather than in cash. That is, instead of receiving money as payment for exported products, the firm receives other products or commodities.

- *Equity or ownership-based international business activities* typically are *foreign direct investment (FDI)* and equity-based *collaborative ventures*. In contrast to home-based international operations, here the firm establishes a physical presence in the foreign market. Usually, presence is established by investing capital in and securing ownership of a factory, subsidiary, or other facility in the foreign market. Collaborative ventures include joint

11.6 Understand foreign market entry strategies.

Importing or global sourcing
The procurement of products or services from independent suppliers or company-owned subsidiaries located abroad for consumption in the home country or a third country.

Exporting
The strategy of producing products or services in one country (often the producer's home country) and selling and distributing them to customers located in other countries.

Countertrade
An international business transaction by which all or partial payments are made in kind rather than in cash.

ventures in which the firm makes similar equity investments abroad but in partnership with another company. We discuss FDI and collaborative ventures in Chapter 14.
- *Contractual relationships* usually take the form of *licensing* and *franchising*, in which the firm allows a foreign partner to use its intellectual property in return for royalties or other compensation. Firms such as McDonalds, Dunkin Donuts, and Century 21 Real Estate use franchising to serve customers abroad. We discuss contractual strategies for foreign market entry in Chapter 15.

Each foreign market entry strategy has advantages and disadvantages. Each places specific demands on the firm's managerial and financial resources. Exporting, licensing, and franchising require a relatively low level of managerial commitment and dedicated resources. By contrast, FDI and equity-based collaborative ventures necessitate a high level of commitment and resources.

When contemplating international expansion, firms often struggle to decide which entry strategy is best. Experienced managers consider the following factors:

- *Goals* and *objectives* of the firm, such as desired profitability, market share, or competitive positioning.
- The degree of *control* the firm desires over the decisions, operations, and strategic assets involved in the venture.
- The specific financial, organizational, and technological *resources* and *capabilities* available to the firm (for example, capital, managers, technology).
- The degree of *risk* that management can tolerate in each proposed foreign venture, relative to the firm's goals.
- The *characteristics of the product or service* to be offered.
- *Conditions in the target country*, such as legal, cultural, and economic circumstances, and the nature of business infrastructure, such as distribution and transportation systems.
- The nature and extent of *competition* from existing rivals and from firms that may enter the market later.
- The availability and capabilities of *partners* in the market.
- The *value-adding activities* the firm is willing to perform itself in the market and what activities it will leave to partners.
- The long-term *strategic importance* of the market.

Although all these factors are relevant, perhaps none is more critical than the degree of control the firm wants to maintain over the venture. *Control* is the ability to influence the decisions, operations, and strategic resources involved in the foreign venture. Without control, the focal firm tends to have trouble carrying out strategy, coordinating actions, and resolving disputes that often arise when two pursue their own interests.[43]

Exhibit 11.12 illustrates another useful way to organize foreign market entry strategies based on the degree of control each strategy affords the focal firm over foreign operations.

On the continuum of control in Exhibit 11.12, the arm's-length buyer-seller relationships of exporting represent little or no control at one extreme, whereas FDI, through a wholly owned subsidiary, represents maximum control at the other extreme.

- *Low-control strategies* are exporting, countertrade, and global sourcing. They provide the least control over foreign operations because the focal firm delegates considerable responsibility to foreign partners, such as distributors or suppliers.
- *Moderate-control strategies* are contractual relationships such as licensing and franchising and project-based collaborative ventures.
- *High-control strategies* are equity joint ventures and FDI. The focal firm attains maximum control by establishing a physical presence, and ownership of key assets, in the foreign market.

EXHIBIT 11.12

A Classification of Foreign Market Entry Strategies Based on Levels of Control, Resource Commitment, Flexibility, and Risk

The arrangement of foreign market entry strategies in Exhibit 11.12 also highlights trade-offs that the focal firm faces when entering foreign markets. In particular, high-control strategies such as FDI imply that the firm must:

- Make substantial *resource commitments*; FDI is costly.
- Establish a relatively permanent base in the market, which limits *flexibility* to reconfigure operations there as market and company conditions evolve over time.
- Endure increased *risk* due to uncertainty in the political and customer environments. Especially important are political risk, cultural risk, and currency risk, which we discussed earlier.

In addition to control, the specific characteristics of the product or service, such as fragility, perishability, and ratio of value to weight, can strongly influence the choice of entry strategy. For example, products with a low value/weight ratio (such as tires and beverages) are expensive to ship long distances, suggesting the firm should internationalize through a strategy other than exporting. Similarly, fragile or perishable goods (such as glass and fresh fruit) may be expensive or impractical to ship long distances because they require special handling or refrigeration. Complex products (such as copy machines and industrial machinery) require significant technical support and after-sales service, which necessitate a substantial presence in the foreign market, often via FDI.

As the firm ventures abroad, managers weigh the potential profits, revenues, and goal achievement of internationalization against the investment of money, time, and other company resources. Because of higher costs and greater complexity, international ventures often take much time to become profitable. Managers' risk-taking preferences determine the firm's initial investments and its tolerance for delayed returns. Risk-averse managers prefer entering safe markets, using conservative entry strategies. They usually target markets with a culture and language similar to the home country. For example, a risk-averse U.S. firm would favor Canada over China. A risk-averse British firm would prefer Australia over Saudi Arabia. Historically, most companies have opted for gradual, incremental international expansion. Even today, most firms internationalize in stages. This is illustrated in Exhibit 11.13. It shows the typical firm's internationalization stages and the justifications for each. Initially, management focuses on only the home market. As it begins to internationalize, management targets low-risk, culturally close markets, using simple entry strategies such as exporting or licensing. As the firm gains experience and competence, management targets increasingly complex markets using more challenging entry strategies such as FDI and collaborative ventures.

Stages of internationalization	Critical management activity or orientation	How the firm behaves
Domestic market focus	Exploit home market opportunities	Firm operates only in its home market due to limited resources or lack of motivation
Pre-internationalization stage	Research and evaluate the feasibility of undertaking international business activity	*Typical triggers from outside the firm:* • The firm receives unsolicited orders from foreign customers. • The firm is contacted by change agents (such as distributors), who want to represent it abroad. *Typical triggers from inside the firm:* • Managers seek to increase the firm's profits or other advantages. • Managers are proactive about international expansion.
Experimental involvement	Initiate limited international business activity, typically through exporting	• Managers consider foreign market opportunities attractive.
Active involvement	Explore international expansion, including entry strategies other than exporting	• Managers' accumulated experience reinforces expectations about the benefits of international business. • Managers commit further resources to international expansion. • Managers dedicate more resources to expand into new foreign markets.
Committed involvement	Allocate resources based on international opportunities	• The firm performs well in various international ventures. • The firm overcomes barriers to doing international business.

EXHIBIT 11.13

Typical Stages in Firm Internationalization

Source: Based on S. Tamer Cavusgil "On the Internationalization Process of Firms," *European Research* 8, No. 6 (1980), pp. 273–281.

An important exception to the stages approach to internationalization are *born global* firms. The rise of these contemporary companies has coincided with globalization and diffusion of technologies such as the Internet that facilitate international business. Born globals internationalize much earlier and faster than firms did in the past. Many reach advanced stages of internationalization within the first few years of their founding.[44]

CLOSING CASE   Global Strategy at Lenovo

The world's top personal computer (PC) producers are Lenovo, HP, Dell, and Acer. Lenovo is the top worldwide PC vendor, ahead of rivals HP and Dell. Lenovo is based in China and generates more than $38 billion in total sales. It holds about 33 percent of the PC market in China, 15 percent in North America, and 20 percent in other countries. Lenovo has experienced rapid growth, even during periods of soft global demand. When Lenovo was founded in modest circumstances in 1984, no one imagined it would evolve into a *Fortune* Global 500 company with a presence in 160 countries. Today, from regional headquarters in each of Beijing, China, and Raleigh, North Carolina, Lenovo offers desktops, laptops, tablets, workstations, servers, and mobile phones to customers across the globe.

Company Strategy

The PC industry has reached maturity, especially in the advanced economies. Computers have become commodities, and their profit margins are thin. The industry is global, which means firms compete with each other, and cater to customer needs, on a global scale. PC firms are under pressure to ensure company survival and success.

Key to Lenovo's success is ensuring organizational learning to optimize the firm's value-chain activities continuously. Lenovo uses mergers and acquisitions (M&As) to acquire needed knowledge and other assets from partner firms and to expand into markets worldwide. In 2005, Lenovo acquired the PC business of IBM. The deal instantly established Lenovo as the number-three PC maker worldwide. In 2011, Lenovo formed a merger with NEC, the largest PC vendor in Japan, to access the huge Japanese PC market better. The merger increased Lenovo's scale economies in manufacturing and marketing. In 2014, Lenovo acquired the telecommunications firm Motorola Mobility. This provided Lenovo with a strong footing in the global smartphone business.

Lenovo follows a protect-and-attack strategy. While protecting its core business, especially the Chinese market, Lenovo is aggressively growing its market share in emerging markets and advanced economies. It is rapidly growing new product categories such as tablets and smartphones. The push into emerging markets benefits from Lenovo's deep knowledge of doing business in China. Lenovo now obtains about 20 percent of its revenues from emerging markets outside China.

Senior management emphasizes global innovation, global products and branding, global human resources, and creation of a corporate culture conducive to global success. Let's examine these strategies in detail.

Global Innovation

The acquisition of IBM's PC business allowed Lenovo to tap world-class technological know-how. It leverages top-notch innovative capabilities from R&D facilities in Beijing, Raleigh, and Yokohama, Japan. Lenovo is a leading PC developer. Each facility has its own distinctive talent capability. Lenovo owns more than 6,500 international patents. *BusinessWeek* ranked Lenovo one of the "Top 50 Most Innovative Companies." It constantly invests in R&D for breakthrough technologies and innovative products. Lenovo can count on capital infusions from China's government, which maintains partial ownership in the firm.

At the annual Consumer Electronics Show in Las Vegas, Lenovo has unveiled many products, including a Windows-based smartphone, a half-tablet, a half-notebook, a smart TV, and a thin and lightweight ultrabook PC. Lenovo's marketing research capability enables the firm to foresee better what consumers desire in information technology products. For example, Lenovo's Yoga is an ultrathin PC that doubles as a tablet.

Lenovo is increasingly on the leading edge of green technologies. ThinkPad PCs are built from up to 30 percent post-consumer content, using recycled material such as old water jugs. PCs meet the latest high-energy efficiency standards and rank high on eco-friendliness. PCs are shipped in 100 percent recycled packaging that can be tossed into a recycling bin.

Global Products and Branding

In developing its products, Lenovo emphasizes modular architecture—suppliers manufacture interchangeable components and modules, which are then snapped into PC cases rolling down assembly lines. The same parts—power supply units, processors, graphics cards, hard drives, and others—can be used to produce various PC models. Interfaces are standardized to facilitate production of PCs that are simultaneously differentiated but use standard parts and components. This minimizes the cost of manufacturing computers and of designing new ones. Products are standardized worldwide, but elements such as keyboards and software are customized to respond to local language needs.

Marketing also responds to local conditions. For example, Lenovo is the most popular PC brand in rural China, where the firm established a complex distribution network extending to small cities and towns. Prices are adapted to fit the buying power of low-income consumers. Lenovo adjusts marketing to fit local traditions. In rural China, the firm markets wedding computers, which come in red, the luckiest color to Chinese. Rural families often pool their money to buy a bride and groom their first PC as a wedding gift.

By purchasing IBM's PC business, Lenovo acquired the IBM brand name and the ThinkPad product brand. Lenovo leveraged the IBM name to build brand awareness on a global scale. Lenovo's "For Those Who Do" global branding campaign is engaging consumers worldwide. The firm is leveraging the power of global social media to target marketing campaigns to youth 18 to 25 years old. Its retailing websites look identical worldwide but are adapted for language differences.

Global Human Resources

Lenovo worked hard to integrate Chinese business methods with an international workforce of 27,000 employees. Blending the distinctive national and organizational culture of IBM required hiring managers with a global mind-set and strong international background. Lenovo recruits globally savvy executives from other high-tech firms and hires talented graduates of top universities to incubate them as future company leaders.

Lenovo created a global training program that provides accelerated development opportunities for employees. The firm's human resources group works with managers to construct career maps and pipelines for every high-potential employee. All employees are asked to examine their career aspirations and the training they need to attain their goals. The career maps are linked to job slots around the world, and employees have much latitude to achieve their dreams. Lenovo employees are ambitious, and senior management is serious about helping them develop their careers.

Global Culture

In 1994, Lenovo's founder, Liu Chuanzhi, forecast that the firm would become a great, global company. At the time, there were very few global Chinese firms, and Chuanzhi's strategic vision stood out. It is Lenovo's strategic vision that draws so many talented managers to work for the firm. Aiming to foster a global spirit, Lenovo's executive team meetings rotate among Beijing, Hong Kong, Singapore, Paris, and North Carolina. The firm's official language is English.

Senior management has instituted processes aimed at socializing young managers into the Lenovo organizational culture. Nationality doesn't matter. If an employee demonstrates capability and vision, there are no limits. Socialization creates broad, tacitly understood rules for appropriate action by managers at all levels in global operations. Lenovo managers become well acquainted with the firm's culture and goals. Wherever they operate, managers feel a strong connection to the firm. This guides decisions on company activities and facilitates global knowledge exchange. Connectedness builds trust and cooperation. It encourages communication and interaction. It facilitates the integration and assimilation of new knowledge and capabilities. Lenovo management values the diversity of global cultures and the learning that accrues from foreign business environments. Key employees need to function with a global mind-set and cosmopolitan values.

Manufacturing and Value-Chain Management

Lenovo concentrates manufacturing at sites in China, Argentina, India, Mexico, and Poland. Production in these low-cost countries generates cost efficiencies and economies of scale. Regional headquarters in the United States and operations in low-cost countries helps diversify sales across advanced economies and emerging markets. While investing huge sums in R&D and innovative product features, senior management maintains a sharp focus on keeping manufacturing costs low. Sourcing of parts and components is done on a global scale. Sourcing from hundreds of high-quality suppliers ensures flexibility in logistics and production.

The diversity of partners and international environments helps Lenovo acquire new technical and managerial knowledge, new product ideas, improved R&D, and better partnering skills. Lenovo leverages the power of global information systems to share important knowledge among the firm's subsidiaries worldwide.

Lenovo aims for a leadership position in which it attains a double-digit share in each of the markets where it does business. Management also aims to maintain a sharp focus on its customers, providing them with the most innovative products worldwide.

AACSB: Reflective Thinking Skills

Case Questions

11-4. What is strategy? How does Lenovo use strategy to succeed in the global marketplace? What strategies does Lenovo employ to maximize company efficiency and flexibility? What does Lenovo management do to foster organizational learning?

11-5. Describe Lenovo's organizational culture. What are the characteristics of Lenovo's culture? How does the culture help Lenovo achieve its international goals?

11-6. What is the nature of Lenovo's international strategy? Is the firm's strategy primarily multidomestic or global? Justify your answer. What advantages does Lenovo derive from the particular international strategy(s) that it pursues?

11-7. Examine Lenovo in terms of the integration-responsiveness framework. What are the pressures that Lenovo faces for local responsiveness? What are the pressures that Lenovo faces for global integration? What advantages do local responsiveness and global integration each bring to Lenovo?

Sources: Eva Dou, "Lenovo Expects Motorola Will Give a Big Boost to Smartphone Shipments," *Wall Street Journal*, January 9, 2015, p. B4; Adi Ignatius, "I Came Back Because the Company Needed Me," *Harvard Business Review*, July/August 2014, pp. 104–108; Lucy Handley, "Lenovo Plots Global Push to Vie with Dell and Apple," *Marketing Week*, March 31, 2011, p. 4; Leslie Norton, "Protect and Attack," *Barron's*, February 6, 2012, p. 17; Chuck Salter, "Protect and Attack: Lenovo's New Strategy," *Fast Company*, November 22, 2011, www.factcompany.com; Elizabeth Woyke, "Lenovo CEO Keeps Focus on Hardware, Eyes PC Market Crown," *Forbes*, January 10, 2012, p. 34; Liu Xiaohui and Trevor Buck, "The Internationalisation Strategies of Chinese Firms: Lenovo and BOE," *Journal of Chinese Economic & Business Studies* 7, No. 2 (2009), pp. 167–181.

Betty Feng and Lawrence Yu wrote this case under the supervision of S. Tamer Cavusgil.

END OF CHAPTER REVIEW

 MyManagementLab

Go to **mymanagementlab.com** to complete the problems marked with this icon .

Key Terms

Summary

In this chapter, you learned about:

- **Strategy in international business**

  Strategy is a planned set of actions that managers employ to make best use of the firm's resources and core competencies to gain a competitive advantage. The firm that aspires to become globally competitive must simultaneously seek three key strategic objectives—efficiency, flexibility, and learning.

- **Building the global firm**

  Managers who exhibit **visionary leadership** possess an international mind-set, cosmopolitan values, and a globally strategic vision. They motivate and lead company personnel toward important organizational goals and engage in strategic thinking, committing resources and human assets to realizing a global approach to business. Advanced international firms value global competence and cross-cultural skills, adopt a single language, and promote interdependency among headquarters and the firm's subsidiaries. They adopt an international organizational culture. They subscribe to globally accepted ethical standards and responsible citizenship. International **organizational processes** include global teams and global information systems.

- **The integration-responsiveness framework**

  The integration-responsiveness (IR) framework describes how internationalizing firms simultaneously seek global integration and local responsiveness. **Local responsiveness** refers to managing the firm's value-chain activities, and addressing diverse opportunities and risks, on a country-by-country basis. **Global integration** describes efforts to coordinate the firm's value-chain activities cross-nationally to achieve worldwide efficiency, synergy, and cross-fertilization to take maximum advantage of similarities across countries.

- **Strategies based on the integration-responsiveness framework**

  The IR framework presents four alternative strategies. Using **home replication strategy**, the firm views international business as separate from, and secondary to, its domestic business. Products are designed with domestic consumers in mind, and the firm is essentially a domestic company, with some foreign activities. **Multidomestic strategy** is a more committed approach, in which managers recognize and emphasize differences among national markets. They treat individual markets on a stand-alone basis, with little cross-national integration of company efforts. **Global strategy** aims to integrate the firm's major objectives, policies, and activities into a cohesive whole, targeted primarily to the global marketplace. Senior management performs sourcing, resource allocation, market participation, and competitive moves on a global scale. Using **transnational strategy**, the firm strives to be more responsive to local needs while retaining maximum global efficiency and emphasizing global learning and knowledge transfer. The strategy aims to combine the major benefits of both multidomestic and global strategies while minimizing their disadvantages.

- **Organizational structure in international business**

  Organizational structure consists of the reporting relationships in the firm between people, functions, and processes that facilitate carrying out international operations. It determines where key decisions are made, the relationship between headquarters and subsidiaries, and the nature of international staffing. Firms develop organizational structures to manage international operations. The **export department** is the simplest organizational structure, in which a unit within the firm manages all export operations. Slightly more advanced is the **international division structure**, in which all international activities are centralized within one organizational unit, separate from the firm's domestic units. The **geographic area structure** features control and decision making that are decentralized to the level of individual geographic regions. Using the **product structure**, decision making and management of international operations are centralized and organized by major product line. The **functional structure** organizes decision making by functional activity, such as production and marketing. The **global matrix structure** blends the geographic area, product, and functional structures in an attempt to leverage the benefits of a purely global strategy and maximize global organizational learning while keeping the firm responsive to local needs.

- **Foreign market entry strategies**

  Market entry strategies consist of *exporting, sourcing,* and *foreign direct investment* as well as *licensing, franchising,* and *nonequity alliances*. Each strategy has advantages and disadvantages. To select a strategy, managers must consider the firm's resources and capabilities, conditions in the target country, risks inherent in each venture, competition from existing and potential rivals, and the characteristics of the product or service to be offered in the market. **Importing** is buying products and services from sources located abroad for use at home. It is also called **global sourcing**, global purchasing, or global procurement.

Test Your Comprehension   AACSB: Reflective Thinking Skills

11-8. Define visionary leadership. What are the traits of a manager who has visionary leadership?

⭐ **11-9.** Describe the distinction between multidomestic and global industries.

11-10. What do you understand by the term home replication strategy?

11-11. What is the difference between global strategy and multidomestic strategy? Visit the Dell Computer website (www.dell.com). Does Dell generally apply a global strategy or a multidomestic strategy? How can you tell?

11-12. Define transnational strategy. Give examples of firms that apply a transnational strategy.

11-13. What is the difference between a centralized and a decentralized organizational structure? Why do firms often prefer to have a centralized structure?

11-14. What are the different organizational structures for international operations? Which structure(s) is most associated with global strategy?

⭐ **11-15.** Some organizations have export departments and others have an international division. Why might an organization opt for this approach?

⭐ **11-16.** What is the functional structure? What are the advantages and disadvantages of this approach?

Apply Your Understanding   AACSB: Communication Abilities, Reflective Thinking Skills, Ethical Understanding and Reasoning Abilities

11-17. Are there any real differences between importing and global sourcing or purchasing?

11-18. Barbie is the best-selling doll, produced by Mattel, a U.S. company. Mattel is targeting Barbie to foreign markets but struggles to find the right strategy because of cultural differences. In Muslim countries, Barbie faces competition from doll producers that offer Islamic alternatives that feature conservative styling. In Latin America, competitors offer dolls with tanned skin and dark hair. In Asia, many girls prefer dolls with Asian features. The fun-loving image that Barbie projects in the U.S. market is often inappropriate abroad. In marketing Barbie abroad, should Mattel management apply a strategy that is global or multidomestic? What are the advantages and disadvantages of each approach? Is it possible to reach a compromise? Elaborate and justify your answer.

11-19. *Ethical Dilemma:* You were recently hired as a manager for international operations of Despoyle Chemical Corporation, a major manufacturer of dyes, fertilizers, and other industrial chemicals. Despoyle has chemical production plants in 28 countries, including many developing economies. It has a decentralized organizational structure, and managers in individual countries operate their plants independently of headquarters. After visiting various Despoyle plants, you find the firm follows local environmental protection standards in different countries. In India, Despoyle allows pollutants to flow freely into local rivers. In Mexico, it generates pollution in local landfills and production sites. In Nigeria, Despoyle's factory emits air pollution that exceeds levels acceptable in more advanced countries. As a new manager, you are surprised by the firm's lax environmental practices around the world. What should you do? Do you complain to senior management and risk angering your superiors? Do you try to modify Despoyle's environmental standards in different countries? What solution, if any, do you propose to address Despoyle's practices? Use the ethical framework in Chapter 4 to formulate your answer.

 **globalEDGE | INTERNET EXERCISES**
(www.globalEDGE.msu.edu)

Refer to Chapter 1, page 54, for instructions on how to access and use globalEDGE™.

11-20. Visit the websites for Toyota (www.toyota.com) and Procter & Gamble (www.pg.com). From what you can gather, how do these two firms organize their international activities? Do they seem to be applying multidomestic strategy or global strategy in their sourcing, manufacturing, product development, and marketing activities? How and why might an internationalizing firm evolve its approaches to internationalization over time?

11-21. Multinational firms play a key role in globalization. Various news organizations prepare classifications and rankings of MNEs (e.g., *Financial Times, Bloomberg BusinessWeek, Forbes, Fortune*). Find two such rankings and identify the criteria used to rank the top global firms. What countries are home to the great majority of MNEs on these lists? For each list, how global are the top three firms? That is, in what countries do they operate? Conduct a search for rankings.

11-22. You work for an MNE that makes and markets cellular telephones. Senior managers want to begin selling the phones in Latin America. To pursue a transnational strategy, management wants to minimize adaptation of the phones. They have asked you for a briefing. Focusing on three Latin American countries, prepare a brief report that identifies the common features of Latin American markets that management should consider when developing the cell phones the firm will sell there. For example, what language should be used in the cell phones? What pricing should management use? You may wish to consult the country commercial guides, Country Insights, and market research reports available through globalEDGE™. In addition, the U.S. Department of Commerce (www.export.gov) is a useful resource.

 CAREER TOOLBOX

Preparing for International Negotiations

Negotiations are often tricky in international business because they rely on cross-cultural communication and interaction. Cultural differences determine how the negotiators think and act. Miscommunications arise from various sources. Perhaps the most important is a failure to understand the mind-sets and motives of the negotiating parties. In many cultures, it is useful to become acquainted with each other and establish a comfort level. To help ensure success, the negotiator should do advance research to develop an understanding of counterparts' national and cultural backgrounds.

In this exercise, you will learn:

- The importance of acquiring advance knowledge about cultural dimensions prior to commencing international negotiations.
- How to recognize important cultural dimensions, negotiating styles, and other factors in international negotiations.
- Acquire research skills to prepare for and optimize international negotiations.

To complete this exercise, assume you are the team leader at an international firm that will engage in negotiations with businesspeople from Mexico and Saudi Arabia. Such a scenario is likely in the oil industry, for example, because both countries are top oil producers. To ensure success, you are to perform advance research about the cultural characteristics of the people with whom you will be negotiating.

To complete this exercise in your MyLab, go to the Career Toolbox.

Background

Negotiations are an essential component of international business transactions, whether selling goods, forming a joint venture, or licensing intellectual property. Communication is the foundation of successful negotiations. The potential for cross-cultural misunderstandings is ever present. Goals of the parties may differ; they may even be diametrically opposed. Parties employ numerous techniques, such as persuasion, coercion, and even manipulation. Developing skills in international negotiations can determine the success of collaborations, contractual relations, and everyday encounters in international business.

Differences in negotiating styles are driven by cultural factors. When negotiating, for example, Americans tend to be aggressive and eager to begin discussions, with little time devoted to socializing. Germans tend to stress clarity, precision, and literal interpretation of contracts. They may emphasize self-interests and concede very little. People from Spain tend to emphasize the social dimension. Choosing the right restaurant or wine can speak louder than words. Spaniards bargain hard and may communicate through nonverbal cues. The British tend to resent aggressive, direct demands. Sensitive issues are best broached over an informal dinner or through intermediaries.

MyManagementLab **Try It!**

The simulation Managing in a Global Environment accompanies this exercise.

 MyManagementLab

Go to **mymanagementlab.com** for Auto-graded writing questions as well as the following Assisted-graded writing questions:

 11-23. What are the primary strategic objectives in international business?

 11-24. Describe the requisite dimensions that characterize truly successful, contemporary international firms.

 11-25. MyManagementLab Only—comprehensive writing assignment for this chapter.

Endnotes

1. S. Tamer Cavusgil, Sengun Yeniyurt, and Janell Townsend, "The Framework of a Global Company: A Conceptualization and Preliminary Validation," *Industrial Marketing Management* 33 (2004), pp. 711–716; G. T. Hult, S. Deligonul, and S. Tamer Cavusgil, "The Hexagon of Market-Based Globalization: An Empirical Approach Towards Delineating the Extent of Globalization in Companies," in *New Perspectives in International Business Thought*, A. Lewin, ed. (London: Palgrave, 2006); George Yip, *Total Global Strategy II* (Upper Saddle River, NJ: Prentice Hall, 2003).

2. Christopher A. Bartlett and Sumantra Ghoshal, *Managing Across Borders: The Transnational Solution* (Boston, MA: Harvard Business School Press, 1989).

3. Christopher A. Bartlett and Sumantra Ghoshal, *Transnational Management: Text, Cases, and Readings in Cross-Border Management*, 3rd ed. (Boston, MA: Irwin/McGraw-Hill, 2000), p. 273.

4. Ibid.

5. Bruce Kogut, "Designing Global Strategies: Profiting from Operational Flexibility," *Strategic Management Journal* 27 (1985), pp. 27–38.

6. L. Bryan and D. Farrell, "Leading Through Uncertainty," *McKinsey Quarterly*, December 2008, http://www.mckinseyquarterly.com.

7. Cavusgil, Yeniyurt, and Townsend (2004); Hult, Deligonul, and Cavusgil (2006); Yip (2003).

8. Hult, Deligonul, and Cavusgil (2006); Ben L. Kedia and Akuro Mukherji, "Global Managers: Developing a Mindset for Global Competitiveness," *Journal of World Business* 34 (1999), pp. 230–251; Robert Waterman, Tom Peters, and J. R. Philips, "Structure Is Not Organization," *Business Horizons* 23, No. 3 (1980), pp. 14–26.

9. Vikram Balla, J. Caye, P. Haen, D. Lovich, C. Ong, M. Rajagopalan, and S. Sharda, *The Global Leadership and Talent Index* (Boston: Boston Consulting Group, 2015).

10. Haig Simonian, "Climber Scales the Health Peak," *Financial Times*, August 21, 2006, p. 8.

11. "Chasing the Grey Yen," *Economist*, April 11, 2015, pp. 60-61; "The Grey Market: Hey, Big Spender," *Economist*, December 3, 2005, pp. 59–60.

12. J. Soble, "Toyota Appoints Founder's Grandson as Next Chief Executive," *Financial Times*, January 21, 2009, p. 18; B. Shafiulla, "Tata Nano to Tata No-No," *IUP Journal of Marketing Management* 13, No. 1 (2014), pp. 78–86; Alex Taylor, "Tata Takes on the World Building an Auto Empire in India," May 2, 2011, pp. 86–92.

13. Joel Nicholson and Yim-Yu Wong, "Culturally Based Differences in Work Beliefs," *Management Research News* 24, No. 5 (2001), pp. 1–10; Edgar H. Schein, *Organizational Culture and Leadership*, 2nd ed. (San Francisco: Jossey-Bass, 1997).

14. Clay Chandler, "Canon's Big Gun," *Fortune*, February 6, 2006, pp. 92–98; *Forbes*, "Canon: Growing Through Strategic Innovation," January 19, 2015, pp. 4–5; Juro Osawa, "At Canon, Elder Gains Wider Leadership Role," *Wall Street Journal*, January 31, 2012, p. B5.

15. David Aaker, "Remove Negatives to Remain Relevant," *Marketing News*, January 31, 2012, p. 14; Alex Taylor III, "Hyundai Smokes the Competition," *Fortune*, January 18, 2010, pp. 62–71.

16. Stephen Chen, Ronald Geluykens, and Chong Ju Choi, "The Importance of Language in Global Teams," *Management International Review* 46, No. 6 (2006), pp. 679–696; Robert T. Keller, "Cross-Functional Project Groups in Research and New Product Development: Diversity, Communications, Job Stress, and Outcomes," *Academy of Management Journal* 44 (2001), pp. 547–555; Mary Maloney and Mary Zellmer-Bruhn, "Building Bridges, Windows and Cultures," *Management International Review* 46 (2006), pp. 697–720.

17. Martha L. Maznevski and Nicholas A. Athanassiou, "Guest Editors' Introduction to the Focused Issue: A New Direction for

Global Teams Research," *Management International Review* 46 (2006), pp. 631–646.

18. Terence Brake, *Managing Globally* (New York: Dorling Kindersley, 2002).

19. Bartlett and Ghoshal (1989); Gary Hamel and C. K. Prahalad, "Do You Really Have a Global Strategy?" *Harvard Business Review* 63 (July–August 1985), pp. 139–149; T. Hout, Michael Porter, and E. Rudden, "How Global Companies Win Out," *Harvard Business Review* 60 (September–October 1982), pp. 98–105; Robert T. Moran and John R. Riesenberger, *The Global Challenge* (London: McGraw-Hill, 1994); Kenichi Ohmae, "Planning for a Global Harvest," *Harvard Business Review* 67 (July–August 1989), pp. 136–145.

20. Bartlett and Ghoshal (1989); Timothy Devinney, David Midgley, and Sunil Venaik, "The Optimal Performance and the Global Firm: Formalizing and Extending the Integration-Responsiveness Framework," *Organization Science* 11 (2000), pp. 674–695; Yves L. Doz, Christopher Bartlett, and C. K. Prahalad, "Global Competitive Pressures and Host Country Demands: Managing Tensions in MNCs," *California Management Review* 23 (1981), pp. 63–74; Yadong Luo, "Determinants of Local Responsiveness: Perspectives from Foreign Subsidiaries in an Emerging Market," *Journal of Management* 26 (2001), pp. 451–477; C. K. Prahalad, *The Strategic Process in a Multinational Corporation*, Unpublished doctoral dissertation (Graduate School of Business Administration, Harvard University, Cambridge, MA, 1975).

21. Bartlett and Ghoshal (2000); Anna Jonsson and Nicola Foss, "International Expansion Through Flexible Replication: Learning from the Internationalization Experience of IKEA," *Journal of International Business Studies* 42, No. 9 (2011), pp. 1079–1102.

22. Bartlett and Ghoshal (2000); G. Ghislanzoni, R. Penttinen, and D. Turnbull, "The Multilocal Challenge: Managing Cross-Border Functions," *McKinsey Quarterly*, 2008, http://www.mckinsey-quarterly.com.

23. L. Chang, "Nestlé Stumbles in China's Evolving Market," *Wall Street Journal*, December 8, 2004, p. A10; G. Chazan, "Foreign Products Get Russian Makeovers," *Wall Street Journal*, January 16, 2001, p. A23; Nestlé Corporation, "Key Facts and History," 2009, http://www.nestle.com; Greg Steinmetz and Tara Parker-Pope, "All Over the Map: At a Time When Companies Are Scrambling to Go Global, Nestlé Has Long Been There," *Wall Street Journal*, September 26, 1996, p. R4.

24. Moran and Riesenberger (1994).

25. Bartlett and Ghoshal (2000); Janell Townsend, S. Tamer Cavusgil, and Marietta Baba, "Global Integration of Brands and New Product Development at General Motors," *Journal of Product Innovation Management* 27, No. 1 (2010), pp. 49–65.

26. Bartlett and Ghoshal (1989); Hamel and Prahalad (1985); Hout, Porter, and Rudden (1982); Levitt (1983); Moran and Riesenberger (1994); Ohmae (1989).

27. Bong Choi, Jongweon Kim, Byung-hak Leem, Chang-Yeol Lee, and Han-kuk Hong, "Empirical Analysis of the Relationship Between Six Sigma Management Activities and Corporate Competitiveness: Focusing on Samsung Group in Korea," *International Journal of Operations & Production Management* 32, No. 5 (2012), pp. 528–550; Evan Ramstad and Jung-Ah Lee, "Samsung's Profit Hits Fast Track," *Wall Street Journal*, April 9, 2012, p. B6.

28. Bartlett and Ghoshal (2000).

29. Roland Bel, "Innovating in China: Lessons for Global Companies," *Global Business & Organizational Excellence* 34, No. 2 (2015), pp. 34–50; Katrin Hille, "Back to the Future for Lenovo," *Financial Times*, February 12, 2009, p. 17; Jane Spencer and Loretta Chao, "Lenovo Goes Global, But Not Without Strife," *Wall Street Journal*, November 4, 2008, p. B1; Elizabeth Woyke, "Lenovo CEO Keeps Focus on Hardware, Eyes PC Market Crown," *Forbes*, January 10, 2012, p. 34.

30. Pankaj Ghemawat, "Regional Strategies for Global Leadership," *Harvard Business Review* 83 (December 2005), pp. 98–106.

31. Moran and Riesenberger (1994); Franklin Root, *Entry Strategies for International Markets* (San Francisco: Jossey-Bass, 1998).

32. Moran and Riesenberger (1994).

33. Alfred D. Chandler, *Strategy and Structure* (Cambridge, MA: MIT Press, 1962).

34. Moran and Riesenberger (1994).

35. Ibid.

36. Ibid.

37. Ibid.

38. Ibid.

39. Bartlett and Ghoshal (1989); Moran and Riesenberger (1994); G. T. Hult, Deligonul, and Cavusgil (2006).

40. Deborah Ball, "Despite Revamp, Unwieldy Unilever Falls Behind Rivals," *Wall Street Journal*, January 3, 2005, pp. A1, A5; Unilever corporate profile at http://www.hoovers.com; "Unilever's Vital Shift in Direction," *Strategic Direction* 28, No. 2 (2012), pp. 6–8; Joan Voight, "Unilever's Keith Weed: Saving the World at Scale," *Adweek*, March 23, 2015, pp. 24–27.

41. Wouter Aghina, Aaron De Smet, and Suzanne Heywood, "The Past and Future of Global Organizations," *McKinsey Quarterly*, No. 3 (2014), pp. 97–106; Philip Atkinson, "Managing Chaos in a Matrix World," *Management Services*, November 2003, p. 8; Jennifer Pellet, "Fine-Tuning Philips," *Chief Executive*, March/April 2009, pp. 12–13.

42. Moran and Riesenberger (1994).

43. Erin Anderson and Hubert Gatignon, "Modes of Foreign Entry: A Transaction Cost Analysis and Propositions," *Journal of International Business Studies* 17 (Fall 1986), pp. 1–26; William H. Davidson, *Global Strategic Management* (New York: Wiley, 1982).

44. S. Tamer Cavusgil and Gary Knight, "The Born-Global Firm: An Entrepreneurial and Capabilities Perspective on Early and Rapid Internationalization," *Journal of International Business Studies* 46, No. 1 (2015), pp. 3–16.

Chapter 12

Global Market Opportunity Assessment

Learning Objectives *After studying this chapter, you should be able to:*

12.1 Understand analyzing organizational readiness to internationalize.

12.2 Determine the suitability of products and services for foreign markets.

12.3 Describe screening countries to identify target markets.

12.4 Understand assessing industry market potential.

12.5 Explain about choosing foreign business partners.

12.6 Know about estimating company sales potential.

Estimating Demand in Emerging Markets

Estimating the demand for products or services in emerging markets and developing economies is a challenging task for managers. These countries have unique commercial environments. They may be limited in terms of reliable data, market research firms, and trained interviewers. Consumers in some of these countries may consider surveys an invasion of privacy. Survey respondents may try to please researchers by telling them what they want to hear rather than providing honest answers to their questions.

Three of the largest emerging markets—China, India, and Brazil—have a combined GDP of more than $15 trillion. Africa is among the biggest markets for mobile phone sales, growing to more than 100 million users in just a few years. Automakers are doing substantial business selling economy cars throughout Latin America, South Asia, and Eastern Europe. In short, emerging markets and developing economies are huge markets for products and services.

Estimating demand in such countries requires managers to use innovative research methods to gain insights or data. Let's consider two firms trying to estimate the demand for wallpaper and adhesive bandages in Morocco.

In Morocco, wealthy people tend to live in villas and condominiums and are a target market for wallpaper sales. The government usually measures wallpaper imports by weight and value. Such information is little use for estimating wallpaper sales because firms sell wallpaper by the roll, and different designs have different weights.

One wallpaper company examined data from various sources to estimate demand. First, managers reviewed a recent study of the number of water heaters purchased in Morocco. From experience, they knew that if households purchased this modern convenience, they would likely buy wallpaper too. Second, managers reviewed government statistics on domestic wallpaper sales, discretionary income by type of household, and home construction data. Third, they studied the lifestyle of a sample of local consumers and found that Moroccans typically shop for wallpaper to complement wall-to-wall carpets. Among married couples, the wife

Source: readytogo/Fotolia

usually decides on decorations for the home. Customers are usually well-off. They include professionals, merchants, and high-ranking administrators. The company made a reasonable estimate of demand for wallpaper by triangulating data from these sources and using its own judgment.

In the case of adhesive bandages, available data revealed that 70 percent of demand for pharmaceutical items, including bandages, was met by wholesalers concentrated in Casablanca, Morocco's capital city. The country imported all its adhesive bandages. Demand was growing quickly, due to rapid population growth, free medication for the needy, and reimbursement programs for medical expenses. Although the government published import statistics, the information was confusing. The data on bandage imports was incomplete and mixed with data about other types of adhesives. Widespread smuggling and gray marketing through unofficial distribution channels complicated demand estimates.

Researchers interviewed bandage salespeople from Curad, Johnson & Johnson, and other firms to gather more information. They visited retail stores to ask about sales, prevailing prices, competitive brands, and consumer attitudes. They found that consumers tend to be price-sensitive and rely on doctors and pharmacists to recommend bandage brands. Researchers also tallied statistics from the United Nations Development Program and other aid agencies that donate medical supplies to developing countries. They eventually arrived at a reasonable estimate of bandage sales by assimilating data from these various sources.

Questions

12-1. Why is it challenging to estimate demand in emerging markets?

12-2. What types of products are in greatest demand in emerging markets?

12-3. Why do researchers often need to use innovative approaches to estimate demand in emerging markets?

SOURCES: Nicolas Hamelin, Meriam Ellouzi, and Andrew Canterbury, "Consumer Ethnocentrism and Country-of-Origin Effects in the Moroccan Market," *Journal of Global Marketing* 24, No. 3 (2011), pp. 228–244; Lyn Amine and S. Tamer Cavusgil, "Demand Estimation in a Developing Country Environment: Difficulties, Techniques, and Examples," *Journal of the Market Research Society* 28, No. 1 (1986), pp. 43–65; Erik Simanis and Duncan Duke, "Profits at the Bottom of the Pyramid," *Harvard Business Review*, October 2014, pp. 86–93; U.S. Department of Commerce, *Doing Business in Morocco: Country Commercial Guide 2014*, http://www.buyusainfo.net; World Bank, *Global Economic Prospects*, (Washington DC: World Bank, January 2015).

Management choices determine the future of the firm. Making good choices depends on having objective evidence and hard data about how best to configure value-chain activities and about what products and services to offer and where to offer them. The more managers know about an opportunity, the better equipped they will be to exploit it. This is particularly true in international business, which usually entails more uncertainty than domestic business.[1] To navigate foreign markets skillfully, managers require substantial information about potential threats and opportunities and how to conduct business abroad.[2] Managers devise strategies as part of planned actions to optimize the firm's competitive advantages. Planning involves estimating, forecasting, and problem solving and therefore requires substantial information inputs.

Central to a firm's research is identifying and defining the best business opportunities in the global marketplace. A **global market opportunity** is a favorable combination of circumstances, locations, and timing that offers prospects for exporting, investing, sourcing, or partnering in foreign markets. Under such conditions, the firm may perceive opportunities to:

Global market opportunity
Favorable combination of circumstances, locations, and timing that offers prospects for exporting, investing, sourcing, or partnering in foreign markets.

- Sell its products and services.
- Establish factories or other production facilities to produce offerings more cheaply or competently.
- Procure raw materials, components, or services at lower cost or of better quality.
- Enter beneficial collaborations with foreign partners.

Global market opportunities can enhance company performance, often far beyond what the firm can achieve in its home market.[3]

In this chapter, we discuss six key tasks that managers should perform to define and pursue global market opportunities. Exhibit 12.1 illustrates the tasks, objectives, and procedures associated with each task. The process is especially appropriate for pursuing marketing or collaborative venture opportunities abroad. The six tasks are:

- Analyze organizational readiness to internationalize.
- Assess the suitability of the firm's products and services for foreign markets.
- Screen countries to identify attractive target markets.
- Assess the industry market potential, or the market demand, for the product(s) or service(s) in selected target markets.
- Choose qualified business partners, such as distributors or suppliers.
- Estimate company sales potential for each target market.

In carrying out this systematic process, the manager will need to employ objective *selection criteria* by which to make choices, as listed in the final column of Exhibit 12.1. Let's examine each task in detail.

Analyzing Organizational Readiness to Internationalize

12.1 Understand analyzing organizational readiness to internationalize.

Before undertaking an international venture the firm should conduct a formal assessment of its readiness to internationalize. An evaluation of organizational capabilities is useful both for companies new to international business and for those with considerable experience. Such a self-audit is similar to a SWOT analysis—that is, an evaluation of the firm's strengths, weaknesses, opportunities, and threats.

Task	Objective	Procedure
1. Analyze organizational readiness to internationalize	To provide an objective assessment of the company's preparedness to engage in international business activity.	● Examine company strengths and weaknesses, relative to international business, by evaluating the availability in the firm of key factors, such as: — appropriate financial and tangible resources — relevant skills and competencies — commitment by senior management to international expansion ● Take action to eliminate deficiencies in the firm that hinder achieving company goals.
2. Assess the suitability of the firm's products and services for foreign markets	To conduct a systematic assessment of the suitability of the firm's products and services for international customers; to evaluate the degree of fit between the product or service and foreign customer needs.	● For each possible target market, identify those factors that may hinder market potential. Determine how the product or service may need to be adapted for each market. Specifically, for each potential market, assess the firm's products and services with regard to such factors as: — foreign customer characteristics and preferences — relevant laws and regulations — requirements of channel intermediaries — characteristics of competitors' offerings
3. Screen countries to identify target markets	To reduce the number of countries that warrant in-depth investigation as potential target markets to a manageable few.	● Identify the five or six country markets that hold the best potential for the firm by assessing each candidate country market with regard to such criteria as: — size and growth rate — 'market intensity' (customers' buying power) — 'consumption capacity' (size and growth rate of the middle class) — receptivity to imports — infrastructure for doing business — degree of economic freedom — country risk
4. Assess industry market potential	To estimate the most likely share of industry sales within each target country; to investigate and evaluate any potential barriers to market entry.	● Develop 3- to 5-year forecast of industry sales for each target market. Specifically, assess industry market potential in each market by examining such criteria as: — market size and growth rate — relevant trends in the industry — degree of competitive intensity — tariff and nontariff trade barriers — relevant standards and regulations — availability and sophistication of local distribution intermediaries — specific customer requirements and preferences — industry-specific market potential indicators — industry-specific market entry barriers

(continues)

EXHIBIT 12.1

Key Tasks in Global Market Opportunity Assessment

| 5. Choose foreign business partners | To decide on the type of foreign business partner, clarify ideal partner qualifications, and determine appropriate market entry strategy. | • Determine what value-adding activities must be performed by foreign business partners.
• Based on needed value-adding activities, determine the most desirable attributes in foreign business partners.
• Assess and select foreign business partners. That is, evaluate each potential business partner based on criteria such as:
— specific industry expertise
— commitment to the international venture
— access to local distribution channels
— financial strength
— technical expertise
— quality of staff
— appropriate facilities and infrastructure |
| 6. Estimate company sales potential | To estimate the most likely share of industry sales the company can achieve, over a period of time, for each target market. | • Develop 3- to 5-year forecast of company sales in each target market. Estimate the potential to sell the firm's product or service, based on criteria such as:
— capabilities of partners
— access to distribution
— competitive intensity
— pricing and financing
— market penetration timetable of the firm
— risk tolerance of senior managers
• Determine the factors that will influence company sales potential |

EXHIBIT 12.1
(*continued*)

When assessing the firm's readiness to internationalize, managers examine their organization to determine the degree to which it has the motivation, resources, and skills necessary to engage in international business successfully. In such an assessment, managers measure the firm's

- Degree of international experience.
- Goals and objectives it envisions for internationalization.
- Quantity and quality of skills, capabilities, and resources available for internationalization.
- Actual and potential support the firm's network of relationships provides.

If one or more key resources is lacking, management must acquire or develop them *before* allowing the contemplated venture to go forward. Organizational culture plays an important role because key employees should possess the motivation and commitment to expand the firm's activities into foreign markets.

Managers also examine conditions in the external business environment by studying opportunities and threats in target markets. They research the specific needs and preferences of buyers as well as the nature of competing products and the risks inherent in such markets.

A formal analysis of organizational readiness to internationalize requires managers to address the following questions:

- *What do we hope to gain from international business?* Objectives might include increasing sales or profits, following key customers who locate abroad, challenging competitors in their home markets, or pursuing a global strategy of establishing production and marketing operations at various locations worldwide.

- *Is international expansion consistent with other firm goals now or in the future?* The firm should evaluate and manage internationalization in the context of its mission and business plan to ensure that it represents the best use of company resources.

- *What demands will internationalization place on firm resources,* such as management, human resources, and finance as well as production and marketing capacity? How will the firm meet such demands? Management must ensure that it has sufficient production and marketing capacity to serve foreign markets. Channel members become frustrated when inadequate capacity prevents the firm from fulfilling customer orders abroad.

- *What is the basis of the firm's competitive advantage?* Companies seek competitive advantages by doing things better than their competitors. Competitive advantages can be based on strong R&D, superior input goods, cost-effective or innovative manufacturing capacity, skillful marketing, highly effective distribution channels, or other capabilities.

Diagnostic tools help managers audit the firm's readiness to internationalize. One of the best known is CORE (Company Readiness to Export, developed by Tamer Cavusgil in the 1990s; see www.globalEDGE.msu.edu). CORE has been widely adopted by individual firms, consultants, and the U.S. Department of Commerce. Because it was developed from extensive research on factors that contribute to successful exporting, it is also an ideal tutorial for self-learning and training.

CORE asks managers questions about their organizational resources, skills, and motivation to assess the firm's readiness to engage in exporting successfully. It generates assessments of both organizational and product readiness to identify the useful assets managers have and the additional ones they need to make internationalization succeed. The assessment emphasizes exporting because it is the typical entry mode for most newly internationalizing firms.

Source: Andrew Paul Travel/Alamy

Products that already sell well at home are among those most likely to succeed abroad. As a manager, given Starbuck's positioning, would you have supported opening this store in China?

Assessing the Suitability of Products and Services for Foreign Markets

Once management has confirmed the firm's readiness to internationalize, it next determines the suitability of its products and services for foreign markets. Most companies produce a portfolio of offerings, some or all of which may be suitable for selling abroad. In other cases, firms develop products specifically for promising international markets.

12.2 Determine the suitability of products and services for foreign markets.

Products or services with the best international prospects tend to have one or more of the following characteristics:

- *Sell well in the domestic market* Offerings received well at home are likely to succeed abroad, especially where similar needs and conditions exist.

- *Cater to universal needs* For example, buyers worldwide demand personal-care products, medical devices, and banking services. International sales may be promising if the product or service is unique or has important features that are appealing to foreign customers and are hard for foreign firms to duplicate.

- *Address a need not well served in particular foreign markets* Potential may exist in countries where the product or service does not currently exist or where demand is just starting to emerge.
- *Address a new or emergent need abroad* Demand for some products and services may arise suddenly from a disaster or emergent trend. In Haiti, for example, an earthquake created an urgent need for easy-to-build housing. In emerging markets, growing affluence is spurring demand for restaurants and hospitality services.

One of the simplest ways to find out whether a product or service will sell abroad is to ask intermediaries in the target market about likely local demand for it. Managers also might attend an industry trade fair in the target market and interview prospective customers or distributors. Because trade fairs often draw participants from entire regions, such as Asia or Europe, this approach is efficient for learning about the market potential of several countries at once. Larger firms typically hire global market research firms to evaluate the suitability of their products or services for international sales. Large MNEs undertake systematic research to assess sales potential of their offerings in specific foreign markets.

To deepen knowledge about the international market potential of a product or service, managers should obtain answers to the following questions:

- *Who initiates purchasing?* Homemakers are usually the chief decision makers for household products. Professional buyers make purchases on behalf of firms.
- *Who uses the product or service?* Children consume various products, but their parents may be the actual buyers. Employees consume products bought by the firms where they work.
- *Why do people buy the product or service?* What specific needs does it fulfill? Such needs vary worldwide. In advanced economies, for example, consumers use Honda's gas-powered generators for recreational purposes; in developing economies households buy them for everyday heating and lighting.
- *Where do people purchase the product or service?* Once the researcher understands where the offering is typically purchased, it is useful to visit likely vendors to assess sales potential, whether the good should be adapted for the market, and how best to price, promote, and distribute it.
- *What economic, cultural, geographic, and other factors in the target market may limit sales?* Countries vary substantially in terms of buyer income levels, preferences, climate, and other factors that can inhibit or facilitate purchasing behavior.

In China, numerous companies are pursuing opportunities to serve the emerging health care market. Demand for medications, medical devices, and health care services is booming due to an aging population, a growing middle class able to afford these treatments, and widespread dissatisfaction with existing health care options. Pharmaceutical firms such as Bayer HealthCare and Novo Nordisk count China among their top markets with enormous growth potential. Medical equipment firms such as GE Healthcare and Philips are targeting numerous opportunities to serve the country's emergent hospital market. Johnson & Johnson and Medtronic have established R&D centers and manufacturing sites to understand and exploit blossoming opportunities better. In total, China is expected to reach $1 trillion in total health care spending by 2020.

Screening Countries to Identify Target Markets

12.3 Describe screening countries to identify target markets.

Screening to identify the best countries is an essential task. It is especially important in the early stages of internationalization. For most firms, it is also the most time-consuming part of opportunity assessment. Failure to choose the right countries not only results in financial loss; it also incurs opportunity costs, tying up resources the firm might have used more profitably elsewhere. Exporting, foreign direct investment (FDI), and sourcing each requires a different set of screening criteria. Let's see why.

Screening Countries for Exporting

Exporters first examine such criteria as population, income, demographic characteristics, government stability, and nature of the general business environment in individual countries. Statistics that span several years help determine which markets are growing and which are shrinking. The exporter can buy research reports from market research firms that provide assessments and key statistics on specific markets. National governments provide much useful information. Many provide some research services free of charge or at very low cost. In the United States, for example, the Department of Commerce (www .export.gov) conducts and publishes numerous market surveys. Examples include *The Water Supply and Wastewater Treatment Market in China, Automotive Parts and Equipment Industry Guide in France*, and *Country Commercial Guide for Brazil*.

Some firms target countries that are psychically near—that is, countries similar to the home country in culture, legal environment, and other factors. Such countries fit management's comfort zone. Australian firms often choose Britain, New Zealand, or the United States as their first foreign market. As managerial experience, knowledge, and confidence grow, firms expand into more complex and culturally distant markets, such as China or Japan.

Other firms are more venturesome and target nontraditional, higher-risk countries. The born-global companies exemplify this trend. Ongoing globalization, as well as advances in communication and transportation technologies, have reduced the foreignness of most countries, hence the cost and risk of entering them. Even small firms now routinely reach out to culturally distant countries, including emerging markets and developing economies.

Information needed for country screening varies by product type or industry. In marketing consumer electronics, for example, the researcher emphasizes countries with large populations, discretionary income, and ample electricity. For farming equipment, the best targets are countries with substantial agricultural land and farmers. Health insurance companies target countries with many doctors and hospitals and the means to purchase health insurance.

Often, the firm may target a geographical region or a group of countries rather than individual countries. This approach is usually more cost effective, particularly in markets with similar characteristics. The European Union includes 27 countries that are relatively similar in income levels, regulations, and infrastructure. When entering Europe, firms often devise a pan-European strategy that considers many EU member countries simultaneously rather than planning separate efforts in individual countries.

In other cases, the firm may target so-called *gateway countries*, or regional hubs, that serve as entry points to nearby or affiliated markets. Singapore is the gateway to Southeast Asian countries, Hong Kong is

Source: MasterLu/Fotolia

When deciding on target markets, internationalizing firms often choose regional hubs, which serve as critical entry points for important national or regional markets. Pictured here is Hong Kong, an important entry hub for China.

EXHIBIT 12.2

Most Promising Export Markets in Incremental Contribution to World GDP, 2015 through 2020, Percent and Dollar Volume in US$ Billions

Source: Based on World Economic Outlook Databases, International Monetary Fund, at www.imf.org.

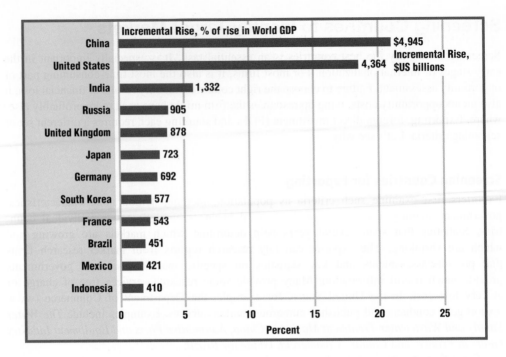

an important gateway to China. Turkey is a good platform for the central Asian republics. Firms base their operations in a gateway country so they can serve the larger adjacent region.

Growing national GDP is among the most important indicators of capacity to purchase products and services. Exhibit 12.2 portrays the world's most promising export markets, based on aggregate GDP growth. The exhibit highlights the countries most expected to grow their GDPs through 2020 and their expected incremental contribution to world GDP. China is in the lead. It is expected to contribute $4,945 billion or more than 20 percent of the rise in global GDP by 2020. Note that most countries in the exhibit are emerging markets. Brazil, Russia, India, and China, known collectively as the BRIC countries, show remarkable potential as target markets in coming years. They will contribute about one-third of the total increase in world GDP by 2020.

SCREENING METHODOLOGY FOR POTENTIAL COUNTRY MARKETS   It is expensive and impractical to target all the nearly 200 countries worldwide. Management must choose markets that offer the best prospects. Two basic methods for doing this are *gradual elimination* and *indexing and ranking*.

Gradual elimination The researcher who uses *gradual elimination* starts with a large number of prospective target countries and gradually narrows the choices by examining increasingly specific information. As indicated in Exhibit 12.1, the researcher aims to reduce the number of countries that warrant in-depth investigation as potential target markets to a manageable five or six. Because research is expensive, it is essential to eliminate unattractive markets quickly. Targeting a less-crowded economy with a product that is not yet widely available may be more profitable than targeting saturated and more competitive markets in Europe, Japan, and North America.

In the early stages, the researcher first obtains general information on macro-level indicators such as population, income, and economic growth before delving into specific information. GlobalEDGE™ (www.globalEDGE.msu.edu) and numerous other sources provide broad screening data. The researcher then employs more specific indicators, such as import statistics, to narrow the choices. Import statistics help reveal the size of the market, the presence of competitors, and the market's viability for new sales. The researcher should also examine the level of the country's exports because some countries, such as Panama and Singapore, function as major transit points for international shipments and may not be actual product users.

Indexing and ranking A second method for choosing the most promising foreign markets is *indexing and ranking*, in which the researcher assigns scores to countries based on their overall market attractiveness. For each country, the researcher first identifies a comprehensive set of market-potential indicators and then uses one or more of them to represent a variable. Weights are assigned to each variable to establish its relative importance. The more important a variable, the greater its weight. The researcher uses the resulting weighted scores to rank the countries.

ASSESSING THE EXPORT POTENTIAL OF EMERGING MARKETS   China, India, and numerous other emerging markets offer huge potential. For example, John Deere & Company saw an opportunity to sell small tractors to India's 300 million small farmers. After conducting extensive research, the firm developed four small tractor models for the market and is now doing significant business there.[4]

The indexing and ranking method for identifying promising markets is illustrated by the Market Potential Index, developed by Tamer Cavusgil[5] and featured at globalEDGE™ (www.globalEDGE.msu.edu).[6] Presented in Exhibit 12.3, the index ranks countries on a collection of variables. We focus on emerging markets. From it, a manager would conclude that China, Hong Kong, and Singapore are attractive markets. China has steadily risen in the index over time, as have Poland and the United Arab Emirates. The data are also helpful for decisions on entry by FDI and for sourcing.

Exhibit 12.4 defines the variables and relative weights in the index. The assigned weights can be adjusted up or down to fit the unique characteristics of any industry. For example, in evaluating market size, food industry firms attach more weight to market size, whereas firms in the telecommunications equipment industry emphasize infrastructure and country risk. The researcher can add variables or countries to refine the tool for greater precision.

The size and growth rate of the middle class are often critical indicators of promising targets. The *middle class* is measured by the share of national income available to middle-income households. These consumers are good prospects for most firms because the wealthier class in most emerging markets is relatively small and the poorest segment has little disposable income. The size of the middle class as a percentage of world population has consistently increased over time, thanks to rising affluence in emerging markets and developing economies. Recent research indicates the global middle class will continue to expand over time. Most of this increase will arise in the Asia Pacific region, especially China.[7] Note, however, that measures of per-capita income may underestimate the true potential of emerging markets due to imprecise measurement methods and the existence in many countries of a large, informal economy.

The relative size of the middle class, and the pace of its growth, also indicate how national income is distributed in a country. If income distribution is very unequal, the size of the middle class will be limited and the market will be less attractive.

In Exhibit 12.3, an analysis of the rankings for each of the dimensions reveals some interesting patterns. China scores highest in market size but much lower in terms of market intensity and market receptivity. This reveals there are always *trade-offs* in selecting target countries. No single country is attractive on all dimensions. Along with desirable features, the researcher also must contend with less desirable ones. For example, both Singapore and Hong Kong are favorable in terms of market receptivity, but they are city-states with small populations.

According to the index in Exhibit 12.3, the top five countries are all in Asia. In recent years, they have made tremendous strides in market liberalization, industrialization, and modernization. South Korea has grown tenfold in the past 40 years. South Korean firms have become world leaders in many industries such as shipbuilding, telecommunications, and consumer electronics. They use pioneering technologies years ahead of their competitors and are overtaking other countries in broadband and mobile technologies. Asia's rapid economic development is one of the remarkable features of contemporary globalization.[8]

Country rankings like those in Exhibit 12.3 are not static; they evolve in the wake of macroeconomic events or country-specific developments. Although India ranks relatively high, its ranking may fall dramatically if a future government reverses market liberalization. The accession of Bulgaria and Romania into the European Union is improving the economic prospects of these countries. The introduction of modern banking systems and legal infrastructure should increase Russia's attractiveness as an export market. Chile has achieved substantial progress in economic reforms and higher living standards, whereas economic stagnation has reduced Argentina's attractiveness.

The variables suggested by ranking indicators are only a general guide for identifying promising countries in the early stages of research. After identifying a few high potential markets,

EXHIBIT 12.3 Market Potential Index for Emerging Markets, 2014

Country	Rank	Overall Score	Market Size	Market Intensity	Market Growth Rate	Market Consumption Capacity	Commercial Infrastructure	Market Receptivity	Economic Freedom	Country Risk
China	1	100	100	4	100	98	56	9	23	80
Hong Kong	2	56	2	100	62	31	96	100	100	95
Singapore	3	50	2	76	76	33	83	89	70	100
India	4	46	37	36	77	57	14	9	47	64
South Korea	5	41	10	59	67	60	78	21	63	83
United Arab Emirates	6	38	2	66	91	37	88	43	43	74
Russia	7	36	19	41	71	51	81	8	28	64
Brazil	8	34	14	48	62	41	58	6	50	69
Mexico	9	31	10	61	62	39	40	23	54	70
Qatar	10	31	1	59	79	30	73	31	45	80
Poland	11	31	4	58	57	47	70	14	65	75
Latvia	12	31	1	61	64	41	98	19	61	59
Chile	13	30	3	61	85	18	56	17	76	79
Slovakia	14	30	1	57	53	48	69	25	64	75
Lithuania	15	30	1	65	40	38	99	24	70	75
Malaysia	16	29	4	34	80	30	66	26	52	85
Turkey	17	29	7	68	65	47	52	10	50	54
Saudi Arabia	18	28	5	20	90	37	84	17	29	75
Slovenia	19	27	1	60	37	45	98	21	61	67
Indonesia	20	27	11	32	82	42	28	8	47	64

Note: Only the top 20 countries are provided here; consult www.globalEDGE.msu.edu for a more complete list.

Source: Market Potential Index (MPI) – 2014, globalEDGE™ (www.globalEDGE.msu.edu/resourcedesk/mpi).

EXHIBIT 12.4 Variables Used in the Market Potential Index

Dimension	Definition	Weight	Measures Used
Market Size	Country's population	25/100	• Urban population (million) • Electricity consumption (billion kwh)
Market Intensity	Buying power of the country's residents	15/100	• GNI per-capita estimates using PPP (U.S. dollars) • Private consumption as a percentage of GDP (%)
Market Growth Rate	Pace of industrialization and economic development	12.5/100	• Average annual growth rate of primary energy use (%) • Real GDP growth rate (%)
Market Consumption Capacity	Size and growth rate of the country's middle class	12.5/100	• Consumer expenditure (U.S. dollars) • Income share of the middle class (%)
Commercial Infrastructure	Ease of access to marketing, distribution, and communication channels	10/100	• Cellular mobile subscribers (per 100 habitants) • Households with Internet access (per 100 habitants) • Main telephone lines (per 100 habitants) • Number of PCs (per 1000 habitants) • Paved road density (km per million people) • Population per retail outlet • Percentage of households with color TV
Market Receptivity	Extent of country's openness to imports	10/100	• Per-capita imports from the United States (U.S. dollars) • Trade as a percentage of GDP (%)
Economic Freedom	Degree to which the country has liberalized its economy	7.5/100	• Economic Freedom Index • Political Freedom Index
Country Risk	Level of political risk	7.5/100	• Business risk rating • Country risk rating • Political risk rating

Source: Market Potential Index—2014, globalEDGE™ (www.globaledge.msu.edu/mpi).

the researcher must do more detailed analyses. Eventually, the researcher will supplement the indicators for specific industries. For medical equipment, for example, the researcher must gather specific data on healthcare expenditures and the number of physicians and hospital beds per capita. Firms in the financial services sector require specific data on commercial risk, interest rates, and density of banks. Depending on the industry, researchers may also apply different weights to each market-potential indicator. Population size is relatively less important for a firm that markets yachts than for one that sells footwear.

Country Screening for Foreign Direct Investment

FDI investments in plant, equipment, and other productive assets are costly and usually undertaken for the long term. Choosing the right targets is critical, and different variables apply than for exporting. For example, with FDI the availability of skilled labor and managerial talent in the target market is often very important.

Researchers identifying the best locations for FDI usually consider the following variables:

• Long-term prospects for growth and substantial returns

• Cost of doing business, based on the price and availability of commercial infrastructure, tax rates and wages and high-level skills and capital markets

• Country risk, including regulatory, financial, political, and cultural barriers and the legal environment for intellectual property protection

• Competitive environment and intensity of competition from other firms

• Government incentives such as tax holidays, subsidized training, grants, or low-interest loans

When screening countries for FDI, numerous sources provide useful information, such as the United Nations Conference on Trade and Development (UNCTAD; www.unctad.org) and the World Bank (www.worldbank.org). The consulting firm A. T. Kearney prepares the *Foreign Direct Investment Confidence Index* (www.atkearney.com), which tracks how political, economic, and regulatory changes affect the FDI preferences of the world's top 1,000 firms. By surveying executives, the index captures the most important variables for the 65 countries that receive more than 90 percent of global FDI investment.

Country Screening for Sourcing

Global sourcing and offshoring describe the practice of procuring finished products, intermediate goods, and services from suppliers located abroad. When seeking foreign sources of supply, managers examine such factors as cost and quality of inputs, stability of exchange rates, reliability of suppliers, and the presence of a workforce with superior technical skills.

Firms increasingly source services from abroad to obtain various advantages. A. T. Kearney, a consulting firm, compares the factors that make countries attractive as potential locations for offshoring service activities such as IT, business processes, and call centers. The following dimensions are relevant.

- *Financial attractiveness* accounts for compensation costs (average wages), infrastructure costs (for electricity and telecom systems), and tax and regulatory costs (tax burden, corruption, and fluctuating exchange rates).
- *People skills and availability* account for suppliers' experience and skills, labor-force availability, education and language proficiency, and employee-attrition rates.
- *Business environment* assesses economic and political aspects of the country, commercial infrastructure, cultural adaptability, and security of intellectual property.

12.4 Understand assessing industry market potential.

Assessing Industry Market Potential

The methods for screening countries discussed so far provide insights on individual markets and reduce the complexity of choosing appropriate foreign locations. Once the number of potential countries has been reduced to a manageable few, the next step is to conduct an in-depth analysis of each. In earlier stages, the researcher examined macro-level indicators. Now, because market potential is industry-specific, the researcher narrows the focus to industry-level indicators.

Industry market potential

An estimate of the likely sales for all firms in a specific industry during a particular period.

Industry market potential is an estimate of the likely sales for all firms in a specific industry during a particular period. It is different from *company sales potential*, the share of industry sales the focal firm itself can expect during a given year. Most firms forecast both industry market potential and company sales potential at least three years into the future.

Estimating industry market potential enables the researcher to refine the analysis and identify the most attractive countries for the firm's product or service. It also provides industry-specific insights and understanding into how the firm needs to adapt its product and marketing approaches.

To estimate industry market potential, managers obtain data and insights on the following variables for each country:

- Size and growth rate of the market and trends in the specific industry.
- Tariff and nontariff trade barriers to market entry.
- Standards and regulations that affect the industry.
- Availability and sophistication of distribution for the firm's offerings in the market.
- Unique customer requirements and preferences.
- Industry-specific market potential indicators.

In addition to generic determinants of demand, each industry sector—from air conditioners to zippers—has its own *industry-specific potential indicators* or *distinctive drivers of demand*. Marketers of cameras, for example, examine climate-related factors such as the average number of sunny days in a typical year. A manufacturer of heavy machinery might examine the rate of industrialization and dependence on hydroelectricity. A marketer of cooling equipment and industrial filters will consider the number of institutional buyers such as restaurants and hotels. These are all industry-specific market potential indicators.

The researcher also evaluates factors that affect the marketing and use of the product, such as consumer characteristics, culture, distribution channels, and business practices. Because intellectual property rights vary worldwide, it is important to protect the firm's critical assets by examining regulations, trademark rules, and product liability. The researcher should also investigate subsidy and incentive programs from home and foreign governments that reduce the cost of foreign market entry.

Source: Aleksandra Gigowska/123RF

Camera makers account for climate in their estimates of demand, since most pictures are taken outdoors. What other industry-specific variables might they consider?

Growth rates tend to be relatively high in new or rapidly innovating industries. The researcher should bear in mind that the product is likely to be in a different phase of its life cycle in each country. Countries in which the product is not currently available or in which competitors have only recently entered are often promising targets.

Managers use various methods to estimate industry market potential.

- *Simple trend analysis.* This method quantifies the total likely amount of industry market potential by examining aggregate production for the industry as a whole, adding imports from abroad and deducting exports. Trend analysis provides a rough estimate of the size of current industry sales in the country.

- *Monitoring key industry-specific indicators.* The manager examines unique industry drivers of market demand by collecting data from various sources. The earth-moving equipment company Caterpillar examines the volume of announced construction projects, number of issued building permits, growth rate of households, and infrastructure development to anticipate sales of its construction equipment.

- *Monitoring key competitors.* Here, the manager investigates the degree of major competitor activity in the countries of interest. If Caterpillar is considering Chile as a potential market, its managers investigate the current involvement of its main competitor, the Japanese firm Komatsu, in Chile and gather competitive intelligence to anticipate Komatsu's likely future moves in Chile.

- *Following key customers around the world.* Automotive suppliers can anticipate their future markets by monitoring the international expansion of their customers such as Honda or Mercedes-Benz. Caterpillar follows its current customers such as Bechtel and Fluor as they bid for contracts or establish operations in specific markets.

- *Tapping into supplier networks.* Many suppliers serve multiple clients and can be a major source of information about competitors. Firms gain valuable leads from current suppliers by asking them about the activities of competitors as long as the questions are ethical and don't expose competitors' trade secrets and other proprietary information.

- *Attending international trade fairs.* By attending a trade fair in the target country, the manager can learn much about market characteristics and other factors that indicate industry sales potential. Trade fairs also help identify potential distributors and other business partners.

Source: atm2003/Fotolia LLC.

Demand is growing in Europe for environmental technologies and green products. These workers are installing solar panels on a house in Italy.

Data Sources for Estimating Industry Market Potential

For each target country, the manager seeks data that directly or indirectly report levels of industry sales and production and the intensity of exports and imports in the product category of interest. Exhibit 12.5 summarizes sites useful for estimating industry market potential and describes various statistics for conducting market opportunity assessment and other research.

One useful source in the United States is the market research section at export.gov (www.export.gov/marketsearch). Specific reports available at this site include:

- *Best Markets and Market Updates* reports that provide extensive industry, country, and market research to pinpoint top export markets and entry strategies.
- *Country Commercial Guides*, which comprehensively profile the political, economic, and commercial environment of some 150 countries.
- *Industry Overviews* and *Industry/Regional Reports* that describe conditions in specific industries.

Managers often must be creative in finding and consulting resources that shed light on the task at hand. Data and resources in international research are rarely complete or precise. Consider Teltone Inc. The firm wished to enter Mexico with its inexpensive brand of cellular telephones and needed to estimate industry-wide demand. It consulted numerous sources, including reports by the International Telecommunications Union (in Geneva, Switzerland),

EXHIBIT 12.5 A Sampling of Sites for Conducting International Business Research

Site	Address	Description
globalEDGE™	www.globalEDGE.msu.edu	Data, information, search engines, and diagnostic tools on a full range of international business topics
Export.gov	www.export.gov	Country commercial guides and other United States government resources to support exporting and other international business activities
UK Trade and Investment	www.uktradeinvest.gov.uk	United Kingdom data and resources to support international business
Industry Canada	www.ic.gc.ca	Canada data and resources to support international business
United Nations Conference on Trade and Development (UNCTAD)	www.unctad.org	Country fact sheets and statistics for analysis of international trade, FDI, and economic trends
World Trade Organization (WTO)	www.wto.org	Statistics on tariffs, government intervention, and economic conditions worldwide
World Bank	www.worldbank.org	National and international statistics, financial and technical information, sectoral data, trends in the world economy
World Bank Doing Business	www.doingbusiness.org	Reports on doing business in various countries
International Monetary Fund (IMF)	www.imf.org	Data and statistics on countries and economic and financial indicators
A.T. Kearney	www.atkearney.com	Various indices, including the Foreign Direct Investment Confidence Index

NATASHA BROWN

Natasha's major: Computer Information Systems
Objectives: Happiness, personal and career growth, travel, and the opportunity to give back
Internships during college: AT&T Network Operations
Jobs held since graduating:

- Technical Consultant, Hewlett Packard, Alpharetta, Georgia
- Pre-sales Solutions Architect, Hewlett Packard Enterprise, New York City

Natasha Brown always had a strong interest in technology and travel. She is passionate about solving problems and helping others. In college, Natasha sought the advice of mentors, executives, and fellow students. She invested much energy in building a network of contacts and advisors. Eventually she fell in love with her university's "Global Business and Media" program. In her third year, a study abroad program piqued her interest, but Natasha lacked funding for the trip. She applied for scholarships and took a job as a resident assistant at school. Natasha's efforts paid off; she was accepted for a one-month study program in Hungary and Turkey. There she visited the local operations of firms such as CNN, Coca-Cola, and Turkcell. She learned about the importance of understanding international cultures on various levels before doing business abroad.

Natasha credits her time in Hungary and Turkey with providing her the most growth in her time at school. Natasha found the trip inspiring. Witnessing the differences in culture and business abroad opened her mind to endless possibilities. She says, "It's a special feeling when international executives take the time to not only meet with you but also inquire about your life. It was humbling how genuinely interested they were in someone like me. All the opportunities I gained on the program gave me more confidence in my studies and who I could be as a professional."

Natasha's Advice

After graduation, Natasha took a job at Hewlett Packard Enterprise. Working as a solutions architect, Natasha's study abroad program in college gave her enormous confidence to interact with clients. Her global business coursework revealed how technology varies around world but also connects people internationally. "My coursework and international travel gave me hands-on experience.... It expanded my curiosity and my way of thinking about the world. I always wanted to learn another language, but going to Turkey helped me learn about a language I would not have researched myself. Through my professors, I've been able to connect with international business grads from my alma mater who are now working abroad. Staying in contact with them can help me to one day work internationally as well. When you consider all the benefits, studying abroad and taking international business classes are well worth the investment. Every student should consider it." Natasha says that having international experience on her resume has enhanced her prospects for securing a position in Hewlett Packard's international operations. She wants to travel overseas again as soon as possible.

Source: Courtesy of Natasha Brown.

Export.gov, and several United Nations publications. Managers researched the size of the Mexican upper class and its average income, the nature of support infrastructure for cellular systems in Mexico, and the nature and number of retail stores that could handle cell phones. They also accessed statistics from the National Telecommunications Trade Association on the number of competitors active in Mexico and their sales volumes. From these sources, Teltone was able to make a rough estimate of market size for telephones and prices in Mexico.

The *You Can Do It: Recent Grad in IB* feature profiles Natasha Brown, who was inspired to pursue international opportunities after doing a study abroad program in Hungary and Turkey.

Choosing Foreign Business Partners

12.5 Explain about choosing foreign business partners.

Business partners are critical to international business success. Key partners include distribution-channel intermediaries, facilitators, suppliers, and collaborative venture partners such as joint venture partners, licensees, and franchisees. Once the firm has selected a target market, it must identify the types of partners it needs for its foreign market venture, negotiate terms with them, and support and monitor their conduct.

Licensing
Arrangement in which the owner of intellectual property grants a firm the right to use that property for a specified period of time in exchange for royalties or other compensation.

Franchising
Arrangement in which the firm allows another the right to use an entire business system in exchange for fees, royalties, or other forms of compensation.

International collaborative venture
Cross-border business alliance whereby partnering firms pool their resources and share costs and risks to undertake a new business venture; also referred to as an international partnership or an international strategic alliance.

Exporters tend to collaborate with foreign market intermediaries such as distributors and agents. Firms that choose to sell their intellectual property, such as know-how, trademarks, and copyrights, may work through foreign licensees. These **licensing** partners are independent businesses that apply intellectual property to produce products in their own country. In **franchising**, the foreign partner is a franchisee, an independent business abroad that acquires rights and skills from the focal firm to conduct operations in its own market (such as in the fast-food or car-rental industries). The focal firm can also internationalize by initiating an **international collaborative venture**, a business activity undertaken jointly with other firms. Such collaborations may be project-based or require equity investments. Other types of international partnerships include global sourcing, contract manufacturing, and supplier partnerships. We describe these in detail in later chapters.

Criteria for Choosing a Partner

The focal firm must identify the ideal qualifications of potential foreign partners. The firm should seek a good fit in terms of both strategy (common goals and objectives) and resources (complementary core competencies and value-chain activities). It is helpful to anticipate the likely synergy with the prospective partner for the intermediate term, three to six years into the future.

Take the case of Brunswick Corporation (www.brunswick.com), a manufacturer of recreational goods such as boats and bowling equipment. When screening for potential foreign distributors, this firm looks for:

- Financial soundness and resourcefulness to ensure that the venture receives the appropriate level of support initially and in the long run.
- Competent and professional management, with qualified technical and sales staff.
- Solid knowledge of the industry with access to distribution channels and end users in the marketplace.
- Reputation in the marketplace and good connections with local government (political clout is often helpful, especially in emerging markets).
- Commitment, loyalty, and willingness to invest in the venture and grow it over time.

Firms also seek partners with complementary expertise. For example, although the focal firm may bring engineering and manufacturing expertise to the partnership, the local distributor may bring knowledge of local customers and distribution channels.

Desirable characteristics are not always available in prospective partners. If a company enters a foreign market late, it may have to pick the second-best or even less-qualified partner. The firm should then be ready and able to strengthen the partner's capabilities by transferring appropriate managerial skills, technical know-how, and other resources.

Searching for Prospective Partners

The process of screening and evaluating business partners can be overwhelming. Commercial banks, consulting firms, and trade journals, as well as country and regional business directories such as *Kompass* and *Dun and Bradstreet*, are helpful in developing a list of partner candidates. National governments offer inexpensive services that assist firms in finding partners in specific markets. The knowledge portal globalEDGE™ (www.globalEDGE.msu.edu) provides additional resources, including diagnostic tools, to help managers systematically choose partner candidates.

Onsite visits and research from independent sources and trade fairs are crucial in the early stages of assessing a partner. Many firms ask prospective partners to prepare a formal business plan before entering an agreement. The quality of the plan illuminates the prospective partner's capabilities and level of commitment.

Source: Stephen Coburn/Shutterstock
Firms seeking a foreign business partner emphasize qualifications, including common goals and competent management.

Estimating Company Sales Potential

12.6 Know about estimating company sales potential.

Once managers have identified several promising country markets, verified industry market potential, and assessed the availability of qualified business partners, the next step is to determine **company sales potential** in each country. Company sales potential is an estimate of the share of annual industry sales the firm expects to generate in a particular target market. Estimating it can be especially challenging because of the need to obtain detailed information from the market and make fundamental assumptions to project the firm's revenues and expenses three to five years into the future. Estimates of company sales potential are rarely precise. They usually require the researcher to make judgment calls and think creatively.

Company sales potential
An estimate of the share of annual industry sales that the firm expects to generate in a particular target market.

When estimating company sales potential in a foreign market, managers collect and review various research findings and assess the following:

- *Intensity of the competitive environment* Local or third-country competitors are likely to intensify their own marketing efforts when confronted by new entrants. Their actions are often unpredictable and not easily observed.

- *Pricing and financing of sales* The degree to which pricing and financing are attractive to both customers and channel members is critical to initial entry and ultimate success.

- *Financial resources* Sufficient capital is a prerequisite for any project. International ventures are often costly.

- *Human resources* Management must ensure that it has personnel with sufficient capabilities in language, culture, and other areas to do business in target markets.

- *Partner capabilities* The competencies and resources of foreign partners, including channel intermediaries and facilitators, influence how quickly the firm can enter and generate sales in the market.

- *Access to distribution channels* The ability to establish and make best use of channel intermediaries and distribution infrastructure in the target market determines sales.

- *Market penetration timetable* A key decision is whether managers opt for gradual or rapid market entry. Gradual entry gives the firm time to develop and leverage resources and strategies but may cede market share to competitors. Rapid entry can ensure first-mover advantages but also tax the firm's resources and capabilities.

- *Risk tolerance of senior managers* Results depend on the level of resources top management is willing to commit, which in turn depends on management's tolerance for risk.

- *Special links, contacts, and capabilities of the firm* The extent of the focal firm's network in the market—its existing relationships with customers, channel members, and suppliers—can strongly affect venture success.

- *Reputation* The firm can succeed faster in the market if target customers are already familiar with its brand name and reputation.

Estimating company sales typically starts from multiple angles and converges on an ultimate estimate that relies heavily on judgment. Exhibit 12.6 provides a framework to estimate company sales. After combining information about customers, intermediaries, and competition, the researcher decides whether the result points to a reasonable estimate. Managers may make multiple estimates based on best-case, worst-case, and most-likely case scenarios. They will usually make assumptions about the degree of firm effort, price aggressiveness, possible competitive reactions, degree of intermediary effort, and so on. The firm's sales prospects also hinge on factors both controllable by management (such as prices charged to intermediaries and customers) and uncontrollable (such as the intensity of competition). Ultimately, estimating company sales potential is more art than science.

Practical Approaches to Estimating Company Sales Potential

When estimating sales potential, it is best to begin with the factors suggested in Exhibit 12.6.

Customer characteristics
- Demographics
- Growth of demand
- Size of customer segment
- Intensity
- Purchasing power

Customer receptivity
- Perceived benefits of product
- Promotional effort directed to customers

Competitive positioning of focal brand
- Unique selling proposition of product
- What are its superior features compared to competitive offerings

Company Sales Potential

Channel effort and productivity
- Margins and incentives offered to distribution intermediaries

Competition
- Intensity
- Relative strength
- Potential reactions to market entrants

Pricing
- The cost of product landed in the foreign market (a function of international shipping costs, tariffs, etc.)
- Customary margins for distributors
- Whether the firm pursues a penetration versus skimming pricing

EXHIBIT 12.6

A Framework for Estimating Company Sales Potential in the Foreign Market

The following activities are especially helpful for estimating company sales potential.

- *Survey of end users and intermediaries.* The firm can survey a sample of customers and distributors to determine the level of potential sales.

- *Trade audits.* Managers may visit retail outlets and question channel members to assess competitors' strengths and price levels. In this approach, managers estimate market potential through the eyes of intermediaries (distributors) responsible for handling the product in the market. The trade audit can also indicate opportunities for alternative distribution approaches and clarify the firm's standing relative to competitors.

- *Competitor assessment.* The firm should benchmark itself against principal competitor(s) in the market and estimate how much sales it can attract away from them. If top competitors are large and powerful, competing head-on might prove too costly. Even in countries dominated by large firms, however, research may reveal untapped or underserved market segments that can be attractive, particularly for smaller firms.

- *Estimates from local partners.* Collaborators such as distributors, franchisees, or licensees already experienced in the market are often best positioned to develop estimates of market share and sales potential.

- *Limited marketing efforts to test the waters.* Some companies may choose to engage in a limited entry in the foreign market—a sort of test market—to gauge sales potential or better understand the market. From these early results, it is possible to forecast longer-term sales.

In developing economies and emerging markets, where information sources are often lacking, two other techniques are useful for estimating company sales potential. These are *analogy* and *proxy indicators*. We illustrated these approaches in the opening case.

- *Analogy* Using this method, the researcher draws on known statistics from one country to gain insights into the same phenomenon for another, similar country. For example, if the researcher knows the total consumption of citrus drinks in Hungary, then—assuming citrus drink consumption patterns do not vary much in neighboring Romania—a rough estimate of Romania's consumption can be made, adjusting, of course, for the difference in population. If a firm knows X number of bottles of antibiotics are sold in a country with Y number of physicians per thousand people, it can assume the same ratio (of bottles per number of physicians) will apply in a similar country.
- *Proxy indicators* With proxy indicators, the researcher uses known information about one product category to infer potential about another product category, especially if the two are complementary. A proxy indicator of demand for professional hand tools might be the level of construction activity in the country; for a particular piece of surgical equipment, it might be the total number of surgeries performed.

A firm contemplating a major market entry by FDI should make its market research especially comprehensive. When Britain's huge retailer Tesco assessed its entry into the United States, researchers investigated every detail of the country's in-store offerings and grocery buyer behavior. The firm set up a mock store in Los Angeles and invited groups of 250 customers in to watch how they shopped, then asked for feedback. The researchers moved into 60 California families' homes for two weeks, sifting through their cupboards and refrigerators, shopping and cooking with them, and keeping diaries of their every movement, from how they got their kids to school to what they did at night. Such research has helped make Tesco a top food retailer worldwide.[9]

 MyManagementLab **Watch It!**

If your professor has assigned this, go to the Assignments section of **mymanagementlab.com** to complete the video exercise titled Emerging Markets: Spotlight on India and Mexico

In Conclusion

Some firms are attracted to foreign markets by the promise of revenues and profits, others by the prospect of increasing production efficiency. Still others internationalize to subdue competitive pressures or keep pace with rivals. Whatever the rationale, when companies fail in international ventures, it is often because they neglect to conduct a systematic and comprehensive assessment of global market opportunity.[10]

Although we have presented the six tasks of global market opportunity assessment in a sequence, firms do not necessarily pursue them that way. They may pursue two or more simultaneously. The process is dynamic—market conditions change, partner performance fluctuates, and competitive intensity may increase. These events require managers to evaluate their decisions and commitments constantly, remaining open to course changes as circumstances dictate.

Some choices that managers make are interrelated. For example, the choice of a business partner is a function of the country. The type of distributor to use varies from market to market—say, for example, between the Netherlands and Nigeria. The degree of country risk may imply a need for a politically well-connected business partner. In nontraditional markets, such as Vietnam, the firm may need a partner that can serve as both distributor and cultural adviser.

Even the most attractive country cannot compensate for a poor partner. Despite growing availability of information on individual countries, many firms struggle to identify qualified and interested business partners, especially in emerging markets. The most qualified partners may already represent other foreign firms. This necessitates recruiting second- or even third-best candidates and then committing adequate resources to ensure their success.

CLOSING CASE   Advanced Biomedical Devices: Assessing Readiness to Export

Dr. Richard Bentley, a well-known British surgeon who developed a medical device that helps the wound-healing process, was so committed to the groundbreaking technology that he left his surgical practice to found Advanced Biomedical Devices, Inc. (ABD). ABD is headquartered in the eastern United States. ABD plans to initiate exporting activities and just completed the process of assessing its readiness, using CORE (COmpany Readiness to Export).

ABD's product line includes several innovative devices called Speedheal that promote healing and reduce postsurgical pain by keeping the wound area from swelling. Speedheal oxygenates the wound area by pulsing electrons through the bandage covering the wound. The devices are very small and portable. Versions exist for different types of surgeries: hand surgery, face lifts, abdominal procedures, and so on.

Dr. Bentley launched ABD with a skillful management team whose members have worked extensively in the European market, the Pacific Rim, and Latin America. ABD's manufacturing director is from Germany, and another manager lived in France and Malaysia for several years.

Thanks to high demand, Speedheal sales increased rapidly, primarily through medical product distributors that sold to hospitals and clinics throughout the United States. Growth approached 20 percent in some years, and the staff grew to 85 people. The firm's success stimulated the entry of competitors offering similar products, but rivals never achieved the degree of miniaturization in ABD's products. Miniaturization thus remains one of Speedheal's competitive advantages. Management's projections for ABD's future growth remain positive.

Dreams of International Expansion

ABD had received unsolicited orders from abroad and learned a great deal about handling international transactions, including foreign exchange, letters of credit, and logistics. Though ABD's plan to internationalize was in its early stages, management intended to expand beyond occasional export sales to target key world markets. Its managers preferred dealing with psychically close markets—those with familiar culture, business customs, and legal and banking systems. They were willing to consider others, especially large and fast-growing markets and those promising superior profitability.

One expected benefit was the opportunity for ABD to learn from global competitors and markets. Many trends that start in foreign markets eventually reach the home country, and often the best way to track them is to do business internationally. Management also believed it could reduce ABD's overall risks by diversifying sales to various foreign markets. Finally, internationalization would help preempt competitors in particular foreign markets.

International Strategic Intent

Dr. Bentley and his management team formulated some questions to clarify ABD's internationalization goals. They knew that answering the questions would help clarify ABD's strategic intent for going international. Management also wanted to develop a comprehensive strategic plan that would lay the foundation for international

success. Following a series of meetings, the team reached consensus on the following key elements of ABD's initial strategic direction.

- Senior management will strongly commit to internationalization, and ABD will pursue foreign markets aggressively. The firm will hire a vice president for international sales in the coming year.
- ABD will invest up to 20 percent of company earnings in export opportunities.
- ABD will begin building distributor relationships in a number of countries.
- ABD will establish a marketing subsidiary in at least one foreign location within three to five years and hire salespeople who select and manage the distributors in their market area.
- Management will seek to ensure that all international ventures reach profitability within two years of their launch.
- Management will develop international marketing plans for each target market, each with its own budget.
- Plans call for international sales to reach 35 percent of total sales within four years.
- ABD will establish an annual budget of $220,000 to finance international activities for each of the first three years. Of that, about $60,000 will be devoted to market research to determine the best target markets and understand competitors.

Product Readiness for Export

Following approval of ABD's strategic intent, Dr. Bentley and his management team addressed questions about the challenges of internationalization. The first dealt with training sales representatives in foreign markets to sell medical devices to hospitals and clinics, the primary end markets for ABD products. Sales reps require training because they deal with doctors, nurses, and other professionals who are deeply involved in decision making about purchases of hospital supplies. Because training costs can be high in foreign markets, Dr. Bentley wanted to ensure that ABD was prepared to make this investment.

Dr. Bentley also raised the issue of after-sales service, which can be challenging in foreign markets. Because ABD's products were seldom defective, the solution for a defective product was to replace it rather than trying to make a repair. U.S. customers counted on a ready backup stock in the event of product defects. ABD planned to employ the same solution for its foreign operations, and management assumed there would be no need for a separate staff to deal with after-sales service. Because Speedheal devices are small and lightweight (though valuable), per-unit transportation costs are very low. In fact, in urgent situations abroad, ABD already made it a practice to ship a replacement device by air.

Although management well understood pricing in the United States, there was much it did not know about foreign pricing. Dr. Bentley and several managers had attended trade fairs in Europe and concluded that ABD's prices were not too high, particularly since no other firms offered similar products. In fact, ABD had filled unsolicited orders from Europe and found that customers never challenged its pricing. In the end, however, management decided research was needed to refine ABD's pricing approach.

Next, the team discussed foreign inventory management. Because the devices were cheap to transport by air freight, distributors could replenish inventories quickly and economically, a significant benefit because they would not have to maintain much inventory to support sales. On the other hand, Speedheal devices were sensitive to changes in temperature and humidity and functioned best when warehoused in climate-controlled facilities. Such warehousing was increasingly common, so ABD should have no problem locating the right warehousing in Europe and elsewhere.

ABD's management realized the firm's flexible packaging put them in a good position to enter foreign markets, and they were also prepared to modify the product in various ways to meet worldwide standards and regulations. Two in particular were the CE mark, a mandatory safety mark required on toys, machinery, and low-voltage equipment, and ISO standards, which aim to make development and manufacturing of products efficient, safe, and clean.

Knowledge, Skills, and Resources

In a subsequent meeting, the ABD team considered less tangible aspects of the firm's readiness to internationalize. Management knew critical self-assessment was vital to long-term success, and internationalization would require additional working capital for foreign warehousing, longer shipping times, and larger inventories abroad. Other costs included legal help, freight forwarding, international transportation, customs duties, bank charges, rent for foreign offices, and approval for certain regulatory issues. ABD's management was not completely clear on the amount of these costs, but it was willing to learn. Although it would use letters of credit when first opening new markets, ABD would opt for open-account payment systems (payable in 30 or 60 days, depending on the market).

Dr. Bentley also considered the appropriate growth rate for the firm. A company's business could increase rapidly, demanding more product than the firm could reasonably supply. Or domestic sales could drop sharply, requiring management to divert all efforts to rescuing domestic operations, thus disrupting the export program.

Competitive intelligence was another concern. A key incentive for venturing abroad was to learn more about foreign competitors. Some major medical device manufacturers marketed their products in the United States, whereas others were based strictly abroad. ABD would have to research and understand the strategies and marketing practices of the important competitors. Dr. Bentley recognized the importance of getting patent coverage on his inventions around the world and of protecting the intellectual property rights of his firm. He planned to retain legal counsel, at home and abroad, to protect ABD's critical assets from patent infringements; to develop suitable distribution and agent agreements, sales agreements, and licensing; and to ensure compliance with local employment laws.

Management believed ABD's initial foreign markets would be Australia, Canada, Western Europe, and Japan because of their large proportion of affluent consumers with the ability to pay for sophisticated medical care. Thus, ABD had gathered information about the markets and competition in those countries but recognized that it needed to do much more.

Managerial Capabilities for Long-Term Internationalization

One concern was whether management would be able to cope with deepening internationalization. In the end, the ABD team members recognized that they were right to take painstaking efforts to determine the firm's readiness to export. Extensive meetings and preliminary research provided the basis for developing initial strategies and action programs as well as for identifying improvements to make the company stronger in the coming years.

AACSB: Reflective Thinking Skills, Analytic Skills

Case Questions

12-4. Do you believe ABD's products are in a state of readiness to begin exporting to Europe? Why or why not? Are the products ready for exporting to emerging markets (e.g., China, Mexico, Russia)? Why or why not? What factors suggest Speedheal products might enjoy demand in all types of foreign markets?

12-5. Does management at ABD possess the appropriate knowledge, skills, and capabilities for internationalization? Justify your answer. What steps should management take to prepare the firm, managers, and employees better to internationalize?

12-6. How well did ABD complete the key tasks in global market opportunity assessment? Evaluate whether it accomplished each task well or poorly. Did ABD achieve each of the objectives set out for the tasks?

12-7. If you were a member of ABD's management team, what countries would you recommend targeting first? As a manager, you would need to justify your recommendation. A good approach is to investigate key characteristics of specific countries through globalEDGE™ (www.globalEDGE.msu.edu) or similar websites.

12-8. What approaches could ABD employ to estimate the firm's sales potential for markets in Europe and other affluent economies? Justify your answer.

This case was written by Myron M. Miller, Michigan State University (retired), in association with Professor S. Tamer Cavusgil. ABD is a fictitious company.

END OF CHAPTER REVIEW

 MyManagementLab

Go to **mymanagementlab.com** to complete the problems marked with this icon .

Key Terms

Summary

In this chapter, you learned about:

- **Analyzing organizational readiness to internationalize**

  A **global market opportunity** is a favorable combination of circumstances, locations, or timing that offer prospects for exporting, investing, sourcing, or partnering in foreign markets. The firm may perceive opportunities to sell, establish factories, obtain inputs of lower cost or superior quality, or enter collaborative arrangements with foreign partners that support the focal firm's goals. Managers perform six key tasks in defining and pursuing global market opportunities. As the first task, management assesses the firm's readiness to internationalize. It assesses the strengths and weaknesses in the firm's ability to do international business and the external business environment by conducting formal research on the opportunities and threats that face the firm. The firm must develop resources it lacks. Diagnostic tools, such as CORE (COmpany Readiness to Export), facilitate a self-audit of readiness to internationalize.

- **Assessing the suitability of products and services for foreign markets**

  Products and services that are good candidates for selling abroad sell well in the domestic market, cater to universal needs, address a need not well served in the target market, or address a new or emergent need abroad. Management should ask the following questions: Who initiates purchasing in the market? Who uses the offering? Why do people buy it? Where is the product or service purchased? What economic, cultural, geographic, and other factors can limit sales?

- **Screening countries to identify target markets**

  Whether the firm is engaged in importing (sourcing from abroad), investing, or exporting, the choice of country is critical, particularly in the early stages of internationalization. The best markets are large and fast-growing. The nature of information necessary for country screening varies by product type and industry. There are two basic screening methods: gradual elimination and ranking and indexing.

- **Assessing industry market potential**

  Once a firm reduces the number of potential country targets to five or six, the next step is to conduct in-depth analyses of each. **Industry market potential** is an estimate of the likely sales for all firms in the specific industry for a particular period. Each industry sector also has its own *industry-specific potential indicators*. Among the methods for assessing industry market potential are performing simple trend analysis, monitoring key industry-specific indicators, monitoring key competitors, following key customers around the world, tapping into supplier networks, and attending international trade fairs.

- **Choosing foreign business partners**

  International business partners include distribution channel intermediaries, facilitators, suppliers, joint venture partners, licensees, and franchisees. Some partners undertake **licensing, franchising**, and **international collaborative ventures**. Management in the focal firm must decide the types of partners it needs, identify suitable partner candidates, negotiate the terms of relationships with chosen partners, support the partners, and monitor their performance.

- **Estimating company sales potential**

  Company sales potential is the share of annual industry sales the firm can realistically achieve in the target country. Estimating company sales potential requires the researcher to obtain highly refined market information. Among the most influential determinants of company sales potential are partner capabilities, access to distribution channels in the market, intensity of the competitive environment, pricing and financing of sales, quality of human and financial resources, timetable for market entry, risk tolerance of senior managers, the firm's contacts and capabilities, and its reputation in the market.

Test Your Comprehension AACSB: Reflective Thinking Skills

12-9. How would a business assess the suitability of its products for an overseas market?

12-10. How does a business use diagnostic tools such as CORE?

12-11. How does an organization assess the industry market potential of an overseas market?

12-12. An organization wants in depth information about the international market potential of a product, what needs to be asked?

12-13. What are the typical variables used in indexing and ranking?

12-14. What types of variables should the researcher consider when screening for each of the following: export markets, foreign direct investment, and global sourcing?

12-15. What tasks does assessing industry market potential entail?

12-16. What are the major issues to consider when selecting foreign business partners?

Apply Your Understanding AACSB: Communication Abilities, Reflective Thinking Skills, Ethical Understanding and Reasoning Abilities

12-17. Target® is a large retailer with about 1,800 stores in the United States but very few in other countries. It has a reputation for merchandising thousands of trendy yet inexpensive products for the home, including apparel, furniture, electronics, toys, and sporting goods. Management wants to open stores in major European cities but will have limited floor space there. Target hires you as a consultant to decide which products to offer in Europe. Write a brief report in which you describe the selection criteria you will use and offer some examples to back up your ideas. Be sure to justify your answer, using the advice and other information included in this chapter.

12-18. Upon graduation, you are hired by Pullman Corporation, a manufacturer of accessories for luxury cars. Management wants you to conduct research to locate foreign markets with the best sales potential. You discover that markets are fairly saturated in advanced economies, but you are aware of numerous *emerging markets* that the industry has overlooked. Using your knowledge of Exhibit 12.3, Market Potential Index, develop a list of the top five emerging markets that Pullman should target. Be sure to justify your choice, based on indicators from this chapter such as market size, market growth rate, market intensity, and market consumption capacity.

12-19. *Ethical Dilemma:* Steven Sanchez is the export manager at Leon Industries, a manufacturer of office furnishings. He has identified Russia as a promising market and decides to attend a furniture trade fair in Moscow. As he prepares for the fair, a consultant suggests hiring two female models in revealing clothing to work the company's booth. The consultant says the models will create buzz and increase Leon's visibility at the crowded fair. Sanchez is skeptical and seeks advice from two colleagues. One colleague says the idea "amounts to exploiting women and could invite sexual harassment charges.... It is sex discrimination. The booth workers' gender and good looks are a condition for their employment." Another colleague tells Sanchez that hiring the models is no problem. He says those who oppose such a practice "perpetuate stereotypes of women as delicate creatures who cannot decide what's best for themselves." Besides, he continues, "Russia is a male-dominated society and people are not offended by such practices." What do you think? Using the ethical framework in Chapter 4, analyze the issue and make a recommendation.

globalEDGE | INTERNET EXERCISES

(www.globalEDGE.msu.edu)

AACSB: Reflective Thinking Skills, Use of Information Technology

Refer to Chapter 1, page 54, for instructions on how to access and use globalEDGE™.

12-20. China is a huge, attractive market with growing affluence. Before exporting to China, most firms conduct market research to understand the Chinese market better. Two useful research sites are the China Business Information Center (CBIC; www.export.gov/china) and UK Trade and Investment (www.uktradeinvest.gov.uk). At the CBIC, for example, firms can find out whether they are China-ready. They can access trade leads and read current news about business in China. Suppose you are hired by a firm that wants to begin exporting to China three products: (a) breakfast cereal, (b) popular music on CDs, and (c) laptop computers. For each of these product categories, using the preceding websites and globalEDGE™, prepare a list of the information that the firm should gather prior to making a decision to export to China.

12-21. Walmart is a huge retailer but gets only about a quarter of its sales from outside the United States. Coles is one of the largest retailers in Australia and gets very little of its sales outside Australia. Assess the international retailing sector using online resources such as globalEDGE™ and A. T. Kearney

(www.atkearney.com). Based on your research: (a) what factors should these top retailers consider in choosing countries for internationalizing their operations? (b) What are the best markets for these firms to target for foreign expansion? (c) What types of questions should management at each firm ask in assessing its readiness to internationalize?

12-22. The United States Bureau of the Census tracks foreign trade statistics. Visit the site at www.census.gov/foreign-trade and find the most recent versions of the "Profile of U.S. Exporting Companies" report by entering this title in the search engine. Peruse the report and address the following questions: (a) What types of firms export from the United States? That is, what is the breakdown by company type of U.S. exporters? For example, are the exporters mainly large or small firms? Do they operate mainly in the manufacturing, agricultural, or services sectors? (b) What is the role of small and medium-sized exporters in U.S. trade? What percent of U.S. exporters are these types of firms, and for what proportion of total exports do they account? (c) What countries are the three favorite targets of U.S. exporters? According to the report, what factors make these countries the top markets for U.S. firms?

CAREER TOOLBOX

Assessing Markets for Cancer Insurance

A life-threatening disease, cancer is often expensive and difficult to treat. Medical bills may run to hundreds of thousands of dollars. Worldwide, people buy health insurance to pay for medical care. In other cases, governments provide tax-funded health insurance. However, a typical insurance policy may be insufficient to cover the high cost of treating cancer fully.

Insurance companies such as American International Group (AIG) and AFLAC specialize in supplemental policies to cover specialized cancer care. When they market health insurance abroad, such firms identify markets with the best prospects for sales. Managers conduct research on the available choices.

In this exercise, assume you work for a health insurance company like AIG or AFLAC. Your task is to assess various countries and identify the most promising one to target for sales of supplemental cancer insurance. You will examine variables that help estimate the size of industry sales in each of three possible target countries. Your

assessment will be based on industry-specific indicators of demand for cancer insurance.

Background

Worldwide, few people have adequate health insurance against cancer. Thus, people often purchase supplemental health insurance. The market for cancer insurance around the world is very substantial.

Health insurance companies such as AIG and AFLAC specialize in supplemental policies to cover specialized cancer care. Supplemental cancer insurance is usually sold through insurance agents and insurance brokers. A typical agent establishes a sales office that customers can easily visit. Occasionally, agents contact potential customers directly by telephone or in their homes to sell insurance. Insurance is sometimes sold over the Internet.

To complete this exercise in your MyLab, go to the Career Toolbox.

MyManagementLab

Go to **mymanagementlab.com** for Auto-graded writing questions as well as the following Assisted-graded writing questions:

⭐ **12-23.** Why is it important for the firm to assess its readiness to internationalize?

⭐ **12-24.** Summarize the screening methodology for identifying potential country markets.

⭐ **12-25.** MyManagementLab Only—comprehensive writing assignment for this chapter.

Endnotes

1. Peter Liesch, Lawrence Welch, and Peter Buckley, "Risk and Uncertainty in Internationalisation and International Entrepreneurship Studies," *Management International Review* 51, No. 6 (2011), pp. 851–873.

2. L. Bryan and D. Farrell, "Leading Through Uncertainty," *McKinsey Quarterly*, December 2008, http://www.mckinseyquarterly.com.

3. Sara Sarasvathy, K. Kumar, Jeffrey York, and Suresh Bhagavatula, "An Effectual Approach to International Entrepreneurship: Overlaps, Challenges, and Provocative Possibilities," *Entrepreneurship Theory & Practice* 38, No. 1 (2014), pp. 71–93.

4. Shruti Singh and Ganesh Nagarajan, "Small Is Beautiful for John Deere," *Bloomberg Businessweek*, September 26, 2011, pp. 33–34.

5. S. Tamer Cavusgil, "Measuring the Potential of Emerging Markets: An Indexing Approach," *Business Horizons* 40 (January–February 1997), pp. 87–91.

6. GlobalEDGE™, *Market Potential Index (MPI) – 2014*, globalEDGE™ (www.globalEDGE.msu.edu/resourcedesk/mpi).

7. "Burgeoning Bourgeoisie: A Special Report on the New Middle Classes in Emerging Markets," *Economist*, February 14, 2009, Special Section; Homi Kharas, *The Emerging Middle Class in Developing Countries* (Paris: OECD Development Centre, 2010); Olga Kravets and Ozlem Sandikci, "Competently Ordinary: New Middle Class Consumers in the Emerging Markets," *Journal of Marketing* 78, July (2014), pp. 125–140.

8. Lee Chi-Ho, "Korea's IT Industry in Transition," *SERI Quarterly*, January 2012, pp. 22–29.

9. C. Miller and P. Olson, "Tesco's Landing," *Forbes*, June 4, 2007, pp. 116–118.

10. Peter Enderwick, "The Imperative of Global Environmental Scanning," *Insights* 11, No. 1 (2011), pp. 12–15.

Chapter 13

Exporting and Global Sourcing

Learning Objectives *After studying this chapter, you should be able to:*

13.1 Understand exporting as a foreign market entry strategy.

13.2 Describe how to manage export-import transactions.

13.3 Explain identifying and working with foreign intermediaries.

13.4 Understand outsourcing, global sourcing, and offshoring.

13.5 Describe the benefits and risks of global sourcing.

13.6 Understand global sourcing strategies and supply-chain management.

Maersk and the global container business

Despite huge technological change over recent decades, including advances in aviation technology, some 90% of traded goods are still shipped in large standard-sized containers. Indeed, the shipping container itself is one of the key innovations of the past century. Invented by US trucking magnate Malcolm McLean in 1956, containers meant that goods were no longer shipped loose in wooden crates. This ability to ship goods in huge volumes has slashed costs for exporters. This has driven global sourcing and offshoring of production, and led to the globalisation of supply chains, with resulting sharp reductions in production costs and prices to consumers.

Container shipping companies are key intermediaries in the exporting process, and have made this an extremely attractive market entry strategy. The giant of this sector is Maersk Line, transporting some 15% of global seaborne container freight. Founded in Denmark in 1904, Maersk is a conglomerate with activities across the transport and energy sector, subsidiaries and offices in over 135 countries and some 89,000 employees.

The resilience of the shipping container in an era of very rapid technological change is a testimony to its dramatic impact on export-import transactions. Nonetheless the sector is vulnerable to downturns in global trade, and fluctuating oil prices. Indeed, Maersk has consolidated its dominant position as an intermediary for exporters during the financial crisis. It has exploited its size to take advantage of overcapacity and buy ships at a discount; and optimising route networks. This allows it to operate at the lowest possible costs, passing on some of these efficiencies to customers through reduced prices, and forcing rivals to operate at a loss to compete.

However, this resilience does not necessarily mean that the dominance of container shipping will continue. Enormous cargo ships emit huge amounts of greenhouse gases, and are

Source: soleg/Fotolia

likely to come under increasing pressure to be more environmentally friendly. Indeed, pressure to be more fuel-efficient is affecting the speed at which vessels travel, which is slowing down shipping times considerably.

While Maersk's management share the pessimism that exists elsewhere in the sector about the future of container shipping, it is positioning itself to remain competitive. It has ordered a new fleet of state of the art larger ships in a bid to cut costs further. However, it faces the threat of rivals seeking to exploit its tactics, which risks eroding its dominance over coming years.

Container ships can still transport vastly greater volumes of goods than air, rail and road alternatives. This means there is little prospect of the container ceasing to be the key tool in managing global supply chains. This means that Maersk will remain a key intermediary for exporters around the world.

However, for it to continue to withstand competition as a result of improved infrastructure and technological innovation that bolster alternatives, the container shipping business will need to innovate. Its challenge over coming decades is likely to be building larger and faster vessels that at the same time emit drastically reduced levels of greenhouse gases.

Questions

13-1. Why has container shipping been such a revolutionary and resilient phenomenon?

13-2. How has Maersk gained a competitive edge in this sector, and what are the key threats it is likely to face over the short- to medium-term?

13-3. Why might container shipping be more useful and important for exporters in some sectors than others?

SOURCES: Maersk (http://www.maersk.com/en/industries/transport); "Why have containers boosted trade so much?," The Economist, May 21, 2013 (http://www.economist.com/blogs/economist-explains/2013/05/economist-explains-14); "About Us – The Maersk Group, " (http://www.maersk.com/en/the-maersk-group/about-us); "Denmark's Maersk Line sticks to its market-leading course," Financial Times, July 8 2015 (http://www.ft.com/cms/s/0/4a171548-2558-11e5-bd83-71cb60e8f08c.html#axzz3oo9t8ckx); "High-tech shipping containers: Boxing clever," The Economist, March 1, 2014 (http://www.economist.com/news/science-and-technology/21597878-engineers-are-trying-upgrade-humble-shipping-container-boxing-clever); "True scale of CO2 emissions from shipping revealed," The Guardian, February 13, 2008 (http://www.theguardian.com/environment/2008/feb/13/climatechange.pollution); "Modern cargo ships slow to the speed of the sailing clippers," The Guardian, July 25, 2010 (http://www.theguardian.com/environment/2010/jul/25/slow-ships-cut-greenhouse-emissions); "Grim outlook for container sector," Splash 24/7, October 9, 2015 (http://splash247.com/grim-outlook-for-container-sector/); "Fast container ships: How to shrink the world," The Economist, August 13, 2001 (http://www.economist.com/node/738336)

Most economic activity takes place outside the home country; thus, it makes sense for firms to engage in international business. Internationalization helps companies grow and become more competitive. When management at firms decides to internationalize, it must choose the most appropriate entry strategy. Recall that such strategies include global sourcing, exporting, licensing, joint ventures, and foreign direct investment. Young companies like Vellus prefer exporting because it is generally the simplest approach and provides many advantages.

In this chapter, we provide a detailed overview on exporting. We examine the advantages and disadvantages of exporting and the steps that experienced firms follow to ensure success. We explore the nature of export intermediaries and examine the various methods that buyers use to pay for imported goods. We also examine exporting's counterpart: importing and global sourcing. Firms access enormous advantages by sourcing parts, finished products, and services from suppliers around the world. Let's begin by examining exporting.

13.1 Understand exporting as a foreign market entry strategy.

Exporting
The strategy of producing products or services in one country (often the producer's home country), and selling and distributing them to customers located in other countries.

Exporting as a Foreign Market Entry Strategy

Exporting refers to the strategy of producing products or services in one country (often the producer's home country) and selling and distributing them to customers located in other countries.

Because it entails limited risk, expense, and knowledge of foreign markets and transactions, most companies prefer exporting as their primary foreign market entry strategy. Typically, the focal firm retains its manufacturing activities in its home market but conducts marketing, distribution, and customer service activities in the export market. The firm can perform these latter activities itself or it can have them performed by an independent distributor in the market.

Exporting is the entry strategy responsible for the massive inflows and outflows that constitute global trade. Exporting generates enormous foreign-exchange earnings for nations. Japan has benefited from export earnings for years. China has become the leading exporter in various sectors, providing huge revenues to its economy. Smaller economies such as Belgium and Finland also add much to their foreign-exchange reserves from exporting and use them to pay for their sizable imports of foreign goods.

Exporting is a common entry strategy even among firms that have extensive international operations. Some of the largest exporters in the United States include aircraft manufacturers Boeing and Lockheed Martin Aero. Big trading companies that deal in commodities, such as Cargill and Marubeni, are also large-scale exporters. Large manufacturing firms typically account for the largest overall value of exports and make up about three-quarters of the total value of exports from the United States. However, most exporting firms—more than 90 percent in most countries—are small and medium-sized enterprises (SMEs) with fewer than 500 employees.

As an entry strategy, exporting is very flexible. The exporter can both enter and withdraw from markets fairly easily with minimal risk and expense. Firms can develop production facilities at various foreign locations and export products to other countries.

The volume of world exports has grown enormously.[1] In the United States, some industries generate two-thirds or more of their total sales from foreign markets. These industries include computers, electronic products, chemicals, medical devices, pharmaceuticals, and motor vehicle parts. Foreign markets account for 63 percent of 3M Company's sales. The figure is 65 percent for Apple and 75 percent for Dow Chemical. Another large group of industries generates about half of its total sales from international markets. These include industries in aerospace, communications equipment, food, beverages, plastics, apparel, and electrical equipment. Pepsico and General Electric obtain 50 percent, and Nike gets 55 percent, of their sales internationally.

Service Sector Exports

In most advanced economies, services are the largest component of economic activity. Services marketed abroad include travel, construction, engineering, education, banking, insurance, and entertainment. Hollywood film studios earn billions by exporting their movies and videos. Construction firms send their employees abroad to work on major construction projects. Accountants and engineers often provide their services through the Internet, by telephone and mail, and by visiting customers directly in their home countries. Insurance packages are created in a central location, such as London, and then exported by mail and the Internet to customers in other countries.

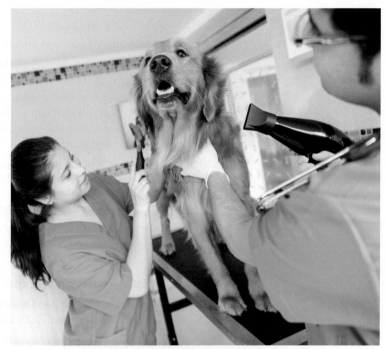

Source: Andres Rodriguez/123RF

Vellus Products Inc. is a U.S.-based producer of grooming products for dogs, and exports to countries worldwide. It is one of many small- and medium-sized enterprises that find success by internationalizing their unique products.

However, many *pure* services cannot be exported because they cannot be transported. You cannot box up a haircut and ship it overseas. Most retailing firms, such as Home Depot and Marks & Spencer, offer their services by establishing retail stores in their target markets. They internationalize through FDI because retailing requires direct contact with customers. Many services firms export *some* of what they produce but rely on other entry strategies to provide other offerings abroad. For example, Ernst & Young (www.ey.com) exports *some* accounting services by sending its employees abroad. It also undertakes FDI by setting up offices overseas and hiring local personnel to perform local accounting services.

International travel is usually considered a service export. When a Canadian citizen stays in a hotel in Brazil, the hotel is said to have exported its service to the foreigner. When an Australian citizen visits India to undergo a cataract operation—a trend known as medical tourism—it is counted as exporting in India's national accounts. In France and the United States, tourism generates more foreign exchange than exports of most categories of merchandise.[2]

Most services are delivered to foreign customers either through local representatives or agents or in conjunction with other entry strategies such as FDI, franchising, or licensing. The Internet provides the means to export some types of services, from airline tickets to architectural services. The Internet has helped make services the fastest-growing exporting sector.[3]

Advantages of Exporting

- Increases overall sales volume, improve market share, and generate profit margins that are often more favorable than in the domestic market.
- Increases economies of scale, reducing per-unit costs of manufacturing.
- Diversifies customer base, reducing dependence on home markets.
- Stabilizes fluctuations in sales associated with economic cycles or seasonality of demand.
- Minimizes the cost of foreign market entry; the firm can use exporting to test new markets before committing greater resources through FDI.
- Minimizes risk and maximizes flexibility compared to other entry strategies.
- Leverages the capabilities of foreign distributors and other business partners located abroad.

Disadvantages of Exporting

- Exporting offers fewer opportunities to learn about customers, competitors, and other unique aspects of the foreign market because the firm does not establish a physical presence there (in contrast to FDI).

- With exporting, the firm must acquire and dedicate capabilities to conduct complex transactions, which can strain organizational resources. Exporters must become proficient in international sales contracts and transactions, new financing methods, and logistics and documentation.

- Exporting exposes the firm to tariffs and other trade barriers as well as fluctuations in exchange rates. Exporters can be priced out of foreign markets if shifting exchange rates make their products too costly to foreign buyers. For example, the U.S. dollar lost 10 percent in value against the Japanese yen in 2010–2011. As the yen became more expensive in dollar terms, U.S. buyers reduced their imports of Japanese goods.

A Systematic Approach to Exporting

Experienced managers use a systematic approach to successful exporting. Exhibit 13.1 highlights the steps in this process. Let's examine each in detail.

STEP ONE: ASSESS GLOBAL MARKET OPPORTUNITY As a first step, management assesses the various global market opportunities available to the firm. Managers analyze the readiness of the firm to carry out exporting. They screen for the most attractive export markets. They identify qualified intermediaries and other foreign business partners. They estimate industry market potential and company sales potential. Participating in foreign trade shows is useful for identifying market potential and foreign intermediaries. We explained Global Market Opportunity Assessment (GMOA) in Chapter 12.

STEP TWO: ORGANIZE FOR EXPORTING Next, managers ask: What types of managerial, financial, and productive resources should the firm commit to the export venture? What timetable should the firm follow to achieve exporting goals? To what degree should the firm rely on domestic and foreign intermediaries to implement exporting?

Exhibit 13.2 illustrates alternative organizational arrangements in exporting. **Indirect exporting** is accomplished by contracting with intermediaries located in the firm's home market. Smaller exporters, or those new to international business, typically hire an export management company or a trading company based in their home country. These intermediaries assume responsibility for finding foreign buyers, shipping products, and getting paid. For most firms, indirect exporting's main advantage is the ability to internationalize with lower risk, less complexity, and at lower cost, than direct exporting.

Indirect exporting
Exporting that is accomplished by contracting with intermediaries located in the firm's home market.

EXHIBIT 13.1

A Systematic Approach to Exporting

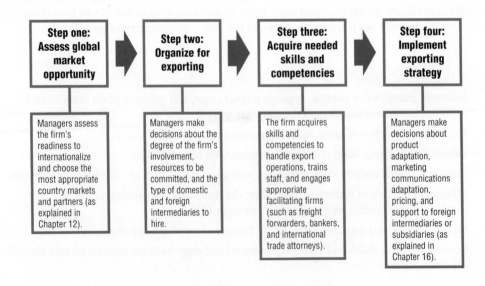

Step one: Assess global market opportunity	Step two: Organize for exporting	Step three: Acquire needed skills and competencies	Step four: Implement exporting strategy
Managers assess the firm's readiness to internationalize and choose the most appropriate country markets and partners (as explained in Chapter 12).	Managers make decisions about the degree of the firm's involvement, resources to be committed, and the type of domestic and foreign intermediaries to hire.	The firm acquires skills and competencies to handle export operations, trains staff, and engages appropriate facilitating firms (such as freight forwarders, bankers, and international trade attorneys).	Managers make decisions about product adaptation, marketing communications adaptation, pricing, and support to foreign intermediaries or subsidiaries (as explained in Chapter 16).

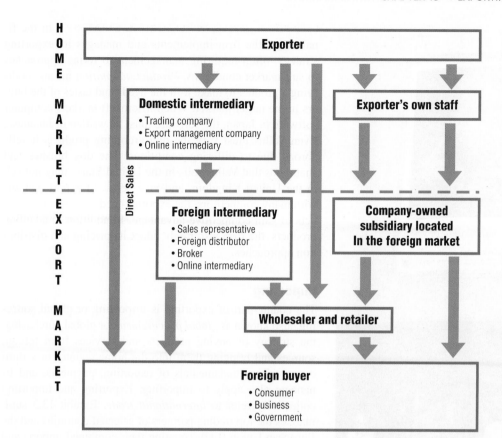

EXHIBIT 13.2

Alternative Organizational Arrangements for Exporting

In contrast, **direct exporting** is typically achieved by contracting with intermediaries located in the foreign market. The foreign intermediaries serve as an extension of the exporter, negotiating on behalf of the exporter and assuming such responsibilities as local supply-chain management, pricing, and customer service. The main advantage of direct exporting is that it gives the exporter greater control over the export process, and potential for higher profits, as well as a closer relationship with foreign buyers and the marketplace. However, the exporter also must dedicate substantial time, personnel, and corporate resources to developing and managing export operations.

Key considerations for choosing between direct or indirect exporting are:

- The time, capital, and expertise that management is willing to commit.
- Strategic importance of the foreign market.
- Nature of the firm's products, including the need for after-sales support.
- Availability of capable foreign intermediaries in the target market.

Note that many firms do both direct and indirect exporting.

At a more advanced stage, the firm may establish a sales office or a **company-owned subsidiary** in the foreign market to handle marketing, physical distribution, promotion, and customer service activities. Such a subsidiary allows the firm to manage major tasks in the market directly, such as attending trade fairs, doing market research, engaging distributors, and finding and serving customers. Companies tend to establish subsidiaries in markets that are large or strategically important. At the extreme, the firm may establish distribution centers and warehouses or a full-function marketing subsidiary staffed with a local sales force.

STEP THREE: ACQUIRE NEEDED SKILLS AND COMPETENCIES Export transactions require specialized skills and competencies in areas such as product development, distribution, logistics, finance, contract law, and currency management. Also useful are foreign language skills and the ability to interact well in foreign cultures. Fortunately, *facilitators* are available to assist firms that lack specific competencies. They include companies such as banks, freight forwarders, and international trade consultants.

Direct exporting
Exporting that is accomplished by contracting with intermediaries located in the foreign market.

Company-owned subsidiary
A representative office of the focal firm that handles marketing, physical distribution, promotion, and customer service activities in the foreign market.

Source: Chris Christoforou/Rough Guides/Dorling Kindersley

China is a major exporter of machinery, furniture, and other goods. El Corte Ingles and other department stores worldwide source much of their apparel and footwear from exporting manufacturers in China.

STEP FOUR: IMPLEMENT EXPORTING STRATEGY In the final stage, the firm implements and manages its exporting strategy, often requiring management to refine approaches to suit market conditions. *Product adaptation* means modifying a product to make it fit the needs and tastes of the buyers in the target market. When Microsoft markets computer software in Japan, the software must be written in Japanese. Even Vellus must vary the dog-grooming products it sells abroad due to differing conditions. The dog brushes and shampoos that Vellus sells in the United States may not sell in the United Kingdom, and vice versa. In export markets with many competitors, the exporter needs to adapt its products to gain competitive advantage. In addition to adapting products, the firm also might adapt its pricing and distribution approaches.

Importing

The counterpart of exporting is **importing** or **global sourcing**, also known as *global procurement*, or global purchasing, the strategy of buying products and services from foreign sources and bringing them into the home country or a third country. The fundamentals of exporting, payments, and financing also apply to importing. Exporting and importing collectively refer to *international trade*. Exhibit 13.3 summarizes the top trading partners of selected countries and the European Union (EU), counting their combined imports and exports. As single countries, Canada and the United States are each other's top trading partners, suggesting that much international trade is regional rather than global. China is a top trading partner with the United States, mostly due to its massive merchandise exports. The EU trades most with China and the United States. Overall, the exhibit reveals that most international trade occurs among the advanced economies and increasingly between the advanced economies and emerging markets.

13.2 Describe how to manage export-import transactions.

Importing or global sourcing
The procurement of products or services from independent suppliers or company-owned subsidiaries located abroad for consumption in the home country or a third country

Documentation
Official forms and other paperwork required in export transactions for shipping and customs procedures.

Managing Export-Import Transactions

When comparing domestic and international business transactions, key differences arise in documentation and shipping.

Documentation

Documentation refers to the official forms and other paperwork required in export transactions for shipping and customs procedures. The exporter usually first issues a *quotation* or *pro forma invoice* upon request by potential customers. It informs them about the price and description of the exporter's product or service. The *commercial invoice* is the actual demand for payment the exporter issues when a sale is made.

Firms typically distribute exported goods by ocean transport, although some use air transport. The *bill of lading* is the basic contract between exporter and shipper. It authorizes a shipping company to transport the goods to the buyer's destination and serves as the importer's receipt and proof of title for purchase of the goods. The *certificate of origin* is the birth certificate of the goods being shipped and indicates the country of origin. In addition, exporters usually must provide a full description of the products being shipped. Government authorities use this

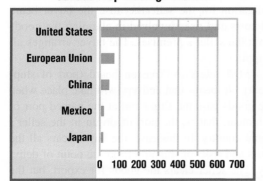

Canada: Top Trading Partners

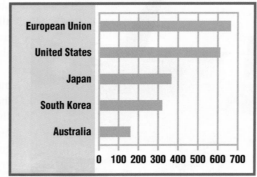

China: Top Trading Partners

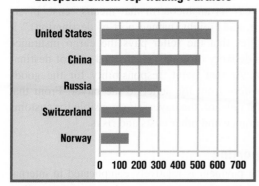

European Union: Top Trading Partners

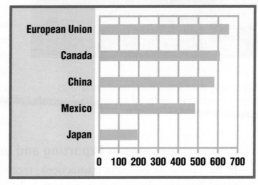

United States: Top Trading Partners

EXHIBIT 13.3

Top Trading Partners of Selected Countries

Note: Values shown represent the sum of merchandise exports and imports in billions of U.S. dollars for 2014.

Sources: European Commission at http://ec.europa.eu; Statistics Canada at http://www.statcan.gc.ca/tables-tableaux/sum-som/l01/cst01/gblec02a-eng.htm; U.S. Department of Commerce at http://www.census.gov/foreign-trade/Press-Release/2014pr/aip/related_party/rp14.pdf; U.S.–China Business Council at http://www.uschina.org; World Trade Organization, at http://stat.wto.org

information to find out the content of shipments, to control exports, and to compile statistics on the goods entering and leaving the country. Exporters usually purchase an *insurance certificate* to protect the exported goods against damage, loss, pilferage (theft), and, in some cases, delay. The exporter typically entrusts the preparation of documents to an international freight forwarder. Freight forwarders function like travel agents for cargo.

Shipping and Incoterms

Export transactions involve shipping products from the exporter's factory to a nearby seaport or airport. From there they travel by ship or airplane to a foreign port and are then transferred to land-based transportation and delivered to the customer. Some shipments to bordering countries are transported entirely overland by rail or truck. Exporters incur transportation costs and carry insurance against damage or loss during transit.

In the past, disputes sometimes arose over who should pay the cost of freight and insurance in international transactions, the foreign buyer or the seller (that is, the exporter). To eliminate such disputes, the International Chamber of Commerce (www.iccwbo.org) developed a system of universal, standard terms of sale and delivery, known as **Incoterms** (short for "International Commerce Terms"). Commonly used in international sales contracts, Incoterms specify how the buyer and the seller share the cost of freight and insurance and at which point the buyer takes title to the goods.

For example, *EXW* is an incoterm that refers to "ex works (named place)". It implies that delivery of the goods takes place at the seller's premises or another named place, such as a

Incoterms
Universally accepted terms of sale that specify how the buyer and the seller share the cost of freight and insurance in an international transaction and at which point the buyer takes title to the goods.

Source: robepco/Fotolia

Exporting is the entry strategy responsible for global trade and generates enormous earnings. Airbus is Europe's leading exporter of commercial aircraft. This Airbus jet is taking on airfreight.

factory or a warehouse. EXW represents minimal obligation for the seller because the buyer bears all costs and risks involved in claiming the goods from the seller's premises. The buyer arranges all shipping.

FOB refers to "free on board (port of shipment)." It means that delivery will take place when the goods pass the ship's rail at the named port of shipment, that is, the port of origin in the seller's home country. In this case, the buyer bears all the costs and risks of shipping from the point of delivery. The seller clears the goods for export, but the buyer must arrange shipping from the port of shipment and onward.

CIF is an incoterm that means "cost, insurance, and freight (named port of destination)." It implies that the seller pays the cargo insurance and delivery of goods to a named port of destination. At that point, responsibility for the goods transfers from the seller to the buyer. From that point onward, the buyer is responsible for customs clearance and other costs and risks.

Payment Methods in Exporting and Importing

In the course of business transactions, receiving payment is relatively complicated in international business. Foreign currencies may be unstable. Governments may be reluctant to allow funds to leave the country. In the event of disputes, local laws and enforcement systems may favor local companies over foreign firms.

In advanced economies and many emerging markets, firms may extend credit to buyers with the assurance that they will be paid. It is typical for exporters to allow these customers several months to make payments or to structure payment on *open account*. In trading with some developing economies, however, exporters extend credit cautiously because of the risk that some customers may fail to pay.

There are several payment methods in international business. Listed roughly in order from most to least secure from the exporter's perspective, they are: *cash in advance, letter of credit, open account*, and *countertrade*. We explain each of these payment methods next.

CASH IN ADVANCE   When the exporter receives cash in advance, payment is collected before the goods are shipped to the customer. This approach is advantageous to the exporter, which need not worry about collection problems and can access the funds almost immediately upon concluding the sale. From the buyer's standpoint, however, cash in advance is risky and may cause cash-flow problems. The buyer may hesitate for fear the exporter will not follow through with shipment, particularly if the buyer does not know the exporter well. For these reasons, cash in advance is unpopular with buyers and tends to discourage sales. Exporters who insist on it tend to lose out to competitors who offer more favorable payment terms.

Letter of credit

Contract between the banks of a buyer and a seller that ensures payment from the buyer to the seller upon receipt of an export shipment.

LETTER OF CREDIT   A documentary letter of credit, or simply a letter of credit, resolves most of the problems associated with cash in advance. Letter of credit is popular with experienced exporters because it protects the interests of both seller and buyer. Essentially, a **letter of credit** is a contract between the banks of the buyer and the seller that ensures payment from the buyer to the seller upon receipt of an export shipment. It amounts to a substitution of each bank's name and credit for the name and credit of the buyer and the seller. The system works because virtually all banks have established relationships with correspondent banks around the world.

An *irrevocable letter of credit* cannot be canceled without agreement by both buyer and seller. The selling firm will be paid as long as it fulfills its part of the agreement. The letter of credit immediately establishes trust between buyer and seller. The letter of credit also specifies the documents the exporter is required to present, such as a bill of lading, commercial invoice, and certificate of insurance. Before making a payment, the buyer's bank verifies that all

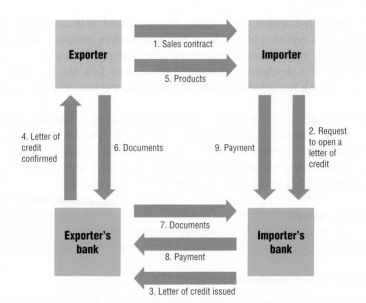

EXHIBIT 13.4
Letter of Credit Cycle

documents meet the requirements the buyer and seller agreed to in the letter of credit. If not, the discrepancy must be resolved before the bank makes the payment.

Exhibit 13.4 presents the typical cycle of an international sale through a letter of credit. As shown in the exhibit:

1. An Exporter signs a contract for sale of goods to a foreign buyer, the Importer.
2. The Importer asks its bank (the Importer's Bank) to open a letter of credit in favor of the Exporter, the beneficiary of the credit.
3. The Importer's Bank notifies the Exporter's Bank that a letter of credit has been issued.
4. The Exporter's Bank confirms the validity of the letter of credit.
5. The Exporter prepares and ships the products to the Importer as specified in the letter of credit.
6. The Exporter presents the shipment documents to its bank, the Exporter's Bank, which examines them to ensure that they fully comply with the terms of the letter of credit. The documents typically include an invoice, bill of lading, and insurance certificate, as specified in the letter of credit.
7. The Exporter's Bank sends the documents to the Importer's Bank, which similarly examines them to ensure that they comply fully with the letter of credit.
8. Upon confirmation that everything is in order, the Importer's Bank makes full payment for the goods to the Exporter through the Exporter's Bank.
9. The Importer makes full payment to its bank within the time period granted, which, in many countries, can extend to several months.

A related payment method is the *draft*. Similar to a check, the draft is a financial instrument that instructs a bank to pay a precise amount of a specific currency to the bearer on demand or at a future date. For both letters of credit and drafts, the buyer must make payment upon presentation of documents that convey title to the purchased goods and confirm that specific steps have been taken to prepare the goods and their shipment to the buyer. Letters of credit and drafts can be paid immediately or at a later date. In addition, the exporter can sell any drafts and letters of credit in its possession to avoid having to wait weeks or months to be paid for its exports.

OPEN ACCOUNT When the exporter uses an *open account*, the buyer pays the exporter at some future time following receipt of the goods. It is similar to the way a retail customer pays a department store on account for products he or she has purchased. Because of the risk involved, exporters use this approach only with customers of long-standing or excellent credit, or with a subsidiary the exporter owns. The exporter simply bills the customer, who is expected to pay under agreed terms at some future time. Open accounts are risky, and the firm should structure such payment methods with care.

COUNTERTRADE **Countertrade** refers to paying for goods or services using other goods or services when conventional means of payment are difficult or unavailable. Similar to barter,

Countertrade
An international business transaction where all or partial payments are made in kind rather than cash.

countertrade is especially common when dealing with governments in developing economies and emerging markets. In a typical deal, the focal firm is a Western company, say General Electric (GE). It wishes to sell its products or technology—for example, jet engines—to a developing-country government. If a developing economy's government falls short of hard currency, for example, it may require a foreign seller to accept some local products as partial payment for purchased goods.

Typically, the products that companies in developing countries offer are commodities such as agricultural grains, minerals, or manufactured goods. If a firm agrees to take these products, it must arrange to sell them to convert the goods to cash. Compared to transactions in which buyers pay with cash, countertrade is complicated. Transactions can take years to complete. Philip Morris exported cigarettes to Russia for which it received industrial chemicals as payment. It shipped the chemicals to China and received glassware in exchange that it then sold for cash in North America.

Some experts claim that countertrade accounts for as much as one-third of all world trade. Countertrade deals are common in large-scale government procurement projects. Firms based in developing economies that want to do international business often need to develop countertrade capabilities.

There are four main types of countertrade:

Barter

A type of countertrade in which goods are directly exchanged without the transfer of any money.

Compensation deals

A type of countertrade in which payment is in both goods and cash.

Counterpurchase

A type of countertrade with two distinct contracts. In the first, the seller agrees to a set price for goods and receives cash from the buyer. This first deal is contingent on a second in which the seller agrees to purchase goods from the buyer for the same amount as in the first contract or a set percentage of same.

Buy-back agreement

A type of countertrade in which the seller agrees to supply technology or equipment to construct a facility and receives payment in the form of goods the facility produces.

- **Barter** is the direct exchange of goods without any money. Though less common today, barter is still used (even in domestic trade) in straightforward, one-shot deals. It requires a single contract (rather than two or more contracts typical of other forms), has a short time span (other countertrade deals may stretch over several years), and is less complicated (other forms usually require managerial commitment and additional resources).
- **Compensation deals** include payment in both goods and cash. For example, a company may sell its equipment to the government of Brazil and receive half the payment in hard currency and the other half in Brazilian merchandise.
- **Counterpurchase**, also known as a back-to-back transaction or offset agreement, requires two distinct contracts. In the first, the seller agrees to a set price for goods and receives cash from the buyer. This first deal is contingent on a second contract in which the seller also agrees to purchase goods from the buyer (or produce and assemble a certain proportion of goods in the buyer's country) for the same cash amount as the first transaction or a set percentage of it. If the two exchanges are not of equal value, the difference can be paid in cash. Counterpurchase is common in the defense industry in sales of military hardware.
- **Buy-back agreement** arises when the seller agrees to supply technology or equipment to construct a facility and receives payment in the form of goods the facility produces. For example, the seller might design and build a factory in the buyer's country to manufacture tractors. The seller is compensated by receiving finished tractors from the factory it built, which it then sells in world markets. In essence, the original transaction trades goods and services that produce other goods and services, which are then received in payment. Product buy-back agreements may require several years to complete and therefore entail substantial risk.

Firms can encounter numerous problems in countertrade.

- The goods the customer offers may be inferior in quality, with limited sales potential in international markets.
- Putting a market value on the goods the customer offers may prove difficult, especially if they are commodities or of low quality. In addition, the buyer may not have the opportunity to inspect the goods or analyze their marketability before the sale.
- The parties to countertrade transactions tend to pad their prices. As a result, the cash the seller receives upon selling received goods may prove less than expected.
- Countertrade is usually complex, cumbersome, and time-consuming. Deals are often difficult to bring to conclusion.
- Government rules can make countertrade highly bureaucratic and often prove frustrating for the exporting firm.

If countertrade is so risky, why do many firms use it? First, the alternative may be no trade at all. For example, some national governments require countertrade as a means of obtaining needed goods. Some firms use countertrade to get a foothold in new markets or to access new sources of supply. In the mining industry, for example, certain types of minerals are available only in developing economies. Mining rights may be available only to firms willing to countertrade. Finally, many firms use countertrade as a way to repatriate profits frozen in a foreign subsidiary's blocked accounts. Otherwise unable to access its funds, the firm will scout the local market for products it can successfully export. General Motors' former Motors Trading subsidiary was created to generate trade credits—that is, sell its vehicles in return for contributing to exports of merchandise originating from that country.

Financing

Exporters often need to obtain financing to support international sales. Financing implies that the buyer or seller obtains a short-term loan to fulfill an export sale. The ability to offer attractive payment terms is often necessary to generate sales. If an SME receives a large order from a foreign buyer, access to the working capital provided from financing can determine the firm's ability to fill the order.

Exporters typically obtain financing from commercial banks, distribution intermediaries, buyers, or suppliers. In some cases, the exporter can sell its accounts receivable to a specialized financial institution, a process known as *forfaiting*.

Large exporters with foreign subsidiaries often employ *intracorporate financing*. The MNE may allow its subsidiary to retain a higher-than-usual level of its own profits to finance export sales. The parent firm may provide loans, equity investments, and trade credit (such as extensions on accounts payable) as funding for the international selling activities of its subsidiaries. The parent can also guarantee loans obtained from foreign banks by its subsidiaries. Finally, large MNEs can often access equity financing by selling corporate bonds or shares in stock markets.

Numerous government agencies offer programs to assist exporters with their financing needs. Some provide loans or grants to the exporter. Others offer guarantee programs that require the participation of a bank or other approved lender. Under such arrangements, the government pledges to repay a loan a commercial bank makes if the importer cannot repay.

In the United States, the *Export-Import Bank* (Ex-Im Bank; www.exim.gov) is a government agency that issues credit insurance to protect firms against default on exports sold under short-term credit. Canada's *Export Development Corporation* (www.edc.ca), India's Export Credit & Guarantee Corporation (www.ecgc.in), and Argentina's *Compania Argentina de Seguros de Credito* (www.casce.com.ar) provide services similar to those of the Ex-Im Bank. Government assistance programs are especially useful to SMEs, which often cannot obtain financing from other sources. For example, the U.S. *Small Business Administration* (www.sba.gov) helps small exporters obtain trade financing.

Four key factors influence the ability of an exporter or importer to obtain financing for export sales.

- *Creditworthiness of the exporter.* Small or inexperienced firms may encounter difficulty in obtaining bank financing, especially large loans.
- *Creditworthiness of the importer.* Some buyers, particularly from developing economies or countries with currency controls, may be unable to secure financing.
- *Riskiness of the sale.* Banks are reluctant to loan funds for risky transactions. International sales are usually more risky than domestic ones. Riskiness depends the value and marketability of the good being sold, uncertainty of the sale, conditions in the buyer's country, and likelihood that the loan will be repaid.
- *Timing of the sale* influences the cost of financing. The exporter usually wants to be paid as soon as possible, whereas the buyer prefers to delay payment. Banks may hesitate to finance a sale if the time to complete it is considerable.

Creditworthiness, risk, and timing also affect the cost of financing, which in turn affects the pricing and profitability of sales and the payment terms the exporter can offer.

13.3 Explain identifying and working with foreign intermediaries.

Identifying and Working with Foreign Intermediaries

Success in exporting usually depends on establishing strong relationships with distributors, sales representatives, and other foreign market intermediaries. Distribution channel intermediaries are physical distribution and marketing service providers in the value chain for focal firms. They move products and services in the home country and abroad and perform key downstream functions in the target market. For most exporters, relying on an independent foreign distributor is a low-cost way to enter foreign markets. The intermediary's intimate knowledge, contacts, and services in the local market can provide a strong support system, especially for small or inexperienced exporters. Intermediaries can be based in the foreign target market or in the home country, or they might operate through the Internet.

Most intermediaries are based in the exporter's target market. They provide many services, including conducting market research, appointing local representatives, exhibiting products at trade shows, arranging local transportation for cargo, and clearing products through customs. Intermediaries organize local marketing activities, including product adaptation, advertising, selling, and after-sales service. Many finance sales and extend credit. In short, intermediaries based in the foreign market can function like the exporter's local partner, handling all needed local business functions.

Foreign distributor

A foreign market-based intermediary that works under contract for an exporter, takes title to, and distributes the exporter's products in a national market or territory, often performing marketing functions such as sales, promotion, and after-sales service.

A **foreign distributor** is a foreign market–based intermediary that works under contract for an exporter. The foreign distributor takes title to and distributes the exporter's products in a national market or territory. It often performs marketing functions such as sales, promotion, and after-sales service. Foreign distributors are essentially independent wholesalers that purchase merchandise from exporters (at a discount) and resell it after adding a profit margin. They promote, sell, and maintain an inventory of the exporter's products in the foreign market. They also typically maintain substantial physical resources and provide financing, technical support, and after-sales service for the product, relieving the exporter of these functions abroad.

Manufacturer's representative

An intermediary contracted by the exporter to represent and sell its merchandise or services in a designated country or territory.

A **manufacturer's representative** is an intermediary contracted by the exporter to represent and sell its merchandise or services in a designated country or territory. Manufacturer's representatives go by various names—agents, sales representatives, or service representatives. In essence, they act as contracted sales personnel in a designated target market on behalf of the exporter. They are usually given broad powers and autonomy. Manufacturer's representatives do not take title to the goods they represent and are most often compensated by commission. They do not maintain physical facilities, marketing, or customer support capabilities, so the exporter must handle these functions.

Some intermediaries are domestically based. Wholesaler importers bring in products or commodities from foreign countries for sale in the home market, re-export, or use in the manufacture of finished products. Manufacturers also import a range of raw materials, parts, and components used in the production of higher value-added products. They may also import a complementary collection of products and services to supplement or augment their own product range. Retailers such as department stores, specialized stores, mail-order houses, and catalogue firms import many of the products they sell. A trip to retailers such as Best Buy, Canadian Tire, or Marks & Spencer reveals that most of their offerings are sourced from abroad, especially from low labor-cost countries.

Trading company

An intermediary that engages in import and export of a variety of commodities, products, and services.

A **trading company** serves as an intermediary that engages in import and export of various commodities, products, and services. It assumes the international marketing function on behalf of producers, especially those with limited international business experience. Manufacturers that lack the will or resources to sell their products internationally often employ trading companies. Large trading companies operate much like agents, coordinating sales of countless products in markets worldwide. Typically, they are high-volume, low-margin resellers compensated by adding profit margins to what they sell. In Japan, large trading companies are known as *sogo shosha*. In Japan and China alike, trading companies usually engage in both exporting and importing and are specialists in low-margin, high-volume trading.

Export management company (EMC)

A domestically based intermediary that acts as an export agent on behalf of a client company.

A domestically based intermediary is the **export management company (EMC)**, which acts as an export agent on behalf of a (usually inexperienced) client company. In return for a commission, an EMC finds export customers on behalf of the client firm, negotiates terms of sale, and arranges for international shipping. Although typically much smaller than a trading company, some EMCs have well-established networks of foreign distributors in place that allow exported products immediate access to foreign markets. Because of the indirect nature of the export sale, the manufacturer runs the risk of losing control over how its products are marketed abroad, with possible negative consequences for its international image.

Some focal firms use the Internet to sell products directly to customers rather than going through traditional wholesale and retail channels. By eliminating traditional intermediaries, companies can sell their products more cheaply and faster. This benefits SMEs in particular because they usually lack the often substantial resources needed to undertake conventional international operations.

Countless online intermediaries broker transactions between buyers and sellers worldwide. Emergent technologies offer—and sometimes require—new roles that intermediaries have not taken previously. Many traditional retailers establish websites or link with online service providers to create an electronic presence. The electronic sites of retailers such as Tesco (www.tesco.com) and Walmart (www.walmart.com) complement existing physical distribution infrastructure and bring more customers into physical outlets.

Source: Ulrich Mueller/123RF

Export transactions generally ship products through seaports and other maritime facilities, such as the Panama Canal.

Finding Foreign Intermediaries

Direct exporters often struggle to find appropriate intermediaries in target countries. Various sources are available for finding intermediaries abroad, including:

- Country and regional business directories, such as Kompass (Europe), Bottin International (worldwide), and the Japanese Trade Directory.
- Trade associations that support specific industries, such as the National Furniture Manufacturers Association or the National Association of Automotive Parts Manufacturers.
- Government departments, ministries, and agencies charged with assisting economic and trade development, such as Austrade in Australia (www.austrade.gov.au), Export Development Canada (www.edc.ca), and the International Trade Administration of the U.S. Department of Commerce (www.trade.gov).
- Commercial attachés in embassies and consulates abroad.
- Freight forwarders and trade consultants with specific knowledge about the exporter's target markets.

The exporter should consider attending a trade fair in the target country. Trade fairs are not only excellent sites to meet potential intermediaries, they also provide the means to become familiar with key players in the local industry and generally to learn about the target market. Visiting the target market is often the best way to identify and qualify intermediaries. On-site visits afford managers direct exposure to the market and opportunities to meet prospective intermediaries. Managers can also inspect the facilities as well as gauge the capabilities, technical personnel, and sales capabilities of prospective intermediaries. Once they have narrowed the choices, experienced exporters often request prospective intermediaries to prepare a business plan for the proposed venture. Its quality and sophistication provide a basis for judging the candidate's true capabilities.

Source: Simon clay/Alamy

Working closely with foreign intermediaries helps green car manufacturers sell electric vehicles around the world. These Mini e electric cars are awaiting shipment from BMW's Cowley Plant in Oxford, England.

Working with Foreign Intermediaries

In exporting, the most typical intermediary is the foreign-based independent distributor. The exporter relies on the distributor for much of the marketing, physical distribution, and customer service activities in the export market. Experienced exporters go to great lengths to build relational assets—that is, high-quality, enduring business and social relationships—with key intermediaries and facilitators abroad. Sharon Doherty succeeded in exporting by developing close relationships with qualified foreign distributors. Although competitors can usually replicate the exporter's other competitive attributes, such as product features or marketing skills, strong ties with competent foreign intermediaries are built over time and provide the exporter with an enduring competitive advantage.

The firm should strive to cultivate mutually beneficial, bonding relations with key intermediaries. To create a positive working relationship, the exporter should be sensitive to the intermediary's objectives and aspirations. The exporter should build solidarity by demonstrating solid commitment, remaining reliable, and building trust. This requires developing a good understanding of the intermediary's needs and working earnestly to address them. In general, foreign intermediaries expect exporters to provide:

- Good, reliable products for which there is a ready market.
- Products that provide significant profits.
- Opportunities to handle other product lines.
- Support for marketing communications, advertising, and product warranties.
- A payment method that does not unduly burden the intermediary.
- Training for intermediary staff and the opportunity to visit the exporter's facilities (at the exporter's expense) to gain firsthand knowledge of the exporter's operations.
- Help establishing after-sales service facilities, including training of local technical representatives and the means to replace defective parts, as well as a ready supply of spare parts, to maintain or repair the products.

The exporter in turn has expectations its intermediaries should meet. Exhibit 13.5 summarizes the selection criteria that experienced exporters use to qualify prospective intermediaries.

EXHIBIT 13.5 Criteria for Evaluating Export Intermediaries

Intermediary Dimension	Evaluation Criteria
Organizational Strengths	• Ability to finance sales and growth in the market • Ability to provide financing to customers • Management team quality • Reputation with customers • Connections with influential people or government agencies in the market
Product-Related Factors	• Knowledge about the exporter's product • Quality and superiority of all product lines handled by the intermediary • Ability to ensure security for patents and other intellectual property rights • Extent to which intermediary handles competing product lines
Marketing Capabilities	• Experience with the product line and target customers • Extent of geographic coverage provided in the target market • Quality and quantity of sales force • Ability to formulate and implement marketing plans
Managerial Commitment	• Percent of intermediary's business consisting of a single supplier • Willingness to maintain inventory sufficient to fully serve the market • Commitment to achieving exporter's sales targets

Sources: Based on *Business International*, "How to Evaluate Foreign Distributors," pp. 145–149 (May 10, 1985); S. Tamer Cavusgil, Poh-Lin Yeoh, and Michel Mitri, "Selecting Foreign Distributors: An Expert Systems Approach," *Industrial Marketing Management* 24, No. 4 (1995), pp. 297–304; International Trade Administration, *Basic Guide to Exporting: The Official Government Resource for Small and Medium-Sized Businesses* (Washington, DC: International Trade Administration, 2011); Franklin Root, *Entry Strategies for International Markets* (Hoboken, NJ: Jossey-Bass, 1983/1998).

When Intermediary Relations Go Bad

Despite good intentions, disputes can arise between the exporter and its intermediaries on issues such as compensation, marketing practices, after-sales service, inventory levels, and adapting the product for local customers. In anticipation of such disagreements, exporters generally establish a contract-based, legal relationship with the partner. Some firms require candidate intermediaries to undergo a probationary period during which they evaluate performance. If it is suboptimal or if disputes appear likely to emerge, the exporter may impose special requirements or even end the relationship.

The contract between an exporter and its intermediary contains various elements. A typical contract specifies the:

- Duration of the relationship between the exporter and the intermediary.
- Sales territory granted to the intermediary.
- Manner in which the intermediary is expected to handle the product (e.g., regarding adaptation, pricing, advertising).
- Tasks and performance goals that the intermediary is expected to achieve.
- Tasks and responsibilities that the exporter is expected to perform.
- Process to be followed for resolving disputes.
- Conditions under which the relationship with the intermediary can be terminated.

Exporters should find out about the legal requirements for termination in advance and specify the intermediary's rights for compensation. In many countries, commercial regulations favor local intermediaries and may require the exporter to indemnify—that is, compensate—the intermediary even if there is just cause for termination. In some countries, legal contracts may prove insufficient to protect the exporter's interests. Many countries in Africa and Latin America lack strong legal frameworks, which can make contracts hard to enforce.

Just as in their domestic operations, exporters occasionally encounter problems with buyers or intermediaries who default on payment. In terms of payment mechanisms, cash in advance or a letter of credit is usually best. The exporter can also buy insurance to cover commercial credit risks. If a default happens, the exporter's best recourse is to negotiate with the offending party. At the extreme, the exporter may pursue litigation, arbitration, or other legal means for enforcing payment on a sale.

Outsourcing, Global Sourcing, and Offshoring

13.4 Understand outsourcing, global sourcing, and offshoring.

When firms import needed goods or services, they engage in global sourcing. Before delving into this important topic, let's first review outsourcing. Specifically, **outsourcing** refers to the procurement of selected value-adding activities, including production of intermediate goods or finished products, from external independent suppliers. Firms outsource because they are not superior at performing *all* value-chain activities, and it is more cost effective to outsource these activities. For example, Harley Davidson sources motorcycle helmets from suppliers in China.

Outsourcing
The procurement of selected value-adding activities, including production of intermediate goods or finished products, from independent suppliers.

Business process outsourcing (BPO) refers to the procurement of services. When firms engage in BPO, they procure services such as accounting, human resource functions, IT services, or technical support, from external suppliers.[4] Firms contract with third-party service providers to reduce the cost of performing service tasks. Typically, such tasks fall outside the firm's core competencies or are not critical to maintaining its competitive position in the marketplace. BPO can be divided into two categories. *Back-office activities* include internal, upstream business functions such as payroll and billing. *Front-office activities* include downstream, customer-related services such as marketing or technical support.

Business process outsourcing (BPO)
The outsourcing to independent suppliers of business service functions such as accounting, payroll, human resource functions, travel services, IT services, customer service, or technical support.

In undertaking outsourcing, managers face two key decisions: which, if any, value-chain activities should be outsourced; and where in the world these activities should be performed. Let's consider these choices.

Decision 1: Outsource or Not?

Managers must decide between *internalization* and *externalization*—whether each value-adding activity should be conducted in house or by an external, independent supplier. In business, this is traditionally known as the *make* or *buy* decision: "Should we make a product or perform a value-chain activity ourselves, or should we obtain it from an outside contractor?"

Firms usually internalize those value-chain activities they consider part of their *core competencies*, those that they perform particularly well or that use proprietary knowledge they want to control. Canon uses its core competencies in precision mechanics, fine optics, and microelectronics to produce some of the world's best cameras, printers, and copiers. It usually performs R&D and product design itself to reduce the risk of divulging proprietary knowledge to competitors and to generate continuous improvement in these competencies. By contrast, firms will usually source from *external* suppliers when they can obtain non-core products, components, or services at lower cost or from suppliers specialized in providing them.

Decision 2: Where in the World Should Value-Adding Activities Be Located?

A second key decision that firms face is whether to keep each value-adding activity in the home country or locate it in a foreign country. **Configuration of value-adding activity** refers to the pattern or geographic arrangement of locations where the firm carries out value-chain activities.[5] Instead of concentrating value-adding activities in their home country, many firms configure them across the world to save money, reduce delivery time, access factors of production, or extract maximum advantages relative to competitors.

This helps explain the migration of manufacturing industries from Europe, Japan, and the United States to emerging markets in Asia, Latin America, and Eastern Europe. Depending on the firm and the industry, management may decide to concentrate certain value-adding activities in just one or a handful of locations while dispersing others to numerous countries. External suppliers are typically located in countries characterized by low-cost labor, competent production processes, and specific knowledge about relevant engineering and development activities.[6]

German automaker BMW (www.bmw.com) operates 17 factories in 6 countries to manufacture sedans, coupes, and convertibles. Workers at the Munich plant build the BMW 3 Series and supply engines and key body components to other BMW factories abroad. BMW has plants in the United States, China, and India, where it manufactures automobiles from imported parts and components. Management configures BMW's sourcing at the best locations worldwide to minimize costs (for example, by producing in China), hire skilled people (by producing in Germany), remain close to key markets (by producing in China, India, and the United States), and succeed in the intensely competitive global car industry.[7]

Global Sourcing

Global sourcing relies on a contractual relationship between the buyer (the focal firm) and a foreign source of supply. It is also called 'importing', 'global procurement', or 'global purchasing'. Dell (www.dell.com) relies on a manufacturing network composed largely of independent suppliers located around the world. Exhibit 13.6 details how Dell assembles components from suppliers in numerous locations for its Dell Inspiron notebook computer.[8]

Global sourcing is a low-control strategy in which the focal firm sources from independent suppliers through contractual agreements as opposed to the high-control strategy of buying from company-owned subsidiaries. Global sourcing frequently represents the firm's initial involvement in international business. For many firms, it increases management's awareness about other international opportunities.

An established business practice, global sourcing has gained momentum in the current phase of globalization.[9] Retailers usually obtain a substantial portion of their merchandise from foreign suppliers. Retailers such as Carrefour, Canadian Tire, and Home Depot are large-scale importers. Walmart accounts for a substantial proportion of U.S. imports from China, more than $30 billion per year. Steinway procures parts and components from a dozen foreign countries to manufacture grand pianos. HP provides technical support to its customers from call centers based in India.

In many cases, firms move entire sections of their value chains abroad, such as R&D, manufacturing, or technical support. In the sports apparel industry, firms such as Nike and Reebok subcontract nearly all their athletic shoe production to lower-cost foreign manufacturers. Clothing retailer Gap sources more than 80 percent of its apparel from suppliers in Asia. The Gap, Nike, and Reebok function primarily as brand owners and marketers, not as manufacturers. Apple sources some 70 percent of its production from abroad while focusing internal resources on continuously improving its software and product designs. This allows Apple management to optimize usage of the firm's finite capital resources and focus on its core competencies.

Configuration of value-adding activity
The pattern or geographic arrangement of locations where the firm carries out value-chain activities.

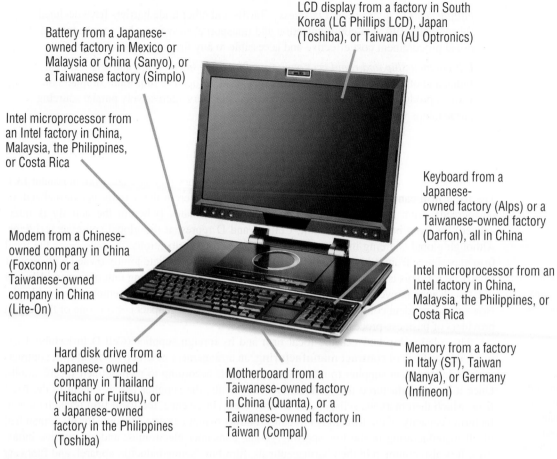

Battery from a Japanese-owned factory in Mexico or Malaysia or China (Sanyo), or a Taiwanese factory (Simplo)

LCD display from a factory in South Korea (LG Phillips LCD), Japan (Toshiba), or Taiwan (AU Optronics)

Intel microprocessor from an Intel factory in China, Malaysia, the Philippines, or Costa Rica

Keyboard from a Japanese-owned factory (Alps) or a Taiwanese-owned factory (Darfon), all in China

Modem from a Chinese-owned company in China (Foxconn) or a Taiwanese-owned company in China (Lite-On)

Intel microprocessor from an Intel factory in China, Malaysia, the Philippines, or Costa Rica

Hard disk drive from a Japanese- owned company in Thailand (Hitachi or Fujitsu), or a Japanese-owned factory in the Philippines (Toshiba)

Motherboard from a Taiwanese-owned factory in China (Quanta), or a Taiwanese-owned factory in Taiwan (Compal)

Memory from a factory in Italy (ST), Taiwan (Nanya), or Germany (Infineon)

EXHIBIT 13.6

Sourcing for the Dell Inspiron Notebook Computer

Sources: Based on "Dell's Current Suppliers," 2015, www.dell.com; Thomas Friedman, *The World Is Flat 3.0* (New York: Picado, 2007);

The total worldwide sourcing market for product manufacturing and services now exceeds $1 trillion. Global sourcing employs more than 500,000 people in the Philippines. Worldwide, the most frequently outsourced business processes include logistics and procurement, sales and marketing, and customer service, followed by finance and accounting. Global sourcing by the private sector now accounts for more than half of all imports by major countries. Contractors such as Softtek in Mexico help U.S. banks develop customized software, manage IT systems, and perform support and maintenance for commercial finance operations. Softtek (www.softtek.com) has 3,500 employees, mostly engineers. Its outsourcing facilities are located in Brazil, Colombia, and Peru.

India is the current leader in the processing of advanced economies' relocated business services. The country has 2.5 million people working in the BPO industry. Indian BPO service providers have developed business relationships with 75 percent of *Fortune* 500 companies. The recent economic turndown is expected to pressure advanced-economy firms to seek further ways to reduce costs, to the benefit of service suppliers in India.

The growth of global sourcing has been driven by three key factors.

• *Technological advances in communications, especially the Internet and international telecommunications*   Access to vast online information means focal firms can quickly find suppliers that meet specific needs, anywhere in the world. Firms can communicate continuously with foreign suppliers at very low cost.

- *Falling costs of international business* Tariffs and other trade barriers have declined substantially. Efficient communication and transportation systems have made international procurement cost effective and accessible to any firm.
- *Entrepreneurship and rapid economic transformation in emerging markets* China, India, and other emerging markets have quickly developed as important suppliers of various products and services. Entrepreneurial suppliers aggressively pursue sourcing partnerships with foreign buyers.

The decisions about whether and where to outsource are shown in the framework in Exhibit 13.7. The focal firm can source from independent suppliers (wherein the activity is externalized, or outsourced), from company-owned subsidiaries and affiliates (wherein the activity is internalized), or from both. In the exhibit, Cells C and D represent the global sourcing scenarios. Although global sourcing implies procurement from foreign locations, in some cases the focal firm may source from its own wholly owned subsidiary or an affiliate jointly owned with another firm (Cell C). This is **captive sourcing**. Genpact was a captive sourcing unit of General Electric (GE), with annual revenues of more than $1 billion and more than 37,000 employees worldwide. Now an independent company based in India, Genpact (www.genpact.com) is one of the largest providers of business-process outsourcing services.[10]

Captive sourcing
Sourcing from the firm's own production facilities.

The relationship between the focal firm and its foreign supplier (Cell D in Exhibit 13.7) may take the form of **contract manufacturing**, an arrangement in which the focal firm contracts with an independent supplier to manufacture products according to well-defined specifications. Once it has manufactured the products or components, the supplier delivers them to the focal firm, which then markets, sells, and distributes them. In essence, the focal firm rents the manufacturing capacity of the foreign contractor. Contract manufacturing accounts for more than half of all manufacturing in the toy, sporting goods, consumer electronics, and automotive industries. It is also common in the pharmaceuticals, furniture, semiconductor, apparel, and footwear industries.[11]

Contract manufacturing
An arrangement in which the focal firm contracts with an independent supplier to manufacture products according to well-defined specifications.

Have you ever heard of Taiwan's Hon Hai Precision Industry Company? Also known as Foxconn, Hon Hai is a leading contract manufacturer in the global electronics industry, with annual sales of more than $100 billion. Hon Hai (www.foxconn.com) works under contract for many well-known companies, churning out PlayStations for Sony; iPods, iPhones, and iPads for Apple; printers and PCs for Hewlett-Packard; and thousands of other products. The firm employs more than one million people in dozens of contract factories worldwide, from Malaysia to Mexico.[12]

EXHIBIT 13.7 The Nature of Outsourcing and Global Sourcing

	Value-adding activity is internalized	Value-adding activity is externalized (outsourced)
Value-adding activity kept in home country	A Keep production in-house, in home country	B Outsource production to third-party provider at home
Value-adding activity conducted abroad (global sourcing)	C Delegate production to foreign subsidiary or affiliate (captive sourcing)	D Outsource production to a third-party provider abroad (contract manufacturing or global sourcing from independent suppliers)

Sources: Based on B. Kedia and D. Mukherjee, "Understanding Offshoring: A Research Framework Based on Disintegration, Location and Externalization Advantages," *Journal of World Business* 44, No. 3 (2009), pp. 250–261; *Information Economy Report 2009* (New York: United Nations, 2009); *World Investment Report 2004* (New York: UNCTAD, 2004).

Offshoring is the relocation of a business process or entire manufacturing facility to a foreign country. It is common in the service sector, including banking, software code writing, legal services, and customer-service activities.[13] Large legal hubs have emerged in India that provide services such as drafting contracts and patent applications, conducting research and negotiations, and performing paralegal work, all on behalf of Western clients. With lawyers in Europe and North America costing $300 an hour or more, law firms in India can cut Western companies' legal bills by up to 75 percent.[14]

Offshoring
The relocation of a business process or entire manufacturing facility to a foreign country.

Industries that benefit most from global sourcing are characterized by:

- Large-scale manufacturing whose primary competitive advantage is efficiency and low cost.
- High labor intensity in product and service production, such as garment manufacturing and call centers.
- Uniform customer needs and standardized technologies and processes in production and other value-chain activities, such as automobiles and machine parts.
- Established products with a predictable pattern of sales, such as components for consumer electronics.
- Information intensity whose functions and activities can be easily transmitted through the Internet, such as accounting, billing, and payroll.
- Outputs that are easily codified and transmitted over the Internet or by telephone, such as software preparation, technical support, and customer service.

Companies headquartered in the advanced economies outsource the most services by volume. Emerging markets and developing economies are the most popular destinations by far, especially India, China, Mexico, Indonesia, Egypt, Chile, and the Philippines. Key criteria for evaluating destinations include the availability of an appropriate labor force, wage rates, worker skill level, language and culture compatibility, quality of infrastructure, the country's legal system, economic environment, tax rates, and regulatory costs. In addition to large firms, global sourcing provides big benefits for small and medium-sized enterprises (SMEs). SMEs from car dealerships to real estate firms increasingly farm out accounting, support services, and design work to suppliers around the world.[15]

Exhibit 13.8 explains the strategic implications of sourcing and location decisions. The exhibit portrays a typical value chain, ranging from R&D and design to customer service. The first row indicates the degree to which management considers each value-adding activity a strategic asset to the firm. The second row indicates whether the activity tends to be internalized inside the focal firm or outsourced to a foreign supplier. The third row indicates where management typically locates an activity.

Running a business as far-flung as DHL's package delivery service requires support offices around the world. This delivery boat travels the Amstel River in Amsterdam. DHL has tracking centers in three time zones that are 8 hours apart, allowing it to offer 24-hour worldwide tracking service.

Source: Danita Delimont/Alamy.

 MyManagementLab   Watch It! I
If your professor has assigned this, go to the Assignments section of **mymanagementlab.com** to complete the video exercise titled Toyota: Outsourcing and Logistics.

	R&D, Design	Manufacturing of Parts, Components	Manufacturing or Assembly of Finished Products	Marketing and Branding	Sales and Distribution	Customer Service
Importance of this activity to the firm as a strategic asset	High importance	Low importance	Low to medium importance	High importance	Medium importance	Medium importance
Likelihood of internalizing rather than outsourcing this activity	High	Low	Low to medium	High	Low to medium	Low to medium
Geographic configuration: Overall tendency to locate activity at home or abroad	Usually concentrated at home	Usually dispersed across various markets	Usually concentrated in a few markets	Branding concentrated at home; Marketing concentrated or dispersed to individual markets	Dispersed to individual markets	Dispersed to individual markets, except call centers, which are often concentrated

EXHIBIT 13.8

Typical Choices of Outsourcing and Geographic Dispersion of Value-Chain Activities Among Firms

13.5 Describe the benefits and risks of global sourcing.

Benefits, Risks, and Responsibilities of Global Sourcing

Global sourcing brings enormous benefits to firms, primarily leading to improved performance and superior competitive advantages. However, global sourcing also entails various risks. Firms that undertake global sourcing are confronted with challenges and opportunities for corporate social responsibility.

Benefits of Global Sourcing

The main benefits of global sourcing are cost efficiency and the ability to achieve strategic goals. Let's examine these.

COST EFFICIENCY   The primary rationale for global sourcing is to reduce the firm's costs of inputs and operations. Exhibit 13.9 reveals typical labor cost per hour of workers in various countries. Labor costs in the emerging markets, such as Indonesia and Mexico, are far less expensive than in the advanced economies. A worker in Indonesia earns only about one dollar per hour. The rate in Mexico is around two dollars per hour. In India, the rate approaches $2.50 per hour. This wage discrepancy explains why MNEs source inputs from emerging markets. Note, however, that wages have been rising rapidly in China. This is helping raise living standards in China but also makes the country less attractive as a sourcing destination.[16]

ABILITY TO ACHIEVE STRATEGIC GOALS   The strategic view of global sourcing is called *transformational outsourcing*. It suggests that just as the firm achieves cost efficiencies, it also obtains the means to restructure operations, speed up innovation, and fund otherwise-unaffordable development projects.[17] Global sourcing allows the firm to free expensive analysts, engineers, and managers from routine tasks to spend more time on important tasks. These tasks include researching, innovating, managing, and generally undertaking high-value-adding activities that contribute more productively to increasing company performance.[18] Global sourcing becomes a catalyst to overhaul organizational processes and company operations and increase the firm's overall competitive advantages. It allows the firm to achieve large, longer-term strategic goals.

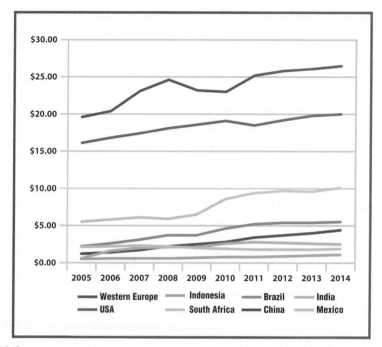

EXHIBIT 13.9

Average Labor Cost Per Hour of Workers, in U.S. Dollars

Sources: Based on Eurostat: Hourly Labor Costs, at ec.europa.eu; International Labour Organisation (ILO), Statistics and Databases, www.ilo.org; Labour Bureau, Government of India, at http://labourbureau.nic.in.

The clothing company Liz Claiborne sold its sourcing operations, which handle all aspects of production from finding materials to manufacturing garments, to Li & Fung Group, based in Hong Kong. Li & Fung (www.lifung.com) specializes in managing the supply chains of dozens of brands and retailers worldwide, including Walmart and Target. Claiborne management took the step to shift the firm's business model dramatically and focus on its core competencies, such as marketing and distribution.[19]

The twin objectives of cost efficiency and strategic goal achievement are often both present in a particular global sourcing activity. Global sourcing can provide other benefits as well, including:

- *Faster corporate growth.* Firms can focus their resources on performing more-profitable activities such as R&D or building relationships with customers. For example, they can expand their staff of engineers and researchers while keeping constant their cost of product development as a percentage of sales.
- *Access to qualified personnel abroad.* Countries such as China, India, and Ireland offer abundant pools of educated engineers, managers, and other specialists to help firms achieve their goals. Disney has much of its animation work done in Japan, home to world-class animators.
- *Improved productivity and service.* Manufacturing productivity and other value-chain activities can be improved by suppliers that specialize in these activities. Penske Truck Leasing improved its efficiency and customer service by outsourcing dozens of business processes to Mexico and India.

Source: Vasily Smirnov/Shutterstock

Global automobile companies outsource much of their production to manufacturers in China. Global sourcing helps reduce costs, improves productivity, and facilitates the redesign of critical value-chain activities.

- *Business process redesign.* By reconfiguring their value-chain systems or reengineering their business processes, companies can improve their production efficiency and resource usage. MNEs see offshoring as a means to overhaul outdated company operations.[20]
- *Increased speed to market.* By shifting software development and editorial work to India and the Philippines, the U.S.-Dutch publisher Wolters Kluwer was able to produce a greater variety of books and journals and publish them faster. Pharmaceutical firms get new medications to market faster by outsourcing clinical drug trials.
- *Access to new markets.* Sourcing provides an entrée to the market, an understanding of local customers, and the means to initiate marketing activities there. By moving many of its R&D operations to Russia, the telecommunications firm Nortel gained an important foothold in a market that needs telephone switching equipment and other communications infrastructure.[21]
- *Technological flexibility.* Leveraging independent suppliers abroad provides firms the flexibility to quickly change sources of supply, employing whichever suppliers offer the most advanced technologies. In this way, sourcing provides greater organizational flexibility and faster responsiveness to evolving buyer needs.[22]

Combined, these benefits give firms the ability to renew their strategic positions continuously. Outsourcing specialists such as Accenture and Genpact meticulously dissect the workflow of other firms' human resources, finance, or IT departments. This helps the specialists build new IT platforms, redesign all processes, and administer programs, acting as virtual subsidiaries to their client firms. The specialists then disperse work among global networks of staff from Asia to Eastern Europe and elsewhere.[23]

Risks of Global Sourcing

In addition to potential benefits, global sourcing also brings unexpected complications. As many as half of all outsourcing arrangements are terminated earlier than planned. Global sourcing entails the following major risks.[24]

- *Lower-than-expected cost savings* International transactions are often more complex and costly than expected. Conflicts and misunderstandings may arise from differences in the national and organizational cultures between the focal firm and foreign supplier. Establishing an outsourcing facility can be surprisingly expensive, due to the need to upgrade poor infrastructure or locate it in a large city to attract sufficient skilled labor.[25]
- *Environmental factors* Environmental challenges include currency fluctuations, tariffs and other trade barriers, high energy and transportation costs, adverse macroeconomic events, labor strikes, and natural disasters. Firms that source from countries whose currencies are strengthening experience higher costs. Many countries suffer from poor public infrastructure, as exemplified by power outages and poor road and rail networks. In 2012, a massive power outage in India left several hundred million people without power and disrupted businesses and transport systems.
- *Weak legal environment* Many popular locations for global sourcing (for example, China, India, and Russia) have weak intellectual property laws and poor enforcement, which can erode key strategic assets. Inadequate legal systems, red tape, convoluted tax systems, and complex business regulations complicate local operations in many countries.
- *Inadequate or low-skilled workers* Some foreign suppliers may be staffed by employees who lack appropriate knowledge about the tasks with which they are charged. Other suppliers suffer rapid turnover of skilled employees. In 2011, customer complaints about the quality of service led the U.K. subsidiary of Banco Santander to move its call centers from India back to the United Kingdom.[26]
- *Overreliance on suppliers* Unreliable suppliers may put earlier work aside when they gain a more important client. Suppliers occasionally encounter financial difficulties or are acquired by other firms with different priorities and procedures. Management at the focal firm may find itself scrambling to find alternate suppliers. Overreliance can reduce the focal firm's control of important value-chain tasks.
- *Risk of creating competitors* As the focal firm shares its intellectual property and business-process knowledge with foreign suppliers, it also runs the risk of creating future rivals.

Schwinn, long the leader in the global bicycle industry, transferred much of its production and core expertise to lower-cost foreign suppliers, which acquired sufficient knowledge to become competitors, eventually forcing Schwinn into bankruptcy (from which it later recovered).

- *Erosion of morale and commitment among home-country employees* Global sourcing can leave employees caught in the middle between their employer and their employer's clients. When outsourcing forces retained and outsourced staff to work side by side, tensions and uncertainty may diminish employee commitment and enthusiasm.

Dissatisfaction with global sourcing has led many companies to return their production operations to the home country. Numerous American firms, for example, have reestablished manufacturing in the United States, following disappointing experiences sourcing inputs from suppliers located abroad. The tendency, known as *reshoring,* underscores the importance of carefully weighing the pros and cons of global sourcing. It also highlights the importance of following a strategic approach to global sourcing.[27]

Corporate Social Responsibility

The business community sees global sourcing as a way to maintain or increase business competitiveness and enhance long-term company sustainability. Others view it negatively, focusing on the loss of local jobs. After IBM workers in Europe went on strike against offshoring, shareholders at IBM's annual meeting argued for an anti-offshoring resolution. In the United States, 27,000 Boeing machinists went on strike to protest the aircraft company's decision to outsource jobs globally in the production of the 787 Dreamliner jet.[28]

Critics of global sourcing point to three potential problems.

- Job losses in the home country
- Reduced national competitiveness
- Declining standards of living

Regarding the last two concerns, critics worry that, as more tasks are performed at lower cost with comparable quality in other countries, high-wage countries will lose their national competitiveness. Long-held knowledge and skills will eventually drain away to other countries, they fear, and the lower wages paid abroad will eventually pull down wages in the home country, leading to lower living standards.

A major concern is job losses. The advanced economies have outsourced millions of jobs to emerging markets in the past decade. Job losses rise when companies increase their sourcing of input and finished goods from abroad. Walmart sources as much as 70 percent of its finished merchandise from abroad. This has led citizens to form a protest group called Walmartwatch.com, which claims millions of U.S. jobs have been lost due to Walmart's global sourcing.[29] Job losses are occurring in developing economies as well. For example, in the textile industry, Honduras, Indonesia, and Turkey have seen jobs gradually transferred to India and Pakistan.[30]

Outsourcing and offshoring represent a process of *creative destruction*, a concept first proposed by the Austrian economist Joseph Schumpeter.[31] According to this view, firms' innovative activities tend to make mature products obsolete over time. The introduction of personal computers essentially eliminated the typewriter industry, the DVD player eliminated the VCR, and so on. Just as offshoring results in job losses and adverse effects for particular groups and economic sectors, it also creates new advantages and opportunities for firms and consumers alike. Sourcing usually enhances company sustainability for the long term. New industries created through creative destruction will create new jobs and innovative products.

Source: Roger Bamber/Alamy

Global sourcing has sparked protests in many countries. Here, trade union members at Lloyds TSB bank in the United Kingdom protest the outsourcing of jobs to India.

MyManagementLab   **Watch It! 2**

If your professor has assigned this, go to the Assignments section of **mymanagementlab.com** to complete the video exercise titled Bringing Jobs Back to the United States.

13.6 Understand global sourcing strategies and supply-chain management.

Global Sourcing Strategies and Supply Chain Management

Firms can reduce much of the risk in global sourcing by employing appropriate strategies. Skillful supply chain management reduces the costs and enhances the advantages available from global sourcing.

Managerial guidelines for global sourcing

- *Go offshore for the right reasons.* The best rationale is strategic. Most companies cite cost cutting as the main reason for global sourcing. After the first year, however, the amount of money saved tends to decline. Global sourcing provides the means to achieve more beneficial, long-term goals. Management should analyze its value-chain activities and outsource those in which it is relatively weak, that offer relatively little value to the bottom line, or that can be performed more effectively by others, yet are not critical to the firm's core competencies.

- *Get employees on board.* Global sourcing can demoralize employees and other organizational stakeholders. Senior management should seek employee support by reaching a consensus of managers and labor, developing alternatives for redeploying laid-off workers and soliciting employee help in choosing foreign partners.

- *Choose carefully between a captive operation and contracting with outside suppliers.* Managers should be vigilant about striking the right balance between the organizational activities they retain inside the firm and those they source from outside. Many firms establish their own sourcing operations abroad to maintain control of outsourced activities and technologies.

- *Choose suppliers carefully.* Finding and managing foreign suppliers is complex. The focal firm may have limited influence over suppliers' manufacturing and processes. Suppliers may engage in opportunistic behavior or act in bad faith. To ensure the success of sourcing ventures, the focal firm must exercise great care to identify and screen potential suppliers and then monitor the activities of those suppliers from which it sources.

- *Emphasize communications and collaboration with suppliers.* Global sourcing may fail if buyers and suppliers spend too little time getting well acquainted. Rushing into a deal before clarifying each other's expectations produces misunderstandings and poor results. Managers at the focal firm may need to monitor manufacturing processes closely. Partners must share necessary information.[32] Close collaboration with suppliers in development activities enables the focal firm to tap ideas for new products, technologies, and improvements. Efforts to build strong relationships foster a moral contract between the focal firm and the supplier, often more effective than a formal legal contract.

- *Safeguard interests.* The focal firm should protect its interests in the supplier relationship. It can advise the supplier against engaging in activities that harm the firm's reputation. The firm can share costs and revenues by building a stake for the supplier so that, in case of failure to meet expectations, the supplier also suffers costs or forgoes revenues. Management should maintain flexibility by keeping open its options for finding alternate partners if needed. The focal firm should withhold access to intellectual property and key assets. If conflicts are unresolved by negotiations, one option is to acquire full or partial ownership of the supplier.

Public policy should strive to mitigate the potential harm global sourcing can cause.[33] Governments can use economic and fiscal policies to encourage the development of new technologies by helping entrepreneurs reap the financial benefits of their work and keeping the cost of capital for financing R&D low. A strong educational system, including technical schools and well-funded universities, supplies engineers, scientists, managers, and knowledge workers. A strong educational system provides firms with pools of high-quality labor.

Global Supply-Chain Management

A key reason sourcing products from distant markets has become a major business phenomenon is the efficiency with which goods can be physically moved from one part of the globe to another.

A **global supply chain** is the firm's integrated network of sourcing, production, and distribution, organized on a worldwide scale and located in countries where competitive advantage can be maximized. Global supply-chain management includes both upstream (supplier) and downstream (customer) flows.

The concepts of supply chain and value chain are related but distinct. Recall that the value chain is the collection of activities intended to design, produce, market, deliver, and support a product or service. By contrast, the supply chain is the collection of logistics specialists and activities that provides inputs to manufacturers or retailers.

Skillful supply-chain management serves to optimize value-chain activities. Sourcing from numerous suppliers scattered around the world is neither economical nor feasible without an efficient supply-chain system. Casual observers are impressed by the vast collection of products in a supermarket or department store that originated from dozens of countries. The speed with which these products are delivered to end users is equally impressive.

Source: Fredrik Renander/Alamy

Minimizing the risks of global sourcing entails several critical strategies. Following a careful selection process, the focal firm should invest in collaborating and communicating with suppliers. Pictured is a call center in New Delhi, India.

Global supply chain
The firm's integrated network of sourcing, production, and distribution, organized on a worldwide scale and located in countries where competitive advantage can be maximized.

Consider a customer in Canada who orders a Dell laptop computer. The order is typically routed to the Dell factory in Malaysia, where workers must access 30 distinct component parts that originate with Dell suppliers scattered around the world. Indeed, the total supply chain for a typical Dell computer, including multiple tiers of suppliers, typically includes some 400 companies in Asia, Europe, and the Americas. Dell is so skilled at managing all this complexity that customers typically receive their computers within two weeks of submitting an order.

Networks of supply-chain hubs and providers of global delivery service are an integral part of global supply chains. Many focal firms delegate supply-chain activities to such independent logistics service providers as DHL, FedEx, and TNT. Consulting firms that manage the logistics of other firms are called *third-party logistics providers (3PLs)*. Using a 3PL is often the best solution for international logistics, especially for firms that produce at low volumes or lack the resources and expertise to create their own logistics network.

Exhibit 13.10 illustrates the stages, functions, and activities in the supply chain. It reveals how suppliers interact with the focal firm and how these, in turn, interact with distributors and retailers.

Costs of physically delivering a product to an export market may account for as much as 40 percent of the good's total cost. Skillful supply-chain management reduces this cost while increasing customer satisfaction. Firms use information and communications technologies (ICTs) to streamline supply chains, reducing costs and increasing distribution efficiency. For example, *electronic data interchange (EDI)* automatically passes orders directly from customers to suppliers through a sophisticated ICT platform. ICTs enhance information sharing and improve efficiency by allowing the firm to track international shipments and clear customs. In efficient systems, suppliers are connected through automated, real-time communications. The focal firm and its supply-chain partners continuously share information to meet marketplace demands constantly.

Logistics physically moves goods through the supply chain. It incorporates information, transportation, inventory, warehousing, materials handling, and similar activities associated with the delivery of raw materials, parts, components, and finished products. Managers seek to reduce moving and storage costs by using just-in-time inventory systems. Internationally, logistics are complex due to wide geographic distances, multiple legal environments, and the often inadequate and costly nature of distribution infrastructure in individual countries. The more diverse the firm's global supply chain, the greater the cost of logistics.

EXHIBIT 13.10

Stages, Functions, and Activities in the Global Supply Chain

	Suppliers	Focal Firm	Intermediaries and/or Retailers
Stage in supply chain	Sourcing, from home country and abroad	Inbound materials; outbound goods and services	Distribution to domestic customers or foreign customers (exports)
Major functions	Provide raw materials, parts, components, supplies, as well as business processes and other services to focal firm	Manufacture or assemble components or finished products, or produce services	Distribute and sell products and services
Typical activities	Maintain inventory, process orders, transport goods, deliver services	Manage inventory, process orders, manufacture or assemble products, produce and deliver services, distribute products to customers, retailers, or intermediaries	Manage inventory, place or process orders, produce services, manage physical distribution, provide after-sales service

Competent logistics management is critical, especially for just-in-time inventory systems. The California ports of Los Angeles (www.portoflosangeles.org) and Long Beach (www.polb.com) handle more than 40 percent of imports into the United States, processing more than 24,000 shipping containers per day. Infrastructure deficiencies and increasing demand can result in long delays, which translate into longer transit times and higher costs for U.S. importers. Because of delays, Toys "R" Us had to build 10 extra days into its supply chain.[34] As a result of poor supply-chain planning, the Microsoft Xbox 360 games console sold out soon after launch. Scarcity led to high prices in unofficial channels. On eBay, Xbox consoles sold for as much as $1,000, compared with the official price of about $400.[35]

International logistics usually use multiple *transportation modes*, including land, ocean, and air transport. Land transportation is conducted on highways and railroads, ocean transport is by container ships, and air transport is on commercial or cargo aircraft. Transportation modes involve several trade-offs. The three main considerations are *cost, transit time* to deliver the goods, and *predictability*, the match between anticipated and actual transit times.

Comparison of ocean, land, and air transport

- Ocean transport accounts for about 90 percent of international shipments. It is slower than air but far cheaper. It was revolutionized by the development of 20- and 40-foot shipping containers, the big boxes that sit atop seagoing vessels. A modern ship's ability to carry thousands of containers yields economies of scale, making ocean transport very cost effective, often accounting for only 1 percent of a product's final price.

- Land transport is usually more expensive than ocean transport but cheaper than air. Exporters often opt for ocean shipping even when land transport is available. For example, some Mexican firms send goods to Canada by ship.

- Air transport is fast and extremely predictable but expensive. It is used mostly to transport perishable products (such as food and flowers), products with a high value-to-weight ratio (such as fine jewelry and laptop computers), and urgently needed goods (such as medicines and emergency supplies). Although the use of air freight has increased because of gradually declining cost, it still accounts for only 1 percent of international shipments.

CLOSING CASE Barrett Farm Foods: A Small Firm's International Launch

Philip Austin, general manager of Barrett Farm Foods, was thrilled after returning from the food industry trade fair in Cologne, Germany—the largest food and beverage fair in the world. Barrett Farm Foods, based in Melbourne, Victoria, is Australia's sixth-largest food company. It distributes both bulk agricultural commodities and processed food products. Among others, it sells macadamia nuts, cereal bars, garlic, ginger, dried fruits, and honey throughout Australia. Barrett has had a healthy rate of growth over the past decade, and its sales reached USD $215 million last year. Although Barrett is well known in the domestic market, its international experience has been limited to responding to occasional, unsolicited orders from foreign customers. In completing these export orders, Barrett has relied on intermediaries in Australia that provided assistance for international logistics and payments. Yet Austin is enthusiastic about substantially expanding the export business over the next few years.

Recognizing an Opportunity

What prompted Austin to attend the Cologne fair was a report from Austrade, the Australian government's trade promotion agency, which highlighted the potential of Australian foodstuffs exports. According to Austrade, Australian food exports exceeded AU $30 billion last year. Austrade believes processed foodstuffs are the coming trend and wants to boost exports.

This raises a dilemma. Much of Australia's current exports are primarily raw foods, not processed foods. If just 10 percent of processed food value-adding were done in Australia, the country's balance of trade would improve. For example, instead of exporting raw grains to Europe, Austrade wants Australian producers to process the grains into bread and other bakery products, thereby creating jobs for Australians. Austrade believes meat, cereal, sugar, dairy commodities, and marine products have the most potential for food processing.

Meeting with Potential Export Customers at the Cologne Fair

At the Cologne fair, Barrett's nut-and-honey cereal bars and butter-like spread were a hit. Luigi Cairati, a senior executive with the Italian supermarket chain Standa, was keen on doing business with Barrett. He pointed out that, over the past decade, there has been an explosion of interest among European supermarkets for exotic foods and vegetables, with each group competing to display produce from around the world. Standa was seeking new products from other countries, partly to meet off-season demand for fruit and vegetables. Gabrielle Martin, purchasing manager for French food group Fauchon, also confirmed her interest in showcasing exotic and high-quality food in Fauchon stores. She added that Europeans view Australia as exotic and pollution-free and as a producer of quality products. In addition, the market for canned fruit is opening up as the fruit crop from trees in Europe declines over time.

Austin also met Peter Telford, an agent from the United Kingdom who showed interest in representing Barrett in the European Union (EU). Telford emphasized his knowledge of the market, extensive contacts, and prior business experience. He noted that other Australian firms, such as Burns Philip, Elders-IXL, and Southern Farmers, are already doing business in Europe. He pointed to several success stories, including Sydney-based pastry manufacturer, C & M Antoniou, which established a small plant in Britain to avoid the wall of agricultural duties in the EU market. The company now supplies several British supermarket chains, including Marks & Spencer, Tesco, and Sainsbury's. Another Australian group, Buderim Ginger, expanded its operations from Britain into continental Europe by opening an office in Germany.

Creating a Task Force

After the fair, Austin created a three-person task force among his senior managers and charged them with implementing an export drive. He felt an export volume of USD $30 million for the first year was reasonable. To identify the most promising exports, Barrett would examine its current product offerings. It would appoint an agent, such as Peter Telford, to facilitate EU sales. The people Austin met at the Cologne fair were potential customers to contact for immediate sales. Barrett could also forward some product and company literature to European importers, identify and appoint one or more distributors in Europe that have access to supermarkets and other large-scale buyers, and revamp its website to attract export business.

Although Barrett senior managers shared Austin's enthusiasm about exporting to Europe, they did not share his optimism. Barrett had little internal expertise to deal with the complexities of international shipping, export documentation, and receiving payments from export customers. In addition, they knew export transactions take time to complete, and the firm would have to arrange for financing of export sales. Most important, senior managers felt they would have to invest in creating a small export team and hire or train employees in export operations.

Food is a complex business, in part because it is perishable, often requiring special equipment for distribution. Europe also has many differences in national tastes, regulations, and market structures. Whereas Australians love Vegemite—a brown, salty breakfast spread made from yeast—the product enjoys little popularity outside Australia. With no name recognition in Europe, Barrett may have to resort to store branding, which will generate lower profit margins.

Barrett would have to rely on foreign intermediaries with access to well-known supermarket chains to distribute its products. Is Peter Telford the right choice? What is the appropriate commission structure for compensating intermediaries? With many larger, more experienced competitors in the EU, Barrett must keep its pricing competitive, although the complexity of pricing can overwhelm inexperienced managers. Barrett's senior managers also realize that prices strongly affect sales and profits. The euro, Europe's common currency, simplified pricing strategy, but numerous challenges remain. Prices are affected by transportation costs, buyer demand, exchange rates, tariffs, competitors' pricing, regulatory compliance, and the costs of marketing and physical distribution.

AACSB: Reflective Thinking Skills, Analytic Skills

Case Questions

13-4. Do you see any problems with Philip Austin's plan for European expansion? Do you support his entrepreneurial approach to exporting? What should be the features of a more systematic approach to exporting?

13-5. Why did Barrett choose exporting as its entry strategy for Europe, as opposed to foreign direct investment or licensing? What advantages does exporting provide to Barrett? What are the potential drawbacks of exporting for Barrett?

13-6. What challenges can Barrett expect in its export drive? What types of new capabilities does the firm need to acquire to manage its export transactions?

13-7. How should Barrett choose between direct and indirect exporting? What are the ideal characteristics of European intermediaries for Barrett? Where can Barrett turn for financing its export sales?

13-8. There are already numerous companies selling processed foods in Europe. What can Barrett do to compete successfully against these firms?

13-9. Why does Austrade want Australian firms to focus on exporting processed foods? Why is exporting high value–added products good for Australia?

Barrett is a fictitious company.

END OF CHAPTER REVIEW

 MyManagementLab

Go to **mymanagementlab.com** to complete the problems marked with this icon .

Key Terms

barter   384
business process outsourcing
   (BPO)   389
buy-back agreement   384
captive sourcing   392
company-owned subsidiary   379
compensation deals   384
configuration of value-adding
   activity   390
contract manufacturing   392

counterpurchase   384
countertrade   383
direct exporting   379
documentation   380
exporting   376
export management company
   (EMC)   386
foreign distributor   386
global sourcing   380
global supply chain   399

importing   380
Incoterms   381
indirect exporting   378
letter of credit   382
manufacturer's representative   386
offshoring   393
outsourcing   389
trading company   386

Summary

In this chapter, you learned about:

- **Exporting as a foreign market entry strategy**

Exporting is producing at home and then shipping products abroad, to be sold and delivered to foreign customers through intermediaries. It is the strategy most firms favor when they first internationalize. It is also a relatively flexible entry strategy, allowing the firm to withdraw readily in case of problems in the target market. A systematic approach to exporting requires managers to perform a global market opportunity

assessment, make organizational arrangements for exporting, acquire needed skills and competencies, and design and implement the export strategy. Among the organizational arrangements for exporting are **indirect exporting, direct exporting**, and establishing a **company-owned subsidiary**.

- **Managing export-import transactions**

Management must become familiar with customs clearance, international goods transportation, and **documentation**, the required forms and other paperwork used to conclude international sales. The exporter typically entrusts preparation of documents to a freight forwarder. **Incoterms** are universally accepted terms of sale that effectively specify what is and is not included in the price of a product sold internationally. Exporting also requires knowledge of payment methods, such as cash in advance, **letter of credit**, open account, and countertrade. For most firms, letter of credit is best because it establishes immediate trust and protects both buyer and seller. Intense competition drives exporters to offer attractive payment terms to their customers.

- **Identifying and working with foreign intermediaries**

  Managers can identify intermediaries, such as sales representatives and distributors, from a variety of public and private information sources. It is best to develop long-term relationships with these business partners, who perform a variety of functions abroad on behalf of the exporter by cultivating mutually beneficial bonds, genuinely responding to distributor needs, and encouraging loyalty.

- **Outsourcing, global sourcing, and offshoring**

  Global sourcing refers to the procurement of products or services from suppliers or company-owned subsidiaries located abroad for consumption in the home country or a third country. **Business process outsourcing** refers to the outsourcing of business functions such as finance, accounting, and human resources. Procurement can be from either independent suppliers or company-owned subsidiaries or affiliates. **Offshoring** refers to the relocation of a business process or entire manufacturing facility to a foreign country. Managers make two strategic decisions regarding value-adding activities: whether to *make* or *buy* inputs and where to locate value-adding activity—that is, the geographic **configuration of value-adding activity**.

- **Benefits and risk of global sourcing**

  Global sourcing aims to reduce the cost of doing business or to achieve other strategic goals. Global sourcing has provided the means to turn around failing businesses, speed up the pace of innovation, or fund development projects that are otherwise unaffordable. Risks include failing to realize anticipated cost savings, dealing with environmental uncertainty, creating competitors, engaging suppliers with insufficient training, relying too much on suppliers, and eroding the morale of existing employees.

- **Global sourcing strategies and supply-chain management**

  Firms should develop a strategic perspective in making global sourcing decisions. In addition to cost cutting, global sourcing is also a means to create customer value and improve the firm's competitive advantages. The efficiency with which goods can be physically moved from one part of the globe to another makes global sourcing feasible. **Global supply chain** refers to the firm's integrated network of sourcing, production, and distribution, organized on a world scale and located in countries where competitive advantage can be maximized.

Test Your Comprehension AACSB: Reflective Thinking Skills

13-10. What is exporting? What are its advantages and disadvantages?

13-11. Describe the organizing framework for exporting. What steps should the firm follow to ensure exporting success?

13-12. Why is knowledge of incoterms important to importers and exporters?

13-13. Explain the payment methods that exporters typically use. What is the most reliable payment method, and how do exporters carry it out?

13-14. Explain the nature, role, and risks involved in countertrade.

13-15. What steps should the exporter take to ensure success in working with intermediaries?

13-16. Identify the benefits that companies receive from global sourcing. Why do firms outsource to foreign suppliers?

13-17. What are the implications for company strategy and performance of business process outsourcing?

13-18. What are the risks that firms face in global sourcing?

⭐ **13-19.** What are the main benefits to a business of global sourcing?

13-20. Is it the case that global sourcing is really about cost-cutting?

⭐ **13-21.** How can global sourcing help ensure a competitive advantage?

Apply Your Understanding   AACSB: Communication Abilities, Reflective Thinking Skills, Ethical Understanding, and Reasoning Abilities

13-22. Moose & Walrus (M&W) is a manufacturer of a popular line of clothing for young people. M&W is firmly established in its home market, which is relatively saturated and has little prospects for future sales growth. Top management has decided to export M&W's clothing line to Japan, Turkey, and various European countries. Suppose M&W hires you to assist with internationalization. Prepare a briefing for senior managers that describes:

- The advantages and disadvantages of exporting.
- A systematic approach to exporting.
- A systematic approach to managing export-import transactions.
- Export payment methods.

What factors should M&W consider regarding the possible need to adapt its clothing styles for its target markets?

13-23. Antenna Communications Technologies, Inc. (ACT) is a small satellite technology communications firm. Its product is a multibeam antenna that allows customers in the broadcast industry to receive signals from up to 35 satellites simultaneously. The firm has little international business experience. ACT recently hired you as its export manager and, based on extensive research, you find substantial demand for the product in Africa, China, Russia, and Saudi Arabia. Having followed most of the steps in the organizing framework for exporting, you decide direct exporting is the best entry strategy for ACT. Your next task is to find distributors in the target markets. How will you approach this task? What resources should you access to find distributors in these markets? Once established, what is the best way to maintain solid relations with foreign distributors? Finally, what payment method should ACT use for most of its prospective markets?

13-24. *Ethical Dilemma:* Suppose EcoPure Industries, a manufacturer of components for hybrid motor vehicles, hires you. EcoPure emphasizes social responsibility in its business dealings and uses three foreign market entry strategies: exporting, joint ventures, and FDI. Exporting implies the sale of products to customers located abroad, usually under contract with foreign intermediaries that organize marketing and distribution activities in local markets. Using joint ventures, EcoPure partners with foreign firms to access their technology, expertise, production factors, or other assets. Using FDI, EcoPure invests funds to establish factories or other subsidiaries overseas. Each of the strategies—exporting, joint venture, and FDI—is vulnerable to particular types of ethical dilemmas, and top management has directed you to identify and describe the most typical ones. Using the ethical framework and other material in Chapter 4 as a guide, what types of ethical problems might arise in each type of entry strategy? Which entry strategy most likely gives rise to ethical problems? Be sure to justify your answer.

globalEDGE | INTERNET EXERCISES
(www.globalEDGE.msu.edu)

AACSB: Communication Abilities, Reflective Thinking Skills

Refer to Chapter 1, page 54, for instructions on how to access and use globalEDGE™.

13-25. You work for a firm that manufactures children's toys. Despite little international experience, management wants to start exporting. Your boss understands the importance of using strong distributors abroad but knows little about how to find them. You are aware that many national governments offer programs that help new exporters find intermediaries in foreign countries. Examples include trade missions, trade shows, and matchmaker programs (in which the exporter is matched with foreign intermediaries). In the United States, the International Trade Administration (ITA) provides various services to help exporters find foreign distributors. Visit the ITA website (www.ita.doc.gov), or the main trade support agency of your country (through globalEDGE™), and see what programs are available. Then prepare a memo to your boss in which you describe specific programs to help your firm get started in exporting.

13-26. Suppose you work for a major trading company exporting timber from Canada, petroleum from Britain, and processed food products from the United States. To enhance your career prospects, you want to learn more about the export of these goods from their respective countries. Visit globalEDGE™ and research current international news about these industries in the countries indicated. Based on your findings, prepare a brief report on the status of each in the context of your firm's exporting efforts.

13-27. Suppose your employer wants to export its products and be paid through letter of credit (LC). You have volunteered to become the company's LC expert. One way to accomplish this is to visit globalEDGE™ and do a search on the keywords "letter of credit." Another is to visit the websites of major banks to learn about procedures and instructions to receive payment through LC. Visit the websites of CIBC (www.cibc.com), the National Australia Bank (www.nab.com.au), and HSBC (www.hsbc.com) to see what you can learn about LCs. For each bank, what are the requirements for getting an LC? What services does the bank offer regarding LCs? Can you get training in LCs from these banks?

13-28. International labor standards are complex and closely related to global sourcing. In particular, the use of sweatshops has attracted much attention. A sweatshop is a factory characterized by very low wages, long hours, and poor working conditions. Some sweatshops employ children in unsafe conditions. Pro-labor groups advocate for minimum labor standards in foreign factories. Suppose your future employer wants to outsource a portion of its production to certain developing countries but is concerned about the possibility of employing sweatshop labor. Visit the websites of groups that encourage minimum standards in labor conditions (for example, www.workersrights.org, www.usas.org, or www.corpwatch.org or enter the keywords "labor conditions" at globalEDGE™) and prepare a memo to your employer that discusses the major concerns of those who advocate minimum labor standards.

CAREER TOOLBOX

Identifying an Attractive Export Market

Exporters seek the best markets for their products and services. Managers do market research to identify potential export markets. They examine such factors as market size, growth rate, economic status, competition, and the degree of political stability. The task of choosing the best export markets is complex. What makes an ideal market? What market potential indicators should be considered? Many firms follow a systematic process of international market research. In this exercise, you will learn the important indicators used to assess potential export markets, access information needed to develop international business plans, and research country-level barriers that firms face in exporting.

Background

Exporting is the most widely used entry mode. This is especially true for smaller firms or those new to international business. Research is

To complete this exercise in your MyLab, go to the Career Toolbox.

vital to small and medium-sized enterprises, which usually lack the resources to sustain significant losses from failed exporting efforts.

Successful exporting requires developing knowledge about appropriate target markets. It involves identifying market opportunities and understanding the characteristics and conditions of target markets. Research provides insights about customer requirements, competitor activity, and appropriate ways of doing business.

Exporters need to learn about the technology level of potential target markets. In countries with low technological knowledge, distributors or customers may need to be trained in the product's features and usage. A country's attractiveness as a target market is reduced if distributors and customers require extensive training.

In this exercise, assume you work for a firm that makes and markets microwave ovens. Initially, the firm wants to sell compact microwave oven models. Assume they retail for about $50.

MyManagementLab   **Try It!**

The simulation Offshoring accompanies this exercise.

 MyManagementLab

Go to **mymanagementlab.com** for Auto-graded writing questions as well as the following Assisted-graded writing questions:

 13-29. What roles do distribution channel intermediaries play for exporting firms?

 13-30. Describe the characteristics and advantages of letter of credit as a payment method in exporting.

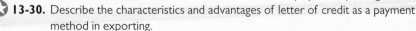 **13-31.** MyManagementLab Only—comprehensive writing assignment for this chapter.

Endnotes

1. UNCTAD, *Review of Maritime Transport 2015* (New York: United Nations).

2. Austan Goolsbee, "Jeremy Lin and America's 'New Exports'," *Wall Street Journal,* February 22, 2012, p. A15; Anne Smith, "Health Care Bargains Abroad," *Kiplinger's Personal Finance,* January 2012, pp. 65–68.

3. UNCTAD, *International Trade Statistics Yearbook 2014,* (New York: United Nations, 2015).

4. "Outsourcing: Time to Bring It Back Home?" *Economist*, March 5, 2005, p. 63.

5. Michael E. Porter, *Competition in Global Industries* (Boston: Harvard Business School Press, 1986).

6. Benito Arrunada and Xose H. Vazquez, "When Your Contract Manufacturer Becomes Your Competitor," *Harvard Business Review,* September 2006, pp. 135–145.

7. Jamil Anderlini, "BMW Plans to Boost China Output After Demand Surge," *Financial Times*, November 13, 2009, p. 19; Neal Boudette and William Boston, "BMW Readies U.S. Factory Expansion," *Wall Street Journal*, March 25, 2014, www.wsj.com; BMW Group, *Company Profile: Locations*, www.bmw.com, June 1, 2015.

8. Thomas Friedman, *The World Is Flat 3.0: A Brief History of the Twenty-First Century* (New York: Picador, 2007).

9. Deloitte, *Outsourcing, Today and Tomorrow: Insights from Deloitte's 2014 Global Outsourcing and Insourcing Survey,* www.deloitte.com; UNCTAD (2015).

10. Andrew Baxter, "GE Unit Plugs into the Outside World," *Financial Times*, September 28, 2005, p. 8; *Marketline*, Genpact Limited, August 30, 2012, www.marketline.com.

11. UNCTAD (2015).

12. Ruth Alexander, "Which Is the World's Biggest Employer?" *BBC News Magazine*, March 19, 2012, www.bbc.co.uk; Bruce Einhorn, "A Juggernaut in Electronics," *BusinessWeek,* June 18, 2007, p. 46; Lorraine Luk, "Hon Hai Shifts Its Chinese Work Force," *Wall Street Journal*, August 19, 2010, p. B8.

13. Masaaki Kotabe, Janet Murray, and Rajshekhar Javalgi, "Global Sourcing of Services and Market Performance: An Empirical Investigation," *Journal of International Marketing* 6 (1998), pp. 10–31; Masaaki Kotabe and Janet Murray, "Outsourcing Service Activities," *Marketing Management* 10 (2001), pp. 40–46.

14. Joshua Freedman, "Distance Earning," *Lawyer*, November 21, 2011, pp. 14–16; Amy Kazmin, "Outsourcing: Law Firms Fuel the Demand for Offshore Services," *Financial Times*, January 30, 2009, http://www.ft.com.

15. Richard Frasch and Charlotte Westfall, "Sourcing Goods and Suppliers In China: A How-To Guide For Small Businesses," *Forbes,* January 26, 2014, www.forbes.com. Poh-Lin Yeoh, "Internationalization and Performance Outcomes of Entrepreneurial Family SMEs," *Thunderbird International Business Review* 56, No. 1 (2014), pp. 77–96.

16. International Labour Organization, *Global Wage Report 2014/15* (Geneva: International Labour Organization, 2015).

17. *BusinessWeek* (2003).

18. Pete Engardio, "The Future of Outsourcing," *BusinessWeek*, January 30, 2006, pp. 50–64.

19. Bruce Einhorn, "How Not to Sweat the Retail Details," *BusinessWeek*, May 25, 2009, pp. 52–54; Turloch Mooney, "Sourcing to Selling," *China Economic Review*, March 2011, p. 22.

20. *BusinessWeek* (2003).

21. "Indian Call Center Lands in Ohio," *Fortune*, August 6, 2007, p. 23.

22. Hokey Min, *The Essentials of Supply Chain Management* (Upper Saddle River, NJ: Pearson FT Press, 2015).

23. Engardio (2006).

24. Masaaki Kotabe and Janet Murray, "Global Sourcing Strategy and Sustainable Competitive Advantage," *Industrial Marketing Management* 33 (2004), pp. 7–14; Min (2015).

25. Harold Sirkin, Michael Zinser, and Douglas Hohner, *Made in America, Again* (Boston: Boston Consulting Group, August 2011).

26. BBC News, "Santander Brings Call Centres Back to UK," July 7, 2011, www.bbc.co.uk; Jackie Range, "India Faces a Homegrown Staffing Issue: Not Enough Talent," *Wall Street Journal*, July 16, 2008, p. B8.

27. James Hagerty and Mark Magnier, "Companies Tiptoe Back Toward 'Made in the U.S.A.'," *Wall Street Journal*, January 13, 2015, www.wsj.com; Katy George, Sree Ramaswamy, and Lou Rassey, "Next-shoring: A CEO's Guide," *McKinsey Quarterly*, January 2014, www.mckinsey.com.

28. J. Lynn Lunsford, "Outsourcing at Crux of Boeing Strike," *Wall Street Journal*, September 8, 2008, pp. B1, B4.

29. "To Start Up Here, Companies Hire Over There," *USAToday*, February 11, 2005, pp. 1B–2B.

30. John Thoburn, Kirsten Sutherland, and Thi Hoa Nguyen, "Globalization and Poverty: Impacts on Households of Employment and Restructuring in the Textiles Industry of Vietnam," *Journal of the Asia Pacific Economy* 12, No. 3 (2007), pp. 345–362.

31. Joseph A. Schumpeter, *Capitalism, Socialism, and Democracy* (New York: Harper, 1942).

32. David Craig and Paul Willmott, "Outsourcing Grows Up," *McKinsey Quarterly* (February 2005), web exclusive, http://www.mckinseyquarterly.com.

33. Tyson (2004).

34. Barney Gimbel, "Yule Log Jam," *Fortune*, December 13, 2004, pp. 164–170; Jeffrey Sparshott, "Trade Gap Shrinks by Most in 6 Years," *Wall Street Journal,* June 4, 2015, p. A2.

35. Alison Maitland, "Make Sure You Have Your Christmas Stock In," *Financial Times*, December 19, 2005, p. 11.

Chapter 14

Foreign Direct Investment and Collaborative Ventures

Learning Objectives *After studying this chapter, you should be able to:*

14.1 Understand international investment and collaboration.

14.2 Describe the characteristics of foreign direct investment.

14.3 Explain the motives for FDI and collaborative ventures.

14.4 Identify the types of foreign direct investment.

14.5 Understand international collaborative ventures.

14.6 Discuss the experience of retailers in foreign markets.

Huawei's Investments in Africa

Africa is the world's second most populous continent, with a population just over one billion. Africa is troubled by poor economic conditions. Most people in sub-Saharan Africa live on less than two dollars per day. Recently, Africa has begun to grow economically in part due to increased investment from abroad.

China is investing billions of dollars in Africa. The investments are targeting extractive industries, such as petroleum and mining, as well as higher-value industries, such as textiles and telecommunications. African demand for mobile communications is growing rapidly. In Ghana, Kenya, and South Africa, for example, about 85 percent of citizens own a cell phone, compared to 90 percent in the United States.

Huawei Technologies is China's largest telecommunications equipment manufacturer, with annual revenues of $32 billion. The firm generates about 70 percent of its sales outside of China. It is a key player in African development. Huawei (pronounced who-ah-way) employs more than 140,000 people, including 7,000 in Africa. Huawei established a presence in Africa in the 1990s. It has developed cell

phone networks throughout the continent. In the past decade, Huawei has invested more than $1.5 billion in Africa. The region now accounts for about 12 percent of Huawei's annual revenue.

Huawei leveraged foreign direct investment (FDI) and collaborative ventures in Africa to establish two R&D facilities, four regional headquarters, six training centers, and 20 representative offices. Despite various challenges, Huawei's operations there have proven very profitable. The firm leverages economies of scale, inexpensive labor, and numerous other advantages to keep costs low. Efficient operations allow Huawei to price its cell phones lower than Ericsson, Nokia, and other competitors. The ability of Chinese firms to operate profitably in poor countries is a primary reason China's companies are outpacing firms from Europe, Japan, and North America in expanding their presence in Africa.

In Uganda, Huawei developed a government data center and several large-scale projects connecting agencies to a central network. In Ghana, Huawei invested more than $100 million to develop telecom facilities. In Northern

Source: Nicolas De Corte/123RF

Africa, Huawei entered a joint venture with ZTE Corporation to expand mobile networks in nine cities and build 800,000 phone lines. In Algeria, Huawei established a mobile network to complement a cell network completed by ZTE. In 2015, Huawei and Global Marine Systems formed a joint venture to develop telecommunications infrastructure in Africa.

In addition to developing telecommunications infrastructure, Huawei's investments contribute directly to economic development. The expansion of cell networks allows Africans, many of whom live in isolated areas, to find jobs and interact with important contacts. Connecting to the Internet further enhances commercial growth. China's Africa investments benefit not only Africans, but also European and U.S. firms. These companies benefit from the roads, railways, telephony, energy systems, and other infrastructure that Chinese firms have helped to develop.

As manufacturing costs in China rise and the African middle class expands, Chinese firms will likely invest much more in Africa. China is playing a key role by financing and providing needed development expertise. Various African countries are streamlining regulations and creating business-friendly environments, increasing their attractiveness for more FDI.

Questions

14-1. What are the main characteristics of Africa as a market for mobile telephones?

14-2. What benefits does foreign investment bring to Africa?

14-3. Describe the various ways Huawei has invested in Africa.

SOURCES: *Africa Monitor: Southern Africa*, "China: Future Partnership," January 2012, p. 12; *Africa Research Bulletin*, "Telecommunications: Africa," January 16, 2013, pp. p19850C–19851C; *Economist*, "Trying to Pull Together," April 23, 2011, pp. 73–75; Huawei Technologies Company, "Africa Fact Sheet," December 10, 2011, www.huawei.com; Andrea Marshall, "China's Mighty Telecom Footprint in Africa," *eLearning Africa News Portal*, February 21, 2011, www.elearning-africa.com; Olusegun Ogundeji, "Huawei Leads New Efforts to Develop Cable Infrastructure in Africa," *PCWorld*, March 19, 2015, www.pcworld.com; Pew Research Center, "Cell Phones in Africa: Communication Lifeline," April 15, 2015, www.pewglobal.org; Hejuan Zhao and Zhang Yuzhe, "China's Telecoms and Wireless Drums for Africa," *Caixin Online*, February 22, 2012, english.caixin.com.

The opening case highlights the benefits of foreign direct investment (FDI) and collaborative ventures, to both firms and nations. The worldwide spread of capital and ownership through FDI is one of the remarkable facets of globalization.

Consider Tata Motors (www.tatamotors.com), India's largest automaker. Tata earns about 65 percent of its sales from abroad. Tata in 2008 paid $2.3 billion to purchase Jaguar and Land Rover from Ford Motor Company. Tata owns many Jaguar and Land Rover car factories in Asia and Europe. Tata developed the Nano–the world's cheapest car. Renault and Nissan partnered with Tata to distribute the Nano in Europe. Tata also acquired 50 percent of Miljo, a Norwegian electric vehicle maker. In South Korea, Tata purchased Daewoo Commercial Vehicle Company, a leading manufacturer of trucks and tractors.[1]

Internationalizing through FDI enables the firm to maintain a physical presence in key markets, secure direct access to customers and partners, and perform critical value-chain activities in the market. FDI is an equity or ownership form of foreign market entry. It is the entry strategy most associated with large MNEs—such as Bombardier, Ford, and Unilever—that have extensive physical operations around the world. As they venture abroad, firms that specialize in products usually establish manufacturing plants. Firms that offer services, such as banks, cruise lines, and restaurant chains, usually establish agency relationships and retail facilities.

In this chapter, we examine the nature of FDI and collaborative ventures. We explain the motives that drive companies to use these entry strategies. We highlight numerous companies engaged in FDI as well as best practices for investment and partnering success. We also examine retailers, a distinctive category of foreign investors in the services sector.

14.1 Understand international investment and collaboration.

Foreign direct investment (FDI)
An internationalization strategy in which the firm establishes a physical presence abroad through acquisition of productive assets such as capital, technology, labor, land, plant, and equipment.

International portfolio investment
Passive ownership of foreign securities such as stocks and bonds to generate financial returns.

International Investment and Collaboration

Foreign direct investment (FDI) is an internationalization strategy by which the firm establishes a physical presence abroad through direct ownership of productive assets such as capital, technology, labor, land, plant, and equipment. FDI is the most advanced and complex foreign market entry strategy. Firms use FDI to establish manufacturing plants, marketing subsidiaries, or other facilities in target countries. Because this involves investing substantial resources to establish a physical presence abroad, FDI is riskier than other entry strategies.

Do not confuse FDI with **international portfolio investment**, which refers to passive ownership of foreign securities, such as stocks and bonds, to generate financial returns. International portfolio investment is a form of international investment, but it is not FDI, which seeks ownership control of a business abroad and represents a long-term commitment. The United Nations uses the benchmark of at least 10 percent ownership in the enterprise to differentiate FDI from portfolio investment. However, this percentage may be misleading because control is not usually achieved unless the investor owns at least 50 percent of a foreign venture.

An **international collaborative venture** is a cross-border business partnership in which collaborating firms pool their resources and share costs and risks of a new venture. Here the focal firm partners with one or more companies to pursue a joint project or initiative. International collaborative ventures are also sometimes called international partnerships or international strategic alliances.

A **joint venture** is a form of collaboration between two or more firms to create a new, jointly owned enterprise. Unlike collaborative arrangements in which no new entity is created, the partners in a joint venture typically invest money to create a new enterprise. Joint ventures (JVs) may last for many years. A partner in a joint venture may enjoy minority, equal, or majority ownership.

Consider the following example from the beer industry. In 2002, South African Breweries (www.sabmiller.com) established a major presence in the U.S. beer market by buying Miller Brewing. It changed its name to SABMiller plc. The firm next acquired 97 percent of Bavaria S.A., South America's second-largest brewer. In 2011, SABMiller acquired Foster's, Australia's largest brewer. SABMiller entered a joint venture with China's CR Snow Breweries, helping make SABMiller the largest brewer in China. In 2015, SABMiller acquired Britain's Meantime Brewing in an effort to enter the craft brewing industry.[2] Through numerous FDI and collaborative ventures, SABMiller has become the world's second-largest brewer and now has operations in more than 80 countries.[3]

International collaborative venture

A cross-border business alliance in which partnering firms pool their resources and share costs and risks to undertake a new business venture; also referred to as an international partnership or an international strategic alliance.

Joint venture

A form of collaboration between two or more firms to create a new, jointly owned enterprise.

Volume of Foreign Direct Investment and Collaborative Ventures

Literally hundreds of cross-border direct investments and collaborative ventures take place each year. In 2014, more than 220 such investments or acquisitions valued at over $1 billion each were concluded. The top five recipients of FDI were China, the United States, Singapore, Brazil, and the United Kingdom.[4] Recent examples of cross-border investments include:

- Volkswagen spent $1 billion to build a factory in Poland to manufacture delivery vans.
- The British pharmaceutical firm GlaxoSmithKline purchased the global Vaccines division of Switzerland's Novartis in 2015 for $5.25 billion.
- Denmark's Lego Group spent more than 100 million euros to build a toy factory in China.
- SABIC Corporation, a Saudi Arabia firm, paid $11.6 billion to acquire GE Plastics from General Electric.
- After acquiring the chocolatier Godiva, the Turkish food company Yildiz paid $3.2 billion in 2014 to acquire UK-based United Biscuits, a large snack food company.
- Japan's Toshiba formed a joint venture with the U.S. firm United Technologies to establish R&D centers in Europe and India to support joint innovation in the heating and air conditioning industry.

These and other examples illustrate several trends:

- Firms from both advanced economies and emerging markets are active in FDI.
- Destination or recipient countries for such investments are both advanced economies and emerging markets.
- Companies use various strategies to enter foreign markets, including acquisitions and collaborative ventures.
- Firms from all types of industries, including services, are active in FDI and collaborative ventures. Retailers began expanding abroad in the 1970s, including Metro AG (Germany), Royal Ahold (Netherlands), Tesco (United Kingdom), and Walmart (United States).
- Direct investment by foreign firms occasionally inflames citizens' patriotic feelings. In the United States, for example, Chinese oil company CNOOC attempted to buy Unocal Corporation. The action raised concerns about a Chinese state enterprise gaining control of a key U.S. firm in the energy sector. Strong opposition drove the U.S. Congress to ban the deal.

Most Active Firms in FDI

Exhibit 14.1 provides a sample of leading MNEs engaged in FDI. General Electric, Toyota, and other firms in the exhibit are listed based on the value of factories, subsidiaries, and other assets they own in foreign countries. For example, Toyota has numerous subsidiaries around the world.

EXHIBIT 14.1 World's Most International Nonfinancial MNEs, Based on Value of Foreign Assets

Company	Home Country	Industry	Approximate Sales (billions of U.S. dollars)		Approximate Assets (billions of U.S. dollars)	
			Foreign	Total	Foreign	Total
Toyota Motor	Japan	Motor vehicles	171	256	403	171
General Electric	United States	Electrical & electronic equipment	74	143	331	657
Royal Dutch Shell	United Kingdom & Netherlands	Petroleum	276	451	302	358
Exxon Mobil	United States	Petroleum	237	390	231	347
Total	France	Petroleum	176	228	227	239
BP	United Kingdom	Petroleum	250	379	203	306
Vodafone Group	United Kingdom	Telecommunications	59	69	183	203
Volkswagen Group	Germany	Motor vehicles	211	262	177	447
Chevron	United States	Petroleum	123	212	176	254
Eni Spa	Italy	Petroleum	110	152	141	190

Sources: Based on Hoovers company database at www.hoovers.com, 2015; UNCTAD, "Annex table 28. The World's Top 100 Non-Financial TNCs, Ranked by Foreign Assets," in *World Investment Report 2014* (New York: United Nations, 2015), accessed June 8, 2015, at www.unctad.org.

Individual Toyota subsidiaries engage in various value-chain activities, including R&D, manufacturing, marketing, sales, and customer service. The most internationally active MNEs are in the automotive, oil, and telecommunications industries.

Service Firms and FDI

Most companies in the services sector, such as retailing, construction, and personal care, must offer their services where they are consumed. This usually requires establishing either a permanent presence through FDI (as in retailing) or a temporary relocation of the service company personnel (as in the construction industry).[5] Management consulting is a professional service usually embodied in experts who interact directly with clients to provide advice. To reach their customers, consulting firms such as McKinsey and Accenture establish offices in key international markets. Many support services, such as advertising, insurance, accounting, legal work, and overnight package delivery, are also best provided at the customer's location. FDI is vital for internationalizing services.[6]

Intrawest, Inc., has established offices and other facilities in China where it aims to build ski resorts. HSBC Bank has established branches around the world because banking services are usually provided directly to customers wherever banks do business. Exhibit 14.2 portrays the world's most globalized financial institutions and the breadth of their international operations. The firms are ranked based on the number of foreign subsidiaries and affiliates and the number of countries where they do business. For example, Citigroup has representative offices in 160 countries.

Leading Destinations for FDI

Advanced economies such as Australia, Canada, Japan, Netherlands, the United Kingdom, and the United States long have been popular destinations for FDI. These countries all share high per capita GDP, strong GDP growth, high density of knowledge workers, and superior business infrastructure, such as telephone systems and energy sources.[7] In recent years, however, developing economies and emerging markets have gained much appeal as FDI destinations. This is illustrated by data from the United Nations Conference on Trade and Development.

EXHIBIT 14.2 Leading Global Financial Institutions, Based on Breadth of Worldwide Operations

Company	Home Country	Industry	Approximate Sales (billions of U.S. dollars)		Approximate Number of Subsidiaries and Affiliates		Approximate Number of Host Countries
			Foreign	Total	Foreign	Total	
Citigroup	United States	Banking	64	93	725	1,020	160
HSBC Bank	United Kingdom	Banking	63	97	680	1,050	80
Allianz SE	Germany	Insurance	103	138	600	800	71
AXA	France	Insurance	125	166	620	780	60
UBS	Switzerland	Banking	24	31	430	460	51
ABN AMRO	Netherlands	Banking	16	22	700	940	48
ING	Netherlands	Insurance	45	63	300	400	41
Banco Santander	Spain	Banking	45	56	280	380	41
Société Générale	France	Banking	20	30	340	520	40
BNP Paribas	France	Banking	81	127	420	660	40

Sources: Based on Hoovers company database at www.hoovers.com, 2015, and annual reports at websites of the listed companies.

It suggests that, between 2007 and 2014, the volume of FDI flowing into advanced economies fell, whereas the amount flowing into developing economies and emerging markets increased. This continuing trend bodes well for less-developed economies because FDI is a key determinant of economic development and living standards.[8]

According to A. T. Kearney's FDI Confidence Index, China ranks among the top destinations for foreign investment (www.atkearney.com). China is popular because of its size, rapid growth rate, and low labor costs. It is an important platform where MNEs manufacture products for export to key markets in Asia and elsewhere.[9] China also holds strategic importance for its long-term potential as a target market and source of competitive advantage.

Factors to Consider in Choosing FDI Locations

Exhibit 14.3 lists the criteria firms use to evaluate countries as potential targets for FDI projects. Suppose Taiwan-based Acer (www.acer.com) wants to build a new computer factory. Its managers will research the best country in which to build it, looking at country and regional factors, infrastructural factors, political factors, profit retention factors, and human resource factors.

As an example, consider the attractiveness of Eastern European nations as FDI destinations. Several of the selection criteria noted in Exhibit 14.3 have attracted foreign firms to these countries. In the Czech Republic, giant Chinese electronics manufacturer Sichuan Changhong (www.changhong.com) built a $30 million factory that produces up to one million flat-screen televisions per year. Numerous automakers, from Ford to Nissan, have built factories in the region. Wages in Eastern Europe are relatively low; engineers in Slovakia earn half of what Western engineers make, and assembly-line workers one-third to one-fifth. In addition, East European governments offer incentives, from financing to low taxes, as in Slovakia, where all

Source: SpectrumBlue/Fotolia

Business-friendly Ireland is one of the world's top FDI destinations. Shown is the North Wall Quay complex in Dublin, which houses key European operations of Citigroup and numerous other international banks.

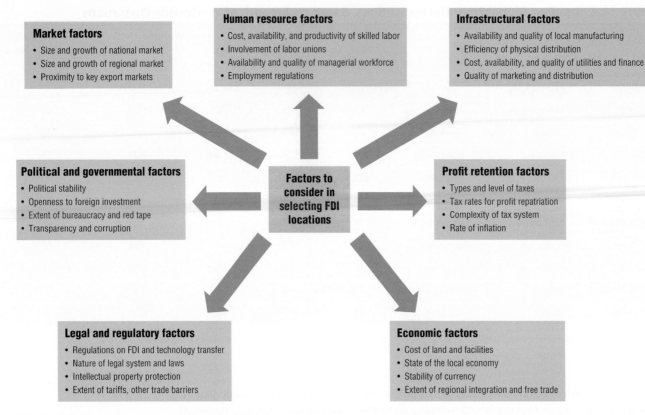

EXHIBIT 14.3

Factors to Consider in Selecting Foreign Direct Investment Locations

Sources: John H. Dunning, *Explaining International Production* (New York: Routledge, 2015); Daniel Hoi Ki Ho and Peter Tze Yiu Lau, "Perspectives on Foreign Direct Investment Location Decisions: What Do We Know and Where Do We Go from Here?," *International Tax Journal*, 33 No. 3 (2007), pp. 39–48; Robert Green and William Cunningham, "The Determinants of US Foreign Investment: An Empirical Examination," *Management International Review*, 15 No. 2-3 (1975), pp., 113-20; Franklin Root, *Entry Strategies for International Markets*, (Hoboken, NJ: John Wiley & Sons, 1994).

income taxes add up to a simple 19 percent. By comparison, personal income tax rates often exceed 30 percent in Germany. Eastern Europe also provides ready access to the huge EU market.[10] Managers examine a combination of criteria when making decisions about where in the world to establish operations through FDI.

14.2 Describe the characteristics of foreign direct investment.

Characteristics of Foreign Direct Investment

FDI is an advanced form of foreign market entry with distinctive characteristics. Key features of FDI include:

- *Substantial resource commitment.* As the ultimate internationalization strategy, it is far more taxing on the firm's resources and capabilities than any other entry strategy. For example, the U.S. firm General Electric owns more than $300 billion in factories, subsidiaries, and other operations outside the United States.[11]
- *Local presence and operations.* With FDI, the firm establishes itself directly in the market, leading to direct contact with customers, intermediaries, facilitators, and governments. Some firms concentrate operations in one or a few locations; others disperse their FDI among many countries. The MNE network may become so extensive that the firm effectively loses its nationality. Nestlé, for example, is based in Switzerland but generates more than 90 percent of its sales from abroad. The Indian MNE Tata Consultancy Services generates most of its revenues in North America, whereas rival IBM, a U.S. company, obtains nearly two-thirds of its sales from abroad.[12]

- *Investment in countries that provide specific comparative advantages.* Managers invest in countries based on the advantages these locations offer. Thus, firms tend to perform R&D in countries with leading-edge knowledge for their industry, source from countries home to suppliers that provide superior goods, build factories in locations with low labor costs, and establish marketing subsidiaries in countries with excellent sales potential.

- *Intense dealings in the host market.* Firms that enter through FDI necessarily deal more intensely with culture and other aspects of the host country. MNEs with high-profile, conspicuous operations are especially vulnerable to close public scrutiny of their actions. To minimize potential problems, managers often favor investing in countries that are culturally and linguistically familiar. When setting up shop in continental Europe, for example, U.S. firms frequently choose the Netherlands because English is widely spoken there.[13]

Source: Albina Glisic/Shutterstock

Vodafone is one of the most international firms due to its very extensive FDI activities. This mobile phone service provider invests to establish retail outlets in Africa, Asia-Pacific, Europe, the Middle East, and the Americas.

- *Substantial risk and uncertainty.* Establishing a permanent, fixed presence abroad makes the firm vulnerable to country risk and intervention by local governments. In addition to local labor practices, direct investors also must contend with local economic conditions such as inflation and recessions. French automaker Renault recently acquired a 25 percent stake in Russian automaker AvtoVAZ to produce Lada brand cars in Russia. However, the 40-year-old AvtoVAZ plant is plagued by inefficient operations, a slow workforce, and a history of organized crime.[14] Business in Russia often requires paying bribes, and the country has a history of high inflation and other macroeconomic concerns. The Russian government often intervenes in the private sector.

Even a large, well-established company such as Disney (www.disney.com) experienced several failures in its foreign investing.[15] When Disney established Tokyo Disneyland, its management assumed the Disneyland experience could not be successfully transferred to Japan. So instead of investing, Disney opted to license rights in Japan for nominal profits. Tokyo Disneyland proved to be a huge success. Not wanting to repeat the same mistake, management opted for an FDI stake in its next theme park—Disneyland Paris. However, it proved to be a financial sinkhole. Having learned from these experiences, Disney made its Hong Kong Disneyland park more successful. Disney owns 47 percent of the venture, making the Hong Kong government the major partner. Management wants to expand the park, but negotiations with the Hong Kong government have been tense and complicated. After receiving permission from the Chinese government, Disney in 2016 launched its most recent theme park, Shanghai Disneyland. Management is worried about intellectual property violations in China, which may reduce profits from licensing Disney movies, animated characters, and other valuable properties.[16]

Ethics, Social Responsibility, and FDI

Companies that internationalize through FDI are often criticized for ethical lapses and irresponsible behavior because such firms can exert substantial power in the markets where they are most heavily invested. For example, some MNEs operate foreign factories under harsh working conditions. Others engage in bribery to advance their interests. Some MNEs market shoddy products or employ questionable marketing practices through their foreign subsidiaries.

At the same time, the strong local presence implied by FDI offers opportunities to conduct business in ways that ensure high ethical standards and social responsibility. Many MNEs invest in local communities and seek to establish global standards of fair treatment for workers.

Unilever (www.unilever.com), the giant Dutch-British producer of consumer products, demonstrates its corporate social responsibility (CSR) by:

- Operating a free community laundry in a slum in São Paulo, Brazil.
- Funding a hospital that offers free medical care to the needy in Bangladesh.
- Teaching palm oil producers to reuse plant waste in Ghana.
- Providing small loans to help women in remote villages start small-scale businesses in India.[17]

Many MNEs are responding to global *sustainability* agendas. For example, automakers such as Toyota, Renault, and Volkswagen are investing in fuel-efficient and clean technologies. Nokia is a leader in phasing out toxic materials. Dell was among the first to accept old PC hardware from consumers and recycle it for free. Suncor Energy assists Native Americans to deal with social and ecological issues in Canada's far north.

Ethical Connections

FDI offers numerous benefits to recipient countries. However, FDI may produce side effects that harm the natural environment, especially in countries with weak environmental laws. Pollution and ecological destruction may result alongside rapid economic growth. One MNE, a manufacturer of food additives, allowed untreated wastewater to flow into the ThiVai River in Vietnam. Resulting pollution nearly destroyed the livelihood of thousands of downstream farmers. Firms must behave responsibly in their international dealings. Governments must not allow development goals to compromise citizens' well-being.

14.3 Explain the motives for FDI and collaborative ventures.

Motives for FDI and Collaborative Ventures

The ultimate goal of FDI and international collaborative ventures is to enhance company competitiveness in the global marketplace. Various motives explain why firms pursue these entry strategies. In Exhibit 14.4, we classify the motives for FDI and collaborative ventures into three categories: market-seeking, resource- or asset-seeking, and efficiency-seeking.[18] In many cases, firms aim to satisfy several motives simultaneously. Let's examine these motives in more detail.

Market-Seeking Motives

Managers may seek new market opportunities as a result of either unfavorable developments in their home market (that is, they may be pushed into international markets) or attractive opportunities abroad (they may be pulled into international markets). There are three primary market-seeking motivations.

- *Gain access to new markets or opportunities* The existence of a substantial market motivates many firms to produce offerings at or near customer locations. Local production

EXHIBIT 14.4

Firm Motives for Foreign Direct Investment and Collaborative Ventures

improves customer service and reduces the cost of transporting goods to buyer locations. Coca-Cola, IBM, Samsung, and Siemens all generate more sales abroad than in their home markets. The opening case highlights Huawei Technologies, a Chinese firm that has invested billions in Africa to gain access to fast-growing mobile phone markets there.

- *Follow key customers* Firms often follow their key customers abroad to preempt other vendors from serving them. Establishing local operations also positions the firm to serve customer needs better. Tradegar Industries supplies the plastic that its customer, Procter & Gamble, uses to manufacture disposable diapers. When P&G built a plant in China, Tradegar followed P&G there, establishing production in China as well.

- *Compete with key rivals in their own markets* Some MNEs may choose to confront current or potential competitors directly, in the competitors' home market. The strategic purpose is to weaken the competitor by forcing it to expend resources to defend its market. In the earth-moving equipment industry, Caterpillar entered a joint venture with Mitsubishi to put pressure on the market share and profitability of their common rival, Japan's Komatsu. The need to spend substantial resources to defend its home market reduced Komatsu's ability to expand abroad.[19]

Resource- or Asset-Seeking Motives

Firms frequently want to acquire production factors that are more abundant or less costly in a foreign market. They may also seek complementary resources and capabilities of partner companies headquartered abroad. Specifically, FDI or collaborative ventures may be motivated by the firm's desire to attain the following assets.

- *Raw materials needed in extractive and agricultural industries.* Firms in the mining, oil, and crop-growing industries have little choice but to go where the raw materials are. In the wine industry, companies establish wineries in countries suited for growing grapes, such as France and Chile. Oil companies establish refineries in countries with abundant petroleum reserves such as Kuwait.

- *Knowledge or other assets.*[20] By establishing a local presence through FDI, the firm is better positioned to deepen its understanding of target markets. FDI provides the foreign firm better access to market knowledge, customers, distribution systems, and control over local operations. By collaborating in R&D, production, and marketing, the focal firm can benefit from the partner's know-how. When Whirlpool entered Europe, it partnered with Philips to benefit from the latter's well-known brand name and distribution network. Royal Dutch Shell and PetroChina established a $1.3 billion joint venture to extract gas and oil from the Changbei gas field in China. Through this venture, PetroChina is acquiring knowledge about Shell's advanced technologies for extracting fossil fuels from deep shale deposits. In turn, Shell gained access to the gas field and is learning from PetroChina how to navigate the complex Chinese energy market.[21]

- *Technological and managerial know-how.*[22] The firm may benefit by establishing a presence in a key industrial cluster. Examples include the robotics industry in Japan, chemicals in Germany, fashion in Italy, and software in the United States. Companies can obtain many advantages from locating at the hub of knowledge development and innovation in a given industry. Denmark, Finland, Israel, New Zealand, Sweden, and the United States are considered ideal for R&D in the biotechnology industry because they have abundant biotech knowledge workers.[23] Many firms enter a collaborative venture abroad as a prelude to wholly owned FDI. Collaboration with a local partner reduces the risks of entry and provides the entrant local expertise before launching operations of its own in the market.

Efficiency-Seeking Motives

International expansion enables the firm to achieve *economies of scale*. International expansion allows the firm to increase sales and employ company assets across a larger number of products and markets. As the quantity of productive output increases, the per-unit cost of production tends to decline. In turn, profits rise as the firm's average cost of operations falls. Similarly, with increasing output, the per-unit cost of other productive activities declines—R&D, marketing, distribution, and customer support.

When firms expand into international markets, they obtain economies of scale. This occurs for various reasons.

- *Falling fixed costs.* Many industries and productive tasks have high per-unit fixed costs that decline the more the task is performed. For example, imagine the per-unit cost of the first car that rolls off an assembly line—production cannot occur unless the firm builds a factory. To increase international sales, the firm must produce more cars. As more cars are produced, the cost to build the factory is amortized across many cars, and the average cost per car declines.

- *Managerial resource efficiencies.* International expansion implies that the firm must employ a relatively fixed number of headquarters staff across more subsidiaries and affiliates. In this way, managerial talent is used more efficiently.

- *Specialization of labor.* When productive output increases, the firm hires more workers, who become more specialized in their tasks. As they specialize, workers become more efficient and produce more output per hour worked.

- *Volume discounts.* Suppliers usually offer discounts for large-quantity purchases. Per-unit sourcing costs fall as the firm buys more parts, components, and other inputs.

- *Financial economies.* Compared to small firms, large companies usually can access capital at lower cost. This arises because large firms are relatively powerful and tend to borrow large sums.

Internationalization also increases *economies of scope.* Economies of scope refers to the cost-savings that arise from using a relatively fixed base of managerial talent, facilities, and other company assets across a larger marketplace. For example, Unilever uses the same base of managers and marketing experts at its Netherlands headquarters to develop advertising for numerous product lines for many countries in Europe. This is more efficient than delegating the task to individual managers in each European country. The cost-reducing benefits of doing business in numerous countries simultaneously are substantial. MNEs frequently concentrate production in only a few locations to increase the efficiency of manufacturing.[24] Many firms develop global brands to increase the efficiency of marketing activities.

In addition to attaining economies of scale and scope, firms engage in international business to achieve four major efficiency-seeking goals:

Source: spectrumblue/Fotolia

Firms in the wine industry engage in foreign direct investment and collaborative ventures to access raw materials, in this case, farm land suitable for cultivating wine grapes. Pictured is a vineyard in New Zealand.

- *Reduce sourcing and production costs by accessing inexpensive labor and other cheap inputs to the production process.*[25] This motive accounts for the massive investment by foreign firms in factories and service-producing facilities in China, Mexico, Eastern Europe, and India. MNEs establish factories in such locations to reduce production costs.

- *Locate production near customers.* In industries that need to be especially sensitive to customer needs or in which tastes change rapidly, companies often locate factories or assembly operations near important customers. H&M and Zara locate much of their garment production close to customers in Europe. Compared to costs in China or Latin America, manufacturing clothing in Europe is more expensive. But the clothing gets into shops faster and more closely represents the latest fashion trends.[26]

- *Take advantage of government incentives.* In addition to restricting imports, governments frequently offer subsidies and tax concessions to foreign firms to encourage them to invest locally. Governments encourage inward FDI because it provides local jobs and capital, increases tax revenue, and transfers skills and technologies.[27]

• *Avoid trade barriers.* Companies often enter markets through FDI to avoid tariffs and other trade barriers because these usually apply only to exporting. By establishing a physical presence inside a country or an economic bloc, the foreign company obtains the same advantages as local firms. Partnering with a local firm also helps overcome regulations or trade barriers and satisfy local content rules. The desire to avoid trade barriers helps explain why numerous Japanese automakers established factories in the United States. However, this motive is declining in importance because trade barriers have fallen substantially in many countries.

Types of Foreign Direct Investment

14.4 Identify the types of foreign direct investment.

We can classify FDI activities by form (greenfield versus mergers and acquisitions), nature of ownership (wholly owned versus joint venture), and level of integration (horizontal versus vertical).

Greenfield Investment versus Mergers and Acquisitions

Greenfield investment occurs when a firm invests to build a new manufacturing, marketing, or administrative facility as opposed to acquiring existing facilities. As the name *greenfield* implies, the investing firm typically buys an empty plot of land and builds a production plant, marketing subsidiary, or other facility there for its own use. This is exactly what Ford did when it established its large factory in Rayong, Thailand, to manufacture small cars for emerging markets.

An **acquisition** is the purchase of an existing company or facility. When Home Depot entered Mexico, it acquired the stores and assets of an existing retailer of building products, Home Mart.[28] The Chinese personal computer manufacturer Lenovo made an ambitious acquisition of IBM's PC business, which now accounts for some two-thirds of its annual revenue. The deal provided Lenovo with valuable strategic assets such as brands and distribution networks and helped it rapidly extend its market reach and become a global player.[29]

A **merger** is a special type of acquisition in which two companies join to form a larger firm. Like joint ventures, mergers can generate many positive outcomes, including inter-partner learning and resource sharing, increased scale economies, cost savings from eliminating duplicative activities, a broader range of products and services for sale, and greater market power.

Greenfield investment
Direct investment to build a new manufacturing, marketing, or administrative facility as opposed to acquiring existing facilities.

Acquisition
Direct investment to purchase an existing company or facility.

Merger
A special type of acquisition in which two firms join to form a larger enterprise.

Cross-border mergers confront many challenges due to national differences in culture, competition policy, corporate values, and operating methods. Success requires substantial advance research, planning, and commitment. *Merger and acquisition* (M&A) activity is substantial in international business. The largest international M&As in recent years include the Kraft Foods (United States) merger with Cadbury (United Kingdom), Suntory's (Japan) purchase of Beam (United States) in the liquor industry, and Telefonica's (Spain) purchase of Brasilcel (Brazil) in the telecommunications sector.[30]

Multinational enterprises may favor acquisition over greenfield FDI because, by acquiring an existing company, they gain ownership of existing assets such as plant, equipment, and human resources as well as access to existing suppliers and customers. Unlike greenfield FDI, acquisition provides an immediate stream of revenue and accelerates the MNE's return on investment. However, host-country governments often pressure MNEs to undertake greenfield FDI. Greenfield FDI creates new jobs and production capacity, facilitates technology and

Source: Inge Hogenbijl/123RF

More companies are investing in Africa to develop power plants and renewable energy. In addition to providing capital for local economies, such investments supply needed infrastructure. This solar panel station is in southern Africa.

EXHIBIT 14.5

Toyota's Direct Investments in Manufacturing Plants in the United States

Sources: Based on Alex Taylor, "America's Best Car Company," *Fortune*, March 19, 2007, pp. 98–101; Toyota Operations 2015, www.toyota.com; Toyota, "Fast Facts," 2015, www.toyota.com.

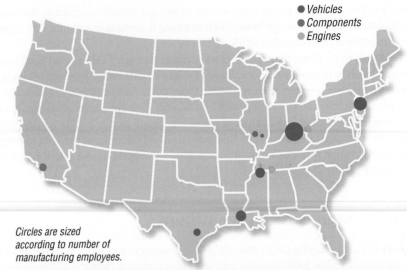

● Vehicles
● Components
● Engines

Circles are sized according to number of manufacturing employees.

Vehicle plants currently operating	Start of production	Models produced	Manufacturing employees
1. Georgetown, Kentucky	1986	Avalon, Camry, Lexus	7,000
2. Lafayette, Indiana	1987	Camry	3,600
3. Princeton, Indiana	1996	Sequoia, Sienna, Highlander	4,800
4. San Antonio, Texas	2003	Tundra, Tacoma	1,850
5. Blue Springs, Mississippi	2010	Corolla	2,000

know-how transfer to locals, and improves linkages to the global marketplace. Many governments offer incentives to encourage greenfield investments. They may be sufficient to offset the advantages of acquisition-based entry.

The Nature of Ownership in FDI

Foreign direct investors also choose their degree of control in the venture. This is accomplished through full or partial ownership, resulting in a commensurate degree of control over decision making on such issues as product development, expansion, and profit distribution. Firms can choose between a wholly owned or joint venture to secure control, which also determines the extent of their financial commitment. If the focal firm is pursuing partial ownership in an existing firm, this is known as **equity participation or equity ownership**.

Wholly owned direct investment is FDI in which the investor assumes 100 percent ownership of the business and secures complete managerial control over its operations. Foreign auto makers, for example, typically established fully owned manufacturing plants in the United States to serve the large U.S. market from within.[31] Exhibit 14.5 maps the location of Toyota's U.S. plants and the year of establishment.

In contrast to wholly owned direct investment, an **equity joint venture** is a type of partnership in which a separate firm is created through the investment or pooling of assets by two or more parent firms that gain joint ownership of the new legal entity.[32] A partner in a joint venture may hold majority, equal (50–50), or minority ownership. Minority ownership provides little control over the operation.

A joint venture is an attractive entry strategy because many foreign markets are complex. Collaborating with a local partner enhances the foreign entrant's ability to navigate the local market. Collaborative ventures benefit small and medium-sized enterprises by providing

Equity participation or equity ownership
Acquisition of partial ownership in an existing firm.

Wholly owned direct investment
A foreign direct investment in which the investor fully owns the foreign assets.

Equity joint venture
A type of partnership in which a new firm is created through the investment or pooling of assets by two or more parent firms that gain joint ownership of the new legal entity.

them with needed capital and other assets. For example, Shanghai-based Tri Star International acquired a majority stake in Illinois-based Adams Pressed Metals, a manufacturer of parts for tractors and other earth-moving equipment. The cash infusion saved 40 jobs at Adams and gave Tri Star access to the U.S. market and marketing know-how.[33]

A joint venture with a local partner may sometimes be the only entry strategy available to the focal firm. This can occur when the government of a target country seeks to protect its important industries by prohibiting 100 percent foreign ownership in local enterprises. Mexico's government, for example, requires foreign MNEs to form joint ventures with local Mexican firms when entering the country's oil industry, which is considered vital to Mexico's economic security. However, governments are relaxing such regulations in most industries, and most are receptive to FDI.

Vertical versus Horizontal Integration

A third way of classifying FDI is by whether integration takes place vertically or horizontally. **Vertical integration** is an arrangement whereby the firm owns, or seeks to own, multiple stages of a value chain for producing, selling, and delivering a product or service. The firm may acquire:

- *downstream* value-chain facilities, such as marketing and selling operations, or
- *upstream* value-chain facilities, such as factories or assembly plants.

Horizontal integration is an arrangement in which the firm owns, or seeks to own, the activities performed in a single stage of its value chain. Microsoft's primary business is developing computer software. In addition to producing word processing and spreadsheet software, it has developed foreign subsidiaries that make other types of software, such as a Montreal-based firm that produces software for creating movie animations. Horizontal integration implies that the firm invests in its own industry to expand its capacity and activities.

Let's illustrate the difference between vertical and horizontal integration. In 2014, Korean appliance manufacturer Samsung Electronics acquired Quietside Corporation, a leading distributor of air conditioners in North America. Samsung bought Quietside to enhance its ability to distribute its own air conditioners in a key foreign market. The acquisition exemplifies downstream vertical integration because appliance distribution is outside Samsung's normal sphere of operations. In 2012, by contrast, Samsung acquired the manufacturing plants of Amica, a home appliance company in Poland. This acquisition represents horizontal integration because Samsung Electronics' core business is manufacturing appliances and electronic products. By buying Amica's manufacturing plants, Samsung invested in its own industry to expand its production capacity.[34]

Read the "You Can Do It: Recent Grad in IB" profile featuring Jennifer Knippen. She acquired valuable international business experience by working for a foreign-owned company in her home country.

Vertical integration
An arrangement whereby the firm owns, or seeks to own, multiple stages of a value chain for producing, selling, and delivering a product or service.

Horizontal integration
An arrangement whereby the firm owns, or seeks to own, the activities performed in a single stage of its value chain.

International Collaborative Ventures

Collaborative ventures, sometimes called *international partnerships* or *international strategic alliances*, are essentially partnerships between two or more firms.[35] They help companies overcome together the often substantial risks and costs involved in achieving international projects that might exceed the capabilities of any one firm operating alone. Groups of firms sometimes form partnerships to accomplish large-scale projects such as developing new technologies or completing major undertakings such as power plants. By collaborating, the focal firm can draw on a range of complementary technologies, accessible only from other companies, to innovate and develop new products. Advantages such as these help explain why such partnerships have become enormously popular in recent decades.[36]

Although collaboration can take place at similar or different levels of the value chain, it is typically focused on R&D, manufacturing, or marketing. International collaborative ventures greatly increase R&D productivity in high-technology sectors such as robotics, semiconductors, aircraft manufacturing, medical instruments, and pharmaceuticals.

Two basic types of collaborative ventures are equity joint ventures and project-based, non-equity ventures. *Equity joint ventures* are traditional collaborations of a type that has existed

14.5 Understand international collaborative ventures.

JENNIFER KNIPPEN

Jennifer's majors: Economics and International Business
Jobs held since graduating:
- Sales Engineer, KONE, Inc.

Jennifer Knippen was inspired to pursue an international career after participating in a study-abroad program in Valencia, Spain. After graduating with dual majors in economics and international business, she returned to Spain for five months of intensive training in Spanish and traveled through various regions to broaden her education.

When she returned home, Jennifer attended a career fair, which led to a sales engineer position with the U.S. subsidiary of KONE, Inc., a leading manufacturer of elevators and escalators based in Finland. Her experience at KONE was both challenging and inspiring. Jennifer had to learn a technical product in the demanding construction industry.

As a sales engineer, she consulted architects in the design stages of a project—cost analysis, equipment specifications, building integration, and code compliance. She next generated a proposal to the general contractor working on the project. She managed the project through completion (more than a year). Jennifer managed multiple projects at a time while still meeting annual and quarterly sales budgets.

Managers at KONE praised Jennifer's strong presentations and relationship-building skills. She began working on high-rise projects with some of the top architectural and construction firms. Through pre-selling, with KONE's global support and resources, Jennifer stimulated substantial demand. Eventually, she was awarded Best in Class for the highest-volume sales in her region.

Jennifer experienced the benefits and challenges that come with working for a local subsidiary of an international parent company. KONE has enjoyed big success in Europe and other parts of the world and has applied a similar approach in the United States. One of the challenges Jennifer faced was strict U.S. building code regulations. She also had to monitor fluctuations in the euro–dollar exchange rate because these greatly affect the sales price of imported equipment.

What's Ahead?

Jennifer returned to school to complete an MBA in international business. She thought her experience, coupled with an advanced degree in international management, would position her well for an exciting international career. Jennifer is excited about what lies ahead.

Success Factors for a Career in International Business

Foreign travel and a study-abroad program in college inspired Jennifer to pursue an international career. Learning Spanish enhanced her credentials to secure an international business job. Jennifer set career goals and worked hard to achieve them.

Source: Photo by Tamer Cavusgil. Courtesy of Jennifer Knippen.

---

for decades. Recent years have seen a proliferation of nonequity, *project-based collaborations*. Let's examine these ventures in detail.

Equity Joint Ventures

Joint ventures are normally formed when no one party possesses all the assets needed to exploit an available opportunity. In a typical international deal, the foreign partner contributes capital, technology, management expertise, training, or some type of product. The local partner contributes the use of its factory or other facilities, knowledge of the local language and culture, market navigation know-how, useful connections to the host-country government, or lower-cost production factors such as labor or raw materials. Western firms often seek joint ventures to gain access to markets in Asia. The partnership allows the foreign firm to access key market knowledge, gain immediate access to a distribution system and customers, and attain greater control over local operations.

Procter & Gamble (P&G) is in a joint venture with Dolce & Gabbana, an Italian fashion house. Under the deal, P&G produces perfumes, and the Italian firm markets them in Europe, leveraging the local strength of its brand name.[37] The partnership provides both firms superior access to each other's strategic assets in R&D, production, branding, distribution, and market knowledge.

Samsung, the Korean electronics firm, began internationalizing in the 1970s through joint ventures with foreign-technology suppliers such as NEC, Sanyo, and Corning Glass Works. The partnerships allowed Samsung to acquire product designs and marketing outlets and gave management increasing confidence in foreign operations. As its capabilities grew, Samsung ventured into international production. Its earliest foreign manufacturing effort was a joint venture in Portugal, launched in 1982. In the 1990s, Samsung formed a joint venture with British supermarket chain Tesco to establish a chain of hypermarkets in South Korea. Samsung's 2013 joint venture with the U.S. company Corning produces glass displays for televisions.[38]

Project-Based, Nonequity Ventures

Increasingly common in cross-border business, the **project-based, nonequity venture** is a collaboration in which the partners create a project with a relatively narrow scope and a well-defined timetable, without creating a new legal entity. Combining staff, resources, and capabilities, the partners collaborate on new technologies or products until the venture bears fruit or they no longer consider collaboration valuable. Such partnering reduces the enormous fixed costs of R&D, especially in technology and knowledge-intensive industries, and helps firms catch up with rivals. For example, Russia's Rusnano and U.S. firm Crocus Technology entered a venture to research and produce advanced versions of MRAM chips in 2013. These chips function as memory chips in smart electronics such as digital cameras and smartphones.[39]

In 2015, Hewlett-Packard formed a nonequity joint venture with Taiwanese contract manufacturer Foxconn to conduct research on hyperscale computing and storage technologies. The venture reflects HP's desire to gain market share in the large-scale data center market. The venture is a strategic commercial agreement that aims to produce advanced computer servers for customers such as Amazon, Google, and Facebook. Such Internet service companies operate large-scale data centers to run their applications for online sales, search services, cloud storage, and social networking. For example, Facebook uses hyperscale technology to store images in its monstrous photo archive. Amazon uses the technology to store information about millions of its customers. The nonequity venture will leverage the computing and brand leadership of HP with the high-volume design and low-cost manufacturing expertise of Foxconn. HP and Foxxconn jointly will design and eventually manufacture the hyperscale storage technologies.[40]

Project-based, nonequity venture A collaboration in which the partners create a project with a relatively narrow scope and a well-defined timetable, without creating a new legal entity.

Differences Between Equity and Project-Based, Nonequity Ventures

In contrast to traditional equity joint ventures, project-based collaborations share the following distinctive characteristics:

- No new legal entity is created. Partners carry on their activity within the guidelines of a contract.
- Parent companies do not necessarily seek ownership of an ongoing enterprise. Instead, they contribute their knowledge, expertise, staff, and monetary resources to derive knowledge or other benefits.
- Collaboration tends to have a well-defined timetable and end date; partners go their separate ways once they have accomplished their objectives or have no further reason for continuation.
- Collaboration is narrower in scope than in equity joint venturing, typically emphasizing a single project, such as development, manufacturing, marketing, or distribution of a new product.
- Exhibit 14.6 highlights advantages and disadvantages of the two types of international collaborative ventures.

EXHIBIT 14.6 Advantages and Disadvantages of International Collaborative Ventures

	Advantages	Disadvantages
Equity joint ventures	• Afford greater control over future directions • Facilitate transfer of knowledge between the partners • Common goals drive the joint venture	• Complex management structure • Coordination between the partners may be a concern • Difficult to terminate • Greater exposure to political risk
Project-based, nonequity ventures	• Easy to set up • Simple management structure; can be adjusted easily • Takes advantage of partners' respective strengths • Can respond quickly to changing technology and market conditions • Easy to terminate	• Knowledge transfer may be less straightforward between the partners • No equity commitment; thus, puts greater emphasis on trust, good communications, and developing relationships • Conflicts may be harder to resolve • Division of costs and benefits may strain relationship

Consortium

Consortium
A project-based, nonequity venture initiated by multiple partners to fulfill a large-scale project.

A **consortium** is a project-based, usually nonequity venture initiated by multiple partners to fulfill a large-scale project. It is typically formed with a contract that delineates the rights and obligations of each member. Work is allocated to the members on the same basis as profits. In a three-partner consortium, for example, if each party performs one-third of the work, then each earns one-third of the profits. Consortia are popular for innovation in industries such as commercial aircraft, computers, pharmaceuticals, and telecommunications, where the costs of developing and marketing a new product often reach hundreds of millions of dollars and require wide expertise. Boeing, Fuji, Kawasaki, and Mitsubishi joined forces to design and manufacture major components of the Boeing 767 aircraft. In China, South Korea's Doosan Group and the U.S. firm Westinghouse partnered with China's State Nuclear Power Technology Corporation to build nuclear power plants. Westinghouse is majority owned by Japan's Toshiba Corporation.[41]

Often, several firms pool their resources to bid on a major project such as building a power plant or a high-tech manufacturing facility. Each brings a unique specialty to the project but would be unable to win the bid on its own. No formal legal entity is created; each firm retains its individual identity. In this way, if one party withdraws, the consortium can continue with the remaining participants. iNavSat is a consortium formed among several European firms to develop and manage Europe's global satellite navigation system.

Cross-Licensing Agreements

Cross-licensing agreement
A type of project-based, nonequity venture in which partners agree to access licensed technology developed by the other on preferential terms.

A **cross-licensing agreement** is a project-based, nonequity venture in which the partners agree to allow access to licensed intellectual property developed by the other on preferential terms. Microsoft entered such an agreement with Japan's JVC to share patented knowledge on software and other products. Two firms also might enter a cross-distribution agreement, in which each partner has the right to distribute products or services produced by the other on preferential terms. The Star Alliance is an agreement among more than 25 airlines—including Air Canada, United, Lufthansa, SAS, Singapore Airlines, and Air New Zealand—to market each other's airline flights (www.staralliance.com).

Potential Risks in Collaboration

Firms that collaborate have decided partnering is preferred to going it alone. In short, the potential benefits outweigh potential risks. In analyzing a possible collaboration, management should address the following questions.

- Are we likely to grow dependent on, or become dominated by, the partner firm?
- By partnering, will we stifle growth and innovation in our own organization?
- Will we share our competencies excessively, to the point that corporate interests are threatened? How can we safeguard our core competencies?
- Will we be exposed to significant commercial, political, cultural, or currency risks?
- How effectively can we integrate the cultures and operations of the partner firms?
- Will we close off any growth opportunities by participating in this venture?
- Will managing the venture place an excessive burden on our corporate resources, such as managerial, financial, or technological resources?

The potential partner may be a current or potential competitor, is likely to have its own agenda, and will likely gain important competitive advantages from the relationship.[42] Management must protect its hard-won capabilities and other organizational assets to preserve its bargaining power and ability to compete. The firm does not want to become too dependent on its partner. Harmony is not necessarily the most important goal, and accepting some conflict and tension between the partners may be preferable to surrendering core skills. For example, Westinghouse shared thousands of technical documents and other intellectual property during its partnership with Chinese firms to build nuclear reactors in China. Intellectual property rights in China are weaker than in some other countries, and the Chinese aim to become major developers of nuclear energy. Western industrial knowledge is certain to seep out to potential competitors, which will hurt future prospects of Westinghouse and other non-Chinese firms in the market.[43]

Managing Collaborative Ventures

The initial decision in internationalization is to choose the most appropriate target market because the market determines the characteristics needed in a business partner. If the firm plans to enter an emerging market, for example, it may need a partner with political clout or connections. In this way, country targeting and partner selection are interdependent choices.

Exhibit 14.7 outlines the process for identifying and working with a suitable business partner.[44] It reveals that managers need to draw on their cross-cultural competence, legal expertise, and financial planning skills.

When managers first contemplate internationalization through FDI, they usually think in terms of a wholly owned operation. Many are accustomed to retaining the control and sole

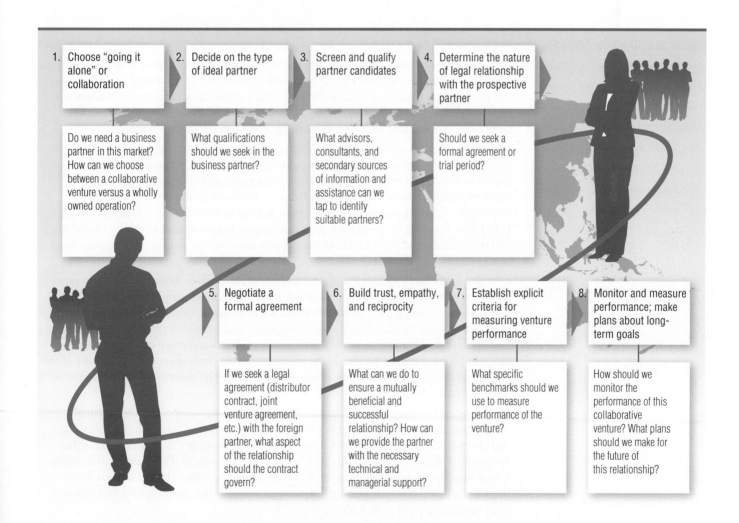

EXHIBIT 14.7

A Systematic Process for International Business Partnering

access to profits that come with 100 percent ownership. Although the nature of the industry or product can make partnering less desirable, management should consider collaboration an option. Typically, the firm enters a collaborative venture when it discovers a weak or missing link in its value chain and chooses a partner that can remedy the deficiency. China is an increasingly popular venue for collaboration in the Internet service-provider industry. Both Microsoft and Google entered this huge market through joint ventures with local partners, but eBay and Yahoo! entered China primarily through wholly owned FDI. Each firm chose the entry strategy most appropriate for its situation.[45]

About half of all collaborative ventures fail within the first five years of operation because of unresolved disagreements, confusion about venture goals, and other problems. International ventures are particularly challenging because, in addition to complex business issues, managers must contend with differences in culture and language as well as in political, legal, and economic systems. The failure rate of collaborative ventures is higher in developing economies than in advanced economies. Companies as diverse as Avis, Daewoo, General Motors, and Sainsbury's have experienced such failures.[46]

French food giant Danone (www.danone.com) terminated its joint venture with a local Chinese partner after years of contentious relations. Danone had formed the partnership at a time when the Chinese government often required such ventures from foreign firms.[47] In later years, however, the Chinese partner established a mirror business in which it sold, on the side, the same products the joint venture was marketing. The partner claimed that contract terms were unfair and accused Danone of trying to gain control of its other businesses.

Success in collaborative ventures is attained by following several guidelines.

- *Be cognizant of cultural differences.* International collaborations require both parties to learn and appreciate each other's corporate and national cultures. Cultural incompatibility can cause anger, frustration, and inefficiency. The partners may never arrive at a common set of values and organizational routines, especially if they are from very distinct cultures—say, Norway and Nigeria. Establishing cultural compatibility is a must.

- *Pursue common goals.* When partners have differing goals for the venture, or their goals change over time, they can find themselves operating at cross-purposes. Japanese firms tend to value market share over profitability, whereas U.S. firms value profitability over market share. Because different strategies are required to maximize each of these performance goals, a joint venture between Japanese and U.S. firms may fail. To overcome such challenges, partners need to interact regularly and communicate at three levels of the organization: senior management, operational management, and the workforce.

- *Give due attention to planning and management of the venture.* Without agreement on questions of management, decision making, and control, each partner may seek to control all the venture's operations, which can strain the managerial, financial, and technological resources of both. In some cases, equal governance and a sense of shared enterprise are best because they help partners view themselves as equals and reach consensus. In other cases, having a dominant partner in the relationship helps ensure success. When one of the partners is clearly the driver or the leader in the relationship, there is less likelihood of a stalemate or prolonged negotiations.

- *Safeguard core competencies.* Collaboration takes place between current or potential competitors that must walk a fine line between cooperation and competition. Volkswagen and General Motors succeeded in China by partnering with the Chinese firm, Shanghai Automotive Industry Corporation (SAIC; www.saicmotor.com). The Western firms transferred much technology and know-how to their Chinese partner. Having learned much from them, SAIC is now becoming a significant player in the global automobile industry and even a competitor to its earlier partners.[48]

> • *Adjust to shifting environmental circumstances.* When environmental conditions change, the rationale for a collaborative venture may weaken or disappear. An industry or economic downturn may shift priorities in one or both firms. Cost overruns can make the venture untenable. New government policies or regulations can increase costs or eliminate anticipated benefits. Flexibility is key for adjusting to changing conditions.

MyManagementLab   **Watch It!**

If your professor has assigned this, go to the Assignments section of **mymanagementlab.com** to complete the video exercise titled Entering the Chinese Market.

The Experience of Retailers in Foreign Markets

14.6 Discuss the experience of retailers in foreign markets.

Retailers represent a special case of international service firms that internationalize substantially through FDI and collaborative ventures. Retailing takes various forms and includes department stores (Marks & Spencer, Macy's), specialty retailers (Body Shop, Gap), supermarkets (Sainsbury, Safeway), convenience stores (7-Eleven, Tom Thumb), discount stores (Zellers, Target), and big-box stores (Home Depot, IKEA). Walmart has more than 240 stores and tens of thousands of employees in China. It sources almost all its merchandise locally, providing jobs for thousands more Chinese.[49]

The major drivers of retailer internationalization include saturation of home–country markets, deregulation of international investment, and opportunities to benefit from lower costs abroad. Home Depot expanded abroad because the home improvement market in Canada and the United States is becoming saturated.[50] Most emerging markets exhibit pent-up demand, fast economic growth, a growing middle class, and increasingly sophisticated consumers. In densely populated developing countries, consumers are flocking to discount retailers that sell a wide selection of merchandise at low prices.

Retailers usually choose between FDI and franchising as a foreign market entry strategy. The larger, more experienced firms, such as Carrefour, Royal Ahold, and Walmart, tend to internationalize through FDI. They typically own their stores and maintain direct control over operations and proprietary assets. Smaller and less internationally experienced firms such as Anytime Fitness tend to rely on networks of independent franchisees. In franchising, the franchisee adopts a business system from, and pays an ongoing fee to, a franchisor. Other firms may employ a dual strategy—using FDI in some markets and franchising in others. Although franchising facilitates rapid internationalization, compared to FDI, it affords the firm less control over its foreign operations, which can be risky in countries with unstable political or economic situations or weak intellectual property laws.

Many retailers have floundered in foreign markets.[51] When the French department store Galleries Lafayette opened in New York City, it could not compete with the city's numerous posh competitors. In its home market in the United Kingdom, Marks & Spencer succeeds with store layouts that blend food and clothing offerings in relatively small spaces, a formula that translated poorly in Canada and the United States. IKEA experienced problems in Japan where consumers value high-quality furnishings, not

Source: Demetrio Carrasco/Dorling Kindersley

Retailers are a distinctive category of international service firms that usually internationalize through FDI and collaborative ventures. Pictured is a department store in Russia.

the low-cost products IKEA offers. Most recently, Home Depot abandoned the Chinese market after only a few years there.

As another example, Walmart (www.walmart.com) is the world's largest retailer but failed in Germany because it could not compete with local competitors and eventually exited the market. In Mexico, Walmart constructed massive U.S.-style parking lots for its new super centers. However, most Mexicans don't have cars, and city bus stops were too far away, so shoppers could not haul their goods home. In Brazil, most families do their big shopping once a month on payday. Walmart built aisles too narrow and crowded to accommodate the rush and stocked shelves in urban São Paulo with some items that were not needed such as leaf blowers. Walmart's red, white, and blue banners, reminiscent of the U.S. flag, offended local tastes in Argentina. Sam's Club, Walmart's food discounting operation, failed in Latin America partly because its huge multipack items were too big for local shoppers with low incomes and small apartments. Today Walmart is one of Latin America's most successful retailers. It took Walmart many years to learn to adapt to local market needs.[52]

So, what are the typical challenges faced by retailers when they expand overseas?

Challenges of International Retailing

- *Culture and language* are a significant obstacle. Compared to most businesses, retailers are close to customers. They must respond to local market requirements by customizing their product and service portfolio, adapting store hours, modifying store size and layout, training local workers, and meeting labor union demands.

- Consumers tend to develop strong *loyalty to indigenous retailers*. As Best Buy in Turkey, Home Depot in China, and Walmart in Germany discovered, local firms usually enjoy great allegiance from local consumers.

- Managers must address *legal and regulatory barriers* that can be idiosyncratic. Germany limits store hours, and most retailers are closed on Sundays. Japan's Large-Scale Store Law required foreign warehouse and discount retailers to get permission from existing small retailers before setting up shop. Although it has been relaxed in recent years, the law was a major obstacle to the entry of stores such as Toys "R" Us. IKEA has been wary of entering India due to excessive restrictions placed on foreign retailers.[53]

- When entering a new market, retailers must develop *local sources* for thousands of products, including some that local suppliers may be unwilling or unable to provide. When Toys "R" Us entered Japan, local toy manufacturers were reluctant to work with the U.S. firm. Some retailers end up importing many of their offerings, which requires establishing complex and costly international supply chains.

International Retailing Success Factors

The most successful retailers pursue a systematic approach to international expansion. Initially, *advanced research and planning is essential*. A thorough understanding of the target market, combined with a sophisticated business plan, allows the firm to anticipate potential problems and prepare for success. In the run-up to launching stores in China, management at the giant French retailer Carrefour spent 12 years building up its business in Taiwan, where it developed a deep understanding of Chinese culture. It also learned how to forge alliances with local governments. These preparations helped Carrefour become China's biggest foreign retailer, rapidly developing a network of hypermarkets in 25 cities.[54]

In addition, international retailers need to *establish efficient logistics and purchasing networks* in each market where they operate. Scale economies in procurement are especially critical. Retailers need to organize sourcing and logistical operations to ensure that they always maintain adequate inventory while minimizing the cost of operations.

International retailers should *assume an entrepreneurial, creative approach to foreign markets*. Virgin Megastore is a good example. Starting from one London location in 1975, founder

Richard Branson expanded Virgin to numerous markets throughout Europe, North America, and Asia. The stores were big, well lit, and stocked music albums in a logical order, all innovations at the time. Sales turnover was much faster than that of smaller music retailers.

Retailers also must be willing to *adjust their business model to suit local conditions.* Home Depot offers merchandise in Mexico that suits the small budgets of do-it-yourself builders. It has introduced payment plans and promotes the do-it-yourself mind-set in a country where most cannot afford to hire professional builders.[55] The major dimensions along which retailers differentiate themselves abroad include selection, price, marketing, store design, and the ways in which goods are displayed. They must proceed cautiously while adapting to local conditions to avoid diluting or destroying the unique features that first made them successful.

IKEA, the world's largest furniture retailer, has enjoyed great success, launching over 200 furniture megastores in dozens of countries. Superior performance derives from strong leadership and skillful management of human resources and from the careful balancing of global integration of operations with responsiveness to local tastes. In each store, IKEA (www.ikea.com) offers as many standardized products as possible while maintaining sufficient flexibility to accommodate specific local conditions. In the United States, for example, IKEA increased the size of its beds to suit American tastes better. In China, IKEA cut its prices to accommodate customer income levels better. IKEA tests the waters first and learns in smaller markets before entering big markets. For example, IKEA perfected its retailing model in German-speaking Switzerland before entering Germany.[56]

CLOSING CASE China's Going Out Strategy

Chinese OFDI: A General Outlook

There have been a lot of discussions, especially after China's entry into the WTO, about the continuous increase of outward foreign direct investments (OFDIs) from China into every area of the globe, a phenomenon that has been defined as "China's going-out strategy."

According to the Chinese Ministry of Commerce (MOFCOM, online, 2015), in 2014 China's outbound FDI flows attained the absolute high of US $ 102.9 billion, up by 14.1% year-on-year, and placing China among the world's three largest source of FDIs, after USA and Japan and with a global share of 7.6%.Chinese FDIs, which have been pouring into the different sectors and countries more or less copiously, have not always been welcomed in the same positive way. This is due to a complex series of reasons.

First of all the typology of the sectors these investments have targeted, which in some cases have attracted worried that, behind them, there was a clear political strategy of the Chinese government to take control in sensitive sectors. This has been, for example, the case of some tentative acquisitions by China blocked in recent years, targeting strategic materials and critical infrastructures. This has been, for instance, the case of the United States where, over the past 10 years, Chinese companies have been seen by block Congress a series of acquisitions. There are a few examples that can be mentioned here – with the famous UNOCAL in the energy sector that constitute one of the best-known cases. The US showed caution in this sense. Among other countries that have proved to be suspicious of Chinese FDIs in strategic sectors there has been Australia, with the famous case of Lynas, a company active in the REEs (rare-earth elements) and which acquisition by Chinalco has been vetoed on the same grounds.

On the other hand, Europe, and especially the EU, has only recently begun to examine this complex issue, and the interest shown in debates is certainly related to the recent increase in Chinese investments, traditionally cautious in entering the EU market; an upward trend, this, that had continued through the global financial crisis and sovereign debt crisis, and it is still ongoing.

In order to analyze the importance and characteristics of Chinese FDIs in Europe, it will be useful is to compare them with the US market, given that two phenomena seem to be connected, when not influencing each other, since 2008.

As shown in the chart, after a different start in terms of amount and timeframe, the two flows have taken two different directions, with Europe which saw an amount of incoming FDI almost double of the one directed to the US in 2011–2012. This trend was due, according to the analysts, the numerous business opportunities arising from the sovereign debt crisis in the euro zone and that opened interesting opportunities to Chinese shoppers.

Chinese OFDI in Europe

An important question here is therefore to examine the character of the Chinese FDIs in Europe over the years, from their modest start to their present surge, and to determine if there is a grand strategy of the Chinese government to occupy strategic locations in Europe or if this renovated interest from the Asian giant is purely dictated by commercial motivations, and pursued independently by Chinese companies. And in order to answer this question, it's important, first of all, to quantify this presence, and gauge how it has been changing over the years.

As a matter of fact, Chinese investments in Europe are a recent phenomenon. They were not substantial until 2004, amounting at less than US $1 billion annually. The surge started in 2008, and in 2009 FDIs reached in flows US $ 3 billion, before tripling in 2010, reaching the level of more than $10 billion. A better idea of their consistence can be obtained by looking at them in terms of stock.

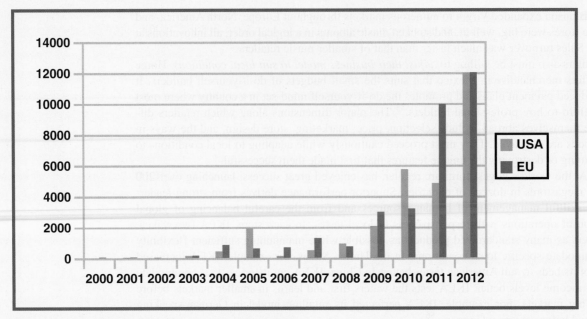

Chinese FDIs to USA and the EU (in US $ million)
(Source: Author's elaboration on: ICE, 2013; Rhodium Group 2013; MOFCOM 2013)

In five years (2009–2014) the committed amount was of US $ 55 billion, and this trend doesn't seem destined to dwindle any time soon. The latest data give incoming FDIs from China reaching US $18 billion in 2014 in terms of flow, surpassing the last record of US $12 billion in 2012.

Chinese investors, in particular, have taken the opportunity to enter the capital of companies short of cash, but able to guarantee stable returns over the long-term, as it is normally the case with infrastructure and public services. In terms of geographic presence, four countries have been consistently present over the years as preferred target countries – namely UK, Italy, Netherlands, and Germany – even though this has been somehow changing more recently.

From the individual sectors, it is easy to notice that energy seemed to be one of favorite targets, with US $17billion in stock between 2000 and 2014. This should not come as a surprise, considering that natural resources have always represented one of the primary objectives of Chinese investment abroad. In Europe, Chinese companies have spent about 5 billion euro for companies of the oil and gas, including upstream and exploration JVs (as in the case of Sinopec-Talisman), refineries (PetroChina-INEOS) and projects with a broader scope (Sinopec-Emerald Energy).

It is, however, in sectors like food, real estate, manufacturing and public utilities where this penetration has been more intense in the last three years, and this is one of the main differences with the policy of Chinese acquisitions in the United States. The motivations of Chinese FDIs here have been not of a resource seeker, but more in terms of acquisition of technologies to modernize Chinese domestic enterprises and to advance in the global value chain. In this sense, the economic crisis in Europe has given to the Chinese companies a precious opportunity to acquire know-how and technology indispensable for their future. There are a few examples in this sense, like in the sector of mechanical engineering, especially automotive that, with US $7.7billionin the period 2000–2014, is the second most popular sector for OFDI from China. Other sectors that have attracted Chinese interest are transports and infrastructure -as in the case of participation announced by the sovereign fund Chinese, CIC into Heathrow Airport in November 2012.

The EU's position on Chinese investments

Over the last decade the EU has generally welcomed Chinese investments, and cases of regulatory vetoes to acquisitions are unheard of. It is also true, however, that the EU lacks a coherent policy and, instead of a regulatory framework at the Commission's level, there is a fragmentary approach where each member state decides on its own. Moreover, and partly due to this reason, not all countries have benefited from Chinese money in the same way. As a matter of fact, the countries that more have implemented a transparent legislation, such as Germany, Sweden and the United Kingdom, have also been more successful into attracting foreign capitals – and China is only one country among many.

However, this enhanced interest and growing Chinese presence has reignited the debate, at European level, over FDIs, even though it has generally been more in the sense of devising and implementing a more consistent policy of attracting Asian investments in Europe than to restrict them, as it has been the case in other extra-EU countries.

According a general view, the Chinese approach in Europe seems driven primarily by the search of commercial gains, and therefore not threatening at a strategic level. Moreover, it is generally left to the initiative of individual companies, and not politically directed by the Chinese government. This was also noted in the case of public enterprises in China, which have shown a clear tendency to act according to the logic of profit.

Scenarios

The latest data, mentioned above, showed that Chinese FDIs has kept flowing to the EU even though the economic and financial situation of the EU is now better. They have been changing characters, however, and, in the latest data, there has been an increase in Greenfield investments with significant capital expenditure, such as food plants in France and machinery production in Germany, and targeting small and medium enterprises, generally left outside this kind of acquisitions. Finally, it's important to point out that, despite this upward trend, the economic importance of Chinese investment in the EU is still somehow limited (about 2% of the European total), and further efforts by both parts is needed to align investments to the level of importance of the foreign trade between the two partners.

Case Questions

14-4. Analyze Chinese FDIs overall trend, and compare the case of USA and the EU. How do the two trends relate one to another, if any?

14-5. Take into considerations Chinese FDIs in Europe: what are the motivating factors of Chinese presence in Europe? How does it compare to the FDI doctrine studied in the rest of the chapters?

14-6. What are the main countries and sectors where Chinese FDIs have been concentrated in the last five years? What are the reasons behind these choices?

14-7. Now look at the latest trends as analyzed in the last section. Why, in your opinion, are Greenfield investments are on the rise? Which other novelties can be expected in the coming years regarding Chinese presence in Europe?

14-8. Over the last decade Chinese investments in the EU have been welcomed. How would you assess the EU's likely attitude to Chinese investment in the longer term?

Sources: china.org.cn, Australia rejects China Nonferrous's acquisition of Lynas, 25 September 2009, http://www.china.org.cn/business/highlights/2009-09/27/content_18609842.htm; World Resource Institute, China's Overseas Investments, Explained in 10 Graphics, January 28, 2015, http://www.wri.org/blog/2015/01/china%E2%80%99s-overseas-investments-explained-10-graphics ; Baker&McKenzie, Chinese investment into Europe hits record high in 2014, 11 February 2015, http://www.bakermckenzie.com/news/Chinese-investment-into-Europe-hits-record-high-in-2014-02-11-2015/; Ministry of Commerce of the People's Republic of China, National Bureau of Statistics of the People's Republic of China, State Administration of Foreign Exchange. (2014). 2013 Statistical Bulletin of China's Outward Foreign Direct Investment. Beijing, China: China Statistics Press EU Website, Foreign direct investment statistics 2014, http://ec.europa.eu/eurostat/statistics-explained/index.php/Foreign_direct_investment_statistics

END OF CHAPTER REVIEW

 MyManagementLab

Go to **mymanagementlab.com** to complete the problems marked with this icon: ⭐.

Key Terms

acquisition 419	foreign direct investment (FDI) 410	joint venture 411
consortium 424	greenfield investment 419	merger 419
cross-licensing agreement 424	horizontal integration 421	project-based, nonequity venture 423
equity joint venture 420	international collaborative venture 411	vertical integration 421
equity participation 420	international portfolio investment 410	wholly owned direct investment 420

Summary

In this chapter, you learned about:

• **International investment and collaboration**

Foreign direct investment (FDI) is an internationalization strategy by which the firm establishes a physical presence abroad through ownership of productive assets such as capital, technology, labor, land, plant, and equipment. An **international collaborative venture** is a cross-border business alliance in which partnering firms pool their resources and share costs and risks of the venture. A **joint venture** is a form of collaboration between two or more firms that leads to minority, equal, or majority ownership.

• **Characteristics of foreign direct investment**

FDI is the most advanced and complex entry strategy and involves establishing manufacturing plants, marketing subsidiaries, or other facilities abroad. For the firm, FDI requires substantial resource commitment, local presence and operations in target countries, and the ability to access comparative advantages. It also entails greater risk compared to other entry modes. FDI is most commonly used by MNEs—large firms with extensive international operations. Services are intangible and typically cannot be exported. Services are usually location-bound and require firms to establish a foreign presence, generally through FDI. International portfolio investment is passive ownership of foreign securities such as stocks and bonds.

- **Motives for FDI and collaborative ventures**

Firms employ FDI for various reasons, including *market-seeking motives*, to enter new markets and gain new customers; *resource/asset-seeking motives*, to acquire production factors that may be cheaper or more abundant in foreign markets; and *efficiency-seeking motives*, to enhance the efficiency of the firm's value-adding activities. These motives often occur in combination. Motivations for international collaborative ventures include the ability to gain access to new markets, opportunities, or knowledge; to undertake international activities too costly or risky for one firm alone; to reduce costs; to meet government requirements; and to prevent or reduce competition.

- **Types of foreign direct investment**

FDI can be wholly owned direct investment, in which the firm owns 100 percent of foreign operations, or an equity joint venture with one or more partners. Firms may engage in **greenfield investment** by building a facility from scratch or by acquiring an existing facility from another firm through **acquisition**. With **vertical integration**, the firm seeks to own multiple stages of its value chain. With **horizontal integration**, the firm seeks to own activities involved in a single stage of its value chain. A **merger** is a special type of acquisition in which two companies join to form a new, larger firm.

- **International collaborative ventures**

Joint ventures (JVs) are normally formed when no one party possesses all the assets needed to exploit an opportunity. Joint ventures are an example of ownership-based collaborations. The **project-based, nonequity venture** emphasizes a contractual relationship between the partners and is formed to pursue certain goals or meet an important business need while the partners remain independent. A **consortium** is a project-based, nonequity venture initiated by multiple firms to undertake a large-scale activity that is beyond the capabilities of the individual members. Collaboration requires management to define its goals and strategies clearly. It requires much research and analysis up front as well as strong negotiation skills. Decisions are made regarding allocation of responsibilities in management, production, finance, and marketing as well as how to handle day-to-day operations and plans for the future. Because many collaborative ventures fail prematurely, firms should choose their partners carefully and follow a systematic process.

- **The experience of retailers in foreign markets**

Because retailing requires intensive customer interaction, it is particularly susceptible to culture, income levels, and other conditions abroad. Success depends on adapting to local conditions while maintaining the retailer's unique features and value proposition. International retailers face cultural and language barriers, strong customer loyalty to local retailers, legal and regulatory barriers, and the need to develop local supply sources. Retailer success also depends on advanced research and planning, establishing efficient logistics and purchasing networks, using an entrepreneurial and creative approach to foreign markets, and adjusting the business model to suit local needs.

Test Your Comprehension AACSB: Reflective Thinking Skills, Analytic Skills

⭐ **14-9.** What are the three different options as far as joint ventures are concerned?

14-10. How can FDI be seen as efficiency seeking?

14-11. Delineate the types of firms involved in FDI. Are there any types of companies that can internationalize only by FDI? Elaborate.

14-12. Identify the different types of collaborative ventures. What type of venture is best for entering a culturally distant market such as Malaysia or Uzbekistan? For the next generation of products in its industry? For undertaking a short-term project, such as building infrastructure (e.g., highway, dam) abroad?

14-13. What are the major motives for undertaking FDI for a small firm whose sales are dwindling in its home market? For a firm that wants to enter a country with high trade barriers? For a firm with high manufacturing costs in its home market? For a hotel chain? For a large, diversified firm seeking to enter various markets worldwide for a variety of reasons?

14-14. What factors should management consider when deciding where in the world to establish a factory? A marketing subsidiary? A regional headquarters?

14-15. What is a project based non-equity venture and how are the partners' independence protected?

⭐ **14-16.** How can a global retailer seek to ensure that they adapt to conditions in an overseas market whilst retaining their unique features and value proposition?

Apply Your Understanding AACSB: Communication Abilities, Reflective Thinking Skills, Ethical Understanding, and Reasoning Abilities

14-17. Suppose you get a job at MobileTV, a small manufacturer of TV sets installed in cars and boats. Business has declined recently, foreign rivals from emerging markets are increasing competition, and management is worried. Because MobileTV does all its manufacturing in Canada and the United Kingdom, it lacks cost advantages, and its prices are relatively high. After studying the problem, you conclude that MobileTV should move much of its production to Mexico, but senior management knows little about FDI. Prepare a report to management detailing the advantages of establishing a production base in Mexico. Why should the firm be interested in foreign manufacturing? Recommend which type of FDI MobileTV should use in Mexico. Finally, what advantages and disadvantages should the venture expect from manufacturing in Mexico?

14-18. Suppose you work for Aoki Corporation, a producer of processed foods. Your boss, Hiroshi Aoki, heard there is a big market for processed foods in Europe but does not know how to enter or do business there. You recommend entering Europe through a joint venture with a local European firm. Prepare a memo to Aoki explaining the objectives and risks of internationalizing through collaborative ventures. Explain why a collaborative venture might be a better entry strategy than wholly owned FDI. Keep in mind that processed food is a culturally sensitive product that entails various complexities in marketing and distribution. What type of European partner should Aoki seek?

14-19. *Ethical Dilemma*: Censorship standards vary worldwide. What is acceptable in some countries, such as nudity on television, criticizing authority, or revealing government secrets that affect national security, is unacceptable in others. Google is an Internet service multinational that used FDI to establish operations in China. Google enjoyed growing market success for several years. Eventually, however, Chinese government officials blocked Google from the market because Google refused to censor links to websites on sensitive topics such as independence for Taiwan and criticism of the Chinese government. Government censorship requirements eventually forced Google to withdraw from mainland China, a move that ceded market share to Chinese competitors and hurt Google's profits. Suppose you are an international manager at Google. Should Google have exited China, or should it reestablish its presence there and comply with Chinese censorship rules? Using the ethical framework in Chapter 4, analyze the arguments for and against Google's withdrawal from China. What can Google do to address the problem effectively?

 **globalEDGE** | **INTERNET EXERCISES**
(www.globalEDGE.msu.edu)

AACSB: Communication Abilities, Reflective Thinking Skills, Use of Information Technology

Refer to Chapter 1, page 54, for instructions on how to access and use globalEDGE™.

14-20. Suppose your company wants to establish a factory in Latin America to make and sell products in the region. It has narrowed the pool of candidate countries to Argentina, Brazil, and Chile. Your task is to write a report that compares the FDI environments of these countries. One approach is to obtain the country fact sheet for each nation from UNCTAD (www.unctad.org), a United Nations agency that gathers FDI data. You can access this data either through globalEDGE™ or the UNCTAD site. By examining the fact sheets, answer each of the following questions individually for Argentina, Brazil, and Chile.

a. What nations are the major trading partners of each country in the region? (This indicates the size and stability of existing trading relationships with key partners.)

b. Which companies are the leading firms now pursuing FDI in each country? (This helps identify key competitors.)

c. What is each country's rating on the FDI Performance Index? (This rating indicates the performance that typical firms have experienced when investing in each country.)

d. What is the level of merger and acquisition activity in each country? (This shows the maturity of each country for acquisition-based FDI.) Elaborate and justify your findings.

14-21. Suppose your firm wants to identify prospective countries for direct investment. Your boss has requested a report on the attractiveness of alternative locations based on their potential FDI return. A colleague mentions a tool called the FDI Confidence Index. Consult this resource and write a report in which you identify the top FDI destinations as well as the criteria used to construct the index. The Confidence Index is published by the consulting firm A. T. Kearney, based on an annual survey of CEOs at the world's top MNEs. Access the index by entering "FDI Confidence Index" at globalEDGE™ or directly at www.atkearney.com. Download the PDF file to do your research.

14-22. Assume you own a company that manufactures medical products in the biotechnology industry. You want to establish a foreign plant to manufacture your products and are seeking countries with a high concentration of knowledge workers. Thus, you decide to collect information about the knowledge economy abroad. The World Bank highlights the state of the knowledge economy in various countries. The data are accessible by visiting the World Bank site (www.worldbank.org) and entering the keywords "Knowledge Economy Index" in the search engine. You will be able to find several articles and retrieve information about these countries. Visit the site and prepare a report on the knowledge economy for each of the following: Singapore, South Korea, and Spain.

CAREER TOOLBOX

Selecting a Site for a Manufacturing Plant

Manufacturing involves various activities, including developing products, managing the inflow of parts and other inputs, organizing logistics, maintaining quality standards, and actual manufacturing operations. To gain comparative advantages, firms use foreign locations to manufacture the products that they offer their customers. For firms that manufacture abroad in company-owned factories, the most important first step is to find the right location to build a factory.

Decisions regarding where to locate factories are complex. For large production projects, numerous decision-makers perform complex analyses. Building or acquiring a foreign factory involves FDI, usually the most expensive foreign entry strategy. Given limited resources, managers establish factories in locations that maximize organizational advantages. The best approach to selecting a location is to narrow the possible countries by using a systematic research process.

In this exercise, assume you work for a company (e.g., Grohe, Kohler) that makes bathroom fixtures, for example, sinks, bathtubs, and shower systems. Your firm wants to expand its presence in the huge European market with these products. The European Union is very attractive due to 500 million affluent consumers in a concentrated area. To serve this region better, companies establish manufacturing plants in Europe through direct investment. However, because production costs are high in Western Europe, many firms establish plants in Eastern Europe, home to lower-cost, high-quality labor. Your task is to identify the most suitable Eastern European country to establish a manufacturing plant.

Background

Finding the best location to establish a foreign factory requires much research and planning. Initially, companies establish factories at foreign locations to minimize production costs. Other objectives include the ability to improve the value added to products, to be close to key foreign customers, and to access production factors not available at home. In a world of intense competition, manufacturing in countries that offer low-cost, high-quality labor makes the firm more competitive and helps it survive and thrive.

Management wants to access low-cost labor that has sufficient knowledge and skills to carry out manufacturing in ways that meet quality standards and performance objectives. Often the most important criteria for establishing foreign production is the level of workforce productivity. *Productivity* implies that the firm can generate maximal output of production for minimal cost. Productivity hinges on various factors, including the skill level of workers.

In the research phase, management accounts for numerous factors, including those related to each country's economy, political system, level of government intervention, legal protections, quality and cost of labor, presence of labor unions, and the level of infrastructure in the target country. In general, the firm wants to locate its manufacturing in countries where factors are optimal.

To complete this exercise in your MyLab, go to the Career Toolbox.

MyManagementLab

Go to **mymanagementlab.com** for Auto-graded writing questions as well as the following Assisted-graded writing questions:

⭐ **14-23.** Governments often provide incentives to encourage foreign firms to invest within their national borders. Why do governments encourage inward FDI?

⭐ **14-24.** Explain what steps a firm should take to launch a collaborative venture with a foreign partner successfully.

⭐ **14-25.** MyManagementLab Only—comprehensive writing assignment for this chapter.

Endnotes

1. Company profile of Tata at http://www.hoovers.com; P. Beckett, "Tata Chairman Doesn't Sweat the Timing on Global Expansion," *Wall Street Journal*, November 18, 2009, p. B1; Peter Harrop, "India Buys More of the UK Electric Vehicle Industry Cambridge, UK," *Automotive Industries*, January 2012, www.dallasnews.com; Andrew Saunders, "Jaguar Land Rover's Indian Adventure," *Management Today*, February 2014, pp. 30–34.

2. Ben Martin, "SABMiller Buys UK Craft Brewer Meantime," *Telegraph*, May 15, 2015, www.telegraph.co.uk.

3. "Datamonitor, MarketWatch Drinks Company Spotlight: SABMiller," December 2011, pp. 18–24; company profile of SABMiller at http://www.hoovers.com; SABMiller, "Who We Are," 2015, www.sabmiller.com.

4. UNCTAD, *Global Investment Trends Monitor* (New York: United Nations, January 29, 2015), www.unctad.org.

5. M. K. Erramilli and C. P. Rao, "Service Firms' International Entry-Mode Choice: A Modified Transaction-Cost Analysis Approach," *Journal of Marketing* 57 (July 1993), pp. 19–38; J. Li and S. Guisinger, "The Globalization of Service Multinationals in the 'Triad' Regions: Japan, Western Europe, and North America," *Journal of International Business Studies* 23 (1992), pp. 675–696; United Nations, *The Transnationalization of Service Industries* (New York: Transnational Corporations and Management Division, Department of Economic and Social Development, 1993).

6. Rajshekhar Javalgi, David A. Griffith, and D. Steven White, "An Empirical Examination of Factors Influencing the Internationalization of Service Firms," *Journal of Services Marketing* 17 (2003), pp. 185–201.

7. A. T. Kearney, *FDI Confidence Index* (Alexandria, VA: Global Business Policy Council, 2015); UNCTAD (2015).

8. UNCTAD (2015).

9. A. T. Kearney (2015).

10. Federation of European Employers, *Pay in Europe* (London: Federation of European Employers, 2013), www.fedee.com.

11. UNCTAD, *World Investment Report 2014* (New York: United Nations, 2015).

12. Steve Hamm, "IBM vs. Tata: Which Is More American?" *BusinessWeek*, May 5, 2008, p. 28.

13. Thomas C. Head and P. Sorensen, "Attracting Foreign Direct Investment: The Potential Role of National Culture," *Journal of American Academy of Business* 6 (2005), pp. 305–309.

14. *Business Eastern Europe*, "Russia: The Joke Misfires," March 14, 2011, p. 9; Carol Matlack, "Carlos Ghosn's Russian Gambit," *BusinessWeek*, March 17, 2008, pp. 57–58.

15. Clay Chandler, "Mickey Mao," *Fortune*, April 18, 2005, pp. 170–178.

16. Thomas Burrows, "How's This for a Magic Kingdom?" *Daily Mail*, February 8, 2015, www.dailymail.co.uk; Kimburley Choi, "Disneyfication and Localisation: The Cultural Globalisation Process of Hong Kong Disneyland," *Urban Studies* 49, No. 2 (2012), pp. 383–397.

17. "Beyond the Green Corporation," *BusinessWeek*, January 29, 2007, pp. 50–64.

18. John Dunning, *International Production and the Multinational Enterprise* (London: Allen and Unwin, 1981).

19. Farok Contractor and Peter Lorange, eds., *Cooperative Strategies in International Markets* (Lexington, MA: Lexington Books, 1988); Gary Hamel, Yves Doz, and C. K. Prahalad, "Collaborate with Your Competitors—and Win," *Harvard Business Review* 67 (January–February 1989), pp. 133–139; *International Construction*, "Equipment Revenues Down –2.6% in 2014," April 2015, p. 6; Vern Terpstra and Bernard Simonin, "Strategic Alliances in the Triad," *Journal of International Marketing* 1 (1993), pp. 4–25.

20. Lilach Nachum and Srilata Zaheer, "The Persistence of Distance? The Impact of Technology on MNE Motivations for Foreign Investment," *Strategic Management Journal* 26 (2005), pp. 747–767.

21. Stanley Reed and Dexter Roberts, "What's Shell Doing in China?" *Bloomberg Businessweek*, November 21–27, 2011, pp. 88–93.

22. Wilbur Chung and Juan Alcacer, "Knowledge Seeking and Location Choice of Foreign Direct Investment in the United States," *Management Science* 48 (2002), pp. 1534–1542.

23. Anders Lotsson, "Tomorrow: A Sneak Preview," *Business 2.0* (August 2005), pp. 77–84.

24. Lilach Nachum and Cliff Wymbs, "Product Differentiation, External Economies and MNE Location Choices: M&As in Global Cities," *Journal of International Business Studies* 36 (2005), pp. 415–423.

25. Nachum and Zaheer (2005).

26. "Retailing: Storm Clouds Over the Mall," *Economist,* October 8, 2005, pp. 71–72.

27. Mariasole Bannò, Lucia Piscitello, and Celeste Varum, "Determinants of the Internationalization of Regions: The Role and Effectiveness of Public Policy Measures," *Regional Studies* 49, No. 7 (2015), pp. 1208–1222.

28. Andrew Ward, "Home Depot in Mexico," *Financial Times*, April 6, 2006, p. 8.

29. Eva Dou, "Lenovo to Focus on Integrating Acquisitions," *Wall Street Journal*, www.wsj.com.

30. UNCTAD (2015).

31. Alan Ohnsman, "Surprise! Carmakers Are a Recovery Bright Spot," *Bloomberg Businessweek*, November 7–13, 2011, pp. 19–20.

32. In this book, we adopt the customary definition of "joint venture" when it is assumed to carry equity interest by the parent firms that founded it. That is, a joint venture is always an equity venture. Nevertheless, in popular literature, the term *equity venture* incorrectly refers to all types of collaborative ventures, including project-based collaborations. Therefore, we will use the term *equity joint venture* rather than simply *joint venture* to avoid miscommunication.

33. Paul Kaihla, "Why China Wants to Scoop Up Your Company," *Business 2.0*, June 2005, pp. 29–30.

34. *Air Conditioning Heating & Refrigeration News*, "Samsung Electronics America to Acquire Quietside," September 8, 2014, pp. 1–14; *Appliance Design*, "News Watch," February 2010, pp. 4–10.

35. Farok Contractor and Peter Lorange, *Cooperative Strategies and Alliances* (Oxford, England: Elsevier Science, 2002); Janell Townsend, "Understanding Alliances: A Review of International Aspects in Strategic Marketing," *Marketing Intelligence & Planning* 21 (2003), pp. 143–158.

36. Donald Fites, "Make Your Dealers Your Partners," *Harvard Business Review* 74 (1996), pp. 84–91; Masaaki Kotabe, Hildy Teegen, Preet Aulakh, Maria Cecilia Coutinho de Arruda, Roberto Santillan-Salgado, and Walter Greene, "Strategic Alliances in Emerging Latin America: A View from Brazilian, Chilean, and Mexican Companies," *Journal of World Business* 35 (2000), pp. 114–132.

37. Ellen Byron and Rachel Dodes, "P&G Flirts with Luxury Cosmetics," *Wall Street Journal,* March 9, 2009, p. B1.

38. "Business Digest," *Chemistry & Industry*, January 2012, p. 14; Y. Kim and K. Ahn, "Samsung Tesco Homeplus and Corporate Social Responsibility," *Richard Ivey School of Business Case Collection*, July 29, 2009; Tess Stynes, "Corning and Samsung in Accord," *Wall Street Journal*, October 23, 2013, p. B7.

39. Don Clark, "Chip Start-Up Joins with Russia in Memory Deal," *Wall Street Journal*, May 17, 2011, p. B7.

40. Eva Dou, "H-P, Foxconn Start Server Joint Venture," *Wall Street Journal*, May 1, 2014, p. B5.

41. Suresh Kotha and Kannan Srikanth, "Managing a Global Partnership Model: Lessons from the Boeing 787 'Dreamliner' Program," *Global Strategy Journal* 3, No. 1 (2013), pp. 41–66; Power Engineering, "Pressure Vessel for AP1000 Nuclear Reactor in China Put in Place," November 2011, Special section p. 6.

42. Ibid; Gang Li, Huan Fan, Peter Lee, and T. Cheng, "Joint Supply Chain Risk Management: An Agency and Collaboration Perspective," *International Journal of Production Economics*, vol. 164 June (2015), pp. 83–94.

43. Dexter Roberts and Stanley Reed, "China Wants Nuclear Reactors—Fast," *Bloomberg Businessweek*, December 6–12, 2010, pp. 15–17.

44. S. Tamer Cavusgil, "International Partnering: A Systematic Framework for Collaborating with Foreign Business Partners," *Journal of International Marketing* 6 (1998), pp. 91–107.

45. "Asian Alliances: New Ties for VW, GM and Peugeot Citroen," *Economist*, December 12, 2009, p. 72; "China: The Great Internet Race," *BusinessWeek*, June 13, 2005, pp. 54–55; Sing Keow Hoon-Halbauer, "Managing Relationships Within Sino-Foreign Joint Ventures," *Journal of World Business* 34 (1999), pp. 334–370.

46. Cavusgil (1998); Kandemir, Yaprak, and Cavusgil (2006); *Strategic Direction*, "Sainsbury's Egyptian Misadventure" 31, No. 3 (2015), pp. 4–6.

47. James Areddy, "Danone Pulls Out of Disputed China Venture," *Wall Street Journal*, October 1, 2009, p. B1.

48. "Asian Alliances" (2009).

49. Laurie Burkitt and Sarah Nassauer, "Wal-Mart Says It Will Go Slow in China," *Wall Street Journal,* April 30, 2015, p. B3; Mei Fong, "Retailers Still Expanding in China," *Wall Street Journal*, January 22, 2009, p. B1.

50. Andrew Ward, "Home Depot in Mexico," *Financial Times*, April 6, 2006, p. 8.

51. Andrew Roberts and Carol Matlack, "Once Wal-Mart's Equal, Carrefour Falls Behind," *Bloomberg Businessweek*, October 24–30, 2011, pp. 22–23.

52. David Agren, Thierry Ogier, and Joachim Bamrud, "Walmart: Latin American Success," *Latin Trade*, July/August, 2011,

pp. 24–27; Adrienne Sanders, "Yankee Imperialist," *Forbes*, December 13, 1999, p. 56; WWD: Women's Wear Daily, "Wal-Mart Alters Course in Latin America," April 21, 2014, p. 2.

53. Amol Sharma, "IKEA Wary of Entering India," *Wall Street Journal*, January 24, 2012, p. B4.

54. Clay Chandler, "The Great Wal-Mart of China," *Fortune*, July 25, 2005, pp. 104–116; Ming-Ling Chuang, James Donegan, Michele Ganon, and Kan Wei, "Walmart and Carrefour Experiences in China: Resolving the Structural Paradox," *Cross Cultural Management* 18, No. 4 (2011), pp. 443–463.

55. Andrew Ward, "Home Depot in Mexico," *Financial Times*, April 6, 2006, p. 8.

56. Valerie Chu, Alka Girdhar, and Rajal Sood, "Couching Tiger Tames the Dragon," *Business Today*, July 21, 2013, p. 92–96; Beth Kowitt, "It's IKEA's World*," *Fortune*, March 15, 2015, pp. 166–175; Hilary Potkewitz, "Can Your Relationship Handle IKEA?" *Wall Street Journal*, April 23, 2015, pp. D1–D2.

Licensing, Franchising, and Other Contractual Strategies

Learning Objectives *After studying this chapter, you should be able to:*

15.1 Explain contractual entry strategies.

15.2 Understand licensing as an entry strategy.

15.3 Describe the advantages and disadvantages of licensing.

15.4 Understand franchising as an entry strategy.

15.5 Explain the advantages and disadvantages of franchising.

15.6 Understand other contractual entry strategies.

15.7 Understand infringement of intellectual property, a global problem.

How LEGO Built Global Value in the Toy Industry — Block By Block

From putting together a bright red fire-fighting engine to a medieval castle or a railway station, millions of children have honed over several decades their imagination and mechanical skills using small, colorful plastic cubes: the LEGO sets. With over 60 billion assembling bricks produced per year, LEGO, a family company in Billund, Denmark, remains the most trusted toymaker in the building-block toy sector with 85% market share worldwide. Production quality, adaptation to buyer preferences and a careful licensing strategy are the key driver's of the company's spectacular success in the US $ 151.1 (€ 133) billion toy industry. More than a third of the sales of toys and non-electronic games worldwide are generated through licenses.

LEGO is a late entrant in the contractual licensing. Its management decided in 1999 that the company's traditional audience was changing in many respects. First, pre-school and school-age users wanted themes that reminded them of their favored heroes from action movies and video games. Second, adults were increasingly attracted towards life-size interlocking constructions, such as cars, tractors, or even caravans! LEGO had the technology to respond. What it lacked was themes and the capabilities to design them. This is where licensing was opening a new window of opportunity, which other toy makers, like Mattel and Hasbro, had already exploited. LEGO was late to join the race, but a quick mover: very soon it began making and distributing the Dungeon and the Desert Outpost of *Minecraft,* Luke and Darth Vader of *Star Wars. Indiana Jones, Harry Potter* and *The Lord of the Rings* settings, the Vet Clinic of *Friends,* or the Treetop Hideaway of the *Elves* are now part of its catalogue of brick-based constructions.

Source: iordani/Shutterstock

Hollywood is now an indispensable partner of toy makers, as it constantly provides new ideas for sets and characters that stimulate the imagination of the users. Most toy manufactures, Mattel and Hasbro included, acquire properties from studios and grant licenses to regional or local production and marketing companies. LEGO has followed a similar pattern. Its first property acquisition was *Star Wars*, a license by Lucasfilm. Its licensing strategy is two-fold: inbound and outbound. Inbound licenses refer to themes developed by third parties, like Disney or Warner Bros. Outbound licenses are issued by LEGO to companies, which want to use its patents, trademarks, logo, and *The LEGO Movie* for their own end-products. DK publishing, Merlin Entertainment Plc, and LEGOLAND theme parks are among such licensees. These represented in 2015 less than 2% of LEGO's total revenues of US $ 4.4 (€ 3.8) billion, but they have since been increasing by 20% annually.

Licensing of games has in the past decade become vital for the industry. In the U.S., 27% of all traditional toys and games sold are licensed, generating a value of US $ 6 (€ 5.3) billion. The rate is, however, higher in Asia, Latin America and Turkey, where licensing ranges from 30 to 40% of total sales and is expected to reach 60% by 2019. The average annual spending per buyer in these regions is US $ 28 (€ 24)—far below the $ 439 (€ 387) toy expenditure per child of the UK. For LEGO, which operates factories in Europe, Mexico and China, and is present in 130 countries through a combination of own offices, licensed producers and distributors, the Emerging Markets offer the most promising opportunity for growth through licensing. They are also fraught with challenges: IPR protection. LEGO has already lost a few legal battles in this field, as some of its original patents have expired.

Companies drive a hard bargain in licensing-out their properties, and Hollywood studios are notoriously demanding. For example, Hasbro, the second major competitor of LEGO after Mattel, recently paid to Marvel Comics a basic fee of US $ 100 (€ 88) million, with a potential for an additional US $140 (€ 123) million in royalties. LEGO's outbound

Contractual entry strategies in international business
Cross-border exchanges in which the relationship between the focal firm and its foreign partner is governed by an explicit contract.

Intellectual property
Ideas or works that individuals or firms create, including discoveries and inventions; artistic, musical, and literary works; and words, phrases, symbols, and designs.

Intellectual property rights
The legal claim through which the proprietary assets of firms and individuals are protected from unauthorized use by other parties.

Licensing
Arrangement by which the owner of intellectual property grants a firm the right to use that property for a specific time period in exchange for royalties or other compensation.

Royalty
A fee paid periodically to compensate a licensor for the temporary use of its intellectual property, often based on a percentage of gross sales generated from the use of the licensed asset.

15.1 Explain contractual entry strategies.

Franchising
Arrangement by which the firm allows another the right to use an entire business system in exchange for fees, royalties, or other forms of compensation.

licensing conditions are relatively modest—less than 100 million base fees plus variable royalties—as the company wants to maintain strict control over the quality of its licensees. But in licensing-in, it is as powerless as its competitors.

The global monetary value of licensed toys and games is expected to grow annually at the rate of 2-3% until 2020. LEGO says it is determined to secure a fair share, without compromising its mission: to "redefine play and re-imagine learning."

Questions

15-1. How does LEGO generate royalties by using contractual entry strategies?

15-2. What are the advantages of licensing as described in the case?

15-3. What risk(s) does LEGO face from licensing its brand, logo, toy patents, and *LEGO Movie*?

SOURCES: LEGO Group A/S company information, www.lego.com September 2015; www.LEGOFoundation.com September 2015; www.kirkbi.com September 2015; LEGO Group A/S Annual Report 2014, pp 1-54; Jens Hansegard, "Oh, Snap! Lego Sales Surpass Mattel", *The Wall Street Journal,* September 4, 2014; Michael Paterniti, "How Lego Built the Coolest Company in the World", *Popular Mechanics,* March 19, 2015 www.popularmechanics.com; Graham Pomphrey, "Rebuilding Lego", *License!Global,* November 1, 2006 www.licensemag.com; Jonathan Ringen, "How Lego Became the Apple of Toys", *Fast Company,* January 8, 2015 www.fastcompany.com; Andy Robertson, "New York Toy Fair: the best Lego sets", *Wired,* February 18, 2015 www.wired.co.uk; Sam Thielman, "How Lego Became the Most Valuable Toy Company in the World", *AdWeek,* April 15, 2013 www.adweek.com; Joint Press Release by Warner Bros, Interactive Entertainment, TT Games and the LEGO Group, *Business Wire,* April 9, 2015 www.businesswire.com; "Key Global and Regional Trends Shaping Toys Licensing", *Euromonitor International.* September 2015, pp. 6, 10, 16; Statista www.statista.com.

Licensing—granting the right to others to use a legally protected property (a name, trademark, logo, design, etc.) —has grown enormously in international business. Such transactions imply a contractual relationship between those who own the property and those given permission to use it. For companies that own licensable properties such as technology, artistic works, logos, and business systems, licensing can be a very lucrative business around the world.

In this chapter, we address licensing, franchising, and other types of cross-border contractual relationships. **Contractual entry strategies in international business** are cross-border exchanges in which the relationship between the focal firm and its foreign partner is governed by an explicit contract. **Intellectual property** describes ideas or works that individuals or firms create, including discoveries and inventions; artistic, musical, and literary works; and words, phrases, symbols, and designs. Harry Potter is a leading example. As explained in Chapter 4, intellectual property is safeguarded through **intellectual property rights**, the legal claim through which proprietary assets are protected from unauthorized use by other parties.[1]

Contractual Entry Strategies

Two common types of contractual entry strategies are licensing and franchising. **Licensing** is an arrangement by which the owner of intellectual property grants another firm the right to use that property for a specific time period in exchange for *royalties* or other compensation. As described in the opening case, a **royalty** is a fee paid periodically to compensate a licensor for the temporary use of its intellectual property. The royalty is usually a percentage of the gross sales generated from use of the licensed asset. As an entry strategy, licensing requires neither substantial capital investment nor extensive involvement of the licensor in the foreign market. Licensing is a relatively inexpensive way for the firm to establish a presence in foreign markets. Firms that use licensing often can avoid expensive entry as is usually required in foreign direct investment (FDI).

Franchising is an advanced form of licensing in which the firm allows another the right to use an entire business system in exchange for fees, royalties, or other forms of compensation.

The preceding types of contractual relationships are common in international business and allow companies to transfer their knowledge assets to foreign partners routinely. Professional service firms such as those in architecture, engineering, advertising, and consulting extend their international reach through contracts with foreign partners. Similarly, retailing, fast food, car rental, television programming, and animation firms rely on licensing and franchising agreements. The retailer 7-Eleven (www.7-eleven.com) operates the world's largest chain of convenience stores, with more than 55,000 stores in 16 countries. Although the parent firm in Japan owns most of them, entrepreneurs operate several thousand stores in Canada, Japan, Mexico, and the United States through franchising arrangements.

Unique Aspects of Contractual Relationships

Cross-border contractual relationships share several common characteristics.

- *They are governed by a contract that provides the focal firm with a moderate level of control over the foreign partner.* Control refers to the ability of the focal firm to influence the decisions, operations, and strategic resources of the foreign venture and ensure that the partner undertakes assigned activities and procedures. In such an arrangement, the focal firm relies largely or entirely on independent agents abroad to perform business activities on its behalf. Thus, compared to FDI, entry by a contractual agreement affords the focal firm substantially less control over its foreign operations.

- *They typically include the exchange of intangibles and services.* Intangibles that firms exchange include various intellectual property, production processes, technical assistance, and know-how. Firms also may supply products or equipment to support the foreign partner.

- *Firms can pursue them independently or in conjunction with other entry strategies.* In pursuing international opportunities, firms may employ contractual agreements alone, or they may combine them with FDI and exporting. The use of such agreements is context specific. The firm may use a contractual relationship with certain customers, countries, or products but not others. Whereas licensing is common for certain types of products, it is not appropriate for others.

- *They provide dynamic, flexible choice.* Some focal firms use contractual agreements to make their initial entry in foreign markets. Then, as conditions evolve, they switch to another, often more advanced entry strategy. For example, franchisors such as McDonald's or Coca-Cola occasionally acquire some of their franchisees and bottlers. In doing so, they switch from a contractual approach to a direct investment strategy.

- *They often reduce local perceptions of the focal firm as a foreign enterprise.* A contractual relationship with a local firm allows the focal firm to blend into the local market. This attracts less attention and less of the criticism sometimes directed at firms that enter through more visible strategies such as FDI.

- *They generate a consistent level of earnings from foreign operations.* In comparison to FDI, contractual arrangements are less susceptible to volatility and risk. Such arrangements tend to bring both parties a predictable stream of revenue.

Contractual relationships emphasize the exchange of intellectual property, which includes various types.

- A *patent* gives an inventor the right to prevent others from using or selling an invention for a fixed period—typically, up to 20 years.[2] It is granted to those who invent or discover a new and useful process, device, manufactured product, or an improvement on these.

- A *trademark* is a distinctive design, symbol, logo, word, or series of words placed on a product label. It identifies a product or service as coming from a common source and having a certain level of quality. Examples include Honda's H-shaped symbol, McDonald's golden arches, and Izod's alligator mark.

- A *copyright* protects original works of authorship, giving the creator the exclusive right to reproduce the work, display and perform it publicly, and authorize others to perform these activities. Copyrights cover music, art, literature, films, and computer software.

- An *industrial design* describes the appearance or features of a product. The design is intended to improve the product's aesthetics and usability as well as increase its production efficiency, performance, or marketability. The Apple iPod is a well-known industrial design.

- A *trade secret* is confidential expertise or information that has commercial value. Trade secrets include production methods, business plans, and customer lists. The formula to produce Coca-Cola is a trade secret.
- A *collective mark* is a logo belonging to an organization whose members use it to identify themselves and associate their products with a level of quality or accuracy, geographical origin, or other positive characteristic. DIN is the collective mark for the German Institute for Standardization, typically found on home appliances in Europe.

Intellectual property rights derive from legally protected patents, trademarks, copyrights, and other protections associated with intellectual property. Such rights provide inventors with a monopoly advantage for a specified period of time, so they can exploit their inventions not only to recoup their investment costs and create commercial advantage, but also to acquire power and market dominance free of direct competition. The availability and enforcement of these rights vary from country to country. Without such legal protection and the assurance of commercial rewards, most firms and individuals would have little incentive to invent.[3]

15.2 Understand licensing as an entry strategy.

Licensing as an Entry Strategy

A licensing agreement specifies the nature of the relationship between the owner of intellectual property, the *licensor*, and the user of the property, the *licensee*. High-technology firms routinely license their patents and know-how to foreign companies. For example, Germany's Cognitec licensed the use of its face recognition technology to U.S. chip manufacturer Intel, which will use the technology to control access to laptops, tablets, and similar devices.[4]

Warner licenses images from the Harry Potter books and movies to companies worldwide. Disney (www.disney.com) licenses the right to use its cartoon characters to shirt and hat manufacturers in China. It also licenses its trademark names and logos to manufacturers of apparel, toys, and watches for sale worldwide. Licensing allows Disney to create synergies with foreign partners, who can then adapt materials, colors, and other design elements to suit local tastes and market a product similar to one Disney already may offer in the United States.

Exhibit 15.1 illustrates the nature of the licensing agreement.[5] Upon signing a licensing contract, the licensee pays the licensor a fixed amount up front *and* an ongoing royalty of

EXHIBIT 15.1

Licensing as a Foreign Market Entry Strategy

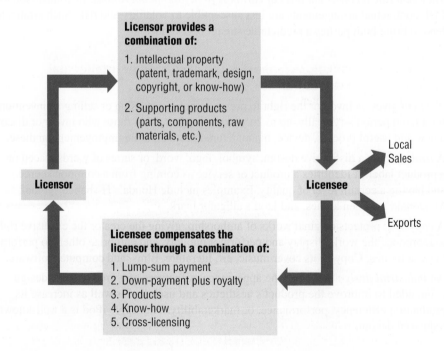

Licensor provides a combination of:

1. Intellectual property (patent, trademark, design, copyright, or know-how)
2. Supporting products (parts, components, raw materials, etc.)

Licensor

Licensee

Local Sales

Exports

Licensee compensates the licensor through a combination of:

1. Lump-sum payment
2. Down-payment plus royalty
3. Products
4. Know-how
5. Cross-licensing

typically 2 to 5 percent of gross sales generated from using the licensed asset. The fixed amount covers the licensor's initial costs of transferring the licensed asset to the licensee, including consultation, training in how to deploy the asset, engineering, or adaptation. Certain types of licensable assets, such as copyrights and trademarks, may have lower transfer costs. The royalty percentage may escalate with increasing sales.

A typical licensing contract runs five to seven years and is renewable at the option of the parties. Initially, the licensor provides technical information and assistance to the licensee. Once the relationship has been established and the licensee fully understands its role, the licensor usually plays an advisory role but usually has no direct involvement in the market and provides no ongoing managerial guidance. Most firms enter into *exclusive agreements*, in which the licensee is not permitted to share the licensed asset with any other company within a prescribed territory. In addition to operating in its domestic market, the licensee also may be permitted to export to other countries.

If the licensor is an MNE, it may enter a licensing arrangement with its own wholly or partly owned foreign affiliate. In this case, licensing is an efficient way to compensate the foreign affiliate, especially when it is a separate legal entity, and transfer intellectual property to it within a formal legal framework.

In the fashion industry, Hugo Boss, Pierre Cardin, and other strong brands generate substantial profits from licensing deals for jeans, fragrances, and watches. Saks Inc. entered China by licensing its Saks Fifth Avenue name for a flagship department store in Shanghai. Saks generates revenue from the agreement and controls which merchandise is sold in China but has no other involvement. Licensing brings greater awareness of Saks Fifth Avenue to Asia without requiring Saks itself to operate the store, thereby reducing its risk.[6]

The national origin of some popular brands might surprise you. Planters and Sunkist are food and beverage brands owned by U.S. companies and sold in Singapore and the United Kingdom through licensing agreements with local companies. Kit Kat chocolate bars are owned by Switzerland's Nestlé and distributed in the United States through a licensing agreement with Nestlé's competitor, Hershey. Game shows such as *Price Is Right* and *Family Feud* are owned by FremantleMedia, a United Kingdom company that licenses these programs for broadcast around the world.

There are two major types of licensing agreements: (1) trademark and copyright licensing and (2) know-how licensing. Let's review each.

Trademark and Copyright Licensing

Trademark licensing grants a firm permission to use another firm's proprietary names, characters, or logos for a specified period of time in exchange for a royalty. Trademarks appear on such merchandise as clothing, games, food, beverages, gifts, novelties, toys, and home furnishings. Organizations and individuals with name-brand appeal benefit from trademark licensing, such as Disney, Nickelodeon, FIFA, Harley-Davidson, LeBron James, and even your favorite university. A famous trademark such as Harry Potter can generate millions of dollars for the owner. Worldwide retail sales of licensed merchandise exceed $175 billion annually.[7]

In Canada, the United States, and numerous other countries, firms acquire rights to trademarks through first use and continuous usage. In other countries, however, rights to trademarks are acquired through registration with government authorities. Many firms register their trademarks in the countries where they do business to protect the asset. When a firm registers its trademark, it formally notifies government authorities that it owns the trademark and is entitled to intellectual property protection. Many countries require local use of the registered mark to maintain the registration.

The convention of gaining ownership to a trademark simply through registration has caused concerns for many firms. When it sought to enter South Africa, McDonald's was frustrated to learn a local businessperson had already registered the McDonald's trademark for his own use. In a court case, the South African Supreme Court ruled in favor of the local entrepreneur. McDonald's eventually won on appeal but only after spending a significant

Source: Malcolm Fairman/Alamy

The Japanese firm Sanrio licenses its trademark characters to apparel and accessory manufacturers worldwide, generating substantial revenue. Shown here is the Hello Kitty store in Osaka, Japan.

sum in legal fees. In China, French apparel company Hermes lost the right to the Chinese version of its name because a local company had already registered it.[8]

Winnie the Pooh (winniethepooh.disney.com) is one of the biggest success stories of trademark licensing. Introduced as a character in children's literature in 1926, Pooh evolved into a multibillion-dollar licensing property. Disney acquired it in 1961. Pooh is the second-highest earning fictional character of all time, behind only Mickey Mouse. The Pooh image is licensed to many manufacturers for inclusion on a range of products from baby merchandise to textiles to gardening products. There are roughly 1,000 Pooh licensees in Europe alone.[9]

In many countries, a copyright gives the owner the exclusive right to reproduce the work, prepare derivative works, distribute copies, or perform or display the work publicly. Original works include art, music, and literature as well as computer software. The term of protection varies by country, but the creator's life plus 50 years is typical. Because many countries offer little or no copyright protection, it is wise to investigate local copyright laws before publishing a work abroad.[10]

Know-How Licensing

Know-how agreement
Contract in which the focal firm provides technological or management knowledge about how to design, manufacture, or deliver a product or a service.

Gaining access to technology is an important rationale for licensing. A **know-how agreement** is a contract in which the focal firm provides technological or management knowledge about how to design, manufacture, or deliver a product or a service to a licensee in exchange for a royalty. The royalty may be a lump sum, a *running royalty* based on the volume of products produced from the know-how, or a combination of both.

In some industries, such as pharmaceuticals and semiconductors, inventions and other intellectual property are acquired in reciprocal licensing arrangements between firms in the same or similar industries. Known as *cross-licensing*, the practice is common in industries with rapid technological advances that often build on each other. Technology licensing from competitors reduces the cost of innovation by avoiding duplication of research while reducing the risk of excluding any one firm from access to new developments.

AT&T (www.att.com) once held most of the key patents in the semiconductor industry. As more firms entered the industry and the pace of research and development (R&D) quickened, AT&T risked being surpassed by competitors in Europe, Japan, and the United States, where thousands of semiconductor patents were being awarded. In such a complex network of patents, few firms would have succeeded without obtaining licenses from competitors. AT&T, Intel, Siemens, and numerous other competitors began licensing their patents to each other, creating synergies that greatly accelerated innovation in semiconductors.

In the pharmaceutical industry, the R&D expense to develop new drugs can reach billions of dollars. Pharmaceutical firms want to launch new medicines as quickly as possible to recoup these costs and to expedite product development. Thus, the firms frequently cross-license technologies to each other, exchanging scientific knowledge about producing specific products as well as the right to distribute them in certain geographic regions.[11] In other industries, firms may license technology and know-how from competitors to compensate for insufficient knowledge, fill gaps in their product lineups, enter new businesses, or save time and money.

The World's Top Licensing Firms

Exhibit 15.2 lists the world's leading licensing firms by annual revenues. The greatest amount of licensing occurs in the apparel, games, and toy industries. In 2009, Disney acquired Marvel Entertainment for $4 billion, greatly expanding Disney's inventory of licensed assets. Licensing sales have benefited immensely from the emergence of large-scale retailers such as Carrefour, Walmart, and Amazon.com.

15.3 Describe the advantages and disadvantages of licensing.

Advantages and Disadvantages of Licensing

Exhibit 15.3 summarizes the advantages and disadvantages of licensing from the perspective of the licensor. Let's highlight some key points.

EXHIBIT 15.2 Leading Licensors Ranked by Licensing Revenues (total retail sales of licensed products)

Rank	Firm Name	Annual Licensing Revenues (U.S. $ billions)	Typical Deals
1	The Walt Disney Company	$45.1	Toy and apparel licensing for Disney movies such as *Little Mermaid* and *Toy Story* and characters such as Winnie the Pooh and Frozen Princess
2	PVH Corporation	18.0	Apparel licensing for such brands as Tommy Hilfiger and Calvin Klein
3	Meredith	17.7	Bedding, furniture, and other products related to the *Better Homes and Gardens* brand
4	ICONIX	13.1	Apparel licensing for such brands as OP, Umbro, and Danskin
5	Mattel	9.0	Toy manufacturer and licensor of iconic toy and game brands such as Barbie, Hot Wheels, and UNO
6	Sanrio	6.5	Toys and apparel tied to the Hello Kitty character
7	Warner Bros. Consumer Products	6.0	Toy and apparel licensing from movies such as Batman, Harry Potter, and The Hobbit
8	Major League Baseball	5.5	Baseball-related video games, apparel, toys
9	Nickelodeon	5.5	Toy and apparel licensing for TV programs such as SpongeBob SquarePants and Teenage Mutant Ninja Turtles
10	Hasbro	5.1	Toy and apparel licensing for TV programs and movies such as *My Little Pony* and *Transformers*

Sources: Based on annual reports of the individual firms; Company profiles at www.hoovers.com; Avanstar, *Global License!*, "The Top 150 Global Licensors," May 1, 2015, pp. T1–T47, www.licensemag.com.

EXHIBIT 15.3 Advantages and Disadvantages of Licensing to the Licensor

Advantages	Disadvantages
• Does not require capital investment or presence of the licensor in the foreign market • Ability to generate royalty income from existing intellectual property • Appropriate for entering markets that pose substantial country risk • Useful when trade barriers reduce the viability of exporting or when governments restrict ownership of local operations by foreign firms • Useful for testing a foreign market prior to entry via FDI • Useful as a strategy to preemptively enter a market before rivals	• Revenues are usually more modest than with other entry strategies • Difficult to maintain control over how the licensed asset is used • Risk of losing control of important intellectual property, or dissipating it to competitors • The licensee may infringe the licensor's intellectual property and become a competitor • Does not guarantee a basis for future expansion in the market • Not ideal for products, services, or knowledge that are highly complex • Dispute resolution is complex and may not produce satisfactory results

Advantages of Licensing

Licensing requires neither substantial capital investment nor direct involvement of the licensor in the foreign market. Unlike other entry strategies, the licensor need not establish a physical presence in the market or maintain inventory there. Simultaneously, the licensee benefits by gaining access to a key technology at a much lower cost and in less time than if it had developed the technology itself.[12] Licensing makes entry possible in countries that restrict foreign ownership in security-sensitive industries such as defense and energy. Licensing also facilitates entry in markets that are difficult to enter because of trade barriers, tariffs, and bureaucratic requirements, which usually apply only to exporting or FDI.

Licensing can be used as a low-cost strategy to test the viability of foreign markets. By establishing a relationship with a local licensee, the foreign firm can learn about the target market and devise the best future strategy for establishing a more durable presence there. For example, Swiss pharmaceutical manufacturer Roche entered a licensing agreement with Chugai Pharmaceuticals in Japan, where success requires substantial knowledge of the local market and the drug approval process. The relationship accelerated Roche's penetration of the huge Japanese market.[13] Licensing can also help the firm develop its brand name in a target market and preempt the later entry of competitors.

Disadvantages of Licensing

From the licensor's standpoint, licensing is a relatively passive entry strategy. However, the licensor must take steps to enforce the licensing agreement. The licensor needs to ensure that licensees are paying the appropriate royalties and are not violating the licensor's intellectual property. Profits tend to be lower than those from exporting or FDI. Licensing does not guarantee a basis for future expansion. To earn royalties, the licensor must rely on the licensee's sales and marketing prowess. A weak partner will generate only meager royalties. Also, licensing provides limited control over how the licensor's asset is used. If the licensee produces a substandard product, the licensor's reputation can be harmed. To avoid such problems, experienced firms require foreign licensees to meet minimum quality and performance standards. For example, Budweiser beer is made and distributed in Japan through a licensing arrangement with Kirin (www.kirin.co.jp/company/english). Kirin is one of Japan's most reputable brewers and produces the beer according to Budweiser's strict standards.

If the licensee is very successful, the licensor may regret not entering the market through a more lucrative entry strategy. This happened to Disney, which developed Disneyland Tokyo through a licensing arrangement with a Japanese partner. When the theme park proved more successful than originally forecast, Disney management wished it had used FDI to develop Disneyland Tokyo itself. In Mexico, Televisa (www.televisa.com), the largest producer of Spanish-language TV programming, opted for a licensing arrangement with California-based Univision to enter the U.S. market. Although there are approximately 40 million native Spanish speakers in the United States, Televisa received only a fraction of Univision's Spanish market advertising revenue.

Because licensing requires sharing intellectual property with other firms, the risk of creating a future competitor is substantial.[14] The rival might exploit the licensor's intellectual property by entering third countries or creating products based on knowledge gained in the relationship. This has occurred in the automobile, computer chip, and consumer electronics industries in Asia as Western firms have transferred process technologies to firms in China, Japan, and South Korea. Japan's Sony (www.sony.com) originally licensed transistor technology from U.S. inventor Bell Laboratories to make hearing aids. But instead, Sony used the technology to create small, battery-powered transistor radios and soon grew to become a global leader in this product category.[15]

The U.S. toymaker Mattel licensed rights to distribute the Barbie doll to the Brazilian toymaker Estrela (www.estrela.com.br). Once the agreement expired, Estrela developed its own Barbie look-alike—Susi—which surpassed sales of Barbie dolls in Brazil. Estrela then launched the Susi doll throughout South America to great success. In Japan, Mattel entered a licensing agreement with local toymaker Takara (www.takaratomy.co.jp), which adapted the Barbie doll for Japanese girls. When the agreement expired, Takara continued to sell the doll under the name "Jenny," becoming a competitor to Mattel in the world's second-biggest toy market.[16]

Source: Eddie Gerald/Alamy

Licensors run the risk of creating competitors, as Mattel discovered when it granted a license to a Brazilian firm to market Barbie dolls. The latter firm went on to create a competitor to Barbie, the Susi doll.

Franchising as an Entry Strategy

Franchising is an advanced form of licensing in which the focal firm, the *franchisor*, allows an entrepreneur, the *franchisee*, the right to use an entire business system in exchange for compensation. As with licensing, an explicit contract defines the terms of the relationship. McDonald's, Subway, Hertz, and FedEx are well-established international franchisors. Others that use franchising to expand abroad include Benetton, Body Shop, Yves Rocher, and Marks & Spencer. Franchising is common in international retailing. However, some retailers such as IKEA and Starbucks favor direct investment and internationalize through company-owned outlets. Ownership provides these firms with greater control over foreign operations but also typically restricts their ability to expand more rapidly abroad.

Franchises generate the biggest volume of sales in advanced economies such as the United States, Europe, and Japan. However, a large number of franchises are found in countries that are less economically developed in Asia. Many of these are *micro-franchises*, operated by one or two people. Franchising is a major job creator in developing economies in Asia and Latin America, helping to raise living standards. A large proportion of franchises in Africa and less-developed Asia are international.[17]

Exhibit 15.4 shows the nature of the franchising agreement. Most firms undertake *business format franchising* (sometimes called *system franchising*).[18] The franchisor transfers to the franchisee a total business method, including production and marketing methods, sales systems, procedures, and management know-how, as well as the use of its name and usage rights for products, patents, and trademarks.[19] The franchisor also provides the franchisee with training, ongoing support, incentive programs, and the right to participate in cooperative marketing programs.

In return, the franchisee pays some type of compensation to the franchisor, usually a royalty representing a percentage of the franchisee's revenues. The franchisee may be required to purchase certain equipment and supplies from the franchisor to ensure standardized products and consistent quality. Burger King and Subway require franchisees to buy food preparation equipment from specified suppliers.

Whereas licensing relationships are often short-lived, franchising parties normally establish an ongoing relationship that may last many years. This results in a more stable long-term entry strategy. In addition, franchisors often combine franchising with other entry strategies. For example, about 70 percent of Body Shop's approximately 2,500 stores in some 60 countries are operated by franchisees. Body Shop (www.thebodyshop.com) headquarters owns the rest. Large retailers such as Carrefour often employ both franchising and FDI when expanding abroad.

15.4 Understand franchising as an entry strategy.

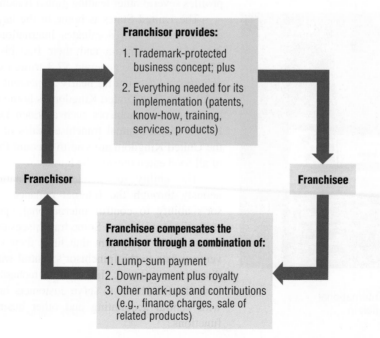

EXHIBIT 15.4

Franchising as a Foreign Market Entry Strategy

Franchising is more comprehensive than licensing because the franchisor prescribes virtually all of the business activities of the franchisee. The franchisor tightly controls the business system to ensure consistent standards. International franchisors employ globally recognized trademarks and attempt to guarantee the customer a uniform retail experience and consistent product quality.

Completely standardized business activities, however, are difficult to replicate across diverse markets. Differences in local tastes, available ingredients, and physical space may necessitate changes to the franchise formula. McDonald's offers teriyaki burgers in Japan, wine in France, and a McPork sandwich in Spain. In China, KFC offers shredded carrots, fungus, and bamboo shoots instead of the coleslaw it sells in Western countries.[20] Limited land in Japan forced KFC to reconfigure its cooking equipment from a wide horizontal design to a narrower, more vertical design that saves space. Japanese KFCs are often multistoried restaurants to save on the high cost of land. The challenge is to strike the right balance, adapting the format to respond to local markets without affecting the overall image and service of the franchise.[21]

Some focal firms may choose to work with a single, coordinating franchisee in a particular country or region. In this **master franchise** arrangement, an independent company is licensed to establish, develop, and manage the entire franchising network in its market. The master franchisee has the right to sub-franchise to other independent businesses and thus assume the role of the local franchisor. McDonald's is organized this way in Japan. By delegating the responsibilities of identifying and working with its franchisees directly, the focal firm gives up considerable control over its foreign market operations. From the focal firm's perspective, however, the arrangement is the least capital- and time-intensive.

Master franchisees prefer this arrangement because it provides them with an exclusive, large, predefined territory (often an entire country) and substantial scale economies from operating numerous sales outlets simultaneously. They gain access to a proven retailing and marketing concept and partnership with a corporate headquarters and master franchisees in other territories, which typically provide support, know-how, and the latest innovations in the field. Master franchising accounts for as much as 80 percent of international franchising deals. Sbarro, Inc., the pizza chain, operates through master franchises in Belgium, Canada, Guatemala, Kuwait, the Philippines, and the United Kingdom.[22]

Master franchise
Arrangement in which an independent company is licensed to establish, develop, and manage the entire franchising network in its market and has the right to sub-franchise to other franchisees, assuming the role of local franchisor.

Who Are the Top Global Franchisors?

Franchising is a global phenomenon and accounts for a large proportion of international trade in services, especially fast-food outlets, professional business services, home improvement, and various types of retailers. Yum! Brands, Inc., owns the KFC, Pizza Hut, and Taco Bell brands of franchised restaurants. KFC has approximately 5,000 stores in China, and Pizza Hut has roughly 1,600 stores in China, making Yum! one of the largest retail developers in China.[23] Exhibit 15.5 profiles several other leading global franchisors.

The United States is home to the largest number of franchisors and dominates international franchising. U.S. franchisors and their franchisees employ 21 million people, generate $2.3 trillion of economic activity, and account for nearly 50 percent of total U.S. retail sales. The United Kingdom is home to numerous home-grown franchisors such as Eden Delicious and Perfect Pizza. Annual franchised sales of fast food in the United Kingdom are said to account for 30 percent of all food eaten outside the home.[24]

The ability to exchange information instantaneously through the Internet enhances the franchisor's ability to control international operations and saves time and money. Some franchisees use electronic point-of-sale equipment that links their sales and inventory data to the franchisor's central warehouse and distribution network. Information technology also allows the franchisor to serve customers or franchisees with central accounting and other business process functions.

Source: RosaIreneBetancourt 7/Alamy

Franchising accounts for a large proportion of international retailing. This 7-Eleven store is in a subway station in Shanghai, China.

EXHIBIT 15.5 Leading International Franchisors

Franchisor	Type of Business	International Profile	Example Markets
Hertz	Car rental and dealer agencies	11,555 franchises in 150 countries	China, Germany, Mexico, Russia
McDonald's	Hamburger restaurants	36,260 restaurants in 120 countries	Canada, France, United Kingdom, Australia, China
KFC	Chicken, sandwiches, pot pies restaurants	17,000 outlets in 119 countries	Brazil, China, Japan, France
Subway	Submarine sandwiches, bagels, salad restaurants	44,000 restaurants in 110 countries	Canada, Australia, United Kingdom, New Zealand, Germany
Pizza Hut	Pizza, pasta, chicken wings restaurants	15,600 outlets in 90 countries	China, Brazil, Canada, Japan
Burger King	Hamburger restaurants	13,000 franchises in 87 countries	Denmark, Ecuador, South Africa, Thailand
Wyndham Hotels and Resorts	Hotels, including Days Inn, Howard Johnson, Ramada, Super 8	7,670 locations in 70 countries	Brazil, China, France, South Korea
Dunkin Donuts	Coffee and donut shops	18,000 restaurants in 60 countries	China, Japan, Taiwan
Curves	Women's fitness and weight-loss centers	10,000 centers in 60 countries	Brazil, France, Mexico, Australia, Ireland, United Kingdom
7-Eleven	Convenience stores	47,700 stores in 16 countries	Japan, Thailand, Mexico, United States

Sources: Based on Entrepreneur.com; Hoovers.com; Franchise Direct, "The Top 100 Global Franchises," 2015, www.franchisedirect.com; company websites and reports.

As markets in Europe and other advanced economies become saturated, franchisors are expanding to emerging markets. Subway is doing big business in Eastern Europe. Avis car rental enjoys much success in Latin America. Ben & Jerry's ice cream is a favorite in Thailand and Turkey. About 70 percent of the countries where KFC does business are developing economies.

Estimates suggest international franchised companies provide more than 2.4 million jobs in developing economies. Franchises help provide needed modernization in business methods, distribution networks, and commercial infrastructure. They help build local capabilities and skills by both bringing in expatriate staff and training local personnel. Because franchising is less risky, it is often preferred over FDI for entering developing economies.[25]

Advantages and Disadvantages of Franchising

15.5 Explain the advantages and disadvantages of franchising.

In an ideal relationship, franchisor and franchisee complement each other. The franchisor possesses economies of scale, a wealth of intellectual property, and know-how about its industry; the franchisee has entrepreneurial drive and substantial knowledge about the local market and how to run a business there. A large pool of well-chosen franchisees greatly enhances the speed and quality of the franchisor's performance abroad.[26] For example, KFC internationalized quickly and performed well worldwide by developing franchisees in more than 115 countries with some 17,000 restaurants serving more than 12 million customers per day.

The Franchisor Perspective

Exhibit 15.6 highlights the advantages and disadvantages of franchising to the franchisor. Firms prefer franchising when they lack the capital or international experience to establish themselves abroad through FDI or when offering the product through exporting or basic licensing is ineffective as an internationalization strategy. Foreign markets often provide greater profitability than the home market. For example, the Beijing KFC store has generated more sales than any

EXHIBIT 15.6 **Advantages and Disadvantages of Franchising to the Franchisor**

Advantages	Disadvantages
• Entry into numerous foreign markets can be accomplished quickly and cost effectively • No need to invest substantial capital • Established brand name encourages early and ongoing sales potential abroad • The firm can leverage franchisees' knowledge to efficiently navigate and develop local markets	• Maintaining control over franchisee may be difficult • Conflicts with franchisee are likely, including legal disputes • Preserving franchisor's image in the foreign market may be challenging • Requires monitoring and evaluating performance of franchisees, and providing ongoing assistance • Franchisees may take advantage of acquired knowledge and become competitors in the future

other KFC outlet worldwide partly due to the novelty and popularity of the offering and the lack of direct competition. Governments in host countries often encourage franchising by foreign entrants because most of the profits and investment remain in the local economy.

For the franchisor, franchising is a low-risk, low-cost entry strategy. It offers the ability to develop international markets relatively quickly and on a larger scale than possible for most nonfranchise firms. The franchisor can generate profit with only incremental investments in capital, staff, production, and distribution.

The major disadvantages include the need to maintain control over potentially thousands of outlets worldwide and the risk of creating competitors. When the franchising agreement is terminated, some franchisees leverage their newly acquired knowledge to remain in business, often by slightly altering the franchisor's brand name or trademark. Franchisees may also jeopardize the franchisor's image by not upholding its standards. Dunkin' Donuts experienced problems in Russia when it discovered some franchisees were selling vodka along with donuts.

When the franchisor depends heavily on a foreign partner as master franchisee, it is critical to cultivate friendly, durable relationships. However, even experienced franchisors encounter major problems. In 2010, nearly 30 years after opening its first outlet in Japan, restaurant chain Wendy's could not reach a new agreement with its Japanese master franchisee, Zensho Company, and chose to close its restaurants there. The move disappointed countless Japanese fans, who formed long lines in front of Wendy's outlets in the days before the chain shut down. By 2013, however, Wendy's reestablished itself in Japan through a joint venture with Higa Industries.[27]

Another major challenge is to become familiar with foreign laws and regulations. The European Union has strict laws that favor the franchisee, sometimes hampering the franchisor's ability to maintain control over operations. Laws and foreign exchange circumstances affect the payment of royalties.

The Franchisee Perspective

Exhibit 15.7 highlights the advantages and disadvantages of franchising from the franchisee's perspective. Entrepreneurs that open a franchised store benefit from the franchisor's established formula. Customers are more likely to patronize a well-known franchise, which helps the franchisee succeed more quickly. Franchising is especially beneficial to SMEs, many of which lack substantial resources and strong managerial skills. The big advantage is the ability to launch a business by using a tested business model. In essence, franchising amounts to cloning best practices. It greatly increases the small firm's chances for success by duplicating a tried-and-true business format.[28]

However, starting a franchise is usually costly and may require the franchisee to build a shop or invest in expensive equipment. Unlike independent store owners, franchisees must satisfy the franchisor's demands. This can be problematic for international franchisees when the franchisor knows little about foreign markets or how to do business there.

EXHIBIT 15.7 Advantages and Disadvantages of Franchising to the Franchisee

Advantages	Disadvantages
• Gain a well-known, recognizable brand name • Acquire training and know-how; receive ongoing support from the franchisor • Operate an independent business • Increase likelihood of business success • Become part of an established international network	• Initial investment or royalty payments may be substantial • Franchisee is required to purchase supplies, equipment, and products from the franchisor only • The franchisor holds much power, including superior bargaining power • Franchisor's outlets may proliferate in the region, creating competition for the franchisee • Franchisor may impose inappropriate technical or managerial systems on the Franchisee

Managerial Guidelines for Licensing and Franchising

Licensing and franchising are complex undertakings and require skillful research, planning, and execution. The focal firm must conduct advance research on the host country's laws on intellectual property, repatriation of royalties, and contracting with local partners. Key challenges of the focal firm include establishing whose national law takes precedence for interpreting and enforcing the contract, deciding whether to grant an exclusive or nonexclusive arrangement, and determining the geographic scope of territory to be granted to the foreign partner.

As with other entry strategies, the key to success is often finding the right partner abroad. The focal firm should carefully identify, screen, and train potential partners who are unlikely to become competitors in the future. The most qualified franchisees tend to have entrepreneurial drive, access to capital and prime real estate, a successful business track record, good relationships with local and national government agencies, strong links to other firms (including facilitators), a pool of motivated employees, and a willingness to accept oversight and follow company procedures. In emerging markets, a knowledgeable, locally connected partner can help sort through various operational problems. In China and Russia, partnering with a state-owned enterprise may be necessary to gain access to key resources and navigate legal and political environments.

For franchisors, developing capable partners in local supply chains is also a prerequisite. Franchisees need a reliable supply chain to obtain input products and supplies. In developing economies and emerging markets, host-country suppliers may be inadequate for providing a sufficient quantity or quality of input goods. In Turkey, Little Caesars pizza franchisees found it difficult to locate dairy companies that could produce the cheese varieties they required. In other countries, KFC developed its own supply-chain network, ensuring dependable delivery of chicken and other critical inputs. In Russia and Thailand, McDonald's had to develop its own supply lines for potatoes to ensure the quality of its french fries. When McDonald's first entered India, it faced resistance from the government. Relations improved as the government recognized that McDonald's would work with Indian farmers to improve the country's agricultural practices and was committed to being a good corporate citizen.

Other Contractual Entry Strategies

15.6 Understand other contractual entry strategies.

Licensing and franchising are especially salient contractual entry strategies. In addition, firms employ other contract-based approaches to venture abroad. Global sourcing is a specific type of international contracting that we addressed in Chapter 13. Other types of contractual agreements deal with building major construction projects, manufacturing products under contract, providing management and marketing services, or leasing major assets. Here, we discuss turnkey contracting, build-operate-transfer arrangements, management contracts, and leasing.

Turnkey contracting
Arrangement in which the focal firm or a consortium of firms plans, finances, organizes, manages, and implements all phases of a project abroad and then hands it over to a foreign customer after training local workers.

Build-operate-transfer (BOT)
Arrangement in which the firm or a consortium of firms contracts to build a major facility abroad, operate it for a specified period, and then transfer control to the project sponsor, typically the host-country government or public utility.

Turnkey Contracting

Turnkey contracting is an arrangement in which the focal firm or a consortium of firms plans, finances, organizes, manages, and implements all phases of a project abroad and then hands it over to a foreign customer after training local workers.

Contractors are typically firms in construction, engineering, design, and architectural services. In a typical turnkey project, a contractor builds a major facility (such as a nuclear power plant or a subway system), puts it into operation, and then hands it over to the project sponsor, often a national government. The contractor may provide follow-up services such as testing and operational support.

Among the most popular turnkey projects are extensions and upgrades to metro systems. These include bridges, roadways, and railways and the construction of airports, harbors, refineries, and hospitals. Such projects are financed largely from public budgets. Most large-scale infrastructure projects are in the Mideast and East Asia, where industrialization and growing affluence are driving demand. In Abu Dhabi, a collection of companies received a multibillion-dollar contract to build an integrated processing plant for natural gas. The team included JGC of Japan, Tecnimont of Italy, and Hyundai Engineering & Construction of South Korea. HDEC has built industrial, infrastructure, commercial, and multifamily residential projects in about 50 countries.[29]

Other examples are Hochtief AG of Germany and Skanska AB of Sweden. These top construction companies have undertaken some of the world's most important infrastructure projects, such as the Three Gorges Dam in China and the Chunnel linking England to France. California-based Bechtel participated in projects such as the renovation of London's 140-year-old subway, the cleanup of the Chernobyl nuclear plant in Russia, and construction of nuclear power plants in South Korea. In Russia, a consortium of firms is building a huge power plant in the Arkhangelsk region to support the thriving mining industry there.[30]

Source: Zharastudio/Fotolia

The spectacular Petronas Twin Towers complex in Kuala Lumpur, Malaysia, was a turnkey project built by Bovis Lend Lease, a leading project management and construction company. Among the firms with offices in the Towers are Accenture, Al Jazeera English, Huawei Technologies, Microsoft, and Reuters.

Build-Operate-Transfer Arrangements (BOT)

Under a **build-operate-transfer (BOT)** arrangement, a firm or consortium of firms contracts to build a major facility abroad, such as a dam or water treatment plant; operates it for a specified period; and then transfers ownership to the project sponsor. The project sponsor is typically a government or public utility in the host country. In contrast to turnkey contracting, a unique feature of the BOT arrangement is that, instead of transferring control of the completed facility to the project sponsor, the builder first operates it for a number of years.

Although the consortium operates the facility, it can charge user fees, tolls, and rentals to recover its investment and generate profits. Or the host-country government can pay the BOT partner for services provided by the facility, such as water from a treatment plant, at a price calculated over the life of the contract, to cover its construction and operating costs and provide a reasonable return.

Governments often grant BOT concessions to get needed infrastructure built cost effectively. Typical projects include sewage treatment plants, highways, airports, mass transit systems, and telecommunications networks. In Vietnam, rapid growth in industry and tourism has greatly increased demand for electric power. The Vietnamese government commissioned the construction of the 720 megawatt *Phu My 3* power plant, the country's first privately owned major energy facility, as a BOT project by Siemens Power Generation (Germany). It is owned by a consortium that includes BP (United Kingdom) and Kyushu Electric Power (Japan).[31]

Management Contracts

Under a **management contract**, a contractor supplies managerial know-how to operate a hotel, hospital, airport, or other facility in exchange for compensation. The client organization receives assistance in managing local operations, and the management company generates revenues without having to make a capital investment. Much of Disney's income from its theme parks in France and Japan comes from providing management services for the parks, which are largely owned by other interests. BAA Limited manages the retailing and catering operations of various airports in Europe and the United States. Using management contracts, Marriott and Four Seasons corporations run, but do not own, numerous luxury hotels around the world.

Management contracts can help foreign governments with infrastructure projects when the country lacks local people with the appropriate skills to operate them. Occasionally the offering of a management contract is the critical element in winning a bid for other types of entry strategies, such as BOT deals and turnkey operations. A key disadvantage of management contracts is that they involve training foreign firms that may become future competitors.[32]

Management contract
Arrangement in which a contractor supplies managerial know-how to operate a hotel, hospital, airport, or other facility in exchange for compensation.

Leasing

In international leasing, another contractual strategy, a focal firm (the lessor) rents out machinery or equipment to corporate or government clients abroad (lessees), often for several years at a time. The lessor retains ownership of the property throughout the lease period and receives regular payments from the lessee. From the perspective of the lessee, leasing helps reduce the costs of using needed machinery and equipment. A major advantage for the lessor is the ability to gain quick access to target markets while putting assets to use earning profits. In some countries, firms opt to lease rather than buy needed equipment due to tax benefits. International leasing benefits developing economies that may lack the financial resources to purchase needed equipment.

Amsterdam-based ING Lease International Equipment Management owns and leases Boeing commercial aircraft to clients such as Brazil's Varig airlines. Dubai-based Oasis Leasing leases aircraft to Air New Zealand, Virgin Express, and Macedonian Airlines. One of the top leasing firms is Japan's ORIX (www.orix.co.jp), which leases everything from computers and measuring equipment to aircraft and ships. The firm operates 2,000 offices worldwide and generated more than $13 billion in sales in 2014.

The Special Case of Internationalization by Professional Service Firms

Professional services include such industries as accounting, advertising, market research, consulting, engineering, legal counsel, and IT services. Firms in these industries have internationalized rapidly during the past three decades. Some have simply followed their key clients abroad. The Internet supports the international spread of some business process services such as software engineering, which is increasingly centralized in cost-effective locations such as India and Eastern Europe.

When they internationalize, professional service firms encounter three unique challenges.

- Professional qualifications that allow firms to practice law, dentistry, medicine, or accounting in the home country are rarely recognized by other countries. If you are a licensed accountant in your country and want to practice accounting in some other country, you usually must earn local certification there.
- Professionals who work abroad for long periods generally must obtain employment visas in the countries where they are employed.
- Professional services often require intensive interaction with the local public, which necessitates language and cultural skills.[33]

Professional service firms employ a mix of direct investment and contractual strategies to enter foreign markets. Publicis Groupe is an advertising agency headquartered in France. It maintains a network of company-owned branches and enters contractual relationships with independent local firms around the world. Focal firms in professional services are likely to serve their major markets with direct investment and operate company-owned offices there. In small markets, however, they will enter contractual relationships with independent partner firms in the same line of business, typically known as *agents, affiliates,* or *representatives.* PriceWaterhouseCoopers, a leading accounting firm, contracts with indigenous accounting firms in smaller markets where it chooses not to have its own offices. Focal firms with limited international experience often prefer to employ foreign partners that can provide international business know-how.

 MyManagementLab   **Watch It!**

If your professor has assigned this, go to the Assignments section of **mymanagementlab.com** to complete the video exercise titled MyGym (Mexico): Entry Strategy and Strategic Alliances.

15.7 Understand infringement of intellectual property, a global problem.

Infringement of intellectual property
Unauthorized use, publication, or reproduction of products or services protected by a patent, copyright, trademark, or other intellectual property right.

Infringement of Intellectual Property: A Global Problem

We have seen that working with independent partners through contractual arrangements provides the focal firm with only moderate control over foreign partners. Safeguarding intellectual property and foreign operations under contractual arrangements is usually challenging. Laws that govern contractual obligations are not always clear, conflicts arise due to cultural and language differences, and contract enforcement abroad is often costly or unattainable.

Infringement of intellectual property is the unauthorized use, publication, or reproduction of products and services protected by a patent, copyright, trademark, or other intellectual property right. Such a violation amounts to piracy—production and distribution of counterfeit goods. Counterfeiting and piracy can be particularly troublesome in emerging markets and developing economies, where intellectual property laws are often weak or poorly enforced.[34]

The International Chamber of Commerce estimates the total annual value of counterfeit and pirated goods crossing borders and traded online worldwide may be as much as $1.7 trillion.[35] The most commonly counterfeited goods include jewelry and accessories, apparel, consumer electronics, pharmaceutical drugs, and optical media such as CDs and DVDs. For example, annual piracy losses in CDs and music exceed $100 million in Brazil, and losses in business software exceed $1 billion in Russia.[36] Counterfeiters may use a product name that differs only slightly from that of a well-known brand; it is similar enough that buyers associate it with the genuine product but just different enough so that prosecution is hampered. Although firms such as Rolex and Tommy Hilfiger are well-known victims, counterfeiting is also common in such industrial products as medical devices and car parts. Counterfeiters even have faked entire motor vehicles. Authorities uncovered 23 unauthorized Apple stores in southeast China, selling fake iPads and counterfeit smartphones.[37]

Cisco Systems sued its Chinese joint venture partner, Huawei Technologies Co., for pirating its networking software and infringing patents. The lawsuit also cited Huawei, the largest telecommunications equipment manufacturer in China, for illegally using technical documentation that Cisco had copyrighted in its own product manuals.[38] Although Microsoft Windows and Office products dominate the software market, the firm receives no payment when unauthorized parties copy and distribute its software. Up to 90 percent of computer software in Russia may be pirated. As a result, Microsoft sells its products mainly to corporate customers. The firm has battled piracy even among the employees in its Russian subsidiary.[39]

Ethical Connections

Counterfeiting is not confined to lower-income countries. Raids of retail outlets in the United States net millions of dollars' worth of counterfeit products every year. In 2014, for example, city and federal authorities in New York arrested numerous people on charges of possessing millions of dollars in counterfeit fashions, including Gucci watches, Louis Vuitton handbags, North Face jackets, and much more.

Source: WWD: Women's Wear Daily, "Raid by N.Y. Police and Feds Nets $2 Million in Fakes," December 10, 2014, p. 1.

The Internet has added a new dimension to international piracy. In Russia, websites sell popular music downloads for as little as 5 cents each or less than $1 for an entire CD. The sites are easily accessed by shoppers in countries where they are outlawed under intellectual property laws and use low prices to attract music fans worldwide. Fake medications sold through the Internet account for a significant percentage of prescription drugs sold online. Consumers have died from consuming fake medications.[40]

When consumers buy counterfeit goods, payments accrue not to the firm that invented the product but, rather, to illicit enterprises. Counterfeiting negatively affects consumer attitudes about the branding and quality of legitimate goods. The quality of counterfeit goods is almost always inferior to that of the original, proprietary goods that they duplicate. In these and other ways, counterfeiting and piracy erode the firm's brand equity and competitive advantage. Where counterfeiting and piracy are commonplace, companies are reluctant to invent, innovate, and market legitimate products, which reduces consumer choices and ultimately lowers living standards.

Guidelines for Protecting Intellectual Property

In advanced economies, intellectual property is usually protected within established legal systems and methods of recourse. A firm can initiate legal action against someone who infringes on its intellectual assets and will usually achieve a satisfactory remedy. Advanced economies have taken the lead in signing treaties that support international protection of intellectual property, including the Paris Convention for the Protection of Industrial Property, the Berne Convention for the Protection of Literary and Artistic Works, and the Rome Convention for the Protection of Performers and Broadcasting Organizations. The World Intellectual Property Organization (WIPO; www.wipo.int) is an agency of the United Nations that administers these multilateral agreements.

The World Trade Organization (WTO; www.wto.org) created the Agreement on Trade-Related Aspects of Intellectual Property Rights (TRIPS), a comprehensive international treaty that lays out remedies, dispute-resolution procedures, and enforcements to protect intellectual property. The WTO is pressuring member countries to comply with the accord and can discipline violators through the dispute settlement mechanism. At the same time, TRIPS provides exceptions that benefit developing economies, such as the ability to access needed patent medication for ailments such as AIDS.

Although most countries are signatories to WIPO, TRIPS, and various treaties, intellectual property infringements remain a huge problem. Rights granted by a patent, trademark registration, or copyright apply only in the country where they are obtained; they confer no protection abroad. Enforcement depends on the attitudes of local officials, substantive requirements of the law, and court procedures. As a result, former licensees and franchisees can launch illicit businesses using proprietary knowledge to which they are no longer entitled.

Experienced firms devise sophisticated approaches to reduce the likelihood of intellectual property violations and help avoid their adverse effects, especially in countries with weak property rights protection.[41]

Protecting Intellectual Property (IP)
To protect its IP, the firm should:

- Research to understand IP laws and protections in target countries.

- Register core IP in each country where it does business.

- Separate value-chain activities to maintain IP secrecy. For example, keep R&D and manufacturing separate so suppliers cannot learn the entire production process.

- Emphasize leading-edge or hard-to-understand technologies. The latest know-how is usually harder to imitate than older technologies.

- Hire employees who maintain high ethical standards.

- Collaborate with ethical partners. Choose reputable suppliers with no history of IP violations.

- Regularly educate employees and partners about the harm of violating IP rights.
- Include provisions in partner contracts that protect IP.
- Develop trusting relations with partners.
- Perform audits to ensure that partners meet their responsibilities to protect the firm's IP.
- Pursue IP violators through prosecution and other legal means.
- Educate customers about the harm of infringing on IP.
- Cultivate contacts in local and national governments involved in IP laws and enforcement.
- Lobby governments for stronger IP protections.

Let's elaborate on some key strategies. Before undertaking contractual entry strategies abroad, management needs to understand local intellectual property laws and enforcement procedures, particularly when exposed assets are valuable. The firm should register patents, trademarks, trade secrets, and copyrights with local governments, especially in countries with weak antipiracy laws. Some companies lobby national governments and international organizations for stronger intellectual property laws and more vigilant enforcement, albeit with limited success.

Management must ensure that licensing and franchising agreements provide for oversight to ensure that intellectual property is used as intended. Licensing contracts should include provisions that require the licensee to share improvements or technological developments on the licensed asset with the licensor.[42] Noncompete clauses in employee contracts help prevent employees from serving competitors for some years after leaving the firm.[43]

Monitoring franchisee, distribution, and marketing channels for asset infringements helps avoid problems. The firm should monitor the activities of local business partners for potential leaks of vital information and assets.[44] Trade secrets must be guarded closely. Using password-based security systems, surveillance, and firewalls limits access to intellectual property. Intel and Microsoft release only limited information about key technologies to partner firms. The firm can deter much potential piracy by aggressively pursuing criminal prosecution or litigation against those who pilfer its logos, proprietary processes, and other key assets. Mead Data Central, Inc., owner of the Lexis-Nexis brand of computerized legal research services, sued Toyota when the Japanese firm began selling its new luxury automobiles under the Lexus name. The suit failed, but it showed Mead's determination to protect its assets.[45]

The firm should leverage technological approaches to minimize counterfeiting. Many companies build biotech tags, electronic signatures, or holograms into their products to differentiate them from fakes. In the long run, the best way to cope with infringement is to update technologies and products continuously. The firm that regularly renews its technologies can stay ahead of counterfeiters by marketing products that counterfeiters cannot imitate fast enough. Even when licensing violations occur, the firm is protected because the stolen property rapidly becomes obsolete.

Ultimately, when contractual strategies prove undesirable or ineffective, management may opt to enter target markets by FDI, through which the firm acquires ownership and, thus, greater control over important assets.

CLOSING CASE   Subway's Franchising Challenges in China

Subway, the sandwich and salad fast-food chain, operates the largest number of restaurants worldwide—more than 44,000 stores in 110 countries. Subway generates more than $19 billion in annual revenues and has more than 25 million Facebook fans.

The franchising chain opened its first international restaurant in Bahrain in 1984. Since then, Subway (www.subway.com) has expanded worldwide and generates about one-fifth of its annual revenues internationally. The firm expects foreign markets to contribute much of its future growth.

Subway is one of the most successful fast-food chains in China. Fish and tuna salad sandwiches are the top sellers. By 2006, Subway had opened about 40 stores in China. The franchise had its share of initial setbacks. Subway's master franchisee in Beijing, Jim Bryant, lost money to a scheming partner and had to teach the franchising concept to a country that had never heard of it. Until recently, there was no word in Chinese for *franchise*.

Cultural problems are still an ongoing challenge. After Bryant opened his first Subway shop, customers stood outside and watched for a few days. When they finally tried to buy a sandwich, many were confused so Bryant printed signs explaining how to order. Some didn't believe the tuna salad was made from fish because they could not see the head or tail. Others didn't like the idea of touching their food, so they would gradually peel off the paper wrapping and eat the sandwich like a banana. To make matters worse, few customers liked sandwiches. Subway has had to create menu items that suit local tastes, such as Roasted Duck Sub.

Subway—or Sai Bei Wei (Mandarin for "tastes better than others")—has forged ahead. Bryant has recruited numerous committed franchisees that he monitors closely to maintain quality. He recruited local entrepreneurs, trained them to become franchisees, and served as liaison between them and Subway headquarters. For this work, he received half of their $10,000 initial fee and one-third of their 8 percent royalty fees. Today, there are about 500 Subway stores in China.

Other multinational franchisors still face significant challenges in China, particularly in dealing with the ambiguous legal environment, finding appropriate partners, and identifying the most suitable marketing, financing, and logistics strategies. Famous brands such as A&W, Dunkin' Donuts, and Rainforest Cafe have all experienced these issues.

Why China for Franchising?

Franchising is an advanced form of licensing. On the surface, franchising in China is attractive because of its huge market, long-term growth potential, and dramatic rise in disposable income among its rapidly expanding urban population. Fast-food sales in China are around $150 billion per year. China's urban population, the target market for casual dining has expanded rapidly, a trend expected to continue. Increasingly hectic lifestyles have led to an increase in meals the Chinese eat outside the home. Surveys reveal that Chinese consumers are interested in sampling non-Chinese foods.

Market researchers have identified several major benefits to franchising in China.

- *A win–win proposition* Franchising in China combines the Western expertise of franchisors with the local market knowledge of franchisees. Many Chinese have strong entrepreneurial instincts and are eager to launch their own businesses.
- *Minimal entry costs.* Because much of the cost of launching a restaurant is borne by local entrepreneurs, franchising minimizes the costs to franchisors of entering the market.
- *Rapid expansion* By leveraging the resources of numerous local entrepreneurs, the franchisor can get set up quickly. Franchising is superior to other entry strategies for rapidly establishing many outlets throughout any new market.
- *Brand consistency* Because franchisors are required to adhere strictly to company operating procedures and policies, brand consistency is easier to maintain.
- *Circumvention of legal constraints* Franchising allows the focal firm to avoid trade barriers associated with exporting and FDI, common in China.

Challenges of Franchising in China

China's market also poses many challenges for franchisors.

- *Knowledge gap* Despite the likely pool of potential franchisees, Chinese entrepreneurs may have limited knowledge about how to start and operate a franchise business. There is still much confusion about franchising among lawmakers, entrepreneurs, and consumers. Focal firms must educate government officials, potential franchisees, and creditors on the basics of franchising, a process that consumes energy, time, and money.
- *Ambiguous legal environment* Franchisors need to examine China's legal system closely regarding contracts and intellectual property rights. China's legal system on franchising is evolving and has loopholes and ambiguities. Some critical elements are not covered. The situation has led to diverse interpretations of the legality of franchising in China. Franchisors must be vigilant about protecting trademarks. A local imitator can quickly dilute or damage a trademark a focal firm has built up through much expense and effort. Branding is important to franchising success, but consumers become confused if several similar brands are present. Chinese imitators have launched restaurants that use similar logos and menus and even accept coupons from Subway when consumers mix up the two stores.
- *Escalating start-up costs* Ordinarily, entry through franchising is cost effective. However, various challenges, combined with linguistic and cultural barriers, can increase the up-front investment and resource demands of new entrants in China and delay profitability. The franchisor may have to invest in store equipment and lease it to the franchisee, at least until the franchisee can afford to buy it. Franchisors must be patient. McDonald's has been in China since the early 1990s and has devoted substantial resources to building its brand, but few firms have its resources.

Perhaps the biggest challenge of launching franchises in China is finding the right partners. It is paradoxical that entrepreneurs with the capital to start a restaurant often lack the franchising business experience or entrepreneurial drive, whereas entrepreneurs with sufficient drive and expertise often lack the start-up capital. Subway's franchise fee of $10,000 is equivalent to two years' salary for the average Chinese. The banking system in China is still developing. Capital sources for small businesses are limited. Entrepreneurs often borrow funds from family members and friends to launch business ventures. Fortunately, Chinese banks are increasingly open to franchising. The Bank of China established a comprehensive credit line of $12 million for Kodak franchisees.

Availability and financing of suitable real estate are major considerations as well, particularly for initial showcase stores where location is critical. According to established Chinese law, local and foreign investors are allowed to develop, use, and administer real estate. But in many cases, the Chinese government owns real estate that is not available for individuals to purchase. Private property laws are underdeveloped, and franchisees occasionally risk eviction. Fortunately, a growing number of malls and shopping centers are good locations for franchised restaurants.

The Chinese authorities maintain restrictions on the repatriation of profits to the home country. Strict rules discourage repatriation of the initial investment, making this capital illiquid. To avoid this problem, firms make initial capital investments in stages to minimize the risk of not being able to withdraw overinvested funds. Fortunately, China is gradually relaxing its restrictions, and franchisors have been reinvesting their profits back into China to continue to fund the growth of their operations. Reinvesting profits also provides a natural hedge against exchange rate fluctuations.

Learning from the Success of Others

Experience has shown that new entrants to China often benefit from establishing a presence in Hong Kong and then moving inland to the southern provinces. Before it was absorbed by mainland China, Hong Kong was one of the world's leading capitalist economies. It is an excellent pro-business location to gain experience for doing business in China. In other cases, franchisors have launched stores in smaller Chinese cities, gaining experience there before expanding into more costly, competitive urban environments such as Beijing and Shanghai.

Franchisors typically must adapt offerings to suit local tastes. Appropriate suppliers and business infrastructure are often lacking. Franchisors spend much money to develop supplier and distribution networks. They also may need to build logistical infrastructure to move inputs from suppliers to individual stores. McDonald's has replicated its supply chain, bringing its key suppliers, such as potato supplier Simplot, to China. There is no one best approach in China. For instance, TGI Friday's imports roughly three-quarters of its food supplies, which helps maintain quality, but heavy importing is expensive and exposes profitability to exchange rate fluctuations.

AACSB: Reflective Thinking Skills, Multicultural and Diversity Understanding

Case Questions

15-4. Why might an organization enter into a know-how agreement rather than another form of entry strategy?

15-5. What do you think about Subway's method and level of compensating its master franchisee and regular franchisees in China? Is the method satisfactory? Is there room for improvement?

15-6. What are the advantages and disadvantages of franchising in China from Jim Bryant's perspective? What can Bryant do to overcome the disadvantages? From Subway's perspective, is franchising the best entry strategy for China?

⭐**15-7.** What is a master franchise and why might it be more valuable?

Sources: Carlye Adler, "How China Eats a Sandwich," *Fortune*, March 21, 2005, pp. F210B–F210D; Laurie Burkitt, Loretta Chao, Melissa Powers, and Yoli Zhang, "Made in China: Fake Stores," *Wall Street Journal*, August 3, 2011, pp. B1–B2; A. Dayal-Gulati and Angela Lee, *Kellogg on China: Strategies for Success* (Evanston, IL: Northwestern University Press, 2004); William Edwards, "The Pros and Consequences of Franchising in China," *Chinabusinessreview.com*, July–September, 2011, pp. 41–43; Richard Gibson, "Foreign Flavors: When Going Abroad, You Should Think of Franchising as a Cookie-Cutter Business; Unless, of Course, You Want to Succeed," *Wall Street Journal*, September 25, 2006, p. R8; Leslie Patton, "Subway's DeLuca Sees Sandwich Chain Expanding to 50,000 Shops," *Bloomberg Business*, February 27, 2013, www.bloomberg.com; Subway corporate website at www.subway.com; Kit Tang, "Time for Chinese Fast Food Chains to Shine?" *CNBC*, July 27, 2014, www.cnbc.com.

This case was prepared by Professor Erin Cavusgil, University of Michigan Flint, for classroom discussion.

END OF CHAPTER REVIEW

 MyManagementLab

Go to **mymanagementlab.com** to complete the problems marked with this icon ⭐.

Key Terms

Summary

In this chapter, you learned about:

• **Contractual entry strategies**

Contractual entry strategies in international business grant foreign partners permission to use the focal firm's **intellectual property** in exchange for a continuous stream of payments. **Intellectual property rights** are the legal claims through which the proprietary assets of firms and individuals are protected from unauthorized use by other parties. Firms run the risk of disclosing their intellectual property to outside partners. **Licensing** grants a firm the right to use another firm's intellectual property for a specified period of time in exchange for royalties or other compensation. **Franchising** allows one firm the right to use another's entire business system in exchange for fees, royalties, or other forms of compensation. A **royalty** is a fee paid to the licensor at regular intervals to compensate for the temporary use of intellectual property. Under a **know-how agreement**, the focal firm provides technological or managerial knowledge about how to design, manufacture, or deliver a product or service.

- ### Licensing as an entry strategy

  The agreement between the licensor and the licensee is for a specific time period in a specific country or region. The licensor may enter an exclusive agreement with the licensee to minimize competition with other licensees in the same territory. Once the relationship is established and the licensee fully understands its role, the licensor has little additional input. Licensing is widely used in the fashion and toy industries.

- ### Advantages and disadvantages of licensing

  Licensing's main advantage to the licensor is that it does not require substantial capital investment or physical presence in the foreign market. The licensor can avoid political risk, government regulations, and other risks associated with FDI. However, licensing generates lower profits and limits the firm's ability to control its intellectual property. The licensee may become a competitor when the licensing agreement expires.

- ### Franchising as an entry strategy

  Franchisors employ widely identifiable trademarks and attempt to guarantee the customer a consistent retail experience and product quality. A **master franchise** is an arrangement whereby a franchisee obtains the rights to, and is responsible for, developing franchised outlets to serve a country or a region. Franchising is common in international retailing but difficult to replicate across diverse markets.

- ### Advantages and disadvantages of franchising

  Franchising allows franchisees to gain access to well-known, well-established brand names and business systems, allowing them to launch successful businesses with minimal risk. The franchisor can rapidly internationalize by leveraging the drive and knowledge of local franchisees but risks disseminating its intellectual property to unauthorized parties.

- ### Other contractual entry strategies

  Under **build-operate-transfer (BOT)** arrangements, the firm contracts to build a major facility, such as a power plant, which it operates for a period of years and then transfers to the host-country government or other public entity. In turnkey contracting, one or several firms plan, finance, organize, and manage all phases of a project which, once completed, they hand over to a host-country customer. **Management contracts** occur when a company contracts with another to supply management know-how in the operation of a factory or service facility such as a hotel. With leasing, the firm rents machinery or equipment, usually for a long period, to clients located abroad.

- ### Infringement of intellectual property: A global problem

  Infringement of intellectual property rights takes place through counterfeiting and piracy, which cost companies billions of dollars per year. Several hundred billion dollars' worth of counterfeit and pirated goods cross national borders every year. The Internet facilitates much piracy worldwide. Counterfeiting affects many of the most well-known multinational firms, hurting company performance by eroding competitive advantage and brand equity. Managers must proactively safeguard their proprietary assets by registering patents, trademarks, and other assets in each country and minimizing operations in major counterfeiting countries and countries with weak intellectual property laws. Managers must also train employees and licensees in the proper legal use of intellectual property and vigilantly track down and prosecute violators.

Test Your Comprehension   AACSB: Reflective Thinking Skills

⭐ **15-8.** In a build operate transfer agreement how does the business that built the facility ensure that they profit from the agreement?

15-9. Outline the challenges facing professional service firms when they internationalize.

15-10. What are the advantages and disadvantages of franchising from the perspective of franchisors and franchisees?

15-11. Name the industries that rely the most on franchising to tap foreign markets.

15-12. Define and distinguish the following contractual entry strategies: build-operate-transfer, turnkey projects, management contracts, and leasing.

⭐ **15-13.** What are the best practices in managing international contractual relationships?

Apply Your Understanding AACSB: Communication Abilities, Reflective Thinking Skills

15-14. Warner Brothers is doing a thriving business by licensing images of Harry Potter characters. Firms that manufacture software, games, clothing, and other products enter into licensing agreements with Warner, paying the firm ongoing compensation to produce goods that feature Potter images. However, some illicit operators produce products that feature Potter images *without* entering a licensing agreement with Warner. What steps can Warner take to address this problem? Some nations lack substantial intellectual property protections and are characterized by significant, ongoing counterfeiting of corporate assets. What can Warner do to protect Harry Potter properties from intellectual property infringement in such countries? Intellectual property violations are especially common in China. Should Warner avoid licensing Potter in China? Justify your answer.

15-15. Suppose upon graduation you get a job with Hitachi America, Ltd. (www.hitachi.us), the U.S. subsidiary of the giant Japanese firm. Hitachi uses various contractual entry strategies in its international operations. These include build-operate-transfer and turnkey projects in the infrastructure development sector, management contracts to run nuclear power plants, and leasing of heavy earthmoving equipment to foreign governments. Hitachi America wants to extend its reach into Latin America. Prepare a brief report for senior management in which you explain the various ways to implement its existing entry strategies in this region.

15-16. *Ethical Dilemma:* You are the president of Dynamic Publishing, a firm that publishes textbooks. During an overseas trip, you assess the prospects for marketing Dynamic's textbooks abroad. Upon visiting a university in a developing country, you discover that many students use photocopied or locally reproduced versions of Dynamic's books. Upon investigation, you are advised that most students could not afford to attend college if they were required to pay full price for the books. You are dismayed by the clear violation of intellectual property rights. You believe Dynamic cannot maintain profitability if its intellectual property is infringed. You also feel obligated to protect the rights of the authors of Dynamic's textbooks. At the same time, however, you are sympathetic to the students' plight. Using the ethical framework in Chapter 4, analyze the dilemma presented here. Should you try to enforce Dynamic's intellectual property rights, or should you look the other way and allow the illicit photocopying to continue? Is there a creative solution to this problem?

 **globalEDGE** | **INTERNET EXERCISES**
(www.globalEDGE.msu.edu)

AACSB: Reflective Thinking Skills

Refer to Chapter 1, page 54, for instructions on how to access and use globalEDGE™.

15-17. Suppose you get a job at the office of the International Intellectual Property Alliance (IIPA; www.iipa.com). You learn that worldwide piracy of products is rampant. Your boss assigns you to draft a brief policy memo in which you address the following questions:

- What is the worldwide scope of piracy? What industries are most affected by piracy, and what is the financial loss from piracy in each of these industries?
- What are the top five countries that are the greatest sources of piracy?
- What strategies do you recommend for combating piracy?

In addition to globalEDGE™ and the IIPA portal, other useful sites for this exercise are the Office of the United States Trade Representative (www.ustr.gov), United Nations (www.un.org), and the Business Software Alliance (www.bsa.org).

15-18. Suppose you are an international entrepreneur and want to open your own franchise somewhere in Europe. You decide to conduct research to identify the most promising franchise and learn how to become a franchisee. Entrepreneur.com publishes an annual list of the top 200 franchisors seeking international franchisees. Visit www.entrepreneur.com for the list or search for "franchising" at globalEDGE™. Choose the franchise that interests you most (for example, Subway, Spar, Century 21, Benetton) and visit its corporate website. Based on information from the website, as well as globalEDGE™ and Hoovers.com, address the following questions.

- How many franchised operations does this firm have outside its home country?
- What are the major countries in which the firm has franchises? Are there any patterns in terms of the countries where this firm is established?
- According to the application information provided at the

corporate site, what qualifications is the firm seeking in new franchisees?

- What types of training and support does the firm provide for its franchisees?

15-19. The International Licensing Industry Merchandisers' Association (LIMA; www.licensing.org) is an organization with offices worldwide. It supports merchandise licensing through education, networking, and professional standards development. Suppose you work for an animation company that has developed several popular cartoon characters that have licensing potential in the same way that Disney licenses its cartoon characters. Your company wants to learn more about how to license its cartoon characters. Visit the LIMA website and write a memo that addresses the following:

- Who are the major members of LIMA?
- What are the major trade shows that your firm can attend to exhibit its licensable products and learn more about licensing?
- What types of seminars and training are available to learn more about becoming a licensor?
- Based on the information provided at the site, what can you learn about anti-counterfeiting activities and challenges in licensing?

MyManagementLab

Go to **mymanagementlab.com** for Auto-graded writing questions as well as the following Assisted-graded writing questions:

⭐**15-20.** What are the advantages and disadvantages of licensing?

⭐**15-21.** Distinguish between licensing and franchising. What are the main types of franchises?

⭐**15-22.** MyManagementLab Only—comprehensive writing assignment for this chapter.

Endnotes

1. International Centre for Trade and Sustainable Development (ICTSD), *Property Rights: Implications for Development Policy, Policy Discussion Paper*, Intellectual Property Rights & Sustainable Development Series (Geneva, Switzerland: ICTSD, and New York: UNCTAD, 2003).

2. ICTSD (2003).

3. International Chamber of Commerce, *Roles and Responsibilities of Intermediaries: Fighting Counterfeiting and Piracy in the Supply Chain* (Paris: International Chamber of Commerce, April 2015); Kay Millonzi and William Passannante, "Beware of the Pirates: How to Protect Intellectual Property," *Risk Management* 43 (1996), pp. 39–42.

4. *Marketwatch*, "Intel Licenses Cognitec's Face Recognition Technology for Device Access," December 3, 2014, www.marketwatch.com.

5. Daniel Gervais, *International Intellectual Property: A Handbook of Contemporary Research* (Northampton, MA: Edward Elgar, 2015); Robert W. Gomulkiewicz, Xuan-Thao Nguyen, and Danielle Conway-Jones, *Licensing Intellectual Property: Law & Application*, 2nd ed. (New York: Wolters Kluwer, 2011).

6. Vanessa O'Connell and Mei Fong, "Saks to Follow Luxury Brands into China," *Wall Street Journal*, April 18, 2006, p. B1.

7. Marc Lieberstein, Stephen Feingold, Christine James, and Paul Rosenblatt, "Current Developments and Best Practices in Trademark Licensing (Part I)," *Licensing Journal*, February 2011, pp. 20–28.

8. "Management Brief: Johannesburgers and Fries," *Economist*, September 27, 1997, pp. 113–114; Gervais (2015); WWD: Women's Wear Daily, "Hermès' China Challenge," February 29, 2012, p. 1

9. "History of Merchandising," *Licensing Journal*, April 2009, p. 23; U.S. Department of Commerce, *A Basic Guide to Exporting* (Washington, DC: U.S. Government Printing Office, 1992).

10. Doug Desjardins, "Winnie the Pooh Out of Hibernation," *License! Global*, June 2010, p. 40.

11. Edward Safarian and Gilles Bertin, *Multinationals, Governments and International Technology Transfer* (New York: Routledge, 2014); Piero Telesio, *Technology Licensing and Multinational Enterprises* (New York: Praeger, 1979).

12. Ibid.

13. "Roche Gains a Stronghold in Elusive Japanese Market," *Chemical Market Reporter*, December 17, 2001, p. 2.

14. Safarian and Bertin (2014); Telesio (1979).

15. Gervais (2015); Akio Morita, Edwin Reingold, and Mitsuko Shimomura, *Made in Japan: Akio Morita and Sony* (New York: EP Dutton, 1986).

16. Jan Golab, "King Barbie: How I Gussied Up America's Favorite Toy and Turned My Struggling Company into a Megatoyopoly," *Los Angeles Magazine*, August 1, 1994, p. 66; Mattel, Inc., annual reports (various years); Helen Wang, "Why Barbie Stumbled in China and How She Could Re-invent Herself," *Forbes*, October 24, 2012, www.forbes.com.

17. UNCTAD, *World Investment Report* (New York: United Nations, 2012).

18. F. Burton and A. Cross, "International Franchising: Market versus Hierarchy," in *Internationalisation Strategies*, G. Chryssochoidis, C. Millar, and J. Clegg, eds., pp. 135–152 (New York: St. Martin's Press, 2001).

19. Hachemi Aliouche and Udo Schlentrich, "Towards a Strategic Model of Global Franchise Expansion," *Journal of Retailing* 87, No. 3 (2011), pp. 345–365; Tendai Chikweche and Richard Fletcher, "Franchising at the Bottom of the Pyramid (BOP): An Alternative Distribution Approach," *International Review of Retail, Distribution & Consumer Research* 21, No. 4 (2011), pp. 343–360; Bill Merrilees, "International Franchising: Evolution of Theory and Practice," *Journal of Marketing Channels* 21, No. 3 (2014), pp. 133–142.

20. Carlye Adler, "How China Eats a Sandwich," *Fortune*, March 21, 2005, pp. F210.

21. K. Fladmoe-Lindquist, "International Franchising," in *Globalization of Services*, Y. Aharoni and L. Nachum, eds., pp. 197–216 (London: Routledge, 2000); Merrilees (2014).

22. Merrilees (2014); C. Steinberg, "A Guide to Franchise Strategies," *World Trade* 7 (1994), pp. 66–70.

23. Lawrence Strauss "How Do You Say Yum in Chinese?" *Barron's*, January 28, 2012, pp. 36–37; Laurie Burkitt and Ilan Brat, "Yum's Novelty Fades in China," *Wall Street Journal*, April 22, 2015, p. B4.

24. David Kaufmann, "The Big Bang: How Franchising Became an Economic Powerhouse the World Over— Franchise 500®," *Entrepreneur*, January 2004, http://www.entrepreneur.com; Melih Madanoglu, Kyuho Lee, and Gary Castrogiovanni, "Franchising and Firm Financial Performance Among U.S. Restaurants," *Journal of Retailing* 87, No. 3 (2011), pp. 406–417; UNCTAD, *World Investment Report* (New York: United Nations, 2012).

25. UNCTAD (2012).

26. Aliouche and Schlentrich (2014); Barry Quinn and Anne Marie Doherty, "Power and Control in International Retail Franchising," *International Marketing Review* 17 (2000), pp. 354–363.

27. Cheng Shinn and Eleanor Warnock, "Wendy's Goes Beyond the Dollar Menu in Japan," *Bloomberg Businessweek*, January 9, 2012, pp. 25–26; "Wendy's Shuts Doors in Japan," *New York Times*, January 2, 2010, p. B3; Brian Mertens, "Hawaiian Ernie Higa Reintroduces Wendy's Hamburgers to Japan," *Forbes Asia*, December 10, 2012, p. 11.

28. K. Fladmoe-Lindquist, "International Franchising," in *Globalization of Services*, Y. Aharoni and L. Nachum, eds., pp. 197–216 (London: Routledge, 2000); Merrilees (2014).

29. "Public Funds and Turnkey Contracts Fuel Growing Global Subway Work," *ENR*, October 25, 2004, p. 32; "Abu Dhabi Awards $9 Billion in Gas Project Contracts," *Oil & Gas Journal*, July 27, 2009, pp. 32–33; Caroline Winter, "Who's Building the Big Projects," *Bloomberg Businessweek*, May 31–June 6, 2010, p. 12.

30. "MAN Power for a Diamond Project," *Modern Power Systems*, February, 2012, p. 24.

31. Robert Peltier, "Phu My 3 Power Plant, Ho Chi Minh City, Vietnam," *Power*, August 2004, p. 42.

32. Richard Clough, Glenn Sears, S. Keoki Sears, Robert Segner, and Jerald Rounds, *Construction Contracting: A Practical Guide to Company Management* (Hoboken, NJ: Wiley, 2015); Farok Contractor and Sumit Kundu, "Modal Choice in a World of Alliances: Analyzing Organizational Forms in the International Hotel Sector," *Journal of International Business Studies* 29 (1998), pp. 325–356; V. Panvisavas and J. S. Taylor, "The Use of Management Contracts by International Hotel Firms in Thailand," *International Journal of Contemporary Hospitality Management* 18 (2006), pp. 231–240.

33. Lloyd Downey, "Marketing Services: How TPOs Can Help," *International Trade Forum* 4 (2005), pp. 7–8; Geoffrey Jones and Alexis Lefort, "McKinsey and the Globalization of Consultancy," Harvard Business School case study 9–806–035 (Cambridge, MA: Harvard Business School, 2006).

34. Carter Dougherty, "One Hot List You Don't Want to Be On," *BloombergBusiness*, March 5, 2015, http://www.bloomberg.com; Xiaobai Shen, "Developing Country Perspectives on Software," *International Journal of IT Standards & Standardization Research* 3 (2005), pp. 21–43.

35. International Chamber of Commerce, "BASCAP: Intermediaries Can Do More to Combat Counterfeiting and Piracy," March 26, 2015, http://www.iccwbo.org.

36. CBP Office of International Trade (2015), *Intellectual Property Rights: Fiscal Year 2014 Seizure Statistics*, Washington DC: U.S. Immigration and Customs Enforcement, http://www.cbp.gov/sites/default/files/documents/2014%20IPR%20Stats.pdf; U.S. Customs and Border Protection, "CBP, ICE HSI Report $1.2 Billion in Counterfeit Seizures in 2014," April 2, 2015, http://www.cbp.gov/newsroom/national-media-release/2015-04-02-000000/cbp-ice-hsi-report-12-billion-counterfeit-seizures, April 2, 2015; P. B. Jayakumar, "Patently Justified," *Business Today,* March 15, 2015, pp. 58–64.

37. Gervais (2015); Murray Hiebert, "Chinese Counterfeiters Turn Out Fake Car Parts," *Wall Street Journal*, March 3, 2004, p. A14; Joon Muller, "Stolen Cars," *Forbes*, February 16, 2004, p. 58; Brendan Murphy, Andy Sun, Philip Warden, Ana Damonte, and Raj Davoe, "IP Problems Don't Just Need IP Solutions," *Managing Intellectual Property*, March 2012, p. 17.

38. Matthew Hamblen, "Cisco, Huawei Look to Settle Software-Copying Lawsuit," *Computer World*, October 6, 2003, p. 19.

39. BBC, "Russia Beefs Up Antipiracy Laws," May 1, 2015, www.bbc.com; B. Cassell, "Microsoft Battles Piracy in Developing Markets," *Wall Street Journal*, December 23, 2004, p. B4.

40. Jonathan Rockoff, "When Buying Drugs Online, First Consider the Source," *Wall Street Journal*, April 3, 2012, p. D2; Vauhini (2005), p. 59; Jack Goldsmith and Tim Wu, *Who Controls the Internet: Illusions of a Borderless World* (Oxford, England: Oxford University Press, 2006).

41. Meagan Dietz, Sarena Shao-Tin Lin, and Lei Yang, "Protecting Intellectual Property in China," *McKinsey Quarterly* 3 (2005), pp. 6–10.

42. A. Dayal-Gulati and Angela Lee, *Kellogg on China: Strategies for Success* (Evanston, IL: Northwestern University Press, 2004).

43. International Chamber of Commerce (2015); Millonzi and Passannante (1996).

44. Dietz, Shao-Tin Lin, and Yang (2005).

45. Ibid.

Chapter 16

Marketing in the Global Firm

Learning Objectives *After studying this chapter, you should be able to:*

16.1 Explain global market segmentation.

16.2 Understand standardization and adaptation of international marketing.

16.3 Describe global branding and product development.

16.4 Explain international pricing.

16.5 Understand international marketing communications.

16.6 Describe international distribution.

Uber Technologies Inc.: Available locally, expanding globally ride service

Uber was founded in 2009 by Garrett Camp and Travis Kalanick as a start-up to address the taxi problems by splitting the cost of a ride through smartphone applications. The system works as a technology that connects drivers with app users. Starting in January 2010 Uber has expanded significantly since then, currently operating in more than 250 cities from 60 countries. Now Uber enjoys revenues of about $ 10 billion with total valuation of $ 51 billion.

Uber's products are all technology-based and available through the multiple brands. Multiple products are offered separately in different markets depending on the demand conditions and external environment in each location. Thus Uber tries to outreach to all possible segments.

Uber's distribution strategy is based on local strategic partnerships utilizing their resources and domestic knowledge of the market. Uber partners with Baidu in China, Times Internet in India, Sberbank in Russia, Golden Pay in Azerbaijan, AmericaMovil throughout the Latin America, etc. In some countries Uber contracts taxi companies, car rental companies and private drivers, in others – only companies. Legislative requirements and regulation are among the main reasons for such a diverse strategy.

Uber is flexible in pricing depending on the market conditions. It also utilizes "peak pricing" charging fees according to the demand. The extent of pricing is criticized as some believe Uber's strategy is "price gouging" rather than "peak pricing".

Source: Hugo Felix/Shutterstock

In cases of mass events or emergency situations (e.g. hostage crisis in Sydney, Australia) prices increased up to 8%.

Uber has been involved in a number of promotional efforts globally. Buzz marketing is one of the strategies applied. What is common for a Uber promotion strategy is use of celebrities and partnering with the major events and conventions. Uber was also advertising its advantages as compared to their rivals.

Uber did not follow a traditional way of market expansion. After two cities in the US, it targeted the European and Canadians markets starting with Paris and Toronto. Uber has never used the standard marketing approach to its global market strategies, adapting to the uniqueness of each city, its transportation services, regulation, economic environment and culture. In some locations some services are offered, ignored in others, or priced differently. Uber is in constant search of new opportunities markets, recently focusing on the ones with booming technological infrastructure and growing incomes, but relatively unsophisticated market and lack of regulatory burden (e.g. Russia, Azerbaijan, UAE). Uber has been adapting to the peculiarities of developing economies, for example adding a cash payment option in India, and possibly other countries of Asia and Latin America.

Uber has faced a number of challenges - complaining drivers, unsatisfied customers, growing competition offering the similar rides-for-share services (Lyft, Curb, Sidecar, etc.), unpredictable market demand, legal and regulatory challenges domestically and globally. The latter has been recently the most serious obstacle for Uber, undermining its otherwise successful international expansion. Uber attempts to differentiate itself from the taxi services serving as an agent of its individual contractors, which is not the common view of many courts around the world that force Uber to comply with licensing requirements or even ban its operations. Uber must address the above-mentioned challenges to ensure its public trust, customer satisfaction, contractors' satisfaction to maintain the long-term success.

Questions

16-1. Which international marketing strategies have been crucial for Uber's global success?

16-2. Describe the role of strategic partnerships in app-based ride sharing technology business.

16-3. Given Uber's business model and strategy, what are the challenges and risks it needs to address to maintain success?

SOURCES: Chloe Albanesius, "Uber Rolling Out On-Demand Ice Cream Trucks," *PC Magazine*, July 12, 2012, http://www.pcmag.com/article2/0,2817,2407069,00.asp; James Garrett Baldwin. "Ways to Invest in Uber before It Goes Public". *Investopedia*, October 14, 2015 http://www.investopedia.com/articles/investing/101415/ways-invest-uber-it-goes-public.asp#ixzz3ovw6omLi; Manu Balachandran. "To grow in emerging markets, Uber goes low-tech", *Quartz India* May 19, 2015 http://qz.com/403910/to-grow-in-emerging-markets-uber-goes-low-tech/; Joshua Brustein, "Uber's Other Legal Mess: Drivers Sue Over Missing Tips," *Bloomberg*, August 29, 2013, http://www.bloomberg.com/bw/articles/2013-08-29/ubers-other-legal-mess-drivers-sue-over-missing-tips; Susan Decker and Serena Saitto, "Uber Seeks to Patent Pricing Surges That Critics Call Gouging," *Bloomberg*, December 18, 2014, http://www.bloomberg.com/news/articles/2014-12-18/uber-seeks-to-patent-pricing-surges-that-critics-call-gouging; Cotton Delo, "In Quest for Ride-Sharing Supremacy, Uber Takes on Lyft with Facebook Ads," *Advertising Age*, January 17, 2014, http://adage.com/article/digital/uber-takes-lyft-facebook-attack-ads/291158/; Josh Horwitz, "Uber's Growing Pains: Head of Operations Ryan Graves on the Challenges of Building A Global Startup". *TNW Blog*. 30 July, 2013 http://thenextweb.com/asia/2013/07/30/ryan-graves-head-of-operations-at-uber-talks-asia-expansion-and-strategy; Vsevolod Salnikov, Renaud Lambiotte, Anastasios Noulas, Cecilia Mascolo. "OpenStreetCab: Exploiting Taxi Mobility Patterns in New York City to Reduce Commuter Costs". in *Proceedings of Conference on the Scientific Analysis of Mobile Phone Datasets (NetMob2015)*. Boston, MA, USA. April 2015; "Sberbank, Uber agree on financial technology partnership", *The Paypers*, September 22 2015, http://www.thepaypers.com/online-mobile-banking/sberbank-uber-agree-on-financial-technology-partnership/761452-12 "Uber gains popularity in Azerbaijan," August 3, 2015, http://abc.az/eng/news/89910.html; "Uber signs Latin America tie-up with Slim's America Movil", Reuters, December 2, 2014. http://www.reuters.com/article/2014/12/02/us-uber-americamovil-idUSKCN0JG1ZY20141202; Uber website, https://www.uber.com/

In international business, marketing is concerned with identifying, measuring, and responding to market opportunities abroad. In this chapter, we examine company marketing activities aimed at meeting international customer needs. Marketing is a critical activity because it is the primary conduit through which the firm finds and interacts with customers abroad.

Exhibit 16.1 provides a framework for marketing activities and previews the topics of this chapter. The outer ring represents the cultural, social, political, legal, and regulatory environment of foreign markets. These environmental conditions influence the way the firm develops and adapts products. It affects product pricing, distribution, and promotional activities. In high-inflation countries, for example, management must review prices frequently. The firm must adapt the positioning or selling propositions of its products to suit local customer expectations across diverse cultures. It must ensure that its products comply with local government regulations.

The middle ring in Exhibit 16.1 represents **global marketing strategy**—a plan of action the firm develops for foreign markets that guides managerial decision making on:.

- How to position itself and its offerings.
- Which customer segments to target.
- Standardizing versus adapting marketing program elements.[1]

We investigate the balance between marketing standardization and adaptation and the development of global brands as well as the critical roles that elements of the marketing mix play. We begin by examining global market segmentation.

Global marketing strategy
A plan of action for foreign markets that guides the firm in deciding how to position itself and its offerings, which customer segments to target, and the degree to which it should standardize or adapt its marketing program elements.

16.1 Explain global market segmentation.

Global Market Segmentation

Market segmentation is the process of dividing the firm's total customer base into homogeneous clusters in a way that allows management to formulate unique marketing strategies for each group. Within each market segment, customers exhibit similar characteristics, including income level, lifestyle, demographic profile, and desired product benefits. Take earthmoving equipment as an example. Caterpillar develops distinct marketing approaches for several major market segments—farmers, construction firms, the military, and others. In setting prices, Caterpillar creates

The Environment of International Business

Diverse Cultural, Political, Legal, Monetary, and Financial
Environment of the Firm

Global Marketing Strategy

Targeting Customer Segments and Positioning

**International Marketing Program
Standardization and Adaptation**

Global Branding and Product Development	International Pricing
International Distribution	International Marketing Communications

EXHIBIT 16.1

Organizing Framework for Marketing in the International Firm

value-priced tractors for farmers, moderately priced earthmoving equipment for construction firms, and high-priced, heavy-duty vehicles for the military. Caterpillar formulates relatively unique advertising and distribution approaches for each segment as well.

In international business, firms frequently formulate market segments by grouping countries based on macro-level variables, such as level of economic development or cultural dimensions. Many MNEs group Latin American countries based on a common language (Spanish) or European countries based on similar economic conditions. This approach has proven most effective for product categories in which governments play a key regulatory role (such as telecommunications, medical products, and processed foods) or where national characteristics prevail in determining product acceptance and usage.[2]

Today, firms increasingly target global market segments. A **global market segment** is a group of customers who share similar characteristics across many national markets. Firms target such buyers by using a relatively uniform marketing strategy and marketing programs. For example, the music network MTV targets a relatively homogenous youth market that exists in most of the world. This segment generally follows global media, is quick to embrace new fashions and

Global market segment

A group of customers who share common characteristics across many national markets.

Source: Corepics VOF/Shutterstock

Popular music stars such as Ed Sheeran and Taylor Swift target the global market segment of young adults who love music.

trends, and has significant disposable income. Another global market segment is frequent business travelers. They are affluent, eager consumers of premium hotels, clothing, jewelry, and other products that represent luxury and style.

A key objective in pursuing global market segments is to create a unique position in the minds of target customers. *Positioning* is a marketing strategy in which the firm develops both the product and its marketing to evoke a distinct impression in the customer's mind, emphasizing differences from competitors' offerings. In the theme park business, Disney positions itself as standing for family values and "good, clean fun" to attract families around the world.[3] Starbucks positions its products to attract customers with sophisticated tastes who do not mind paying several dollars for a cup of coffee.

In the automobile industry, BMW positions its cars as luxurious, powerful, and superior quality. Volvo positions its vehicles as good quality, safe, family-oriented, and sophisticated. Honda positions its cars as good quality, affordably priced, fuel efficient, and environmentally friendly. Hyundai cars are positioned as affordable, value-priced, reliable, and stylish.

Positioning may also evoke the specific *attributes* that consumers associate with a product. Diet Coke elicits an image of someone who wants to lose or maintain weight. When Coca-Cola first entered Japan, research revealed that Japanese women do not like products labeled "diet," nor is the population considered overweight. Thus, management altered the product's positioning in Japan by changing the name to Coke Light.

Internationalizing firms aim for a *global positioning strategy*, which positions the offering similarly in the minds of targeted buyers worldwide. Starbucks, Volvo, and Sony successfully use this approach. Consumers worldwide view these strong brands in the same way. Global positioning strategy reduces international marketing costs by addressing the shared expectations of a global customer market segment.[4]

Standardization and Adaptation of International Marketing

16.2 Understand standardization and adaptation of international marketing.

In addition to guiding targeting and positioning, a global marketing strategy also clarifies the degree to which the firm's marketing program should vary between different foreign markets. **Adaptation** refers to modifying one or more elements of the firm's international marketing program to accommodate specific customer requirements in a particular market. **Standardization** refers to making the marketing program elements uniform with a view to targeting entire regions, or even the global marketplace, with the same product or service.

In the center of Exhibit 16.1, we identify the key elements of the marketing program (sometimes referred to as the *marketing mix*) affected by the standardization/adaptation decision. These are:

Adaptation
The firm's efforts to modify one or more elements of its international marketing program to accommodate specific customer requirements in a particular market.

Standardization
The firm's efforts to make its marketing program elements uniform with a view to targeting entire regions, or even the global marketplace, with the same product or service.

- Global branding.
- Product development.
- International pricing.
- International marketing communications.
- International distribution.

In the international context, marketing strategy tackles the complexity of having both global and local competitors as well as cross-national differences in culture, language, living standards, economic conditions, regulations, and quality of business infrastructure. A key challenge is to resolve the trade-offs between standardization and adaptation.

When they enter international markets, managers undertake a broad corporate strategy in which they attempt to strike an ideal balance between *global integration* and *local responsiveness*. As discussed in Chapter 11, global integration seeks cross-national synergy in the firm's value-chain activities to take maximum advantage of similarities between countries, whereas local responsiveness aims to meet the specific needs of buyers in individual countries. How the firm resolves the balance between global integration and local responsiveness also affects how it makes standardization and adaptation decisions in its marketing program elements.

Exhibit 16.2 highlights the trade-offs between standardization and adaptation in international marketing. Let's examine the advantages of each approach.

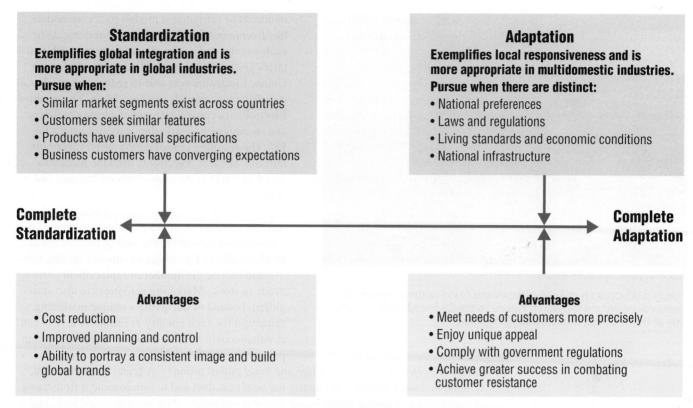

EXHIBIT 16.2

Trade-Offs Between Adaptation and Standardization of International Marketing Program

Standardization

Standardization represents a tendency toward global integration and is more likely to be pursued in global industries such as aircraft manufacturing, pharmaceuticals, and credit cards. Airbus, Pfizer, and MasterCard use a standardized marketing strategy with great success. Their offerings are largely uniform across many markets worldwide. A standardized marketing approach is most appropriate when market segments and customer needs are consistent across numerous countries. Products that feature universal specifications are also candidates for a standardized approach. In industrial sales, businesses often prefer parts and components of similar specifications, quality and performance, and other product attributes.

The feasibility of standardization varies across industries and product categories. Commodities, industrial equipment, and technology products lend themselves to a high degree of standardization. Popular consumer electronics such as Apple's iPhone, Samsung's Galaxy smartphone, and Canon digital cameras, as well as well-known fashion accessories such as Rolex watches and Michael Kors handbags, are largely standardized around the world. Automotive parts, building materials, dinnerware, and basic food ingredients are other products that require little or no adaptation.

Advertising may be standardized too. One TV ad featured an attractive 25-year-old British woman eagerly anticipating a scoop of Haagen-Dazs ice cream. The same ad was broadcast worldwide, with voice-overs in French, Portuguese, Spanish, and Mandarin Chinese.[5] Gillette sells shaving products, uses uniform marketing in all the countries where it does business, and often introduces them with simultaneous global launches under universal brand names such as Sensor and Fusion. Gillette's global approach has achieved an impressive 70 percent global market share while minimizing marketing and distribution costs.[6]

When managers build on commonalities in customer preferences and attempt to standardize their international marketing program, they can expect at least three major benefits.

● *Cost reduction*   Standardization reduces costs by making possible economies of scale in design, sourcing, manufacturing, and marketing. Offering a similar marketing program to the global marketplace or across entire regions is more efficient than having to adapt products for each market. Electrolux (based in Sweden, www.electrolux.com) once made

Source: Bargotiphotography/Shutterstock

Luxury products such as Rolex watches and Gucci clothing are largely standardized around the world. Pictured is the Champs-Élysées in Paris, one of France's most luxurious shopping streets.

Global brand

A brand whose positioning, advertising strategy, look, and personality are standardized worldwide.

hundreds of refrigerator models to accommodate the diverse tastes and regulatory requirements of each country in Europe. As product standards and tastes gradually harmonized across the European Union, Electrolux was able to reduce the number of its refrigerator models to a few dozen. This enabled Electrolux to consolidate manufacturing facilities and streamline its marketing activities across the EU. The resulting consolidation saved Electrolux millions of euros. Electrolux used the money to invest in R&D to develop advanced features and superior technology.

- *Improved planning and control* Standardization reduces the complexity of planning and control of value-adding activities. The ability to offer fewer products allows Electrolux to simplify quality control and reduce the number of replacement parts it needs to stock. Marketing activities are also simplified. Instead of designing a unique marketing campaign for each country in Europe, the firm can simultaneously offer a relatively standardized campaign for numerous countries.

- *Ability to portray a consistent image and build global brands* A brand is a name, sign, symbol, or design intended to identify the firm's product and to differentiate it from those of competitors. A **global brand** is one whose positioning, advertising strategy, look, and personality are standardized worldwide. Global branding increases customer interest and reduces the confusion that can arise when the firm offers numerous adapted products and marketing programs.[7]

Read the *You Can Do It: Recent Grad in IB* story about John Dykhouse to learn how working in brand strategy and marketing can provide the basis for an exciting international business career.

Adaptation

Although firms usually prefer to standardize their products, adaptation is often necessary due to differences across countries in language, culture, regulation, economic conditions, and other factors. Adaptation is useful in *multidomestic industries* such as publishing and software, which tailor their offerings to suit individual markets. It may be as straightforward as translating labels, instructions, or books into a foreign language or as complex as completely modifying a product to fit unique market conditions. Local adaptation can provide the marketer with important advantages. When the firm emphasizes adaptation in international marketing, it seeks to meet the needs of local customers more precisely and create unique appeal for its products. The presence of numerous local competitors may force the firm to accommodate local consumer needs more closely. Adaptation also is frequently driven by the need to comply with local regulations. Let's delve more deeply into the specific rationale that drives firms to adapt marketing program elements.

- *Differences in national preferences* Companies adapt their products to suit the specific, unique wants and needs of customers in individual markets. For example, Häagen-Dazs operates more than 900 ice cream shops in 50 countries. In Japan, customers favor green tea–flavored ice cream. In Latin America, *dulce de leche* flavor is preferred. Customers in France enjoy ice cream chocolate fondue. In China, shops feature ice cream and mooncakes to celebrate the lunar festival popular in Chinese culture.[8]

  When *The Simpsons* cartoon series was broadcast in Saudi Arabia, it was adapted for language and local Islamic culture. The show was renamed *Al Shamshoon*, Homer Simpson's name was changed to "Omar," and Bart Simpson became "Badr." In addition to translating the show into Arabic, producers had to address the way the Simpson daughter and mother dress. Producers removed references to potentially offensive practices such as consuming pork and beer. They changed Homer Simpson's Duff beer to soda, hot dogs to

You Can Do It | RECENT GRAD IN IB

JOHN DYKHOUSE

John's major Bachelor of Business Administration (International Business, Marketing)

Objectives Inspiration, business success, adventure, a global outlook on life, community involvement, and helping others achieve their goals

Internships during college Nonprofit marketing; business innovations for a large consumer packaged goods firm

Jobs held since graduating

- Associate Brand Manager, Amway Corporate Marketing, Nutrition Brands
- Brand Manager, Amway Corporate Marketing, Nutrition Brands
- Trade Development Manager, Amway Global, Health Brands

A single decision made in the blink of an eye can shape your life. As an undergraduate, John Dykhouse decided to study abroad in Grenoble, France, for one year. John notes, "For the first time, I understood that learning a new culture and language doesn't open doors just to communication, but to a new way of thinking."

Upon graduation, the combination of international experience and several marketing-related internships helped John obtain a position at Amway Corporation. Over time, he became Associate Brand Manager with Nutrilite, a brand of vitamins, minerals, and dietary supplements sold in many countries worldwide. His job responsibilities included managing several product categories within the brand, managing a global product portfolio, marketing communications, and pricing, to name a few.

Within two years, John was offered the position of Brand Manager. With this new role came a shift into the world of athletic sponsorships. The position gave John the chance to work with professional athletes and their agencies to develop their brands further through awareness-generating sponsorships and events around the world. His work brought John back to Europe many times, as well as to Korea and Japan, to perform various functions in the corporate strategy he helped create. In his newest position, John is working in trade development to create training tools, product campaigns, and digital strategies.

John's Advice for Career Success

- Be a good communicator. With international work, think about when to use simplified English and be brief.
- Be persistent. Many people give up on the first, second, or even third try. You will likely make a few blunders during an international career. Treat these as learning experiences and move on—just don't make them again.

- Find a great mentor and learn from him or her.
- Be a team player. You will likely work with people who come from cultures you don't completely understand. Make sure you explore what is behind their opinions, be respectful, and at times, be cautious.
- Be curious. Take in the sights, sounds, people, and even some smells of the places you visit.
- Don't skip lunch. Although it's tempting to sit at a desk to work through lunch, it is better to lunch with mentors and colleagues—you will have very productive discussions, helping you navigate through challenges in your career.

In the coming years, John plans to complete an MBA with an emphasis on brand management and international business.

Source: Photo courtesy of John Dykhouse.

Egyptian beef sausages, and donuts to the popular Arab cookies called *kahk*. Moe's Bar was edited out of the show. As one Arab viewer told ABC News, "We are a totally different culture, so you can't talk about the same subject in the same way."[9]

McDonald's has been able to standardize its hamburgers across most world markets, but not all. Some cultures and religions shun the consumption of beef. McDonald's substitutes lamb or chicken in its burgers in some markets such as India. It also adds additional items such as *Kofte* burgers (hamburger with special spices) in Turkey. In Hong Kong, burgers are sandwiched between buns made of glutinous rice. McDonald's outlets in Norway serve McLaks, a grilled salmon sandwich with dill sauce. In Berlin, consumers can savor a beer with their double cheeseburgers and fries. In some Arab countries, the McArabia, a spicy chicken filet on flatbread, has been a success. Customers in France can get a burger on a baguette bun.[10]

- *Differences in living standards and economic conditions* Because income levels vary greatly worldwide, firms frequently adjust the pricing and the complexity of their product offerings for individual markets. In China, IKEA reduced prices on its furniture to make it more affordable for lower-income segments.[11] Dell sells less-expensive, simplified versions of its computers in developing economies. Inflation and economic recessions also influence pricing policy. A recession signals a drop in consumer confidence, and the firm may need to reduce prices to generate sales. High inflation can rapidly erode profits even as prices rise. Exchange rate fluctuations also necessitate adjustments. When the importing country currency is weak, the purchasing power of its consumers is reduced.

- *Differences in laws and regulations*   Germany, Norway, and Switzerland are among the countries that restrict advertising directed at children. Packaged foods in Europe are often labeled in several languages, including English, French, German, and Spanish. In Quebec, Canada's French-speaking province, local law requires product packaging to be in both English and French. In some markets, the use of certain sales promotion activities such as coupons and sales contests is restricted.

- *Differences in national infrastructure*   The quality and reach of transportation networks, marketing intermediaries, and overall business infrastructure influence the marketing communications and distribution systems that firms employ abroad. Infrastructure is poor in many rural parts of developing economies. This necessitates innovative approaches for getting products to customers. Road and rail networks in many parts of western China are underdeveloped. Firms use small trucks to reach retailers in the outlying communities of these areas. Undeveloped media also require substantial adaptations to carry marketing communications. In rural regions of Vietnam, most consumers cannot access television, magazines, or the Internet. Radio, billboards, and brochures are favored for targeting low-income buyers.

Adaptation also provides managers an opportunity to explore alternate ways of marketing the product or service. What they learn in the process can guide R&D efforts, often leading to superior products for sale abroad and at home. Products developed or modified for foreign markets sometimes prove so successful that they are launched as new products in the firm's home market. After developing an inexpensive, battery-powered electrocardiograph machine for doctors in China and India, General Electric realized the device's potential for advanced economies and began marketing it to rural clinics and visiting nurses in the United States.[12]

Source: Richard Ellis/Alamy

Popular consumer electronics such as Apple's iPad can gain a worldwide following and require little adaptation from country to country. These commuters are awaiting a bus in central Hong Kong.

Standardization and Adaptation: A Balancing Act

A managerial decision about standardization and adaptation is not an either-or-decision but, rather, a balancing act. There are good arguments and outcomes that favor both options; it is up to senior marketing managers and the global new-product planning team to sort out the trade-offs, given the distinctive environments where the firm operates.

Perhaps the most important distinction between standardization and adaptation is that standardization helps the firm cut costs, whereas local adaptation helps the firm more precisely cater to local needs and requirements. However, adaptation is costly and time-consuming, often requiring substantial modifications to product design, manufacturing, pricing, distribution, and communications. Thus, managers usually prefer standardization. Many firms adapt marketing program elements *only when necessary* to respond to local customer preferences and mandated regulations. Unilever streamlined the number of its brands from more than 1600 to about 400 and focused attention on a dozen or so global ones. However, the firm had to retain many local adaptations to suit individual markets.[13]

In many cases, for a given product or service, managers both standardize and adapt in varying degrees. Some marketing mix elements are standardized, some are localized, and others require a team-based solution developed among corporate, regional, and local decision makers. For example, the firm might offer a standardized product worldwide but modify its pricing or advertising for different markets. Management decides not only *what* elements to adapt, but also *how much* to adapt them. IKEA offers uniform products across its markets while modifying, say, the size of beds or chests of drawers in individual countries. It emphasizes its catalog as the principal promotional tool worldwide but supplements it with local TV advertising in some major markets.

Companies rarely find it feasible or practical to follow a one offering–one world strategy across *all* dimensions of the marketing program. Automakers tried for years to market a world car that met customer preferences everywhere and that complied with various governments' safety specifications. Ambitious experiments such as the Ford Mondeo failed to meet the approval of customers and regulatory bodies around the world. Ford was forced to modify its design to accommodate climate and geography (which affected engine specifications), government emissions standards, gas prices, and customer preferences for frills such as cupholders.

As a compromise, some firms pursue standardization as part of a *regional* strategy, formulating international marketing elements to exploit commonalities across a geographic region instead of the whole world. General Motors markets distinctive car models for China (Excelle, Sail), Europe (Corsa, Mokka), and North America (Silverado, Escalade). A regional marketing approach is often appropriate in industries where the following conditions are present.

- Buyer preferences and product standards have converged at the regional level.
- Media and distribution channels are organized on a regional basis.
- Countries in target regions have formed regional economic integration blocs.[14]

Global Branding and Product Development

16.3 Describe global branding and product development.

Global marketing strategy poses unique challenges and opportunities for managers, especially in branding and product development. Let's examine these topics.

Global Branding

A key outcome of a global positioning strategy is the development of a global brand. Well-known global brands include Hollywood movies (*Spider-Man*), pop stars (Lady Gaga), personal care products (Gillette Fusion), toys (Barbie), credit cards (Visa), food (Cadbury chocolate), beverages (Coca-Cola), furniture (IKEA), and consumer electronics (iPad).[15] Consumers frequently prefer globally branded products because global branding provides a sense of trust and confidence in their purchasing.[16]

A strong global brand:

- Increases the efficiency and effectiveness of marketing programs.
- Stimulates brand loyalty.
- Allows the firm to charge premium prices.
- Increases the firm's leverage with intermediaries and retailers.
- Enhances the firm's competitive advantage in global markets.[17]

The firm can reduce its marketing and advertising costs by concentrating on a single global brand instead of on numerous national brands. The strength of a global brand is best measured by its *brand equity*—the market value of the brand. Exhibit 16.3 provides brand equity figures for selected global brands.

The most successful global brands tend to have several of the following characteristics.

- High, conspicuous visibility such as consumer electronics and jeans
- Status symbols, such as cars and jewelry
- Widespread appeal, due to innovative features that seem to fit everyone's lifestyle, such as mobile phones, credit cards, and cosmetics
- Close identification with a particular country such as Levi's (U.S. style) and IKEA furniture (Scandinavian style)

Still, in other cases, global brands reap the benefits of first-mover advantages in offering new and novel products or services. In 1971, the first Starbucks opened in Seattle, Washington, and offered freshly brewed coffee in a comfortable setting that encouraged people to sit and relax. Fashionable shoppers worldwide favor distinctive Louis Vuitton handbags and accessories. Samsung propelled itself into consumer electronics with unique design and leading-edge technology.

EXHIBIT 16.3 Top Global Brands, by Region

Company	Brand Value (US$ billions)	Country of Origin	Main Product or Service
Asian Brands			
Samsung	38	South Korea	Consumer electronics
Toyota	38	Japan	Automobiles
Honda	23	Japan	Automobiles
Hyundai	8	South Korea	Automobiles
Canon	7	Japan	Copiers, cameras
European Brands			
Louis Vuitton	28	France	Fashion accessories
BMW	28	Germany	Automobiles
Mercedes-Benz	23	Germany	Automobiles
Nescafe	17	Switzerland	Beverages
H&M	15	Sweden	Clothing retailing
U.S. Brands			
Apple	145	United States	Consumer electronics
Microsoft	69	United States	Software
Google	66	United States	Internet services, software
Coca-Cola	56	United States	Beverages
IBM	50	United States	Technology, consulting

Sources: Based on Forbes, "The World's Most Valuable Brands: 2015 Ranking," www.forbes.com; Interbrand, www.interbrand.com; and Hoovers.com company profiles, www.hoovers.com.

Developing and maintaining a global brand name is one of the best ways for firms to build global recognition. The Eveready Battery Co. consolidated its various national brand names—such as Ucar, Wonder, and Mazda—into one global brand name, Energizer. The move increased the efficiency of Eveready's marketing efforts worldwide. Although most managers conceive brands for a national market and then internationalize them, the preferred approach is to build a global brand from the beginning with input from all major markets. Several firms have succeeded in this approach, including Japan's Sony Corporation. "Sony" was derived from the Latin for "sound." The Japanese car company Datsun switched its name to Nissan to create a unified global brand worldwide.[18]

Global branding also helps the MNE compete more effectively with popular local brands that appeal to buyers' sense of local tradition, pride, and preference. In Peru, Inca Kola was long a successful local brand that established itself as Peru's Drink. Its experience reveals how local brands can be vulnerable to the market power of strong global brands. Coca-Cola purchased 50 percent of the Inca Kola Corporation. Coca-Cola and Inca Kola each have about 30 percent of the Peruvian market, giving Coca-Cola an edge because it owns half the other brand.

Global Product Development

In developing products with multicountry potential, managers emphasize their commonalities across countries rather than the differences between them.[19] A basic product will incorporate only core features into which the firm can inexpensively implement variations for individual markets. For example, although the basic computers that Dell sells worldwide are essentially identical, the letters on its keyboards and the languages used in its software are unique to countries or major regions. Many firms design products by using *modular architecture*, a collection of *standardized* components and subsystems that they can rapidly assemble in various configurations to suit the needs of individual markets. Honda and Toyota design models such as the Accord and Corolla around a standardized platform to which modular components, parts, and features are added to suit specific needs and tastes.

The cosmetics firm L'Oréal develops new products through its Research and Innovation Group, concentrated at headquarters in Paris. Each year, the center's staff of 80 develops more than 1,000 new products for Lancôme, Armani, Maybelline, and other L'Oréal brands. L'Oréal systematically recruits and builds teams around managers experienced and knowledgeable about the norms and tastes of multiple cultures. For example, a team consisting of three researchers working on women's hair-care products might include a Lebanese-Spanish-American manager in charge of hair color and a French-Irish-Cambodian in charge of hair care. Team members share offices so they can exchange ideas. By centralizing R&D and drawing on knowledge from the firm's six key areas—Europe, United States, Japan, China, Brazil and India—L'Oréal develops new products that reflect tastes in major markets and facilitate global marketing. L'Oréal's centralized teams of multicultural managers leverage continuous knowledge-based interactions to produce a stream of new products every year.[20]

A *global new-product planning team* is a group of managers within a firm that determines which elements of the product will be standardized and which will be adapted locally. The team also decides when to launch products. Launch may be simultaneous across numerous countries or handled on a sequential basis. Sequential release implies launching a product one country at a time and is often preferred for products that require local adaptation. Some firms launch a new product in high-priced markets first and then gradually enter lower-priced markets. This helps reduce potential consumer objections to higher prices.

Global new-product planning teams formulate best practices that the firm implements in all its units worldwide. These teams assemble employees with specialized knowledge and expertise from various geographically diverse units of the MNE. The teams then collaborate to develop products that address needs or problems common to the firm's major international markets. For example, the iXi Bike was designed by a team from France, the United Kingdom, and the United States for France's iXi Bicycle Company. The bike fits easily into the trunk of a small car. The Logiq & Vivid E9 is a mobile ultrasound system developed by a global team from France, Japan, and the United States. Used for medical examinations, the ergonomic equipment offers substantial efficiency with minimal environmental impact. A global new-product planning team from the Netherlands and the United States created the Nuance Syringe, an electronic needle used to repair teeth.[21]

International Pricing

Pricing is complex. It is particularly challenging in international business, with multiple currencies, trade barriers, added costs, diverse regulations, and typically longer distribution channels.[22] Given lower incomes in much of the world, firms often feel pressure to lower prices. Conversely, prices tend to escalate because of tariffs, taxes, and higher markups by foreign intermediaries. Price variations among different markets can lead to **gray market activity**—legal importation of genuine products into a country by intermediaries other than authorized distributors (also known as parallel imports). We discuss gray markets later in this chapter.

Prices influence customers' perception of value, determine the level of motivation of foreign intermediaries, affect promotional spending and strategy, and compensate for weaknesses in other elements of the marketing mix. Let's explore the unique aspects of international pricing.

Factors That Affect International Pricing

Factors that influence international pricing fall into four categories.

- *Nature of the market* Buyers' income level and demographic profile are major factors that influence their ability to pay for products and services. Most consumers in emerging markets and developing economies lack significant disposable income. Firms must set lower prices to generate significant product sales. Local regulation, climate, infrastructure, and other factors often drive the firm to modify products, communications, and other marketing elements. Such adjustments cost money. Food items shipped to hot climates require refrigeration, which drives up costs. In countries with many rural residents or those with poor

16.4 Explain international pricing.

Gray market activity
Legal importation of genuine products into a country by intermediaries other than authorized distributors (also known as parallel imports).

distribution systems, delivering products to widely dispersed customers necessitates higher pricing because of steeper shipping costs. In addition, foreign governments impose tariffs, taxes, or other costs that lead to higher prices. Foreign governments also enforce health rules, safety standards, and other regulations that increase the cost of doing business locally. The federal government in Canada and many countries in Europe impose price limits on prescription drugs, which reduces pharmaceutical firms' pricing flexibility.

- *Nature of the product or industry*   Products with substantial added value—such as cars or high-end computers—usually necessitate charging relatively high prices. A specialized product, or one with a technological edge, gives a company greater price flexibility. When the firm holds a relative monopoly in a product (such as Microsoft operating system software), it can generally charge premium prices.
- *Type of distribution system* Firms that export rely on independent distributors based abroad. Distributors often modify pricing to suit their own goals. Some distributors mark up prices substantially, which can harm the exporter's image and pricing strategy in the market. By contrast, when the firm internationalizes through FDI by establishing company-owned marketing subsidiaries abroad, management maintains control over pricing strategy. Firms that sell directly to end users also control their pricing and can quickly make adjustments to suit local conditions.
- *Location of the production facility* Locating manufacturing in those countries with low-cost labor enables a firm to charge lower prices. Locating factories in or near major markets cuts transportation costs and may reduce problems that foreign exchange fluctuations can create. Daimler established a factory in Hungary to produce Mercedes-Benz cars. Wages are one-fifth those in Germany, Daimler's home country. Major markets in Western Europe are only a few hours away by truck and rail. Achieving lower manufacturing costs helps Daimler compete more effectively with rival BMW.[23]

Exhibit 16.4 lists internal and external factors that influence how firms set international prices. Internally, management accounts for its own objectives regarding profit and market share,

EXHIBIT 16.4

Internal and External Factors That Affect International Pricing

Internal to the Firm
- Management's profit and market share expectations
- Cost of manufacturing, marketing, and other value-chain activities
- The degree of control management desires over price setting in foreign markets

External Factors
- Customer expectations, purchasing power, and sensitivity to price increases
- Nature of competitors' offerings, prices, and strategy
- International customer costs
  - Product/package modification; labeling and market requirements
  - Documentation (certificate of origin, invoices, banking fees)
  - Financing costs
  - Packing and container charges
  - Shipping (inspection, warehousing, freight forwarder's fee)
  - Insurance
- Landed cost
  - Tariffs (customs duty, import tax, customs clearance fee)
  - Warehousing charges at the port of import; local transportation
- Importer's cost
  - Value-added tax and other applicable taxes paid by the importer
  - Local intermediary (distributor, wholesaler, retailer) margins
  - Cost of financing inventory
- Anticipated fluctuations in currency exchange rates

the cost of goods sold, and the degree of control desired over international pricing. Externally, management must account for customer characteristics, competitor prices, exchange rates, tariffs, taxes, and costs related to generating international sales as well as transporting and distributing the goods. Many countries in Europe and elsewhere charge value-added taxes (VATs) on imported products. Unlike a sales tax, which is calculated based on the retail sales price, the VAT is determined as a percentage of the gross margin—the difference between the sales price and the cost to the seller of the item sold. In the EU, for example, VAT rates range between 15 and 25 percent, which adds substantially to local prices.

Framework for Setting International Prices

Managers examine the suitability of prices at several levels in the international distribution channel—importers, wholesalers, retailers, and end users—and then set prices accordingly. Exhibit 16.5 presents a systematic approach for managers to use in setting international prices.[24]

Let's illustrate the international pricing framework with an example. Suppose a leading U.S. musical instrument manufacturer, Melody Corporation, wants to begin exporting electric guitars to Japan and needs to set prices. Melody decides to export its John Mayer brand of guitar, which retails for $2,000 in the United States. Initial research reveals that additional costs of shipping, and insurance, and a 5 percent Japanese tariff will add a total of $300 to the price of each guitar, bringing the total landed price to $2,300. Melody has identified an importer in Japan, Aoki Wholesalers, which wants to add a 10 percent profit margin to the cost of each imported guitar. Thus, the total price once a guitar leaves Aoki's Japan warehouse is $2,530. This is the *floor price*, the lowest acceptable price to Melody, because management doesn't want Japanese earnings to dip below those in the United States.

Next, market research on income levels and competitor prices reveals that Japanese musicians are willing to pay prices about 30 percent above typical U.S. prices for high-quality instruments. Given this information, Melody management believes Japan can sustain a ceiling price for the Mayer guitar of $2,600. Additional research provides estimates for Melody's sales potential at the floor price and at the ceiling price. Managers eventually decide on a suggested retail price of $2,560. Research has revealed this is the most appropriate price in light of factors

Step 1. Estimate the "landed" price of the product in the foreign market by totaling all costs associated with shipping the product to the customer's location.

Step 2. Estimate the price the importer or distributor will charge when it adds its profit margin.

Step 3. Estimate the target price range for end users. Determine:
- Floor price (lowest acceptable price to the firm, based on cost considerations)
- Ceiling price (highest possible price, based on customer purchasing power, price sensitivity, and competitive considerations)

Step 4. Assess the company sales potential at the price the firm is most likely to charge (between the floor price and ceiling price).

Step 5. Select a suitable pricing strategy based on corporate goals and preferences from:
- Rigid cost-plus pricing
- Flexible cost-plus pricing
- Incremental pricing

Step 6. Check consistency with current prices across product lines, key customers, and foreign markets (in order to deter potential gray market activity).

Step 7. Implement pricing strategy and tactics, and set intermediary and end-user prices. Then, continuously monitor market performance and make pricing adjustments as necessary to accommodate evolving market conditions.

EXHIBIT 16.5

Key Steps in International Price Setting

in Japan such as local purchasing power, size of the market, market growth, competitors' prices, and Japanese attitudes on the relationship of price to product quality. Management also feels the price is reasonable given Melody's pricing in other markets, such as Hawaii and Australia. Accordingly, the firm implements the price level for end users and the corresponding price for Aoki, the importer. Melody begins shipping guitars to Japan and monitors the marketplace, tracking demand and the need to adjust prices in light of demand, economic conditions, and other emergent factors.

Step 5 in Exhibit 16.5 identifies three common pricing strategies in international business.

- *Rigid cost-plus pricing* refers to setting a fixed price for all export markets. It is an approach favored by less experienced exporters. In most cases, management simply adds a flat percentage to its domestic price to compensate for the added costs of doing business abroad. The final price to the customer includes a markup to cover transporting and marketing the product as well as profit margins for both intermediaries and the manufacturer. A key disadvantage of this method is that it may fail to account for local market conditions such as buyer demand, income level, and competition.
- *Flexible cost-plus pricing* is used when management includes any added costs of doing business abroad in its final price. Management also accounts for local market and competitive conditions, such as customer purchasing power, demand, competitor prices, and other external variables, as identified in Exhibit 16.4. This approach is more sophisticated than rigid cost-plus pricing because it accounts for specific circumstances in the target market. For example, the fashion retailer Zara uses this approach, adapting prices to suit conditions in each of the countries where it does business.
- *Incremental pricing* refers to setting prices to cover only the firm's variable costs but not its fixed costs. Here, management assumes fixed costs are already paid from sales of the product in the firm's home country or other markets. The approach enables the firm to offer competitive prices, but it may result in suboptimal profits. When carried to an extreme, incremental pricing may invite competitors to accuse a company of dumping—charging a lower price for exported products, sometimes below manufacturing cost, potentially driving local suppliers out of business. Dumping may be regarded as unfair or illegal, leading to sanctions from the World Trade Organization (www.wto.org).

Managing International Price Escalation

International price escalation

The problem of end-user prices reaching exorbitant levels in the export market, caused by multilayered distribution channels, intermediary margins, tariffs, and other international customer costs.

International price escalation refers to the problem of end-user prices reaching exorbitant levels in the export market, caused by multilayered distribution channels, intermediary margins, tariffs, and other international customer costs (identified in Exhibit 16.4). International price escalation means the retail price in the export market can be much higher than the price in the firm's home market, creating a competitive disadvantage for the exporter. Corporations can use five key strategies to combat export price escalation abroad, which we review next.[25]

- *Shorten the distribution channel* to establish a more direct route to reach the final customer by bypassing some intermediaries in the channel. With a shorter channel, there are fewer intermediaries to compensate, which reduces the product's final price.
- *Redesign the product* to remove costly features. Whirlpool developed a no-frills, simplified washing machine that it manufactures inexpensively and sells for a lower price in developing economies.
- *Ship products unassembled,* as parts and components, to qualify for lower import tariffs. Then perform final assembly in the foreign market, ideally by using low-cost labor. Some firms have their product assembled in foreign trade zones, where import costs are lower and government incentives may be available.[26]
- *Reclassify the exported product* to qualify for lower tariffs. Suppose Motorola faces a high tariff when exporting telecommunications equipment to Bolivia. By having the product reclassified as computer equipment, Motorola might be able to export the product under a lower tariff. The practice is possible because imported products often fit more than one product category for determining tariffs.
- *Move production or sourcing to another country* to take advantage of lower production costs or favorable currency rates.

Managing Pricing Under Varying Currency Conditions

In export markets, a strong domestic currency can reduce competitiveness, whereas a weakening domestic currency makes the firm's foreign pricing more competitive. Exhibit 16.6 presents various firm responses to a weakening or appreciating domestic currency.[27]

Transfer Pricing

Transfer pricing, or intracorporate pricing, refers to the practice of pricing intermediate or finished products exchanged among the subsidiaries and affiliates of the same corporate family located in different countries.[28] For example, when the Ford auto parts plant in South Africa sells parts to the Ford factory in Spain, it charges a transfer price for this intracorporate transaction. This price generally differs from the market prices Ford charges its usual customers.

MNEs such as Ford manage their internal prices primarily for two reasons.[29] First, it gives them a way to repatriate—that is, bring back to the home country—the profits from a country that restricts MNEs from taking their earnings out, often due to a shortage of its own currency. High prices charged to its foreign affiliate serve as an alternative means of transferring money out of the affiliate's country. The strategy works because controls imposed on money transferred in this way are not normally as strict as controls imposed on straight repatriation of profits.

Second, transfer pricing can help MNEs shift profits out of a country that has high corporate income taxes into a country with low corporate income taxes to increase companywide profitability. In this case, the MNE may opt to maximize the expenses (and therefore minimize the profits) of the foreign-country affiliate by charging high prices for goods sold to the affiliate. MNEs typically centralize transfer pricing under the direction of the chief financial officer at corporate headquarters.

Consider Exhibit 16.7 for a simple illustration of transfer pricing. A subsidiary may buy or sell a finished or intermediate product from another affiliate below cost, at cost, or above cost. Suppose the MNE treats Subsidiary A as a favored unit. That is, Subsidiary A is allowed to *source at or below cost* and *sell at a relatively high price* when transacting with other subsidiaries. Over time, Subsidiary A will achieve superior financial results at the expense of Subsidiaries

Transfer pricing
The practice of pricing intermediate or finished products exchanged among the subsidiaries and affiliates of the same corporate family located in different countries.

EXHIBIT 16.6 Strategies for Dealing with Varying Currency Conditions

When the exporter gains a price advantage because its home–country currency is weakening relative to the customer's currency, then it should:	When the exporter suffers from a price disadvantage because its home–country currency is appreciating relative to the customer's currency, then it should:
Stress the benefits of the firm's low prices to foreign customers.	Accentuate competitive strengths in nonprice elements of exporter's marketing program, such as product quality, delivery, and services.
Maintain normal price levels, expand the product line, or add more costly features.	Consider lowering prices by improving productivity, reducing production costs, or eliminating costly product features.
Exploit greater export opportunities in markets where this favorable exchange rate exists.	Concentrate exporting to those countries whose currencies have not weakened in relation to the exporter.
Speed repatriation of foreign-earned income and collections.	Maintain foreign-earned income in the customer's currency and delay collection of foreign accounts receivable (assuming the customer's currency likely will regain strength over a reasonable time period).
Minimize expenditures in the customer's currency (for example, for advertising and local transportation).	Maximize expenditures in the customer's currency.

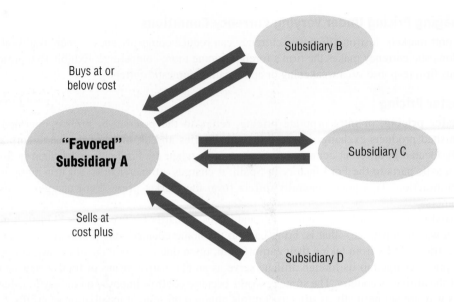

B, C, and D. Why would the MNE headquarters allow this? In general, headquarters would do this to optimize profits of the firm as a whole. A subsidiary would receive such a favorable treatment if it is located in a country with:

- Lower corporate income-tax rates.
- High tariffs for the product in question.
- Favorable accounting rules for calculating corporate income.
- Political stability.
- Little or no restrictions on profit repatriation.
- Strategic importance to the MNE.

Although the subsidiary's financial performance has been boosted in an artificial way, the earnings of the MNE as a whole are optimized. However, this benefit frequently comes at a cost. First, there is the complication of internal control measures. Manipulating transfer prices may make it more difficult to determine the true profit contribution of a subsidiary. Second, some subsidiary managers may react negatively to price manipulation. Third, as local businesses, subsidiaries must abide by local accounting rules. Legal problems will arise if they follow accounting standards the host government doesn't accept. Indeed, governments often scrutinize MNE transfer pricing practices to ensure that foreign firms pay their fair share of taxes by reporting accurate earnings. Thus, transfer pricing must be managed with great care.

Gray Market Activity (Parallel Imports)

Caterpillar, Duracell, Gucci, and Sony all have been the target of gray market activity. Exhibit 16.8 illustrates the nature of flows and relationships in gray market activity—the legal importation of genuine products into a country by intermediaries who are not authorized distributors.[30]

Consider a manufacturer that produces its products in one country and exports them to another, illustrated by the green arrow between countries A and B in Exhibit 16.8. If the going price of the product happens to be sufficiently lower in Country B, then gray market brokers can exploit arbitrage opportunities—buy the product at a low price in Country B, import it into the original source country, and sell it at a high price there, illustrated by the orange arrow.

In this scenario, the first transaction, illustrated by the green arrow, is carried out by authorized channel intermediaries. The second transaction, illustrated by the orange arrow, is carried out by unauthorized intermediaries. Often referred to as *gray marketers*, the unauthorized intermediaries are typically independent entrepreneurs. Because their transactions parallel those of authorized distributors, gray market activity is also called *parallel importation*.

In Canada, government determines pharmaceutical drug prices by imposing price controls. Consequently, drug prices are often lower there than in the United States. Because of

Manufacturer in the source country: Country A

Product is available locally from authorized distributors/retailers at a higher price than export markets

Manufacturer ships the product to authorized distributors in the export market

A gray marketer in the importing country purchases the product, ships it to the exporting country or to a third country, and sells it through unauthorized distributors to customers

Importing country: Country B

Product is available at a lower price from authorized distributors/retailers than the original source country

EXHIBIT 16.8

Illustration of Gray Market Activity

this difference, many U.S. consumers purchase their prescription drugs from online pharmacies in Canada to benefit from lower prices even though it is illegal for individuals to import prescription medications into the United States. Worldwide, gray market activity is common in pharmaceuticals, cameras, watches, computers, perfumes, and even construction equipment.[31]

The root cause of gray market activity is a large enough difference in price of the same product between two countries. Such price differences arise due to (i) the manufacturer's inability to coordinate prices across its markets, (ii) the firm's deliberate efforts to charge higher prices in some countries when competitive conditions permit, or (iii) exchange rate fluctuations that result in a price gap between products priced in different currencies.

Manufacturers of branded products are concerned about gray market activity because it can lead to:

- *A tarnished brand image* when customers realize the product is available at a lower price through alternative channels, particularly less-prestigious outlets.
- *Strained manufacturer–distributor relations* that can arise when parallel imports result in lost sales to authorized distributors.
- *Disruptions in company planning* that occur in regional sales forecasting, pricing strategies, merchandising plans, and general marketing efforts. Managers can pursue at least four strategies to cope with gray market imports.[32]
  - Aggressively cut prices in countries and regions that gray market brokers target.
  - Hinder the flow of products into markets where gray market brokers procure the product. For instance, in dealing with the pharmaceutical gray market between Canada and the United States, the U.S. firm Pfizer could reduce shipment of its cholesterol drug Lipitor to Canada to levels just sufficient for local use by Canadians.
  - Design products with exclusive features that strongly appeal to customers. Adding distinctive features unique to each market reduces the likelihood that products will be channeled elsewhere.
  - Publicize the limitations of gray market channels. Trademark owners publicize the disadvantages of buying gray market goods to potential buyers.

Source: Rob Crandall/Alamy

Toyota is typical of many firms that apply a global, standardized approach to advertising and distribution. This dealership is in South Africa.

International Marketing Communications

Companies use *marketing communications* (also known as *marketing promotion*) to provide information to, and communicate with, existing and potential customers, with the ultimate aim of stimulating demand. The various activities of marketing communications vary substantially around the world. Let's examine them in more detail.

International Advertising

Firms conduct advertising through *media*, which include direct mail, radio, television, cinema, billboards, transit, print media, and the Internet. *Transit* refers to ads placed in buses, trains, and subways; they are particularly useful in large cities. *Print media* are newspapers, magazines, and trade journals. Managers assess the availability and viability of media by examining the amount and types of advertising spending already occurring in each market. In 2015, advertising expenditures on major media were approximately $190 billion in the United States, $100 billion in Western Europe, and $125 billion in the Asia-Pacific region. Total spending on advertising worldwide reached almost $600 billion.[33] Five Western firms—Yum Brands, Pernod Ricard, Avon Products, Colgate-Palmolive, and P&G— typically spend more than 10 percent of their ad budgets in just one country — China.[34] In 2015, the United Kingdom became the world's first country where half of all advertising spending went to digital media.[35]

The availability and quality of media closely determine the feasibility and nature of marketing communications. Exhibit 16.9 provides statistics on media for various countries. The literacy rate indicates the number of people who can read, which is necessary to understand much advertising. Other data reveal the diversity of communication media in selected countries. In developing economies, TV, radio, newspapers, and the Internet are sometimes quite limited. The firm must use creative approaches to advertise in countries with low literacy rates and limited media infrastructure. Certain media selections make sense for some countries but not others. In Mexico and Peru, for example, marketers emphasize television advertising, in Kuwait and Norway, they concentrate on print media, and in Bolivia, firms use a lot of outdoor advertising

EXHIBIT 16.9 Media Characteristics in Selected Countries

	Literacy Rate (percentage of population)	Households with Television (percentage of all households)	Radio Stations (per one million people)	Newspaper Circulation (newspaper copies per one million people)	Internet Users (percentage of population)
Argentina	98%	97%	30.2	32,552	60%
Australia	99	99	25.5	95,439	90
China	96	99	0.5	87,572	46
Ethiopia	43	5	0.1	4,200	2
India	61	66	0.2	88,612	19
Japan	99	100	2.4	371,083	86
Mexico	94	95	11.5	44,033	41
Netherlands	99	99	32.0	226,497	96
Nigeria	68	43	0.7	23,000	38
Saudi Arabia	94	98	2.4	59,000	59
United Kingdom	99	99	14.8	184,977	84
United States	99	99	44.8	133,856	78

Note: Data are for the most recent year available.

Sources: Based on *CIA World Factbook* at http://www.cia.gov; World Bank at www.worldbank.org; Internet World Stats, "Internet Usage Statistics," www.internetworldstats.com; *World Press Trends, 2014* (Paris: WAN-IFRA, 2014).

on billboards and buildings. About half of all advertising funds in Italy are spent on television, more than double the figure for the United Kingdom, where newspapers attract the largest proportion of ad spending.[36]

International advertising expenditures vary depending on the size and extent of the firm's foreign operations. Smaller firms often lack the resources to advertise on TV or to develop a foreign sales force. Differences in culture, laws, and media availability mean it is seldom possible to duplicate in foreign markets the type and mix of advertising used in the home market. For example, the Italian government limits television advertising on state channels to 12 percent of airtime per hour and 4 percent per week. Mexico and Peru require firms to produce commercials for the local audience in their respective countries and use local actors.

Culture determines buyer attitudes toward the role and function of advertising, humor content, the depiction of characters (such as the roles of men and women), and decency standards. Advertising conveys a message encoded in language, symbols, colors, and other attributes, each of which may have distinctive meanings. Buyer receptiveness differs as a function of culture and language. In China, Nike ran an ad in which NBA basketball star LeBron James battles—and defeats—a computer-generated Chinese Kung Fu master. Chinese consumers were offended, and China's national government banned the ad.[37]

Many MNEs employ relatively standardized advertising around the world, an approach that simplifies the communications strategy and saves money. Benetton, the Italian clothing manufacturer, has enjoyed much success by using essentially the same "United Colors of Benetton" ad campaigns in markets worldwide. Levi Strauss's advertising approach is similar around the world, stressing the all-American image of its jeans. One TV ad in Indonesia showed teenagers cruising around a U.S. town in 1960s convertibles. In Japan, Levi Strauss frequently used James Dean, the 1950s U.S. film star, as the centerpiece of its advertising. The dialogue in Levi's ads is often in English worldwide.[38]

Most MNEs employ advertising agencies to create promotional content and select media for foreign markets. The choice is usually from among a home country–based agency with international expertise, a local agency based in the target market, or a *global advertising agency* that has offices in the target market. Exhibit 16.10 identifies leading global advertising agencies. These firms maintain networks of affiliates and local offices around the world. They can create advertising that is both global and sensitive to local conditions while offering a range of additional services such as market research, publicity, and package design.

MyManagementLab: Watch It! I

If your professor has assigned this, go to the Assignments section of **mymanagementlab.com** to complete the video exercise titled International Marketing and Unilever's BOP Strategy.

EXHIBIT 16.10 Large Global Advertising Agencies

Rank	Agency	Headquarters	Worldwide Revenue (billions of dollars)
1	Dentsu	Japan	$22.4
2	WPP	Ireland	19.0
3	Omnicom Group	United States	15.3
4	Publicis	France	9.6
5	Interpublic Group	United States	7.5
6	Hakuhodo	Japan	6.2
7	Havas	France	2.4
8	Young & Rubicam	United States	1.2

Sources: Based on Forbes, "The World's Biggest Public Companies: 2015 Ranking," www.forbes.com; Hoovers.com, company profiles, www.hoovers.com.

International Promotional Activities

Promotional activities are short-term marketing activities intended to stimulate an initial purchase, immediate purchase, or increased purchases of the product and to improve intermediary effectiveness and cooperation. They include tools such as coupons, point-of-purchase displays, demonstrations, samples, contests, gifts, and Internet interfacing.

Greece, Portugal, and Spain permit virtually every type of promotion, and Germany, Norway, and Switzerland forbid or restrict some. Couponing is illegal or restricted in some countries. Other promotional activities, such as giveaways, may be considered unethical or distasteful. In much of the world, such activities are uncommon and may be misunderstood. Promotions usually require a high level of intermediary or retailer sophistication to succeed.

16.6 Describe international distribution.

International Distribution

Distribution refers to the processes of getting the product or service from its place of origin to the customer. Distribution is the most inflexible of the marketing program elements—once a firm establishes a distribution channel, it may be difficult to change it. The most common approaches to international distribution include engaging independent intermediaries (for exporting firms) or establishing marketing and sales subsidiaries directly in target markets (an FDI-based approach). The exporting firm ships goods to its intermediary, which moves the product through customs and the foreign distribution channel to retail outlets or end users.

Ethical Connections

Walmart paid some $24 million in bribes to mayors, zoning officials, and other bureaucrats in Mexico to obtain building permits, clearances, and preferential treatment. The bribes were paid to expedite construction of the firm's huge network of stores in Mexico. Confronted with news of corruption at the firm's Mexican subsidiary, top executives focused on minimizing damage to Walmart's image rather than on rooting out wrongdoing. When the scandal was revealed, Walmart's stock price fell, and the firm exposed itself to prosecution from government officials.

David Barstow, "Vast Mexico Bribery Case Hushed Up by Wal-Mart After Top-Level Struggle," *New York Times*, April 22, 2012, p. A1.

By contrast, the foreign direct investor establishes its own operations in the market and works directly with intermediaries to move offerings through the channel to buyers. Using this approach, the firm will lease, acquire, or set up a sales office, warehouse, or an entire distribution channel directly in the target market. The main disadvantage of direct investment is its high cost. However, direct investment allows the firm to:

- Gain control over marketing and distribution activities in the market.
- Monitor the performance of employees and other actors in the market more effectively.
- Get closer to the market, which is especially helpful when the market is complex or rapidly changing.

Some firms bypass traditional distribution systems altogether by using *direct marketing*—selling directly to end users. It typically implies using the Internet to provide detailed product information and the means for foreigners to buy offerings. Some firms such as Amazon.com are entirely Internet based, with no retail stores. Others, such as Coles, Tesco, and Home Depot, combine direct marketing with traditional retailing.

Channel length refers to the number of distributors or other intermediaries that it takes to get the product from the manufacturer to the market. The longer the channel, the more intermediaries the firm must compensate, and the costlier the channel. For example, Japan is characterized by long distribution channels with numerous intermediaries. High channel costs contribute to international price escalation, creating a competitive disadvantage for the firm.

Distribution is especially challenging in emerging markets and developing economies, where delivery infrastructure is often poor. Nestlé expects nearly half its sales to come from emerging markets by 2020. In South Africa, the firm employs 80 sales personnel to sell baby food, nondairy creamers, and other products in areas characterized by poverty and small-scale retailing. Nestlé has invested almost a billion dollars in Africa to build up supply chains and distribution channels. Delivery is often accomplished by taxi, by bicycle, or on foot. Small-scale retailing accounts for about one-third of Nestlé's distribution in Africa.[39]

Global Account Management

In a gradually globalizing world, foreign customers increasingly seek uniform and consistent prices, quality, and customer service. **Global account management (GAM)** means serving a key global customer in a consistent and standardized manner, regardless of where in the world it operates. Walmart is a key global account for Procter & Gamble, purchasing many different P&G products. Walmart expects consistent service, including uniform prices for the same P&G product regardless of where in the world it is delivered.

Key accounts such as Migros, Zellers, and Walmart typically purchase from a collection of preferred suppliers that meet their specifications. Suppliers target these key customers by shifting resources from national, regional, and function-based operations to GAM, whose programs feature dedicated cross-functional teams, specialized coordination activities for specific accounts, and formalized structures and processes. Private IT-based portals facilitate the implementation of such systems. Each global customer is assigned a global account manager, or team, who provides the customer with coordinated marketing support and service across various countries.[40]

Global account management (GAM)

Serving a key global customer in a consistent and standardized manner, regardless of where in the world it operates.

MyManagementLab: **Watch It! 2**

If your professor has assigned this, go to the Assignments section of **mymanagementlab.com** to complete the video exercise titled Companies Look at the Hispanic American Consumer.

CLOSING CASE   H&M: International Marketing Success Story

H&M is a Swedish clothing retailer specializing in fast fashion and cheap chic styles for men, women, and children. The firm generates about $24 billion in global sales, making it one of the world's largest fashion retailers. The Gap and Zara are key competitors. When H&M opens a new store, it is accompanied by much attention and interest. From New York to Berlin to Tokyo, store openings typically receive massive media coverage. The Pasadena, California, store launch was covered from news helicopters, and numerous people slept outside the store the night before it opened. In May 2015, H&M opened its largest, new flagship store in New York City with a performance by Grammy winner John Legend. Such excitement is typical of H&M store launches worldwide.

The firm began as a women's clothing retailer, Hennes, and later merged with the Swedish men's store Mauritz. Management changed the name to H&M to simplify worldwide perception of the brand.

Initially, H&M was cautious with international expansion, restricting its reach to nearby European countries, where Germany, France, and the United Kingdom became top markets. In 2000, H&M opened its first U.S. store on Fifth Avenue in New York. The firm expanded into China, Japan, Russia, South Korea, and the Middle East. Today, H&M has more than 130,000 employees operating some 3,500 stores in about 55 countries. The retailer's top markets are Europe, Canada, and the United States.

On the heels of the spacious Fifth Avenue store launch, H&M opened several more outlets in the United States. The success of its Manhattan store did not consistently translate to other locations. Some new stores were too big, forcing management to downsize them. In the United States, H&M quickly learned that styles vary between cities and suburban locales. Management focused trendy

fashions in city stores and maintained more conservative items at suburban mall stores. A decision to launch a colorful apparel collection backfired, forcing retreat to traditional styles with subdued shades. Compared to Europe, top management noted that U.S. stores need to be more inviting. U.S. salespeople prefer focusing on a single segment such as children's wear or men's clothing.

Rapid Response Retailing

H&M emphasizes fast turnaround: the ability to take a garment from design to store shelf in three weeks. Although this falls short of competitor Zara's two-week turnaround, H&M's prices are usually lower. Known for its flexibility, H&M constantly monitors sales and restocks stores daily to replenish popular merchandise quickly.

Another cost-saving measure comes from outsourcing apparel manufacturing to 700 independent suppliers through 20 production offices, mainly located in Asia and Europe. Large quantities of materials are ordered from suppliers, allowing economies of scale that are passed on to consumers.

Rapid response retailing means that H&M ensures the right product gets to the right stores at the right time. It requires careful cost control and management of lead times with suppliers, factories, and distributors. The approach results in retail prices that are substantially lower than those of competitors.

Market Segments and Branding

The H&M brand symbolizes "fashion and quality at the best price." Men's and women's collections emphasize innovative styling for fashion-minded people of all ages. Strong branding increases marketing effectiveness, stimulates brand loyalty, and enhances customer confidence in purchase decisions. It helps customers know what H&M stands for—simple, stylish fashions offered at popular prices. The brand drives management decisions about how to design products and where and how to launch new stores.

Most H&M stores are located in Europe, where brand awareness is substantial. However, brand awareness is still limited in other parts of the world. In some markets, building a strong brand remains challenging. Weak brand image limits H&M's sales potential and its ability to recruit and retain employees, who are crucial to long-term success.

Marketing

H&M has more than 100 in-house designers who interpret apparel trends and create fashions accessible to everyone. H&M collaborates with well-known designers, offering limited edition clothing lines in some stores. For example, collaboration with Chanel design chief Karl Lagerfeld drew large crowds to H&M stores, selling out the exclusive line in only three days. Other design partners include Stella McCartney, Madonna, and Versace. At the Tokyo store opening, H&M introduced a collection with Comme des Garçons, one of Japan's most respected fashion houses. The initial response exceeded expectations, with customers waiting in line for three days before the launch.

H&M employs unique strategies to reach target markets and attract customers to new stores. Management is careful to choose the location of stores in each city, preferring exclusive shopping districts with high traffic. Stores are intended to be fun, inspiring, and inviting, with interior design and displays that communicate what H&M stands for. Together, the products, shop floors, displays, and staff make up the whole package that communicates the H&M brand.

The firm employs conventional promotional tactics such as print advertisements and catalogues as well as more novel approaches. *H&M Magazine* offers readers a mix of fashion and the latest lifestyle trends. The firm has its own Facebook page and sends out tweets on Twitter, maintaining a social network with fans around the world. The H&M YouTube site offers Fashion TV and inspirational films.

Use of celebrities such as Benicio Del Toro and Molly Sims helps maintain a trendy image. H&M experiments with nontraditional methods to communicate with customers. Partnering with marketing agencies Mobiento and Adiento, H&M launched a mobile marketing campaign targeted to 20- to 40-year-old women. The campaign included banner ads placed on carrier portals and media sites and a website with click-through slideshows and animated images of the firm's latest designs. Beyond promoting new additions to its apparel collection, the campaign drove customers to the H&M Club and its loyalty rewards program. Consumers received alerts and mobile coupons redeemable at nearby stores.

Recently, the firm expanded beyond traditional apparel by venturing into the home textiles business. H&M Home's products, including pillows, towels, curtains, and other textile products, are sold online and by mail. With this addition, H&M now competes with Spanish retailer Zara in the home textile market. Most recently, H&M launched its online sales in several countries to complement its physical stores. It also initiated a new beauty line featuring cosmetics and hair and skin care products.

Global Strategy and Localization

H&M management follows a global approach by emphasizing a uniform global brand and similar apparel in all its stores. Company designers at headquarters draw inspiration from key markets so that different regions' styles are incorporated into apparel designs. The product assortment is 80 percent the same in all markets, and local managers adjust the remaining 20 percent to fit local tastes. Apparel offered in the Tokyo stores is essentially the same as that offered in Europe, but the presentation is modified.

The head office provides substantial guidance on global strategy, and store managers localize tactics to their markets. At individual stores, local managers can adapt pricing, advertising, and product range to suit local conditions. The firm offers smaller sizes in Asia, conservative apparel in Islamic countries, and garments adjusted for seasonal differences between the northern and southern hemispheres. In a fickle industry, H&M has been a smashing success. The firm has applied skillful marketing to triumph in markets around the world.

AACSB: Reflective Thinking Skills

Case Questions

16-4. Visit H&M's website at www.hm.com. What are the characteristics of H&M's global market segment(s)? How does H&M position itself in the minds of target customers around the world?

16-5. How does management at H&M use global branding and global product development to create and offer its fashions? How does the firm use marketing mix elements to market its offerings around the world?

16-6. A key aspect of H&M's strategy is to provide value to customers by maximizing perceived product benefits, minimizing prices, or both. Given this, how can H&M further increase the value of its offerings to customers? That is, what steps can management take to increase the benefits and reduce the prices that its customers encounter when shopping for H&M products?

16-7. How does H&M strike a balance between standardization and adaptation of its marketing program? What advantages does H&M gain from standardization? From adaptation? What factors drive management to adapt offerings in particular markets?

16-8. Increasingly, H&M targets emerging markets such as China, Russia, and Saudi Arabia, which are often characterized by distinctive cultures, lower incomes, and inexperience with leading-edge fashion. In terms of marketing program elements, what can management do to ensure that H&M succeeds in these markets?

Sources: Dan Butcher, "Retail Giant H&M Runs Multifaceted Mobile Marketing Campaign," 2009, http://www.mobilemarketer.com; Patricia Cheng, "H&M Customers, Lured by Madonna Line, Flock to Asia Store Debut," 2009, http://www.bloomberg.com; H&M corporate website at http://www.hm.com; "Clothing Culture: International Designers Cut Their Cloth to Suit Local Tastes: Management Briefing: Japan," *Just-Style*, October 2009, pp. 13–16; Ingrid Giertz-Mårtenson, "H&M: Documenting the Story of One of the World's Largest Fashion Retailers," *Business History* 54, No. 1 (2012), pp. 108–115; Jens Hansegard, "H&M Expansion Pushes Sales Higher," *Wall Street Journal*, January 29, 2015, www.wsj.com; Katie Smith, "The 5 Things Making Zara and H&M Successful," *New Zealand Apparel*, April 2015, p. 28; Marina Strauss, "H&M's Next Move: Taking It to the Streets," *Globe and Mail*, May 22, 2009, http://www.theglobeandmail.com; Stephen Wigley and C. R. Chiang, "Retail Internationalisation in Practice: Per Una in the UK and Taiwan," *International Journal of Retail & Distribution Management* 37, No. 3 (2009), pp. 250–270; *WWD: Women's Wear Daily*, "Versace's H&M Invasion," November 18, 2011, p. 4; *WWD: Women's Wear Daily*, "H&M Eyes Expansion with More U.S. Stores," April 16, 2015, p. 1.

Note: This case was prepared by Professor Erin Cavusgil, University of Michigan, Flint, for classroom discussion.

END OF CHAPTER REVIEW

 MyManagementLab

Go to **mymanagementlab.com** to complete the problems marked with this icon .

Key Terms

adaptation   468
global account management
    (GAM)   485
global brand   470

global market segment   467
global marketing strategy   466
gray market activity   475
international price escalation   478

standardization   468
transfer pricing   479

Summary

In this chapter, you learned about:

- **Global market segmentation**

    Developing a marketing strategy requires managers to assess the unique foreign market environment and then make choices about market segments, targeting, and positioning. **Global marketing strategy** is a plan of action that guides the firm in how to position itself and its offerings in foreign markets, which customer segments to pursue, and to what degree its marketing program elements should be standardized and adapted. A **global market segment** is a group of customers who share common characteristics across many national markets.

- **Standardization and adaptation of international marketing**

    How management balances **adaptation** and **standardization** determines the extent to which the firm must modify a product and its marketing to suit foreign markets. On the whole, firms prefer to standardize their products to achieve scale economies and minimize complexity. A **global market segment** is a group of customers that shares common characteristics across many national markets. *Positioning* strategy involves using marketing to create a particular image of a product or service, especially relative to competitor offerings, among the firm's customers worldwide.

- **Global branding and product development**

    A **global brand** is perceived similarly in all the firm's markets and increases marketing strategy effectiveness, allowing the firm to charge higher prices and deal more effectively with channel members and competitors. In developing products with multicountry potential, managers emphasize the commonalities rather than the differences across countries. The development of global products facilitates economies of scale in R&D, production, and marketing. Innovation and design in international product development are increasingly performed by *global teams*—internationally distributed

groups of people with a specific mandate to make or implement decisions that are international in scope.

- **International pricing**

    International prices are determined by factors both internal and external to the firm that often cause prices to inflate abroad. A special challenge for exporters in pricing is **international price escalation**—the problem of end-user prices reaching exorbitant levels in the export market, caused by multilayered distribution channels, intermediary margins, tariffs, and other international customer costs. **Transfer pricing** is the practice of pricing intermediate or finished products exchanged among the subsidiaries and affiliates of the same corporate family located in different countries. **Gray market activity**, also known as parallel imports, refers to legal importation of genuine products into a country by intermediaries other than authorized distributors.

- **International marketing communications**

    International marketing communications involves the management of advertising and promotional activities across national borders. Managers are often compelled to adapt their international communications due to unique legal, cultural, and socioeconomic factors in foreign markets. Firms must also accommodate literacy levels, language, and available media.

- **International distribution**

    Firms usually engage foreign intermediaries or foreign-based subsidiaries to reach customers in international markets. Some firms bypass traditional distribution systems by using *direct marketing*. *Channel length* refers to the number of distributors or other intermediaries it takes to get the product from the manufacturer to the market. Long channels are relatively costly. In working with key business customers, firms may undertake **global account management (GAM)**—servicing key global customers in a consistent and standardized manner, regardless of where in the world they operate.

Test Your Comprehension AACSB: Reflective Thinking Skills, Ethical Understanding and Reasoning Abilities

16-9. Outline the environment for international business. What dimensions need to be considered by organizations that operate internationally?

⭐ **16-10.** Toledo Glass Sociedad Anónima operates successfully in the Spanish domestic market and across many countries in Latin America. The company struggles to compete elsewhere. What might be the fundamental problems that are preventing the company from being successful elsewhere?

⭐ **16-11.** How does a positioning strategy help an organization differentiate itself from competitors?

16-12. Consider Toshiba's laptop computer division. In terms of the marketing program elements, what attributes of laptop computers does the firm need to adapt and which attributes can it standardize for international markets?

16-13. What is the role of market segmentation and positioning in international marketing? What is a global market segment?

16-14. What are the most important factors to consider when formulating international pricing strategies? What steps would you follow in arriving at international prices?

16-15. Suppose export customers of a consumer product are highly sensitive to price. However, the firm is experiencing substantial price escalation in the market. What factors may be causing this situation? What can management do to reduce the harmful impact of international price escalation?

16-16. What does a global account manager do?

Apply Your Understanding AACSB: Reflective Thinking Skills, Analytic Skills, Ethical Understanding and Reasoning Abilities

16-17. Products must be adapted to accommodate national differences arising from customer preferences and each market's economic conditions, climate, culture, and language. Think about the following products: packaged flour, swimsuits, textbooks, and automobiles. Describe how a firm would need to adapt the marketing for each of these products to suit conditions in China, Germany, and Saudi Arabia. In particular, think about the nature of the product, its pricing and distribution, and the marketing communications associated with it. China is an emerging market with low per-capita income, Saudi Arabia is an emerging market with a conservative culture rooted in Islam, and Germany is an advanced economy with a liberal culture. You may wish to consult globalEDGE™ (www.globalEDGE.msu.edu) to learn more about these specific markets.

16-18. Office Depot (www.officedepot.com) is a North America-based supplier of office equipment and supplies. It has stores in Japan, Mexico, and Poland. Suppose Office Depot decides to launch a line of notebook computers and wants to know how to price them in each of these markets. What factors should Office Depot consider in setting prices in each market? Should the firm standardize

its pricing, or should prices be adapted to each country? Suppose Office Depot's final prices proved to be too high for Mexico; what steps could management take to lower the price and still generate profits from selling notebooks there? Suggest a step-by-step approach to international pricing.

16-19. *Ethical Dilemma:* You just assumed a senior management position with Philip Morris (PM), a major manufacturer of cigarettes. As cigarette sales have declined in the advanced economies, PM has increased its marketing efforts in developing economies and emerging markets, where demand for smoking tobacco remains strong. Because of the enormous population in such countries, PM expects to generate huge sales. However, many of the countries have high illiteracy rates, and people are not very aware of the harmful health effects of smoking cigarettes. Many people become addicted to smoking. Given these factors, is it ethical to target such countries with cigarettes? Using the ethical framework in Chapter 4, analyze the arguments for and against marketing cigarettes to developing economies and emerging markets. As a senior manager, what steps should you take, if any, to address the dilemma?

 **globalEDGE** | **INTERNET EXERCISES**

(www.globalEDGE.msu.edu)

AACSB: Reflective Thinking Skills

Refer to Chapter 1, page 54, for instructions on how to access and use globalEDGE™.

16-20. Global branding is key to international marketing success. Each year *Interbrand* (www.interbrand.com) publishes a ranking of the top 100 global brands. The ranking can be accessed by searching at the *Interbrand* site or by entering Best Global Brands in a Google search. For this exercise, locate and retrieve the most current ranking and answer the following questions:

    a. In your view, what are the strengths and weaknesses of the methodology *Interbrand* uses to estimate brand equity?

    b. What patterns do you detect in terms of the countries and industries most represented in the top 100 list?

    c. According to *Interbrand*, what managerial guidelines will help a company develop a strong global brand?

16-21. Procter and Gamble (P&G) and Unilever are the two leading firms in the consumer products industry for offerings such as soap, shampoo, and laundry detergent. P&G (www.pg.com) is based in the United States, and Unilever (www.unilever.com) is based in Europe. What are the major regional markets of each firm? What products does each firm offer through a global marketing strategy? Structure your answer in terms of the marketing-mix elements. That is, what global strategy approaches does each firm use for the product, its pricing, communications, and distribution?

16-22. *A third-party logistics provider (3PL)* provides outsourced or third-party logistics services to companies for part or all of their distribution activities. Examples include C.H. Robinson Worldwide, Maersk Logistics, and FedEx. Your firm needs to find a 3PL to handle its distribution efforts abroad. Your task is to locate two 3PLs' online and address the following questions:

    a. What logistical services does each firm provide?

    b. What types of customers does each 3PL serve?

    c. Where are their headquarters and branch offices located?

    d. Based on the information provided, which of the two 3PLs would you most likely choose? Why?

 # CAREER TOOLBOX

Developing a Distribution Channel in Japan

A critical step in developing export operations is creating the foreign distribution channel. It provides the means to convey products (and many services) from their point of production to a convenient location where customers can buy them. In the absence of a well-conceived distribution channel, marketing and selling may prove ineffective.

The direct exporting firm should establish a reliable distribution channel in the foreign market from the beginning of export operations. Channels are often costly to set up and, once established, may be difficult to change. Because buyers may view the distributor as the originator of the product or service, the exporter must choose a good distributor. In this exercise, your challenge is to investigate the nature of distribution channels in Japan for a firm that manufactures medical equipment. Managers typically undertake such an investigation in the course of developing a channel in a promising foreign market.

Background

The *Japanese medical equipment and supplies market* is very promising. It is the second largest medical products market in the world and has achieved steady growth in recent years. Japanese distribution channels are usually complex, multilayered, and often inefficient. The market in Japan for medical equipment exceeds $10 billion annually. Imports are about 40 percent of this figure. The Japanese government regulates many medical products because of potential health risks. The government also has established programs to hold down medical product prices. The Japanese often are not the leading producers of medical technologies. Foreign firms see bright prospects for sales of pacemakers, artificial implants, and interventional cardiology devices. Sales of software and other products used in medical information and communications systems are also promising.

Various types of intermediaries provide distribution, including merchant distributors, agents, trading companies, and export management companies. Trading companies are common in Japan. However, because they deal in thousands of imported goods, large trading companies often do not give products individual attention. The direct exporter typically engages one or more independent intermediaries in the market.

To complete this exercise in your MyLab, go to the Career Toolbox.

MyManagementLab **Try It!**

The simulation Global Marketing accompanies this exercise.

 MyManagementLab

Go to **mymanagementlab.com** for Auto-graded writing questions as well as the following Assisted-graded writing questions:

⭐**16-23.** Firms frequently adapt their products to suit conditions abroad. What other marketing program elements do firms adapt for international markets?

⭐**16-24.** William Corporation is a manufacturer of high-quality men's and women's fashions. What steps should you take to transform William into a well-recognized global brand?

⭐**16-25.** MyManagementLab Only—comprehensive writing assignment for this chapter.

Endnotes

1. Cem Bahadir, Sundar Bharadwaj, and Rajendra Srivastava, "Marketing Mix and Brand Sales in Global Markets: Examining the Contingent Role of Country-Market Characteristics," *Journal of International Business Studies* 46, No. 5 (2015), pp. 596–619; Shaoming Zou and S. Tamer Cavusgil, "The GMS: A Broad Conceptualization of Global Marketing Strategy and Its Effect on Firm Performance," *Journal of Marketing* 66 (2002), pp. 40–56.

2. H. Gatignon, J. Eliashberg, and T. Robertson, "Modeling Multinational Diffusion Patterns: An Efficient Methodology," *Marketing Science* 8 (1989), pp. 231–243; Salah Hassan and Stephen Craft, "Examining World Market Segmentation and Brand Positioning Strategies," *Journal of Consumer Marketing* 29, No. 5 (2012), pp. 344–356.

3. G. Fowler and M. Marr, "Disney's China Play," *Wall Street Journal*, June 16, 2005, pp. B1, B7; Kimburley Choi, "Disneyfication and Localisation: The Cultural Globalisation Process of Hong Kong Disneyland," *Urban Studies* 49 No. 2 (2012), pp. 383–397.

4. George Yip, *Total Global Strategy II* (Upper Saddle River, NJ: Prentice Hall, 2003).

5. David Kaplan and Bill Powell, "General Mills' Global Sweet Spot," *Fortune*, May 23, 2011, pp. 23–25.

6. Yip (2003); Ellen Byron, "Gillette Sharpens Its Pitch for Expensive Razor," *Wall Street Journal*, October 6, 2008, p. B9.

7. Roger Calantone, S. Tamer Cavusgil, Jeffrey Schmidt, and Geon-Cheol Shin, "Internationalization and the Dynamics of Product Adaptation—An Empirical Investigation," *Journal of Product Innovation Management* 21 (2004), pp. 185–198; Berk Talay, Janell Townsend, Sengun Yeniyurt, "Global Brand Architecture Position and Market-Based Performance: The Moderating Role of Culture," *Journal of International Marketing* 23, No. 2 (2015), pp. 55–72.

8. Kaplan and Powell (2011).

9. J. Tapper and A. Miller, "'The Simpsons' Exported to Middle East," October 18, 2005, *ABC News*, http://abcnews.go.com/wnt.

10. Brian Bremner, "McDonald's Is Loving It in Asia," *BusinessWeek*, January 24, 2007, http://www.businessweek.com; Marion Issard, "To Tailor Burgers for France, McDonald's Enlists Baguette," *Wall Street Journal*, February 24, 2012, p. B4.

11. Beth Kowitt, "It's IKEA'S World*," *Fortune*, March 15, 2015, pp. 166–175.

12. Reena Jana, "Inspiration from Emerging Economies," *BusinessWeek*, March 23, 2009, p. 38; Ian Rowley, "Will Japan Fall in Love with Lexus?" *BusinessWeek*, July 11, 2005, p. 49.

13. Mark Ritson, "Coke's 'One Brand' Strategy Highlights One of the Great Marketing Themes of Our Lifetime," *Marketing Week*, March 11, 2015, p. 1; Gabriele Suder and David Suder, "Strategic Megabrand Management: Does Global Uncertainty Affect Brands?" *The Journal of Product and Brand Management* 17, No. 7 (2008), pp. 436–445.

14. Patrick Regnér and Udo Zander, "International Strategy and Knowledge Creation: The Advantage of Foreignness and Liability of Concentration," *British Journal of Management* 25, No. 3 (2014), pp. 551–569; Yip (2003).

15. Douglas Holt, John Quelch, and Earl Taylor, "How Global Brands Compete," *Harvard Business Review* (September 2004), pp. 68–75; Jennifer Rooney, "Forbes Corporate Approval Ratings," *Forbes*, October 24, 2011, pp. 30–32.

16. John Egan, *Marketing Communications* (Thousand Oaks, CA: Sage, 2015); Rajshekhar Javalgi, Virginie Pioche Khare, Andrew Gross, and Robert Scherer, "An Application of the Consumer Ethnocentrism Model to French Consumers," *International Business Review* 14 (2005), pp. 325–344; Plavini Punyatoya, Ashish Sadh, Sushanta Mishra, "Role of Brand Globalness in Consumer Evaluation of New Product Branding Strategy," *Journal of Brand Management* 21, No. 2 (2014), pp. 171–188.

17. David Aaker, *Managing Brand Equity* (New York: The Free Press, 1991); Cheng Lu Wang and Jiaxun He, *Brand Management in Emerging Markets: Theories and Practices* (Hershey, PA: IGI Global, 2014); Yen-Tsung Huang and Ya-Ting Tsai, "Antecedents and Consequences of Brand-Oriented Companies," *European Journal of Marketing* 47, No. 11/12 (2013), pp. 2020–2041.

18. Egan (2015); Yip (2003).

19. Ibid.

20. Hae-Jung Hong and Yves Doz, "L'Oréal Masters Multiculturalism," *Harvard Business Review* 91, No. 6 (2013), pp. 114–119; L'Oréal, "A Network That Is Open to the World," L'Oréal company website, www.loreal.com, accessed July 8, 2015; L'Oréal, "Product Development: From Dreams to Reality," L'Oréal company website, www.loreal.com, accessed July 18, 2015.

21. Alexander Brem and Florian Freitag, "Internationalisation of New Product Development and Research & Development," *International Journal of Innovation Management* 19, No. 1 (2015), pp. 1–32; *Proofs*, "Philips Wins International Design Award," January 2012, p. 27; Helen Walters, "IDEA 2009: Designing a Better World," *BusinessWeek*, July 29, 2009, http://www.businessweek.com.

22. Deepa Chandrasekaran, Joep Arts, Gerard Tellis, and Ruud Frambach, "Pricing in the International Takeoff of New Products," *International Journal of Research in Marketing* 30, No. 3 (2013), pp. 249–264; Matthew B. Myers, "Implications of Pricing Strategy-Venture Strategy Congruence: An Application Using Optimal Models in an International Context," *Journal of Business Research* 57 (2004), pp. 591–690.

23. Chris Reiter and Edith Balazs, "Daimler's Billion-Dollar Bet on Hungary," *Bloomberg Businessweek*, April 9, 2012, pp. 29–30.

24. S. Tamer Cavusgil, "Pricing for Global Markets," *Columbia Journal of World Business* (Winter 1996), pp. 66–78.

25. S. Tamer Cavusgil, "Unraveling the Mystique of Export Pricing," *Business Horizons* 31 (1988), pp. 54–63; Cavusgil (1996).

26. William McDaniel and Edgar Kossack, "The Financial Benefits to Users of Foreign-Trade Zones," *Columbia Journal of World Business* 18 (1983), pp. 33–41.

27. Cavusgil (1988); Nergiz Dincer and Magda Kandil, "The Effects of Exchange Rate Fluctuations on Exports," *Journal of International Trade & Economic Development* 20, No. 6 (2011), pp. 809–837.

28. Thomas Pugel and Judith Ugelow, "Transfer Prices and Profit Maximization in Multinational Enterprise Operations," *Journal of International Business Studies* 13 (Spring–Summer 1982),

pp. 115–119; Nilufer Usmen, "Transfer Prices: A Financial Perspective," *Journal of International Financial Management & Accounting* 23, No. 1 (2012), pp. 1–22.

29. Ralph Drtina and Jane Reimers, "Global Transfer Pricing: A Practical Guide for Managers," *S.A.M. Advanced Management Journal* 74, No. 2 (2009), pp. 4–12.

30. S. Tamer Cavusgil and Ed Sikora, "How Multinationals Can Counter Gray Market Imports," *Columbia Journal of World Business* 23 (1988), pp. 75–86; Chun-Hsiung Liao and I. Hsieh, "Determinants of Consumer's Willingness to Purchase Gray-Market Smartphones," *Journal of Business Ethics* 114, No. 3 (2013), pp. 409–424.

31. Ernst Berndt, "A Primer on the Economics of Re-Importation of Prescription Drugs," *Managerial and Decision Economics* 28 (2007), pp. 415–435; Margaret Kyle, "Strategic Responses to Parallel Trade," *Journal of Economic Analysis & Policy* 11, No. 2 (2011), pp. 1–32.

32. Cavusgil and Sikora (1988); Liao and Hsieh (2013).

33. *eMarketer*, "Advertisers Will Spend Nearly $600 Billion Worldwide in 2015," December 10, 2014, www.emarketer.com; *Marketing Week*, "Global Ad Spend Forecast to Outpace Economic Growth," December 8, 2011, p. 10.

34. Laurel Wentz and Bradley Johnson, "Top 100 Global Advertisers Heap Their Spending Abroad," *Advertising Age*, November 30, 2009, pp. 1–2.

35. Mark Sweney, "UK First Country in World Where Half of All Ad Spend Is on Digital Media," *The Guardian*, March 27, 2015, www.theguardian.com.

36. T. Melewar, D. Pickton, S. Gupta, and T. Chigovanyika, "MNE Executive Insights into International Advertising Programme Standardization," *Journal of Marketing Communications* 15, No. 5 (2009), pp. 345–365; Charles R. Taylor and Shintaro Okazaki, "Do Global Brands Use Similar Executional Styles Across Cultures?" *Journal of Advertising* 44, No. 3 (2015), pp. 276–288.

37. F. Balfour and D. Kiley, "Ad Agencies Unchained," *BusinessWeek*, April 25, 2005, pp. 50–51.

38. Egan (2015); Yip (2003).

39. Devon Maylie, "By Foot, by Bike, by Taxi, Nestlé Expands in Africa," *Wall Street Journal*, December 1, 2011, pp. B1, B16.

40. Linda Shi, Shaoming Zou, J. Chris White, Regina McNally, and S. Tamer Cavusgil, "Executive Insights: Global Account Management Capability," *Journal of International Marketing* 13 (2005), pp. 93–113; Sengun Yeniyurt, S. Tamer Cavusgil, and Tomas Hult, "A Global Market Advantage Framework: The Role of Global Market Knowledge Competencies," *International Business Review* 14 (2005), pp. 1–19.

Chapter 17

Human Resource Management in the Global Firm

Learning Objectives *After studying this chapter, you should be able to:*

17.1 Understand the strategic role of human resources in international business.

17.2 Explain international staffing policy.

17.3 Know about preparation and training of international employees.

17.4 Discuss performance appraisal and compensation of international employees.

17.5 Understand international labor relations.

17.6 Describe diversity in the international workforce.

Etisalat Egypt: Attracting and Maintaining the Best Employees

Etisalat is an Emirates-based telecommunications company, which is now operating in 19 countries in the Middle East, Asia, and Africa. Their biggest claim to excellence is that within their first 50 days of operations in Egypt, Etisalat was able to attract 1 million subscribers. Simply put, they believe they are the best, and they believe that in order to maintain their standing as an outstanding service provider, they need to ensure that each aspect of the business is able to uphold the quality of service which is expected from such a global company.

Operating in such a dynamic and labor-intensive industry and having the experience of operating in several countries around the world, Etisalat understands the need to uphold the highest standards when it comes to their employees. In fact, they recognize that the core of their success stems directly from the performance of their employees.

Being the third mobile operator to open in Egypt, with both competitors trying to out-do each other in the market, Etisalat's focus on hiring the best telecom employees and continuously inspiring them to be the best was, no doubt, one of the reasons why Etisalat was able to build up a strong consumer base in a short number of years, despite the fierce competition present in the telecom industry.

Etisalat realizes that operating in the service sector necessitates that it ensures its people are highly skilled, motivated, and talented employees in order to ensure providing the best service possible. In order to promote such employee behavior, Etisalat has focused on creating a corporate culture that incorporates the following values;

- Proudly Etisalat: a combination of customer focus as well as passion to be the best.

Source: View Stock/Alamy

- Respectful: towards one another, respected within the organization and feeling a sense of ownership of the business.
- Outstanding: a winning, fighter's attitude, in addition to taking initiative and going the extra mile whenever possible.
- Unique: leading by example, being an inspiration to others and creating opportunities for innovation.
- Delivering: proactively, ambitiously and with a sense of responsibility for delivering on individual and team promises.

Etisalat is a company that truly believes in the power its employees have on affecting their performance as a company. They understand that the customer experience is not only affected by the technical aspects of the service, but, more importantly, by the services they receive from the employees they interact with. Therefore, it is essential for them to ensure that their employees around the globe are not only aware of their impact on the consumer's perception of the business, but actively work towards continuously enhancing customer satisfaction across the board in all the various consumer interaction channels.

Questions

17-1. Emaar's slogan for their HR is "Satisfied Employees Create Satisfied Customers". What does this mean?

17-2. How does Etisalat ensure that their employees have access to quality career development programs?

17-3. Suggest how a corporation like Etisalat could create an comprehensive training program.

SOURCES: http://etisalat.com.eg/etisalat/Etisalat_Portal_En/about/why_etisalat.htm and http://etisalat.com.eg/etisalat/Etisalat_Portal_En/about/culture_values.htm

---

Human resources refer to the employees who make up the workforce of a business or other organization. The organizational function that oversees such assets is called *human resource management* (HRM, or simply HR). Leading-edge companies refer to their employees as "human talent," "human capital," or "intangible assets," emphasizing that they represent a strategic investment rather than a cost. This is especially true in knowledge-intensive industries such as management consulting, banking, advertising, engineering, and architecture. Without problem solvers, knowledge workers, and other creative personnel, firms such as McKinsey, Pixar, Gucci, Nokia, and many others would have great difficulty competing globally.

Managers recognize that their employees and the knowledge they possess are among their most important strategic assets.[1] Recruiting, managing, and retaining human resources are especially challenging at firms with global operations.

For example, consider Siemens, the German MNE. In 2015, Siemens employed more than 350,000 people in some 200 countries. These included 200,000 people throughout Europe; 80,000 in North and South America; 60,000 in the Asia-Pacific region; and 10,000 in Africa, the Middle East, and Russia. Like Siemens, Hutchison Whampoa, IBM, ArcelorMittal, Nestlé, Matsushita, McDonald's, Unilever, Volkswagen, and Walmart each has more than 100,000 employees working outside their home countries.

In this chapter, we examine the critical role of human resources in the multinational enterprise. We describe the planning and training that firms undertake to recruit and prepare employees to work in international operations. We explain the complexities of compensating managers who work abroad, the complex nature of international labor relations, and the value of maintaining a diverse global workforce. We begin by examining the strategic role that managers and the workforce play in company operations around the world.

17.1 Understand the strategic role of human resources in international business.

International human resource management (IHRM)
The planning, selection, training, employment, and evaluation of employees for international operations.

The Strategic Role Of Human Resources In International Business

International human resource management (IHRM) refers to the planning, selection, training, employment, and evaluation of employees for international operations.[2] Management struggles with a wide range of challenges in hiring and managing workers within the distinctive cultural and legal frameworks that govern employee practices around the world. International human resource managers, usually located at corporate or regional headquarters, support subsidiary managers by providing IHRM guidelines and by hiring, training, and evaluating employees for international operations.

For example, a Canadian MNE may employ Italian citizens in its subsidiary in Italy (HCNs), send Canadian citizens to work in the Asia-Pacific region on assignment (PCNs), or assign Swiss employees to its subsidiary in Turkey (TCNs).

In a firm with multicountry operations, there are generally three types of managers.

- **Parent-country nationals (PCNs).** These managers are citizens of the country where the MNE is headquartered. They are also called "home–country nationals."
- **Host–country nationals (HCNs).** They are citizens of the country where the MNE's subsidiary is located. They are typically the largest proportion of workers hired abroad and usually work in manufacturing, assembly, basic service activities, clerical work, and other nonmanagerial functions.
- **Third-country nationals (TCNs).** They are citizens of countries other than the home or host country. They typically work in management and are usually hired because of their special knowledge or skills.

Employees in any of the three categories assigned to work and reside in a foreign country for an extended period, usually a year or longer, are called **expatriates** (sometimes shortened to *expat*). A U.S. firm might employ a German manager in its subsidiary in France or transfer a Japanese executive to its U.S. headquarters.[3] Both these managers are expatriates. Although expatriates comprise only a small percentage of the workforce in most MNEs, they perform many critical functions.

For IHRM managers, the ultimate challenge is to ensure that the right person is in the right position at the right location with the right pay scale. In some countries, it is easier to get work visas for employees with specific specialized skills. For example, the financial services and information technology sectors in southern India have experienced a shortage of mid- and senior-level managerial talent. Managers from as far away as Eastern Europe can obtain work visas and gain posts in India, receiving compensation packages that are now competitive by advanced economy standards.[4]

Differences Between Domestic and International HRM

International human resource management is usually more complex than domestic human resource management. Exhibit 17.1 illustrates six factors that drive this complexity.[5] Let's examine each in turn.

- *New HR responsibilities*   IHRM managers encounter numerous factors not necessarily present at home, including foreign taxation issues for expatriates, international relocation and orientation, expatriate support, host government relations, language translation services, and repatriation (returning the expatriate to his or her home country).
- *Need for a broader, international perspective*   Management must account for all its PCNs, HCNs, and TCNs, who may be nationals of numerous countries. In an emerging market, such as Vietnam, compensation may need to include allowances for housing, education, and other facilities not readily available there. Large MNEs are often challenged by the

---

Parent-country national (PCN)
An employee who is a citizen of the country where the MNE is headquartered.

Host–country national (HCN)
An employee who is a citizen of the country where the MNE subsidiary or affiliate is located.

Third-country national (TCN)
An employee who is a citizen of a country other than the home or host country.

Expatriate
An employee assigned to work and reside in a foreign country for an extended period, usually a year or longer.

EXHIBIT 17.1

Factors That Increase the Complexity of Human Resource Management in International Business

need to establish a fair and comparable compensation scale for employees, regardless of nationality. For example, an Australian posted to Brazil can be subject to income tax from both countries. Tax equalization—ensuring that there is no tax disincentive to take an international assignment—is complex.

- *Greater involvement in employees' personal lives*   Human resource professionals help expatriates and their families with housing arrangements, health care, children's schooling, safety, and security. Some expatriates may require additional temporary compensation because of higher living costs in some foreign locations.
- *Managing the mix of expatriates and locals*   Foreign subsidiaries may be staffed from the home country, the host country, and/or third countries. The mix of staff depends on several factors, including the firm's level of international experience, cost of living in the foreign location, and availability of qualified local staff.
- *Greater risk exposure*   Employee productivity, labor union activism, employee turnover, and other human resource phenomena are often more pronounced abroad. Exposure to political risk and terrorism are major concerns for IHRM professionals and may require greater compensation and security arrangements for employees and their families.
- *External influences of the government and national culture*   Employees must be hired, evaluated, and compensated in ways consistent with country and regional customs and regulations. Laws govern work hours, the firm's ability to dismiss or lay off employees, and severance pay. In many countries, labor unions are active in managing the firm. In France, Germany, and Spain, employees may work no more than a set number of hours per week, sometimes as few as 35. Italy's labor regulations are so complex that many companies delay hiring new workers.[6]

Key Tasks in International Human Resource Management

Exhibit 17.2 outlines six key tasks of international human resource managers.

- *International staffing policy*, activities related to recruiting, selecting, and placing employees.

EXHIBIT 17.2 Key Tasks and Challenges of International Human Resource Management

Task	Strategic Goals	Illustrative Challenges
International staffing policy	• Choose between home–country nationals, host–country nationals, and third-country nationals • Develop global managers • Recruit and select expatriates	• Avoid country bias, nepotism, and other local practices • Cultivate global mind-set
Preparation and training of international employees	• Increase effectiveness of international employees, leading to increased company performance • Train employees with an emphasis on area studies, practical information, and cross-cultural awareness	• Minimize culture shock and expatriate assignment failure
International performance appraisal	• Assess, over time, how effectively managers and other employees perform their jobs abroad	• Strike the right balance between standardized and localized employee performance benchmarks
Compensation of employees	• Develop guidelines and administer compensation (e.g., base salary, benefits, allowances, and incentives)	• Avoid double taxation of employees
International labor relations	• Manage and interact with labor unions, engage in collective bargaining, handle strikes and other labor disputes, wage rates, and possible workforce reduction	• Reduce absenteeism, workplace injuries due to negligence, and the occurrence of labor strikes
Diversity in the international workforce	• Recruit talent from diverse backgrounds to bring specific knowledge and experience to the firm's problems and opportunities	• Achieve gender diversity

- *Preparing and training international employees.*
- *International performance appraisal*, providing feedback necessary for employees' professional development.
- *Compensation of employees,* including benefits packages that may vary greatly from country to country.
- *International labor relations*, including interacting with labor unions and collective bargaining.
- *Diversity in the international workforce.*

The remainder of this chapter is devoted to examining these tasks.

International Staffing Policy

17.2 Explain international staffing policy.

A critical task for MNEs is to decide the ideal mix of employees in the firm's foreign subsidiaries and affiliates.[7] The ideal mix varies by location, industry, stage in the value chain, and availability of qualified local workers. Country laws may dictate how many employees can come from nonlocal sources.

Exhibit 17.3 shows the criteria and rationale for hiring each type of employee.[8] Firms usually post PCNs abroad to take advantage of their specialized knowledge, especially in upstream value-chain operations, or to maintain local control over foreign operations. PCNs can also help develop local managers.

Firms prefer HCNs when the host–country environment is complex and their specialized knowledge or local connections are required in the local marketplace. HCNs often perform downstream value-chain activities, such as marketing and sales, which require extensive local knowledge.[9] It is usually less costly to compensate them than PCNs or TCNs.

Firms often prefer TCNs when senior management wants to transfer specific knowledge or corporate culture from third countries to host–country operations. Worldwide staffing with TCNs helps firms develop an integrated global enterprise.

EXHIBIT 17.3

Criteria for Selecting Employees for Foreign Operations

Staff with Parent-Country Nationals (PCNs) When...	Staff with Host–Country Nationals (HCNs) When...	Staff with Third-Country Nationals (TCNs) When...
Headquarters wants to maintain strong control over its foreign operations.	The country is distant in terms of culture or language (such as Japan), or when local operations emphasize downstream value-chain activities such as marketing and sales, as HCNs usually understand the local business environment best.	Top management wants to create a global culture among the firm's operations worldwide.
Headquarters wants to maintain control over valuable intellectual property that is easily dissipated when accessible by HCNs or TCNs.	Local connections and relations are critical to operational success (such as relations with the government in Russia).	Top management seeks unique perspectives for managing host–country operations.
Knowledge sharing is desirable among headquarters and the subsidiaries, particularly for developing local managers or the host–country organization.	The local government requires the MNE to employ a minimum proportion of local personnel, or tough immigration requirements prevent the long-term employment of expatriates.	Headquarters wants to transfer knowledge and technology from third countries to host–country operations.
Foreign operations emphasize R&D and manufacturing, because PCNs are usually more knowledgeable about such upstream value-chain activities.	Cost is an important consideration; salaries of PCNs, especially those with families, can be up to four times those of HCNs.	The firm cannot afford to pay the expensive compensation typical of PCNs.

Source: Eléonore H/Fotolia

Successful expatriates have family members who cope well in new environments. This family is touring Istanbul, Turkey.

Recruiting, Selecting, and Developing Talent

Recruitment is searching for and finding potential job candidates to fill the firm's needs. *Selection* is gathering information to evaluate and decide who should be employed in particular jobs. A big challenge for most MNEs is finding talented managers willing and qualified to work outside their home countries. Schlumberger Ltd. (www.slb.com) is a Texas oil company with operations worldwide. Schlumberger's human resources department is a strategic asset for finding and developing talent, especially engineers, around the world. Among other initiatives, Schlumberger assigns high-level executives as ambassadors to important engineering schools, such as Kazakhstan's Kazakh National Technical University, Beijing University, Massachusetts Institute of Technology, and Universidad Nacional Autónoma de México. IBM, Nokia, and Unilever are also proactive in finding and developing international talent.[10]

Developing talent is a multistep collaboration between human resource managers and executive management. Together, they need to:

- Analyze the firm's growth strategies and the mission-critical roles needed to achieve them.
- Define the desired skills, behaviors, and experiences for each role.
- Examine the firm's current supply of talent and create a plan to acquire needed talent.
- Develop talent internally and acquire existing or potential talent from outside the firm.
- Assess current and potential talent according to each individual's performance over time, willingness to learn, learning skills, and commitment to career advancement.[11]

Cultivating Global Mind-Sets

Some firms are staffed by ethnocentric managers at headquarters who believe their ways of doing business are best and can be easily transferred to other countries.[12] More sophisticated MNEs have a *geocentric orientation*—they staff headquarters and subsidiaries with the most competent people, regardless of national origin. A geocentric orientation is synonymous with a *global mind-set*. Managers with a global mind-set are open to multiple cultural and strategic realities on both global and local levels.[13] They do not force headquarters business methods on foreign subsidiaries. However, most employees lack the skills, traits, or global mind-set needed for expatriate positions. Many managers prefer to remain at home.

Managers best suited to working in foreign environments typically have the following characteristics:

- *Job knowledge*   In distant locations, managers need sufficient knowledge of the administrative and technical dimensions of their job and organization to fulfill company goals and objectives.
- *Self-reliance*   Having an entrepreneurial orientation, a proactive mind-set, and a strong sense of innovativeness are important because expatriate managers frequently function with increased independence abroad and limited support from headquarters.
- *Adaptability*   The manager should adjust well to foreign cultures. The most important traits are cultural empathy, flexibility, diplomacy, and a positive attitude for overcoming stressful situations.
- *Interpersonal skills*   The best candidates get along well with others. Building and maintaining relationships is key, particularly for managers who interact with numerous colleagues, employees, local partners, and government officials.

- *Leadership ability*   The most successful managers view change positively. They skillfully manage threats and opportunities that confront the firm. They collaborate with employees to implement strategies and facilitate successful change.
- *Physical and emotional health*   Living abroad can be stressful. Expatriates must learn to adapt to the local culture. Medical care is often different and may be difficult to access.
- *Spouse and dependents prepared for living abroad*   The candidate's spouse and other family members need the desire and ability to cope with unfamiliar environments and cultures.

Employees with a global mind-set strive to understand organizational and group dynamics to create consensus on a team.[14] Members of a *global team* require specialized training to work effectively with others from different cultures and life experiences.

Cultural Intelligence

Human resource managers need to prepare expatriates and their families to live and work effectively in new cultural environments. Employees should be trained to understand local government regulations, cultural norms, and language differences and to adapt to local customs such as gift giving and business dining.

Cultural intelligence is an employee's ability to function effectively with those from different cultural backgrounds or in different cultural contexts.[15] It has four dimensions.

Source: Terry Carter/Dorling Kindersley, Ltd.

Cultural intelligence implies the ability to function well in complex cultural environments.

Cultural intelligence
An employee's ability to function effectively in situations characterized by cultural diversity.

- *Strategy* describes how an employee makes sense of cross-cultural experiences through her or his judgments.
- *Knowledge* is the employee's understanding of cultural dimensions such as values, social norms, religious beliefs, and language.
- *Motivation* measures the employee's interest in interacting with people from different cultures and confidence in doing so effectively.
- *Behavioral flexibility* is the employee's ability to adopt verbal and nonverbal behaviors appropriate in different cultures.[16]

Expatriate Assignment Failure and Culture Shock

What happens when things go wrong for the employee working abroad? **Expatriate assignment failure** describes the employee's premature return from an international assignment. It occurs when the employee is unable to perform well or because his or her family has difficulty adjusting. Such failure is costly to company productivity and goals and adds to the costs of relocating. Failure can also affect expatriates themselves, leading to diminished careers or problems in their family lives. As many as one-third of foreign assignments end prematurely due to expatriate assignment failure. The rate is high among employees assigned to countries with large culture and language differences.

A leading cause of expatriate assignment failure is **culture shock**—confusion and anxiety experienced by a person who lives in a foreign culture for an extended period.[17] It can affect the expatriate or family members and results from an inability to cope with the differences experienced in a foreign environment. Inadequate language and cross-cultural skills tend to worsen

Expatriate assignment failure
An employee's premature return from an international assignment.

Culture shock
Confusion and anxiety experienced by a person who lives in a foreign culture for an extended period.

culture shock because the expatriate is unable to function effectively in the foreign environment or fails to communicate well with locals.[18] Most expatriates and their families who experience culture shock overcome it, usually within a few months, but a few give up and return home early.

Preparation and Training of International Employees

Preparation is crucial to help employees better understand, adapt, and perform well in foreign environments?[19] International human resource managers must assist subsidiary management in assessing the needs of host–country workers and devise training programs that enable them to achieve their work responsibilities. These include manufacturing, marketing, sales, after-sales services, or business processes such as accounting and records management.

Exhibit 17.4 highlights key features of preparation and training programs for international workers. Training consists of three components.

Area studies
Factual knowledge of the historical, political, and economic environment of the host country.

Practical information
Knowledge and skills necessary to function effectively in a country, including housing, health care, education, and daily living.

Cross-cultural awareness
Ability to interact effectively and appropriately with people from different language and cultural backgrounds.

- **Area studies**—factual knowledge of the historical, political, and economic environment of the host country.
- **Practical information**—knowledge and skills necessary to function effectively in a country, including housing, health care, education, and daily living.
- **Cross-cultural awareness**—the ability to interact effectively and appropriately with people from different language and cultural backgrounds.[20]

Employees benefit from training in the host–country language and learning to communicate more effectively with local colleagues and workers, suppliers, and customers. Language skills allow them to monitor competitors, recruit local talent, and improve relations with host–country officials and organizations. Language skills also increase employee insights and enjoyment of the local culture.[21]

Cross-cultural awareness training increases intercultural sensitivity and effectiveness. Managers need to be well versed in how best to supervise and communicate with local employees, negotiate with customers and suppliers, and adapt to the local culture. Training should help employees avoid the *self-reference criterion*—the tendency to view other cultures through the lens of your own culture.

Training methods vary. They include videos, lectures, assigned readings, case studies, books, web-based instruction, critical incident analyses, simulations, role-playing, language training, field experience, and long-term immersion. In role-playing and simulations, the employee acts out typical encounters with foreigners. *Critical incident analysis* examines an episode in which tension arises between employee and foreign counterpart due to a cross-cultural misunderstanding. Field experience is a visit to the host country, usually for one or two weeks. Long-term

Goal		Desirable employee qualities		Training emphases		Training methods
Increase manager's effectiveness abroad; increase company performance		Technical competence, self-reliance, adaptability, interpersonal skills, leadership ability, physical and emotional health, spouse and dependents prepared for living abroad		• *Area studies*–host–country historical, political, economic, and cultural dimensions • *Practical information*–skills necessary to work effectively in host country • *Cultural awareness*–cross-cultural communication; negotiation techniques; reduction of ethnocentric orientation and self-reference criterion; language skills		Videos, lectures, assigned readings, case studies, critical incident analysis, simulations and role-playing, language training, field experience, long-term immersion

EXHIBIT 17.4

Key Features of Preparation and Training for International Employees

immersion puts the employee in the country for several months or more, often for language and cultural training. In choosing training methods, the firm must balance between rigor and the degree of interaction required abroad.[22]

Preparing Employees for Repatriation

Repatriation is the expatriate's return to his or her home country following completion of a foreign assignment. Like expatriation, it requires advance preparation, this time to help the employee avoid problems upon returning home. Some expatriates report financial difficulties upon returning, such as higher housing costs. Some find their international experience is not valued, and they may be placed in less important positions than they held abroad. Others experience reverse culture shock, difficult readjustment to home–country culture. For those who have spent several years abroad, and for their families, adjustment to life back home may be stressful. As many as one-quarter of expatriates leave their firm within one year of returning home. Others refuse to undertake subsequent international assignments.[23]

International human resource managers can help reduce repatriation problems by providing counseling on the types of problems employees face upon returning home. While the expatriate is abroad, the firm can monitor his or her compensation and career path. After repatriation, the firm can provide bridge loans and other interim financial assistance, as well as counseling, to address both career and psychological needs. The firm needs to ensure that the expatriate has a career position equal to, or better than, the one held before going abroad.[24]

Charting Global Careers for Employees

Many firms create career development programs that provide high-potential employees with opportunities to gain experience both at headquarters and in the firm's operations around the world. They do this because, as the firm generates an increasing proportion of sales and earnings from abroad, it needs globally experienced employees capable of managing company operations worldwide. This approach broadens the pool of global talent for managerial positions and visibly demonstrates top management's commitment to its global strategy.

For example, employees at Unilever (www.unilever.com) cannot advance far professionally without substantial international experience. This Anglo-Dutch firm has numerous programs to develop international leadership skills. Managers are rotated through various jobs and locations around the world, especially early in their careers. Unilever maintains a **global talent pool**—a searchable database of employees that profiles their international skills and potential for supporting the firm's global goals. Human resource managers search the database for the recruit with ideal qualifications, regardless of where he or she works in Unilever's global network. They identify the best global talent and present candidates to the appropriate business managers for final selection.[25]

Performance Appraisal and Compensation of International Employees

Performance appraisal is a formal process for assessing how effectively employees perform their jobs. Appraisals help a manager identify problem areas where an employee needs to improve and additional training is needed. Performance appraisals are typically conducted annually.

In appraising performance, managers compare mutually agreed-upon objectives with actual performance. MNEs typically devise diagnostic procedures to assess the performance of individual employees, see whether problems are attributable to inadequate skill levels, provide additional training and resources as needed, and terminate employees who consistently fail to achieve prescribed goals.

Firms assign employees duties or goals that vary from unit to unit. A new foreign subsidiary might be charged with establishing relationships with key customers and rapidly increasing sales. A manufacturing plant might be tasked with ensuring high productivity or maintaining

---

Repatriation
The expatriate's return to his or her home country following the completion of a foreign assignment.

Global talent pool
A searchable database of employees, profiling their international skill sets and potential for supporting the firm's global aspirations.

17.4 Discuss performance appraisal and compensation of international employees.

Performance appraisal
A formal process for assessing how effectively employees perform their jobs.

Source: Alliance/Fotolia

Learning about host-country culture, history, politics, and practical skills is critical to help expatriates succeed in international assignments and prepare their families for life abroad. This mother and child are visiting Venice, Italy.

high-quality output. When a subsidiary performs poorly, the local manager must resolve problems and get the unit back on track.

The following factors make performance evaluations more complex in the international context.[26]

- The problem of *noncomparable outcomes* arises because of differences in economic, political, legal, and cultural variables. For example, the firm should not punish a Mexican subsidiary manager because worker productivity is half that of home–country operations. Senior management must account for worker conditions, factory equipment, and other factors in Mexico that may cause lower productivity.[27] Different accounting rules may make financial results appear more favorable than under different accounting rules used in the home country.

- *Incomplete information* may result because headquarters is separated from foreign units by both time and distance. Headquarters staff often cannot directly observe employees working in foreign subsidiaries. To address this problem, two evaluators—one from headquarters and one based abroad—might assess subsidiary managers.

- Performance outcomes may be affected by the *maturity* of foreign operations. Relatively new subsidiaries may not achieve the same level of results as older subsidiaries staffed with more experienced personnel.

To avoid inaccurate or biased assessments, management needs to consider the presence of unique circumstances when appraising the performance of foreign subsidiaries, affiliates, and employees.[28]

Compensation

Compensation packages vary across nations because of differences in legally mandated benefits, tax laws, cost of living, local tradition, and culture. Exhibit 17.5 presents the cost of living in selected cities. Some world business capitals are expensive. Employees posted at foreign sites often expect to be paid at a level that allows them to maintain their usual home–country standard of living. This can add substantially to company costs. Managers typically consider four elements when developing compensation packages for employees working abroad.

- Base remuneration or wages.
- Benefits.
- Allowances.
- Incentives.

Base remuneration represents the salary or wages the employee typically receives in his or her home country. A local factory worker in Poland would receive wages equivalent to what average factory workers receive in the particular industry in Poland. A Japanese manager working in Singapore would receive a base salary comparable to that paid to managers at the same level in Japan. Expatriate salaries are usually paid in the home currency, the local currency, or some combination of both.

Benefits include health care plans, life insurance, unemployment insurance, and paid vacation days. They typically account for one-third of the total compensation package but vary as a function of local regulation, industry practice, and taxability. Expatriates usually receive the benefits normally accorded to home–country employees.

Allowance is an additional payment that allows the expatriate to maintain a standard of living similar to that at home. It is intended to pay for the added costs of housing and, sometimes,

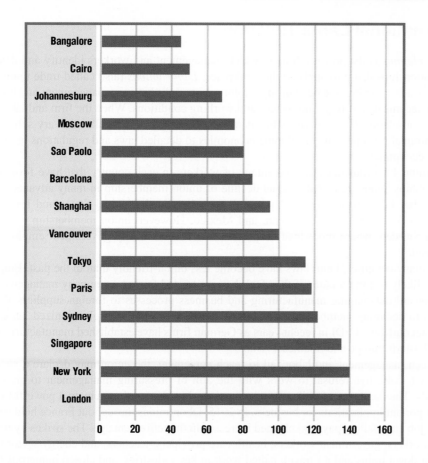

EXHIBIT 17.5

Cost of Living Index in Various Cities, 2015 (Index scale: Vancouver, Canada = 100)

Sources: Based on *Economist,* "Cost-of-Living Index," March 2, 2015, www.economist.com; Expatistan, *Expatistan Cost of Living Index,* 2015, www.expatistan.com; International Monetary Fund, "World Economic Outlook Database April 14, 2015," www.imf.org.

food, transportation, and clothing in the relocation country. Additional support may be provided to cover relocation, children's education, travel, and business-related entertainment. Firms may provide additional hardship allowances to employees who work in countries with civil strife or other dangers or in developing economies that lack essential housing, education, and other facilities.[29]

Given the potential hardships of working abroad, many MNEs also provide *incentives* to expatriate employees. The incentive is similar to a bonus. It is intended to motivate the employee to undertake extraordinary efforts to accomplish company goals abroad, particularly in new foreign markets. It is typically a one-time, lump-sum payment.[30]

In expatriate compensation, tax equalization is a special consideration. Expatriates may face two tax bills for the same pay, one from the host country and one from the home country. Most parent–country governments have devised regulations that allow the expatriate to minimize double taxation or pay income tax in only one country. When the employee incurs additional taxes, the employer will frequently reimburse her or him for this extra tax burden.

Ethical Connections

Executive compensation varies around the world. In China, the annual compensation of the president of a big bank is typically $300,000. In the United Kingdom, the pay may reach $3 million. In the United States, the compensation may exceed $10 million. Ethics experts argue that CEOs should not earn salaries hundreds of times greater than entry-level employees. Lopsided compensation can hurt employee morale. Others argue that pay should be tied to company profitability; firms cannot attract top talent unless they pay top salaries. What is your view?

 MyManagementLab: **Watch It! I**

If your professor has assigned this, go to the Assignments section of **mymanagementlab.com** to complete the video exercise titled Joby: Global HR Management.

17.5 Understand international labor relations.

Collective bargaining
Joint negotiations between management and hourly labor and technical staff regarding wages and working conditions.

International Labor Relations

Labor relations is the process through which management and workers identify and determine job relationships that will apply in the workplace. *Labor unions* (also called trade unions) provide a means for **collective bargaining**—joint negotiations between management and hourly labor and technical staff regarding wages and working conditions. When the firm and labor union negotiate a relationship, they formalize it with a contract. Labor regulations vary substantially, from minimal rules in some developing economies to detailed laws and regulations in many advanced economies.

Exhibit 17.6 illustrates the percentage of workers in each country that have formal union memberships. Note the recent gradual decline of union membership in many advanced economies. It has fallen to less than 12 percent of workers in the United States and less than 18 percent in Australia, Germany, Japan, and Mexico. However, union membership is relatively high in Sweden, where more than 65 percent of workers, mostly government employees, are unionized.[31]

In many countries, labor laws have become less union-friendly than in the past. Employees are less likely to form a union if they feel they are treated fairly by company management. The trend toward outsourcing manufacturing and business processes to foreign suppliers also contributes to declining membership.[32] Germany has a strong tradition of unionized labor. It has seen a net outflow of FDI in recent years as German firms have established manufacturing facilities in Eastern Europe and Southeast Asia.

When management and labor fail to reach agreement, the union may declare a *strike*—an organized, collective refusal to work with the aim of pressuring management to grant union demands. The incidence of strikes has declined worldwide, but they remain a powerful weapon with important implications for business. In 2015, labor unions throughout France held strikes to protest job cuts, falling pay, and planned increases in the retirement age. The strikes by transportation workers, government workers, health care providers, teachers, and energy sector personnel shut down trains and air travel, halted work in key industries, and closed numerous schools

EXHIBIT 17.6

Percentage of Workers Who Belong to Labor Unions, 2003 and 2013

Source: Adapted from *Organisation for Economic Cooperation and Development,* "Trade Union Density," accessed at http://www.oecd.org.

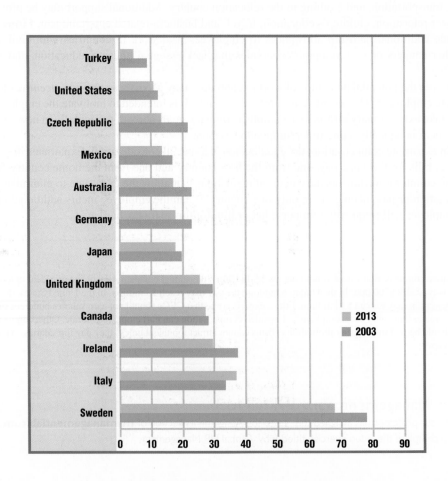

nationwide. A strike by workers at a Wintek factory in China delayed production of products for Apple. Chinese workers participate increasingly in labor unions and strike to protest issues ranging from low pay to poor working conditions.[33]

If a strike lasts more than a few days, a *mediator* or an *arbitrator* may be called in to negotiate between labor and management to end the dispute. A mediator is an expert in labor-management relations who brings both sides together and helps them reach a mutually acceptable settlement. An arbitrator is an expert third party who delivers a judgment in favor of one side or the other after assessing arguments presented by both sides.

Distinctive Features of Labor Around the World

Countries follow different approaches to labor, depending on their history, culture, tradition, and other local factors. In the United States, unionization is concentrated in such industries as automobiles and steel and among public-sector employees such as police and teachers. Union membership in the United States peaked in the 1950s, and the unionized labor force in various traditional industries has fallen in recent years. Globalization, capital mobility, and mass emigration from Mexico have affected the power of organized labor, leading to workforce restructuring. However, U.S. labor unions remain an important political force. Collective bargaining centers on wages, benefits, and workplace conditions and on representing members if management attempts to violate contract provisions.[34]

Labor activism and dispute resolution through unions have grown significantly in China in recent years. Given close ties between Chinese labor and government, Western managers usually deal extensively with China's national and local governments in managing labor relations. Walmart had to accept employee unions in its stores in China —something it does not normally do. China has a developing independent labor movement. Workers have staged thousands of strikes and protests there to demand better wages and working conditions.

Unions are a factor in reducing the occurrence of sweatshops and other poor working conditions in China.[35] The government has launched several initiatives to protect workers' rights better, including new legislation. A campaign by the All-China Federation of Trade Unions (ACFTU), the world's largest labor federation with more than 130 million members, is seeking to unionize workers at all foreign firms operating in China. The ACFTU functions largely to bridge labor demands and the interests of the Chinese government.[36]

Unions in Europe often represent not only factory workers but white-collar workers such as physicians, engineers, and teachers. They hold considerable political power and may be allied with a particular political party, usually the Labor Party. A unique feature in Europe, especially in Germany and the Scandinavian countries, is labor union participation in determining wage rates, bonuses, profit sharing, holiday leaves, dismissals, and plant expansions and closings. The European Union requires even small enterprises to inform and consult employees about a range of business, employment, and work organization issues.[37] In Sweden, labor plays a significant role in shop-floor decisions and participates in such issues as product quality standards and how to organize the factory for greater efficiency and safety. In Sweden and Germany, labor participation in management may be mandated, and workers often sit on corporate boards, a practice known as **codetermination**.[38] By contrast, in South Korea, the United Kingdom, and the United States, relations between management and labor unions are often adversarial.

Codetermination
An industrial relations practice in which labor representatives sit on the corporate board and participate in company decision making.

Cost, Quality, and Productivity of Labor

Worker wages vary greatly worldwide. So do the quality and productivity of worker efforts. Advanced economies tend to pay relatively higher wages. Hourly wages are particularly high in Northern Europe. Lower wages in emerging markets and developing economies are commensurate with the lower costs of living in those countries. Firms typically pay wages consistent with what local living standards and market conditions require.

Exhibit 17.7 displays the typical hourly wage rates of manufacturing workers in various countries. Firms from the advanced economies often prefer to manufacture their products in countries with lower wages. In the decade through 2013, U.S.-based multinational firms cut more than 800,000 jobs in the United States. They added about 1.6 million workers and 400,000 workers to their payrolls in Asia and Latin America, respectively. The most popular destinations for creating jobs included China, India, Brazil, and Mexico. In total, U.S. firms employ more than 1.5 million employees in Asia and about 1 million in Mexico. More than 1 million people

EXHIBIT 17.7

Wage Rate of Manufacturing Labor, in U.S. Dollars per Hour

Source: Based on Euromonitor International, "Wages per Hour in Manufacturing," www.euromonitor.com; International Labour Organization, Labour Cost statistics, www.ilo.org; Organisation for Economic Cooperation and Development, *Hourly Earnings, Manufacturing, 2015*, www.oecd.org; World Bank, *Doing Business 2015*, www.doingbusiness.org.

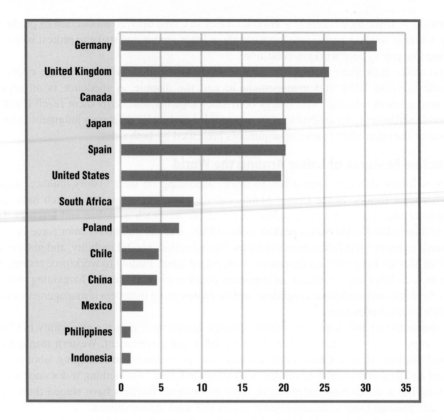

work for U.S. firms in the United Kingdom. France and Germany are also popular job sites—in each country, more than 500,000 locals work for U.S.-based firms.[39]

When firms hire workers abroad, they consider quality and trainability of labor as well as wage rates. Well-educated and skilled labor pools are scarce in some countries. Low productivity, poor work quality, and the cost of training offset some of the benefits of paying low wages. Firms must consider wages in the context of worker productivity. All else being equal, a worker in Romania who is paid half the wage of a comparable worker in Germany but is only half as productive provides no additional value. When outsourcing work to foreign suppliers, managers must ensure that worker productivity in the host country meets acceptable levels. Firms may outsource or offshore work abroad only to discover the local level of productivity is less than expected.

Workforce Reduction and Employee Termination

When firms experience downturns or rising input costs, they may resort to workforce reduction to maintain profitability. In the recent global financial crisis, deteriorating economic conditions forced countless firms to lay off workers. Ford closed three factories in Europe as part of a restructuring of global operations. It closed a body and assembly plant in Genk, Belgium, that had employed some 5,000 workers and moved the jobs to other, lower-cost Ford facilities.[40] From 2009 to 2013, several hundred thousand employees in the financial services industry lost work as banks, insurers, and money management firms shed jobs around the world.[41]

Laying off workers (or making them redundant, as it is called in some countries) requires management to consider various factors, including local norms, regulations, and labor unions. Local custom obligates firms in Japan to avoid layoffs or find positions for dismissed workers in supplier organizations. Most European countries restrict firms' ability to lay off workers.

International human resource and legal managers need a full understanding of local country labor and worker dismissal laws and regulations. In the United States, declaring bankruptcy enables a firm to decrease the number of employees more easily. Auto parts manufacturer Delphi Corporation gained concessions from the United Auto Workers union on wages, benefits, and plant closings. Delphi reduced hourly wages from approximately $27 to $16 per hour.[42]

Many countries require *just cause* to terminate an employee. In most cases, just cause is satisfied if the employee becomes permanently disabled, is terminated within a probationary period (usually one to six months), or is found guilty of incompetence, theft, or disclosure of confidential information. If the firm cannot demonstrate just cause, local courts may require it to pay substantial compensation to the employee upon termination. In most countries, the employee is considered the weaker party; thus, ambiguous cases are usually settled in the employee's favor.[43]

International Labor Trends

Labor is increasingly mobile across national borders thanks to the growing integration of national economies, the rapid expansion of multinational firms, and the rise of international collaborative ventures. As more countries liberalize their economies, many governments are eliminating or reducing protectionist policies that restrict work permits for foreigners.

Many countries are seeing an influx of immigrants, both legal and illegal, who compete with established workers. They provide low-cost labor. Knowledge workers also flock to other nations, seeking work in specialized fields. Recent economic distress drove thousands of skilled professionals from Europe to Australia, Asia, and the Americas. Greece, Ireland, Spain, and Portugal saw thousands of their workers depart for such destinations. Thanks to a construction boom, Brazil lured engineers, architects, and other specialists to help carry out housing, energy, and infrastructure projects. The Brazilian government subsidized much of this construction. Australia has proven an attractive destination to workers from Greece and other European countries.[44] Many nations, especially those with labor shortages or rapidly growing economies, loosen entry requirements to encourage legal immigration. Persian Gulf countries have long retained large labor pools from abroad. By contrast, Japan discourages worker immigration, a policy that, combined with a low birth rate and aging population, likely will result in labor shortages.

Formation of global alliances by national labor unions is another recent trend. To help counter weakening union power, labor organizations have lobbied supranational organizations, such as the International Labour Office (a United Nations agency), to require MNEs to comply with labor standards and practices worldwide. Some national labor unions are joining forces with unions in other countries, forming global unions to equalize compensation and working conditions for workers in different geographical areas.[45] Subsidiaries of European firms in the United States have signed union-organizing agreements that compel their U.S. units to comply with European labor standards.[46] A few unions have succeeded in creating global agreements that affect all the subsidiaries of numerous MNEs. The UNI Global Union represents 900 unions with 20 million members around the world. Firms that have signed global agreements with the UNI include Carrefour (France), H&M (Sweden), Metro AG (Germany), and Telefonica (Spain).[47]

Firm Strategy in International Labor Relations

Labor relations differ markedly around the world. Many MNEs delegate the management of labor relations to their foreign subsidiaries. However, this can be a mistake because of the potential *global* impact of labor relations in any one country. Cross-border linkages give rise to complex interactions among differing national labor systems. Wage levels or labor unrest in one country affect the firm's activities in other countries. For example, a strike by 500 workers at an auto-parts factory in South Korea forced Hyundai to halt production temporarily of Santa Fe and Tucson sport utility vehicles, which the firm sells in North America. Yoosung Enterprise makes piston rings and other parts for Hyundai, General Motors, and Renault. A work stoppage threatened vehicle production and sales in various countries.[48] Because unions influence the cost of labor, productivity, worker morale, and firm performance, and because labor agreements made by foreign subsidiaries can create precedents for negotiations in other countries, managing labor relations on a global scale is often needed.

Skillful development and management of international human resource policies at headquarters helps ensure consistency. Many firms use a centralized information system on the company's intranet to provide continuous data on labor developments among subsidiaries. The approach helps managers anticipate employee concerns and resolve potential threats in cross-national labor relations. It is often easier to negotiate with labor unions when they understand the challenges that confront the firm.

Diversity in the International Workforce

17.6 Describe diversity in the international workforce.

Highly developed MNEs embrace employees from diverse backgrounds and nationalities who bring vast knowledge and experience to the firm. Workers from various countries bring perspectives that management should leverage to perform better in markets worldwide. A multicultural workforce helps the firm develop a global mind-set, especially critical to companies with multinational ambitions.

Many internationally experienced personnel possess maturity and sophistication beyond that of employees who lack such experiences. International experience tends to enhance:

- Cross-cultural awareness and sensitivity.
- Confidence, initiative, and independence.
- Problem-solving and crisis management skills.
- Communication skills, including foreign language ability.
- A greater ease in traveling on foreign assignments.

Obtaining substantial international experience, whether as an employee or a student, enhances prospects for an interesting career.

Women in International Business

Organizational effectiveness is strongly correlated with gender diversity. Companies benefit from gender diversity in leadership positions.[49] Country culture, traditions, and regulations impose various roles on men and women. Some restrict women to a limited set of work roles and grant them fewer legal rights than men. In traditional societies, women are usually economically dependent on men. In Latin America, employers might consider a woman's marital status in hiring. Some firms avoid hiring young married women with no children on the assumption that they will soon leave to start families. In Asia and the Middle East, female managers are often mistaken for the wife or secretary of a male manager. In other countries, women have few opportunities to work outside the home or advance their own economic interests.

Female senior managers in international business are still more the exception than the norm.[50] Exhibit 17.8 presents the proportion of women working in senior management positions. The exhibit is based on findings of a survey of some 10,000 senior executives in firms worldwide. Representation by women in senior management is highest in Russia and the Philippines. Among senior positions, women worldwide work most often as human resource directors and chief financial officers.[51]

Exhibit 17.8 suggests women still do not have equal access to senior management positions in most countries. Even in the advanced economies, they are sometimes not afforded the same opportunities for education and training as their male colleagues. Although evidence suggests just as many women seek international positions as men, relatively few are asked to fill expatriate positions.[52]

There are several reasons for this. First, senior managers may assume women do not make suitable leaders abroad or that foreign men do not like reporting to female managers. Firms hesitate to send women to countries where traditional gender roles are the norm. Even obtaining a work visa can prove problematic in some male-dominated countries. In many countries, male managers drink together, go to sports events, or enjoy nightlife. Some women feel uncomfortable in such all-male settings.[53]

Having children and other family obligations can disrupt career paths. Although flexible and part-time work policies are often beneficial to women's progress up the corporate ladder, many firms do not provide such opportunities. Finally, because women currently occupy

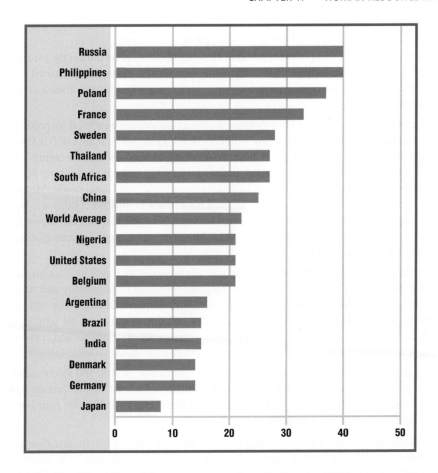

EXHIBIT 17.8

Average Percentage of Women in Senior Management Positions

Sources: Based on Grant Thornton International Ltd., "Women in Business: The Path to Leadership," *International Business Report 2015*, www.grantthornton.global.

relatively few senior management positions (in Europe, they hold only 15 to 25 percent of senior executive posts), there are fewer women with sufficient experience to send abroad for important positions.[54]

Yet the situation for working women is improving. In the advanced economies, more women are in the workforce than ever before. In the European Union, women have filled the majority of new jobs created since 2000. In the United States, unemployment rates are lower for women than for men. Better-educated women are more likely to obtain jobs.[55]

More women are obtaining university degrees in business. They account for about one-third of students in business masters programs in Europe and the United States. About half the recruits who join European firms are female university graduates.[56] In the United States, 140 women enroll in higher education each year for every 100 men. In Sweden, the rate is as high as 150.[57] Businesswomen increasingly form their own networks. In the United Kingdom, a group of women established *Women Directors on Boards*, which improves prospects for women to reach top management jobs. The *Association of Women in International Trade* is a U.S. organization that promotes the interests of women working in international business (www.wiit.org).

In the European Union, proposed legislation would require women to occupy at least 40 percent of seats on the corporate boards of publicly listed companies by 2020. However, a similar law passed in Norway in 2003 has had very little effect on increasing the number of women in business generally.[58]

Source: Konstantin Sutyagin/Shutterstock

Educated women increasingly succeed in international business in environments that were once the domain of men.

IHRM and Corporate Social Responsibility

Corporate actions affect employees, whether they work directly or indirectly for the firm. Corporate social responsibility (CSR) means the firm should be responsive to all its stakeholders and operate in socially acceptable ways, including when hiring, contracting with, and managing employees.

Apparel and footwear company Nike (www.nike.com) outsources nearly all its production to foreign contractors. Nike relies on many suppliers that employ more than 1,000,000 workers, especially in Vietnam, Indonesia, and China. Nike long had been accused of caring little for the welfare of its contract workers abroad. In the early 1990s, employees in some Nike factories in Asia were paid wages insufficient to sustain even basic nutritional needs. Many plants operated like *sweatshops*, where workers labored long hours in difficult conditions. Nike executives deflected the accusations by arguing that because Nike did not own the factories, it was not responsible for conditions in them. However, Nike became a target for anti-globalization and anti-sweatshop movements.

To understand the situation better, Nike systematically assessed its suppliers' foreign factories. In the mid-2000s, it announced CSR goals to integrate corporate responsibility and sustainability into its business strategies and long-term growth. Nike demanded better working conditions from its suppliers. It set benchmarks to improve labor conditions and eliminate long work hours. It developed auditing tools to measure compliance with new labor standards and approved supplier plans to invest in worker development and ensure that its standards were followed.

Nike began requiring suppliers to meet minimal environmental, health, and safety standards. Today, Nike examines country-level factors such as quality of infrastructure, human rights, and economic and political conditions and aims to ensure that factory workers are paid fair wages. Nike is working hard to meet its CSR.

Sources: Shelly Banjo, Patrick Barta, and Ben Otto, "Inside Nike's Struggle to Balance Cost and Worker Safety," *Wall Street Journal*, April 22, 2014, pp. A1, A12; David Doorey, "The Transparent Supply Chain: From Resistance to Implementation at Nike and Levi-Strauss," *Journal of Business Ethics* 103, No. 4 (2011), pp. 587–603; Eugenia Levenson, "Citizen Nike," *Fortune*, November 24, 2008, p. 165; Richard Locke, *The Promise and Perils of Globalization: The Case of Nike* (Cambridge: Massachusetts Institute of Technology, 2007); Peter Lund-Thomsen and Neil Coe, "Corporate Social Responsibility and Labour Agency: The Case of Nike in Pakistan," *Journal of Economic Geography* 15, No. 2 (2015), pp. 275–296; Khalid Nadvi, "Global Standards, Global Governance and the Organization of Global Value Chains," *Journal of Economic Geography* 8 (2008), pp. 323–343; Nike, "Nike CSR," 2007 press release, www.nike.com; Nike, "Global Manufacturing," 2015 company information, www.nike.com.

A survey by Mercer Human Resource Consulting (www.mercer.com) found that companies are substantially increasing the number of women on foreign assignments. About half the surveyed firms believe the number of female expatriates will continue to rise. At the same time, 15 percent of companies said they would not send women to male-oriented locations such as the Middle East. The survey included more than 100 multinational companies with nearly 17,000 male and female expatriates.[59]

Success Strategies for Women Managers in International Business

Johnson & Johnson links a portion of managers' compensation to efforts to hire minorities, women, and people from varied cultural backgrounds. In many countries, being a female expatriate can be an advantage for developing and leveraging strengths as a woman and as a manager. In the long run, managerial competence wins out over prejudice.[60]

Many women have found ways of overcoming senior management bias against sending females abroad. Obtaining foreign assignments is easier if you speak a foreign language or have other international skills. Substantial experience as a domestic manager or in short international assignments improves prospects for working abroad. Garnering strong support from senior management increases credibility. Once abroad in traditional societies, most women report the first reaction of surprise is often replaced by professionalism and respect. Some female graduates highlighted in the "You Can Do It: Recent Grads in IB" feature in this book fit this trend.

Firms help ensure that women achieve greater equality in international business in various ways.

- Provide training programs to develop female managerial talent.
- Fill leadership roles in foreign assignments with qualified women.
- Fill a minimal percentage of senior international executive posts with female employees.
- Set targets for the number of women on executive boards.
- Have female executives serve as mentors and role models for aspiring women.

In addition, many firms have restructured promotion practices to accommodate workers raising children. Most firms in Germany and Sweden offer flexible work hours, allowing employees to arrange schedules around children's needs. Leading firms understand the need to forge a new standard of diverse and internationally successful female managers. Organizations such as Accenture, Ernst & Young, and Vinson & Elkins all sponsor programs that assist women to advance in the global workplace.

MyManagementLab: **Watch It! 2**

If your professor has assigned this, go to the Assignments section of **mymanagementlab.com** to complete the video exercise titled Root Capital: Human Resource Management and Operations.

CLOSING CASE   Human Resource Challenges at Sony

The Japanese electronics giant, Sony, employs 132,000 people worldwide. Sony makes and markets PlayStation home video game systems, televisions, digital and video cameras, laptop computers, personal music players, and semiconductors. Japan produces about one-third of Sony's annual sales. Europe and North America account for another 20 percent each. China and other Asian countries generate 10 percent each. The remainder comes from the rest of the world. The firm has several entertainment divisions, including Epic and Sony Pictures Entertainment. Sony has plants in China, Japan, Malaysia, Mexico, Spain, the United Kingdom, and the United States.

Sony has struggled in recent years because of the impact of the strong yen and the global recession. PlayStation faces serious competition from Nintendo's Wii system. Amazon's Kindle and now iPad have pressured the Sony Reader. The iPod and iPhone displaced Sony's music-player business.

The Manufacturing Workforce

In the past decade, senior management has substantially reorganized Sony. It has closed more than a dozen factories, cut 20,000 jobs, and shifted component and product manufacturing to low-cost countries. In 2010, the firm closed its remaining plant in the United States. It laid off 500 workers and moved production to Mexico.

Sony tries to maintain strong labor relations and tries to avoid worker layoffs. Factories in the United Kingdom manufactured cathode-ray tubes. These components became obsolete with

introduction of the flat-screen TV. Sony worked with unions to create enhanced severance packages and find new job opportunities for many employees. Management successfully restructured the plants to produce high-definition broadcast cameras. Sony built strong customer relationships, developed talent, created a new corporate culture, and aligned employees to the new strategy. The plants reinvented themselves by emphasizing best-in-class efforts to achieve preferred supplier status.

Sony's numerous plants and R&D centers in China employ many expatriates. China's attractions are its low-cost labor and superior worker skills, particularly for high-tech projects. Sony's R&D center in northern China employs more than 20,000 software engineers. Nearby universities and technical institutes churn out thousands of engineering graduates each year. The high concentration of foreign firms in China (including Dell, Hitachi, IBM, and NEC) has created significant competition for local talent.

Human Resource Philosophy

Sony has a highly developed approach to international human resource management. When recruiting new employees, executives seek candidates who have an entrepreneurial spirit, think creatively, and have strong communications skills. Sony's former chairman, Norio Ohga, was also an opera singer, an orchestral conductor, and a licensed jet pilot. His education in music and the arts, alongside science and engineering, strongly influenced the development of the firm's most successful products. In all areas, Sony encourages employees to structure their roles to make best use of their individual strengths.

In Sony's foreign subsidiaries, human resource managers spend time with executives and employees, linking the firm's objectives and strategies to employee capabilities. Senior managers identify key jobs for realizing the firm's objectives and analyze whether they have the best people in the most strategically important jobs and what talent they need to acquire.

When Sony Europe had to reinvent itself, the human resource group focused on identifying and leveraging the key strengths of managers to enhance corporate performance. The firm introduced mentoring projects that encouraged employees to focus on what they do best and maximize their contribution to increasing firm performance.

Training and Talent Development

Sony offers management trainee programs for its most promising recruits. Trainees are counseled to follow their passions and use their distinctive talents to advance the firm. They complete formal courses and training tailored to individual demands and career aspirations. The firm established a mentoring and coaching network across all its talent pools. Executives coach their potential successors, who in turn act as mentors to younger upper-management candidates.

Sony develops global managers and does succession planning for top management jobs. Senior management grooms executives with strong analytical and intellectual qualities who are driven and not shy about taking risks. Programs stress visionary leadership, emotional intelligence, people skills, and the ability to influence others.

Sony implemented an extensive talent pipeline running vertically through the organization, developing and supporting high-potential employees from entry level all the way to senior levels of the firm. Management has a system of exhaustive interviews and assessments for identifying potential talent within Sony's own ranks. Executive candidates must be fluent in English and two other languages, have significant international experience, and possess the drive and ambition to take on international leadership roles.

Senior managers are required to scan the employee pool continuously to identify and groom potential talent. Recently the firm, long bound by its Japanese culture, launched initiatives to groom more English-speaking executives as a way to transform itself and remain on the cutting edge. Former CEO Howard Stringer appointed numerous non-Japanese leaders who are much younger than the traditional, seasoned Japanese management. Having a non-Japanese CEO helped shift the firm toward a geocentric staffing policy.

Corporate Social Responsibility

Sony pursues an integrity approach to foreign manufacturing operations and attempts to maintain workplace standards that exceed local requirements. As the firm expands internationally, management knows that actions today may be crucial for entry to new markets tomorrow. Exploiting low workplace standards in one country can ruin a reputation and jeopardize entry to new markets. Sony learned a lesson from its experiences in Mexico, where human rights groups accused it of violating worker rights.

Rather than simply following local standards in host countries, MNEs should strive to develop global standards for company operations. Sony has taken steps to standardize workplace norms so that management can benchmark internal performance, transfer expertise among countries, and apply holistic, cohesive planning and practices in operations worldwide. Sony is aiming for a universal employment standard, offering superior working conditions and locally relevant wages and benefits at all locations. Wages in foreign factories should provide a fair standard of living to all workers.

AACSB: Reflective Thinking Skills, Ethical Understanding and Reasoning Abilities, Multicultural and Diversity Understanding

Case Questions

17-4. Traditionally, Japanese MNEs followed an ethnocentric orientation in international staffing, in which managers from headquarters held key subsidiary positions. Sony is shifting away from this model. What approach should Sony follow for staffing its subsidiaries? When recruiting expatriates for foreign operations, what characteristics should Sony emphasize to ensure that its managers are adept at living and working abroad?

17-5. Sony faces challenges in finding suitable talent for its operations in China and Europe. What steps should it take to ensure that it has an adequate pool of international managers and other talent for worldwide operations? What should Sony do to promote global mind-sets?

17-6. What is your view of Sony's training efforts? What steps could Sony take to improve its training in light of its multicountry operations?

17-7. Sony has experienced labor relations problems in Indonesia and elsewhere. What strategies should management follow to improve labor relations? What can it do to reduce the number and severity of labor difficulties the firm might face in the future?

17-8. What is your view of Sony's efforts at corporate social responsibility (CSR) in international operations? What steps can Sony take to improve CSR in organizing and managing its operations around the world, particularly in developing countries and emerging markets?

Sources: Ishneet Dhillon and Sonam Gupta, "Organizational Restructuring and Collaborative Creativity: The Case of Microsoft and Sony," *IUP Journal of Business Strategy* 12, No. 1 (2015), pp. 53–65; Hoover's profile of Sony, 2015, http://www.hoovers.com; Rebecca Johnson, "Can You Feel It?" *People Management* 13, No. 17 (2007), pp. 1–4; Takashi Mochizuki and Eric Pfanner, "Sony Completes Its Restructuring; Outlook Improves," *Wall Street Journal* May 1, 2015, p. B4; Richard Siklos, "Sony: Lost in Transformation," *Fortune*, July 6, 2009, p. 68; "Game On," *Economist*, March 7, 2009, p. 73; Daisuke Wakabayashi and Yoshio Takahashi, "Sony's New CEO Vows to 'Revive' Company," *Wall Street Journal*, April 13, 2012, p. B4; Roy White, "Building on Employee Strengths at Sony Europe," *Strategic HR Review*, July/August 2006, pp. 28–31; *Works Management*, "Sony Workers Rally After Site Is Torched in London Riots," September 2011, p. 7.

END OF CHAPTER REVIEW

 MyManagementLab

Go to **mymanagementlab.com** to complete the problems marked with this icon .

Key Terms

area studies 500
codetermination 505
collective bargaining 504
cross-cultural awareness 500
cultural intelligence 499
culture shock 499

expatriate 495
expatriate assignment failure 499
global talent pool 501
host–country national (HCN) 495
international human resource
    management (IHRM) 494

parent-country national (PCN) 495
performance appraisal 501
practical information 500
repatriation 501
third-country national (TCN) 495

Summary

In this chapter, you learned about:

- **The strategic role of human resources in international business.**

    International human resource management (IHRM) is the selection, training, employment, and motivation of employees for international operations. IHRM is more complex than its domestic counterpart. The firm must develop procedures, policies, and processes appropriate for each country where it does business. A **parent-country national (PCN)** is an employee who is a citizen of the country where the MNE is headquartered. A **host–country national (HCN)** is an employee who is a citizen of the country where the MNE subsidiary or affiliate is located. A **third-country national (TCN)** is an employee who is a citizen of a country other than the home or host country. An **expatriate** is an employee who is assigned to work and reside in a foreign country for an extended period, usually a year or longer. There are six key tasks in IHRM: international staffing policy; preparation and training of international employees; international **performance appraisal**; compensation, including formulation of benefit packages that vary from country to country; international labor relations; and managing diversity in the international workplace.

- **International staffing policy.**

    IHRM managers determine the ideal mix of employees to work in the firm's subsidiaries and affiliates abroad. Managers best suited for working abroad typically have technical competence, self-reliance, adaptability, interpersonal skills, leadership ability, physical and emotional health, and, if present, a family prepared for living abroad. **Expatriate assignment failure** is the unplanned early return home of an employee or the failure of an expatriate to function effectively abroad. It is not unusual for expatriates to experience culture shock.

- **Preparation and training of international employees.**

    Proper training and orientation of managers improves firm performance. Training for foreign assignments includes **area studies, practical information**, and **cross-cultural awareness**. Training includes methods such as videos, lectures, readings, simulations, and field experience. Acquiring language skills provides managers with numerous advantages. **Repatriation** is the return of the expatriate to the home country and requires advance preparation. Training is also important for the nonmanagerial workforce abroad.

- **Performance appraisal and compensation of international employees.**

    International performance appraisals involve providing feedback on how well employees are doing their jobs, identifying problems and areas where more training is needed, and providing a basis to reward superior performance. Firms must develop systems to measure foreign unit performance. Various factors in the foreign environment can impede effective performance appraisal. Compensation packages vary internationally because of differences in legally mandated benefits, tax laws, cost of living, local tradition, and culture. Expatriates expect to maintain their usual standard of living, which can be costly in some locations. Typical expatriate compensation includes four components: base salary, benefits, allowances, and incentives. Tax equalization must be considered because expatriates may face two tax bills for the same pay, from the host and home countries.

- **International labor relations.**

  MNEs employ many nonmanagerial employees abroad, often represented by *labor unions*, to work in factories and perform other tasks. Management must ensure effective labor relations and take care when reducing the workforce. Along with the cost of labor, the quality and productivity of the workforce are important considerations. **Codetermination**, the participation of workers on boards of directors, is common in some countries. Labor unions are sometimes at odds with the realities of global competition and the influx of immigrants in many countries. Leading MNEs establish an information system on labor developments, communicate with all employees, and formulate a standard policy on employment and working conditions worldwide.

- **Diversity in the international workforce.**

  Experienced MNEs include people from diverse backgrounds, nationalities, and gender who bring a wealth of experience and knowledge to addressing the firm's problems and opportunities. Employee cultural diversity increases the complexity of interaction. Success comes from understanding and accepting differences and then using them to enhance planning, strategy, and the firm's operations. In most countries, female managers in international business are still somewhat rare. Firms can take several steps to ensure that women achieve more equality in international business.

Test Your Comprehension AACSB: Reflective Thinking Skills, Ethical Understanding and Reasoning Abilities

17-9. What is international human resource management (IHRM)? Why is it important to internationalize firms? What is the role of IHRM in company strategy?

17-10. Under what circumstances would an MNE staff itself with (a) parent-country nationals, (b) host–country nationals, and (c) third-country nationals?

17-11. What is expatriate assignment failure? Provide a suitable example.

⭐ **17-12.** What are the benefits of delivering cross-cultural training to expatriates?

⭐ **17-13.** What is the value to an organization of maintaining a global talent pool?

17-14. What are incomparable outcomes in the context of international performance evaluations? Give a suitable example.

17-15. Suppose you are working abroad as an expatriate for an MNE. What are typical components you would expect to have in your compensation package?

17-16. What are some key trends affecting international labor?

17-17. What measures can firms take to enhance the prospects of placing women in international business jobs?

Apply Your Understanding AACSB: Communication Abilities, Reflective Thinking Skills, Ethical Understanding, and Reasoning Abilities

17-18. Nissan Motor Co. is Japan's second-largest automotive company, with annual sales of more than USD $100 billion. The firm makes Maxima and Sentra cars, Altima and Infiniti upscale sedans, Frontier pickups, and the Xterra and Pathfinder SUVs. Some years ago, Nissan was on the verge of bankruptcy. Then Carlos Ghosn was installed as the firm's CEO. He closed inefficient factories, reduced purchasing costs, and introduced new products. Suppose Nissan asked you to advise it on IHRM issues. What specific human resource strategies would you recommend to enhance the firm's performance further? In particular, how would you advise top management on development of global managers, preparation and training of employees, and how best to integrate the diversity of Japanese and Western managers who come from distinct cultural backgrounds?

17-19. Global Wannabe (GW), a manufacturer of musical instruments, is eager to internationalize. New to international business, within the coming four years, senior management wants GW to generate at least one-third of its sales from abroad by establishing foreign marketing subsidiaries and production bases in low-cost countries to cut manufacturing costs. GW's president, Larry Gerber, has appointed you to the task force charged with recruiting managers who can run GW's operations abroad. What guidelines would you offer to GW to recruit and select expatriates while avoiding the problem of expatriate assignment failure and evaluating the performance of employees posted abroad?

17-20. *Ethical Dilemma:* In China, factory people often work long hours with low pay. Some factories lack heating or air-conditioning, and employees may work with hazardous materials. Workers may be fired if they complain. However, a growing labor union movement is taking hold in China. Despite management resistance, firms such as Tesco and Walmart are being forced to allow Chinese workers to unionize. Unions demand better working conditions and higher wages, and occasionally they go on strike. Management at some MNEs has prevented the workforce from unionizing. Other MNEs are establishing operations in Eastern Europe and Latin America, where labor unions are relatively weak. The Chinese government worries that unionization is hurting inward FDI by scaring foreign companies away from China. Suppose you work for Tesco or Walmart in China. Is it acceptable for your firm to prevent its workers from forming a union? What factors should management consider when determining the appropriateness and role of unions? To whom is your firm accountable—its employees or its shareholders? Can companies reach a fair compromise with workers? Analyze this dilemma by using the ethical framework in Chapter 4.

 **INTERNET EXERCISES**
(http://www.globalEDGE.msu.edu)

AACSB: Communication Abilities, Reflective Thinking Skills, Use of Information Technology

Refer to Chapter 1, page 54, for instructions on how to access and use globalEDGE™.

17-21. Lifestyle factors such as the cost of living vary worldwide. One job of international human resource managers is to develop appropriate compensation packages for managers working abroad. The U.S. Department of State provides information firms can use to calculate compensation around the world. Prepare a report on the factors relevant to developing a compensation package for expatriates working in Prague and Tokyo, including *Living Costs Abroad*, by accessing the State Department through globalEDGE™ (keywords Travel/Living Abroad) or directly at aoprals.state.gov.

17-22. Stryker Inc. manufactures medical devices and wants to establish a factory in continental Europe. For the location, management must decide between France, Germany, and Poland. You have been assigned to research and recommend the best country from the three choices. Management prefers the country with the best overall profile of productive and low-cost workers. Good data sources for your research are the U.S. Bureau of Labor Statistics (www.bls.gov), the European Commission (http://ec.europa.eu), and the OECD (www.stats.oecd.org). Prepare a recommendation on which country—France, Germany, or Poland—would be the best choice to locate the factory. (Note: Such decisions are normally much more complex than implied here, but a preliminary analysis is a starting point for decision making.)

17-23. Executive Planet™ provides information for traveling managers and expatriates on how to live and do business in various countries. Suppose that you work for Virgin, the British airline, and are assigned to work in Virgin's office in an emerging market (choose an emerging market such as Argentina, India, Russia, Mexico, South Africa, or Turkey). You need to learn how to be effective in dealing with customers and colleagues in the chosen country. Select three topics (such as making appointments, business dress guidelines, or gift giving) and prepare an executive summary on how to behave regarding the topics you selected for your chosen country. You can find Executive Planet™ online through globalEDGE™ or by visiting the site directly at www.executiveplanet.com.

CAREER TOOLBOX

Evaluating International Locations for Quality of Life

Companies establish subsidiaries around the world to manage foreign operations. Globalization means that more companies are transferring their employees abroad. MNEs may require employees to live and work abroad for long periods. For managers and their families, expatriate life can be stressful, leading to occasional assignment failures. A manager may leave the company if assigned to an undesirable location. The most experienced firms use a systematic approach to relocate employees abroad.

Employees are sometimes reluctant to relocate abroad unless life quality is satisfactory. Before moving employees to a given country, the firm should research and consider factors that ensure that transferred employees will succeed there. Success means the transferee remains in the new position and performs well.

In this exercise, you will (i) learn the important indicators used to assess the quality of life in various international locations; (ii) understand the types of information needed about living conditions abroad; and (iii) understand factors that firms consider when relocating managers abroad for establishing a regional headquarters or subsidiary.

Background

MNEs often require managers to live abroad for extended periods. An expatriate is a person who goes to live temporarily or permanently in a foreign country. Expatriates expect to maintain a living standard similar to the one they have at home.

Europe is one of the world's most attractive markets. Eastern Europe enjoys numerous advantages, including low-wage, high-quality workers. Many firms are anxious to relocate their employees to Europe. However, management need to make such moves carefully. A failed expatriate relocation harms the employee and is costly to the firm.

Numerous measurable features, such as commuting times, tax rates, and housing cost can affect the expatriate's move to a foreign city and the ease of settling in. The firm should consider quality of life factors that will help ensure the transferee and family assimilate and achieve a comfortable lifestyle.

In this exercise, assume that you work for a company that is relocating management staff to Europe. Your task is to investigate three European cities as possible relocation destinations. Consider the quality of life for moving as an expatriate to each city. The task is not easy because there are shortcomings to every city, no matter how seemingly attractive. There are always trade-offs. Take Paris, France, for example. France is a power house in the European Union and has attracted much interest from foreign firms establishing operations abroad. Paris is a world hub of style and fashion and a popular tourist destination. However, the cost of living in Paris is high. The tax burden in France is substantial. Up to 60 percent of your gross pay may be diverted to the French government. During the winter months, Paris is grey and sometimes depressing. Parisians are sometimes rude to foreigners.

To complete this exercise in your MyLab, go to the Career Toolbox.

MyManagementLab

Go to **mymanagementlab.com** for Auto-graded writing questions as well as the following Assisted-graded writing questions.

 17-24. What steps can senior managers take to develop global managers?

 17-25. In what ways might an employee experience expatriate assignment failure?

17-26. MyManagementLab Only—comprehensive writing assignment for this chapter.

Endnotes

1. Vicar Ballad et al., *The Global Leadership and Talent Index* (Boston: Boston Consulting Group and World Federation of People Management Associations, March 2015), www.bcg.com.

2. Peter Dowling, Marion Festing, and Allen Engle, *International HRM: Managing People in a Multinational Context*, 5th ed. (London: Thomson Learning, 2008).

3. Ibid.

4. Jo Johnson, "More Westerners Take Top Posts in India as Locals' Pay Demand Soars," *Financial Times*, May 30, 2007, p. 1.

5. Dowling, Festing, and Engle (2008).

6. MSNBC, "Italy Labor Market Reform Moves Ahead," April 4, 2012, www.msnbc.msn.com; *Wall Street Journal*, "Italy's Economic Suicide Movement," October 27, 2014, p. A18.

7. James Neelankavil, Anil Mathur, and Yong Zhang, "Determinants of Managerial Performance: A Cross-Cultural Comparison of the Perceptions of Middle-Level Managers in Four Countries," *Journal of International Business Studies* 31, No. 1 (2000), pp. 121–141.

8. Dowling, Festing, and Engle (2008); Anne-Wil Harzing, "Of Bears, Bumble-Bees, and Spiders: The Role of Expatriates in Controlling Foreign Subsidiaries," *Journal of World Business* 36, No. 4 (2008), pp. 366–379.

9. Anne-Wil Harzing, "Who's in Charge? An Empirical Study of Executive Staffing Practices in Foreign Subsidiaries," *Human Resource Management* 40, No. 2 (2001), pp 139–145.

10. Wayne Finger, "The 'Crew Change' Challenge Facing Us All," *World Oil*, September 2012, pp. R139–R141; Debbie Lovewell, "Employer Profile: World Order," *Employee Benefits*, September 2009, p. 50; Jean-Marie Rousset and Pierre Bismuth, "Learning HR lessons from the Past," *Petroleum Economist*, April 13, 2015, p. 6.

11. Bhalla et al. (2015); Nanette Byrnes, "Star Search," *BusinessWeek*, October 10, 2005, p. 68; Deloitte Consulting LLP, *Global Human Capital Trends 2014: Engaging the 21st-Century Workforce* (Deloitte University Press, 2014), www.dupress.com; David Pollitt, "Unilever 'Raises the Bar' in Terms of Leadership Performance," *Human Resource Management International Digest* 14, No. 5 (2006), pp. 23–25; Philip Harris, Robert Moran, and Sarah Moran, *Managing Cultural Differences*, 6th ed. (Burlington, MA: Elsevier Buttermann-Heinemann, 2007).

12. Robert T. Moran and John R. Riesenberger, *The Global Challenge* (London: McGraw-Hill, 1994).

13. Deloitte Consulting LLP (2014); Ben L. Kedia and Akuro Mukherji, "Global Managers: Developing a Mindset for Global Competitiveness," *Journal of World Business* 34, No. 3 (1999), pp. 230–251; Orly Levy, Schon Beechler, Sully Taylor, and Nakiye Boyacigiller, "What We Talk About When We Talk About 'Global Mindset'—Managerial Cognition in Multinational Corporations," *Journal of International Business Studies* 38, No. 2 (2007), pp. 231–258.

14. Jeanne Brett, Kristin Beyfar, and Mary Kern, "Managing Multicultural Teams," *Harvard Business Review* 84, No. 11 (2007), pp. 84–92.

15. S. Ang, L. Van Dyne, and C. K. S. Koh, "Personality Correlates of the Four Factor Model of Cultural Intelligence," *Group and Organization Management* 31 (2006), pp. 100–123; Brent MacNab, Richard Brislin, and Reginald Worthley, "Experiential Cultural Intelligence Development: Context and Individual Attributes," *International Journal of Human Resource Management* 23, No. 7 (2012), pp. 1320–1341.

16. Ibid.

17. Dowling, Festing, and Engle (2008).

18. Anne-Wil Harzing and Claus Christensen, "Expatriate Failure: Time to Abandon the Concept?" *Career Development International* 9, No. 6/7 (2004), pp. 616–620; Ann Murdoch and Eugene Kaciak, "Culture Shock Re-Visited: What Features of the Polish Culture Most Bother Expatriates in Poland?" *Journal of Applied Business Research* 27, No. 2 (2011), pp. 87–104.

19. M. Mendenhall, E. Dunbar, and G. Oddou, "Expatriate Selection, Training and Career Pathing: A Review and Critique," *Human Resources Management* 26 (1987), pp. 331–345.

20. Priscilla Cuevas et al., "Lessons from Fred Bailey's Expatriate Experience in Japan: Proactively Preparing Employees for International Assignments," *Journal of Business Studies Quarterly* 2, No. 4 (2011), pp. 40–52; Harris, Moran, and Moran (2007).

21. Stephen Rhinesmith, *A Manager's Guide to Globalization* (Homewood, IL: Business One Irwin, 1998); David C. Thomas and Mila B. Lazarova, *Essentials of International Human Resource Management: Managing People Globally* (Thousand Oaks, CA: Sage, 2013).

22. Thomas and Lazarova (2013); Hong Ren, Dilek Yunlu, Margaret Shaffer, and Katherine Fodchuk, "Expatriate Success and Thriving: The Influence of Job Deprivation and Emotional Stability," *Journal of World Business* 50, No. 1 (2015), pp. 69–78; Rosalie Tung, "Expatriate Assignments: Enhancing Success and Minimizing Failure," *Academy of Management Executive* 1 (1987), pp. 117–126.

23. J. Black, H. Gregersen, and M. Mendenhall, "Toward a Theoretical Framework of Repatriation Adjustment," *Journal of International Business Studies* 23 (1992), pp. 737–760; David Collings, Hugh Scullion, and Michael Morley, "Changing Patterns of Global Staffing in the Multinational Enterprise: Challenges to the Conventional Expatriate Assignment and Emerging Alternatives," *Journal of World Business* 42, No. 2 (2007), pp. 198–213.

24. Harris, Moran, and Moran (2007).

25. George Yip, *Total Global Strategy II* (Upper Saddle River, NJ: Prentice Hall, 2003).

26. Peter Dowling, Denice Welch, and Randall Schuler, *International Human Resource Management*, 3rd ed. (Cincinnati, OH: South-Western, 1999); Thomas and Lazarova (2013).

27. Ibid.

28. Ibid.

29. Richard Hodgetts and Fred Luthans, *International Management: Culture, Strategy, and Behavior*, 5th ed. (Boston: McGraw-Hill Irwin, 2003); Thomas and Lazarova (2013).

30. Ibid.

31. David Blanchflower, "International Patterns of Union Membership," *British Journal of Industrial Relations* 45, No. 1 (2007), pp. 1–28; Organisation for Economic Cooperation and Development, "Trade Union Density," www.oecd.org.

32. Ibid.; Guglielmo Meardi, "Multinationals' Heaven? Uncovering and Understanding Worker Responses to Multinational Companies in Post-Communist Central Europe," *International Journal of Human Resource Management* 17, No. 8 (2006), pp 1366–1378.

33. Charles Duhigg and David Barboza, "In China, Human Costs Are Built into an iPad," *New York Times*, January 25, 2012, http://www.nytimes.com; Jamey Keaten, "Huge French Protests as Strikes Close Schools, Eiffel Tower," *Yahoo News!*, April 9, 2015, news.yahoo.com; Dexter Roberts and Bruce Einhorn, "Using Propaganda to Stop China's Strikes," *Bloomberg Businessweek*, December 19–25, 2011, pp. 15–16.

34. M. Dubofsky and F. R. Dulles, *Labor in America: A History*, 8th ed. (Hoboken, NJ: Wiley-Blackwell, 2010).

35. "Membership Required: Trade Unions in China," *Economist*, August 2, 2008, p. 55; Kai Chang and Fang Lee Cooke, "Legislating the Right to Strike in China: Historical Development and Prospects," *Journal of Industrial Relations* 57, No. 3 (2015), pp. 440–455.

36. Chang and Cooke (2015); Ying Zhu, Malcolm Warner, and Tongqing Feng, "Employment Relations 'with Chinese Characteristics': The Role of Trade Unions in China," *International Labour Review* 150, No. (2011), pp. 127–143.

37. John Gennard, "Development of Transnational Collective Bargaining in Europe," *Employee Relations* 31, No. 4 (2009), pp. 341–346; Wenzel Matiaske and Gerd Grözinger, "The Future of Trade Unions in Europe. Part I," *Management Revue* 23, No. 1 (2012), pp. 5–6.

38. Alberto Alesina and Francesco Giavazzi, *The Future of Europe: Reform or Decline* (Boston: MIT Press, 2006).

39. Scott Thurm, "U.S. Firms Add Jobs, But Mostly Overseas," *Wall Street Journal*, April 27, 2012, pp. B1–B4; Suddep Reddy, "Domestic-Based Multinationals Hiring Overseas," *Wall Street Journal*, April 19, 2013, p. A2; David Wessel, "U.S. Firms Eager to Add Foreign Jobs," *Wall Street Journal*, November 22, 2011, p. B1.

40. Marietta Cauchi and Mike Ramsey, "Ford to Shut 3 Europe Plants," *Wall Street Journal*, October 26, 2012, p. B2; Robin Emmott and Robert-Jan Bartunek, "As Ford Closes, European Rust Belt Seeks New Ideas," *Yahoo News!*, December 21, 2014, www.news.yahoo.com.

41. Max Abelson and Ambereen Choudhury, "After Massive Job Cuts, Wall Street's a Different Place," *Bloomberg Businessweek*, December 5–11, 2011, pp. 55–57.

42. Jeffrey McCracken, "GM, Chrysler Face Some Messy Surgery," *Wall Street Journal*, April 1, 2009, p. B3; Ashby Monk, "The Knot of Contracts: The Corporate Geography of Legacy Costs," *Economic Geography* 84, no. 2 (2008), pp. 211–35.

43. Peter J Dowling, Marion Festing, and Allen Engle, *International Human Resource Management*, 6th ed. (Boston: Cengage Learning, 2013).

44. Richard Boudreaux and Paulo Prada, "Exodus of Workers from Continent Reverses Old Patterns," *Wall Street Journal*, January 14–15, 2012, pp. A1, A8.

45. C. Mako, P. Csizmadi, and M. Illessy, "Labour Relations in Comparative Perspective," *Journal for East European Management Studies* 11, No. 3 (2006), pp. 267–287.

46. Jessica Marquez, "Unions' Global End Run," *Workforce Management*, January 30, 2006, pp. 1–4.

47. John Gennard, "A New Emerging Trend? Cross Border Trade Union Mergers," *Employee Relations* 31, No. 1 (2009), pp. 5–8.

48. BBC, "South Korea Police Break Up Yoosung Hyundai Strike," May 24, 2011, www.bbc.co.uk; Kyong-Ae Choi, "Riot Police Break Up Strike at Hyundai Supplier," *Wall Street Journal*, May 24, 2011, www.wsj.com.

49. Julia Sperling et al., *Women Matter 2014: GCC Women in Leadership—From the First to the Norm* (McKinsey & Co., 2014), www.mckinsey.com.

50. "The Conundrum of the Glass Ceiling," *Economist*, July 23, 2005, pp. 63–65; Grace Thomson, "Breaking the Glass Ceiling: Female Leaders in the Global Marketplace," *Journal of Entrepreneurship Development* 8, No. 1 (2011), pp. 51–63.

51. Sandrine Devillard et al., *Women Matter 2013: Gender Diversity in Top Management: Moving Corporate Culture, Moving Boundaries* (McKinsey & Co., 2013), www.mckinsey.com; Grant Thornton International Ltd., "Women in Business: The Path to Leadership," *International Business Report 2015*, www.grantthornton.global.

52. Nancy Adler, *International Dimensions of Organizational Behavior*, 5th ed. (Cincinnati, OH: Thomson South-Western, 2008); Harris, Moran, and Moran (2007).

53. Robert T. Moran, Phillip R. Harris, and Sarah V. Moran, *Managing Cultural Differences, Global Leadership Strategies for the 21st Century*, 7th ed. (Oxford, UK: Elsevier, 2007); Jeanine Prime, Karsten Jonsen, Nancy Carter, and Martha Maznevski, "Managers' Perceptions of Women and Men Leaders: A Cross Cultural Comparison," *International Journal of Cross Cultural Management* 8, No. 2 (2008), pp. 171–180.

54. Georges Desvaux, Sandrine Devillard-Hoellinger, and Mary Meaney, "A Business Case for Women," *McKinsey Quarterly*, September 2008, www.mckinseyquarterly.com; Sandrine Devillard et al., *Women Matter 2013: Gender Diversity in Top Management: Moving Corporate Culture, Moving Boundaries* (McKinsey & Co., 2013), www.mckinsey.com; Lynda Gratton, "Steps That Can Help Women Make It to the Top," *Financial Times*, May 23, 2007, p. 13; Chris Rowley, Jean Lee, and Luh Lan, "Why Women Say No to Corporate Boards and What Can Be Done: 'Ornamental Directors' in Asia," *Journal of Management Inquiry* 24, No. 2 (2015), pp. 205–207; Susan Shortland, "The 'Expat Factor': The Influence of Working Time on Women's Decisions to Undertake International Assignments in the Oil and Gas Industry," *International Journal of Human Resource Management* 26, No. 11 (2015), pp. 1452–1473; Julia Sperling et al., *Women Matter 2014: GCC Women in Leadership—From the First to the Norm* (McKinsey & Co., 2014), www.mckinsey.com.

55. *Economist*, "Female Power," January 2, 2010, pp. 49–51; Jasen Lee, "Women in International Business Growing," *Deseret News*, November 8, 2011, www.deseretnews.com.

56. Ibid.; "Conundrum of the Glass Ceiling" (2005); Ruth Simpson and Afam Ituma, "Transformation and Feminisation: The Masculinity of the MBA and the 'Un-Development' of Men,"

Journal of Management Development 28, No. 4 (2009), pp. 301–316.

57. "Women and the World Economy: A Guide to Womenomics," *Economics*, April 12, 2006, p. 80; Matthew Brannan and Vincenza Priola, "Between a Rock and a Hard Place: Exploring Women's Experience of Participation and Progress in Managerial Careers," *Equal Opportunities International* 28, No. 5 (2009), pp. 378–397; Rowley, Lee, and Lan (2015).

58. Toko Sekiguchi, "Abe Wants to Get Japan's Women Working," *Wall Street Journal,* September 12, 2014, www.wsj.com.

59. Mercer Human Resource Consulting, "More Females Sent on International Assignment than Ever Before, Survey Finds," October 12, 2006, http://www.mercerhr.com.

60. Joanna Barsh and Lareina Yee, "Unlocking the Full Potential of Women at Work," Special Report, April 30, 2012, McKinsey & Co., www.mckinsey.com; Rowley, Lee, and Lan (2015).

> Glossary

Absolute advantage principle A country benefits by producing only those products in which it has an absolute advantage or that it can produce using fewer resources than another country.

Acculturation The process of adjusting and adapting to a culture other than one's own.

Acquisition Direct investment to purchase an existing company or facility.

Adaptation Firm's efforts to modify one or more elements of its international marketing program to accommodate specific customer requirements in a particular market.

Advanced economies Post-industrial countries characterized by high per capita income, highly competitive industries, and well-developed commercial infrastructure.

Agent An intermediary (often an individual or a small firm) that handles orders to buy and sell commodities, products, and services in international business transactions for a commission.

Antidumping duty A tax imposed on products deemed to be dumped and causing injury to producers of competing products in the importing country.

Arbitragers Currency traders who buy and sell the same currency in two or more foreign-exchange markets to profit from differences in the currency's exchange rate.

Area studies Factual knowledge of the historical, political, and economic environment of the host country.

Balance of payments The annual accounting of all economic transactions of a nation with *all* other nations.

Barter A type of countertrade in which goods are directly exchanged without the transfer of any money.

Bond A debt instrument that enables the issuer (borrower) to raise capital by promising to repay the principal along with interest on a specified date (maturity).

Born global firm A young entrepreneurial company that initiates international business activity very early in its evolution, moving rapidly into foreign markets.

Build-operate-transfer (BOT) Arrangement in which the firm or a consortium of firms contracts to build a major facility abroad, operate it for a specified period, and then hand it over to the project sponsor, typically the host-country government or public utility.

Business process outsourcing (BPO) The outsourcing to independent suppliers of business service functions such as accounting, payroll, human resource functions, travel services, IT services, customer service, or technical support.

Buy-back agreement A type of countertrade in which the seller agrees to supply technology or equipment to construct a facility and receives payment in the form of goods produced by the facility.

Capital flight The rapid sell-off by residents or foreigners of their holdings in a nation's currency or other assets, usually in response to a domestic crisis that causes investors to lose confidence in the country's economy.

Captive sourcing Sourcing from the firm's own production facilities.

Central bank The monetary authority in each nation that regulates the money supply and credit, issues currency, and manages the exchange rate of the nation's currency.

Codetermination An industrial relations practice in which labor representatives sit on the corporate board and participate in company decision making.

Collective bargaining Joint negotiations between management and hourly labor and technical staff regarding wages and working conditions.

Commercial risk Firm's potential loss or failure from poorly developed or executed business strategies, tactics, or procedures.

Common market A stage of regional integration in which trade barriers are reduced or removed; common external barriers are established; and products, services, and *factors of production* are allowed to move freely among the member countries.

Company-owned subsidiary A representative office of the focal firm that handles marketing, physical distribution, promotion, and customer service activities in the foreign market.

Company sales potential An estimate of the share of annual industry sales that the firm expects to generate in a particular target market.

Comparative advantage Superior features of a country that provide unique benefits in global competition, typically derived from either natural endowments or deliberate national policies.

Comparative advantage principle It can be beneficial for two countries to trade without barriers as long as one is relatively more efficient at producing goods or services the other needs. What matters is not the absolute cost of production but rather the relative efficiency with which a country can produce the product.

Compensation deal A type of countertrade in which payment is in both goods and cash.

Competitive advantage Distinctive assets or competencies of a firm that are difficult for competitors to imitate and are typically derived from specific knowledge, capabilities, skills, or superior strategies.

Configuration of value-adding activity The pattern or geographic arrangement of locations where the firm carries out value-chain activities.

Consolidation The process of combining and integrating the financial results of foreign subsidiaries into the financial statements of the parent firm.

Consortium A project-based, nonequity venture initiated by multiple partners to fulfill a large-scale project.

Contagion The tendency of a financial or monetary crisis in one country to spread rapidly to other countries, due to the ongoing integration of national economies.

Contract manufacturing An arrangement in which the focal firm contracts with an independent supplier to manufacture products according to well-defined specifications.

Contractual entry strategies in international business Cross-border exchanges where the relationship between the focal firm and its foreign partner is governed by an explicit contract.

Corporate governance The system of procedures and processes by which corporations are managed, directed, and controlled.

Corporate social responsibility (CSR) A manner of operating a business that meets or exceeds the ethical, legal, commercial, and public expectations of stakeholders, including customers, shareholders, employees, and communities.

Corruption The abuse of power to achieve illegitimate personal gain.

Counterpurchase A type of countertrade with two distinct contracts. In the first, the seller agrees to a set price for goods and receives cash from the buyer. This first deal is contingent on a second wherein the seller agrees to purchase goods from the buyer for the same amount as in the first contract or for a set percentage of same.

Countertrade An international business transaction by which all or partial payments are made in kind rather than in cash.

Countervailing duty Tariff imposed on products imported into a country to offset subsidies given to producers or exporters in the exporting country.

Country risk Exposure to potential loss or adverse effects on company operations and profitability caused by developments in a country's political and/or legal environments.

Critical incident analysis (CIA) A method for analyzing awkward situations in cross-cultural encounters by developing objectivity and empathy for other points of view.

Cross-cultural awareness Ability to interact effectively and appropriately with people from different language and cultural backgrounds.

Cross-cultural risk A situation or event in which a cultural misunderstanding puts some human value at stake.

Cross-licensing agreement A type of project-based, nonequity venture in which partners agree to access licensed technology, developed by the other, on preferential terms.

Cultural intelligence An employee's ability to function effectively in situations characterized by cultural diversity.

Cultural metaphor A distinctive tradition or institution strongly associated with a particular society.

Culture The learned, shared, and enduring orientation patterns in a society. People demonstrate their culture through values, ideas, attitudes, behaviors, and symbols.

Culture shock Confusion and anxiety experienced by a person who lives in a foreign culture for an extended period.

Currency control Restrictions on the outflow of hard currency from a country or the inflow of foreign currencies.

Currency option A contract that gives the purchaser the right, but not the obligation, to buy a certain amount of foreign currency at a set exchange rate within a specified amount of time.

Currency risk Potential harm that arises from changes in the price of one currency relative to another.

Currency swap An agreement to exchange one currency for another, according to a specified schedule.

Current rate method Translation of foreign currency balance sheet and income statements at the current exchange rate—the spot exchange rate in effect on the day or for the period when the statements are prepared.

521

Customs Checkpoints at the ports of entry in each country where government officials inspect imported products and levy tariffs.

Customs brokers Specialist enterprises that arrange clearance of products through customs on behalf of importing firms.

Customs union A stage of regional integration in which the member countries agree to adopt common tariff and nontariff barriers on imports from nonmember countries.

Debt financing The borrowing of money from banks or other financial intermediaries, or the sale of corporate bonds to individuals or institutions, to raise capital.

Devaluation Government action to reduce the official value of its currency relative to other currencies.

Developing economies Low-income countries characterized by limited industrialization and stagnant economies.

Direct exporting Exporting that is accomplished by contracting with intermediaries located in the foreign market.

Direct quote The number of units of domestic currency needed to acquire one unit of foreign currency; also known as the normal quote.

Distribution channel intermediary A specialist firm that provides various logistics and marketing services for focal firms as part of the international supply chain, both in the home country and abroad.

Documentation Official forms and other paperwork required in export transactions for shipping and customs procedures.

Dumping Pricing exported products at less than their normal value, generally less than their price in the domestic or third-country markets, or at less than production cost.

Economic exposure The currency risk that results from exchange-rate fluctuations affecting the pricing of products, the cost of inputs, and the value of foreign investments.

Economic union A stage of regional integration in which member countries enjoy all the advantages of early stages but also strive to have common fiscal and monetary policies.

Emerging markets Former developing economies that have achieved substantial industrialization, modernization, and rapid economic growth since the 1980s.

Equity financing The issuance of shares of stock to raise capital from investors and the use of retained earnings to reinvest in the firm.

Equity joint venture A type of partnership in which a separate firm is created through the investment or pooling of assets by two or more parent firms that gain joint ownership of the new legal entity.

Equity participation Acquisition of partial ownership in an existing firm.

Ethics Moral principles and values that govern the behavior of people, firms, and governments, regarding right and wrong.

Ethnocentric orientation Using our own culture as the standard for judging other cultures.

Eurobond A bond sold outside the issuer's home country but denominated in its own currency.

Eurocurrency Any currency deposited in a bank outside its country of origin.

Eurodollars U.S. dollars held in banks outside the United States, including foreign branches of U.S. banks.

Exchange rate The price of one currency expressed in terms of another; the number of units of one currency that can be exchanged for another.

Expatriate An employee assigned to work and reside in a foreign country for an extended period, usually a year or longer.

Expatriate assignment failure An employee's premature return from an international assignment.

Export control A government measure intended to manage or prevent the export of certain products or trade with certain countries.

Export department A unit within the firm charged with managing the firm's export operations.

Export management company (EMC) A domestically based intermediary that acts as an export agent on behalf of a client company.

Exporting The strategy of producing products or services in one country (often the producer's home country) and selling and distributing them to customers located in other countries.

Extraterritoriality Application of home-country laws to persons or conduct outside national borders.

Facilitator A firm or an individual with special expertise in banking, legal advice, customs clearance, or related support services that assists focal firms in the performance of international business transactions.

Family conglomerate A large, highly diversified company that is privately owned.

Focal firm The initiator of an international business transaction, which conceives, designs, and produces offerings intended for consumption by customers worldwide. Focal firms are primarily MNEs and SMEs.

Foreign bond A bond sold outside the issuer's country and denominated in the currency of the country where issued.

Foreign direct investment (FDI) An internationalization strategy in which the firm establishes a physical presence abroad through acquisition of productive assets such as capital, technology, labor, land, plant, and equipment.

Foreign distributor A foreign market-based intermediary that works under contract for an exporter, takes title to, and distributes the exporter's products in a national market or territory, often performing marketing functions such as sales, promotion, and after-sales service.

Foreign exchange All forms of money that are traded internationally, including foreign currencies, bank deposits, checks, and electronic transfers.

Foreign-exchange market The global marketplace for buying and selling national currencies.

Foreign trade zone (FTZ) An area within a country that receives imported goods for assembly or other processing and re-export. For customs purposes, the FTZ is treated as if it is outside the country's borders.

Forward contract A contract to exchange two currencies at a specified exchange rate on a set future date.

Forward rate The exchange rate applicable to the collection or delivery of a foreign currency at some future date.

Franchising Arrangement in which the firm allows another the right to use an entire business system in exchange for fees, royalties, or other forms of compensation.

Franchisor A firm that grants another the right to use an entire business system in exchange for fees, royalties, or other forms of compensation.

Free trade Relative absence of restrictions to the flow of goods and services between nations.

Free trade agreement A formal arrangement between two or more countries to reduce or eliminate tariffs, quotas, and barriers to trade in products and services.

Free trade area A stage of regional integration in which member countries agree to eliminate tariffs and other barriers to trade in products and services within the bloc.

Freight forwarder A specialized logistics service provider that arranges international shipping on behalf of exporting firms.

Fronting loan A loan between the parent and its subsidiary, channeled through a large bank or other financial intermediary.

Functional structure An arrangement in which management of the firm's international operations is organized by functional activity, such as production and marketing.

Futures contract An agreement to buy or sell a currency in exchange for another at a specified price on a specified date.

Geocentric orientation A global mind-set that enables the manager to understand a business or market without regard to country boundaries.

Geographic area structure An organizational design in which management and control are decentralized to the level of individual geographic regions.

Global account management (GAM) Serving a key global customer in a consistent and standardized manner, regardless of where in the world it operates.

Global bond market The international marketplace in which bonds are bought and sold, primarily through bond brokers.

Global brand A brand whose positioning, advertising strategy, look, and personality are standardized worldwide.

Global capital market The collective financial markets where firms and governments raise intermediate and long-term financing.

Global equity market The worldwide market of funds for equity financing—stock exchanges around the world where investors and firms meet to buy and sell shares of stock.

Global financial system The collective of financial institutions that facilitate and regulate investment and capital flows worldwide, such as central banks, commercial banks, and national stock exchanges.

Global industry An industry in which competition is on a regional or worldwide scale.

Global integration Coordination of the firm's value-chain activities across countries to achieve worldwide efficiency, synergy, and cross-fertilization to take maximum advantage of similarities between countries.

Global market opportunity Favorable combination of circumstances, locations, and timing that offers prospects for exporting, investing, sourcing, or partnering in foreign markets.

Global market segment A group of customers who share common characteristics across many national markets.

Global marketing strategy A plan of action for foreign markets that guides the firm in deciding how to position itself and its offerings, which customer segments to target, and the degree to which it should standardize or adapt its marketing program elements.

Global matrix structure An arrangement that blends the geographic area, product, and functional structures to leverage the benefits of a purely global strategy while keeping the firm responsive to local needs.

Global money market The collective financial markets where firms and governments raise short-term financing.

Global sourcing The procurement of products or services from independent suppliers or company-owned subsidiaries located abroad for consumption in the home country or a third country.

Global strategy An approach by which headquarters seeks substantial control over its country operations to minimize redundancy and maximize efficiency, learning, and integration worldwide.

Global supply chain The firm's integrated network of sourcing, production, and distribution, organized on a worldwide scale and located in countries where competitive advantage can be maximized.

Global talent pool A searchable database of employees, profiling their international skill sets and potential for supporting the firm's global aspirations.

Global team An internationally distributed group of employees charged with a specific problem-solving or best-practice mandate that affects the entire organization.

Globalization of markets Ongoing economic integration and growing interdependency of countries worldwide.

Gray market activity Legal importation of genuine products into a country by intermediaries other than authorized distributors (also known as parallel imports).

Greenfield investment Direct investment to build a new manufacturing, marketing, or administrative facility as opposed to acquiring existing facilities.

Hedgers Currency traders who seek to minimize their risk of exchange-rate fluctuations, often by entering into forward contracts or similar financial instruments.

Hedging Using financial instruments and other measures to reduce or eliminate exposure to currency risk by locking in guaranteed foreign-exchange positions.

High-context culture A culture that emphasizes nonverbal messages and views communication as a means to promote smooth, harmonious relationships.

Home replication strategy An approach in which the firm views international business as separate from and secondary to its domestic business.

Horizontal integration An arrangement whereby the firm owns, or seeks to own, the activities performed in a single stage of its value chain.

Host-country national (HCN) An employee who is a citizen of the country where the MNE subsidiary or affiliate is located.

Idiom An expression whose symbolic meaning is different from its literal meaning.

Import license Government authorization granted to a firm for importing a product.

Importing or global sourcing Procurement of products or services from suppliers located abroad for consumption in the home country or a third country.

Incoterms Universally accepted terms of sale that specify how the buyer and the seller share the cost of freight and insurance in an international transaction and at which point the buyer takes title to the goods.

Indirect exporting Exporting that is accomplished by contracting with intermediaries located in the firm's home market.

Indirect quote The number of units of foreign currency obtained for one unit of domestic currency.

Individualism versus collectivism Describes whether a person functions primarily as an individual or as part of a group.

Industrial cluster A concentration of businesses, suppliers, and supporting firms in the same industry at a particular location, characterized by a critical mass of human talent, capital, or other factor endowments.

Industry market potential An estimate of the likely sales for all firms in a particular industry over a specific period.

Infringement of intellectual property Unauthorized use, publication, or reproduction of products or services protected by a patent, copyright, trademark, or other intellectual property right.

Intellectual property Ideas or works created by individuals or firms, including discoveries and inventions; artistic, musical, and literary works; and words, phrases, symbols, and designs.

Intellectual property rights The legal claim through which the proprietary assets of firms and individuals are protected from unauthorized use by other parties.

Internalization theory An explanation of the process by which firms acquire and retain one or more value-chain activities inside the firm, minimizing the disadvantages of dealing with external partners and allowing for greater control over foreign operations.

International business Performance of trade and investment activities by firms across national borders.

International collaborative venture Cross-border business alliance whereby partnering firms pool their resources and share costs and risks to undertake a new business venture; also referred to as an "international partnership" or an "international strategic alliance."

International division structure An organizational design in which all international activities are centralized within one division in the firm, separate from domestic units.

International human resource management (IHRM) The planning, selection, training, employment, and evaluation of employees for international operations.

International investment The transfer of assets to another country or the acquisition of assets in that country.

International Monetary Fund (IMF) An international agency that aims to stabilize currencies by monitoring the foreign-exchange systems of member countries and lending money to developing economies.

International monetary system Institutional framework, rules, and procedures by which national currencies are exchanged for one another.

International portfolio investment Passive ownership of foreign securities such as stocks and bonds for the purpose of generating financial returns.

International price escalation The problem of end-user prices reaching exorbitant levels in the export market caused by multilayered distribution channels, intermediary margins, tariffs, and other international customer costs.

International trade Exchange of products and services across national borders, typically through exporting and importing.

Intracorporate financing Funds from sources inside the firm (both headquarters and subsidiaries) such as equity, loans, and trade credits.

Investment incentive Transfer payment or tax concession made directly to foreign firms to entice them to invest in the country.

Joint venture A form of collaboration between two or more firms to create a new, jointly owned enterprise.

Joint venture partner A focal firm that creates and jointly owns a new legal entity through equity investment or pooling of assets.

Know-how agreement Contract in which the focal firm provides technological or management knowledge about how to design, manufacture, or deliver a product or a service.

Legal system A system for interpreting and enforcing laws.

Letter of credit Contract between the banks of a buyer and a seller that ensures payment from the buyer to the seller upon receipt of an export shipment.

Licensing Arrangement in which the owner of intellectual property grants a firm the right to use that property for a specified period of time in exchange for royalties or other compensation.

Licensor A firm that enters a contractual agreement with a foreign partner to allow the partner the right to use certain intellectual property for a specified period of time in exchange for royalties or other compensation.

Local responsiveness Management of the firm's value-chain activities on a country-by-country basis to address diverse opportunities and risks.

Logistics service provider A transportation specialist that arranges for physical distribution and storage of products on behalf of focal firms and controls information between the point of origin and the point of consumption.

Long-term versus short-term orientation Refers to the degree to which people and organizations defer gratification to achieve long-term success.

Low-context culture A culture that relies on elaborate verbal explanations, putting much emphasis on spoken words.

Management contract Arrangement in which a contractor supplies managerial know-how to operate a hotel, hospital, airport, or other facility in exchange for compensation.

Manufacturer's representative An intermediary contracted by the exporter to represent and sell its merchandise or services in a designated country or territory.

Maquiladoras Export-assembly plants in northern Mexico along the U.S. border that produce components and typically finished products destined for the United States on a tariff-free basis.

Masculinity versus femininity Refers to a society's orientation based on traditional male and female values. Masculine cultures tend to value competitiveness, assertiveness, ambition, and the accumulation of wealth. Feminine cultures emphasize nurturing roles, interdependence among people, and care of less fortunate people.

Master franchise Arrangement in which an independent company is licensed to establish, develop, and manage the entire franchising network in its market and has the right to subfranchise to other franchisees, assuming the role of local franchisor.

Mercantilism The belief that national prosperity is the result of a positive balance of trade, achieved by maximizing exports and minimizing imports.

Merger A special type of acquisition in which two firms join to form a new, larger firm.

Monetary intervention The buying and selling of currencies by a central bank to maintain the exchange rate of a country's currency at some acceptable level.

Monochronic A rigid orientation to time, in which the individual is focused on schedules, punctuality, and time as a resource.

Multidomestic industry An industry in which competition takes place on a country-by-country basis.

Multidomestic strategy An approach to firm internationalization in which headquarters delegates considerable autonomy to each country manager, allowing him or her to operate independently and pursue local responsiveness.

Multilateral development banks (MDB) International financial institutions owned by multiple governments within world regions or other groups.

Multilateral netting Strategic reduction of cash transfers within the MNE family through the elimination of offsetting cash flows.

Multinational enterprise (MNE) A large company with substantial resources that performs various business activities through a network of subsidiaries and affiliates located in multiple countries.

National industrial policy A proactive economic development plan the government initiates, often in collaboration with the private sector, to develop or support particular industries within the nation.

New global challengers Top firms from emerging markets that are fast becoming key contenders in world markets.

Nontariff trade barrier A government policy, regulation, or procedure that impedes trade through means other than explicit tariffs.

Normativism The belief that ethical behavioral standards are universal, and firms and individuals should seek to uphold them around the world.

Offshoring The relocation of a business process or entire manufacturing facility to a foreign country.

Organizational culture The pattern of shared values, behavioral norms, systems, policies, and procedures that employees learn and adopt.

Organizational processes Managerial routines, behaviors, and mechanisms that allow the firm to function as intended.

Organizational structure Reporting relationships inside the firm that specify the links among people, functions, and processes.

Outsourcing The procurement of selected value-adding activities, including production of intermediate goods or finished products, from independent suppliers.

Parent-country national (PCN) An employee who is a citizen of the country where the MNE is headquartered.

Performance appraisal A formal process for assessing how effectively employees perform their jobs.

Political system A set of formal institutions that constitute a government.

Polycentric orientation A host-country mind-set in which the manager develops a strong affinity with the country in which she or he conducts business.

Polychronic A flexible, nonlinear orientation to time, whereby the individual takes a long-term perspective and emphasizes human relationships.

Power distance Describes how a society deals with the inequalities in power that exist among people.

Practical information Knowledge and skills necessary to function effectively in a country, including housing, health care, education, and daily living.

Privatization Transfer of state-owned industries to private concerns.

Product structure An arrangement in which management of international operations is organized by major product line.

Project-based, nonequity venture A collaboration in which the partners create a project with a relatively narrow scope and a well-defined timetable without creating a new legal entity.

Protectionism National economic policies designed to restrict free trade and protect domestic industries from foreign competition.

Purchasing power parity (PPP) An adjustment for prices that reflects the quantity of goods that consumers can buy in their home country, using their own currency and consistent with their own standard of living.

Quota A quantitative restriction placed on imports of a specific product over a specified period of time.

Regional economic integration The growing economic interdependence that results when two or more countries within a geographic region form an alliance aimed at reducing barriers to trade and investment.

Relativism The belief that ethical truths are not absolute but differ from group to group.

Repatriation The expatriate's return to his or her home country following the completion of a foreign assignment.

Royalty A fee paid periodically to compensate a licensor for the temporary use of its intellectual property, often based on a percentage of gross sales generated from the use of the licensed asset.

Rule of law A legal system in which rules are clear, publicly disclosed, fairly enforced, and widely respected by individuals, organizations, and the government.

Self-reference criterion The tendency to view other cultures through the lens of one's own culture.

Small and medium-sized enterprise (SME) A company with 500 or fewer employees (as defined in Canada and the United States).

Socialization The process of learning the rules and behavioral patterns appropriate to one's given society.

Sovereign wealth fund (SWF) A state-owned investment fund that undertakes systematic, global investment activities.

Special Drawing Right (SDR) A unit of account or a reserve asset, a type of currency used by central banks to supplement their existing reserves in transactions with the IMF.

Speculators Currency traders who seek profits by investing in currencies with the expectation that their value will change in the future.

Spot rate The exchange rate applied when the current exchange rate is used for immediate receipt of a currency.

Standardization Firm's efforts to make its marketing program elements uniform, with a view to targeting entire regions, or even the global marketplace, with the same product or service.

Strategy A planned set of actions that managers employ to make best use of the firm's resources and core competencies to gain competitive advantage.

Subsidy Monetary or other resources that a government grants to a firm or group of firms, usually intended to encourage exports or to facilitate the production and marketing of products at reduced prices, to ensure that the involved firms prosper.

Sustainability Meeting humanity's needs without harming future generations.

Tariff A tax imposed on imported products, effectively increasing the cost of acquisition for the customer.

Tax haven A country hospitable to business and inward investment because of its low corporate income taxes.

Temporal method Translation of foreign currency balance sheet and income statements at an exchange rate that varies with the underlying method of valuation.

Tenders Formal offers a buyer makes to purchase certain products or services.

Third-country national (TCN) An employee who is a citizen of a country other than the home or host country.

Trade deficit A condition in which a nation's imports exceed its exports for a specific period of time.

Trade surplus A condition in which a nation's exports exceed its imports for a specific period of time.

Trading company An intermediary that engages in import and export of a variety of commodities, products, and services.

Transaction exposure The currency risk firms face when outstanding accounts receivable or payable are denominated in foreign currencies.

Transfer pricing The practice of pricing intermediate or finished products exchanged among the subsidiaries and affiliates of the same corporate family located in different countries.

Transition economies A subset of emerging markets that evolved from centrally planned economies into liberalized markets.

Translation exposure The currency risk that results when a firm translates financial statements denominated in a foreign currency into the functional currency of the parent firm as part of consolidating international financial results.

Transnational strategy A coordinated approach to internationalization in which the firm strives to be relatively responsive to local needs while retaining sufficient central control of operations to ensure efficiency and learning.

Transparency The degree to which companies regularly reveal substantial information about their financial condition and accounting practices.

Turnkey contracting Arrangement in which the focal firm or a consortium of firms plans, finances, organizes, manages, and implements all phases of a project abroad and then hands it over to a foreign customer after training local workers.

Turnkey contractors Focal firms or a consortium of firms that plan, finance, organize, manage, and implement all phases of a project and then hand it over to a foreign customer after training local personnel.

Uncertainty avoidance The extent to which people can tolerate risk and uncertainty in their lives.

Value chain The sequence of value-adding activities the firm performs in the course of developing, producing, marketing, and servicing a product.

Vertical integration An arrangement whereby the firm owns, or seeks to own, multiple stages of a value chain for producing, selling, and delivering a product or service.

Visionary leadership A quality of senior management that provides superior strategic guidance for managing efficiency, flexibility, and learning.

Wholly owned direct investment A foreign direct investment in which the investor fully owns the foreign assets.

World Bank An international agency that provides loans and technical assistance to low- and middle-income countries with the goal of reducing poverty.

World Trade Organization (WTO) A multilateral governing body empowered to regulate international trade and investment.

> Author Index

This index includes names of authors cited. For names of companies, see the Company Index. For terms and topics, see the Subject Index. Page references with e refer to exhibits. Page references with n refer to notes cited by page numbers appearing on.

A

Aaker, David, 322n, 473n
Abelson, Max, 506n
Adele, 467n
Adler, Carlye, 448n, 458n
Adler, Nancy, 508n
Agarwal, James, 101n
Agarwal, Milind, 175n
Agarwal, V., 126n
Aghina, Wouter, 336n
Agren, David, 428n
Aguiar, Marcos, 62n, 254n
Aharoni, Y., 448n, 450n
Ahn, K., 423n
Alcacer, Juan, 417n
Alderman, Liz, 278n
Alesina, Alberto, 505n
Alexander, Philip, 288n
Alexander, Ruth, 392n
Alexander, Yonah, 186n
Aliber, Robert, 297n
Aliouche, Hachemi, 447n, 449n
Allison, Gerald, 387n
Amine, Lyn, 350n
Anderlini, Jamil, 390n
Anderson, Erin, 338n
Anderson, James, 221n
Anderson, Kym, 203n
Ang, Soon, 108n, 499n
Antimiani, Alessandro, 215n
Aoki, Hiroshi, 433
Apud, Salvador, 108n
Areddy, James, 426n
Arnold, Wayne, 277n
Arrunada, Benito, 390n
Arts, Joep, 475n
Athanassiou, Nicholas A., 323n
Atkinson, Philip, 336n
Auerbach, Alan J., 305n
Aulakh, Preet, 421n
Austin, Philip, 401
Axtell, Roger, 90n

B

Baack, Daniel, 102n
Baba, Marietta, 328n
Bachman, S. L., 76n
Badenhausen, Kurt, 156n
Badrtalei, J., 431n
Bahadir, Cem, 466n
Bahnson, Paul, 304n
Bailey, Fred, 500n
Balachandran, Manu, 466n
Balassa, Bela, 215n, 216n
Balazs, Edith, 476n
Baldwin, James Garrett, 466n
Balfour, F., 483n
Ball, Deborah, 336n
Balla, Vikram, 321n
Ballad, Vicar, 494n
Bamrud, Joachim, 428n
Banerjee, Sy, 232n
Banjo, Shelly, 510n
Bannò, Mariasole, 419n

Barber, Andrew, 173n
Barboza, David, 505n
Barro, Robert, 96n
Barsh, Joanna, 510n
Barstow, David, 122n, 484n
Barta, Patrick, 510n
Bartlett, Christopher A., 319, 324n, 326n, 327n, 328n, 329n, 336n
Bartunek, Robert-Jan, 506n
al-Bashir, Omar, 177
Basu, Choton, 45n, 58n
Batson, Andrew, 130n
Baxter, Andrew, 392n
Bazerman, Max, 118n
Bech, Morten, 298n
Beckett, P., 410n
Beechler, Schon, 498n
Beer, Larry, 116n, 117n, 119n, 120n, 122n, 127n, 129n
Behrman, Jack, 237n
Bel, Roland, 330n
Bell, Alex, 225
Bender, Ruth, 51n
Bennett, David, 116n
Benoit, Bertrand, 266n
Bentley, Richard, 368–369
Berman, Phyllis, 184n
Berndt, Ernst, 481n
Berr, Jonathan, 266n
Bertin, Gilles, 444n, 446n
Beshouri, Christopher, 251n
Beyfar, Kristin, 499n
Bhagavatula, Suresh, 350n
Bhalla, Surjit, 76n, 244n, 498n
Bharadwaj, Sundar, 466n
Bhattacharya, A., 247n
Bhattacharya, C., 127n
Bilkey, Warren, 157n
Bismuth, Pierre, 498n
Black, J., 501n
Blanchflower, David, 504n
Blaško, M., 431n
Blewitt, John, 129n
Block, Walter, 221n
Boddewyn, Jean, 214n
Boerner, Hank, 303n
Bolton, Ruth, 101n
Bonini, Sheila, 129n, 131n, 132n, 133n
Boston, William, 390n
Boudette, Neal, 390n
Boudreaux, Richard, 507n
Bouras, Stelios, 42n
Bournay, Emmanuelle, 129n
Boyacigiller, Nakiye, 498n
Boyd, Robert, 106n
Bozer, Ahmet, 43
Brabeck, Peter, 321
Brada, Josef, 268n
Brady, D., 210n
Brake, Terence, 323n
Brannan, Matthew, 509n
Branson, Richard, 103n, 429
Brat, Ilan, 448n
Bray, C., 136n
Brem, Alexander, 475n
Bremner, Brian, 471n
Brett, Jeanne, 499n
Brewer, Benjamin D., 58n
Brislin, Richard, 499n
Brooks, Arthur, 180n
Brown, Mark, 305n
Brown, Natasha, 363
Brustein, Joshua, 466n

Bryan, L., 350n
Bryant, Jim, 456–457, 458
Brzezinski, Zbigniew, 177n
Buck, Trevor, 342n
Buckley, Peter, 161n, 350n
Buell, Todd, 266n
Bughin, Jacques, 62n, 64n, 79n
Burkitt, Laurie, 245n, 427n, 448n, 458n
Burn, Janice, 62n
Burrows, Thomas, 415n
Burton, F., 447n
Bush, Jason, 185n
Busis, Hillary, 109n
Butcher, Dan, 486n
Byrnes, Nanette, 498n
Byron, Ellen, 423n, 469n

C

Cairati, Luigi, 401
Calantone, Roger, 470n
Calkins, Martin, 76n, 123n
Cameron, Doug, 223n
Caminiti, Matthew, 305n
Camp, Garrett, 464
Campano, Fred, 236n
Campbell, Colin, 144n
Cancel, Daniel, 207n
Canterbery, E., 109n
Canterbury, Andrew, 350n
Capell, Kerry, 50n
Carlton, Jim, 202n
Carrasco, Demetrio, 188n
Carter, Meg, 97n
Carter, Nancy, 508n
Cassell, B., 454n
Casson, Mark, 161n
Castrogiovanni, Gary, 448n
Catan, T., 262n
Cauchi, Marietta, 506n
Cavusgil, Erin, 45n, 58n, 129n, 486n
Cavusgil, S. Tamer, 45n, 54, 58n, 62n, 157n, 175n, 188n, 237n, 244n, 247n, 319, 320n, 321n, 328n, 336n, 340n, 342n, 350n, 353, 357, 357n, 369n, 388n, 425n, 426n, 466n, 470n, 477n, 478n, 479n, 480n, 481n, 485n
Caye, J., 321n
Celentani, Marco, 117n, 120n
Cendrowski, Scott, 175n
Chacholiades Ciltiades, 214n
Chacko, Sarah, 184n
Chaffin, Joshua, 223n
Chaiken, Shelly, 89n
Chana, Felix, 301n
Chandler, Alfred D., 331n
Chandler, Clay, 322n, 415n, 428n
Chandrasekaran, Deepa, 475n
Chandy, N., 77n
Chandy, R., 232n
Chang, Dae-Oup, 157n, 159n
Chang, Juichuan, 232n
Chang, Kai, 505n
Chang, L., 328n
Chao, Deng, 292n
Chao, Loretta, 125n, 206n, 245n, 330n, 458n
Chapped, Lindsay, 254n
Chase, Lisa, 127n
Chase-Dunn, C., 58n
Chavez, Hugo, 185, 264
Chazan, G., 202n, 328n
Chen, H., 86n
Chen, Liyan, 73n

> Company Index

This index includes names of companies and commercial banks.
For names of authors, see the Author Index.
For terms and topics, see the Subject Index.
Page references with e refer to exhibits.
Page references with n refer to notes cited by page numbers appearing on.

> Subject Index

This index includes terms and topics.
For names of companies, see the Company Index.
For authors cited, see the Author Index.
Page references with "e" refer to exhibits.
Page references with "n" refer to notes cited
by page numbers appearing on.

A

Absolute advantage principle, 147–148, 147e
  limitations of, 149
Accounting and reporting laws, 190
Account management, global, 485
Acculturation, 88–89
Acquisitions, 340, 419
Active hedging, 301
Adaptability, 498
Adaptation, 108, 468, 470–473, 498
  standardization and, 472–473
Administrative procedures, 204e, 206–207
Ad valorem, 203
Advanced biomedical devices, 368–369
Advanced economies, 233, 234–235e, 236e
  defined, 232
  emergent firms in, 250
  national characteristics of, 238e
  trade conditions in, 237e
Advertising, international, 482–483, 482e, 483e
Affiliates, 454
Afghanistan
  born global firms in, 57
  terrorism and, 186
Africa. *See also countries in*
  banks in, 275
  Chinese investment in, 408–409
  ethical standards in, 118
  globalization and, 78
  population of, 408
  poverty in, 71
  as special case, 251–252
Agents, 454
Air transport, 400
Algeria, Chinese investments in, 409
Alliances with qualified local partners, 191
Allowances, 502
Ambiguity, tolerance for, 108
American option, 301
Analogy, 367
Appreciation of currency, 262
Arab Spring, 63
Arbitrage, 300
Arbitration, 191
Area studies, 500
Argentina
  Compania Argentina de Seguros de Credito
    of, 385
  computer manufacturing in, 341
  hyperinflation in, 266
  as member of MERCOSUR, 221
  trade policies of, 210
Asian values, 104–105
Asia-Pacific Economic Cooperation (APEC), 68, 221
Asociación Interamericana de Contabilidad
  (Interamerican Association of Accounting), 303
Asset-seeking motives, 416e, 417
Association of South East Asian Nations (ASEAN),
  184, 221
Association of Women in International Trade, 509
Attitudes, 89
Australia
  advanced economies in, 232
  born global firms in, 45

focus on present in, 91
foreign direct investment and, 412
idioms in, 95e
as individualistic society, 104
legal system in, 181
living standards in, 179
as masculine society, 104
mixed political systems in, 179
public sector in, 43
trade barriers in, 59
Australia and New Zealand Closer Economic
  Relations Agreement (CER), 221
Austria
  McDonald's in, 50
  as member of EU, 260
Automatic teller machines (ATMs), 46

B

Back-office activities, 389
Back-to-back transaction, 384
Bahamas as tax haven, 306
Balance of payments, 268
Balance of trade, 268
Bangalore, India, as emerging market, 241
Bangladesh
  clothing exports and, 209
  developing economies in, 232
  garments factory workers, 114
  tariffs and, 211
Bank for International Settlements
  global financial system and, 270
  in monetary and financial systems, 275, 276
Banking crisis, 276
Banks
  in Africa, 275
  in Canada, 275
  central, 266, 275
  commercial, 273–275
  correspondent, 298
  investment, 273
  merchant, 273
  offshore, 273
  in Sweden, 275
  in United States, 276
Bartering, 384
Basel Capital Accord, 276
Basel III global regulatory standard, 190
Base remuneration, 502
BBVA (Spain), international monetary system and, 273
Belarus, embargo against, 186
Belgium
  contract law and, 191
  as exporter, 376
  franchising in, 448
  government spending in, 180
  IKEA and, 316
  international trade and, 37
  as member of EU, 260
  national debt in, 277
  uncertainty avoidance and, 104
Benefits, 502
Bid, 299
Bid-ask spread, 301
Big Mac Index, 242, 243e
Bill of lading, 380
Blackmail, 121
Bolivia
  expropriation and, 185
  government in, 185
Bond markets, role of, in monetary and financial
  systems, 273

Bonds, 273, 293
  foreign, 293
Born global firms, 43, 45, 157
  emergence of, 56–58
Botswana, economy of, 251
Boycotts, against firms or nations, 186
Brand equity, 473
Branding, global, 470, 473–474, 474e
Brazil
  accounting in, 190
  bribery in, 121
  cultural metaphors in, 102
  distribution channels in, 162
  economic conditions and, 267
  efficiency in, 149
  as emerging market, 43, 48, 60, 62, 230, 231, 232,
    237, 240, 241, 328, 348
  foreign direct investments in, 60, 411
  income taxes in, 178
  inflation in, 267
  international travel and, 377
  JLR strategy, 253
  as member of MERCOSUR, 221
  poverty in, 71
  refineries in, 162
  retail in, 428
  sustainability and, 129
  trade policies of, 210
Bretton Woods Agreement, 59, 268–270
Bribery, 120, 121–122, 172, 245
BRIC countries, 232, 237
  as emerging markets, 48
British Virgin Islands as low-tax rate country, 306
Buddhism, 96, 100
Build-operate-transfer (BOT) arrangements, 452–453
Bulgaria
  economic crises in, 220
  as member of EU, 357
Bureaucracy, 204e, 206–207, 245
Business houses, 246
Business jargon, 94
Business methods, gaining new ideas about, 46–47
Business process outsourcing (BPO), 389
Buy-back agreement, 384

C

Call option, 301
Cambodia
  born global firms in, 57
  tariffs and, 211
Canada
  accounting in, 190
  as advanced economy, 232, 233
  banks in, 275
  contract law and, 191
  country risk and, 175
  economic environment in, 40
  environment in, 77
  ethical behavior and, 117
  euro and, 261
  Export Development Corporation of, 385
  focus on present in, 91
  foreign direct investment and, 412
  foreign exchanges in, 291
  franchising in, 448
  government in, 183
  as individualistic society, 104
  legal system in, 181
  mixed political systems in, 179
  motorcycles in, 51
  offshoring and, 73